Hospitality and Travel Marketing

Fourth Edition

Join us on the web at

www.hospitality-tourism.delmar.com

Hospitality and Travel Marketing

Fourth Edition

ALASTAIR M. MORRISON, PH. D.

DELMAR
CENGAGE Learning™

Australia • Brazil • Japan • Korea • Mexico • Singapore • Spain • United Kingdom • United States

DELMAR
CENGAGE Learning™

Hospitality and Travel Marketing, 4th Edition
Author: Alastair M. Morrison

Vice President, Career and Professional Editorial: Dave Garza

Director of Learning Solutions: Sandy Clark

Acquisitions Editor: James Gish

Managing Editor: Larry Main

Product Manager: Anne Orgren

Editorial Assistant: Sarah Timm

Vice President, Career and Professional Marketing: Jennifer McAvey

Marketing Director: Wendy Mapstone

Marketing Manager: Kristin McNary

Marketing Coordinator: Scott Chrysler

Production Director: Wendy Troeger

Senior Content Project Manager: Nina Tucciarelli

Art Director: Bethany Casey

Library of Congress Control Number: 2009922623

ISBN-10: 1-4354-8686-2

ISBN-13: 978-1-4354-8686-7

ISE Hospitality & Travel Marketing

Delmar
5 Maxwell Drive
Clifton Park, NY 12065-2919
USA

Cengage Learning is a leading provider of customized learning solutions with office locations around the globe, including Singapore, the United Kingdom, Australia, Mexico, Brazil, and Japan. Locate your local office at: **international.cengage.com/region**

Cengage Learning products are represented in Canada by Nelson Education, Ltd.

To learn more about Delmar, visit **www.cengage.com/delmar**

Purchase any of our products at your local college store or at our preferred online store **www.ichapters.com**

Notice to the Reader

Printed in Canada
1 2 3 4 5 6 7 13 12 11 10 09

CONTENTS

PREFACE

This book began evolving on my very first day as a college teacher at Purdue University. Like many of my peers in hospitality and travel education, there was no introductory marketing textbook that quite fit my needs and those of my students. The existing texts in the field were either too narrowly focused, dealing only with restaurants, hotels, or travel agencies, or were written for practitioners rather than college students. They lacked many of the essentials of an effective college text, including learning objectives, assignments, glossaries, instructor's manuals, test banks, and other ancillaries. The content tended to be slanted in one direction, usually the authors' pet areas, resulting in unbalanced treatment of many other important marketing issues.

Hospitality and Travel Marketing, Fourth Edition, is designed to fill a void in the marketing textbooks for our industry. It is unique because it avoids the compartmentalized thinking characteristic of various segments of our business. In the twenty-first century, the need and value of cooperative marketing efforts among hotels, airlines, restaurants, travel agents, DMOs, and others will increase. This accelerating push for "partnership" is a major theme of *Hospitality and Travel Marketing*, Fourth Edition. Our students are tomorrow's managers and need to share with us a broader perspective of our industry than just restaurants, lodging, or the travel agency business. Surely, marketing is one of the areas of study in which students should be encouraged to take a broad, long-term view of their chosen industry and career field.

The target market for this book is the student in two- or four-year college courses in hotel, restaurant, tourism, or travel industry marketing. It was written with the student in mind and was extensively reviewed by college students as well as college marketing teachers. Several special features are included to increase student learning and interest.

Systematic Sequence of Book

One of the major strengths of *Hospitality and Travel Marketing*, Fourth Edition, is its clear structure and organization. Students new to marketing often fail to grasp how each element fits together and get lost in the jargon of our discipline. This book is organized around the hospitality and travel marketing system model. The model serves as a road map for students in understanding how the various marketing functions and techniques are related. It reflects a simple, common-sense approach to marketing that students can easily follow and comprehend. The text's five parts and twenty chapters follow the chronological flow of the hospitality and travel marketing system.

Part I (Introduction to Marketing) clearly explains marketing and its evolution in our industry. It highlights the important differences between marketing services and marketing products. This part also introduces the hospitality and travel marketing system. Part II (Planning: Research and Analysis) provides a detailed description of the research and analysis techniques that are an essential first step in planning the marketing effort. Part III (Planning: Marketing Strategy and Planning) looks at the alternative marketing approaches available to hospitality and travel organizations. Detailed coverage of market segmentation is included, as well as an extensive review of consumer (demand) and industry (supply) trends. The concept of positioning also receives in-depth treatment. Part IV (Implementing the Marketing Plan) discusses how each element of a marketing plan is developed and implemented. Chapters are devoted to product development and partnership, services and service quality (people), packaging, programming, distribution channels (place), communications, advertising, sales promotion, and merchandising personal selling, public relations and publicity, and pricing. Part V (Controlling and Evaluating the Plan) discusses the final steps in marketing planning and implementation—marketing management, control, and evaluation.

Features

Learning Objectives and Review Questions

Every chapter opens with a comprehensive set of learning objectives addressing the main points covered in the chapter. Review questions at the end of each chapter allow students to review how well they have learned the material related to each objective. The test bank supplied to adopting teachers has been carefully prepared to match the text's learning objectives and review questions.

Key Terms

Marketing is a discipline with a language almost its own. To help students cope with the many new words and ideas, a list of key terms is located at the beginning of each chapter. Every listed item is also boldfaced and defined in the chapter when first mentioned. For easy review of all key terms, a glossary is included near the end of the text.

Industry Players

Ten of the chapters include an *Industry Players* case describing an organization that has enjoyed great success in applying marketing approaches and techniques related to the chapter's topic area. Each case is carefully linked to chapter materials so that students have real-life examples of how organizations in our industry have made excellent applications of the various elements of marketing.

Global Perspective: The Big Picture

Ten of the chapters include *Global Perspective* cases that provide interesting information from around the world on the application of hospitality and travel marketing.

Internet Marketing

This feature provides a glimpse of the latest Internet marketing approaches in hospitality and travel marketing as they relate to the topics covered in individual chapters.

Did You Know?

This feature presents interesting facts and figures in an easy-to-follow format that stimulates interest in chapter materials.

Chapter Assignments

Hospitality and Travel Marketing, Fourth Edition, contains 80 chapter assignments. These are provided to give students another type of learning experience and the opportunity to apply what they have learned in the chapter. Teachers may also find the chapter assignments useful as individual or group projects. Many of the assignments require students to do a combination of secondary (library) and primary research.

Web Resources

This feature acknowledges the important role that technology plays in today's world. Web addresses are provided at the end of each chapter for students who wish to further explore topics presented in the text.

The author and Delmar affirm that the website URLs referenced herein were accurate at the time of printing. However, due to the fluid nature of the Internet, we cannot guarantee their accuracy for the life of the edition.

Supplements

INSTRUCTOR RESOURCES

Online Instructor Resources with PowerPoint® lecture slides and Computerized Test Bank

The Online Instructor Resources includes an Instructor's Manual, which has answers to review questions, assignments and suggested resources, PowerPoint® lecture slides, and a computerized test bank in ExamView® format. The computerized test bank comprises multiple choice and true/false questions for each chapter.

Instructors can use the computerized test bank software to create sample quizzes for students. Refer to the CTB User's Guide for more information on how to create and post quizzes to your school's Internet or Intranet server. Your students may also access sample quizzes created by Delmar from their website for Online Companion™ for Students at http://www.Hospitality-Toursim.delmar.com.

Online Companion

TIP ✪ *The Online Companion™ to accompany the fourth edition of Hospitality and Travel Marketing is your link to hospitality, travel and tourism on the Internet. The Online Companion™ contain many features to help focus your understanding of hospitality and travel marketing:*

- *Chapter Objectives Review—This review provides an overview of the key topics presented in the chapter.*
- *Web Activities—These activities direct you to a website(s) and allow you to conduct further research and apply content related to hospitality and travel marketing.*
- *Web Links—For each chapter, a summarized list of Web links is provided for your reference. A listing of travel trade intermediaries and publications is also provided.*

TIP ✪ *The Online Companion™ icon appears at the end of each chapter to prompt you to go online and take advantage of the many features provided. You can find the Online Companion™ at www.Hospitality-Tourism.delmar.cengage.com or at www.delmarlearning.com/companions.*

New to This Edition

Overall

Every chapter in *Hospitality and Travel Marketing* now includes either an *Industry Players* or *Global Perspective* case study. Sixteen of the 20 case studies are completely new to the fourth edition; and the remaining four have been substantially updated from the previous edition's *Excellence Cases*. A new *Internet Marketing* feature has been added in all 20 chapters. The *Did You Know?* feature provides interesting new tidbits on hospitality and travel marketing, and 18 of these are new to this edition. An almost completely new art program of photographs, website page captures, and drawn figures has been introduced and for the first time the book is published in color. All of the chapter-end website addresses have been updated to the date of publication. Additionally, all of the lists of references have been substantially changed and updated.

The fourth edition has increased global coverage in materials, cases, and examples. While retaining a core focus on North America, more contents have been introduced from Europe, China and Hong Kong, Australia and

New Zealand, Singapore, and other countries. This was done in recognition of the increasing globalization of the hospitality and travel industry.

Chapter 1: Marketing Defined

An increased emphasis has been placed on recent trends such as online marketing, ticketless travel, wireless technologies, green tourism, impacts of terrorism, natural disasters, and economic downturns, and corporate social and environmental responsibility. The environmental protection programs introduced by Royal Caribbean Cruise Lines are presented as a good example of corporate environmental responsibility. New figures have been created and inserted to improve student comprehension of key learning concepts.

Chapter 2: Marketing Hospitality and Travel Services

Updated information has been included on the increasing importance of the service industries in major developed countries. A new *Industry Players* case has been introduced featuring *KFC* and *Skyline Chili*.

Chapter 3: The Hospitality and Travel Marketing System

The section of this chapter dealing with different definitions of hospitality and travel has been rewritten to better reflect the current industry situation. Updated information has been added about the relationships among different sectors of the hospitality and travel industry. A new *Global Perspective* case on *Tourism Jiangsu* in China has been incorporated. As in Chapter 1, new figures have been introduced to improve student learning of key concepts.

Chapter 4: Customer Behavior

A new *Global Perspective* case on *Tourism New Zealand* discusses how that organization targets the "interactive traveler" market. A new Consumer Decision Process model has been introduced to show how customers make purchasing decisions. A new process model for organization buying is featured as well. More updated coverage is provided on Internet use and social information sources on the web (e.g., blogs). New figures are also added in Chapter 4.

Chapter 5: Analyzing Marketing Opportunities

A new *Industry Players* case of the market analyses of indoor waterpark resorts provides a great practical application for Chapter 5. The chapter introduces the concepts of GIS-based market information for the first time. New figures are again added in Chapter 5 to improve understanding.

Chapter 6: Marketing Research

New and recent examples are introduced on the application of marketing research in the hospitality and travel industry. The new *Industry Players* case on the Las Vegas Convention & Visitors Authority supplies an outstanding on a destination marketing organization's research program. New information of external sources of secondary research data and several new figures are added.

Chapter 7: Marketing Strategy: Market Segmentation and Trends

Chapter 7 incorporates a completely new section on demand and supply trends in hospitality and travel. This provides a very contemporary viewpoint on major changes in market preferences and recent development in the industry. Updated information on the PRIZM® segmentation system is presented.

Chapter 8: Marketing Strategy: Strategies, Positioning, and Marketing Objectives

Expanded information on brand extension strategies features is included in this new edition. Chapter 8 has a new *Industry Players* case on Scottsdale Resort & Conference Center. The recent concepts of space tourism and dynamic packaging are introduced for the first time.

Chapter 9: The Marketing Plan and the 8 Ps

The new *Global Perspective* case on the Canadian Tourism Commission represents an outstanding example of effective marketing planning in hospitality and travel. New figures are added that better summarize and depict some of the key chapter contents.

Chapter 10: Product Development and Partnership

This chapter contains a completely new update on all groups and sectors of the hospitality and travel industry. The recent trends in different sectors are identified and explained. Newer concepts such as lifestyle hotels and third-party intermediaries are described. The canal sector is included for the first time in this fourth edition of the book. Once more, new figures give a better visual portrayal of key ideas within Chapter 10.

Chapter 11: People: Services and Service Quality

The concepts of service orientation, service culture, and customer delight are new to this edition. New global service excellence examples are included from Mandarin Oriental, Peninsula Hotels, and Shangri-la Hotels & Resorts, Swiss Tourism, and the Hong Kong Tourism Board. The Total Quality Service (TQS) system provides an interesting further dimension to the discussion on Total Quality Management. New information is supplied on the ISO 9000 and 9001 standards. Materials on employee orientation, internal marketing, and mystery shopping programs are also included.

Chapter 12: Packaging and Programming

The concept of dynamic packaging is introduced for the first time. A new *Global Perspective* case on the World Expos in Japan (2005) and Shanghai, China (2010) provide a great example of programming on a grand scale.

Chapter 13: The Distribution Mix and the Travel Trade

New materials on global distribution systems (GDS) and online travel companies feature in Chapter 13. Also, updated statistics and trends for all the travel trade intermediaries are incorporated.

Chapter 14: Communications and the Promotional Mix

Chapter 14 now places much more emphasis on the Integrated Marketing Communications (IMC) concept and on the blending of the traditional promotional mix elements with Internet marketing. The online promotional strategies of international theme parks are the focus of a new *Global Perspective* case.

Chapter 15: Advertising

The Hong and Shanghai Hotels, Ltd. company is featured in a new *Global Perspective* case in Chapter 15. The new and outstanding advertising campaign by Tourism Australia is also discussed in detail. A newly organized section is provided around all the advertising media alternatives. Up-to-date information on spending on advertising and advertising reach is provided.

Chapter 16: Sales Promotion and Merchandising

Fresh information about the application of specialty advertising items is included. In addition, new materials are added about the effective use of travel trade shows and exhibitions. A new *Global Perspective* case on Hong Kong's Charterhouse Hotel further expands the discussion on these shows and exhibitions. Many new recent examples of sales promotions in hospitality and travel have been detailed. Several new figures are included that give students a clearer visual depiction of key concepts in Chapter 16.

Chapter 17: Personal Selling and Sales Management

The Best Cities Global Alliance is a new *Global Perspective* case that provides a good example of how destination marketing organizations can cooperate around the world to increase sales. The case adds to this chapter's greater emphasis on MICE markets and the role of requests for proposals (RFPs) for meetings and conventions. There is also more attention given to the use of the Internet in hospitality and travel sales.

Chapter 18: Public Relations and Publicity

Chapter 18 gives more attention to the new technologies of PR and publicity including blogging, webcasting, podcasting and RSS feeds, as well as website media and press centers. A number of new diagrams have been designed and incorporated to improve understanding of the key concepts in hospitality and travel public relations.

Chapter 19: Pricing

A fascinating new *Global Perspective* case on low-cost airline carriers (LCCs) appears for the first time in the fourth edition. It explains how these airlines have prospered while the more powerful larger airlines have performed poorly. Expanded coverage is given in Chapter 19 on the concept of revenue management.

Chapter 20: Marketing Management, Evaluation, and Control

Tourism Australia is the focus for a new *Global Perspective* case on marketing evaluation. Chapter 20 discusses emerging new concepts in hospitality and travel marketing, including mobile commerce or m-commerce and evaluation techniques for application in Internet marketing.

Appendices 1 and 2

All of the data in the tables has been updated to either 2007 or 2008 to provide the most current statistical information at the time of publication.

Glossary

This new edition of *Hospitality and Travel Marketing* features several new and contemporary concepts and terms. The already extensive glossary has been significantly expanded to include these new items.

Acknowledgments

A textbook like this one is never a one-person effort but is the result of a variety of creative minds. There are many people who have helped or inspired me in my career as a management consultant and a professor. I would like to offer special thanks to the following individuals:

Rodney Lindsey and Jim Carpenter, former students, who were such a great help in acquiring photographs and advertisements and in reviewing manuscript drafts.

Kimberly Risk, former student, for her insightful comments in reviewing manuscript drafts.

Amy So, David Wimbiscus, Troy Bennett, and Liz Berry, former students, for their help in acquiring photographs and advertisements.

Joe Cioch and Brother Herman Zaccarelli for coaxing me to come to Purdue University. A special thanks is due to Brother Herman for his insightful guidance in choosing the best publishing company.

Patrick Wilson of Hospitality Marketing in Toronto for the initial idea that sparked all five steps in the hospitality and travel marketing system.

I would also like to thank the following reviewers whose helpful comments and suggestions helped shape the final product:

Jeffrey A. Beck, Ph.D.
Michigan State University
East Lansing, Michigan

Ken Myers
University of Minnesota Crookston
Crookston, Minnesota

Dan Creed
Metropolitan State University
St. Paul, Minnesota

F. Allen Powell
University of Arkansas
Fayetteville, Arkansas

Bradford Hudson
Boston University
Boston, Massachusetts

Alastair M. Morrison, Ph.D.
Shanghai, PR China

About the Author

Alastair M.Morrison is the CEO of Belle Tourism International Consulting, based in Shanghai, China. He also holds the title of Distinguished Professor Emeritus of Hospitality and Tourism Management from Purdue University in West Lafayette, Indiana, USA. Dr. Morrison has hospitality and travel industry experience in the United States, Canada, China, United Kingdom, and Australia. He has conducted training programs and provided tourism marketing and development advice in Australia, Bahrain, China, Ghana, Honduras, Hong Kong, India, Italy, Jamaica, Macau, Malaysia, New Zealand, Poland, Scotland, Singapore, Slovenia, Sri Lanka, Thailand, Trinidad & Tobago, and Vietnam. He served as a Visiting Professor at University of Strathclyde in Scotland and at James Cook University in Queensland, Australia.

Dr. Morrison spent several years in Canada as a management consultant specializing in the hospitality and travel industry. He established a private consulting firm called The Economic Planning Group of Canada, now one of the leading companies in the field. This book reflects Dr. Morrison's international background and his unique blend of practical and academic experience. A native of Scotland, he has both lived and worked in five different countries. His work and educational background have given him the basic ingredients for an effective marketing textbook—an in-depth knowledge of marketing theory plus a clear understanding of what actually works in practice.

Dr. Morrison has had extensive experience in publishing, including several years of writing hospitality and travel manuscripts on behalf of Tourism Canada and other government agencies. He is the co-author with Robert Christie Mill of *The Tourism System* and with Philip Pearce and Joy Rutledge of *Tourism: Bridges Across Continents*. He has also written a variety of journal articles related to marketing and market segmentation in the hospitality and travel industry.

INTRODUCTION TO MARKETING

WHERE ARE WE NOW?

WHERE WOULD WE LIKE TO BE?

HOW DO WE GET THERE?

HOW DO WE MAKE SURE WE GET THERE?

HOW DO WE KNOW IF WE GOT THERE?

chapter 1

Marketing Defined
What Is Marketing?

OVERVIEW

Welcome to the dynamic world of hospitality and travel marketing! Make sure you fasten your seat belt as you read more about this fast-moving management function. Why is marketing such a hot topic in today's hospitality and travel industry? Why do companies spend millions each year on marketing? To rev up your engine, this chapter starts at the beginning and explains the evolution of marketing. You will learn about the differences between production and marketing orientations, and the importance of adopting a marketing orientation in today's highly-charged marketplace.

You will become familiar with the core principles of marketing. The benefits of marketing are identified, so you will understand why it's becoming so important in today's hospitality and travel industry. So let's get going then!

OBJECTIVES

Having read this chapter, you should be able to:

- Define marketing and explain the six marketing fundamentals used in this book.

- Explain the PRICE of marketing concept.

- Compare and contrast the roles of marketing during four evolutionary eras and describe the online marketing era.

- Describe the symptoms of a production and sales orientation.

- Explain the marketing myopia concept.

- Describe the characteristics of a marketing (or customer) orientation and its benefits.

- Explain the core principles of marketing.

- Describe the environment for marketing in the hospitality and travel industry.

- Explain the reasons for the increasing importance of marketing in the industry.

K E Y   T E R M S

baby boomers

competitors

core principles of marketing

corporate responsibility (social responsibility)

customers' needs

customers' wants

database marketing

e-commerce

economy

exchange process

external environment

4 Ps (four Ps of marketing)

green marketing

hospitality and travel industry

hospitality and travel marketing environment

Internet

laws and government regulations

market segmentation

marketing

marketing-company era

marketing-company orientation

marketing concept

marketing-department era

marketing environment factors

marketing manager

marketing mix (Ps of marketing)

marketing myopia

marketing orientation

marketing-orientation era

marketing strategy factors

online marketing era

organizational priorities and goals

product life cycle

production orientation

production-orientation era

relationship marketing

sales orientation

sales-orientation era

service industries

societal-marketing-orientation era

society and culture

sustainable development

target markets

technology

value

World Wide Web (the Web)

You are probably new to marketing, wondering how this subject might help further your career objectives. What if you knew that marketing is destined to be the most important management activity in the hospitality and travel industry in the future? What if we told you that every manager will need to be familiar with the basic principles of marketing?

Are you now more interested in marketing? Well, what is so magical and dynamic about this powerful subject? The best place to start seems to be with a definition of the term.

Definition of Marketing

How would you define marketing? Write down your ideas on what you think is involved and compare them later with this book's definition. If you are like most people unfamiliar with marketing, you probably listed such things as the Internet, advertising or commercials, selling, and sales promotions (e.g., coupons, in-store displays). As you will soon realize, these aspects of marketing are only the tip of the iceberg. Even more marketing work goes on behind the scenes. For example, how and why does a company decide to spend millions on advertising? What are the reasons for promotions? Why does each organization do things just a little differently? These are just a few of the many behind-the-scenes marketing decisions that companies must make.

This book's definition is based on the following six marketing fundamentals:

1. **Satisfaction of customers' needs and wants.** The primary focus of marketing is satisfying **customers' needs** (gaps between what customers have and what they would like to have) and **customers' wants** (needs of which customers are aware).
2. **Continuous nature of marketing.** Marketing is a continuous management activity, not a one-time set of decisions.
3. **Sequential steps in marketing.** Effective marketing is a process of following a set of sequential steps.
4. **Key role of marketing research.** Using marketing research to anticipate and identify customer needs and wants is essential for effective marketing.
5. **Interdependence of hospitality and travel organizations.** There are many opportunities for partnerships in marketing among organizations in our industry.
6. **Organization-wide and multi-department effort.** Marketing is not the sole responsibility of one department or division. To be most effective, it requires the efforts of all departments or divisions.

When you combine these six marketing fundamentals, the following definition of **marketing** emerges:

> Marketing is a continuous, sequential process through which management in the **hospitality and travel industry*** plans, researches, implements, controls, and evaluates activities designed to satisfy both customers' needs and wants and their own organization's objectives. To be most effective, marketing requires the efforts of everyone in an organization and can be made more or less effective by the actions of complementary organizations.
>
> ――――――
>
> *A group of interrelated organizations providing personal services and facilities to customers who are away from home.

You may have noticed in this definition that the five management tasks in marketing are planning, research, implementation, control, and evaluation. What do you notice about these five words when arranged in this order? Give yourself a pat on the back if you saw that their first letters spell out the word PRICE. The PRICE of marketing is that all organizations must do planning, research, implementation, control, and evaluation.

THE PRICE OF MARKETING

P	Planning
R	Research
I	Implementation
C	Control
E	Evaluation

Evolutionary Eras of Marketing

Now that you know what marketing is, you might be interested in some historical background of the topic. There are differences between the way marketing evolved in non-service industries and the way it developed in **service industries** (organizations primarily involved in the provision of personal services), which includes the hospitality and travel industry.

Marketing in Non-service Industries

Among manufacturing and packaged-goods companies, marketing evolved through four distinct eras: (1) production, (2) sales, (3) marketing, and (4) societal marketing (Figure 1.1). The changes in management thinking about marketing developed during these four eras because of technological advances, productivity improvements, intensified competition, expanding market demand, increased management sophistication, changing societal values, and other factors.

1. **Production-Orientation Era.** The **production-orientation era** was the first evolutionary stage in the development of marketing. It began with the Industrial Revolution in the 1870s and lasted into the 1920s. During this era, the production capacities of factories could not keep pace with demand. Demand exceeded supply. Every item that was manufactured could be sold, and management's emphasis was on producing as many goods as possible. Customers' needs and wants were of secondary

FIGURE 1.1 The evolution of marketing in non-service industries. (Adapted from Perreault, William D., and E. Jerome McCarthy, *Essentials of Marketing: A Global Managerial Approach*, 10th ed. © 2006 by The McGraw-Hill Companies, Inc. Reproduced with permission of The McGraw-Hill Companies.)

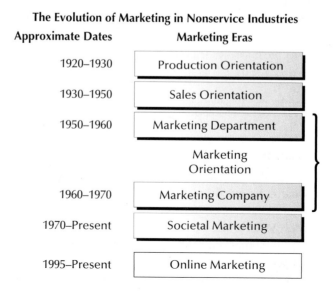

importance. Henry Ford summed up production orientation when he said, "They (customers) can have any color they want, as long as it's black." The Ford Motor Company has come a long way since then. It not only has the Ford, Lincoln, and Mercury brands, but also Jaguar, Land Rover, Mazda, and Volvo—available in many colors (http://www.ford .com/en/default.htm).

2. **Sales-Orientation Era.** Gradually, technological advances in production and increased competition changed the emphasis of marketing. Beginning in the 1930s, there was enough capacity to meet demand. As competition intensified, the emphasis switched from production to selling. Customers' needs and wants were still of secondary importance. Beating the competition by outselling them was first priority. This was the **sales-orientation era**, which lasted until the 1950s.

3. **Marketing-Orientation Era.** The **marketing-orientation era** resulted from even more intense competition and technological advances. Supply now exceeded demand. It was also a result of greater management sophistication and the advancement of marketing as an academic discipline. Organizations began to realize that selling alone did not guarantee satisfied customers and more sales. Customers had more choices than ever before and could select the products and services that best matched their needs. It made good sense to give customers' needs a higher priority than just selling. During this time organizations began adopting the **marketing concept** (acting on the assumption that satisfying customers' needs and wants is first priority).

This era had two stages—the marketing-department era and marketing-company era. In the **marketing-department era**, the need to set up new departments to coordinate marketing activities gained acceptance. Sales departments and divisions were renamed and reorganized, and their responsibilities were expanded to include the related functions of advertising, customer service, and other marketing activities. It was more effective to have all marketing responsibilities in one department, rather than dividing them among several different departments. Marketing was not yet looked at as a long-term activity.

"That's not our problem. It's the marketing department's." This might have been a typical statement of a chef or front-desk supervisor in the marketing-department era. It shows an attitude that satisfying customers' needs is solely a marketing department responsibility and not the concern of other departments.

An organization-wide change of attitude occurred with the onset of the **marketing-company era** in the 1960s. "It's everyone's problem if our customers are not satisfied" is a statement that typifies this attitude. The marketing department might have had the prime responsibility for marketing-related activities, but all departments played a role in and were affected by customer satisfaction levels. Marketing was seen as a long-term, organizational concern. Survival of the company hinged not only on satisfying customer needs in the short term, but also in the long

FIGURE 1.2 Today's marketplace is highly diverse, requiring a strong marketing orientation.

Image copyright Digitalskillet, 2008. Used under license from Shutterstock.com

term. The definition of marketing used in this book is based on a **marketing-company orientation**. As Figure 1.2 shows, the market for hospitality, travel, and tourism is becoming increasingly diverse. This requires that marketing managers have a strong marketing orientation that focuses on the needs of individual markets. In today's marketing, we cannot "be all things to all people."

4. **Societal-Marketing-Orientation Era.** The **societal-marketing-orientation era** is the fourth evolutionary era. Beginning in the 1970s, organizations started to recognize their social responsibility in addition to their profit and customer-satisfaction objectives. A prime example in the hospitality industry is brewers and distillers that use advertising to fight drunk driving, alcoholism, and under-age drinking. Another example is Royal Caribbean International that has created its own environmental management program known as *Save the Waves*. The program includes, among other things, the appointment of an Environmental Officer on each of its cruise ships and measures aimed at reducing waste. Figure 1.3 shows how Royal Caribbean International has designed its ships so carefully to take care of all waste products. Some refer to programs like this as **green marketing**, in which hospitality and travel organizations develop actions to protect the environment and communicate these actions to customers. Almost every hotel in the world encourages its guests to use bath towels more than once to help with environmental conservation. **Sustainable development** is another related concept which has developed during this era of marketing. This means developing hospitality and travel in such a way as not to harm the environment or the culture and lifestyles of local people, so that future generations may enjoy them as they are today.

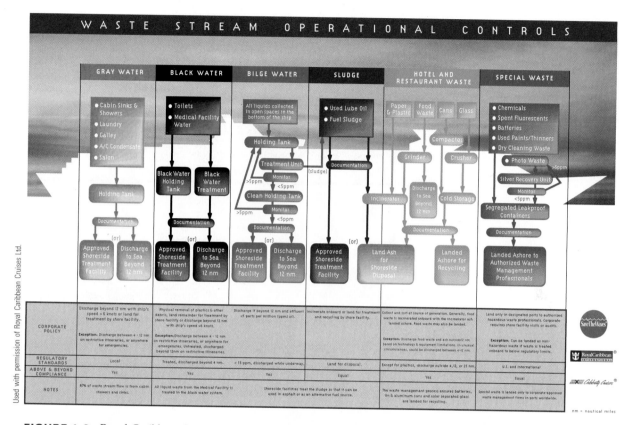

FIGURE 1.3   Royal Caribbean International's *Save the Waves* program is an outstanding example of environmental concern and protection.

5. **Online Marketing Era.** Some industry observers have suggested that the mid-1990s brought another new era of marketing in which digital technologies were rapidly adopted. No doubt you already know that the **Internet** revolutionized the way business was done from about 1995 onwards, causing a huge growth in electronic or **e-commerce** (Figure 1.4). Hospitality and travel marketers are now making heavy use of the **World Wide Web (the Web)** for providing information and accepting reservations. The use of e-mail for communications is a norm in today's marketing environment. Cell or mobile phones are helping marketing and sales people stay in touch with their clients and home offices. PowerPoint, compact discs (CDs), digital videodiscs (DVDs), and blu-ray disks have replaced videotapes in marketing presentations. Personal digital assistants (PDAs) are quickly replacing traditional business calendars and time management systems. Hospitality and travel companies are now podcasting and using RSS and Webcasting to distribute public relations (PR) materials and financial information.

The **online marketing era** is fundamentally changing how travelers get information about hospitality and travel services, and how they book

FIGURE 1.4 The online marketing era has changed how marketing is done in hospitality and travel.

Image copyright Andresr, 2008. Used under license from Shutterstock.com

them. The era of ticketless air travel is almost upon us, as e-tickets have almost completely replaced traditional "hard copy" tickets. Online travel companies like Expedia.com and Travelocity.com are now among the leading players in travel distribution.

Computer software programs are changing how marketers understand and analyze customers, and are leading the transition from mass marketing to **database marketing**. Database management software allows marketers to gather and use information to form closer relationships (relationship marketing) with individual customers and to customize appeals to them. In hospitality and travel, frequent-traveler programs are a key strategy in implementing database marketing and loyalty programs.

Is the online marketing era replacing the societal-marketing-orientation era? The answer is certainly no since most organizations continue to follow their social responsibilities while making greater use of online and other new digital technologies. So when you look back at Figure 1.1, think about the societal marketing and online marketing eras as working in parallel today.

Almost all basic marketing textbooks describe these eras by chronicling the histories of a few major manufacturing companies. After reading these books, you are left with the impression that there are no organizations in existence today with production or sales orientations. This is definitely not true! Another misleading impression you might have is that if an organization has a marketing orientation, it automatically follows that all managers and staff of the organization have the same orientation. This is not always the case. You might also assume that all organizations must have passed through these evolutionary stages, and at roughly the same time. This confusion is caused by mixing two slightly different concepts—the evolutionary stages in the development of marketing as a management activity (which you have just read about) and the orientations of individual organizations and their managers and staff (which are discussed later).

Marketing in the Service Industries

The hospitality and travel industry, along with other service industries, has not exactly followed the same historical evolution in marketing that you have just read about. In fact, the industry has lagged behind manufacturing and packaged-goods firms in its use of marketing by perhaps as much as 10 to 20 years.

Why, you ask, has the hospitality and travel industry let this happen? Many different reasons for this fact are explored in this book, the principal one being that many managers have come up through the ranks. Former chefs and cooks manage restaurants, ex-airline pilots create airline companies, hotel company presidents were front desk clerks, and tour wholesaling company executives used to be tour guides. As these managers advanced, their individual business environments, training, and education stressed operations or the technical details of the business, rather than customers and their needs. Few **marketing managers** (managers responsible for marketing) with manufacturing and packaged-goods firms have ever worked on the floors of their factories. The statement "In order to market this business, you must know it inside out" reflects a common management attitude in our industry. To modify an old saying; "If you don't know how to cook; you shouldn't be in the marketing department."

A second reason that our industry lagged behind is that major technological breakthroughs came later than they did in the manufacturing and packaged-goods industry. The introduction of mass production as a manufacturing concept is normally credited to Henry Ford in the early 1900s. Mass production did not arrive in the hospitality and travel industry until three or four decades later. For example, Pan American offered the first transatlantic passenger flight—in a flying boat—in 1939. The inaugural flight of British Airways, then BOAC, came even later—in 1946. The year 1952 marked the advent of the Holiday Inn concept and the now-familiar golden arches of McDonald's first

INTERNET MARKETING

E-marketing in the Air? Internet and Cell Phones in Planes

- Since around 2005, passengers on long-distance international flights have been able to use wireless Internet in-flight. The airlines in Asia such as Japan Airlines were the first to pioneer this service in the sky.
- Qantas announced in July 2007 that all its new planes would be equipped to provide passengers with wireless Internet service.
- North American airlines were slower to follow this trend. Late in 2007, JetBlue become the first airline to offer limited Internet service in the air. Other major airlines including American Airlines began testing the service in early 2008 in partnership with AirCell.
- In December 2007, Air France and OnAir introduced the first in-flight mobile phone service on its Airbus 318 planes on European routes.
- While this technology is advancing, there is still much public debate about cell phone etiquette in the sky.

Sources: **http://www.onair.aero; http://www.aircell.com**

Student Questions

1. What are the benefits for airlines in giving passengers access to the Internet and their cell or mobile phones when flying?
2. What are the advantages to the passengers?
3. What are the potential drawbacks or problems with providing these services in the sky?
4. How could the airlines and other hospitality and travel marketers use this new in-flight communications access for marketing purposes?

welcomed customers in 1955. That same year, Walt Disney revolutionized the commercial attraction business by opening North America's first theme park—Disneyland in Anaheim, California. The first wide-bodied jet—the Boeing 747—took to the air in 1970.

Because of this technological time lag, our managers have had 30 years or less to perfect their marketing skills while others in the manufacturing and packaged-goods industries have had 60 to 70 years. In addition, a large part of these 30 years has been spent perfecting technology and operating systems in the hospitality and travel industry for greater efficiency and profitability. Now, as we are at the end of the first decade of the 2000s, it seems that the hospitality and travel industry has caught up in its marketing approaches.

Industry Players

Social Responsibility and Sustainability

Ben & Jerry's Homemade Holdings, Inc.

http://www.benjerry.com

Ben & Jerry's cows are a very strong part of its visual images.

Eating ice cream serves a good cause if your favorite brand is Ben & Jerry's. This Vermont-based company manufactures ice cream, frozen yogurt, sorbet, and other novelty products and has 580 franchised ice cream "scoop shops" and PartnerShops worldwide. Now, it is a wholly-owned subsidiary of Unilever after being sold in 2000 at an estimated price of $326 million.

This company is a great example of a societal-marketing orientation in action in the hospitality, travel and tourism industry. Started in 1978 in Burlington, Vermont, with just a $12,000 investment, Ben & Jerry's take their name from the two founders, Ben Cohen and Jerry Greenfield. The company's societal orientation is embedded in its mission statement:

"Ben & Jerry's is founded on and dedicated to a **sustainable corporate concept of linked prosperity**." The company's mission statement has three interrelated parts.

Product

To make, distribute and sell the finest quality all natural ice cream & euphoric concoctions with a continued commitment to incorporating wholesome, natural ingredients and promoting business practices that respect the Earth and the Environment.

(continues)

(continued)

Economic

To operate the Company on a sustainable financial basis of profitable growth, increasing value for our stakeholders and expanding opportunities for development and career growth for our employees.

Social

To operate the company in a way that actively recognizes the central role that business plays in society by initiating innovative ways to improve the quality of life locally, nationally and internationally."

"Central to the mission of Ben & Jerry's is the belief that all three parts must thrive equally in a manner that commands deep respect for individuals in and outside the company and supports the communities of which they are a part."[1]

Courtesy of Ben & Jerry's

Every year Ben & Jerry's conducts a Social & Environmental Assessment.

Ben & Jerry's is one of very few organizations to have a *Social & Environmental Assessment* included as part of its Annual Report. The 2006 report covered eight areas—our company, values-led sourcing, scoop shops, environment, workplace, giving back and community, connecting with consumers, and global business. Ben & Jerry's have four different ways of giving back and helping communities: (1) through the Ben & Jerry's Foundation, (2) Product Donations, (3) Factory Seconds Donations (in Vermont), and (4) Community Action. In 2006, the Ben & Jerry's Foundation received $1,587,917 from Ben & Jerry's Homemade, Inc., based on a percentage of the company's 2005 sales. This was a 9.1 percent increase over 2005.

This societal orientation, along with great ice cream, has paid off handsomely for Ben & Jerry's. The company now has scoop shops in 23 other countries, including Canada, France, Israel, the Netherlands, Peru, and the United Kingdom. A small business that started in 1978

(continues)

(continued)

as an ice cream scoop shop in a renovated garage in Burlington, Vermont, has become a multimillion-dollar global ice cream giant. The next time you see Ben & Jerry's distinctive black-and-white Friesian cow logo, you may remember how a good product mixed with a good amount of corporate caring can be a recipe for a great marketing success story.

Discussion Questions

1. How has Ben & Jerry's demonstrated a societal-marketing orientation?
2. What can other hospitality and travel companies learn from the Ben & Jerry's example?
3. Which other hospitality and travel companies have shown they have a societal orientation and how have they demonstrated this orientation?

Developing a Marketing Orientation

You have probably noticed how many times the words **marketing orientation** have already been used. Being the intelligent person that you are, you may have been alerted to the fact that this is a key aspect of this field of marketing. If we tell you it may also be the key to your future career success, you might like to hear more.

Unfortunately, none of us are born with a marketing orientation! It needs to be learned and polished through constant practice. Surprisingly, some successful managers have never heard of marketing orientation, but they act as if they had. You might wonder how this can be. The answer is simple: A marketing orientation is such a common-sense approach to business today that some people develop it through their experience, knowledge of what works, and natural intuition, without ever reading a single marketing book or coming within 160 kilometers or 100 miles of a business school. Other people are not as lucky. They may be exposed to the same stimuli, but still emerge with a production orientation or sales orientation.

Production and Sales Orientation

Many organizations and managers within the hospitality and travel industry have either a **production orientation** or a **sales orientation**. How can you spot them? Production- and sales-oriented organizations have a very strong internal focus. Their entire world revolves only around what goes on within the walls of their business premises. A production-oriented organization puts most of its emphasis on selling services that are the easiest and most efficient to produce. They tend to emphasize sales rather than profits. These organizations may provide only the services their executives like best or the ones they think customers like based on their managers' opinions.

There are 13 symptoms that can be used to diagnose production and sales orientations:

1. Planning is short term. Little value is attached to long-term planning.
2. Long-term decisions are made only when serious problems are encountered. When things are going well, no such decisions are made.
3. There is a definite reluctance to change.
4. Business growth is seen as being assured and current business volumes are viewed as guaranteed.
5. Providing the best or highest quality service is assumed to be an automatic guarantee of success. This is the "better-mousetrap fallacy."
6. Little is known about the specific characteristics and needs of customers. Research on customers' needs is not given a high priority. Managers assume they know what customers need without any research.
7. Promotions stress service or product features, rather than the customer needs they satisfy.
8. Customers are given only what they ask for and what is normally provided—no more, no less.
9. Decisions are made from a production or sales perspective, not with customers' needs in mind.
10. The organization or department is seen as an island unto itself. Cooperation with other departments and complementary organizations (those providing related hospitality and travel services) is not considered to be very valuable. Only when there is an emergency is the need to cooperate recognized.
11. Departments or divisions have overlapping activities and responsibilities related to marketing. There are open or hidden conflicts between departments concerning these activities and responsibilities.
12. Department or division managers tend to be very defensive and protective of their domains.
13. The organization is set up and the services are offered because the owners themselves like them. This is known as the "share-the-wealth syndrome."

Figure 1.5 shows a set of actual statements from managers in our industry that reflect some of these symptoms. Look at these statements and see if you can spot any of the 13 symptoms of production and sales orientations.

The phrase **marketing myopia** was coined in 1960 to describe many of these 13 symptoms of production- and sales-oriented orientations.[2] Myopia as a medical condition means short-sightedness. In a business sense, myopia is being unable or unwilling to think, see, and plan beyond the short term; or to shut your eyes on the future. Managers often fail to realize there's no such thing as a perpetual growth industry. Those who act as if growth is inevitable run the risk of failure in the long term, because it is not the ability to produce that guarantees success, but being able to identify and adapt to customers' needs and wants.

Can you think of any examples of marketing myopia in the hospitality and travel industry? In fact, there have been many. Our world has seen incredible

Lodging Example

"The demand for rooms will always keep growing in this community. In any case, our rooms and restaurants will be the best available."
- Assumes that growth is inevitable (symptom #4).
- Assumes that having the best or highest quality is a guarantee of success (#5).

Food-Service Example

"My sister and I love French food. We are going to open a French restaurant because there are enough people in every town that share our love for the French cuisine."
- Assumes that customers have the same needs, wants, and preferences as the organization (#6, #13).

Travel Agency Example

"I'm sorry, Mrs. Jones, but that was the airline's fault, not ours. You never asked me to recommend any alternative routes or carriers."
- Assumes that customers view the travel industry as a group of independent suppliers and do not blame all for the mistakes of others (#10).
- Assumes that it is only necessary to provide what customers themselves ask for (#8).

Cruise Line Example

"Our ships are the largest and most expensive to build. These are the features we stress most in our advertising, because we think this is important to our cruise patrons."
- Assumes that stressing product features is of greatest importance. This is not usually the case (#7).

Travel Destination Example

"We really can't handle any more visitors in the summer months, so we're switching all our promotional efforts to other periods of the year."
- Assumes that current success is guaranteed for the future (#1, #2, #4).

changes and events since the 1980s until the present. Major economies have followed "boom-and-bust" cycles, as recessions have followed periods of strong economic growth. Natural disasters and outbreaks of serious diseases have brought our industry to a standstill in many destinations. The constant threat of terrorism targeting airlines, airports, hotels, railways, and tourists has cast a large shadow of the rosy picture of world tourism growth. There have been periods of overbuilding in the lodging sector; new theme parks have been opened, but have failed and closed. Airlines have been started up, but later were grounded and have gone out of business. Many travel agencies in North America have shut down, as their major source of revenues from airline commissions dried up to almost nothing.

There are also frequent cases of marketing myopia in the restaurant business. New concepts rise and fall in popularity at an alarming rate. Management often becomes preoccupied with expansion and production efficiency when demand for a particular concept is rising, but fails to prepare for an eventual downturn in popularity. New and different ways of satisfying customers' needs must be found before the decline occurs.

As these events show, it was a strategic error for management in the hospitality and travel industry to assume that domestic and international travel would always be a growth industry. As Levitt suggested in 1960, without proper planning and an acceptance of change as inevitable, nothing is assured. History has proven the wisdom of his words in our industry. Some of our industry's former giants, including Pan American, Eastern Airlines, and Chi-Chi's are now in our industry's version of *Jurassic Park*.

Production-oriented organizations also define their industries too narrowly and miss lucrative marketing opportunities. For example, if Disney had defined its business as just movies instead of the entertainment industry, it would have missed the opportunity to get into the profitable theme park field. Holiday Inns, now part of the InterContinental Hotels Group (IHG), could have stuck closely to its original formula of providing affordable family accommodations in roadside locations, missing the lucrative extended-stay hotel concept and the Embassy Suites brand (now owned by Hilton Hotels Corp.).

The dangers of a production orientation are serious, the ultimate being eventual organizational failure. The inability to understand customers' needs and changes in these needs is the most serious long-term threat. Loss of market share, falling business volumes, increased customer dissatisfaction, and missed marketing opportunities are some of the results of such an orientation. Management and staff energies tend to be focused inwardly. Profitable opportunities for cooperation between departments and partnerships with complementary organizations are neglected.

Experts use the words *orientation, attitude, philosophy*, and *perspective* interchangeably to describe an organization's or person's view of marketing. Whichever stance managers or their organizations adopt, this view tends to trickle down to all employees. If an organization is production-oriented, then its managers usually follow suit. If managers are production-oriented, their staffs mimic them.

Marketing Orientation

Being marketing oriented is essential in today's competitive environment. It will also be a great help to you in your career! So what does it involve? **Marketing orientation** means acceptance and adoption of the marketing concept—customers' needs are first priority. Marketing-oriented organizations and managers always have a long-term perspective.

How can you spot an organization with a marketing orientation? Just as there are symptoms of production or sales-orientation, there are nine principal characteristics that can be used to identify marketing-oriented organizations (Figure 1.6).

1. **Customers' needs are a first priority and understanding these needs is a constant concern.** Examples of this are a restaurant chain that places an oversized suggestion box near the door of its stores. Another example

FIGURE 1.6
Characteristics of a marketing-oriented organization.

Customer needs are a first priority and understanding these needs is a constant concern.

Marketing research is an ongoing activity assigned a very high priority.

Customers' perceptions of the organization are known.

Frequent reviews are made of strengths and weaknesses relative to competitors.

The value of long-term planning is fully appreciated.

The scope of business or activities is broadly set, and change is seen as inevitable.

Interdepartmental cooperation is valued and encouraged.

Cooperation with complementary organizations is recognized as worthwhile.

Measurement and evaluation of marketing activities are done frequently.

is a travel agency that holds periodic focus group meetings with 10 to 15 of its customers. McDonald's, in its annual *Worldwide Corporate Responsibility Report*, details many actions that it is taking to promote *Balanced Active Lifestyles* and other socially desirable programs.[3] Marriott International's "Spirit to Serve" programs are another excellent example of community and social responsibility.[4] These examples of **corporate responsibility (social responsibility)** clearly show the organizations' concern for customers' feedback and opinions. With such a focus on the customers' needs and their experiences with the organization's services, the result is usually more satisfied customers. Satisfied customers return and tell their friends about their experiences with marketing-oriented hospitality and travel organizations (positive word-of-mouth information). A second benefit is that this gives all departments, managers, and staff a common goal—the satisfied customer.

2. **Marketing research is an ongoing activity assigned a very high priority.** An example of this is a theme park company that interviews hundreds of park guests each week to see if these customers feel they received value for money. Another example is the computerized guest comment system in Marriott's Fairfield Inn properties. A third example is the hotel general manager who drives the airport limousine once or twice a week to find out what guests think of the hotel. One benefit of

this type of ongoing marketing research is that it provides an early warning system for changes in customer needs and expectations. It also gives an accurate indication of how well the organization is satisfying customers' needs.

3. **Customers' perceptions of the organization are known.** It is very important in business to find out customers' images of the organization. As companies such as Ramada Inns and Club Med found out some time ago through customer surveys, customers' perceptions are not always favorable, nor are they always the same as management's image of their own companies. If customers' perceptions are identified, facilities, services, and promotions can be designed to match these images.

4. **Frequent reviews are made of strengths and weaknesses relative to competitors.** One of the biggest dangers in business today is complacency. As Holiday Inn found out, yesterday's strengths (standardized properties, highway locations) can become tomorrow's weaknesses (lack of variety, high gasoline prices). Club Med's wide assortment of recreational activities for its guests (a strength) gave some potential customers the perception that they would be forced to participate in them (a weakness). Future marketing success usually comes from accentuating strengths and eliminating weaknesses.

5. **The value of long-term planning is fully appreciated.** Always thinking "long term" is a key ingredient for success in the hospitality and travel industry. Building lasting relationships with individual customers, distribution channels, and other industry partners—called **relationship marketing**[5]—is much more important than making a one-time sale or deal. The travel agent that finds a customer the lowest-priced cruise package, knowing that a higher-priced package would produce a higher commission, demonstrates an investment in long-term customer satisfaction. As well as building lasting relationships, marketing-oriented organizations are always looking five or more years into the future, deciding how they will adapt to change. In so doing, changes in customer needs are anticipated and acted upon, and marketing opportunities are realized.

6. **The scope of business or activities is broadly set, and change is seen as inevitable.** If the passenger railroad companies throughout the world had defined their business as transportation and not railways, they would probably be operating some of the largest airline companies today. The railways could have been more successful if they had adopted Disney's lead of a broadly set industry definition. Entertainment became Disney's industry definition, not movies. This gave Disney much greater flexibility to adapt to future trends and opportunities. The marketing-oriented organization does not resist but adapts smoothly to change. It capitalizes on opportunities that serve customers more comprehensively or those that tap into related fields.

7. **Interdepartmental cooperation is valued and encouraged.** For marketing to work at its best, all the departments in an organization must play

FIGURE 1.7 Benefits of having a marketing orientation.

- Changes in customer needs and characteristics are known.
- Cooperation among an organization's departments increases.
- Cooperation with complementary organizations increases.
- Customers are more satisfied.
- Departments, managers, and staff share a common goal.
- Effective marketing programs are repeated or enhanced; ineffective ones are dropped.
- Marketing expenditures and human resources are used most effectively.
- More marketing opportunities are realized.
- Services, products, and promotions match the customer's image of the organization.
- Strengths are accentuated and weaknesses addressed.
- Viability of new services and products are identified.

a role. This reflects the marketing-company orientation presented earlier in this chapter. Organizations that make a determined effort to share their marketing plans among all departments or throughout the community if they are destinations demonstrate this marketing orientation characteristic. For example, the Nova Scotia Tourism Partnership Council in Canada translated its tourism marketing plan into a video format and made it available for viewing through its website.

8. **Cooperation with complementary organizations is recognized as worthwhile.** Hospitality and travel is an industry with great opportunities for marketing partnerships between different organizations. It makes sense for organizations to cooperate because each provides only part of the experience that customers desire. The synergy that comes through cooperation normally benefits the customer. The cooperative marketing by the European countries that share the Alps as a tourism destination and by the four Visegrad Group countries (Czech Republic, Hungary, Poland, and Slovakia) are great examples. In addition, the thousands of vacation and tour packages now available to travelers provide much greater customer choice. In short, increased cooperation leads to better services and greater customer satisfaction.

9. **Measurement and evaluation of marketing activities are done frequently.** The marketing-oriented organization always prepares a report card of the successes and failures in its marketing activities. Effective marketing activities are identified and then repeated or enhanced. Ineffective activities are reevaluated or dropped. Doing this ensures that marketing dollars and staff are used as effectively as possible. The successful marketing organizations never take anything for granted.

The benefits of having a marketing orientation are shown in Figure 1.7.

Core Principles of Marketing

Now you are ready to hear about the seven **core principles of marketing** that will be so important to your career. They are shown in Figure 1.8.

FIGURE 1.8   Core principles of marketing.

1. **Marketing Orientation.** Having a **marketing orientation** implies that the manager or organization has accepted the marketing concept and acts according to it. The late J. Willard Marriott, Sr. exemplified customer orientation by reading daily every single comment card from guests staying at Marriott's many properties.

2. **Marketing Concept.** When hospitality and travel managers adopt the **marketing concept**, it means they believe that satisfying customers' needs and wants is first priority. They constantly put themselves in their customers' shoes, and ask, "How would I react if I were one of our customers?" They continually force themselves to put resources and effort toward satisfying customer needs and wants. Walt Disney demonstrated the rich rewards of "wearing his customers' shoes" when he came up with the Disneyland theme park concept. Sitting, rather bored, on a bench in an amusement park watching his two daughters playing on the rides, he realized there was a need for parks with entertainment for the whole family, not just children.

3. **Satisfying Customers' Needs and Wants.** To ensure long-term survival in today's competitive business environment, all hospitality and travel organizations must realize that the key to their existence is the ongoing satisfaction of customers' needs and wants. In this marketing-orientation era, they must always be alert for new opportunities to convert customers' needs and wants into sales.

4. **Market Segmentation.** All customers are not alike. Experts have come up with the term **market segmentation** to describe this concept. It is better to pick out specific groups of people—or **target markets**—and market only to them. Some call this the "rifle approach," as compared with the "shotgun approach." Assuming you are a good shot, you can aim a rifle at a specific target and hit it. If you use a shotgun, you might also hit the target, but a lot of precious buckshot would be wasted. Hospitality and travel marketers can't afford wasted buckshot, because marketing dollars and resources are limited. They must take aim at specific target markets to ensure the highest returns. Contiki, for example, is a tour wholesaler and operator with vacation packages for younger markets with its positioning of *Holidays for 18-35's*.

5. **Value and the Exchange Process.** Value and value for money are terms often used in today's business and in our daily lives. Although easy to say, these terms are hard to define. **Value** represents a mental estimate that customers make of a hospitality or travel service's ability to satisfy

Did You Know?

How are People's Purchases Affected by Causes at Holiday Seasons?

- The Foundation Center defines cause-related marketing as "the public association of a for-profit company with a non-profit organization, intended to promote the company's product or service and to raise money for the non-profit."
- The American Marketing Association conducted a consumer survey at the end of 2007. People were asked if they would be more likely to buy a product or service if they knew that a certain amount of the purchase price would be donated to a cause or campaign.
- One-third (around 33%) of all those surveyed said they would be more likely to make such a purchase.
- The proportion for the 18-24 year age group was much higher at 46%.
- The proportion for women, at 40%, was significantly higher than for men, at 30%.

Reprinted with permission from "It's the Chat Room rather than the Dressing Room where Holiday Purchasing Decisions are being made," published by the American Marketing Association. December 2007 press release titled "American Marketing Association: Social networking and cause related marketing top holiday trends."

their needs and wants. Some customers equate value closely with price; others do not. Price is not the only indicator of value. Marketing is an **exchange process**. Suppliers of hospitality and travel services trade items of value with their customers. The industry provides services and experiences that customers find valuable when they are away from home. In return, customers make reservations and pay money, which satisfies the industry's financial objectives.

6. **Product Life Cycle.** The **product life cycle** idea suggests all hospitality and travel services pass through four predictable stages: (1) introduction, (2) growth, (3) maturity, and (4) decline. Marketing approaches need to be modified with each stage. Avoiding a decline is the key to long-term survival. Atlantic City, New Jersey, is a great example of a travel destination that went through one life cycle (from a fashionable to a rather seedy seaside resort) and then got a completely new lease on life as an exciting gaming destination (Figure 1.9).

FIGURE 1.9 Atlantic City has had two product life cycles. (a) Atlantic City's new life as a casino gambling destination. (b) Atlantic City in pre-casino era.

Courtesy of Atlantic City Convention & Visitors Authority

(a)

Courtesy of the Atlantic City Free Public Library

(b)

FIGURE 1.10
Marketing strategy
factors.

Traditional 4 Ps of Marketing

Product
Place
Promotion
Price

Additional 4 Ps of Hospitality and Travel Marketing

People
Packaging
Programming
Partnership

7. **Marketing Mix**. Every organization has a **marketing mix**. It includes the **marketing strategy factors** (the Ps of marketing) that are used to satisfy the needs of specific customer groups. Traditionally, four such factors are identified. They are product, place, promotion, and price—the **4 Ps**. This book adds another 4 Ps that are especially important in hospitality and travel marketing: people, packaging, programming, and partnership (Figure 1.10).

The Hospitality and Travel Marketing Environment

Marketing success is based both on marketing strategy factors (the marketing mix) and marketing environment factors. These factors make up the **hospitality and travel marketing environment** (all the factors to be considered when making marketing decisions). The marketing mix (8 Ps) can be changed in many different ways. For instance, an organization can switch from magazine to television advertising or from radio advertising to coupon promotions. Time, marketing dollars, and customer response are the limiting factors.

Marketing environment factors are events completely beyond the direct control of the marketing manager. Some people call these events the **external environment** that shapes the way business is done. The six marketing environment factors are shown in Figure 1.11.

1. **Competitors.** Marketing managers can influence the actions of competitive organizations, but they cannot control them. The number and size of competing companies are also uncontrollable. Competition has expanded rapidly in the hospitality and travel industry. There are more lodging and restaurant chains, airlines, theme parks and attractions, tour wholesalers, and destination marketing organizations (DMOs) than ever before. Destinations are pouring more money into attracting visitors. Hospitality and travel's future growth potential has been the main reason for intensifying competition. Competition is also becoming global as more companies expand into foreign countries (Figure 1.12).

   Competition is a dynamic process in the industry. One company will implement a marketing strategy, and then its competitors will react with

FIGURE 1.11 The marketing environment factors.

counter-strategies. One-upmanship seems to be a constant. An airline will introduce Wi-Fi service onboard its planes, and competitive airlines will add it soon after. A hotel chain will add a new brand of lifestyle hotels; competitors will watch how the brand does; and if it appears to be successful, they will then launch their own brands of lifestyle hotels. "If it works for them, we'll copy it" seems to be the rule in the hospitality and travel industry.

FIGURE 1.12 Competition today in tourism is global as Shanghai's skyline clearly reflects.

No one can afford to stand still in our industry. Marketing managers constantly need to keep track of competitors' marketing activities, as well as their own. There has to be enough flexibility to modify an organization's marketing programs to react to competitive moves.

There are three levels of **competition** in the industry: (1) direct competition, (2) substitute services, and (3) indirect competition. What we have been talking about is the most direct type of competition—organizations with similar services competing to satisfy the needs of the same customer groups. The second level of competition comes from substituting certain services and goods for others. Instead of going on vacation, for example, a family could stay at home, maintain the lawn, swim in the backyard pool, watch movies on cable TV, or travel virtually on the Web. A Web conference (or "Webinar") is a substitute for a meeting at a central location. Home-cooked meals compete with trips to fast-food restaurants.

The third level consists of those companies and non-profit organizations that are competing against our industry for the customer's dollar. Mortgage payments; grocery, medical, and dental bills; insurance costs; and home improvement expenses are just some of these indirect competitors. The fight for the individual consumer's disposable income (what is left after taxes) is fierce. Competition for corporate travel and entertainment dollars is no less intense. Companies can spend money in many different ways, including cutting out some of their travel costs. This cutback can be even more devastating than the effects of direct industry competition. Marketing managers must accept the fact that they face both direct and indirect competition. They have to be on top of what competitors are doing and be flexible enough to react to change when the time comes.

2. **Laws and Government Regulations.** Marketing is also affected directly and indirectly by the **laws and government regulations** of the land. There are specific laws concerning how services and products can be advertised, how contests and sweepstakes must be structured, who can and cannot drink, and much more. Marketing must be performed within the bounds of these laws and government regulations, yet these laws are beyond an individual organization's control.

Some pieces of legislation or certain regulations have a greater impact on the hospitality and travel industry than others. Privatization of national airlines and airline deregulation of the airlines has had an enormous impact worldwide. Discounted fares and more commercial airlines including low-cost carriers (LCCs) and more routes are some of the outcomes. Changes in the tax deductibility of travel and entertainment expenses can have major impacts, as do changes in the minimum-age provisions of drinking laws. As mentioned earlier, changes in tax laws regarding hotel investments have had a major impact on the expansion of the lodging sector.

Laws and government regulations dictate how business is done. They directly affect the ways that services and products can be marketed, and they are constantly changing. Sometimes pieces of legislation, such as increased security measures or airline privatization, are passed causing major changes in hospitality and travel. Organizations and marketing managers need to keep up-to-date on legislative and regulatory adjustments. Industry and trade association membership helps achieve this goal, but this association membership has to be backed up with internal monitoring of these trends.

3. **Economy.** The **economy** of a country and its upward and downward trends has a major impact. Inflation, unemployment, and recession are three factors that periodically plague the economies of most developed countries, like the global economic crisis at the end of 2008. They also hurt the hospitality and travel industry. Less money is available for business and pleasure travel, and the dining-out dollar is more tightly guarded in poor economic times. Companies and individuals also tend to look for substitute services and goods. Conference calls and Webcasting replace meetings, national meetings become regional, and staying at home is substituted for vacations.

    There are local, regional, national, and international components of the economic environment. Changes in the local and regional economies can have a very direct impact on hospitality and travel organizations. The opening of new factories can be very positive in bring more corporate business. Industrial closures have the opposite impact. In a one-industry community, a factory closure can be fatal for its hospitality and travel businesses. International economic events have an indirect impact on the industry. Recently, shorter vacation trips closer to home is a predominant trend. In times of very high oil prices, a two- to three-week family touring trip in the family car is no longer affordable and travel by air offers greater value.

4. **Technology.** **Technology** is a constant frontier of change. Hospitality and travel marketers need to watch two aspects of the technological environment. The first aspect is using new technology that may provide a competitive edge. Providing wireless Internet or Wi-Fi services, travel information delivery to cell/mobile phones and PDAs, podcasts and Webcasts, online booking and reservations, and e-ticketing are just a few examples.

    A second aspect is the impact of technology on customers. People are inundated with technological changes. Mobile technologies, in-home entertainment systems, online banking, smart cards, and wireless Internet are just a few examples. A threat on one side, technology is a friend on the other. Advances in home-maintenance-equipment technology have reduced the time required for household chores, making more time available for out-of-home entertainment and travel.

5. **Society and Culture.** There are also two sides to **society and culture**. First, an organization must consider how customers will react to marketing activities based on societal and cultural norms. For example,

showing X-rated movies might be popular with some as in-flight enter-
tainment, but it is socially unacceptable. Although popular in Korea and
China, dog meat still has not found a place at restaurant tables in North
America and Europe.

Second, customers themselves are affected by changes in society and
culture. Casino gambling, now known as *gaming*, was frowned upon a
few decades ago, but now casinos are everywhere. The official tourism
slogan of Las Vegas, *What Happens Here, Stays Here*, a few years ago
would have been judged too risqué, but most now think it's very *cool*.
People are also changing in what they want to do in their discretionary
time. Voluntourism is growing, in which people travel to places where
they can help poorer and needier people. Ambassadors for Children are
a good example of an organization that arranges voluntourism to help
children and their families in underdeveloped areas of the world
(Figure 1.13). Learning vacations are increasing in popularity, in which
people travel to add to their knowledge stores or to acquire new skills.

FIGURE 1.13
Ambassadors for
Children is an
organization that
provides voluntourism
trips to help needy
children.

6. **Organizational Priorities and Goals.** **Organizational priorities and goals** represent the final uncontrollable factor. Marketing is not the only organizational concern, although it is a key to long-term success and survival. Marketing activities need to be weighed against competing priorities for resources. A new brochure might have to go head-to-head with a site on the Web, a proposed sales force against a new call center.

A great marketing idea can run contrary to an organization's objectives or policies. Airlines could capitalize on fatal crashes of competitive jets. Countries promoting tourism could cash in on acts of terrorism and civil disturbances in competing destinations. Restaurants and hotels could criticize specific competitive chains in their media campaigns. These negative approaches are seldom followed because they clash with a company's overall policies and objectives. There is an unwritten code of professional conduct in the industry that discourages these "great" ideas.

Increased Importance of Marketing in the Industry

When you add up what has just been said, it is easy to see that the hospitality and travel industry has undergone rapid change. Continuing change is inevitable and marketing plays a key role in an organization's ability to cope with change.

Marketing is now more important to our industry than ever before. Greater competition, increased market fragmentation and complexity, and more well-traveled and sophisticated customers have created a greater emphasis on marketing. Marketing in the hospitality and travel industry has become more professional and aggressive.

Let's consider increased competition first. There are now more hotels, restaurants, bars, airlines, theme parks, car rental outlets, and cruise lines than there have ever been. Another supply-side trend heating up competition has been the growth of chain, franchise, strategic alliances, and referral/consortium organizations. These groups are present in all parts of the industry. By pooling resources in national and international programs, they have added to their marketing clout, and have increased competition. Mergers and acquisitions are also a constant, tending to put more marketing power through consolidation in the hands of fewer organizations.

The market used to be easy to describe. Vacations meant mother, father, the two kids, and the family car. The business traveler was a man in his 40s who stayed in a Holiday Inn on every trip and ate New York strip steak and French fries. This normal world has turned upside down since then. The advent of the **baby boomers** (those born between 1946 and 1965) changed all the rules. Their search for new experiences in travel caused major changes in our industry. The baby boomers also instigated many changes in our society. Women are now the major growth market in business travel. People are eating far less red meat. Family travel groups have lost ground to couples and singles. Overall, the market has become more segmented. The causes are many: the economy; technology; and social, cultural, and lifestyle changes have all played a role. The hospitality and travel industry has reacted with new services and products, further splintering the market. The end result is that marketers must be more knowledgeable about customer groups and more specific in choosing their targets.

There are more sophisticated travelers and out-of-home eaters in the market today than ever before. They get their sophisticated tastes from traveling and eating out more often than earlier generations did. They have much more experience in sizing up hospitality and travel organizations. These people go to the Web for travel information and see slick promotion and advertising campaigns every day at home, at the office, on the Web, and on the road. To get through to these people requires better quality services and products and more sophisticated marketing.

All of these factors mean that marketing has become increasingly important in the hospitality and travel industry. Success now comes only with the ability to satisfy the needs of particular customer groups, and to do an excellent job of it.

Chapter Conclusion

Marketing in the hospitality and travel industry is maturing and becoming more sophisticated. There is increasing recognition of the importance of marketing to an organization's ultimate success. Although some years behind manufacturing and packaged goods, our industry has now fully adopted the seven core principles of marketing—the marketing concept, marketing orientation, satisfying customers' needs and wants, market segmentation, value, product life cycle, and marketing mix. This has happened because more people understand the benefits of marketing. An emphasis on marketing is also being forced on our industry because of the intensified competition and the effects of marketing environment factors.

New managers entering our industry must have some knowledge of marketing and what it takes to succeed in today's marketplace. Product-related skills and knowledge, although necessary, are not enough.

REVIEW QUESTIONS

1. How is marketing defined in this book and what are the six fundamentals on which it is based?
2. What is the price of marketing?
3. What are the four evolutionary eras of marketing? How has marketing changed in these eras?
4. What is the online marketing era?

5. Has the hospitality and travel industry passed through these eras at the same pace as other industries? Why or why not?
6. What are the 13 symptoms of production and sales orientation?
7. What is marketing myopia and how can it be avoided?
8. What does it mean to have a marketing orientation? Is this the same as a production or sales orientation?
9. What are the characteristics of marketing orientation?
10. What are the benefits of adopting a marketing orientation?
11. What are the seven core principles of marketing?
12. There are six marketing environment factors in the hospitality and travel marketing environment. What are they?
13. Why has marketing increased in importance in the hospitality and travel industry?

CHAPTER ASSIGNMENTS

1. Assume you are the manager of a hotel, travel agency, restaurant, auto rental agency, or other customer-contact, travel-related business. Describe the program you would use to make your supervisors and other staff members more marketing-oriented. Also show how you could act as a role model in this respect.
2. Pick an organization in the part of the hospitality and travel industry in which you are most interested. Arrange an interview with one or more of its executives to discuss the organization's marketing approaches. Does it seem to have a marketing or a production/sales orientation? What symptoms or characteristics led to your conclusions? Have the seven core principles of marketing been applied? If you were asked to make recommendations to the management team based upon what you have found, what would they be?
3. Select three to five major airlines, hotel or restaurant chains, car rental firms, cruise lines, or other hospitality and travel organizations, and analyze how they have adapted their operations and marketing based on the six marketing environment factors. Which company has done the best job in changing with the hospitality and travel environment?
4. Prepare a standardized list of criteria for evaluating the marketing approaches of hospitality and travel organizations based on the information presented in this chapter.

WEB RESOURCES

Atlantic City Convention & Visitors Authority, http://www.atlanticcitynj.com/
Ambassadors for Children, http://ambassadorsforchildren.org/
Ben & Jerry's, http://www.benjerry.com/
British Airways, http://www.britishairways.com/
Club Med, http://www.clubmed.com/
Contiki, http://ww.contiki.com/
Disney, http://corporate.disney.go.com/

Expedia, http://www.expedia.com/
Marriott International, http://www.marriott.com/
McDonald's, http://www.mcdonalds.com/
Ramada Worldwide, http://www.ramada.com/
Royal Caribbean International, http://www.rccl.com/
Travelocity, http://www.travelocity.com/

REFERENCES

1. Perreault, William D., Jr., and E. Jerome McCarthy. 2005. *Essentials of Marketing: A Global Managerial Approach.* 10th ed. Boston: McGraw-Hill/Irwin.
2. Levitt, Theodore. 1960. "Marketing myopia." *Harvard Business Review* 38 (4): 45–56.
3. McDonald's. 2007. *2006 Worldwide Corporate Responsibility Report*, 16–25.
4. Marriott International. 2007. "Spirit to Serve" In Action.
5. McKenna, Regis. 2006. *Relationship Marketing: Successful Strategies for the Age of the Customer.* New York, New York: Basic Books.

chapter 2

Marketing Hospitality and Travel Services
What Is Marketing?

O V E R V I E W

This chapter describes the emerging field of services marketing. It emphasizes that, although product and service marketing are similar in many ways, there are important differences between them. These differences are identified and described. For the hospitality and travel industry, generic, contextual, and specific differences are discussed. The unique marketing approaches required in the service industries are also described. One of the distinct features of the hospitality and travel industry is the dependency that exists among companies and organizations. The chapter ends by reviewing these relationships.

O B J E C T I V E S

Having read this chapter, you should be able to:

- Explain the meaning of services marketing.

- Identify four reasons that marketing in the service industries has lagged behind marketing in other industries.

- List and describe six generic differences between the marketing of services and the marketing of products.

- List and describe six contextual differences between the marketing of services and the marketing of products.

- List and explain eight specific differences affecting the marketing of hospitality and travel services.

- Explain five unique approaches required in hospitality and travel marketing.

- Identify three unique relationships among hospitality and travel organizations.

KEY TERMS

carriers

contextual differences

co-production

destination marketing
   organizations (DMOs)

destination mix

experience clues

generic differences

hospitality and travel
   industry

inseparable

intangible

packaging and programming

partnership

perishability

service industries

services marketing

suppliers

travel trade intermediaries

variability

word-of-mouth (W-O-M)

Now that you know what marketing is, you are probably anxious to learn the steps involved. So what is the point of having to read another introductory chapter on services marketing? Well, not including this material would be like selling you a car without giving you a maintenance manual. You would probably know how to drive the vehicle, but not much about why it operates the way it does and why things sometimes go wrong.

To be an effective marketing manager, you need to understand the big picture. You have to visualize the broad scope of the industry and be aware of the many different organizations within it. Think of our business as a car engine, with many parts working together to ensure high performance. As you know, it takes a problem with only one small car part to give you that sinking feeling when you turn the ignition key and nothing happens. The same is true in our industry. If one of the providers in the chain provides bad service, all suffer.

Take a trip to your local supermarket and then think about the differences between its merchandise and what we provide. You will realize there is no shelf space in the hospitality and travel industry, nor can you put what we produce in a plastic bag. Because of these and other differences, our organizations have to use marketing approaches not required by supermarkets and other product suppliers. You need to understand these differences and unique approaches before moving on.

What Is Services Marketing?

Around the world, the services industries are growing rapidly. In the United States and Canada in 2007, 79 percent and 69.1 percent of Gross Domestic Product (GDP) respectively were created by the service industries. The percentage for the United Kingdom was 75.7 percent and for Australia it was 70.6 percent.[1] Increasing affluence and more leisure time are two of the reasons for the growing economic importance of services.

The **hospitality and travel industry** (a group of interrelated organizations providing personal services to customers who are away from home) is just one part of the **service industries** (organizations primarily involved in the provision of personal services). Other service industries include banking; legal, accounting, and management consulting services; insurance; health care; laundry and dry cleaning; education; and entertainment. National, state, provincial, and local government agencies are also major providers of services. **Services marketing** is a concept based on the recognition of the uniqueness of all services. It is a branch of marketing that specifically applies to the service industries.

Chapter 1 discussed the evolution of marketing in the non-services industries. Services marketing has not developed at the same pace, but has lagged behind by as much as 20 years. Why did this happen? The first reason is that marketing terms and principles were defined with the manufacturing industry in mind. Most marketing textbooks were written for manufacturing and hardly scratched the surface of services marketing. Few marketing textbooks devoted special chapters to services.

We cannot blame only authors and marketing managers in manufacturing for the slow evolution of services marketing. A second reason for the delay involves certain characteristics of the industry and management. Parts of the hospitality and travel industry have been highly regulated. National airlines in many countries have been protected from competition by their governments. Their privatization has opened up the airline sector and it is now more competitive and market-driven.

A third reason is the composition of the hospitality and travel industry. It is dominated by small businesses. Small family-run restaurants, motels, resorts, campgrounds, travel agencies, attractions, and tour wholesalers significantly outnumber larger chain and franchised businesses. Most small businesses cannot afford full-time marketing managers and have limited marketing budgets. Many of them regard marketing as a luxury that only big business can afford.

There were no multinationals in the hospitality and travel industry in 1950, when large manufacturers began using the marketing concept. McDonald's, Burger King, Wendy's, Holiday Inns, Marriott, Ramada, and Best Western—all household names now—did not get going until after 1950. Others like Starbucks arrived even later. Most of the major airlines, travel agencies, rental car firms, tour wholesalers, and theme parks have been in operation for less than 50 years. International and national marketing by destination marketing organizations has only about a 40-year history. For example, VisitBritain (then the British Tourist Authority) only started full-scale operations in the early 1970s. Compared with Pillsbury, Procter & Gamble, General Motors, and the Ford Motor Company, our industry's leaders have had much less time to practice marketing.

As Chapter 1 mentioned, a fourth reason for the lag in services marketing is the historical tendency for technical and operations-oriented people to create and manage hospitality and travel organizations. Few of these people had any formal training in marketing. They learned it on the job. Manufacturers were creating full-blown marketing departments in the 1950s, when our industry was in its infancy.

Why is an understanding of services marketing so important? The answer is simple. Some of the approaches to marketing products need to be modified to fit the service industries. For example, packaging in the hospitality and travel industry is quite different from the packaging of cereals and other packaged goods. A box of cereal serves as a container and visual merchandiser of the product, whereas a hospitality and travel package is a combination of our industry's services. The distribution system for hospitality and travel services is also much different from the physical transportation of products from manufactures to retailers and then to customers. An online travel company, for example, does not physically pass a hotel or air trip to the customer. The customer books the trip on the Web but then must go to the hotel or airport to use the service.

Why Is Services Marketing Different?

The marketing of hospitality and travel services has several unique characteristics. Some are shared with all service organizations (**generic differences**). Others exist because of the ways in which service organizations are managed and regulated (**contextual differences**). Generic differences affect all organizations in the service industries and will never be eliminated. Contextual differences are also unique to service organizations, but they may eventually disappear through changes in management, laws and government regulations. Generic differences are common to all service organizations. Contextual differences vary by type of service organization. There are six generic and six contextual differences that can be seen in Figure 2.1.[2]

FIGURE 2.1 Generic, contextual, and specific hospitality and travel differences affecting marketing.

Generic Differences	Contextual Differences	Hospitality and Travel Differences
• Intangibility • Production methods • Perishability • Distribution channels • Cost determination • Relationships of services to providers	• Narrow definition of marketing • Lack of appreciation of marketing skills • Different organizational structures • Lack of data on competitive performance • Impact of government regulation and deregulation • Constraints and opportunities for nonprofit marketers	• Shorter exposure to services • More emotional buying appeals • Greater importance on managing experience clues • Greater emphasis on stature and imagery • More variety and types of distribution channels • More dependence on complementary organizations • Easier copying of services • More emphasis on off-peak promotions

Generic Differences

Let's now take a closer look at the six generic differences that affect the marketing of services.

1. **Intangibility.** Before you buy products, you can evaluate them in various ways. If you go into a grocery store, you can pick up, feel, shake, smell, and sometimes taste many products. The packaging and contents can be examined closely. In a clothing store, you can try on merchandise for fit and size. Products such as automobiles, laptops and desktop computers can be tested before you buy them. You can do so much evaluation because products are tangible. However, services cannot be tested and evaluated in the same way. They are **intangible** and you have to experience them to know how they work (Figure 2.2). Since customers cannot physically evaluate or sample most services, they tend to rely on other people's experiences with these services. This is usually referred to as **word-of-mouth information (W-O-M)** and is of great importance in the hospitality and travel industry. Customers also place great value on the advice of hospitality and travel experts, such as travel agents and tour wholesalers, who tend to have more previous experience with travel destinations and companies. They may also check out other people's blogs about destinations, hotels, and resorts on the Web.

2. **Production Methods.** Products are manufactured, assembled, and physically transported to the point of sale. Most services are produced and consumed in the same location. Passengers have to board airplanes, guests need to stay in hotels, and people must visit restaurants to experience the services they purchase. The fast-food outlet is the closest thing

FIGURE 2.2 Services have to be experienced to "know if they work."

INTERNET MARKETING

Planning Travel "Down Under": The Use of Interactive Maps on the Internet

- One of the major challenges with hospitality and travel services is their intangibility. However, the Internet now provides many tools and features that tend to make these services more tangible in customers' perceptions. One of these tools is the interactive map.
- A great application of an interactive map is on Tourism Australia's website. Open the site and you are presented with a full-page map of the "land down under."
- Site visitors can click and display a variety of locations on the main map, including attractions, Australian nature, climate, distance and size, and roads and railway lines. The map changes with each click and is highly interactive. For example, by dragging and clicking on the map, the visitor can find the distances between two places.
- Visitors can enlarge the map to show any of Australia's six states and two territories in the same level of detail as the overall map for the country.
- The map can be viewed in several languages, including English, Chinese, French, German, Italian, Japanese, and Korean.

Source: **Tourism Australia. (2008). http://www.australia.com/**

Student Questions

1. What are the customer benefits of having these interactive maps available on destination websites?
2. What types of limitations and potential problems might there be in a destination using interactive maps such as this?
3. In which ways can interactive mapping technologies make places seem more tangible for potential visitors?
4. How can businesses such as hotels and restaurants also take advantage of this type of interactive mapping technology?

our industry has to a manufactured product, but even then the service is consumed on-site or is picked up by the customer. The fast-food outlet that provides a home- or office-delivery service is one step closer. Most services are not mass-produced.

The manufacturing process can be precisely and comprehensively controlled. Checkers, inspectors, and even robots ensure that rigid production and quality standards are met. Factory workers have the equipment and training to produce exactly the same quality and quantity of goods each time. No customers are around to worry about. Quality control of services is neither as precise nor as easy to achieve because of the human factors that are involved in supplying them. All staff members cannot consistently provide the same levels of service as their colleagues. **Variability** of service levels is a fact of life. Although standardized service is an admirable target that all organizations should try to achieve, it is unrealistic. A robot cannot yet provide effective personal service, and the ever-present stare of an inspector would surely take something away from a service experience.

Customers are more involved in the production process of services. Manufacturers keep customers out of their factories for safety and proprietary reasons. Service organizations cannot bar people from their factories. If they did, most companies would be bankrupt before long. Hotels, restaurants, airplanes, theme parks, and cruise ships are some of the "factories" in our business. The behavior of one customer can ruin the service experience of others. A boisterous drunk on an airline flight; a noisy, all-night party in an adjoining hotel room; a smoker in a non-smoking area (Figure 2.3); or a loud quarrel at the next table in a restaurant can result in dissatisfied customers.

In other words, our own customers can stop us from achieving marketing objectives. For example, drunks do enter retail stores, and such stores get their share of quarrels, but shoppers in retail stores do not get as upset by such disruptive behavior as they would if they were celebrating a special occasion in a local restaurant. They can leave their shopping carts, having spent some time but no money in the store. However, customers make a significant emotional, financial, and time investment in most hospitality and travel services. Once a service experience begins, the customer is more committed to completing it. If the

FIGURE 2.3 When customers smoke cigars or cigarettes, this can upset other guests.

experience is spoiled by other customers or service staff, the customer cannot totally recoup the investment, especially its emotional and time components.

Our industry offers various self-service options, including salad and buffet bars, cafeterias, airline boarding card and e-ticket dispensing machines, and so on. This is sometimes called **co-production**.[3] How well customers serve themselves can affect how well they are satisfied with the service (Figure 2.4). Many bars, resorts, restaurants, and amusement and entertainment facilities depend on the behavior of some guests to influence others positively. If guests have a good time, it rubs off on others. People attract people, especially the ones who are visibly enjoying themselves. An empty restaurant parking lot, a beach with no bathers, an empty dance floor, or a theme park ride with no riders is less likely to attract people than ones thronged with customers. Such is human nature.

When customers buy toothpaste in supermarkets, they are almost 100 percent sure that the toothpaste will clean their teeth. When they

FIGURE 2.4
Customers often have to "serve themselves" in hospitality and travel.

Image copyright Stephen Coburn, 2008. Used under license from Shutterstock.com

purchase a service, they have far less assurance. The same standardization cannot be provided. The actions of service staff, other customers, and the customers themselves make the experience much more variable.

3. **Perishability.** Products can be stored for future sale—services cannot. A product such as a laptop computer can be purchased any day the store is open—now, next week, next month, or even next year. Services are subject to **perishability**. They are ephemeral, which means they are transitory and perishable.[4] The unsold "inventory" of services is just like water down the drain. Time cannot be saved. The sale of an empty hotel room, airline seat, cruise ship berth, or convention center meeting room is lost forever (Figure 2.5). Services and, more importantly, the time available to experience them, cannot be stored. There is only one chance to enjoy a summer vacation or holiday in any given year. An anniversary or birthday dinner only has value at a specific time. Their shelf lives are only one day or less. There are no warehouses for service experiences.

4. **Distribution Channels.** Trucks, railroad cars, ships, and airplanes physically transport manufactured goods to warehouses and retailers, and directly to customers. Shipping services deliver products bought online to customers' residences. Marketing managers in manufacturing have to devise distribution strategies for the most effective movement of products. There is no physical distribution system in our industry. Customers, in fact, have to come to the service factory to buy, rather than vice versa. There are a few exceptions to this rule, including home delivery of pizza and other prepared foods.

There are many intermediaries in the hospitality and travel industry. Online travel companies, travel agents, tour wholesalers and operators,

FIGURE 2.5 If not rented, the sale of this lovely hotel room today is lost forever.

corporate travel managers, incentive travel planners, and convention/ meeting planners are examples. The items being purchased, however, are not physically shipped from producers through the intermediaries to customers. They cannot be because they are intangible.

The chain of distribution for most products consists of several distinct locations: a factory, a warehouse, a retail store, and a place of consumption (home or business). There is often only one location involved when hospitality and travel services are bought. For example, customers come to a restaurant (the factory) where food and beverages are merchandised (the retail store), and leave after consuming the food and drinks of their choice (the place of consumption).

Most manufacturers do not own the retail outlets that merchandise their products. The opposite is true in our industry. Chains, franchisors, and other similar groups have direct control over the individual outlets that provide the services.

5. **Cost Determination.** Fixed and variable costs can be precisely estimated for most manufactured goods. Such goods are physical, known commodities. Services are both variable and intangible. Some customers may require more attention than others, and the nature of the service needed may not always be known exactly. Factory output can be carefully programmed and predicted. Business volumes in our industry cannot.

6. **Relationship of Services to Providers.** Services are **inseparable** from the individuals who provide them (Figure 2.6). For example, there are many restaurants whose chefs or owners have developed unique reputations for their food, personalities, or both, like K-Paul's Louisiana Kitchen in New Orleans. Dolly Parton's Dollywood theme park in Tennessee, and

FIGURE 2.6 Services are inseparable from the individuals who provide them.

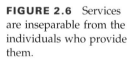
Image copyright Leah-Anne Thompson, 2008. Used under license from Shutterstock.com

---

Did You Know?

How Old Is Bungy Jumping?

- Bungy jumping turned 20 in 2008.
- AJ Hackett from New Zealand introduced it to the world by doing the world's first jump from a building (the Auckland Stock Exchange Tower).
- This is a service that is very much "tied" to one man and his spirit of adventure and willingness to accept a challenge.
- AJ Hackett International has expanded worldwide from its home base in New Zealand to Australia, France, Germany, Bali, Malaysia, and Macau.
- The company in December 2006 introduced the highest bungy jump in the world from the Macau Tower, at 336 meters. The first jump was made by AJ Hackett himself testing a newly engineered bungy cord.

Source: **AJ Hackett International. (2007). http://www.ajhackett.com/welcome.html/**

A J Hackett Bungy in New Zealand are also inseparable. Other examples include tennis camps at resorts hosted by professional stars, shows by famous performers, and tours guided by noted experts in their fields. These individuals are the major attraction. Without them, the services would not have the same appeal.

Contextual Differences

Generic differences between products and services exist because of their inherent natures, production processes, distribution, and consumption. Contextual differences are caused by variations in organizations' management philosophies and practices, and in external environments. Now, let's take a closer look at six common contextual differences that affect the marketing of services (Figure 2.1).

1. **Narrow Definition of Marketing.** Chapter 1 explained that societal marketing and online marketing are the latest eras of marketing. Of course, societal marketing is firmly built upon the marketing-company view, where everybody in an organization feels and acts as if they are part of the marketing team. Some hospitality and travel organizations have not progressed this far. Many have yet to fully adopt a marketing-department orientation. Their so-called marketing departments are really only responsible for promotion (advertising, sales promotion, merchandising, personal selling, public relations, and Internet marketing). Pricing, new site selection, development of new service concepts, and research are still done by other departments or by general managers.

This is changing, and many marketing specialists are reaching top management positions in our organizations.

There is less emphasis on marketing research in the hospitality and travel industry than there should be. Its value to marketing decisions is not yet fully appreciated.

2. **Lack of Appreciation for Marketing Skills.** Marketing skills are not yet as highly valued in our industry as they are in manufacturing. Technical skills such as food preparation, inn-keeping, and destination/supplier knowledge still tend to be held in higher regard. There seems to be a feeling that everybody has the skills to be a marketer, if they really want to be. Marketing skills and talent are not seen as unique, and they are not fully appreciated.

3. **Different Organizational Structures.** Many hospitality and travel organizations are run by persons with the title General Manager or GM for short. Most hotels and other lodging properties follow this pattern. Similar management positions exist in travel agencies, airlines, restaurants, tour wholesaler companies, and attractions. When the businesses belong to chains, general managers usually report to the operations division at the head office. These managers are involved in pricing, developing new services, and managing customer-contact personnel. Marketing or sales managers/directors, who handle other marketing management functions, report to them. In the hotel business, there has been a tendency to name the manager in charge of marketing as the Director of Sales rather than Director of Marketing, or the Director of Sales and Marketing. Many manufacturing companies use a different organizational model, with all marketing activities assigned to one executive and department at both the corporate and field level.

4. **Lack of Data on Competitive Performance.** A large amount of sales data on competitive brands is available for most consumer goods. A packaged-goods manufacturer can access years of sales history on competitive products through various research services. This is not the case in most parts of the hospitality and travel industry. Where data are available, the information tends to be on an aggregated, industry-average basis. Unit sales figures for various companies and their brands are non-existent except for airlines.

5. **Impact of Government Regulation and Deregulation.** Parts of the global hospitality and travel industry have been highly regulated by government agencies. Tight government control has tended to limit the marketing flexibility of many organizations, including airlines, bus companies, travel agencies, and tour wholesalers. Pricing, distribution channels, routes, and even services provided have required government approval. Most manufacturing businesses have not been as comprehensively controlled.

6. **Constraints and Opportunities for Non-profit Marketers.** Non-profit organizations, including most destination marketing organizations (DMOs), play a key role in our industry. They normally have a unique

set of marketing constraints imposed upon them. Politics, particularly what is politically acceptable, tends to influence the marketing decisions made by non-profit organizations—decisions that would be unacceptable or unprofitable for profit-making firms. For example, a state or province may have one tourist attraction or region that draws the vast majority of its visitors. It is usually politically unacceptable for a government DMO to feature only that attraction or region in its promotional campaigns. Favoritism is not tolerated, and all regions and attractions must be promoted. The opposite is true in profit-making organizations, where the philosophy is, push the winners; de-emphasize the losers.

Why Is Hospitality and Travel Services Marketing Different?

Hospitality and travel services have specific characteristics that are not found in other services. It is also true that all hospitality and travel services are not the same. They range all the way from companies that offer mass-produced hamburgers to those that prepare individual, foreign tour (FIT) excursions. There are eight specific differences in hospitality and travel services, shown in Figure 2.1. Let's look more closely at each of these differences.

1. **Shorter Exposure to Services.** Customers are exposed to, and can use, most products and many services that they buy for weeks, months, and sometimes years. Consumer durables such as refrigerators, home entertainment systems, and automobiles are multi-year investments. So are educational programs, residential mortgages, bank accounts, and personal investment consulting. Many items bought at the supermarket can be deep-frozen for months, or, if it is a non-food item, it can be used and stored for a long time. The customer's exposure to most hospitality and travel services is usually shorter. In many cases our services, including trips to fast-food restaurants, short commuter flights, and visits to travel agencies, are consumed within an hour or less. There is less time to make a good or bad impression on customers. Most manufacturers offer warranties and guarantees on their products, sometimes covering several years; however, not many similar assurances of quality are available with hospitality and travel services. Whereas inadequately cooked menu items can be sent back to the restaurant kitchen, many hospitality and travel services that do not work cannot be returned and exchanged for similar ones since they are more intangible.

2. **More Emotional Buying Appeals.** You buy products knowing that they will perform a specific function for you, using rational (logical or fact-based) rather than emotional (feeling-based) reasoning. There are a few exceptions where some people form close emotional bonds with specific products and brands. Harley Davidson motorcycles are a prime example with the very strong bonding shown in its Harley Owners Group® or

HOG. This emotional bonding happens more frequently with hospitality and travel services because, above all else, ours is a people industry. People provide and receive our services. A person-to-person encounter always takes place. Emotions and personal feelings are generated by these service encounters, and they influence future purchase behavior. In our industry, a single employee may determine if a customer uses our services again.

People also tend to buy hospitality and travel services that match their self-images. They fly first class and stay at a Ritz-Carlton, Shangri-La or Four Seasons Hotel because it fits the mental picture of themselves as successful business people. They use a combination of rational (higher level of personal service) and emotional (status or class) reasons when they buy these services.

3. **Greater Importance on Managing Experience Clues.** Whereas a product is basically a tangible object, a service is in essence a performance. Customers cannot see, sample, or self-evaluate services because of their intangibility, but they can see and sense various **experience clues** associated with these services.[5] The combined effect of these experience clues determines their assessment of the service's quality and how well it will meet their needs.

What experience clues do you think are available to hospitality and travel customers when they are deciding what to buy? How do you form an impression of a hotel, restaurant, or airline without having been a customer? You might have guessed that the evidence falls into four categories:

1) Physical environment
2) Price
3) Communications
4) Customers

The physical environment can include the types of furniture, carpeting, wall coverings, staff uniforms, and signs that a hotel or restaurant uses. An enormous crystal chandelier hanging over a beautiful Oriental rug on a gleaming hotel-lobby floor is a clue to a top-quality operation. The price of a service also influences customers' perceptions of quality. High prices are often assumed to indicate luxury and high quality, while low prices reflect lesser luxury and quality. Communications about a company's services come from the company itself, through word-of-mouth information, and through expert advisers such as travel agents. Websites, brochures, and printed advertisements provide customers with tangible evidence, since they picture what the customer can expect. The types of customers a service business currently has provides signals to potential new customers. For example, if an 18- to 25-year-old notices that a local restaurant's customers are mostly elderly, she may not see the restaurant as a good place to dine with her friends. Service marketers must manage these four types of experience clues to ensure that customers make the right decisions. They have to be sure that all the experience clues they provide are consistent and that they are matched by the quality of personal service they provide.

4. **Greater Emphasis on Stature and Imagery.** A related concept is the stature and image of hospitality and travel organizations. Because the services provided are mainly intangible and customers frequently have emotional reasons for buying them, organizations put great effort into creating the desired mental associations.

5. **More Variety and Types of Distribution Channels.** There is no physical distribution system for hospitality and travel services. Instead of a distribution system, our industry has a unique set of travel intermediaries, including travel agents, online travel companies, and companies that put together holiday or vacation packages (tour wholesalers). Products also have intermediaries, but these intermediaries seldom influence customers' purchase decisions. Warehousing and shipping companies have no impact on which products customers select in retail stores or online. In contrast, many travel intermediaries greatly influence what the customer buys. Travel agents and incentive travel and convention planners are looked to for advice on destinations, hotels, attractions, vacation packages, tours, and transportation. Customers see them as experts and take their recommendations seriously.

6. **More Dependence on Complementary Organizations.** A travel service can be extremely complex, beginning when customers notice the advertising for a particular destination. These advertisements may be promotional campaigns funded by destination marketing organizations. Customers may then visit travel agencies or go online for more detailed information and advice. Travel agents may recommend a destination package consisting of round-trip airfare, ground transportation, hotel accommodations, local sightseeing tours, entertainment and attractions, and meals. While on holiday, the customers may go shopping, try a few restaurants, rent a car, buy gas, and visit the hairdresser. What this adds up to is that many different organizations provide the travel service experience. The experience suppliers are interdependent and complementary. Travelers evaluate the overall quality of their experiences based on the performance of every organization involved. If one does not perform up to the standards of others, it reflects badly on all.

7. **Easier Copying of Services.** Most hospitality and travel services are easy to copy. However, products are usually patented or difficult to replicate without detailed knowledge of production processes and materials. Competitors can be kept out of factories to protect industrial secrets. We cannot keep competitors out of our factories, since they are free to visit the places where our services are consumed. Most services our industry provides cannot be patented. Services are provided by people and can be imitated by other people. There are only a handful of situations in which trade secrets have been maintained in the hospitality and travel industry. Colonel Sanders' famous recipe for fried chicken is one of these. And if

FIGURE 2.7 Skyline Chili markets its unique products online.

you know much about Cincinnati, Ohio, then you're probably aware of another one—Skyline Chili. The company's founder, Nicholas Lambrinides, brought the secret recipe to the United States from Greece in 1949 (Figure 2.7).

8. **More Emphasis on Off-Peak Promotion.** Products are promoted most aggressively when there is peak demand. Christmas cards, decorations, and trees in December; garden and pool supplies, suntan oil, and boats in summer; and snow blowers, cold remedies, and warm clothes in winter are all examples. With few exceptions, there is a need for an entirely different schedule of promotions in our industry. Heavy off-peak promotion is the rule, rather than the exception. There are three reasons for this. First, customers make a large emotional investment in their vacations or holidays. These time periods represent precious time away from work and other, everyday responsibilities. They frequently involve major cash outlays. With so much time and money invested, pre-purchase planning is a must and is normally enjoyable. The best time to promote a service is when customers are in this planning stage. To start promoting when their vacation dates arrive is too late.

Second, the capacity to produce is usually fixed. If resorts, hotels, airplanes, ships, and restaurants are full, their capacities cannot be expanded quickly. Factories can run extra shifts and stockpile inventory to cope with above-peak demand. This is impossible in most parts of our industry.

Third, there is more pressure to use available capacity in off-peak periods. Christmas-decoration manufacturers can spend January to November producing and storing inventory. Hospitality and travel services inventories cannot be stored for later sale. They must be consumed when they are available for consumption. There are often wide variations in business volumes during a year, or even a month, week, or day. Since peak capacity is fixed, the emphasis has to shift to promoting the off-peak period. The one notable exception is the fast-food industry, where there is a traditional peak of business from April to September. With such a short time between the decision to buy and to purchase, it makes more sense to promote the hardest when demand is at a peak.

Industry Players

Protecting Trade Secrets in Hospitality and Travel

KFC and Skyline Chili

http://www.kfc.com and http://www.skylinechili.com

Hospitality and travel services are fairly easy to copy, so it is usually very difficult to maintain "trade secrets" for many years. Potential competitors can check in at a hotel, stay in its rooms, and extensively photograph its services. Would-be competitors can eat in a restaurant, take its food home, and even conduct elaborate experiments to determine the ingredients. So, keeping any secrets in hospitality and tourism operations is truly difficult. In fact, there are few cases in which trade secrets have been maintained in the hospitality and travel industry. Colonel Harland Sanders' famous recipe for fried chicken is one of these; Skyline Chili is a second one. The following is some basic information on how these two companies have kept their secrets away from competitors.

Kentucky Fried Chicken's "Secret Recipe"

The secret formula of "11 herbs and spices" has been protected for about 70 years now. Colonel Sanders invented this formula in the 1930s when he was operating the Sanders Court & Cafe restaurant and motel in Corbin, Kentucky.

The recipe is now elaborately protected. One of KFC's suppliers blends a formula of part of the recipe and another spice company blends the other part. In addition, a computer processing system is used to standardize the blending of the products to make sure that no other company has the complete recipe for the "11 herbs and spices."

There are now more than 14,900 KFC outlets in 100-plus countries around the world. This includes 2,140 restaurants in Mainland China, according to Yum! Brands' *Annual Report for 2007*. The Original Recipe® chicken using Colonel Sander's secret recipe has been joined by other products, but undoubtedly has been the main reason for the

(continues)

(continued)

company's success. KFC is now a part of Yum! Brands, Inc., and its four sister brands include Pizza Hut, Taco Bell, A&W All American Food, and Long John Silver's.

Skyline Chili

Skyline Chili's founder, Nicholas Lambrinides, brought the secret recipe to the United States from Greece in 1949. The mixture of "secret spices" helped produce the distinctive dish, now known as Cincinnati-style chili. The company has gone to great lengths to guard the secret for 60 years. The recipe is locked away in a safe and is known by only a few people. The company also prohibits these people from flying together on the same flights.

It's Skyline Time™ The Story of Skyline Chili.

These extreme measures have paid off. Skyline Chili enjoys a cult-like following and can now be bought in grocery stores and online via

(continues)

(continued)

the Web. For the bigger fans of this unique chili, an online order of a case of twenty-four 15 oz. cans might be the most popular. Those with a smaller appetite might want to order just eight cans; while the "Skyline Crave Kit" includes just two cans and a box of Skyline Oyster Crackers.

Skyline Grocery Products.

The most popular dishes at Skyline Chili restaurants are called "ways." Among these, the 3-way Chili is the most favored, and features a dish of spaghetti covered with the secret-recipe chili, and then topped with shredded cheddar cheese. 4-ways and 5-ways are also on the menu, as are the 3-ways plus red beans and/or diced onions. From the first restaurant opened about 60 years ago in Cincinnati by Mr. Lambrinides, Skyline Chili now has grown to about 150 restaurants in four states (Ohio, Kentucky, Indiana, and Florida).

Discussion Questions

1. What steps can hospitality and travel companies take to prevent their competitors from easily copying the services and facilities that they offer?
2. What can other companies and organizations learn from the two examples of KFC and Skyline Chili in keeping their own "trade secrets"?
3. What can tourism destinations do to make sure they are unique and how do they communicate this to potential visitors?

Different Marketing Approaches Needed for Hospitality and Travel

What is the point of talking about all these differences? Basically, it is because products and services cannot be marketed in exactly the same ways. Many of the contextual differences between products and services should disappear in the future. For example, marketing in the hospitality and travel industry is becoming more sophisticated and the industry is steadily becoming less regulated. However, the generic and specific hospitality and travel service differences will remain forever. Time cannot change them. It is because of these ever-present differences that unique marketing approaches are required in our industry. These include the following five unique approaches in hospitality and travel marketing:

1. Use of more than 4 Ps
2. Greater significance of word-of-mouth information
3. More use of emotional appeals in promotions
4. Greater difficulties with new-concept testing
5. Increased importance of relationships with complementary organizations

1. **Use of More Than 4 Ps.** Most books identify the 4 Ps (product, place, promotion, price) as marketing mix elements. One of the assumptions of this book is that there are another 4 Ps in our industry: people, packaging, programming, and partnership.

   a. *People.* Hospitality and travel is a people industry. It is a business of **people** (staff or hosts) providing services to **people** (customers or guests), who share these services with other people (other customers). Industry marketers have to be very selective both in terms of whom they hire—particularly customer-contact staff—and who they target as customers. Some potential employees are just not suitable because their people skills are poor. Some customer groups are not appropriate because their presence conflicts with the enjoyment of others.

   Technically, employees are part of the product offered by hospitality and travel organizations (Figure 2.8). However, they are different enough from inanimate products and of such great importance in marketing that they require separate consideration. Staff recruitment, selection, orientation, training, supervision, and motivation all play an exceptionally important role in our industry.

   Managing the customer mix or portfolio, and how customers behave, are also very important to service marketers.[6] One reason is that customers are often part of the experience purchased. Customers share airplanes, restaurants, hotels, attractions, buses, and resorts with other customers. Who they are, how they dress, and how these customers behave are part of the experience. Customers have to follow stricter dress and behavior codes in most hospitality and travel

FIGURE 2.8 Staff have a major influence on guest satisfaction in hospitality and travel.

businesses than they do in grocery stores. Marketing managers not only have to think about which target markets will produce the best profits, but also if these customers are compatible.

b. *Packaging and Programming.* These two related techniques— **packaging and programming**—are significant for two reasons. First, they are very customer-oriented concepts. They satisfy a variety of customer needs, including the desire for convenience found in all-inclusive packages. Second, they help businesses cope with the problems of matching demand with supply or reducing unsold inventory. Unsold rooms and seats and unused staff time are like pouring a rare wine down the sink. They cannot be recaptured for re-consumption. Packaging and programming can help to stimulate demand. Weekend packages at downtown hotels, early-bird discounts for seniors in restaurants, spa retreats at resorts, and residents' days at theme parks are all good examples. Marketing creativity is at a premium in our industry because of the perishable nature of the services.

c. *Partnership.* Cooperative marketing efforts among complementary hospitality and travel organizations are referred to as **partnerships**. It is suggested as the eighth P because of the interdependence of many organizations in satisfying customers' needs and wants. This complementary nature of organizations can be either positive or negative. Customer satisfaction often hinges on the actions of other organizations over which we have no direct control. Relationships with complementary organizations need to be carefully managed and monitored. It is in the best interests of the industry's **suppliers** (the lodging, restaurant and foodservice, cruise line, car rental, attraction and event, and casino and gaming sectors) to maintain good relations with **travel trade intermediaries** (the retail travel agency, tour operator and wholesaler, corporate travel, incentive travel planning, convention/meeting planning, online travel company, and GDS sectors) and **carriers** (the airline, railway, ferry, bus and motor coach, and canal sectors). The opposite is also true. When various parts of the industry cooperate more effectively, the result is predictable—more satisfied customers. When they do not cooperate, the result is equally obvious.

Marketers also need to understand the value of cooperation and interdependency at the travel destination itself. A travel experience is shaped by many organizations as a destination. When these organizations see that they are all in the same boat, the result again is usually more satisfied customers.

2. **Greater Significance of Word-of-Mouth Information.** The opportunities for customers to sample services prior to purchasing them are limited in the hospitality and travel industry. People have to rent hotel rooms, buy airplane tickets, and pay meal checks to find out if these services meet their needs. The rule is, "You have to buy to try." This places a premium on word-of-mouth or W-O-M (information about a service experience passed from past to potential customers). Because there are few sampling or testing opportunities in our industry, people have to rely partly on the advice of others, including friends, relatives, and business associates (Figure 2.9). Positive word-of-mouth information is crucial to the success of most hospitality and travel organizations.

Providing a consistent quality of service and associated facilities is a key ingredient in getting positive word-of-mouth. It is also a basic fundamental of marketing in this industry. The importance of managing experience clues was discussed earlier. Inconsistent experience clues detract from the quality of a customer's experience. A waitperson with a soiled uniform in a top-quality restaurant or a so-called luxury hotel with few in-room guest amenities are two simple examples of inconsistency. Consistency in these experience clues ensures that customers leave with a consistent impression of an organization's quality standards.

Image copyright Gautier Willaume, 2008. Used under license from Shutterstock.com

FIGURE 2.9 Word-of-mouth has a powerful effect on people's choices of hospitality and travel services.

Consistency is also needed in multi-unit organizations, because customers tend to make decisions about the entire company based on their experiences in individual units. Most packaged-goods firms have successfully developed separate brand images for their products. If customers have bad experiences with one brand, it does not usually carry over to the company's other brands. The customer does not associate the brand with the parent company or its other brands as closely as they do in our industry. A bad experience at one Westin property, for example, can create a negative predisposition to all sister properties in the Starwood chain. Branding as a concept is only in its infancy in our industry.

3. **More Use of Emotional Appeals in Promotions.** Because of the intangible nature of services, customers tend to make more use of emotional appeals when they buy. This means that it is often more effective to emphasize these appeals in promotional campaigns. In order to make a hotel or restaurant chain, airline, travel agency, destination, package, or attraction appeal to customers, it must be given a distinctive personality. It is not enough to talk about the number of guest rooms, aircraft types, ride configurations, and other rational facts and figures. A dash of color and personality must be added. Thus the phrase *The Fun Ships* conjures up the Carnival Cruise name, United Airlines becomes *The Friendly Skies*, and so

on. Companies must be given personalities with which customers can associate.

4. **Greater Difficulties with New-Concept Testing.** Services can be copied more easily than products, and this makes it essential for hospitality and travel organizations to be ever-alert for new and innovative customer services. Leading corporations are aware of this and are constantly test marketing new concepts. With the increasing dynamics of global society, it is unwise to stand still in our business.

5. **Increased Importance of Relationships with Complementary Organizations.** There are three unique relationships among organizations in our industry that have a significant impact on the marketing of hospitality and travel services. These relationships are described in the following paragraphs.

   a. *Suppliers, Carriers, Travel Trade Intermediaries, and Destination Marketing Organizations.* Suppliers are organizations that operate facilities, attractions and events, ground transportation, and other support services within or between travel destinations. Facilities include the lodging, food and beverage, and support services (retail shopping, tour guiding, and recreation). Attractions and events are divided into six categories: natural resource, climatic, cultural, historical, ethnic, and accessible.[7] Ground transportation organizations provide car rental, taxi and limousine, bus, and other related services within destinations. Carriers are those companies providing transportation to the destination. They include airlines and railway, bus and motor coach, ferry, and canal companies. The travel trade contains the intermediaries that suppliers and carriers use to get their services to customers, including retail travel agents and tour wholesales. **Destination marketing organizations (DMOs)** market their cities, areas, regions, counties, states or provinces, and countries to travel trade intermediaries and individual and group travelers. They work on behalf of the suppliers and carriers serving their destinations. Through various types of packages and tours, the services of these four industry groups (suppliers, carriers, travel trade intermediaries, and DMOs) are combined for greater customer appeal and convenience.

   Although some tour or package providers are at greater financial risk than others, all have a stake in the package's success or failure. All are mutually dependent from a marketing standpoint. If the airline or hotel fails to honor reservations, this reflects badly on the travel agent and tour wholesaler. If the travel agent misrepresents the resort's or cruise line's package, the customer develops a negative impression of the resort or cruise ship. Hospitality and travel marketers in different organizations need to appreciate their mutual dependence and to ensure that their partners consistently deliver a level of service that is equal to their own.

b. *The Destination Mix Concept.* The **destination mix** is another unique, relational concept with five components: attractions and events, facilities, infrastructure, transportation, and hospitality resources.[8] Attractions and events play the pivotal role in travel destinations—they draw visitors. There are both business and pleasure travel attractions. Business travelers are drawn to a destination by the industrial and commercial bases in communities, while pleasure travelers are drawn by the six attraction categories mentioned earlier. Facility and ground transportation organizations such as hotels, restaurants, and car rental firms must realize that the demand for their service is derived from the demand for attractions. Without the commercial/industrial base or pleasure-traveler attractions a large portion of their business would disappear.

c. *Visitors and Residents.* A third unique and important relationship exists between visitors and local residents. Both intermingle and share the same services and facilities. Positive resident attitudes are a major plus for the hospitality and travel industry. When developed, this attitude can enhance the marketing efforts of industry organizations. The opposite is equally true if residents have unfriendly or hostile attitudes toward visitors. Non-profit organizations, such as DMOs, need to be especially aware of this important relationship.

Figure 2.10 shows each of the three relationships just discussed. Managing these three relationships is an added role that hospitality and

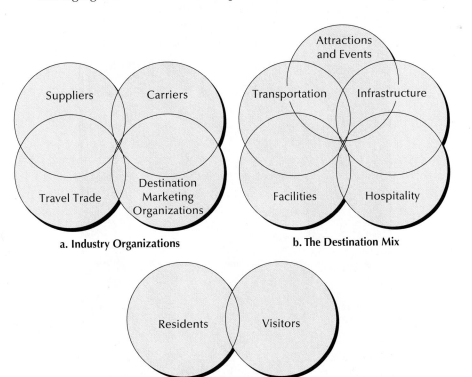

a. **Industry Organizations**

b. **The Destination Mix**

c. **Visitor-Resident Interaction**

FIGURE 2.10 Three unique relationships in hospitality and travel.

travel marketers must play. With the first two relationships, the key is to understand that others outside one's own organization have a direct impact on our customers' satisfaction. We not only have to be consistent in providing our own services, but we must also ensure that other partners do likewise. The third relationship, the interaction of visitors with a destination's residents, must also receive careful attention from marketers. Unfriendly or inhospitable local residents can spoil the visitor's experience (Figure 2.11). Terrorism and serious crimes committed against visitors can have a very adverse effect on tourism. From the resident perspective, increasing tourism can cause a feeling of resentment toward visitors because of the overcrowding of popular attractions, traffic congestion, degradation of natural features, increased commercialization, and increasing crime rates.

FIGURE 2.11 Visitors often ask residents for directions and other information.

Image copyright Factoria singular fotografia, 2009. Used under license from Shutterstock.com

Chapter Conclusion

There is a growing recognition that services marketing is a separate and distinct branch of marketing. This is based on the belief that unique marketing approaches are required in the service industries, of which hospitality and travel are just one element. Services share common features that make them quite different from products. Services are intangible, highly perishable, inseparable from providers, and difficult to cost. They have different production processes and distribution channels.

Marketing in the services industry has evolved at a slower pace than it has in the manufacturing and packaged-goods industry, and in several instances has been influenced by government regulation. Service managers and executives have been more reluctant to adopt the core principles of marketing.

The hospitality and travel industry is, above all, a people industry. Those organizations that have climbed to the top are known for their high concern for both customer and employee satisfaction.

REVIEW QUESTIONS

1. What does services marketing mean?
2. Should services be marketed exactly the same as manufactured products and packaged goods? Why or why not?
3. What are generic and contextual differences between services and products? Explain the meaning of each concept.
4. What are the six generic and six contextual differences between the marketing of services and products?
5. Are these differences expected to continue in the future? Why or why not?
6. What are the eight specific differences affecting the marketing of hospitality and travel services?
7. This book suggests four additional Ps in marketing hospitality and travel services. What are they?
8. What are the four other unique approaches required in hospitality and travel marketing?
9. What are three key relationships among organizations and individuals in the hospitality and travel industry?

CHAPTER ASSIGNMENTS

1. You have just been hired by an automobile manufacturing company that has recently acquired a chain of resort properties. One of your initial tasks is to meet with the company's corporate marketing executives and to explain the difference between marketing resorts and marketing cars. Highlight the points you will make, including the common approaches both types of marketing share and the unique approaches required to market resorts.

2. Your instructor has asked you to visit the local supermarket and other retail stores and to bring back to class some items that demonstrate the generic differences between services and products. What would you collect, and how would you demonstrate the differences?

3. You have been asked to conduct a workshop in your community to highlight the close relationships between various organizations and individuals involved with hospitality and travel. Who would you invite? What things would you emphasize in the workshop and how would you do this? How would the workshop effectively demonstrate the importance of cooperation and mutual dependency among various organizations and individuals?

4. A major manufacturing company has just acquired a chain of travel agencies. You have been hired as the marketing director of the new travel agency division and have been asked to explain the differences between the distribution systems for products and services. What differences would you emphasize and how would you put your points across effectively?

WEB RESOURCES

AJ Hackett, http://www.ajhackett.com/
Best Western, http://www.bestwestern.com/
Burger King, http://www.burgerking.com/
Dollywood, http://www.dollywood.com/
Four Seasons Hotels and Resorts, http://www.fourseasons.com/
Harley Owners Group, http://www.harley-davidson.com/
KFC, http://www.kfc.com/
K-Paul's Louisiana Kitchen, http://www.kpauls.com/
Marriott, http://www.marriott.com
Shangri-La, http://www.shangri-la.com
Skyline Chili, http://www.skylinechili.com/
Starwood Hotels & Resorts Worldwide, http://www.starwoodhotels.com/
United Airlines, http://www.united.com/
VisitBritain, http://www.visitbritain.com/
Wendy's, http://www.wendys.com/
Westin, http://www.starwoodhotels.com/
The World Factbook, Central Intelligence Agency, https://www.cia.gov/library/

REFERENCES

1. Central Intelligence Agency. 2008. *The World Factbook 2008.*
2. Lovelock, Christopher H., and Jochen Wirtz. 2007. *Services Marketing: People, Technology, Strategy.* 6th ed. Pearson International Edition. Upper Saddle River, N.J.: Pearson Education International, 16–21.

3. Lovelock, Christopher H., and Jochen Wirtz. 2007. *Services Marketing: People, Technology, Strategy.* 6th ed. Pearson International Edition. Upper Saddle River, N.J.: Pearson Education International, 19–20.

4. Lovelock, Christopher H., and Jochen Wirtz. 2007. *Services Marketing: People, Technology, Strategy.* 6th ed. Pearson International Edition. Upper Saddle River, N.J.: Pearson Education International, 16.

5. Berry, Leonard L., Lewis P. Carbone, and Stephan H. Haekel. 2002. "Managing the Total Customer Experience." *MIT Sloan Management Review*, 43(3), 85–89.

6. Lovelock, Christopher H., and Jochen Wirtz. 2007. *Services Marketing: People, Technology, Strategy.* 6th ed. Pearson International Edition. Upper Saddle River, N.J.: Pearson Education International, 20.

7. Mill, Robert Christie, and Alastair M. Morrison. 2009. *The Tourism System.* 6th ed. Dubuque, Iowa: Kendall Hunt Publishing Company.

8. Mill, Robert Christie, and Alastair M. Morrison. 2009. *The Tourism System.* 6th ed. Dubuque, Iowa: Kendall Hunt Publishing Company.

chapter 3

The Hospitality and Travel Marketing System
What Is Marketing?

O V E R V I E W

Is there a common way to market all the diverse organizations within the hospitality and travel industry? This chapter starts by exploring this question and suggests that there is a systematic process that everyone can use—the hospitality and travel marketing system. It describes the general characteristics of all systems and identifies the benefits of using a systematic marketing approach. The need for both long- and short-term planning is emphasized. The chapter ends by describing the five-step hospitality and travel marketing system.

O B J E C T I V E S

Having read this chapter, you should be able to:

- Explain the different definitions of the hospitality and travel industry, and why these are insufficient in guiding marketing for our industry.

- Describe what a system is.

- Explain the hospitality and travel marketing system.

- List the four fundamentals of the hospitality and travel marketing system.

- List the benefits of using the hospitality and travel marketing system.

- List and arrange, in order, the five key questions in the hospitality and travel marketing system that must be answered.

- Define long- and short-term marketing planning.

- Distinguish between a strategic market plan and a marketing plan.

KEY TERMS

feedback

hospitality and travel
    marketing system

interdependent

long-term planning

macro-system

marketing plan

micro-system

mission and mission statement

open systems

planning

plans

relationship marketing

short-term planning

strategic market plan

strategic marketing planning

system

vision and vision statement

You may have been attracted to the hospitality and travel industry because of its great diversity. It's a fabulous, exciting, and wide-ranging industry. For example, lodging businesses range from the smallest motels to the mega-hotels and resorts that contain several thousand rooms. Foodservice establishments run the gamut from elegant, table-service restaurants to roadside hamburger stands. There are small, local travel agencies with a staff of three or four, as well as major national brands such as American Express and Carlson Wagonlit Travel. Air services range from global companies such as Lufthansa, KLM, British Airways, American, United, Northwest, Air Canada, Qantas, and Cathay Pacific to one-man bush pilots. Among attractions, there are theme parks such as Disney World and Universal Studios, and small museums with a few hundred attendees a year.

Chapter 1 reviewed core principles of marketing common to all for-profit and non-profit groups. Chapter 2 discussed features shared by all hospitality and travel organizations. Despite this common ground, you are probably still thinking that totally different marketing approaches are needed within our industry. What if we told you that you are both right and wrong? You are right in thinking that businesses as different as hotels and travel agencies need to customize their services, prices, distribution systems, and promotions to fit their guests. But there is a systematic process to marketing that every hospitality and travel organization can use—the **hospitality and travel marketing system**. Think about it. You are going to learn this process and will be able to use it in any facet of our industry. Before describing this system, we thought you should be aware of the confusion that exists in our industry about who we are.

Many Different Approaches to Defining our Industry

What exactly are we marketing then? Unfortunately, the list of definitions for the hospitality and travel industry is almost never-ending. As you travel across this world, these definitions change and it becomes even more confusing.

As someone studying this industry, you might wonder which definition is correct, or if they are all right. Before answering this, let's look at some of these definitions. Once you see them, you will know why a systems approach to hospitality and travel marketing is needed. This is what the author concluded as well after being thoroughly confused like you!

It's the Hospitality Industry!

Many people working in the industry as well as academics call it the hospitality industry, and this is especially true in the United States and in the United Kingdom. You may be studying in a Department of Hospitality Management, or perhaps it's Hospitality and Tourism Management (HTM). The Travel Industry Dictionary defines the hospitality industry as "the hotel, restaurant, entertainment, and resort industry."[1] Most of your professors would probably agree with this and add that the hospitality industry includes lodging, restaurants and foodservice, and casinos and gaming. In the United Kingdom, the British Hospitality Association (BHA) is the national trade association for hotels, restaurants, and caterers. It also includes The Restaurant Association.[2] Cruise lines might also fit in here since they provide beds, meals and beverages. However, the Cruise Lines International Association says it represents the cruise industry.[3]

It's the Travel and/or Tourism Industry!

Other organizations and writers suggest there is either a travel industry, a tourism industry, or a travel and tourism industry. The United Nations World Tourism Organization (UNWTO) states "tourism has become one of the major players in international commerce, and represents at the same time one of the main income sources for many developing countries."[4] So for the UNWTO, it's the tourism industry. The World Travel & Tourism Council (WTTC) identifies its mission as "to raise awareness of the economic and social contribution of Travel & Tourism and to work with governments on policies that unlock the industry's potential to create jobs and generate prosperity."[5] For the WTTC then, it's the travel and tourism industry. The U.S. Travel Association (USTA) states it is "a non-profit trade organization that represents and speaks for the common interests of the $740 billion U.S. travel industry."[6] Then for USTA, it's the travel industry. Travel Weekly agrees with USTA and bills itself as "The National Newspaper of the Travel Industry."[7]

It's the Restaurant or Foodservice or Food Service Industry!

The National Restaurant Association (NRA) in the United States represents the restaurant industry.[8] You might be thinking, is this not part of the hospitality industry that we just defined? The equivalent organization to NRA in Canada is the Canadian Restaurant and Foodservices Association (CRFA). The CRFA says it represents restaurants, bars, cafeterias, and social and contract caterers, as well as accommodation, entertainment, and institutional foodservice.[9]

According to the U.S. Bureau of Labor Statistics, the Food Services and Drinking Places subsector prepares "meals, snacks, and beverages to customer order for immediate on-premises and off-premises consumption. There is a wide range of establishments in these industries. Some provide food and drink only; while others provide various combinations of seating space, waiter/waitress services and incidental amenities, such as limited entertainment. The industries in the subsector are grouped based on the type and level of services provided. The industry groups are full-service restaurants; limited-service eating places; special food services, such as food service contractors, caterers, and mobile food services; and drinking places."[10]

It's the Lodging Industry!

Not to be outdone by their restaurant and foodservice colleagues, there are those who see themselves as part of the lodging industry. Others have an even narrower focus, using such terms as the hotel industry, the resort industry, and the campground industry.

It Depends Where You Are!

If you live outside the United States in places such as Canada, Australia, or New Zealand, you will be exposed to another layer of industry labels. In Canada, Australia, and New Zealand, the term *tourism industry* is well-accepted as the umbrella term for the entire industry, including hospitality businesses.

It's Not an Industry at All!

The definitions that you have just read are all created by people in our industry. However, many economists and statisticians disagree with all of the previous definitions. They have a different way of classifying industries and, in North America, this is known as the North American Industry Classification System (NAICS). The North American Industry Classification System (NAICS), which was developed for the Unites States, Canada, and Mexico, shows that hospitality and travel organizations are scattered among several NAICS codes. Code 72 is Accommodation and Food Services while Code 71 is for Arts, Entertainment, and Recreation, which includes theme parks. Airlines and other transportation carriers are under Code 48 (Transportation), travel agencies and tour operators are within Code 56 (Administrative and Support and Waste Management and Remediation Services), and CVBs fit in either Codes 92 (Public Administration) or 81 (Other Services, except Public Administration).[11]

The NAICS is a very convenient way of looking at the industrial structure of a country. However, by neatly fitting every business or organization into a box, the strong relationships that exist among hospitality and travel organizations are not reflected. This system also ignores situations in which an organization fits into more than one category.

Did You Know?

Why is so Much Tourism Marketing Power "Down Under"?

- Tourism Australia (TA) is responsible for marketing Australia worldwide as a tourism destination. Many experts consider TA to be one of the best destination marketing organizations in the world.
- TA's mission is to stimulate sustainable international and domestic demand for Australian tourism experiences through industry leadership and coordination, and to influence the actions of the industry's tourism and travel marketing by:

  - championing a clear destination marketing strategy;
  - articulating and promoting a compelling tourism destination brand;
  - facilitating sales by engaging and supporting the distribution network;
  - identifying and supporting the development of unique Australian tourism experiences, especially indigenous;
  - promoting Australia as a desirable destination for business events;
  - gathering and communicating reliable market intelligence and insights for improved decision making; and
  - working with partners who can extend Tourism Australia's influence.

Source: Tourism Australia. (2008). *Tourism Australia's Mission.* **http://www.tourism. australia.com/**

No Universally Accepted Definition of the Industry

What can you learn from these different definitions? You should see that there is no universally accepted definition of the industry that this book covers. The word *industry* itself is used very loosely. Both people in the industry and educators have a sense of unity and belonging in using a common definition of the field. Influencing legislation and government policy is another practical reason for dividing the industry into groups that share common characteristics. Thus, airlines belong to the Air Transport Association of America, travel agents to the American Society of Travel Agents, lodging facilities to the American Hotel & Lodging Association, restaurants to the National Restaurant Association, theme parks to the International Association of Amusement Parks and Attractions, cruise lines to Cruise Lines International Association, DMOs to Destination Marketing Association International, and so on.

FIGURE 3.1
Hospitality and travel marketing covers all these sectors of the industry.

SUPPLIER SECTORS	CARRIER SECTORS
• Lodging • Restaurant and Foodservice • Cruise Line • Car Rental • Attraction and Event • Casino and Gaming • (Includes hospitality) 1	• Airline • Railway • Ferry • Bus and Motorcoach • Canal 2
TRAVEL TRADE INTERMEDIARY SECTORS	DESTINATION MARKETING ORGANIZATION (DMO) SECTORS
• Retail Travel Agency • Tour Operator and Wholesaler • Corporate Travel • Incentive Travel Planning • Convention/Meeting Planning • Online Travel Company • Global Distribution System (GDS) 3	• National, state, provincial, and territorial DMO • City and county DMO 4

Figure 3.1 shows how this book defines hospitality and travel. While also not a perfect definition of our industry, it does classify all the groups and sectors by their main function: (1) suppliers, (2) carriers, (3) travel trade intermediaries, and (4) destination marketing organizations (DMOs). You will find a more detailed description of each of these in Chapter 10.

In summary, the hospitality and travel industry seems to be suffering from an "identity disorder." While all of these definitions can be justified in some ways, they are insufficient in guiding the marketing approaches for our industry. They lack a holistic or "big picture" perspective on hospitality and travel. The industry gets splintered into smaller sub-groups, rather than as being viewed as a large, interrelated group of businesses and organizations. This book recommends that the systems approach be used as the basis for effective marketing across the many sectors of the hospitality and travel industry. As you read on, you will see why this approach unites, rather than fragments our industry.

The Systems Approach
Definition

The systems approach is an alternative way of looking at industries and organizations. A **system** is a collection of interrelated parts that work together to achieve common objectives. Our industry consists of a group of interrelated organizations with a common purpose and goals. Likewise, each individual organization is a system—a collection of interrelated departments, divisions, or activities with the same overall purpose and goals. What is it that our industry and its component organizations have in common? It is the satisfaction of customer needs while these customers are out of their homes (eating at a local restaurant) or out of their normal environments (staying at a hotel out of town). Customers may be thousands of miles from home on an overseas trip, or simply down the road at a local fast-food restaurant. Our industry is set up to meet all types of away-from-home needs.

There is a macro-system and many micro-systems in hospitality and travel. The **macro-system** exists at the hospitality and travel industry level. As you saw in Chapter 2, there are a number of unique relationships among hospitality and travel organizations. It might be helpful for you to think of the hospitality and travel macro-system as being like a car. The attractions, for both pleasure and business travelers, are the engine of that car. Without an engine, a car does not run. Without attractions, a hospitality and travel destination is unlikely to draw visitors. However, an engine alone does not constitute a car! A chassis, axles, four tires, a body, seats, and many other parts must be added. Likewise, a hospitality and travel destination needs facilities (hotels, restaurants, shopping), transportation and infrastructure, and hospitality resources to run with the maximum effectiveness. Those who operate attractions and events need help from other suppliers of facilities, transportation carriers, and travel trade intermediaries in attracting customers and meeting customer needs.

Micro-systems are found at the individual organization level. This book primarily deals with micro-systems and discusses how individual hospitality and travel organizations market their services. The term *hospitality and travel marketing system* is used to describe a micro-system—a process for marketing an organization that involves everyone who works for that organization.

Characteristics of Systems in the Hospitality and Travel Industry

To understand marketing, you must know the characteristics of systems. There are six major characteristics of the systems in our industry (Figure 3.2):

1. **Openness.** The industry and its organizations are **open systems**. Unlike mechanical and electrical closed systems, open systems are not rigid, and the system parts are not precisely organized in a definite way. These systems are dynamic, constantly undergoing change. People are always coming up with new and creative ways of marketing hospitality and travel services. Airlines' frequent-flyer and hotels' frequent guest programs are two examples from the 1980s. Global partnerships and strategic alliances among airlines, hotel companies, travel agencies, tour operators, and destination marketing organizations were the hallmark of the 1990s. The Internet and e-commerce started to become a way of life in the mid-1990s. Since 2000, the hospitality and travel industry has been challenged by a string of events well beyond its control, including 9-11 and other terrorist attacks, SARS, the impacts of many hurricanes including Katrina, and tsunamis (including the so-called "financial tsunami" in the second half of 2008). The external, strategic environment

FIGURE 3.2
Characteristics of hospitality and travel systems.

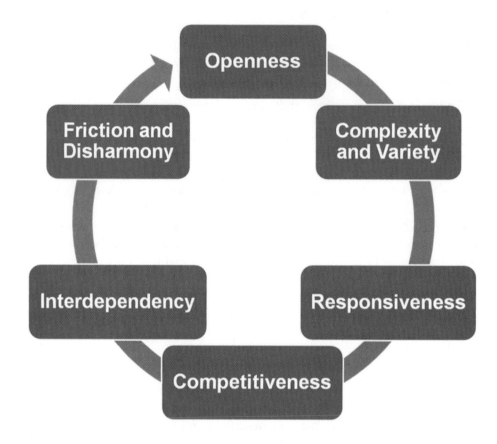

continually affects our systems, reshaping the way we do business. For example, e-tickets developed because of people's need for greater convenience in air travel, and were supported by technology advancements.

This book recommends a carefully sequenced series of steps in marketing—the hospitality and travel marketing system. But it does not suggest a rigid approach to marketing. The steps can be compared to a human skeleton. They are a basic framework required for effective functioning. A skeleton must have body tissue and a mind before it can be considered to be a human being. Likewise, each organization must have a unique personality and set of marketing activities to survive.

2. **Complexity and Variety.** A great variety of hospitality and travel organizations exist. They range from very small businesses to multinational conglomerates. The interrelationships among the different organizations are complex. One prime example is the diversity of distribution channels that exists. A resort can market directly online and offline to potential guests or it can select from a variety of intermediaries, including retail travel agencies, online travel companies, tour wholesalers and operators, convention/meeting planners, and incentive travel planners. There are many different ways to promote, sell, and price hospitality and travel services. No fixed success formula exists.

3. **Responsiveness.** The marketplace is constantly changing. So, too, must our industry and organizations change. We must be responsive to change, or we will not survive. All systems must have **feedback** mechanisms. Information must be gathered from customers and others to make decisions about changes in both customer needs and competitive activities. Standing still in our industry is fatal. Marketing research provides a nourishing supply of information to help us adapt and survive.

4. **Competitiveness.** Ours is an industry of intense competition. New organizations throw their hats into the ring almost daily. Competitive power and intensity increase as large corporations increase in size and market share. Smaller organizations collaborate to improve their competitive positions. They form consortia, referral groups, and marketing cooperatives and make other joint efforts to gain more clout in the marketplace. Change from within the industry macro-system is as important as change caused by external factors. The 1990s saw the true beginning of global competition in the hospitality and travel industry. National boundaries lost importance as organizations formed strategic marketing alliances and partnerships with other organizations both within and outside of the hospitality and travel business. The Star Alliance, **one**world®, and SkyTeam are good examples of major airlines joining together to be more globally competitive. Now in the 2000s, most of the major brand names in hospitality and travel are truly global companies.

5. **Interdependency.** Our industry (the macro-system) includes a variety of **interdependent** and interrelated businesses and organizations involved in serving the needs of customers who are away from home. They include suppliers (lodging, restaurants, theme parks, etc.), carriers (airlines, passenger railways, etc.), and travel trade intermediaries (e.g., retail travel agencies, tour operators, etc.) within the hospitality and travel industry. Other organizations involved are government tourism promotion agencies, convention and visitors bureaus (CVBs), and other destination marketing organizations (DMOs).

   Many people have a myopic view of the scope of our industry. A broader perspective is required. Many businesses and organizations, even countries, are interdependent. They complement one another, working together to produce results greater than the sum of their individual efforts. A travel agent may never book a meal for a customer at a McDonald's restaurant, but may have made the customer's reservation at the nearby hotel. A full understanding of marketing in this industry requires knowledge and acceptance of these interrelationships. **Relationship marketing** is a term that emphasizes the importance of building long-term relationships with customers and with other organizations in the distribution chain.

   Interdependency also exists at the individual organization level. Marketing is not the only function of hospitality and travel managers. Other areas of responsibility are operations, finance and accounting, human resources management, and maintenance activities. Marketing

INTERNET MARKETING

Selling Individual Incentives to Corporations on the Internet

Marriott's website points out that gifts, no matter how nice, are not as powerful as free trips in getting people engaged and motivated. This is the basic idea behind the concept of incentive travel.

- Incentive travel is also a great example of the need for a "whole system" approach to marketing hospitality, travel and tourism since almost all parts of the industry participate to product a satisfied guest.
- Marriott's Individual Incentives are promoted on the company's website toward corporations. These give individual company employees rewards in which they can stay at any of Marriott's 2,700 properties.
- Marriott provides some interesting case studies on companies that have used its individual incentives. For example, British Airways used them to coax their Executive Club frequent flyers to book flights during a difficult time for the worldwide airline industry.
- By providing the basic information on the Internet for corporations to study, the next step is for the companies to contact Marriott's sales staff to discuss how to use the individual incentives.

Source: Marriott. 2008. **http://www.marriott.com/incentives/travel.mi/**

Student Questions

1. What are the advantages for Marriott in using the Internet to introduce its individual incentive programs to corporations?
2. What types of destinations do you think are most attractive to people who are given these individual incentive rewards?
3. Why does it require a "whole system" approach to make these customers have the best experience at a hotel and its surrounding destination?
4. How can hotel chains like Marriott use the Web and e-mail to more effectively market individual incentives to both the companies and potential winners of the rewards?

has to be coordinated with these other areas and is dependent on them for its success.

6. **Friction and Disharmony.** Within both our industry and individual organizations, there are many points of conflict, stresses, and tensions. We do not have perfect systems. They do not perform exactly as we think they should. Airlines and retail travel agencies have had a strained relationship, as the airlines have trimmed costs, and introduced online bookings at airline websites. Lodging companies are increasingly concerned about how much room inventory is controlled by online travel

companies. Hotels and resorts are always on their guard for meetings and conventions that do not fulfill their room blocks. Destinations and businesses that should be cooperating are working against one another.

This imperfect world of hospitality and travel extends to individual organizations. Unhealthy internal competition, personality clashes, and communication problems cause the system to function differently than it should. Marketing can promise the customer something that cannot be delivered due to these types of internal problems. Much of the job of marketing is showing everyone that they are all in the same boat.

The Hospitality and Travel Marketing System

Figure 3.3 shows the hospitality and travel system model. This model applies to all organizations, from the largest to the smallest. Whether we are marketing hotels restaurants, travel agencies, or airlines, five key questions require answers. They are:

1. Where are we now?
2. Where would we like to be?
3. How do we get there?
4. How do we make sure we get there?
5. How do we know if we got there?

FIGURE 3.3
Hospitality and travel marketing system model.

System Fundamentals

Before discussing each of the questions in the system model, you need to have some idea of the system's fundamentals and benefits. There are four fundamentals of the system:

1. Strategic marketing planning
2. Marketing orientation
3. Differences between product and services marketing
4. Understanding customer behavior

1. **Strategic Marketing Planning.** The hospitality and travel industry is very dynamic, and is constantly experiencing change both from within and from outside. Long-term planning is required to guarantee success. "Those who live in the present will perish in the very near future" is a most appropriate statement about our industry. **Strategic marketing planning** is the term used to describe the process of developing long-term (three to five or more years) plans for marketing. It involves selecting a definite course of action for long-term survival and growth. Using strategic marketing planning is the first of the system's fundamentals.

2. **Marketing Orientation.** Adopting a marketing orientation is the second fundamental. This was discussed in Chapter 1. It means that satisfying customer needs and wants must have the top priority in an organization.

3. **Differences between Product and Services Marketing.** There are differences between marketing services and marketing products. Ours is a business of marketing and providing services. Using the hospitality and travel marketing system assumes that we are aware of these differences. Chapter 2 reviewed this subject.

4. **Understanding Customer Behavior.** The fourth fundamental is the need to understand customer behavior. This is the main focus of Chapter 4. The system is most effectively used if we fully appreciate the personal and interpersonal factors that influence customer behavior.

Benefits of Using the System

There are three main benefits for organizations that use the hospitality and travel marketing system:

1. Priority on planning
2. Logical flow of efforts
3. Better balance of marketing activities

1. **Priority on Planning. Planning** is a must in today's volatile business environments. Organizations that use the hospitality and travel marketing system are forced to plan ahead and to anticipate future events. If we can be sure of just one thing, it is that tomorrow will not be exactly like today. Planning one year ahead is not enough. Multi-year, strategic market plans are required.

Whether **plans** are short-term (two years or less) or long-term (more than two years), they have at least six basic purposes:

a. Identifying alternative marketing approaches
b. Maintaining uniqueness
c. Creating desirable situations
d. Avoiding undesirable situations
e. Adapting to the unexpected
f. Facilitating the measurement, monitoring, and evaluation of results

The first purpose is to identify all alternative marketing approaches available. There is always more than one way to achieve objectives. It is essential to consider them all and to pinpoint the most effective approach.

The second purpose is to maintain an organization's uniqueness. Part of the secret of marketing success is having customers perceive that we provide something different. Creating this image means work and maintaining it requires even more effort.

The third purpose is to create desirable conditions. These include maintaining a high awareness of the business or destination among potential customers, making effective and balanced use of marketing resources and techniques, capitalizing on new market opportunities, adding services that increase market share (proportion of total demand available), and taking full advantage of cooperative marketing ventures.

Avoiding undesirable future conditions is the fourth purpose. Typical situations that most organizations want to avoid include losing market share, continuing to provide services that dilute profitability, and conflicting with interrelated organizations and competitors.

The fifth purpose is to be in a better position to adapt to the unexpected. We noted earlier that the hospitality and travel marketing system was an open system. It can be dramatically affected by economic, social, cultural, political/legal, technological, and competitive changes and events. Organizations have to be prepared for the unexpected and forward planning helps.

A good plan facilitates the measurement, monitoring, and evaluation of results, since it incorporates measurable objectives. Success can be judged by determining how close the organization comes to achieving these objectives.

2. **Logical Flow of Efforts.** The second system benefit is that it produces a logical flow of effort. Marketing budgets and human resources are more effectively used because the right questions are asked at the right time. Many organizations become lazy and skip over basic marketing questions such as "Where are we now?" and "Where would we like to be?" They jump into implementing a marketing plan before they consider the basics. Others fail to coordinate and control marketing efforts. They just let things happen. They ignore the question, "How do we make sure we get there?" Often no feedback mechanism is used. The organization has no idea if their marketing is effective or not. They do not ask the question, "How do

we know if we got there?" As you can see, the five key marketing questions in the system logically flow from one to the other.

3. **Better Balance of Marketing Activities.** A better balance in marketing activities results from using the hospitality and travel marketing system. The five questions are given equal priority. All available marketing techniques are carefully considered. There is a constant re-evaluation of activities, rather than a continuous repetition of past efforts.

Effective marketing decisions are based on sound research. The hospitality and travel marketing system assumes that organizations recognize the value of marketing research and realize its great benefits. Pinpointing new marketing opportunities is one of these benefits. Research helps us identify new services and customer groups. It lets us know where we stand relative to competitors. Research assists in measuring the results of marketing activities. It shows us what worked and what did not. Research also helps us understand what has been most effective, and points out our mistakes. We learn how customers look at us. We find different ways to increase their satisfaction. And finally, research provides a constant source of nourishment for the hospitality and travel system.

The system is used continuously and experience is gained from every use. Something different is learned each time.

Steps in the System

Most textbooks suggest that there is a logical and sequential flow to marketing. However, the authors of these books try to outdo one another in the sophistication of the terminology they use for each step and technique. Students are left confused by the jargon of marketing and wonder whose definitions and terms are correct. We will not add to your confusion! The hospitality and travel marketing system uses a more commonsense and practical approach that reduces marketing to five basic steps expressed as questions that have to be answered.

Let's start looking at the system by comparing it to a commercial airline flight. Try to answer the following questions:

1. Does the flight crew of a commercial aircraft know where they are when their plane lands?
2. Does the flight crew know where they are going as their plane takes off?
3. Does the flight crew have a flight plan for each trip?
4. Do the pilot and copilot monitor their progress and make adjustments to their original flight plan as necessary?
5. Does the pilot evaluate each trip and fill in a flight log?

You should have answered yes to all five questions. If you did not, look them over again. We think you will agree that we are right. Why is a commercial airline flight like the marketing of a hospitality or travel organization? The answer is simple. The key questions that ensure a safe and successful flight are identical to those needed for effective marketing. They are shown in Figure 3.4.

FIGURE 3.4 The hospitality and travel marketing system and airline flight analogy

STEPS	HOSPITALITY AND TRAVEL MARKETING	AIRLINE FLIGHT
1. Where are we now?	• Current situation	• Current airport location
2. Where would we like to be?	• Desired future situation	• Destination airport
3. How do we get there?	• Marketing plan	• Flight plan
4. How do we make sure we get there?	• Monitoring and adjusting marketing plan	• Monitoring and adjusting flight plan
5. How do we know if we got there?	• Evaluating and measuring results of marketing plan	• Evaluating flight plan and filling in pilot's log

The hospitality and travel marketing system is a systematic process of planning, researching, implementing, controlling, and evaluating an organization's marketing activities. It is systematic because five questions are repeatedly answered in the same order. Figure 3.5 relates the marketing tasks in the system (the PRICE of marketing—planning, research, implementation, control, and evaluation) to the system's steps or questions.

FIGURE 3.5 Hospitality and travel marketing system tasks and steps. The PRICE of marketing model.

TASKS/FUNCTIONS		STEPS/QUESTIONS
Planning and	**P**	• Where are we now?
Research	**R**	• Where would we like to be?
Implementation	**I**	• How do we get there?
Control	**C**	• How do we make sure we get there?
Evaluation	**E**	• How do we know if we got there?

1. **Where Are We Now?** Every airline pilot and flight deck crew knows their current location and the course they have followed. So, too, must an organization assess where it is and where it has just been. If an organization is to succeed in the long run, it must always be assessing its strengths and weaknesses, and its marketing performance in previous time periods. A great deal must be known about past and potential customers, and about primary competitors. This is similar to putting the organization under a microscope. The day-to-day things that get

FIGURE 3.6 "Where are we now?" Doing a situation analysis to determine marketing strengths and weaknesses.

Image copyright Diego Cervo, 2009. Under License from Shutterstock.com

overlooked are magnified and carefully examined. A technique called the situation analysis and various marketing research tools are used. These help answer the question, "Where are we now?" (Figure 3.6) It is not enough to answer this question once, but it must be answered at least once or twice every two years.

2. **Where Would We Like To Be?** Theodore Levitt said that if an organization does not know where it is going, any route will take it there.[12] An organization that does not know what it wants to achieve is like an aircraft taking off without knowing its destination. There are many alternative marketing routes that an organization can follow. The key is to determine which one is most effective. Every organization must try to identify where it wants to be as a result of its marketing activities. Specific techniques are used to achieve this goal, including market segmentation, target marketing, positioning, marketing mixes (8 Ps), and marketing objectives. These techniques help an organization chart the course that it will take to get where it wants to be (Figure 3.7).

3. **How Do We Get There?** Having decided where it wants to be, the organization must next turn to the question of how it is going to get there. The marketing plan is the key tool here. It acts like a blueprint for action. The marketing plan documents how the organization will use the 4 Ps (product, place, pricing, and promotion) and the other 4 Ps of hospitality and travel marketing (packaging, programming, partnership, and people) to achieve its marketing objectives (Figure 3.8). An organization without a marketing plan is like an aircraft taking off without a flight plan. It does not know exactly how it will get to where it wants to be.

Image copyright James Steidl, 2008. Used under license from Shutterstock.com

FIGURE 3.7 "Where would we like to be?" Researching and planning for the future.

4.   **How Do We Make Sure We Get There?** Having a marketing plan does not automatically guarantee that an organization will be successful. Checks and controls have to be built in to ensure that things go as planned. There is a need for marketing management, budgeting, and controls. Every aircraft that takes off has pre-check and in-flight checking procedures. If an aircraft encounters adverse weather conditions, it may alter its route, speed, or altitude with air traffic control's

Image copyright Kristian Sekulic, 2008. Used under license from Shutterstock.com

FIGURE 3.8 "How do we get there?" Developing the marketing plan.

FIGURE 3.9 "How do we make sure we get there?" Checking the progress of the marketing plan.

permission. If an organization finds that parts of its marketing plan are not working, it may have to make changes to get to where it wants to be (Figure 3.9).

5. **How Do We Know If We Got There?** Many organizations put great effort into developing marketing plans and very little into measuring the results of these plans. This is unfortunate because they can learn from both their mistakes and their successes. Just as an airline pilot evaluates each trip and fills in a flight log, measuring and evaluating results of a marketing plan produce useful information that is fed back into the next attempt to answer the question, "Where are we now?" (Figure 3.10).

FIGURE 3.10 "How do we know if we got there?" Evaluating the success of the marketing plan

The Global Perspective: The Big Picture

Implementing the Hospitality and Travel Marketing System

Tourism Jiangsu (Jiangsu Provincial Tourism Bureau)

http://www.tastejiangsu.com/

Jichang Chinese classical garden, Wuxi, Jiangsu

The province of Jiangsu is located in eastern China, next door to Shanghai and with an extensive coastline on the Yellow Sea. Jiangsu is a major tourism destination for domestic Chinese travelers and for international visitors. In particular, the World Heritage-listed Chinese classical gardens in Suzhou and the capital city of Nanjing are popular with foreign visitors.

Marketing Plan for Europe and North America

In late 2006, Tourism Jiangsu retained the services of Belle Tourism International Consulting (BTI) to prepare a marketing plan for Europe and North America. The consulting company conducted extensive research around the world in completing the plan over a period of approximately one year. The five steps of the hospitality and travel marketing system, as described in this chapter, were closely followed in preparing the plan.

(continues)

(continued)

Courtesy of Jiangsu Provincial Tourism Bureau

Ming Dynasty king's tomb in Xuyu, Huai'an, Jiangsu

Implementing the Hospitality and Travel Marketing System in Jiangsu

Where are we now?

The first step in preparing the plan involved an analysis of Tourism Jiangsu's past marketing programs and activities, together with an assessment of the major tourism attractions in the province's 13 major cities. The major strengths and weaknesses in past marketing were identified. For example, the consultants found that Tourism Jiangsu's English-language website was very weak and suggested that a completely new site had to be developed. In addition, the strengths of Jiangsu's existing tourism attractions were pinpointed. In this case, BTI identified 26 categories of unique selling propositions (USPs) for Jiangsu tourism, including the Chinese classical gardens and Ming Dynasty relics illustrated with photos in this case.

Where would we like to be?

Marketing goals were identified for Tourism Jiangsu for the five-year period of 2008 to 2012. BTI then developed a marketing strategy for Jiangsu's tourism for Europe and North America. The most important target markets for 2008 to 2012 were identified as the USA, UK, Germany, France, Italy, and Canada. The consultants recommended a positioning approach in English for tourism in Jiangsu, including a positioning statement of *"To taste Jiangsu is to know China."*

(continues)

(continued)

How do we get there?

Detailed marketing plans were then developed for 2008 to 2012 inclusive. These included specific marketing objectives for each year and each target market. For example, for 2008 the marketing objectives were for the USA and UK markets. In applying the 8 Ps of hospitality and travel marketing to implement this plan, for example, two of the activities were the development of a new English website and a sales mission and presentations to the travel trade in the USA.

How do we make sure we get there?

To make sure that the marketing plan for 2008 was working, a very detailed set of control and monitoring procedures were developed and included within the marketing plan. Tracking the number of visitors to the new website on a monthly basis was one of the specific procedures, as well as the monthly recording of visitor arrivals from the highest priority target markets.

How do we know if we got there?

The marketing plan described the results expected at the end of each year for each marketing objective. An evaluation of the actual results for the first year's performance on the plan's implementation was completed in early 2009.

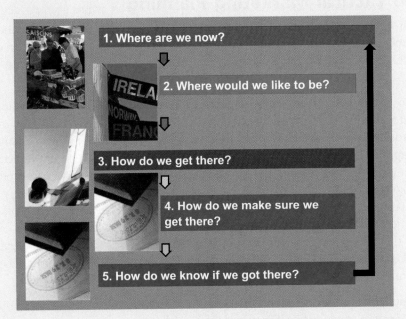

A systematic, five-step approach for marketing hospitality and travel organizations.

(continues)

(continued)

Future Marketing Plans in Jiangsu

As the diagram above shows, just having one marketing plan is not enough. In fact, marketing planning must involve a continuous learning process. The results from one plan need to be fed into the next period's marketing plan. Tourism Jiangsu is the first provincial destination marketing organization (DMO) in China to apply this systematic approach to marketing tourism, and sets an outside example for others to follow.

Discussion Questions

1. How did the marketing plan for Tourism Jiangsu follow the five steps of the hospitality and travel marketing system?
2. What would you do to modify this approach to assist with the marketing of a hotel or restaurant in your local community?
3. Having a written marketing plan is just the first step in being successful with marketing. What steps can the marketing manager use to keep everyone in the organization focused on the achievement of the marketing plan's objectives?

Relationship of the System to Strategic and Tactical Marketing Planning

Most books use the terms *strategic* and *tactical* to refer to the two branches of planning required for effective marketing. We also use *long-term* and *short-term* in this book. **Long-term (strategic) planning** is a period of more than two years. **Short-term (tactical) planning** covers two years or less.

To be most effective, marketing has to be viewed as a long-term management investment and activity. It needs to be planned more than two years ahead. Long-term strategic marketing planning is required. Because change is so rapid in the hospitality and travel industry and events can be unpredictable, short-term, tactical planning is also needed. What is a plan? It is a procedure, worked out in advance, for achieving clearly-stated objectives. In this book, plans are assumed to be written on paper, but not in stone. There are often good reasons to modify plans. What is planning? It is a management activity of looking into the future and developing procedures in advance to achieve objectives. Marketing planning is an activity of marketing managers who try to anticipate future events and develop procedures for realizing marketing objectives.

The term **marketing plan** is widely used in industry to mean a short-term plan for two years or less. Since budget periods are usually for one year ahead, marketing plans normally cover 12 months. A **strategic market plan** is different. It covers three or more years. A marketing plan is short term and needs to be more detailed. A large part of this book is devoted to developing marketing (short-term or tactical) plans. This does not mean that marketing plans are more important than strategic (long-term) market plans. It is just the main focus selected for the book.

Before discussing strategic marketing planning, we need to get some basics out of the way. Above all, you need to realize that there is more to the success of an organization than marketing alone. Marketing is just one of several management functions. Every organization has many different objectives and plans, and ways of accomplishing them.

A hierarchy of objectives and plans exists in all organizations (Figure 3.10). At the foundation of the hierarchy is the organization's vision. A **vision** and **vision statement** describe where the organization wants to be at some future time. A **mission** is a broad statement about an organization's business and scope, services or products, markets served, and overall philosophy. It summarizes the organization's role in society. Overall organizational objectives or goals are next in the hierarchy. They support the **mission statement**. Corporations usually set these as profitability, market share, and sales volume targets. Next are the long-term (strategic) goals for each management function. In our case, these are long-term marketing goals. These must be consistent with the vision, mission, and overall objectives. Last in the hierarchy are the short-term (tactical) goals for each management function. For us, they are short-term marketing objectives.

Planning and plans are needed to achieve objectives. For each level of the objectives hierarchy, there is a corresponding plan. This means that there is a hierarchy of plans as well. Figure 3.11 illustrates this point.

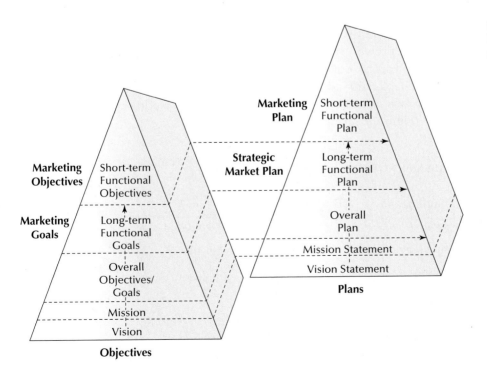

FIGURE 3.11
Hierarchy of objectives and plans.

Where does strategic marketing planning fit? It is the second level from the top in Figure 3.11. Strategic (long-term) marketing planning involves establishing long-term marketing goals and a strategic market plan to achieve them. How does the hospitality and travel marketing system reflect strategic marketing planning? It does so in two ways. First, strategic marketing planning itself uses the process of the system. It addresses the same five questions, but it does so with a longer-term perspective. Second, a strategic market plan is achieved by repeating the system several times.

Let us clarify one more important point. For planning to be most effective, it must be continuous. Strategic market and marketing plans have to be reassessed and adjusted constantly. We do not start on the first day of Year 1 with a strategic market plan and then not touch the plan again until the first day of Year 4. Likewise, it is wrong to start on January 1st with a marketing plan and assume that it need not be changed during the year. We do not begin with a strategic market plan, follow with two or more marketing plans, and then implement a new strategic market plan. Because change can happen almost instantaneously, strategic market and marketing plans are always subject to revision.

Organization of this Book

This book has been written so that it follows the sequential steps in the hospitality and travel marketing system. The first three chapters start with the fundamentals. Chapters 4, 5, and 6 are devoted to the question, "Where are we now?" Chapters 7, 8, and 9 ask, "Where would we like to be?" These six chapters (4 through 9) discuss the planning and research activities that are required for effective marketing. Chapters 10 through 19 answer the question, "How do we get there?" They provide specifics on how marketing activities are carried out. They discuss the implementation part in the PRICE model. Chapter 20 addresses control and evaluation and the questions, "How do we make sure we get there?" and "How do we know if we got there?" (Figure 3.12).

FIGURE 3.12
Orgnization of this book.

TASKS/FUNCTIONS		STEPS/QUESTIONS	CHAPTERS
Planning and	P	• Where are we now?	4–6
Research	R	• Where would we like to be?	7–9
Implementation	I	• How do we get there?	10–19
Control	C	• How do we make sure we get there?	20
Evaluation	E	• How do we know if we got there?	20

Chapter Conclusion

There is a common approach that can be used to market any hospitality and travel organization. It is a five-step process termed the hospitality and travel marketing system. This systematic process involves finding the answers to five questions: "Where are we now?" "Where would we like to be?" "How do we get there?" "How do we make sure we get there?" and "How do we know if we got there?"

Effective marketing requires careful planning, both long-term and short-term. Planning helps organizations identify alternative marketing approaches, maintain uniqueness, create desirable situations, avoid undesirable situations, adapt to the unexpected, and measure success. If used, the hospitality and travel marketing system ensures that the needed priority is given to planning.

REVIEW QUESTIONS

1. What are some of the different definitions for the hospitality and travel industry and why are they insufficient?
2. What are the six characteristics of systems?
3. Why are most definitions of our industry inadequate for marketing purposes?
4. What five key questions make up the hospitality and travel marketing system?
5. What are the four fundamentals of the hospitality and travel marketing system?
6. What are the benefits of following the procedure suggested in the hospitality and travel marketing system?
7. In marketing, how would you define short-term and long-term?
8. Is a strategic market plan the same as a marketing plan? If not, explain the difference.
9. Is there a need for both short-and long-term marketing planning in our industry? Why or why not?

CHAPTER ASSIGNMENTS

1. You have just been hired as the marketing manager of a hospitality or travel organization. You find out quickly that the company has never used a systematic approach to marketing. How would you change the situation, employing the hospitality and travel marketing system? Which departments and individuals would you involve in the process? How would you sell your suggested changes to upper management?
2. Select an existing hospitality or travel organization and examine its marketing procedures and practices. Is the hospitality and travel marketing system being used? If not, what problems exist and what opportunities are being missed? If the system is being used, have any

modifications or additional steps been added? Write a short report summarizing your findings and suggested improvements.

3. This chapter lists the six characteristics of systems in the hospitality and travel industry as openness, complexity and variety, responsiveness, competitiveness, interdependency, and friction and disharmony. Identify three real-life examples or indications of these characteristics in our industry. Use a combination of library and Internet research and interviews with hospitality and travel professionals to prepare your paper.

4. "There is a time for competition, but there is also a time for cooperation." Discuss this statement in the context of the hospitality and travel industry. When does it make sense for organizations to cooperate? Cite at least three actual examples where potentially competitive organizations have joined together in cooperative marketing in our industry. Why do you think they decided to join forces?

WEB RESOURCES

Air Transport Association, http://www.air-transport.org/
American Hotel & Lodging Association, http://www.ahla.com/
American Society of Travel Agents, http://www.astanet.com/
British Hospitality Association, http://www.bha.org.uk/
Canadian Restaurant and Foodservices Association, http://www.crfa.ca/
Cruise Lines International Association, http://www.cruising.org/
International Association of Amusement Parks and Attractions, http://www.iaapa.org/
National Restaurant Association, http://www.restaurant.org/
North American Industrial Classification System (NAICS), http://www.census.gov/epcd/www/naics.html
oneworld®, http://www.oneworld.com/
SkyTeam, http://www.skyteam.com/
Star Alliance, http://www.staralliance.com/
Travel Industry Association, http://www.tia.org/
Travel Weekly, http://www.travelweekly.com/
UN World Tourism Organization, http://www.unwto.org/
World Travel & Tourism Council, http://www.wttc.org/

REFERENCES

1. The Intrepid Traveler. 2009. *The Travel Industry Dictionary*. http://www.hometravelagency.com/index.html, accessed February 14, 2009.
2. British Hospitality Association. 2009. *Welcome to the British Hospitality Association*, http://www.bha.org.uk/, accessed February 14, 2009.
3. Cruise Lines International Association. 2009. *About CLIA*, http://www.cruising.org/, accessed February 14, 2009.

4. United Nations World Tourism Organization. 2009. *About UNWTO. Why Tourism?* http://www.unwto.org/, accessed February 14, 2009, ©UNTWO, 9284404908.

5. World Travel & Tourism Council. 2006. *Progress and Priorities 2006/07.*

6. U.S. Travel Association. 2009. *About TIA. What We Do,* http://www.tia.org/, accessed February 14, 2009.

7. *Travel Weekly.* 2009. Secaucus, N.J.: Northstar Travel Media.

8. National Restaurant Association. 2007. *About the National Restaurant Association,* http://www.restaurant.org/, accessed February 15, 2009.

9. Canadian Restaurant and Foodservices Association. 2009. *About CRFA,* http://www.crfa.ca/, accessed February 15, 2009.

10. Bureau of Labor Statistics. 2008. *Food Services and Drinking Places: NAICS 722,* http://www.bls.gov/iag/tgs/iag722.htm, accessed August 22, 2008.

11. U.S. Census Bureau. 2009. *2007 NAICS Codes and Titles,* http://www.census.gov/, accessed February 15, 2009.

12. Levitt, Theodore. 1960. " Marketing myopia." *Harvard Business Review* 38(4), 56.

NIGERIA
KENYA
BRAZIL
UNITED KINGDOM
GERMANY
JAPAN
IRELAND
NORWAY
CHINA
FRANCE

PLANNING: RESEARCH AND ANALYSIS

WHERE ARE WE NOW?

WHERE WOULD WE LIKE TO BE?

HOW DO WE GET THERE?

HOW DO WE MAKE SURE WE GET THERE?

HOW DO WE KNOW IF WE GOT THERE?

chapter 4

Customer Behavior
Where Are We Now?

O B J E C T I V E S

Having read this chapter, you should be able to:

- List and describe six personal factors that influence customer behavior.

- List and describe four factors that influence customers' perceptions of hospitality and travel services.

- List and explain the role of stimulus factors in perception.

- List and describe five interpersonal factors that influence customer behavior.

- List and describe the seven stages in the customer buying process.

- Explain the three categories of decision processes that customers follow.

- Explain the purchasing process of organizational buyers.

O V E R V I E W

Why do customers behave the way they do? This is a question everyone involved in marketing must answer. If we can understand customers' behavior, we are in a much better position to customize services, prices, promotions, and distribution channels to fit their individual needs and wants.

This chapter explains that people's behavior is influenced both by personal and interpersonal factors. The key factors in each of the two categories are discussed. The relative importance of information from commercial and personal sources is examined. All customers go through a series of stages when they decide to buy hospitality and travel services. This chapter emphasizes that marketers need to understand the decision processes that customers use.

KEY TERMS

AIOs (activities, interests, opinions)	lifestyles	primary groups
buying process	motivation	product adoption curve
cognitive dissonance	motives	psychographics
commercial information sources	need	reference groups
culture	need recognition	secondary groups
customer behavior	non-commercial sources (non marketer-dominated)	self-concept
evoked set	objective criteria	social class
family life-cycle	objectives	social information sources
individual customers	opinion leaders	subcultures
Internal sources	organizational buying behavior	subjective criteria
Interpersonal factors	perception	VALS™
learning	personal factors	wants
	personality	word-of-mouth information (W-O-M)

Have you ever thought about the products and services you buy? What about some of your most prized possessions, such as your laptop computer, car, cell phone or PDA, or MP5? Did you decide to buy these items completely on your own, or did you ask friends for advice? Did you take more time to make these decisions than you do when you choose a fast-food restaurant, for example? Have you ever bought things because you thought your friends would approve of them?

Why are we asking you so many questions? Simple! We want you to realize what a complex decision-making unit you are. If you live in North America, multiply yourself as an individual decision maker by a factor of about 447 million (Canada, Mexico, United States) and you will have some idea of the enormous task that marketing decision makers.[1] If you live in Europe or in the Asia-Pacific region, the market of potential customers is even bigger and more complex. This chapter looks at why people do the things they do.

Marketing managers must understand customers' behavior patterns and why they occur. This means not only knowing how customers act when they are consuming services, but also their pre-purchase and post-purchase behavior.

Behavior of Individual Customers

Customer behavior is the way customers select, use, and behave before and after they have purchased hospitality and travel services. Two types of factors influence

Personal Factors

- Needs, wants, and motivation
- Perception
- Learning
- Personality
- Lifestyle
- Self-concept

Interpersonal Factors

- Cultures and sub-cultures
- Reference groups
- Social classes
- Opinion leaders
- The family

FIGURE 4.1
The personal and interpersonal factors influencing customer behavior.

the behavior of **individual customers**: personal and interpersonal. **Personal factors** are the psychological characteristics of the individual (Figure 4.1).

Personal Factors

1. **Needs, Wants, and Motivation.** Customer needs are the foundation of marketing. Satisfying them is the key to long-term success. But what are needs? A need exists when there is a gap between what customers have and what they would like to have. **Need recognition** is the customer's perception of a difference between the desired state of affairs and the actual situation that is sufficient to arouse and activate the decision process.[2] These gaps or differences may be in customers' needs for food, clothes, shelter, feeling of safety, or their sense of belonging and esteem. Needs result from customers' physiological and psychological persons. Flying first class, staying in the most expensive hotel, or ordering the most expensive dish on the menu may be based on a need for esteem (a psychological need), indicating one's importance to others. Hunger or thirst (two physiological needs) may be the reason for a visit to a fast-food restaurant.

   Wants are the particular modes of consumption that customers select to satisfy their needs.[3] For example, a person may need a sense of belonging and affection but want to visit friends and relatives (VFR). Another customer needs esteem from friends and neighbors but wants to ride first class on the bullet train (*Shinkansen*) in Japan. Whereas people's needs are relatively few, they usually have many more wants. For each need, there can be several wants.

The reasons people give for traveling and dining out in research studies are often insufficient. They do not usually reveal the basic needs they are trying to satisfy. Why? Customers may be unaware of the true reasons or do not want to divulge them.[4] It is easier for people to say they are traveling first class because of the extra services provided, than to say they are looking for esteem. Therefore, surveys of why people select hotels, restaurants, airlines, cruise ships, destinations, and other hospitality and travel services can be incomplete and misleading. Customers are more likely to supply rational (price, cleanliness, facilities, and services) than irrational (emotional) reasons. Would you tell your innermost secrets to a stranger? Marketing managers need to understand both rational and emotional reasons for buying in developing and promoting their services.

An understanding of human **motivation** is essential to knowing how customers become aware of their needs. There are several motivation theories. Before discussing them, we will look at the process of motivation and how the customer and marketer interact.

Every person has needs, both physiological and psychological. He or she may or may not be aware of them, however. Marketers have to make customers recognize their need deficiencies and provide the services or products to eliminate them. Need awareness must exist for customers before they can begin the process of satisfying their needs. A **need** is a conscious or unconscious disparity between a present and desired physiological or psychological state. Marketers are in the business of reminding and making customers aware of their needs.

Customers have to be motivated to act to satisfy their wants. Marketers must trigger this process by supplying objectives and potential motives. **Objectives** are the services that the hospitality and travel industry supplies—hotel accommodations, restaurant meals, destinations, cruises, flights, travel counseling, inclusive tours, and entertainment. **Motives** are customers' personal desires or drives to satisfy their wants. Marketers have to suggest motives to customers involving the use of objectives. For example, Starbucks' website in 2007 carried the invitation of *Let's Meet at Starbucks*. This is a very fine example of creating need awareness (closer relationship with your friends), supplying objectives (good environment to relax and enjoy great conversations with hot and iced coffee drinks and snacks), and suggesting motives (meet at Starbucks). Figure 4.2 illustrates the relationship of needs, wants, motivation, and objectives (i.e., needs → through awareness become → wants that → motivate purchase of → objectives (services) → and satisfy → needs).[5]

Two popular motivational theories have been suggested by Maslow and Herzberg. They partly explain how individual customers are motivated to make purchase decisions.

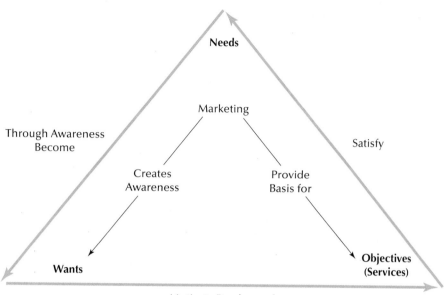

FIGURE 4.2 The relationship of needs, wants, motivation, and objectives.
(Adapted from Mill, Robert Christie, and Alastair M. Morrison. 2009. *The Tourism System.* 6th ed. Dubuque, Iowa: Kendall/Hunt Publishing. Used with permission.)

Maslow's *Hierarchy of Needs* is one of the cognitive theories of human motivation. It suggests that customers attach varying levels of priority to different needs.[6] Maslow suggests five categories of needs:

a. Physiological
b. Safety
c. Belonging (social)
d. Esteem
e. Self-actualization

Physiological needs are the most basic, including the need for food and liquids, shelter, clothing, relaxation, and physical exercise. They must be satisfied before the individual moves on to thinking about other (higher-level) needs. Most people have a strong desire to feel safe and secure and to be free from the unexpected. These are safety needs. The desire to be accepted by various social groups represents our belonging or social needs. You will hear about these later in the discussion on interpersonal factors. Esteem needs represent the desire to attain status, respect, accomplishment, and achievement in one's own and others' eyes. Realizing our growth potential and discovering our own selves are self-actualization needs.

Maslow's hierarchy concept is usually illustrated in the form of a pyramid, as shown on the left side of Figure 4.3. Customers must satisfy the lower-level needs such as physiological and safety needs before moving on to the higher-level, psychological needs of belonging, esteem, and self-actualization. Another way of looking at Maslow's needs hierarchy is to view it as a needs ladder as shown on the right side of Figure 4.3.

FIGURE 4.3 Maslow's
Hierarchy of Needs and
the Needs Ladder.
(From Blackwell. Consumer
Behavior, 10 E © 2006, South-
Western, a part of Cengage
Learning, Inc. Reproduced by
permission. www.cengage.
com/permissions).

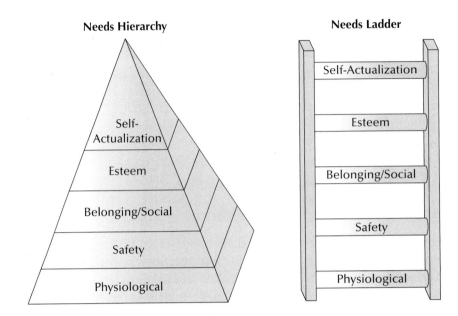

A more detailed description of the motives associated with these needs
and travel is provided in Figure 4.4. Physiological needs are on the lowest rung; they must be satisfied before others can be dealt with. Once
each type of need is satisfied, the person moves on to the next highest
need on the ladder. Maslow believes that once a need level has been satisfied, it no longer serves as a motivator. For example, if customers
perceive that all hotel chains provide a sufficient guarantee of food,
shelter, and security, then physiological and safety needs are no longer
significant to them. What this implies is that it would be more effective
to appeal to the higher-level needs (Figure 4.5). It is generally accepted
that most of society in the developed world has progressed beyond great
concern for physiological and safety needs.

However, recent events in the world and within the hospitality and
travel industry have taught us all an important lesson—a ladder is for
climbing down as well as climbing up! We are constantly driven to
ascend the needs ladder, but problems at the lower levels may cause us
to descend. The aftereffects of the tragic events of 9–11 and the SARS
outbreak severely undermined the perceived safety of air travel. This
made many people climb down the needs ladder to its second-lowest
rung, the need for safety. The Indian Ocean tsunami of 2004, the terrorist
bombings in Bali in 2002–2005, the devastation caused by Hurricane
Katrina in 2005, and the murders of tourists in top international hotels in
Mumbai, India in 2008 riveted the world's attention on important tourism destinations, and shook potential travelers' confidence levels. These
types of events make many people climb down the needs ladder to its
second lowest rung, the need for safety. People's lower-level needs may

NEED	MOTIVE	TRAVEL LITERATURE REFERENCES
Physiological	Relaxation	Escape
		Relaxation
		Relief of tension
		Sunlust
		Physical
		Mental relaxation of tension
Safety	Security	Health
		Recreation
		Keep oneself active and healthy for the future
Belonging	Love	Family togetherness
		Enhancement of kinship relationships
		Companionship
		Facilitation of social interaction
		Maintenance of personal ties
		Interpersonal relations
		Roots
		Ethnic
		Show one's affection for family members
		Maintain social contacts
Esteem	Achievement	Convince oneself of one's achievements
	Status	Show one's importance to others
		Prestige
		Social recognition
		Ego-enhancement
		Professional/business
		Personal development
		Status and prestige
Self-actualization	Be true to one's own nature	Exploration and evaluation of self
		Self-discovery
		Satisfaction of inner desires

FIGURE 4.4 Maslow's needs and motives listed in the hospitality and travel literature.
(Adapted from Mill, Robert Christie, and Alastair M. Morrison. 2006. *The Tourism System.* 5th ed. Dubuque, Iowa: Kendall/Hunt Publishing. Used with permission.)

also be aroused by such events as terrorist attacks, airplane crashes, natural disasters, crimes and fires within hotels, and restaurant food-poisoning incidents. The City of New Orleans lost an estimated $2 billion in income from tourism in the aftermath of Hurricane Katrina in 2005. The marketers in the New Orleans CVB had to reassure travelers that it was safe to come back to New Orleans, and a complete destination re-branding program was developed and launched (Figure 4.6).

Look through any number of travel websites, magazines or in the travel sections of newspapers and you will find many examples of hospitality and travel advertisers drawing the reader's attention to the needs

FIGURE 4.5 Some people travel to "get away from it all" on journeys of self-discovery.

Image copyright Galyna Andrushko, 2008. Used under license from Shutterstock.com

on Maslow's hierarchy. The following are a few examples for you to consider. Try to determine the advertisers' message by studying the wording in the following advertisements:

Physiological	Hawaii World	• *Relax. Renew. Rekindle. Are you ready?*
Safety	American Express Travelers Cheques	• *Travel with peace of mind.*
Belonging	Sheraton Hotels & Resorts	• *You don't just stay here. You belong.*
	Tourism Ireland	• *Your very own Ireland*
Esteem	Windstar Cruises	• *180° from Ordinary*
	Seabourn Cruises	• *The Yachts of Seabourn. Intimate. Luxury.*
Self-actualization	Outward Bound	• *For adventures that last a lifetime*
	AJ Hackett Macau Tower	• *Challenging people & gravity since 1986*

Now let's turn to the second theory of motivation. Herzberg's *two-factor* motivation theory suggests that customers are concerned with *motivators* (things that motivate them) and *hygiene factors* (things that de-motivate them).[7] Herzberg's theory can be explained by the classic hotel swimming pool example. The availability of a swimming pool in a hotel is seldom the primary motivator for its guests' visits, nor will it satisfy their needs. But the absence of a pool can de-motivate, causing guests not to select the hotel without a pool. Another simple example is that although passengers may not select an airline based on the availability of a complimentary food and beverage services, they may decide against airlines that do not provide them.

The implication of Herzberg's theory is that marketers need to know their primary motivators, the services and facilities that meet customers' most important needs. However, that is not enough. They must also identify the common turnoffs or de-motivators, the factors that can repel customers if they are not provided.

Courtesy of New Orleans Convention Visitors Bureau

FIGURE 4.6 New Orleans makes a bold recovery as a tourism destination after Hurricane Katrina.

2. **Perception.** Customers use their five senses—sight, hearing, taste, touch, and smell—to size up hospitality and travel services and the industry's promotional messages. This sizing-up process is known as **perception**. The phrase "perception counts more than reality" expresses a most important customer behavior concept: decisions are made more on how customers perceive the facts than on the facts themselves. Customers must not only be motivated to buy, but they must perceive that a service will satisfy their needs and wants.

Perception is the cognitive impression that is formed of "reality" which in turn influences the individual's actions and behavior toward that object.[8] It is almost impossible to find two people who share the exact same view of the world. Why? Experts talk about four perceptual processes that make the difference:

   a. Perceptual screens or filters
   b. Perceptual biases
   c. Selective retention
   d. Closure

a. *Perceptual Screens or Filters.* People are literally bombarded with stimuli every day, most of them commercially-oriented. The morning radio and television are loaded with commercials. The kids show up at the breakfast table wearing T-shirts promoting their favorite brands of soft drinks, clothes, and hosts of other products and services. Even the cereal box tries to grab our attention. The drive-times to and from work are heavily assaulted by advertising. Radio shows, billboards, and even buses, trains, trucks, vans, and buildings are laden with commercial messages. To supplement the daily diet of commercials, the newspapers, magazines, e-mail and "snail" mail that we read and the evening television that we watch make sure that we get our promotional quotas. Your cell or mobile phone also keeps buzzing with advertising messages. The Web is full of online advertisements and other promotions. The average person is exposed to hundreds or even thousands of advertisements each day. There is just no way that the human brain can register and remember all of these messages.

Customers screen out the majority of the stimuli or messages to which they are exposed. They notice and retain information from only a small portion of these messages. Some experts call this selective attention[9] while others choose the words *perceptual screens* or *filters.* Marketers must do everything in their power to be sure that their services are among the select few that get noticed.

b. *Perceptual Biases.* All customers have perceptual biases; customers twist the information to match their pictures or unique views of the world. Even if an advertising message makes it through perceptual screens, people may alter it so much that it bears no resemblance to what was intended. The reshaped information may run contrary to the advertiser's objectives.

c. *Selective Retention.* Even if messages make it through the perceptual screens and biases intact, they may not be retained for a long time. Customers practice something called selective retention; they hold on longer to information that supports their predispositions, beliefs, and attitudes.

d. *Closure.* Customers tend to see what they want to see. The human brain does not like to deal with incomplete images of objects, people, or organizations. Where information is unavailable to round out an image, the mind adds the missing data, whether the information is right or wrong. A state of psychological tension exists until the missing information is added (closure). Tension forces attention and the marketer can take advantage of temporarily missing information. A few classic examples are United Airline's "Fly the friendly skies of United," American Express' "Don't leave home without it," and McDonald's "I'm lovin' it." Later we will use the title positioning statements for these tag lines. Constant repetition of advertisements using these statements, along with the companies' names, has ingrained them in most people's minds. So familiar are these statements that people automatically add the companies' names, whether or not they are specifically mentioned in the messages. People round out their images of the companies created by advertising. Positioning, covered in Chapter 8, is mostly concerned with trying to create desired images in the customer's mind. Effective positioning relies on the closure concept.

Research has demonstrated a degree of predictability about customer perceptions. Some of the key findings show that customers are more likely to do the following:[10]

- Screen out information with which they are already familiar.
- Notice and retain information related to a need of which they are aware (a want) or one that they are actively trying to satisfy.
- Buy services that match their perceived images of themselves (you will hear about this later under the self-concept theory).
- Notice and retain things that stand out from the norm (e.g., advertisements that are much larger than average).
- See things that they anticipate seeing (e.g., tour brochures in a travel agency).
- Notice information from hospitality and travel organizations and destinations with which they have had successful previous experiences.
- Attach greater credibility to interpersonal rather than commercially generated information.

However, customers are less likely to do the following:

- Use perceptual biases to distort information received from interpersonal sources (family, friends, business associates, reference and social groups).
- Absorb information that is too complicated and requires a great deal of effort to fully comprehend.
- Notice and retain information about competitive hospitality and travel service brands if these customers are satisfied with another brand.

Marketing managers can use a variety of tools and techniques to navigate their way around the perception barrier. They need to know how customers acquire information and how they process that information. Internal and external factors and sources of information influence customers' perceptions. The internal are the personal factors that are the subject of this part of the chapter. They include needs, wants, motives, learning, lifestyle, self-concept, and personality—the customer's individual overall makeup and frame of mind. The external include the marketer-dominated and non-marketer dominated, mainly interpersonal, factors.[11] Marketer-dominated factors are those related to how hospitality and travel services are communicated and promoted, and how they are presented.

Marketer-dominated factors are all actions that hospitality and travel marketers take to inform and persuade customers through communications and promotion. These actions include advertising, websites, personal selling, sales promotion and merchandising, and public relations and publicity. Marketer-dominated factors are also part of the experience clues discussed in Chapter 2. They include how hospitality and travel services and facilities are actually presented to customers. For example, take a look at the image of the lobby of the hotel in Figure 4.7. You will probably agree that the "atmospherics" of this lobby are on the luxury side with nice marble floors and walls. As you just did, customers make deductions using all the clues hospitality and travel organizations give them about the quality, price, and uniqueness of services and facilities. Did you think that this hotel was relatively expensive? Customers use their five senses (sight, hearing, taste, touch, and smell) to evaluate the evidence presented.

Hospitality and travel marketers can use size, color, intensity, movement, position, contrast, isolation, texture, shape, and surroundings

FIGURE 4.7 The "atmospherics" of this hotel lobby give a signal of luxury and quality.

Image copyright David Gilder 2008. Used under license from Shutterstock.com

to support desired customers' perceptions. These factors can also be used simply to get through customers' perceptual screens.

a. *Size.* Many customers equate size with quality. The bigger the hotel or restaurant chain, airline, attraction, cruise line, or tour wholesaler, the better their services are perceived to be. Greater size also usually means greater attention in print advertising. The bigger the billboard, the more likely it will be noticed (Figure 4.8). The larger the magazine or newspaper advertisement, the more likely the reader will see it.

b. *Color.* Color also has perceptual connotations. The use of color in advertisements is far more effective in getting customers' attention than is black and white. Some colors like gold can convey the perception of quality. Rental car companies make extensive use of color to make their services and advertisements stand out (e.g., yellow for Hertz; red for Avis; green for National).

c. *Intensity.* The intensity of an advertising message can attract above-average attention. Many of the public-service commercials aired on television about drugs, AIDS, drunk driving, using seatbelts, helping the hungry, and crimes against people and animals are very strong in intensity. The use of fear appeals in advertisements fits into this category. American Express' series featuring couples who lost their

Copyright 2006, Colorado Tourism Office & Jeff Wack Illustration

FIGURE 4.8 This spectacular advertisement by Colorado Tourism shows the greater impact of size on the viewer's perception.

travelers checks was an excellent use of a fear appeal. Being stranded in a foreign country with no cash before the popularity of ATM machines was not a thought that many travelers relished.

d. *Movement.* As a stimulus, moving objects are more likely to attract attention than stationary objects. This is one of the reasons that television and the Web have become popular advertising media. They display visual movement; print and radio ads do not. Signs and point-of-sale displays with moving parts also are noticed more frequently than stationary ones.

e. *Position.* The position of advertisements, point-of-sale displays, and signs affects their perception. For example, certain pages and parts of pages in newspapers, magazines, and menus are read more frequently than others.

f. *Contrast.* Contrast can also be used effectively to get customers' attention by making a promotional message or service facility stand out from its competitors. Examples include using an exceptionally large headline in a print advertisement, trick photography, or a predominant color that other ads do not feature (e.g., black, silver, or gold).

g. *Isolation.* The use of white space to isolate print advertisements from competing messages is an effective perceptual technique. Actually, it can be white, black, red, yellow, or any other color; the effect is the same. The idea is to provide a visual border, and enough separation from other items on a page, to make the ad stand out.

h. *Texture.* Texture is another factor that affects perception. Chair and wall coverings, carpeting, letterhead stationery, brochure and direct marketing materials, and menu paper stock are just a few of the items that can create an impression with customers.

i. *Shape.* Designing service facilities or promotional pieces in a distinctive or unusual shape can make them stand out from the competition. For example, many restaurants use odd-shaped menus—on bottles, brown paper bags, and carving boards—to make their operations unique.

j. *Surroundings.* Surroundings as a stimulus factor refer to the physical location of service facilities and promotional materials. For example, locating a restaurant or hotel in an exclusive area, or placing an advertisement in a high-class magazine, connotes quality and high prices.

3. **Learning.** We tend to learn a little from everything we do. We then adjust our behavior patterns after each learning experience. Buying hospitality and travel services is similar to reading and writing; it has to be learned through experience. Learning comes through a combination of factors—needs, motives, objectives, cues, responses, and reinforcement. Needs, motives, and objectives were discussed earlier in this chapter. **Learning** is the process by which experience leads to changes in knowledge and behavior.[12]

For cognitive learning to begin, hospitality and travel marketers must get customers' attention. For example, a former advertising campaign by Tourism Australia that certainly got people's attention had the question, *So where the bloody hell are you?* Repeating the message on the Tourism Australia website further reinforced the learning of this unique message. This campaign, however, caused much controversy by its rough tone and was replaced in 2008 by the milder *Come Walkabout* campaign. Airlines and hotel companies encourage frequent travelers to join their membership programs. By receiving the benefits of these programs, travelers learn through experience that these "perks" are of value to them and increase their loyalty to the companies.

4. **Personality.** A customer's **personality** is a combination of most of the factors we have already discussed, including motivations, perceptions, learning, and emotions. It is the individual's unique psychological makeup, which consistently influences how the person responds to his or her environment.[13] It represents all the things that make a person unique, the different ways that every person thinks and acts.

   The two common ways of describing personalities is by traits and types. Individual people tend to react in a similar way to things that happen to them and to stimuli. They have traits, or ways of acting and behaving. The types of personality labels we tend to stick on people include outgoing, self-confident, quiet, domineering, sociable, happy-go-lucky, defensive, flexible, and many others.

   Although psychologists agree that there is a strong link between personalities and buying behavior, research results are inconclusive on the relationship. Using personality traits or types as a predictor of buying behavior is still an inexact science.

5. **Lifestyle.** You will not find the word *lifestyle* in any dictionary published before 1980. But everybody now knows this word very well. People began saying such things as, "That doesn't fit in with my lifestyle," "I'd like to have a better lifestyle," "The lifestyle is quite different in. . .," or "I wouldn't like to have their lifestyle." Asked to define lifestyle, most people would say, "Well, isn't it just the way we live?"

   The answer is "yes"; **lifestyles** are the way we live. And the way we live is a function of our **activities, interests, and opinions or AIOs.** Actions are what people do in their work and leisure time. Our interests are the parts of their lives to which people give the most attention and enthusiasm. These include families, homes, jobs, hobbies, recreational pursuits, communities, clothes, food and drink preferences, and other items. Opinions are beliefs that people have, accurate or inaccurate, about a wide variety of subjects, including the political scene, the economy, the educational system, products, future events, sports, countries, and so on. The interaction of activities, interests, and opinions determines how people live.

   Marketers feel that customers' lifestyles or **psychographics** (an operational technique to measure lifestyles) provide a more comprehensive picture of people's purchase behavior than just their demographic characteristics (age, income, occupation, etc.).[14] However, it is better to use psychographic and demographic segmentation together, since it is difficult to identify people based solely on lifestyles or psychographic groups. One of the companies that pioneered the joint-factor approach was SRI Consulting Business Intelligence (SRIC-BI), which developed the **VALS**™ (Values and Lifestyles) system. The VALS™ segment framework has eight segments and uses the two dimensions of resources on the vertical dimension (high to low) and primary motivation on the horizontal dimension: ideals, achievement, self-expression (Figure 4.9). Each of the eight groups has a composite profile. For example, SRIC-BI describes the Innovators as "successful, sophisticated, take-charge people with high self-esteem. Because they have such abundant resources, they exhibit all three primary motivations in varying degrees. They are change leaders and are the most receptive to new ideas and technologies. Innovators are very active consumers, and their purchases reflect cultivated tastes for upscale, niche products and services."[15]

There are alternative approaches to psychographic segmentation, including PRIZM® NE in North America, and ACORN in the United Kingdom.[16] SRIC-BI has also developed Japan-VALS™.

FIGURE 4.9 The VALS™ Framework and eight segments. (Courtesy of SRI Consulting Business Intelligence (SRIC-BI); www.sric-bi.com/VALS).

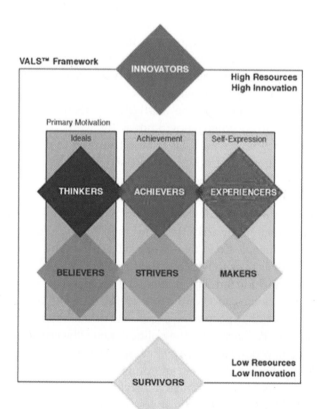

INTERNET MARKETING

Using the Internet to Provide a Customer Profile: The PRIZM NE Zip Code Look-Up Feature

- Claritas is a company that has developed a market segmentation system for every neighborhood in the United States into 66 lifestyle types.
- You can sample PRIZM NE by using MyBestSegments.com at the company's website. At the link below, just enter a five-digit zip code into the box provided, add the security code, and then click on the submit button.
- For example, using the 47906 zip code for West Lafayette, Indiana, the results showed that the five most common PRIZM NE segments are: (1) Blue Highways, (2) City Startups, (3) New Beginnings, (4) Suburban Pioneers, and (5) Suburban Sprawl.
- Here is a description and some of the customer profile for the Suburban Sprawl market segment:

  - Suburban Sprawl is an unusual American lifestyle: a collection of midscale, middle-aged singles and couples living in the heart of suburbia. Typically members of the Baby Boomer generation, they hold decent jobs, own older homes and condos, and pursue conservative versions of the American Dream. Among their favorite activities are jogging on treadmills, playing trivia games, and renting videos.
  - Age group: 45–64
  - Median household income: $49,535
  - Education level: college graduate
  - Employment level: white collar

Source: Claritas Inc. (2008). *Zip Code Look-up.* **http://www.claritas.com/ MyBestSegments/Default.jsp?ID=20**

Student Questions

1. What types of hospitality and travel organizations will get the most value out of pinpointing potential markets with PRIZM NE?
2. How could these organizations best use the information from this analysis?
3. Which factors will change the customer profile in a zip-code area from one year to the next?
4. What are the results when you use a different zip code for this analysis?

6. **Self-concept.** Customers buy things that they perceive as matching their images of themselves. Two psychological processes are at play at the same time—perception and self-concept. A customer's **self-concept** is a mental picture, consisting of four different elements: the real self, ideal

self, reference-group (or looking-glass) self, and self-image. Simply stated, they represent the following:

a. The way we really are (real self)
b. The way we would like to be (ideal self)
c. The way we think other people see us (reference-group self)
d. The way we see ourselves (self-image)

Few people know their real selves, and many do not want to. They are even more reluctant to talk about their real selves to others. However, customers like to think and talk about their ideal selves. The ideal self is a strong motivating influence. We are constantly trying to get closer to this vision of ourselves. How we think others see us is our reference-group self. Reference groups, discussed later in the chapter, are the social groups to which we belong or aspire to belong.

A person's self-image is the most important element of the self-concept theory for marketing. It is usually a combination of the real, ideal, and reference-group selves. We often buy something to make a positive impression on our reference groups; "keeping up with the Joneses" is a favorite activity of many. Staying or dining at the luxurious and 7-star Burj Al Arab Hotel in Dubai could inspire feelings of respect from your family and friends. We also make purchases to get closer to our ideal selves, and sometimes we just plain give in to our real selves.

Interpersonal Factors

Interpersonal factors represent the outside influence of other people. Personal and interpersonal influences are at play at the same time. The interpersonal factors include the following:

1. Cultures and subcultures
2. Reference groups
3. Social classes
4. Opinion leaders
5. The family

1. **Cultures and Subcultures.** A **culture** is a combination of the beliefs, values, attitudes, habits, traditions, customs, and forms of behavior that are shared by a group of people. We are born into a culture, but we are not born with these components of culture. We learn our culture from our parents and others in previous generations. The cultural lessons we absorb affect our decisions about buying hospitality and travel services. They do so by influencing our motivations, perceptions, lifestyles, and personalities, the personal factors we just talked about.

Cultures are the broadest social groups to which customers belong. A culture affects society in a general way, and it also influences society's social groups and individual customers. It dictates what types of behavior and motives are socially acceptable, which social institutions and conventions we adopt, and how we communicate through language and body movements.[17]

Social conventions are practices that tend to be universally followed by people within a culture; for example, sending birthday cards to family and friends, not eating the flesh of certain animals, and bringing gifts to parties. Hospitality and travel providers must be sensitive to these conventions; for example, by not serving pork to people of the Muslim faith.

Each individual customer is affected by the prevailing culture, which determines what is normal and acceptable and what is not. The frenetic pace of life in major cities is quite tolerable and normal to those who live there, but would be unacceptable to people in more rural societies. A culture affects the way we express our feelings. For example, Britons tend to hide their inner feelings with the "stiff upper lip," whereas Americans "let it all hang out" by freely showing their emotions.

Cultures are not static. They constantly have to weather the effects of new generations, as well as economic, technological, environmental, political, and social change. But there are certain threads of a culture that tend to endure, no matter how severe the pressure to adapt. For example, the Puritan or Protestant work ethic is deeply ingrained in U.S. and Canadian society, as is the never-ending quest for material possessions and individual achievement. Chinese people have been deeply influenced by the teachings of Confucius and, therefore, have a deep respect for their elders. Although there have been trends that run counter to these, and they are not valued by everyone, these two values still remain almost intact.

Both the United States and Canada have their distinctive cultures, but their citizens do not share exactly the same beliefs, values, attitudes, habits, and behavior patterns. They are both melting-pot societies made up of a collection of unique **subcultures** (cultures within a culture). The U.S. subcultures include African Americans, Hispanics, Asians, and certain religion-based groups (Mormons, Jews, Mennonites, and others). Canada has French- and English-speaking subcultures, black Canadians, and various religious groups. Today, most European countries and places like Australia are also a mosaic of many different cultures.

In the United States, the total population increased to approximately 304 million in July 2008. The country's minority population has grown steadily; in 2007 one-third of the U.S. population was classified as being minorities according to Census Bureau. The Hispanic population is the largest subculture, at around 15 percent in July 2007 (Figure 4.10). The African American population was 40.2 million and Asian Americans were at 14.9 million.[18] It is dangerous and wrong to assume that all persons within a subculture act exactly the same way. A large proportion of the people in a subculture, however, have certain behavior patterns that are different from the norm. For example, Cohorts® has divided the Hispanic population into 19 different sub-groups.[19]

2. **Reference Groups.** All customers belong to several **reference groups** with which they identify. There are two broad types of reference

FIGURE 4.10 People of Hispanic origin are the largest subculture in the USA.

Image copyright Andresr, 2008. Used under license from Shutterstock.com

groups—primary and secondary. **Primary groups** include a person's family and friends in which there can exist unrestricted direct interaction; **secondary groups** include those at church and work, and ones to which membership dues are paid (e.g., country clubs, hobby societies, service clubs, and professional associations) in which interaction is more sporadic.[20] Most of us are also affected by *aspirational* and *dissociative* groups.[21] Many people wish they were professional athletes or entertainers and will purchase services and products with which their idols are associated (an example of *aspirational* groups). *Dissociative* groups are ones that we want nothing to do with, and we avoid services and products that these groups buy. Now we also have *Internet-based membership groups*, consisting of friends and acquaintances that people make while chatting or surfing on the Internet. Among these are people who frequently write or read *travel blogs* or actively participate in travel discussion groups or forums.

These social units are called reference groups because they have certain codes of behavior to which members adhere. In other words, customers use them as a reference point to determine both acceptable and unacceptable purchase behavior. Reference groups vary widely; some exert much more influence than others. The purchase of hospitality and travel services can be affected by these reference groups. People can come back from vacations with suntans, souvenirs, clothing, videos and photos, art, and miscellaneous other items to show off to other group members. They may feel that they win esteem by having others see these items, or by having been to places or having done things that others have not. Although an intangible service, travel can be made conspicuous to the reference groups with which we closely identify.

3. **Social Classes.** While people today are not quite as class conscious as they were in previous generations, there are definite social classes in existence in most countries. A **social class** is a relatively permanent and homogeneous division in a society into which individuals or families sharing similar values, lifestyles, interests, wealth, status, education, economic positions, and behavior can be categorized.[22] Social class segments differ greatly, but they typically include upper, middle, and lower social classes. A 2005 report by *The New York Times* divided the population of the United States into the Top Fifth, Upper Middle, Middle, Lower Middle, and Bottom Fifth.[23]

    Social class is determined by demographic and socio-economic characteristics such as education, occupation, income, and wealth, with occupation being one of the strongest indicators. People's possessions are influenced by social class, and this includes where and how they travel, and in which activities they participate. Therefore, these social classes are significant to the hospitality and travel industry because of their relationship to leisure activities. Social classes have different media preferences and habits and ways in which individuals communicate with one another.

4. **Opinion Leaders.** Every social group contains **opinion leaders**, who act as channels of information for all members. They set the trend by seeking information or purchasing services and products before others do. There are very few general opinion leaders. Instead, there are several opinion leaders in every social group, each with specialized knowledge and information on different types of hospitality and travel services. For example, in a club of fishing enthusiasts, there may be opinion leaders with knowledge on where to fish for trout, bass, walleye, and pike. In a yacht club, these leaders may be divided into power boating, racing sailboat, and cruising sailboat enthusiasts. Opinion leaders tend to seek out and soak up more information on their specialty area. To be recognized as an expert in the group serves as an incentive to become even more knowledgeable.

    There are two major external sources of information on hospitality and travel services—commercial and social. **Marketer-dominated** or **commercial information sources** are the advertising and other promotional materials designed by corporations and other organizations. **Non marketer-dominated/non-commercial information** or **social information sources** are the interpersonal channels of information, including opinion leaders. Information from commercial sources flows to targeted customers in different ways. Sometimes it goes directly, with no opinion leaders involved. Other information goes to one group of opinion leaders and then is passed on to other customers. This is called a two-step communication flow. Multi-step communication occurs when information is passed through two or more groups of opinion leaders.

How Big is the Foreign Travel Market from China?

- China has a large population of about 1.4 billion people and the number of outbound travelers from China to other countries has boomed in recent years.
- Some 40.95 million Chinese residents traveled outside of their country in 2007 according to information from the China National Tourism Administration (CNTA).
- The number of outbound travelers from China in 2007 was double that for 2003.
- The top 10 destinations for Chinese visitors in 2007 were Hong Kong, Macau, Japan, South Korea, Vietnam, Russia, Thailand, USA, Singapore, and Malaysia.
- Chinese travelers are curious, optimistic, and status-conscious when it comes to long-haul travel. They want to see the world and how the other half lives.
- Chinese travelers are also driven by the status of seeing famous cities and attractions and experiencing something new and different.
- The United Nations World Tourism Organization (UNWTO) predicts that China will become one of the top sources of international tourists in the world in the near future.

Source: China National Tourism Administration. 2008, **http://www.cnta.gov.cn/html/2008-9/2008-9-10-11-35-98624.html**

The **product adoption curve** is a concept closely associated with the subject of opinion leaders and interpersonal communication flows. The curve is like a normal distribution curve that is bell-shaped. The idea of this curve is that the population can be divided into innovators (2.5 percent of the population), early adopters (13.5 percent), early majority (34 percent), late majority (34 percent), and laggards (16 percent).[24] Opinion leaders tend to be among the innovators and early adopters, because they are more ready than others to try out new products and services. Opinion leaders are most important to marketers. Because they influence how others behave, it pays to take time to identify and appeal to them.

5. **The Family.** The family is among the strongest interpersonal influences on customer behavior. The traditional wife-husband-children family unit has been buffeted by many pressures in recent decades, but still remains a significant part of the market for hospitality and travel organizations.

Traditional families pass through predictable stages over time; experts term this the **family life-cycle** concept. Purchasing behavior varies with life-cycle stages. Blackwell, Miniard, and Engel identify 11 family life-cycle stages:[25]

- Young singles
- Newly married couples
- Full nest I (youngest child not of school age)
- Full nest II (youngest child is of school age)
- Full nest III (parents are in mid-40s)
- Married, no kids
- Older singles
- Empty nest I (children have left home)
- Empty nest II (income earners have retired)
- Solitary survivor
- Retired solitary survivor

Free from the responsibilities of child rearing, the single, newly married, and empty nest I groups are less restricted in their vacation and holiday choices and spend more time and money on vacations.

Relative Importance of Social and Commercial Information

You have just read about five non marketer-dominated or interpersonal factors influencing customer behavior: cultures/subcultures, reference groups, social classes, opinion leaders, and the family. These are the social sources of information about services and products, but how important are these social sources of information, compared to the information generated by hospitality and travel organizations?

Interpersonal information is considered to be more objective and accurate than that received from hospitality and travel organizations, because the social source has no vested interest in the information. Socially-relayed information is less likely to be distorted by a person's perceptual biases, again because it is more credible. The more important the purchase, the higher the emphasis customers will attach to interpersonal information about that purchase. The same is true when a customer thinks of trying out a service for the first time or is uncertain about the benefits of alternative services.

Chapter 2 showed that it is more difficult to evaluate services than it is to evaluate products before purchasing them. Thus, customers place more weight on social sources of information when they buy services than they do when they buy products. Most research studies confirm this, and they refer to the information as word-of-mouth. In other words, the information on which the purchase is based is passed orally from social contacts to buyers. The hospitality and travel industry is one of the industries which is most dependent on **word-of-mouth information (W-O-M)**.

The Global Perspective: The Big Picture

Interactive Travelers as a Target Market

Tourism New Zealand

http://www.tourismnewzealand.com/
http://www.newzealand.com/travel/International/

Image copyright Henrique Daniel Araujo, 2008. Used under license from Shutterstock.com

Bungy jumping is an interactive sport that originated in New Zealand.

Profile of interactive travelers

In 2003, Tourism New Zealand announced its intentions to pursue "interactive travelers" as its major international target market. In the *New Zealand Tourism Strategy 2015*, they are defined as regular international travelers who consume a wide range of tourism products and services. They are travelers who seek out new experiences that involve engagement and interaction. Other characteristics of these customers are that they:

- Seek out new experiences that involve interacting with nature, social and cultural environments

(continues)

(continued)

- Respect the environment, culture, and values of others
- Are considered leaders by their peers
- Don't mind planning and booking holidays directly
- Prefer authentic products and experiences
- Are health conscious and like to "connect" with others
- Enjoy outdoor activity
- Are sociable and like to learn
- Have high levels of disposable income

The selection of interactive travelers as a target market was based on careful and in-depth research of international visitors to New Zealand, particularly its *International Visitor Survey* data and studies on customer satisfaction. The specific reasons for pinpointing interactive travelers were: (1) financial constraints required TNZ to precisely focus its marketing programs; (2) these customers most appreciated New Zealand's attractions and resources, and could be offered the highest quality visitor experiences; (3) New Zealand was a highly attractive destination to the customers in the interactive traveler segment; and (4) this group of travelers supported TNZ's other strategic goals including those related to environmental protection and conservation.

Image copyright B.S. Karan, 2008. Used under license from Shutterstock.com

Beautiful scenery and pristine landscapes are a hallmark of tourism in New Zealand.

Benefits of targeting interactive travelers

These travelers are also "interactive" in how they gather travel information and make bookings. They commonly use the Internet to plan, schedule, and book their vacations. Interactive travelers are also highly interested in experiencing the indigenous cultures in their destinations,

(continues)

(continued)

which for New Zealand is the Maori people. According to TNZ's research, these people represent 35 to 50 percent of the long-haul markets in its key origin markets, which include Australia, UK, USA, Japan, China, South Korea, and Germany.

Interactive travelers have higher disposable incomes and this makes them an attractive market in economic terms. The recent focus on this market by TNZ has helped spread tourism arrivals into the shoulder months from the peak season, and this has also been beneficial.

Interactive travelers like to experience the Maori culture in New Zealand.

Promoting to interactive travelers

TNZ is using the positioning and branding approach of *100% Pure New Zealand* in promoting to these travelers. The Internet plays a very important role in the overall campaign to attract interactive travelers.

(continues)

(continued)

A brand new website was launched in 1999, along with the introduction of the *100% Pure New Zealand* theme. This website is both highly attractive and interactive. In 2008, TNZ said that its traffic amounted to over 200,000 user sessions per month.

Satisfying interactive travelers in New Zealand

TNZ conducted the *Visitor Satisfaction Research 2006/07 study* and found that international visitors rate activities as contributing 65 percent to their overall vacation satisfaction while in New Zealand. Reflecting their interactive interests, the rating for "thrill-seeking and adventure activities" was a very high 8.8 out of 10. Physically-active activities and natural wonder activities also each received high evaluations of 8.3. Visits to *marae* (important traditional Maori community facilities), museums and art galleries, and Maori cultural performances earned a high score of 8.5.

Discussion Questions

1. In your opinion, which personal and interpersonal factors most influence the interactive travelers in choosing New Zealand as a vacation destination?
2. What other travel destinations do you think appeal most to interactive travelers, and which other ones would not be popular with these people? Why do you think so?
3. Which features should be designed into a website so that it has the greatest appeal and usefulness to interactive travelers?

Buying Processes of Individual Customers

The customer's buying or decision process describes another important aspect of behavior. This process describes the stages customers go through when making purchases. Understanding the process is most important to marketers, since the effectiveness of different types of advertisements and promotions varies with the **buying process** stage.

Most experts agree that there are distinct buying process stages, but they disagree over their labels and on the exact number of stages. The following 7-stage model is known as the Consumer Decision Process Model and is mostly applicable to hospitality and tourism except for the last step (Figure 4.11).[26]

Customers do not always follow each of the seven stages, however. Sometimes one or more are skipped.

1. **Need Recognition.** For the process to get going there must be a stimulus that leads customers to action; a need must be recognized. Under the

FIGURE 4.11
Consumer Decision
Process Model.

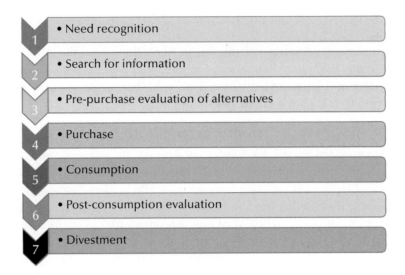

1. • Need recognition
2. • Search for information
3. • Pre-purchase evaluation of alternatives
4. • Purchase
5. • Consumption
6. • Post-consumption evaluation
7. • Divestment

topic of motivation, it was shown that organizations can use promotions (marketer-dominated or commercial information sources) to make potential customers recognize their needs. However, the stimulus might come from an interpersonal (non-marketer) source, such as an opinion leader, friend, relative, or business associate. A third source of the stimulus is an internal or personal drive, such as hunger or thirst. Most people do not need to be told when they are hungry or thirsty. A customer might recognize a need deficiency because of the combined impact of several stimuli.

2. **Search for Information.** When a customer recognizes a need, that need becomes a want. If a want exists, the customer normally begins an information search. Different sources of information may be tapped: marketer-dominated, non marketer-dominated; and internal. Marketer-dominated information sources include websites, other promotions, and the experience clues provided by hospitality and travel organizations. Nowadays the Internet is a major source for finding information about our industry. Non marketer-dominated information includes the interpersonal sources described earlier, as well as independent, objective assessments of hospitality and travel services, such as ratings by the American Automobile Association, Consumer Reports, Mobil, Michelin, restaurant critics, and independent guidebooks. The blogs of other travelers would also be included within non marketer-dominated information. **Internal sources** are those stored in the customer's own memory, including past experiences with a service and recollections of related promotions, and arising from other personal factors as discussed earlier.

Customers become aware of alternative services that might satisfy their needs during their information searches. These alternatives might be vacation destinations, hotels, resorts, airlines, attractions, restaurants, rental car firms, or packaged tours. Not all the alternatives available are always considered. Lack of awareness, perception of prohibitive costs, previous bad experiences, and negative word-of-mouth information are the reasons that some alternatives do not make the customer's final short list. This final list is often called the customer's **evoked set**, the alternatives that are chosen for further consideration.

3. **Pre-purchase Evaluation of Alternatives.** The next stage involves evaluating the short-listed alternatives using the customer's own criteria. Some people write these factors down on paper; others just consider them in their heads. Criteria can be objective or subjective. **Objective criteria** include prices, locations, physical characteristics of facilities and destinations (e.g., number of rooms, diversity of restaurants, availability of swimming pool, major attractions), and services offered (e.g., free breakfast, complimentary limousine service from the airport). **Subjective criteria** are intangible factors, such as the image of the hospitality and travel organization.

    Customers make judgments using their evaluation criteria. They develop attitudes and preferences for each alternative service. They may even rank the services from their first to their last choice. At the end of this process, one service is favored over the others.

4. **Purchase.** Customers now know which hospitality and travel services best meet their criteria. They develop a definite intention to buy these services, but their decision-making process may not be complete. Whether or not they buy can still be influenced by other factors. Customers may discuss their intentions with family members and other social contacts. There may be some people who disagree with their choices. This may lead to postponing the purchase or completely reevaluating it. Customers' personal, employment, or financial circumstances might change. A job may be lost, or there may be an illness in the family. Again, the purchase decision may be delayed.

    Another factor that often holds up purchases is the concept of perceived risk. All purchases involve risk. The risk can be financial (will my money be well spent?), psychological (will it improve my self-image?), or social (will my friends think more of me?). If the risk is considered too high, customers usually do something to reduce it. They may postpone their purchases, keep searching for more information, or choose a hospitality and travel organization with a national image and reputation. Risk can also be reduced by continually using the same organizations or destinations. Marketers have to do everything they can promotionally to reduce perceived risk.

    Various sub-decisions have to be made before a customer makes a purchase. For a family vacation, these sub-decisions might include when to travel, how to pay, how and where to make reservations, how long to stay, how much to spend, how to get there, what routes to take, and what to do at the destination. These decisions are not simple, and several different people may be involved in making them (e.g., mother, father, and children).

5. **Consumption.** This stage represents the travel and hospitality experience itself. Here, of course, the level of service received along with the experience clues influence customer satisfaction.

6. **Post-consumption Evaluation. Cognitive dissonance** is a state of mind that many customers feel after making a booking or after traveling. Customers are unsure whether they have made a good or bad decision. The level of dissonance increases with the importance and dollar value of the purchase. A customer is likely to experience less dissonance having chosen Burger King over McDonald's than when selecting an expensive restaurant for a 25th anniversary dinner. Dissonance is also greater when the purchased service lacks some of the appealing features of the rejected alternatives.

   When customers have used services, they evaluate them against their expectations. Expectations are based on the information they received from commercial (advertising and promotions) and social (family, friends, associates) sources. If expectations are met, customers are satisfied. If not, customers are usually dissatisfied. The secret for the hospitality and travel organization is never to promise more than can be delivered. It is a much better policy to promise less, knowing that you can probably exceed customer expectations.

   When customers are satisfied with services, the payoffs are great. Satisfied customers are much more likely to be repeat buyers. They have learned that the services they purchased meet their needs and expectations. By telling friends, relatives, and acquaintances about their positive experiences, satisfied customers influence others to buy because of word-of-mouth recommendations. The reverse is also true. Dissatisfied customers are less likely to be repeat customers. They will tell others of their experiences, discouraging them from buying.

7. **Divestment.** Hospitality and travel services are mainly intangible sodivestment is not an important decision process step. However, you might be thinking about what consumers do with food containers that they receive "to go" from restaurants, and also what do customers do with souvenirs that they purchased at destinations that they no longer want.

Information from interpersonal sources often carries more weight than that from marketer-dominated sources. Because we provide intangibles in this industry, marketers have to be especially concerned about dissatisfied customers. Chapter 2 mentioned that quality control is much harder to achieve in the service industry than it is in the manufacturing and packaged-goods industry. Ours is a people-to-people business. People and their behavior cannot easily be standardized. Monitoring customer satisfaction is vital. Chapter 6 discusses how this is done through research.

Classification of Decision Processes

Not all buying decisions are the same. They require different levels of effort from customers. Decisions can be broken down into three categories:

1. Routine decisions
2. Limited decisions
3. Extensive decisions

1. **Routine Decisions.** A routine buying decision is one that customers make frequently and with little effort. Customers buy as the result of habit, almost in a mechanical way. One or more of the buying process stages are skipped. Little perceived risk is involved, and little information is needed. The services are inexpensive. Customers know about all alternative services and have set criteria for evaluating them. Choosing a fast-food outlet for hamburgers is a routine decision for many. Most customers have a clear idea of what they will get when they buy a hamburger at McDonald's, Burger King, or Wendy's. They do not need to ask other people for information. Eating at any of these restaurants is inexpensive, and customers tend to make frequent visits.

2. **Limited Decisions.** Limited decision making takes more time and effort because customers go through all the buying process stages when they make a purchase. Although customers do not buy these services frequently, the services, or similar services, have been tried before. The perceived risk and level of spending are higher than they are for routine purchases. Customers know the evaluation criteria and most alternative services, and may ask other people for information on some alternatives. Eating out at a fine-dining restaurant often involves limited decision making. Customers know what kinds of food, service, and ambience they like. But they know they will spend more than they would at a fast-food outlet. They visit fine-dining restaurants less frequently and have less information about them. Limited decision making will also be used if the customer is thinking about trying one of these services for the first time.

3. **Extensive Decisions.** Extensive decision making takes the most time and effort. Customers get heavily involved in the process. The services are expensive and complex; perceived risk is high. Customers start with little information and previous experience and have not yet developed evaluation criteria. All of the stages in the buying process are followed, and the customers conduct an extensive information search among both commercial and social sources. Customers are more inclined to postpone or reevaluate purchase decisions. First-time cruises, holidays and vacations in Europe, honeymoon trips, African safaris, and round-the-world trips are good examples of extensive decisions. Customers will also use the services of experts, including travel agents and DMOs, and may search for information on the Web.

Behavior of Organizational Customers

Most hospitality and tourism organizations are involved in B2C marketing (business to consumer) and B2B marketing (business to business). In B2B marketing, the focus is on organizations rather than individual customers. It is true that organizations and individual customers face similar types of decisions about hospitality and travel services. However, how these decisions are made is quite different. **Organizational buying behavior** tends to have greater complexity because more people are involved in the decision-making processes, competitive bids may be required, and objective factors such as costs and service facility amenities may weigh more heavily than emotional ones. Because of different constraints and influences, these groups do not behave in exactly the same way. For example, an individual pleasure traveler can choose any destination. However, an association convention planner faced with a site rotation policy cannot consider certain destinations.

Organizational buyers include private-sector companies, government agencies, and non-profit organizations including associations and institutions (hospitals, universities, colleges, schools, associations, and other non-profit groups). The hospitality and travel industry itself consists of suppliers, carriers, travel trade intermediaries, and DMOs. Some groups and sectors of the industry market to organizations in other parts of the industry; for example, carriers, suppliers, and DMOs promote to travel trade intermediaries.

Earlier in this chapter, you heard about the buying process for individual customers. For organizational buyers, this process is more complex and may include all of the following steps:[27]

- *Problem recognition*: For example, an association must select a site for its annual convention in a future year. A corporation needs to obtain hotel rooms for its staff members.
- *General need description and product specification*: The association specifies its requirements in terms of a room block (number of rooms needed for convention), meeting and exhibition room needs, audio-visual equipment specifications, etc. The corporation describes the quality of rooms and related hotel services it requires for its staff.
- *Supplier search*: The association identifies destinations, hotels, and convention/exhibition centers that can meet its specifications. The corporation finds hotels and hotel companies that can meet its needs in the destinations where staff members will be staying.
- *Proposal solicitation (RFP)*: The association issues a request for proposals (RFP) to DMOs, hotels, and convention/exhibition centers to those identified in the supplier search. The corporation may also issue an RFP.
- *Proposal development and presentation*: The DMOs, hotels, and convention/exhibition centers develop proposals and present them to the association or corporation.
- *Supplier selection*: The association and corporation develop a set of criteria for evaluating all the proposals; review all the proposals submitted; and make a final selection.
- *Order-routine specification*: The final negotiations take place between the winning bidder and the association or corporation. The final details are specified. Specific agreements may have to be developed and signed, such as the pick-up on the room block.

- *Pre-consumption service*: The successful DMO, hotel, or convention/exhibition center may be required to provide certain services prior to guest arrival, e.g., a booking or reservations desk; providing general travel information, etc.
- *Consumption*: The association holds its convention in the selected destination. The staff members of the corporation stay in the selected hotel.
- *Performance review*: An evaluation is made on the performance of the destination in housing the association's convention, and on the corporation's staff members' satisfaction with the hotel.

As you can see, organizational buying decisions tend to be more complex and objective. Certainly, this is needed as more money is involved, and many people's needs have to be considered. Professional personal selling is required in securing business from organizational buyers, and exhibiting at convention and incentive travel shows may also be desirable. In addition, as Figure 4.12 suggests, it is often important to appeal to the ultimate users of services as

 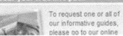 

FIGURE 4.12 Castles and conventions? Convention Scotland demonstrates that destinations have to appeal to both organizational buyers and attendees.

Courtesy of VisitScotland

well as the organizational decision-makers. This is especially true in the MICE markets (meetings, incentives, conventions, exhibitions).

Chapter Conclusion

Understanding how individual customers and organizational buyers behave is a prerequisite for effective marketing. Personal and interpersonal factors influence customers' choices of hospitality and travel services. The personal (internal) factors include needs, wants, and motivation; perception; learning; personality; lifestyle; and self-concept. Interpersonal influences come from cultures and subcultures, reference groups, social classes, opinion leaders, and the family. Customers place more weight on the recommendations they receive from their friends and associates than they do on the information supplied by hospitality and travel organizations. Word-of-mouth information is, therefore, a powerful force in our industry.

Customers go through different stages in making purchase decisions. The actual stages followed, and the sequence of these stages, vary according to the amount of the purchase and the perceived degree of difference between alternatives. To be successful, marketers must understand their customers' decision processes.

REVIEW QUESTIONS

1. Why is it important for a hospitality or travel organization to understand the behavior of its customers?
2. What are the personal (internal) factors that influence customer behavior?
3. What are the interpersonal factors that affect customer behavior?
4. What are marketer-dominated factors and how do they affect customers' perceptions?
5. What stages do customers usually go through when they make decisions about buying hospitality and travel services?
6. Do customers always go through the same stages when they make decisions? Why or why not?
7. Why is it important for marketers to understand the decision process their customers are following?
8. Why are organizational buyers different from individual customers, and how do buying processes compare?

CHAPTER ASSIGNMENTS

1. Take a close look at yourself and your family. What interpersonal factors affect the buying decisions made by members of the family? What personal factors tend to influence these choices? How could a hospitality or travel organization effectively appeal to you and other members of your family?

2. Select a hospitality or travel business and try to characterize the behavior patterns of its customers. What decision stages do its customers go through? What are their demographics, lifestyles, cultural backgrounds, social classes, and family life-cycle stages? How can the business best appeal to these groups?

3. Gather a selection of hospitality and travel advertisements. Which factors have been used in these ads to attract customer attention? How effectively have these factors been used? What could have been done to improve the impact of these ads on customers' perceptions?

4. Think about some major and minor purchases you have made in the past year. Which of the three decision-making processes did you use? How important were social information sources in your decision making? How important were marketer-dominated information sources? How can you apply what you have learned from this assignment to the marketing of hospitality and travel services?

WEB RESOURCES

ACORN, http://www.caci.co.uk/acorn/
American Automobile Association, http://www.aaa.com/
Avis, http://www.avis.com/
Claritas, http://www.claritas.com/
Cohorts, http://www.cohorts.com/
Consumer Reports, http://www.consumerreports.org/
Hertz, http://www.hertz.com/
Michelin Travel Guide, http://www.michelintravel.com/
Mobil Travel Guide, http://www.mobil.com/
Outward Bound, http://www.mobil.com/
SRI Consulting Business Intelligence, http://www.sric-bi.com/VALS/
U.S. Census Bureau, http://www.census.gov/

REFERENCES

1. Central Intelligence Agency. 2008. *CIA World Factbook 2008.*
2. Blackwell, Roger D., Paul W. Miniard, and James F. Engel. 2006. *Consumer Behavior*, 10th ed. Mason, Ohio: Thomson South-Western, 740.
3. Solomon, Michael. 2007. *Consumer Behavior*. 7th ed. Upper Saddle River, New Jersey: Pearson Prentice Hall, 630.
4. Mill, Robert Christie, and Alastair M. Morrison. 2009. *The Tourism System*. 6th ed. Dubuque, Iowa: Kendall/Hunt Publishing.
5. Mill, Robert Christie, and Alastair M. Morrison. 2009. *The Tourism System*. 6th ed. Dubuque, Iowa: Kendall/Hunt Publishing.
6. Blackwell, Roger D., Paul W. Miniard, and James F. Engel. 2006. *Consumer Behavior*, 10th ed. Mason, Ohio: Thomson South-Western, 311.

7. Bassett-Jones, Nigel, and Geoffrey C. Lloyd. 2005. "Does Herzberg's motivation theory have staying power?" *The Journal of Management Development*, 24(10), 929–943.

8. American Marketing Association. 2009. *Dictionary of Marketing Terms*, http://www.marketingpower.com/, accessed February 15, 2009.

9. Kotler, Philip, and Kevin Lane Keller. 2006. *Marketing Management*. 12th ed. Pearson Prentice Hall, 176.

10. Mill, Robert Christie, and Alastair M. Morrison. 2009. *The Tourism System*. 6th ed. Dubuque, Iowa: Kendall/Hunt Publishing.

11. Blackwell, Roger D., Paul W. Miniard, and James F. Engel. 2006. *Consumer Behavior*, 10th ed. Mason, Ohio: Thomson South-Western, 74–79.

12. Blackwell, Roger D., Paul W. Miniard, and James F. Engel. 2006. *Consumer Behavior*, 10th ed. Mason, Ohio: Thomson South-Western, 88.

13. Blackwell, Roger D., Paul W. Miniard, and James F. Engel. 2006. *Consumer Behavior*, 10th ed. Mason, Ohio: Thomson South-Western, 271.

14. Blackwell, Roger D., Paul W. Miniard, and James F. Engel. 2006. *Consumer Behavior*, 10th ed. Mason, Ohio: Thomson South-Western, 278.

15. SRI Consulting Business Intelligence (SRIC-BI). 2007. *Innovators*, http://www.sric-bi.com/VALS/, accessed May 22, 2007.

16. Claritas, *PRIZM® NE*, http://www.claritas.com/; CACI Ltd., *Welcome to the New ACORN*, http://www.caci.co.uk/acorn/

17. Mill, Robert Christie, and Alastair M. Morrison. 2009. *The Tourism System*. 6th ed. Dubuque, Iowa: Kendall/Hunt Publishing.

18. Central Intelligence Agency. 2009. *CIA World Factbook 2008*; U.S. Census Bureau. 2007. *Minority Population Tops 100 Million*, http://www.census.gov/Press-Release/www/releases/, accessed February 15, 2009.

19. Looking Glass Inc. 2009. *Hispanic Cohorts*, http://www.cohorts.com/hispanic.html, accessed February 15, 2009.

20. Blackwell, Roger D., Paul W. Miniard, and James F. Engel. 2006. *Consumer Behavior*, 10th ed. Mason, Ohio: Thomson South-Western, 523.

21. White, Katherine, and Darren W. Dahl. 2006. "To Be or Not to Be? The Influence of Dissociative Reference Groups on Consumer." *Journal of Consumer Psychology*, 16(4), 404–414.

22. Blackwell, Roger D., Paul W. Miniard, and James F. Engel. 2006. *Consumer Behavior*, 10th ed. Mason, Ohio: Thomson South-Western, 468.

23. The New York Times. 2005. *Class Matters. A Special Section.*

24. Rogers, Everett M. 2003. *Diffusion of Innovations*. 5th ed. New York: Free Press.

25. Blackwell, Roger D., Paul W. Miniard, and James F. Engel. 2006. *Consumer Behavior*, 10th ed. Mason, Ohio: Thomson South-Western, 490–493.

26. Blackwell, Roger D., Paul W. Miniard, and James F. Engel. 2006. *Consumer Behavior*, 10th ed. Mason, Ohio: Thomson South-Western, 70–86.

27. Kotler, Philip, and Kevin Lane Keller. 2006. *Marketing Management*. 12th ed. Pearson Prentice Hall, 203–213.

chapter 5

Analyzing Marketing Opportunities
Where Are We Now?

O V E R V I E W

This chapter begins by stressing the importance of research and analysis as the foundation of sound marketing decisions. It looks at three analysis techniques— situation, market, and feasibility analysis. A situation analysis is a very important element of the first of the five systematic steps in the hospitality and travel marketing system.

The benefits and products of preparing a situation analysis are identified. The fact that situation analysis results are the foundation for long- and short-term marketing planning is emphasized. Sample worksheets for a situation analysis are provided.

Situation analyses are used for existing operations. Market and feasibility analyses are used for proposed new or expanding businesses. The relationship among the three analysis techniques is emphasized.

O B J E C T I V E S

Having read this chapter, you should be able to:

- Define the terms *situation analysis, market analysis,* and *feasibility analysis.*

- Explain the relationship and differences between situation, market, and feasibility analyses.

- Explain the five benefits of doing a situation analysis.

- List in order and describe the steps in a situation analysis.

- List in order and describe the six major steps in a market analysis.

- List and describe the four additional steps in a feasibility analysis.

Analysis for Success

We begin this chapter with a catchy heading to get your attention quickly. Analysis for success—what does it mean? The analysis of marketing opportunities and problems is the foundation for starting and sustaining a successful business. No new venture should be launched without a thorough market or feasibility analysis. Likewise, no organization should be without at least an annual situation analysis.

What is a market or feasibility analysis, and why are they different from a situation analysis? A **situation analysis** is similar to a market analysis, but is done for an existing business. It is a study of the marketing strengths, weaknesses, opportunities, and threats of a business or other type of organization. A **market analysis** is a study of the potential demand for a new or expanding hospitality or travel business or other organizational type. It determines whether market demand is large enough. A **feasibility analysis** is a study of the potential demand for and economic feasibility of a business or other organizational type, and it includes a market analysis plus four additional steps. It looks at the total investment required to start a business, and the expected financial returns. Market and feasibility analyses are done for new businesses or other organizations that people are considering starting or expanding.

Most writers talk about either the situation analysis or the feasibility and market analysis. Few of them link all three techniques in an integrated way. Why then put them together in one chapter? The answer is simple; they are related. The first situation analysis should be built upon a market or feasibility analysis. The second situation analysis is founded on the first, and so on (Figure 5.1). If the initial market or feasibility analysis is placed on a shelf and ignored, the business loses an opportunity to use valuable research information and analysis. If each situation analysis does not build on prior ones, effort is wasted. Using these analysis tools has to be a continuous process. Just like marketing itself, performing these analyses must be a long-term activity.

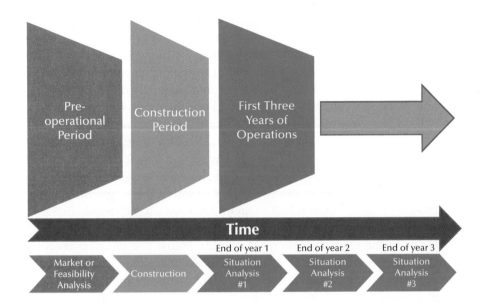

FIGURE 5.1
Relationship of market,
feasibility, and situation
analyses.

Chapter 3 pointed out that long-term marketing planning is a fundamental of the hospitality and travel marketing system. There is a strong link between planning and these analysis techniques. A market analysis should be the basis for a strategic (long-term) market plan. The situation analysis updates the initial market analysis. The new information is then used to prepare the marketing (short-term) plan and to update the strategic (long-term) market plan. The situation analysis does this by answering the question, "Where are we now?" Because the situation analysis is included in the first step in the hospitality and travel system described in Chapter 3, we start with it.

The Situation Analysis

We have already defined a situation analysis as a study of an organization's marketing strengths, weaknesses, opportunities, and threats. It is the first step in the hospitality and travel marketing system. It answers the question "Where are we now?" Sometimes the terms *marketing* or *market audit* and *SWOT analysis* are used instead of *situation analysis.* Before telling you what a situation analysis includes, let's look its five advantages:

1. Focuses attention on strengths and weaknesses
2. Assists with long-term planning
3. Helps in the development of marketing plans
4. Puts a priority on marketing research
5. Has spin-off benefits

1. **Focuses Attention on Strengths and Weaknesses.** The greatest benefit from doing a situation analysis every year is that it continually focuses an organization's attention on its strengths and weaknesses. In busy

organizations it is easy to lose track of the big picture and get caught up in day-to-day operations. It is convenient to accept the status quo and to believe that things will not change. Doing a situation analysis is similar to going to the dentist for a checkup or to the doctor for a physical. Both professionals examine you thoroughly and may tell you to change habits. Although you may not like the advice they give you, you know it will do you good. Giving an organization a routine checkup is just as beneficial and important to the continued health of an organization.

2. **Assists with Long-Term Planning.** The second benefit is that the completed situation analysis contributes to strategic (long-term) marketing planning. The situation analysis makes sure that the long-term planning process remains current. It does so by reviewing recent trends in the marketing environment.

3. **Helps in the Development of Marketing Plans.** The situation analysis plays an important role in structuring marketing plans. The results of the situation analysis are the base upon which plans are built. Preparing a plan without first doing a situation analysis is similar to trying to put a roof on a building with no walls. It is bound to fall flat. Marketing plans must reflect an organization's strengths and opportunities, and the situation analysis identifies them.

4. **Puts a Priority on Marketing Research.** Situation analyses rely heavily on research and place a premium on marketing research results. Research is needed to investigate new marketing opportunities, track customer satisfaction levels, evaluate competitors' strengths and weaknesses, and measure the effectiveness of past marketing plans. The human body continues to function as intended with continual nourishment from food and liquids. Marketing research plays the same role for an organization. The situation analysis focuses attention on the value of research and requires an ongoing research effort.

5. **Has Spin-off Benefits.** The fifth benefit is the by-products of the situation analysis. It provides an inventory, a status report on conditions, and a list of improvements needed in an organization's facilities and services. The inventory is useful for updating website information, and for preparing press or media kits and other information packages, such as those for meeting planners. The more obvious products of the situation analysis are as follows:

   a. An identification of strengths, weaknesses, opportunities, and threats
   b. An identification of primary competitors' strengths and weaknesses
   c. A community profile, including an indication of the opportunities and problems presented
   d. An assessment of the impact of marketing environment factors
   e. An historical record of marketing activities, successes, and failures

Like the marketing plan, the situation analysis should be a written document. It needs to be updated each time a new marketing plan is required.

Steps in a Situation Analysis

A situation analysis includes six steps. The procedure used is much like taking a photograph of someone. It starts by viewing the *big picture* (marketing environment analysis), focuses on the next level (location and community analysis), and then eventually zooms in more tightly on the organization's marketing position and plan. The situation analysis often goes by the name **SWOT analysis**, meaning an analysis of strengths, weaknesses, opportunities, and threats. The sequence in which the situation analysis steps are completed is slightly different than that followed in a market analysis, as can be seen in Figure 5.2.

As you can see, the order of the location and community analysis and the market potential analysis is reversed in these two types of analyses. The reordering of the steps is possible because in a situation analysis the business location is set and information is available on past customers. Since a market analysis is done for a proposed new business or a business expansion, the exact characteristics of customers are not known, and the location may not be established for a new business.

Now let's take a step-by-step look at how the situation analysis is done. Before doing this, you should know that because hospitality and travel organizations are very diverse, their situation analyses can be very different. For example, a hotel may have hundreds of rooms and other physical facilities to evaluate in its services analysis, but a travel agency or tour operator may only have one small office. A cruise line company may have several ships

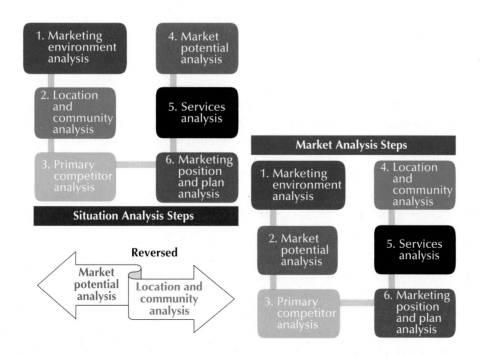

FIGURE 5.2 Situation and market analyses steps.

with thousands of berths among them, whereas a convention and visitors bureau has no physical facilities directly serving the public except for its office space and perhaps a visitor information center. Despite these differences, the same six steps should be followed by all hospitality and travel organizations.

1. **Marketing Environment Analysis.** Marketing is a long-term activity that requires constant planning and updating. Chapter 1 highlighted the need for marketers to carefully consider the marketing environment. No organization totally controls its future direction. Marketing environment factors often dictate the path to follow. A **marketing environment analysis** looks at these factors and their impacts. Chapter 1 identifies six marketing environment factors: competitors, the economy, laws and government regulations, society and culture, technology, and organizational priorities and goals. Analyzing these factors helps highlight long-term marketing opportunities and threats. It can be fatal for an organization to lose sight of the marketing environment that shapes the way future business is done. Checking and rechecking each marketing environment factor during the situation analysis is an effective way to anticipate important future events.

   Let's go back to the basics. What factors, other than an organization's internal operations, affect its marketing success and future direction? We can divide them into controllable and marketing environment factors. Controllables are factors over which complete control is possible. Marketing environment factors are beyond the total control of organizations. The economy, society, culture, government, technology, and population (demographic) trends certainly cannot be controlled. Competitors' and customers' behavior patterns can be influenced but cannot be completely controlled. The same is true of the hospitality and travel industry, suppliers, creditors, distribution channels, and other publics. The marketing mix (8 Ps) and the other elements of the hospitality and travel marketing system are the only items that can be totally controlled.

   What this discussion shows is that the marketing environment has three levels (Figure 5.3). The first level is the internal environment (the hospitality and travel marketing system), which can be controlled. The second is the business and industry environment and it can be influenced, but is uncontrollable. The third level is the marketing environment. It cannot be influenced and is also uncontrollable.

   Preparing a situation analysis for an existing organization takes a combination of research, forecasting, and judgment. Updating a situation analysis is easier if preprinted worksheets are used. This means anticipating the questions that require answers.

   Figure 5.4 is an example of a marketing environment analysis worksheet, which can be modified to suit the needs of individual organizations. The five marketing environment factors, excluding organizational priorities and goals, are listed in the left column. Two or three questions are then supplied to focus attention on the major trends for each factor.

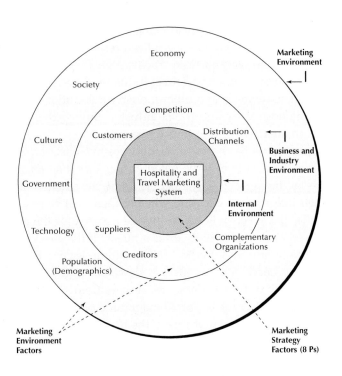

FIGURE 5.3 The hospitality and travel marketing environment.

The people doing the situation analysis respond to these questions by writing in the *"Answers"* and *"Impact Assessment"* columns. They must have an ongoing tracking and research program to supply the answers.

UNCONTROLLABLE FACTORS	QUESTIONS	ANSWERS	IMPACT ASSESSMENT How will this affect our organization?	+	–	Rating (+10 to –10)
1. COMPETITIVE AND INDUSTRY TRENDS	What has been the pattern of growth in the industry?					
	Which parts of the industry have enjoyed the greatest success recently?					
	Are there any new viable substitutes for our types of services?					
2. ECONOMIC TRENDS	What are the economic forecasts for the country?					
	What are the economic prospects for this region?					
3. POLITICAL AND LEGISLATIVE TRENDS	Are there any regulatory or legislative proposals that will directly affect us?					
4. SOCIETAL AND CULTURAL TRENDS	What lifestyles are gaining in popularity?					
	What sections of the population and subcultures are growing fastest?					
	What trends are happening in our target markets?					
5. TECHNOLOGICAL TRENDS	What has been the major technological advances in the country as a whole?					
	What have been the major technological advances in our industry?					
	What new technologies are in their developmental stage?					

FIGURE 5.4 Marketing environment analysis worksheet.

Most information for the analysis comes from secondary (previously published) research. There are specialized research organizations, such as the World Tourism Organization, Pacific Asia Travel Association, European Travel Commission and Travel Industry Association, consulting and research companies, and other industry associations that track major trends in the hospitality and travel industry. Buying their periodic reports is an alternative to in-house research.

Will these trends have a negative or a positive effect on the organization? This is the next item to be noted on the *Marketing Environment Analysis Worksheet* in Figure 5.4. The people doing the situation analysis have to use their judgment in deciding whether there will be any impact at all and whether the effects will be positive or negative. Is the result of the trend viewed as an opportunity or as a threat? If the effect is seen as being positive (an opportunity), the "+" (plus) column is checked. The "−" (minus) column is checked if the effect is viewed as negative (a threat). Next, each opportunity or threat is assigned a score from −10 to +10 in the "rating" column to reflect the expected magnitude of the effect of the trend. The bigger the opportunity or threat, the higher the assigned score.

2. **Location and Community Analysis.** The scope of the situation analysis then narrows to the local community and site location. Although a site location analysis is an accepted part of a market or feasibility analysis, it is seldom mentioned as an element of the situation analysis. However, assuming that a site location's advantages will last forever is dangerous. Changes in highway design, new building construction, new primary competitors, and other factors can all make a site less attractive. Remember that site locations can make or break hospitality and travel businesses. A site's market-related features must constantly be reevaluated. Of particular importance are proximity, accessibility, and visibility for potential customers.

    The **location and community analysis** is a two-part process. Part one is the Community Profile, which summarized the surrounding community's resources. Part two is an assessment of Community Trends and their impact. Figure 5.5 shows a sample *Location and Community Analysis Worksheet*. This form is most suitable for hospitality and travel organizations that derive most of their business either directly or indirectly from surrounding local communities. These businesses include hotels, restaurants, attractions and theme parks, travel agencies, car rental agencies, and shopping facilities. The factors analyzed in Figure 5.5 are the community's industrial and other employment base, population characteristics, residential neighborhoods, transportation system and facilities, visitor attractions and recreational facilities, events, health facilities, educational facilities, and local media and newsmakers.

    The people conducting the situation analysis first complete the community profile by writing answers in the *"Location and Community Profile"* section of Figure 5.5. Much of the required information can be obtained from local economic development agencies, chambers of

LOCATION AND COMMUNITY PROFILE			TRENDS	IMPACT
INDUSTRIAL AND OTHER EMPLOYMENT BASE	Major Employers: 1. _____ 2. _____ 3. _____ 4. _____ 5. _____	Employees (#): _____ _____ _____ _____ _____		
POPULATION CHARACTERISTICS (DEMOGRAPHICS)	Population Size: _____ Age Distribution: _____ Income Distribution: _____ Ethnic Distribution: _____ Sex Distribution: _____ Occupational Distribution: _____ Households: _____ Household Size Distribution: _____			
RESIDENTIAL NEIGHBORHOODS	Single Family: _____ Multi–Unit: _____			
TRANSPORTATION SYSTEM AND FACILITIES	Airport: _____ Expressways: _____ Bus Terminal: _____ Other: _____			
VISITOR ATTRACTIONS AND RECREATIONAL FACILITIES	1. _____ 2. _____ 3. _____ 4. _____ 5. _____			
EVENTS	1. _____ 2. _____ 3. _____ 4. _____ 5. _____			
HEALTH FACILITIES	Hospitals: _____ Medical / Dental Centers: _____ Nursing Homes: _____			
EDUCATIONAL FACILITIES	College / Universities: _____ High Schools: _____ Elementary Schools: _____ Trade Schools: _____			
LOCAL MEDIA AND NEWSMAKERS	Newspapers: _____ Radio: _____ T.V.: _____ Newsmakers: _____			

FIGURE 5.5 Location and community analysis worksheet.

commerce, or convention and visitors bureaus (CVBs). Next, they record in the "*Trends*" column any changes that have occurred in the nine location and community factors since the last situation analysis was completed. For example, this might include the opening of a new factory or the expansion of a local attraction. Finally, the "*Impact*" column is filled out by indicating how each trend is expected to affect the business. Layoffs at local industries might have a negative effect, whereas the construction of a new housing area would be a positive.

3. **Primary Competitor Analysis.** Competition as a whole is considered in the marketing environment analysis. It is also important to take a detailed look at **primary competitors**. These are usually businesses in the local community with a large share of the target markets identified in the market potential analysis. We say usually because there are some hospitality and travel organizations that compete on a broader geographic basis: resorts, theme parks, airlines, tour wholesalers, incentive travel planners, and destination marketing organizations (DMOs). Their primary competitors are more dispersed and may even be located abroad.

Primary competitors are put under the microscope to discover their major strengths and weaknesses. Different information sources are used to make this assessment. The first is obvious! Studying competitors' websites, advertising, and other promotional materials is the best place to start. What facilities, services, and advantages do they promote the most? If their marketing is effective, these are their major strengths. Physical inspection, observation, and sampling should come next. Most hotel and restaurant consultants use a standardized checklist to physically inspect competitive operations. Physically observing business patterns and customers is another technique. What is wrong with counting the cars passing through a competitive restaurant's drive-through or in their parking areas? How about adding up the people inside a competitor's restaurant? These are just two useful tricks among many. Sampling the competitor's services is another good way of evaluating them.

A *Primary Competitor Analysis Worksheet* is provided in Figure 5.6. This particular form has been designed for a lodging facility. By modifying the form in the "*Target Markets and Marketing Activities*" section, it can be adapted for use by restaurants, attractions, travel agencies, car rental agencies, and shopping facilities.

A separate primary competitor analysis worksheet should be completed for each primary competitor. The people doing the situation

NAME: ______
ADDRESS: ______
PHONE NUMBER: ______
OWNER: ______
MANAGER: ______

SITE LOCATION Located close to (check):	Travel Time (min)	PROXIMITY + –	ACCESS + –	VISIBILITY + –	
[ ] Downtown	____	[ ] [ ]	[ ] [ ]	[ ] [ ]	STRENGTHS:
[ ] Major Employers	____	[ ] [ ]	[ ] [ ]	[ ] [ ]	
[ ] Expressway	____	[ ] [ ]	[ ] [ ]	[ ] [ ]	
[ ] Airport	____	[ ] [ ]	[ ] [ ]	[ ] [ ]	
[ ] Suburbs	____	[ ] [ ]	[ ] [ ]	[ ] [ ]	WEAKNESSES:
[ ] Shopping Centers	____	[ ] [ ]	[ ] [ ]	[ ] [ ]	
[ ] Other Shopping Districts	____	[ ] [ ]	[ ] [ ]	[ ] [ ]	
[ ] Restaurant District	____	[ ] [ ]	[ ] [ ]	[ ] [ ]	
[ ] Attraction #1: ______	____	[ ] [ ]	[ ] [ ]	[ ] [ ]	
[ ] Attraction #2: ______	____	[ ] [ ]	[ ] [ ]	[ ] [ ]	
[ ] Attraction #3: ______	____	[ ] [ ]	[ ] [ ]	[ ] [ ]	COMPARISON:
[ ] University / College	____	[ ] [ ]	[ ] [ ]	[ ] [ ]	
[ ] Hospital / Medical	____	[ ] [ ]	[ ] [ ]	[ ] [ ]	
[ ] Other #1: ______	____	[ ] [ ]	[ ] [ ]	[ ] [ ]	
[ ] Other #2: ______	____	[ ] [ ]	[ ] [ ]	[ ] [ ]	
[ ] Other #3: ______	____	[ ] [ ]	[ ] [ ]	[ ] [ ]	

TARGET MARKETS AND MARKETING ACTIVITIES: 1. TARGET MARKETS SERVED:	Guest Rooms	(Percentages) F&B	Convention/Meeting	COMMENTS:	
Target Market #1	[ ]	[ ]	[ ]		STRENGTHS:
Target Market #2	[ ]	[ ]	[ ]		
Target Market #3	[ ]	[ ]	[ ]		
Target Market #4	[ ]	[ ]	[ ]		WEAKNESSES:
Target Market #5	[ ]	[ ]	[ ]		
Target Market #6	[ ]	[ ]	[ ]		
Target Market #7	[ ]	[ ]	[ ]		COMPARISON:
Target Market #8	[ ]	[ ]	[ ]		
Target Market #9	[ ]	[ ]	[ ]		
Target Market #10	[ ]	[ ]	[ ]		

2. MARKETING ACTIVITIES: Major activities:	COMMENTS:	
Advertising ______		STRENGTHS:
Sales Promotion ______		WEAKNESSES:
Personal Selling ______		
Public Relations ______		COMPARISON:
Merchandising ______		
Travel Trade ______		

FIGURE 5.6 Primary competitor analysis worksheet.

analysis should first provide the information on the site location, target markets, and marketing activities of the primary competitor. Completing this form is not just a fact-finding exercise. While the facts are important, their interpretation is even more important. This interpretation is accomplished by filling out the right column in Figure 5.6. What are competitors' major strengths that they use effectively in marketing? What are their weaknesses, and how do we compare these strengths and weaknesses? These are three key questions that the *Primary Competitor Analysis Worksheet* should answer for each primary competitor.

To complete the primary competitor analysis, a form such as that shown in Figure 5.7 (*Services Analysis Worksheet*) should be completed for

FACILITIES AND SERVICES INVENTORY

1. GUEST ROOMS (#):

[ ] Singles
[ ] Twin (Singles)
[ ] Twin (Double)
[ ] Single and Double
[ ] Queens
[ ] Kings
[ ] Suites with Parlors
[ ] Convertible Parlors
[ ] Studios
[ ] Connecting
[ ] Other: ______
[ ] Other: ______

COMMENTS:

STRENGTHS:

WEAKNESSES:

OPPORTUNITIES/ IMPROVEMENTS:

2. FOOD AND BEVERAGE FACILITIES (#):

(# seats)	1	2	3	4
Restaurant	[ ]	[ ]	[ ]	[ ]
Coffee Shop	[ ]	[ ]	[ ]	[ ]
Snack Bar	[ ]	[ ]	[ ]	[ ]
Lounge Bar	[ ]	[ ]	[ ]	[ ]
Pub	[ ]	[ ]	[ ]	[ ]
Cabaret	[ ]	[ ]	[ ]	[ ]
Licensed Patio	[ ]	[ ]	[ ]	[ ]
Other	[ ]	[ ]	[ ]	[ ]

COMMENTS:

STRENGTHS:

WEAKNESSES:

OPPORTUNITIES/ IMPROVEMENTS:

3. CONVENTION, MEETING, AND BANQUET FACILITIES (#):

(# seats)	Banquet	Theatre	Other
Room ______	[ ]	[ ]	[ ]
Room ______	[ ]	[ ]	[ ]
Room ______	[ ]	[ ]	[ ]
Room ______	[ ]	[ ]	[ ]
Room ______	[ ]	[ ]	[ ]
Room ______	[ ]	[ ]	[ ]
Room ______	[ ]	[ ]	[ ]
Room ______	[ ]	[ ]	[ ]
Room ______	[ ]	[ ]	[ ]
Room ______	[ ]	[ ]	[ ]

COMMENTS:

STRENGTHS:

WEAKNESSES:

OPPORTUNITIES/ IMPROVEMENTS:

4. RECREATIONAL FACILITIES (Provided on–site):

INDOOR

[ ] Pool
[ ] Whirlpool / Hot Tub
[ ] Sauna / Steam Room
[ ] Tennis Courts
[ ] Exercise Room
[ ] Games Room
[ ] Squash Courts
[ ] Racquetball / Handball Courts
[ ] Dance Floor
[ ] Jogging Track
[ ] Other ______
[ ] Other ______

OUTDOOR

[ ] Pool
[ ] Whirlpool / Hot Tub
[ ] Golf Course
[ ] Tennis Courts
[ ] Beach
[ ] Boat Rentals
[ ] Boat Docks
[ ] Marina
[ ] Alpine Skiing
[ ] Cross–country skiing
[ ] Other ______
[ ] Other ______

COMMENTS:

STRENGTHS:

WEAKNESSES:

OPPORTUNITIES/ IMPROVEMENTS:

5. GUEST SERVICES:

[ ] Airport Limo
[ ] Complimentary Coffee
[ ] Babysitting
[ ] Bilingual Staff
[ ] Room Service
[ ] Doormen
[ ] Bell Staff
[ ] Beauty / Barber Shop
[ ] Shoe-Cleaning
[ ] Office Center
[ ] Other ______
[ ] Free Parking
[ ] Valet Parking
[ ] Executive Floor (s)
[ ] Executive Lounge
[ ] Wake–up calls
[ ] Massage
[ ] Dry Cleaning
[ ] Turndown Service
[ ] Free Paper
[ ] Other ______
[ ] Other ______

COMMENTS:

STRENGTHS:

WEAKNESSES:

OPPORTUNITIES/ IMPROVEMENTS:

FIGURE 5.7 Services analysis worksheet.

each primary competitor. Again, this form was designed for a lodging facility, but it can be adapted to suit other hospitality and travel businesses. It includes an inventory of competitor's facilities and services (left side) and an analysis of competitive strengths and weaknesses.

4. **Market Potential Analysis.** A **market potential analysis** for an existing hospitality and travel organization considers both the organization's past and potential customers. It is a research study of the market potential, or target markets, upon which the business is built.

Chapter 6 discusses marketing research techniques in detail. In this chapter, these tools are mentioned where they apply. Some important research terminology should be discussed before you go any further. A market potential analysis uses a combination of secondary and primary research. **Secondary research** is already published information available from other sources, either internally (e.g., a hotel's registration database) or externally (e.g., from the local economic development agency or chamber of commerce). **Primary or original research** is data collected for the first time, by a method other than secondary research, to answer specific questions, such as doing a survey.

The situation analysis uses a systematic, seven-step process in preparing the market potential analysis. This process is also used where research is required in other parts of the situation analysis. The seven steps involved are as follows:

a. Decide on research questions
b. Collect and analyze secondary information
c. Design primary research, data collection method, and forms
d. Design sample and collect primary information
e. Analyze and interpret primary information
f. Draw conclusions and make recommendations
g. Present results

Figure 5.8 provides ideas on how this process is applied in a *Market Potential Analysis Checklist.* Listing the key questions for which answers are needed is the starting point for the research. The following seven key research questions about past and potential customers are answered in the market potential analysis.

a. **Who?** Who are the customers?
b. **What?** What needs are they trying to satisfy?
c. **Where?** Where do the customers live and work? Where do they buy?
d. **When?** When do they buy?
e. **How?** How do they buy?
f. **How many?** How many customers are there?
g. **How do?** How do they feel about our organization and about primary competitors?

Figure 5.9 shows the detailed research questions that should be answered in a Market Potential Analysis.

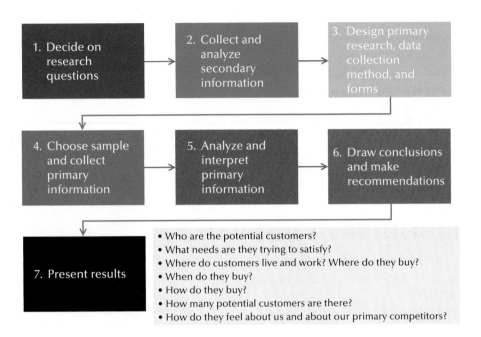

We now know the types of information we need. Next, we have to make a choice. Should we use secondary research, primary research, or a combination of both? The best answer is always a combination of both. Secondary information is less expensive and is more quickly available. Primary research is more difficult to do, is more expensive, and takes longer to gather, but it provides more specific and reliable information.

The best place to start the market potential analysis is by collecting secondary research information. It does not make any sense to reinvent the wheel! If someone has already gathered the data and it is easily available, primary research is not required. Secondary information also helps us plan primary research. It pinpoints information gaps, ways of segmenting the market, and profiles of average customers. It helps in structuring primary research questions. Get smart quick is the key principle in making effective use of secondary information. Chapter 6 looks at major information sources and quick ways of using them.

Now let us take a more detailed look at what is involved in the past customer analysis and the potential customer analysis.

a. *Past Customer Analysis.* Every hospitality and travel organization should have databases that track customer volumes and characteristics. This is essential for measuring success and for planning future marketing activities. Past customers are usually an excellent source of new business. Many become repeat users and influence others to become customers through positive "word of mouth." Knowing as much as possible about past customers is one of the best investments of an organization's time and money. With so much emphasis in business now on relationship marketing and database marketing, it is

STEP 1	Decide on research questions.
[ ]	**WHO?** Who are the customers?
[ ]	**WHAT?** What needs are they trying to satisfy?
[ ]	**WHERE?** Where do the customers live and work? Where do they buy?
[ ]	**WHEN?** When do they buy?
[ ]	**HOW?** How do they buy?
[ ]	**HOW MANY?** How many customers are there?
[ ]	**HOW DO?** How do they feel about our organization and about primary competitors?
STEP 2	**Collect and analyze secondary information.**
[ ]	What information do we have on customers in our own organization's records?
[ ]	What information have other organizations gathered on these customers?
[ ]	Do we need to do any further or new (primary) research?
STEP 3	**Design primary research data collection method and forms.**
[ ]	Which research method should be used to collect data (experimental, observational, survey, or focus groups)?
[ ]	Which specific research techniques should be used (e.g., mail, telephone, personal interview, online, or in-house, self-administered surveys)?
[ ]	What questions and other materials should be included on data collection forms?
[ ]	How should data collection forms be administered and analyzed?
STEP 4	**Design sample and collect primary information.**
[ ]	Who are the research subjects (e.g., in-house customers, corporate travel managers, travel agents, or householders)?
[ ]	How many research subjects are there?
[ ]	What sample selection method and sample size should be used?
STEP 5	**Analyze and interpret primary information.**
[ ]	What procedures should be used for coding, editing, and entering or tabulating the data?
[ ]	Which statistical analysis techniques and programs should be used to analyze the data?
[ ]	What are the results and how should we interpret these results?
STEP 6	**Draw conclusions and make recommendations.**
[ ]	What types of conclusions can we draw from the results?
[ ]	What types of recommendations can we make?
[ ]	What form of report or reports are required?

FIGURE 5.9 Detailed research questions in a market potential analysis.

extremely important to have an in-depth profile of past customers. Figure 5.10 shows a *Past Customer Market Potential Analysis Worksheet*. The people completing the situation analysis provide answers in the lined section on the right of the worksheet and check off each topic after it has been covered.

b. *Potential Customer Analysis.* Organizations constantly have to be alert for new sources of customers. A situation analysis helps achieve this in several different ways. The location and community analysis discovers new market opportunities arising from the site location (proximity)

WHO? 1.   Who are our past customers?

[   ]   Target markets _____

[   ]   Demographic profile _____

[   ]   Purposes of trips _____

[   ]   Lifestyle/psychographic profile _____

[   ]   Party or group sizes _____

[   ]   Number of previous visits or uses of our business _____

WHAT? 2.   What needs have past customers tried to satisfy?

[   ]   Needs _____

[   ]   Benefits sought _____

[   ]   Services purchased _____

[   ]   Dollar volumes purchased _____

WHERE? 3.   Where do past customers live and work?

[   ]   Place of residence _____

[   ]   Place of work _____

[   ]   Location before use _____

[   ]   Location after use _____

WHEN? 4.   When have past customers bought?

[   ]   Day part, daily, weekly, monthly _____

[   ]   Weekday versus weekend _____

[   ]   Lengths of stay or visit _____

HOW? 5.   How have past customers bought?

[   ]   Travel agents, tour operators, and other intermediaries used _____

[   ]   Sources of information _____

[   ]   Internet use _____

[   ]   Decision-makers and influencers _____

[   ]   Reservations methods used _____

[   ]   Routes/transportation used _____

HOW MANY? 6.   How many past customers do we have?

[   ]   Total number of customers _____

[   ]   Number of customers by market segment _____

[   ]   Number of repeat customers _____

[   ]   Customer counts by day part, day, week, month, and year _____

HOW DO? 7.   How do past customers feel about our organization and about primary competitors?

[   ]   How well are we meeting their needs? _____

[   ]   How can we improve to better serve their needs? _____

[   ]   Will they recommend us to others? _____

[   ]   What is different about the way we do business that customers like? _____

[   ]   What image do they have of us? _____

[   ]   How well are competitors meeting their needs? _____

[   ]   What problems have they had with competitors? _____

[   ]   Would they recommend competitors to others? _____

[   ]   What is different about the way competitors do business that customers like? _____

[   ]   How are competitors different from us? _____

FIGURE 5.10   Past customer market analysis worksheet.

and from cooperation with complementary businesses. The primary competitor analysis pinpoints competitors' target markets and successful marketing activities. Businesses can certainly duplicate successful techniques. There is no law against imitation! The services analysis highlights strengths and opportunities, some of which may not have been fully capitalized upon. The past customer analysis may produce methods of increasing repeat use and customer spending. Finally, the marketing environment analysis may indicate new potential markets.

Once identified, potential markets must be researched. This may take place during the situation analysis or at some other time. Researching new markets is a constant activity of a marketing-oriented organization. The situation analysis is one of the best sources of ideas for research programs.

- *Who are the potential customers?* How do we select the potential customers to research? Usually this is done by specifying a market segment or segments in which the organization sees some business potential. Market segmentation is a subject that Chapter 7 reviews in detail. In general, there are many ways to segment a market. Some methods are traditional, having become standard practice in the hospitality and travel industry for years. Dividing lodging customers by purpose of trip is an example. Purpose-of-trip segmentation is also popular with airlines, travel agencies, restaurants, DMOs, and others. Purpose-of-trip segmentation first divides customers into business and pleasure travelers and then subdivides these two segments using factors such as price and group size. Non-traditional, or newer, methods include lifestyle and benefit segmentation. They are more sophisticated and are slowly gaining popularity.
- *What needs are potential customers trying to satisfy?* This is a much more difficult question to answer! It often gets skipped over because it is hard to answer. Remember our Chapter 1 definition of marketing as satisfying customers' needs and wants? How can an organization satisfy potential customers' needs if it does not know what these needs are? It is easy to fall into the trap of assuming that all hospitality and travel organizations in the same industry sector (hotels, restaurants, travel agencies, theme parks, DMOs, etc.) are alike and, therefore, all their customers must also be alike. Secondary research information points the way. But there is only one surefire way of getting good information on potential customers' needs—go right to the source! Using the primary research method, ask potential customers about their needs and the benefits they want.
- *Where do potential customers live and work?* Secondary information comes first in determining where potential customers live and work. A few examples help explain the process. The **GIS (Geographic Information System)** has revolutionized how the industry evaluates the market potential in specific communities.[1] GIS is extensively

INTERNET MARKETING

Using the Internet to Get a Trade Area Analysis: SiteReports

- The Internet has made it easier to do trade area analysis through services like Claritas' SiteReports.
- Reports and maps can be ordered online using a one-, three-, or five-mile radius from the selected site or for a standard geographic unit like a zip-code area.
- Various categories of reports can be ordered and delivered online: (1) Demographic Reports, (2) Business Reports, (3) Retail Reports, (4) Shopping Center Reports, (5) Restaurant Reports, (6) Financial Reports, (7) Segmentation Reports, and (8) Traffic Reports. The Segmentation Reports are based on Claritas' *PRIZM NE* system.
- The Restaurant Reports identify the Top Chain restaurant locations, which can also be shown on a map.

Source: (2008). **http://www.claritas.com/eReports/Default.jsp**

Student Questions

1. Which types of hospitality, travel and tourism marketers would find these trade area analyses to be the most useful?
2. How large of a radius should be used for analyzing the market for a new restaurant business and why?
3. What are the key data or statistics that should be produced from a trade area analysis like this?
4. Should a trade area analysis be repeated and, if so, why is there a need to do so?

used in **trade area analysis**, a research study that analyzes the market within an organization's surrounding trade area. GIS maps demographic and socio-economic characteristics of potential customers within trading areas. **Geo-demographic analysis** is a technique that captures the differences in resident characteristics in specific intra-urban areas (within urban areas).[2] These two tools provide useful data and insights for hospitality and travel businesses that rely heavily on local communities such as restaurants, travel agencies, stores, and amusement and theme parks. They consider customer demographics and socio-economics, are based on census data, and often now use GIS. A restaurant does not usually have to look far for its potential customers; for example, one expert says that 80 percent of a restaurant's customers come from within a 3-mile radius.[3]

- *Where, when, and how do they buy?* To answer these questions, we again get some clues from secondary research, but the most precise answers come from primary research. Primary research is harder to collect and is more expensive and time-consuming: it must be carefully planned. Many primary research tools are available. Choosing the right ones for the job is the key planning task. Chapter 6 discusses the alternatives. It divides these tools into four groups: survey, observational, experimental, and simulation research. The survey method is by far the most frequently used in the analysis of potential customers. Personal, telephone, online, and mail surveys are the most used survey techniques.

Let us carry through with our lodging and restaurant examples to show how a primary research plan is put together. We will assume that the people doing the analysis of potential customers have analyzed the local areas and picked out the biggest business-generating markets (areas). The next step is to conduct interviews with corporate travel managers, convention/meeting planners, and other travel trade intermediaries. An interview is another name for a survey carried out in person or on the telephone. The author's own experience in doing potential customer analyses for lodging facilities indicates that personal interviews (surveys) are more effective than telephone interviews. Some of the key questions that need to be answered in these interviews are the following:

i. Where do they buy?

- To which destinations are trips made?
- What types of lodging formats are preferred (e.g., luxury, upscale, extended-stay, budget)?
- Which types of location are preferred (e.g., downtown/CBD, airport, resort)?
- Which specific lodging properties are used frequently?
- What do travelers like most about these specific properties?
- What major problems or weaknesses have they experienced at these specific properties?

ii. When do they buy?

- When are important booking decisions made?
- When are trips made?

iii. How do they buy?

- Who makes the decision on choices of destinations and specific lodging choices?
- Who else has a say in the decision-making process?
- Are frequent-guest or frequent-flyer programs important?
- Are travel agents used?
- Are other travel intermediaries used?

Figure 5.11 provides a *Potential Customer Market Potential Analysis Worksheet*.

WHO? 1. **Who are the potential customers?**

[   ]   Market segments   _____

[   ]   Demographic profile   _____

[   ]   Lifestyle/psychographic profile   _____

[   ]   Party or group sizes   _____

[   ]   Frequency of visits/uses of business like ours   _____

WHAT? 2.   **What needs are potential customers trying to satisfy?**

[   ]   Needs   _____

[   ]   Benefits sought   _____

[   ]   Services sought   _____

[   ]   Expenditures/spending   _____

WHERE? 3.   **Where do potential customers live and work?**

[   ]   Place of residence   _____

[   ]   Place of work   _____

[   ]   Location before use   _____

[   ]   Location after use   _____

WHEN? 4.   **When do potential customers buy?**

[   ]   Day part, daily, weekly, monthly   _____

[   ]   Weekday versus weekend   _____

[   ]   Lengths of stay or visit   _____

HOW? 5.   **How do potential customers buy?**

[   ]   Use of travel agents, tour operators, and other intermediaries   _____

[   ]   Sources of information   _____

[   ]   Use of Internet   _____

[   ]   Decision-makers and influencers   _____

[   ]   Reservations methods   _____

[   ]   Routes/transportation   _____

HOW MANY? 6.   **How many potential customers are there?**

[   ]   Total number of potential customers   _____

[   ]   Number of potential customers by market segment   _____

HOW DO? 7.   **How do potential customers feel about our organization and about primary competitors?**

[   ]   How well can we meet potential customers' needs?   _____

[   ]   What is different about the way we do business that potential customers   _____
may like?

[   ]   What image do potential customers have of us?   _____

[   ]   How well are competitors meeting potential customers' needs?   _____

[   ]   What problems have potential customers had with competitors?   _____

[   ]   Would potential customers recommend competitors to others?   _____

[   ]   What is different about the way competitors do business that potential   _____
customers like?

[   ]   How are competitors different from us?   _____

FIGURE 5.11   Market potential analysis worksheet: potential customers.

Industry Players

Indoor Waterpark Resorts: Market Analysis

Image copyright Glenda M. Powers, 2008. Used under license from Shutterstock.com

Indoor waterpark resorts offer a fun environment for families irrespective of the weather outside.

An indoor waterpark resort is an entertainment-based hotel property. According to David Sangree, an expert in these types of resorts, they must include a minimum of 10,000 square feet (930 square meters) of indoor waterpark space. These resort hotels cost more to develop than traditional city hotels because of the expense of building the waterpark area. Therefore, before developers "splash out" the money, it is important to conduct thorough market and feasibility analyses.

At the beginning of 2008, there were 169 hotel waterpark resorts in the USA, with another 55 expected to be opened during the rest of the year. This is a hot trend in hotel development in North America (Coy and Haralson, 2008); there were 14 of these hotels in Canada in mid-June 2008. One of the largest of these properties is the Kalahari Resort in Sandusky, Ohio. The resort was expanded in 2007; it now has 884 guest rooms and 173,000 square feet (16,072 square meters) of waterpark area. The Wisconsin Dells area has several large indoor waterpark resorts and the area is generally considered to be the birthplace of the concept in the 1990s. In fact, many of these resorts are located in the Midwest and Ontario where the winter weather tends to be rather cold and harsh.

So, how should a market analysis be completed for these rather expensive, but popular, resorts? As Chapter 5 indicates, this should definitely involve a marketing environment analysis, location and community analysis, primary competitor analysis, and market potential analysis. David Sangree of Hotel & Leisure Advisors (H&LA) recommends that the market analysis should be focused mainly within a 120- to 180-mile (193- to 290- kilometer) radius of the site; about the

(continues)

(continued)

equivalent of a 2- to 3-hour drive. He further suggests that the market analysis should an analysis of economics and demographics, and the hotel and indoor waterpark resort markets within this "catchment area."

Economics and Demographics

- *Population trends:* The size of the population is very important and particularly to determine if the population is growing or declining.
- *Household growth:* The presence of children in households is a critical factor, since these resort hotels specialize in attracting younger families. Is the number of households with children growing or not?
- *Household economics:* The average household income and disposable income levels are key indicators, as they reflect the ability to afford a vacation at a resort like these.
- *Catchment area economics:* The presence of other existing major tourist attractions in the area is a great advantage for an indoor waterpark resort. In addition, having major companies or industries that are growing is a major plus. Of course, assessing the overall economic health of the area and recent economic growth is a must.
- *Catchment area transportation:* Convenient access, especially by highway, is a prerequisite for the success of an indoor waterpark resort. The availability of a major airport is another important factor.

Image copyright Sean/ The Shamen, 2008. Used under license from Shutterstock.com

The Wisconsin Dells is an area where there are several large indoor waterpark resorts.

(continues)

(continued)

- *Comparative data:* Here the analyst should compare the data gathered for the catchment area with similar data for other areas that have successful indoor waterpark resorts. Two such areas are the Wisconsin Dells and Sandusky, Ohio in the United States.

Hotel Market

- *Existing and potential competitors:* How many competitive hotels are there in the area and how have they performed in the past two to three years?
- *Opening of new hotels:* How many new hotels have opened in the past two or three years and how did they affect the hotel market as a whole?
- *Potential new hotels:* Determine the number and types of new hotels likely to be opened in the next three to five years, and their potential impact on the area's hotel market.
- *Market segmentation and market penetration:* Identify and analyze the hotels that have a major focus on the leisure market, as these will be the primary competitors for the proposed new indoor waterpark resort.

Indoor Waterpark Resort Market

- *Existing and potential competitors:* How many existing and proposed new indoor waterpark resorts are there in the area and how have they performed in the past two to three years? Determine their levels of competitiveness with the proposed new indoor waterpark resort.
- *Waterpark pricing and usage:* Here the analyst determines the pricing structures for the hotel guestrooms and the water parks at existing competitive properties. In addition, the total number of guests and other visitors has to be estimated.

Discussion Questions

1. Are there any other questions that you would include in a market analysis for an indoor waterpark resort and why would you add them?
2. What do you feel are the main reasons for the recent popularity of indoor waterpark resort hotels in terms of customer demands and trends?
3. In terms of the economic feasibility of an indoor waterpark resort, what are the main factors that influence its return on investment?

As the follow-up to a trade area and geo-demographic analysis, interviewers may survey people in specific parts of the area. These people may live in a single zip- or postcode area or within a specific radius around the business' location. They may also be selected because of demographic and socioeconomic characteristics such as age, household income, household composition, or occupation. The same *where*, *when*, and *how* questions are asked. For example, the second question becomes "What restaurant format is preferred?"

- *How many potential customers can we attract?* With all the secondary and primary research completed, it is time to draw conclusions and make recommendations. About what? Remember the *who, what, where, when, how, how many*, and *how do* questions? These are the key questions that the research findings must now answer. Answering the *how many* question is particularly important since the answer determines if the potential market is big enough. Whatever the answer, it is only an estimate. The best estimates require a combination of research results, experience with the types of business under consideration, and excellent judgment.

5. **Services Analysis.** What are the organization's strengths and weaknesses? What opportunities and problems do they present? These are the two most important questions the **services analysis** addresses (Figure 5.7). This self-analysis is more realistic and beneficial if it comes after the analysis of primary competitors and market potential. It is a two-part process involving an inventory of facilities and services and a physical inspection of their condition.

6. **Marketing Position and Plan Analysis.** The last situation analysis step draws from all previous ones. It is the culmination of the information-gathering and analysis process. Two key questions are considered: "What position (image) do we occupy in the minds of past and potential customers?" and "How effective is our marketing?" These two topics are discussed in detail later in Chapters 8 and 20 respectively. For now it is sufficient to look at the information requirements and results.

   Figure 5.12 shows a *Market Position and Plan Analysis Worksheet* for a lodging facility. It provides a history of past marketing activities and their effectiveness. In the first part of the worksheet, strengths, unique features, and customer benefits are noted. In the second section, marketing expenditures are entered and an evaluation of effectiveness is made.

The Market Analysis

Let's face the hard facts right now. Not every organization has a market or feasibility analysis. Some owners and executives do not see the value of these analyses. Others perform these analyses, but not for marketing purposes. Often, they are completed only to satisfy a lender's requirements. Still another group does them for marketing reasons and for lenders, but puts the analyses on the shelf on the day their business opens. Why do people not make greater use of this outstanding source of marketing information? There is no logical answer, but such people are wasting a good opportunity.

There are many reasons for doing a market analysis. When a new business is being considered, several groups need to see this analysis, including the

1. MARKET POSITION ANALYSIS	Strengths, Unique Features, and Benefits:
All Target Markets	
Target Market #1	
Target Market #2	
Target Market #3	
Target Market #4	
Target Market #5	
Target Market #6	
Positioning Statement:	

2. PLAN ANALYSIS AND HISTORY

MARKETING MIX ELEMENTS — ACTUAL EXPENSES (19__ , 19__ , 19__ , 19__ , 19__) — TARGET MARKETS (1 2 3 4 5 6) — EVALUATION OF EFFECTIVENESS & OTHER COMMENTS

1. ADVERTISING
a. Newspapers
b. Magazines
c. Travel Guides
d. Trade Publications
e. Yellow Pages
f. Billboards
g. Transit Ads
h. Radio
i. Television
j. Barter Ads
k. Cooperative Ads
l.
m.
n.
Subtotal

2. SALES PROMOTION
a. Direct Mail
b. Brochures
c. Post Cards
d. Newsletters
e. Trade / Travel Shows
f.
g.
h.
Subtotal

3. PERSONAL SELLING
a. Sales Calls
b.
c.
d.
e.
Subtotal

4. PUBLIC RELATIONS AND PUBLICITY
a.
b.
c.
d.
e.
Subtotal

5. MERCHANDISE / IN-HOUSE PROMOTIONS
a.
b.
c.
d.
e.
Subtotal

6. TRAVEL TRADE MARKETING
a.
b.
c.
d.
e.
Subtotal

7. OTHER MARKETING PROGRAMS
a.
b.
c.
Subtotal
TOTAL

FIGURE 5.12 Market position and plan analysis worksheet.

developers and investors. They are the ones putting money into the business, and they want to be sure their money is spent wisely. Sometimes in our industry the developers and investors do not run the business, but hire a management group to do this. Many new hotels operate in this way under a legal arrangement known as a **management contract**. Lenders asked to supply loans or mortgages are also interested in seeing the market analysis. They must be sure that the business will be able to repay the loan amount on the date it is due. A market analysis has the same six steps as a situation analysis:

1. **Marketing Environment Analysis.** How will marketing environment and controllable factors (marketing mix or 8 Ps) affect the organization's direction and success?
2. **Market Potential Analysis.** Is the potential market large enough?
3. **Primary Competitor Analysis.** What are the main strengths and weaknesses of primary competitors?
4. **Location and Community Analysis.** How will the site and community contribute to success?
5. **Services Analysis.** What services and facilities must be provided to match the needs of potential customers?
6. **Marketing Position and Plan Analysis.** How can the new business carve a niche for itself in the potential market? What are the keys to marketing the new business?

Outside experts are usually hired to prepare market and feasibility analyses. Because they have no financial interest in the new business, their opinions and recommendations are objective. They are also very experienced in doing these studies. They have access to information on industry performance and competitors that other interested groups do not. External consultants and researchers have standardized approaches for completing market and feasibility analyses and only do what is asked of them. The marketing managers of the new business often have to do additional analysis. We include this fact so that you will not automatically assume that the outside expert's analysis is the only element of the first strategic market plan.

Completing the six steps in a market analysis is very similar to the process described earlier for the situation analysis. However, there are some differences in the two analysis techniques. Whereas the steps in the marketing environment and primary competitor analyses are almost identical to those used in the situation analysis, the other four analyses are not exactly the same.

1. **Market Potential Analysis.** When conducting a market potential analysis, a forecast of primary competitors' capacities and total market demand must be made. For a new hotel this refers to how many rooms both existing and new competitors will have in the future. Other organizations may be concerned about restaurant seats, retail stores, airplanes, buses, convention space, or other facilities. Growth rates for each market segment will also have to be projected. Comparing future supply and demand shows whether there is a gap that can be filled by the new business under consideration.

   For new lodging properties, data on local hotel market conditions may be purchased from sources such as Smith Travel Research. This company provides US Custom Reports by zip code that can be very helpful in determining the demand levels in the area surrounding the proposed new hotel.[4]

Approaches for determining the size of the potential market for a new business are many and varied. One is to use the pro rata or fair-share method. The total market available to all primary competitors is calculated and then projected 5 to 10 years into the future. The new business is then assigned a share of total market equal to its share of total capacity (e.g., available room nights, restaurant seats, aircraft seats, cars, cruise ship berths, etc.). For example, a new hotel with 20 percent of the available room nights in the community is allocated 20 percent of the projected occupied room nights (expected occupancy percentage times total available rooms). This method is easy to apply and is often used in this or a slightly modified way. However, it is imprecise and should only be used along with more detailed and sophisticated calculations. One involves estimating the demand from each individual market segment and forecasting the new business share of each one. The market shares projected are based on the results of the primary research for each market segment. Each interviewee or respondent is asked to estimate his or her likelihood of using the new business.

2. **Location and Community Analysis.** The right location is a key determinant of the success of a new hospitality and travel business with fixed real-estate sites. The surrounding community is usually a major source of business, and its future prospects influence success. A market analyses must consider these the site location and surrounding community in great detail.

Location and site analysis are extremely important in market analyses for lodging facilities, restaurants, travel agencies, attractions, shopping facilities, and other types of hospitality and travel businesses. For many years it has been accepted that, no matter how good an organization's

---

Did You Know?

What is the ideal site for a Red Lobster restaurant?

- Should have a trade area with a minimum of 125,000 people.
- Average daily traffic adjacent roads of 30,000 vehicles.
- Site needs to be able to accommodate a building of 7,200 square feet and have a land area of 1.2 to 2.4 acres.
- Site must allow for a building 26 feet tall.
- Must be parking for 155 vehicles.
- The area of focus should be prime regional locations, lifestyle and power centers.

Source: Darden Restaurants. (2008). **http://www.darden.com/abt_siteselection.asp/**

marketing is, a poor site can lead to failure. The criteria for evaluating and selecting a site vary with the type of business. Urban hotels need to be close to offices and industrial areas. Motor hotels must have easy access for cars and be close to highways. Restaurants usually need a combination of the two, plus a proximity to residential neighborhoods. Resorts must be near major recreational resources or attractions. Whatever the business, the criteria for selecting a site are divided into three groups: market-related, site-related, and other. Market-related factors are those that affect the customers' convenience in using the business. Site-related criteria deal with the physical characteristics of the site. Other criteria include legal considerations and land costs.

Market-related criteria are of primary importance to marketing. Success for many new businesses requires being as close as possible to their customers. As you read earlier in this chapter, one expert says that 80 percent of a restaurant's business comes from within three miles or five kilometers. New lodging facilities often take market share away from existing properties by locating closer to customers. Without a doubt, the more convenient a location is for customers, the greater its success potential.

Site accessibility and visibility are two other factors related to proximity. How easy is it to get to the site? Is the site clearly visible? The best site location for most hospitality and travel businesses is not only one closest to customers but also one easily accessible and highly visible. Many hotels and restaurants, for example, are highly dependent on their stores' (or their signs') visibility and convenient access.

3. **Services Analysis.** What services can the new business provide to meet the needs of potential customers? This means combining all previous information and judging which services will best satisfy customer needs. Some authors talk about this as a product analysis or the product-service mix. The term *services analysis* better matches the nature of our industry. Combining research findings and a knowledge of what actually works in the business accomplishes this most effectively.

The first step is deciding on the format and quality of the service. Does the market indicate the need for a cafeteria or a table-service restaurant? Will a budget hotel or an extended-stay property better satisfy customer needs? Does the community need a theme park or waterpark? (Figure 5.13). Within each format, different quality levels are possible. Primary research results should be the deciding factor.

The second step is determining the size of the facilities. How big should they be, based on the size of the potential market? For hotels, this means the number of guest rooms, restaurant and bar seats, and convention and meeting rooms. Other interior spaces, such as the lobby and reception area, kitchens, and recreational facilities, are sized and designed next.

4. **Marketing Position and Plan Analysis.** What is the market niche or **marketing position** that the new business will occupy, and how will it

FIGURE 5.13 Before the fun can begin at a theme park, a market analysis should be conducted.

earn this position? These are the last two questions in the market analysis. Again, this step is based on research findings and the judgment of the people completing the market analysis. The answers to these two questions define a number of unique features of the new business that can be used in positioning it. The concept of **positioning** (developing a service and marketing mix to occupy a specific place in the minds of customers within target markets) is discussed in Chapter 8.

The Feasibility Analysis or Study

Four more steps are added when completing a feasibility analysis or study: (1) pricing analysis, (2) income and expense analysis, (3) development cost analysis, and (4) analysis of return on investment and economic feasibility. Figure 5.14 shows the relationship of the feasibility analysis to a marketing analysis. It indicates that part of the feasibility analysis is, in fact, a market analysis.

1. **Pricing Analysis.** What prices or rates can the new business hope to command? This question is answered by carefully considering the prices

```
 FEASIBILITY ANALYSIS

 ┌──────────────────────────────────────────────┐
 │ MARKET ANALYSIS                                │
 │   1.    Environmental Analysis                 │
 │   2.    Market Potential Analysis              │
 │   3.  · Primary Competitor Analysis            │
 │   4.    Location and Community Analysis         │
 │   5.    Services Analysis                       │
 │   6.    Marketing Position and Plan Analysis    │
 └──────────────────────────────────────────────┘

     7.    Pricing Analysis
     8.    Income and Expense Analysis
     9.    Development Cost Analysis
    10.    Analysis of Return on Investment and
           Economic Feasibility
```

FOUR ADDITIONAL
STEPS ARE
INVOLVED IN A
FEASIBILITY
ANALYSIS

FIGURE 5.14
Relationship of market
and feasibility analyses.

of primary competitors, together with the responses of potential customers to price-related questions in the market potential analysis. Again, this usually requires separate analyses for each distinct target market. Hotels, for example, often have special rates for corporate travelers, convention/meeting attendees, people on group tours, and government employees. In addition, prices normally vary according to a specific time period—by time of day for restaurants, day of the week (or weekend) for city hotels, and season for resorts.

This type of pricing exercise takes considerable experience and judgment, as well as in-depth knowledge of the pricing system used in the relevant part of the hospitality and travel industry. This is also a facet of analysis with which independent consultants tend to be very effective because of their knowledge and experience with similar situations.

2. **Income and Expense Analysis.** The next step is to estimate the revenues, operating expenses, and profits for the new business. A **pro forma (projected) income statement** is prepared that generally covers 5 to 20 years. The demand expected from each target market is multiplied by the applicable rate or price to arrive at a sales forecast for each target market. These figures are then totaled to give an aggregate income estimate. Operating expenses are costs incurred directly in running the business, such as labor, food and other materials, energy, administration, marketing, and maintenance.

Secondary information can be useful in preparing estimates of prices, sales volumes, and operating costs. Several organizations publish hospitality and travel industry average operating statistics. Arthur Andersen, Deloitte, Ernst & Young, PKF Consulting, D. K. Shifflet & Associates, HVS, PricewaterhouseCoopers, and Smith Travel Research are firms that produce periodic reports and statistical data on the lodging industry. Smith Travel Research's *US Lodging Review* provides data on occupancy percentages, average daily rates (ADRs), and RevPARs for the top 25 city markets and by state. D. K. Shifflet & Associates' *DIRECTIONS®—Lodging Overview* provides in-depth information about business and pleasure travelers, including demographics, trip purposes, transportation modes, lodging choices, spending levels, and satisfaction with lodging facilities used.[5] Travel Weekly provides the *U.S. Travel Industry Survey* that includes information on U.S. travel agency revenues and revenue sources.[6]

3. **Development Cost Analysis.** How much will it cost to develop the new business? This forecast is often called a **capital budget** (a projection of the capital investment expected in a new hospitality or travel business). In our industry, development costs normally include building construction, equipment, furniture and fixtures, professional fees (e.g., for architects and designers), infrastructure (e.g., roads, electrical and sewerage service), and contingencies. The most accurate capital budgets result when a multidisciplinary team of consultants, architects, engineers, interior designers, and landscape architects is used (Figure 5.15).

   Next, capital-related expenses, including long-term financing, property taxes, depreciation, and insurance charges for fixed assets (e.g., buildings and equipment), are estimated. The capital-related expenses are then deducted from operating profits to arrive at net income and cash-flow figures.

4. **Analysis of Return on Investment and Economic Feasibility.** The final feasibility analysis step involves the calculation of the return on investment and, based on this, the **economic feasibility** of the new business. The net income, cash flow figures, and capital budget forecast are then compared. A

FIGURE 5.15 A feasibility analysis should be completed before the architectural drawings on a new hotel are finalized.

time-value, financial analysis technique such as the net-present-value or internal-rate-of-return method is best for this type of analysis. These techniques indicate the rate of return the new business will produce. If the return is high enough, the business is considered to be economically feasible.

Chapter Conclusion

Good marketing decisions result from research and careful analysis of research findings. A situation analysis is done for an existing business and represents the first step in the hospitality and travel marketing system. The situation analysis focuses an organization's attention on its strengths and weaknesses, assists with long-term planning, helps in developing marketing plans, and puts a priority on marketing research. The six steps involved in such an analysis are environmental, location and community, primary competitor, market potential, services, and market position and plan.

Market and feasibility analyses are the techniques available for determining the optimum approaches for proposed new business or expansions to existing ones. They determine if the market potential is large enough and if the projects will be economically feasible.

REVIEW QUESTIONS

1. What are the differences between market, feasibility, and situation analyses?
2. Are these three analysis techniques related and, if so, how?
3. How often should each of these analyses be conducted?
4. What is the relationship between these three techniques and marketing research?
5. How does a situation analysis fit into the hospitality and travel marketing system?
6. What are the benefits of completing a situation analysis?
7. What are the steps involved in preparing a situation analysis?
8. What are the six components of a market analysis?

CHAPTER ASSIGNMENTS

1. Pick a hospitality and travel organization and decide how you would prepare a situation analysis for it. Where would you gather the necessary research information? Who would you involve in its preparation? If time permits, try to prepare the situation analysis and assess the organization's major strengths, weaknesses, and opportunities.
2. You have been asked to prepare a market analysis for a proposed new hotel, restaurant, attraction, or travel agency in your home town. Prepare a proposal outlining the steps you would follow in doing the analysis. What sources of information would you use? How long would it take to complete? What recommendations will it produce?

3. There are many similarities between market, feasibility, and situation analyses, but there are also important differences. Write a paper comparing these similarities and differences for an organization in a specific part of the hospitality and travel industry. Be sure to explain how each level of analysis builds upon previous ones.

4. A developer has asked you to prepare a feasibility study for a new restaurant, hotel, travel agency, or other hospitality and travel business. The developer asks you to write a detailed proposal describing the steps to be followed in the study. Prepare this proposal, trying to be as specific as possible about the approaches you would use in each feasibility study step.

WEB RESOURCES

Arthur Andersen HotelBenchmark™ Survey, http://www.strglobal.com/

D.K. Shifflet & Associates, http://www.dksa.com/

Deloitte Touche Tohmatsu, Tourism, Hospitality and Leisure, U.S., http://www.deloitte.com/

Ernst & Young, http://www.ey.com/

European Travel Commission, http://www.etc-corporate.org/

HVS International, http://www.hvs.com/

Pacific Asia Travel Association, http://www.pata.org/

PKF Consulting, http://www.pkfc.com/

PKF Consulting Canada-, http://www.pkfcanada.com/

PricewaterhouseCoopers, http://www.pwc.com/

Smith Travel Research, http://www.strglobal.com/

Travel Industry Association of America (TIA), http://www.tia.org/

UN World Tourism Organization, http://www.unwto.org/

U.S. Department of Interior, Geographic Information Systems, http://erg.usgs.gov/

REFERENCES

1. Dramowicz, Ela. 2005. "Retail trade analysis using the Huff model." *Directions Magazine*, July 2, 2005.

2. Gonzalez-Benito, Oscar and Javier Gonzalez-Benito. 2005. "The role of geodemographic segmentation in retail location strategy." *International Journal of Market Research*, Vol. 47, No. 3, 295–316.

3. Allen, Emma. 2006. "How to market a new restaurant." *Caterer & Hotelkeeper*, May 25, 2006.

4. Smith Travel Research. 2009. *US Hotel Review*, http://www.strglobal.com/

5. D.K. Shifflet & Associates. 2009. DIRECTIONS®, http://www.dksa.com/

6. Travel Weekly. 2008. *2008 U.S. Travel Industry Survey*, http://www.travelweekly.com/

chapter 6

Marketing Research
Where Are We Now?

O V E R V I E W

This chapter begins with a discussion of the importance of using research results to make marketing decisions. The reasons for doing and not doing marketing research are covered. The chapter then explains the role of research in each step of the hospitality and travel marketing system, and it presents a systematic, six-step procedure for doing marketing research.

The distinction between primary and secondary research information is described. Various marketing research methods are identified and discussed.

O B J E C T I V E S

Having read this chapter, you should be able to:

- Define marketing research.

- Describe the reasons for doing marketing research (the five Cs) and explain why marketing research is sometimes not done.

- Explain how research is used in each step of the hospitality and travel marketing system.

- List and describe the five key requirements for good research information.

- List in order and explain the six steps in the marketing research process.

- Describe the internal and external sources of secondary research data.

- Explain the differences between primary and secondary research and list their respective advantages and disadvantages.

- List and describe the primary research methods and differentiate between quantitative and qualitative research.

- Explain the advantages and disadvantages of personal interviews, mail, telephone, in-house, self-administered, and online surveys.

- Explain the focus group approach and how it can be used in making effective marketing decisions.

KEY TERMS

accountability research

case study

change

comment cards

competitors

conclusive research

confidence

credibility

customers

databases

direct-response advertising

evaluation research

experimental research

exploratory research

external secondary research
data

five Cs

focus group

frequently asked questions
(FAQs)

individual depth interview (IDI)

internal secondary research
data

log file analyzer programs

marketing research

marketing research process

marketing research program

marketing research projects

non-probability sampling

observational research

online research

online surveys

primary research data

probability sampling

qualitative data

quantitative data

questionnaires

response rate

secondary research data

simulation

survey research

test marketing

Research: Nourishment for Marketing

You are probably wondering what is so nourishing about marketing research. How can a subject so statistical and technique-laden be the lifeblood of the hospitality and travel marketing system? Aren't the creative sides of marketing, such as advertising and the Web, more important? The answer is an emphatic "no"! Good marketing decisions are usually based on marketing research.

The following headlines and quotes will give you a flavor of the importance of research and how it is used in the hospitality and travel industry:

Tourism Australia's research shows that psychographic segmentation is best. "Tourism Australia has undertaken extensive research to identify the ideal visitor segment for Australia which will best help meet key business objectives. This research has challenged the previously held notions that the traveling population was segmented primarily by country of origin and thereafter by mode of travel (long haul, inter-regional, domestic), style of travel (free independent; package; backpacker) and distribution channel. In fact, the key defining characteristics which group people into segments are psychographic and include factors such as personal motivations and lifestyle drivers."[1]

Las Vegas has 32 years of visitor data to guide its marketing programs.

"According to the Las Vegas Convention and Visitors Authority's (LVCVA) 2006 Visitor Profile Study, visitors to the destination are spending more on non-gaming elements such as dining and shopping. For 32 years, the LVCVA has surveyed its visitors to develop the annual Visitor Profile Study, which details their trends, attitudes, behaviors and spending habits while visiting the destination. The report presents the findings from 3,600 personal interviews that were conducted throughout the destination from Jan. 1 to Dec. 31, 2006, and includes comparisons to results from the 2003, 2004 and 2005 studies."[2]

Figure 6.1 shows a great application of the importance of market research information and how it can be distributed globally with the help of the Web. Through its Website, the Las Vegas Convention and Visitors Authority (LCVA) answers many **frequently asked questions (FAQs)** about the hospitality and travel industry. Without a good marketing research program, the LCVA would not be able to distribute this information.

www.LVCVA.com

Vegas FAQ

Top 25 Frequently Asked Questions

Question	2006	2007
1 How many visitors come to Las Vegas?	38,914,889	39,196,761
2 What is tourism's economic impact?	$39.4 Billion	$41.6 Billion
3 How many convention delegates visit?	6,307,961	6,209,253
4 How many conventions are held per year?	23,825	23,847
5 Conventions' non-gaming economic impact?	$8.2 Billion	$8.4 Billion
6 What is Clark County's gaming revenue?	$10.6 Billion	$10.9 Billion
7 What is Las Vegas' gaming revenue?	$8.2 Billion	$8.4 Billion
8 What is the average gambling budget per trip?	$652	$556
9 What is Las Vegas' city-wide occupancy?	89.7%	90.4%
10 What is Las Vegas' hotel occupancy?	93.2%	94.0%
11 What is Las Vegas' motel occupancy?	65.2%	64.5%
12 What is Las Vegas' weekend occupancy?	94.6%	94.3%
13 What is Las Vegas' midweek occupancy?	87.4% r	88.7%
14 What is the US national avg. hotel occupancy? *	63.3% r	63.2%
15 Total enplaned/deplaned airline passengers?	46,304,376 r	47,728,414
16 Avg daily auto traffic: all major highways?	86,961	86,701
17 Avg daily auto traffic: I-15 at NV/CA Border?	40,383	39,808
18 What is the average nightly room rate?	$120	$132
19 How many hotel/motel rooms are in Las Vegas?	132,605	132,947
20 How long is the avg. visitor's trip (in nights)?	3.6	3.5
21 What % of visitors are under 21?	10%	8%
22 What is the average age of a visitor?	48.0	49.0
23 What % are first time visitors?	19%	19%
24 What % of visitors are from So. California?	27%	25%
25 What % of visitors are International?	13%	12%

U.S. avg. hotel occupancy based on data from Smith Travel Research

LAST-UPDATED: 3/08
r=revised

Compiled by the Las Vegas Convention and Visitors Authority, Research Department   Ph: (702) 892-0711

Courtesy of the Las Vegas Convention and Visitors Authority

FIGURE 6.1 The Las Vegas Convention and Visitors Authority uses its research to answer FAQs.

Definition of Marketing Research

According to the American Marketing Association (AMA), **marketing research** is "the function which links the consumer, customer, and public to the marketer through information." This information is used to do the following:

1. Identify and define marketing opportunities and problems.
2. Generate, refine, and evaluate marketing actions.
3. Monitor marketing performance.
4. Improve understanding of marketing as a process.

The AMA definition also states that "marketing research specifies the information required to address issues; designs the method for collecting information; manages and implements the data collection process; analyzes the results; and communicates the findings and their implications."[3]

Reasons for Doing Marketing Research: The Five Cs

Marketing research helps an organization make more effective marketing decisions. This is its primary objective. Good marketing decisions come from being better informed, and research supplies the information. There are five major reasons for doing marketing research and you will notice that these all start with the letter "C"—the **five Cs**:

1. Customers
2. Competitors
3. Confidence
4. Credibility
5. Change

The most important reason for doing marketing research is that it helps an organization develop a detailed knowledge of its **customers**, both past and potential. It gives the organization information on how well it is meeting customers' needs and on the organization's position in the market. Take a look back at the quotes from Marriott to see the importance of customer research. New target markets are investigated through research. New services and facilities are assessed and tested through market and feasibility analyses, test marketing, and other product testing.

Competitive research is also a must in today's intensely competitive hospitality and travel industry. Research identifies primary **competitors** and pinpoints their strengths and weaknesses.

Well-designed research increases the **confidence** of an organization as well as its marketing partners when making marketing decisions. The perceived risk is reduced if the organization has developed an in-depth understanding of customer needs and characteristics as well as competitive strengths and weaknesses.

Research results can be used to add **credibility** to an organization's advertising campaigns. For example, research done by the organization itself or by others can be used effectively to back up marketing program success and

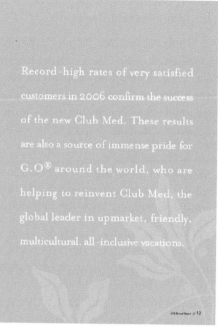

Courtesy of Club Med Sales Inc.

Record-high rates of very satisfied customers in 2006 confirm the success of the new Club Med. These results are also a source of immense pride for G.O® around the world, who are helping to reinvent Club Med, the global leader in upmarket, friendly, multicultural, all-inclusive vacations.

FIGURE 6.2 Club Med's research confirms the success of its new marketing and positioning efforts.

messages delivered in advertising campaigns. Figure 6.2 shows a section of Club Med's 2006 Annual Report that clearly indicates Club Med's new positioning and marketing have been a success.

Domestic and international travel markets are in a constant state of **change**, as is the global hospitality and travel industry. Travelers' needs and expectations are also changing rapidly. Organizations must constantly keep up-to-date with these changes, and research is the primary tool for doing so.

Reasons for Not Doing Marketing Research

Having read this chapter so far, you are probably wondering how an organization survives without marketing research. We want to be totally realistic—many effective marketing decisions have been based on no research at all. We were afraid to say that, but it had to be said. The intuition and judgment of the decision-makers have turned out to be extremely accurate in some cases. Does this mean that marketing research is unnecessary? Is management intuition and judgment an acceptable substitute? The answer is "no" on both counts. Intuition is not a good substitute for research. However, research cannot take the place of intuition and judgment. The best marketing decisions come from a blend of research, intuition, and judgment. Effective marketing managers know the advantages of marketing research and how to use it. They are also aware of the limitations and the need to inject their own intuition and judgment.

Following are reasons for not doing marketing research:

1. Timing
2. Cost
3. Reliability

4. Competitive intelligence
5. Management decision

A research project such as a survey can take several months to complete. The decision for which the research information is needed may have to be made in just a few weeks. Research can be very expensive, and its costs may outweigh its value. There may also be no reliable method available to answer a specific research question. When conclusions such as these are reached rationally and with full information, research may have to be replaced completely by intuition and judgment.

There is another reason why research is not done. A company considering a new service or product may be concerned that doing a research study in full public view might provide valuable information to its closest competitors. These competitors may try to imitate the new service or product offerings.

There are many managers who do not care for research or understand its value. They are content to fly solo and by the seat of their pants, using intuition and judgment to make a decision. A crash landing is usually not too far ahead, as they wear out the seat of their pants quickly! Intuition and judgment tend to be based on past experience. The future often is nothing like the past. These managers seldom see all sides of a problem or opportunity. They frequently fail to identify all alternative approaches. As a result, their marketing decisions may not be as effective as they could have been with some research.

Using Research in the Hospitality and Travel Marketing System Steps

Figure 6.3 indicates that research is done during all five steps in the hospitality and travel marketing system (Chapter 3). It shows the relationship of

	PRICE MODEL TASKS	STEPS IN THE HOSPITALITY AND TRAVEL MARKETING SYSTEM	USES OF MARKETING RESEARCH
M A R K E T I N G	Planning & Research	1. Where are we now? 2. Where would we like to be?	◆ Research for planning and analysis ◆ Research for strategy selection
	Implementation	3. How do we get there?	◆ Research to guide marketing mix (8 Ps) decisions
R E S E A R C H	Control	4. How do we make sure we get there?	◆ Research for monitoring the marketing plan
	Evaluation	5. How do we know if we got there?	◆ Evaluation research

FIGURE 6.3 Relationship of marketing research to the hospitality and travel marketing system.

marketing research to the five marketing tasks (PRICE—planning, research, implementation, control, and evaluation) and to the five steps in the hospitality and travel marketing system.

Now let's take a quick look at how research is used in each step of the hospitality and travel marketing system.

1. Where Are We Now? (Research for Planning and Analysis)

The first step in the hospitality and travel marketing system requires researching and analyzing the marketing environment, location and community, primary competitors, past and potential customers, services, market position, and past marketing plans—the research for a situation analysis. Figure 6.4 shows the research needs and questions for all five steps in the system.

1. WHERE ARE WE NOW? RESEARCH FOR PLANNING AND ANALYSIS

Needs	Research Questions
1. Trends in the marketing environment	• How will marketing environment factors affect the organization's direction and future success?
2. Trends affecting location and community	
3. Strengths and weaknesses of primary competitors	• How will the location and community contribute to the organization's future success?
4. Current target market characteristics and penetration	• What are the strengths and weaknesses of the organization's primary competitors?
5. Characteristics and size of potential target markets	• Who are the organization's customers and what are they like?
6. Current market position	• Should the organization pursue specific new target markets?
7. Evaluation of past marketing plans	• What images do the organization's customers have of the organization?
	• How effective have the organization's past marketing programs been?

2. WHERE WOULD WE LIKE TO BE? RESEARCH FOR STRATEGY SELECTION

Needs	Research Questions
1. Needs and characteristics of overall market	• How should the market be segmented?
2. Market trends by segment	• What recent trends have occurred in each market segment?
3. Benefits and services that match needs of segments' customers	• Which market segments are available to the organization?
4. Likelihood and amount of use by customers in a given target market	• Which market segments should the organization target?
5. Potential effectiveness of alternative approaches to positioning	• How effective are different positioning approaches for the organization likely to be?
6. Potential effectiveness of alternative marketing mix approaches for each target market	• How effective are different marketing mix approaches for each target market likely to be?

(continued)

FIGURE 6.4 Research needs and questions for the steps in the hospitality and travel marketing system.

(continued)

3. HOW DO WE GET THERE? RESEARCH TO GUIDE MARKETING MIX DECISIONS

Needs	Research Questions
1. Potential effectiveness of specific promotional activities or campaigns	• Which promotional activities or campaigns should the organization use?
2. Potential effectiveness of specific distribution mix approaches	• Which distribution channels should the organization use?
3. Potential effectiveness of specific pricing approaches	• Which pricing approaches should the organization use?
4. Potential effectiveness of specific packaging and programming approaches	• Which packaging and programming approaches should the organization use?
5. Potential effectiveness of specific partnership arrangements	• Should the organization cooperate with other organizations in certain marketing programs?
6. Potential effectiveness of specific service quality training programs	• What service quality training approaches and programs should the organization use?

4. HOW DO WE MAKE SURE WE GET THERE? RESEARCH FOR MONITORING THE MARKETING PLAN

Needs	Research Questions
1. Progress in achieving marketing objectives	• Does it look as if the organization will achieve each of the marketing plan's objectives?
2. Progress in using positioning approaches	• Are the selected positioning approaches working as planned?
3. Progress in using specific promotional campaigns and other specific marketing mix activities	• Are the promotional campaigns and other selected marketing mix activities working as planned?
4. Changes in customer satisfaction levels	• How have customer satisfaction levels changed since the service quality training programs were implemented?

5. HOW DO WE KNOW IF WE GOT THERE? RESEARCH FOR EVALUATION

Needs	Research Questions
1. Level of success in achieving marketing objectives for each target market	• To what extent did the organization achieve the objectives for each target market?
2. Success of specific marketing mix approaches, campaigns, and other activities	• To what extent were promotional campaigns and other specific marketing mix activities effective in achieving their objectives?
3. Changes in customer satisfaction levels	• How did customer satisfaction levels change since the implementation of the marketing plan?

FIGURE 6.4 *Continued*

2. Where Would We Like to Be? (Research for Strategy Selection)

Marketing research helps an organization select target markets, marketing mixes (8 Ps), and positioning approaches. It assists with the development of a marketing strategy. Here research looks at the advantages and disadvantages of alternative courses of action, another element of planning. Organizations use this type of research when considering possible new marketing strategies—new target markets and ways of attracting customers in these markets. A restaurant chain may be considering adding a delivery service, whereas a hotel chain may investigate the addition of a new brand of property. Many "What if we did this?" questions can be tackled in this way, using marketing research.

3. How Do We Get There? (Research to Guide Marketing Mix Decisions)

Marketing research assists an organization in the development of the marketing plan by assessing the potential effectiveness of specific promotional campaigns (called pre-testing) and other specific marketing mix activities. This research helps with decisions on how to use the 8 Ps (product, price, place, promotion, packaging, programming, partnership, and people) in the upcoming marketing plan by investigating and testing out alternative approaches.

4. How Do We Make Sure We Get There? (Research for Monitoring the Marketing Plan)

You should realize that once the marketing plan is implemented, marketing research does not stop. It takes great effort to research, analyze, and develop a marketing plan. This effort does not stop on Day 1 of the marketing plan. In fact, a plan must be constantly monitored to see whether its marketing objectives are being achieved and to determine if adjustments are needed. Research is used to check progress at specific times (called *milestones*) during the implementation of the marketing plan.

5. How Do We Know If We Got There? (Research for Evaluation)

Although often overlooked, this is a crucial application of marketing research. A marketing plan is effective only if it achieves stated objectives. Research assists in measuring the results of the plan. This is often referred to as **evaluation research** or **accountability research**.

When the marketing plan comes to an end, one major question must be answered. Did we reach our objectives? Research helps to measure and evaluate the results. The plan's objectives should have been expressed in numbers of customers by target market, in sales volumes, or in a variety of other ways. Measuring the results of a marketing plan is rather like tallying the votes in a political election (but hopefully more accurate and less controversial). But it is not just a simple yes-no process. The results also have to be evaluated. What do the results mean for future marketing plans? How should marketing be adjusted for greater future effectiveness? Which activities worked? Which activities did not work?

Key Requirements for Good Research Information

Before discussing specific techniques, it is important to establish what we mean by good research. The five key requirements are shown in Figure 6.5 and described in detail below.

1. **Utility.** Marketing research can be expensive and time consuming. Money and staff time can be saved by gathering only information that can be used. There is a tendency in many research activities to collect *nice-to-know* as well as *must-know* data. The *nice-to-know* information often has limited value. Having a well defined research problem and clear research objectives is the key here. These objectives are translated into a number of *must-know* questions to be answered. Only the information that specifically addresses these *must-know* questions is collected.

2. **Timeliness.** Timeliness of the research results is also important—the information should be very current and up-to-date. Again, this requires some preplanning to determine when the results are needed for decision making. A decision may be needed by the end of the month, but a

FIGURE 6.5 Five requirements for good research information.

survey would take three months to complete. In this case, the decision makers may have to rely on secondary research, because it is available almost immediately.

3. **Cost-Effectiveness.** Some nationwide research projects cost a huge amount of money. The expense can be justified because the decisions they affect are worth millions or even billions. However, it does not make any sense to conduct a research project on a problem or opportunity worth only less than the total cost of the research. The research cost must be directly related to the expected value of investigating the opportunity or solving the problem. There must be a good return on the investment in the research project.

4/5. **Accuracy and Reliability.** Two related requirements are that research information must be accurate and reliable. Accuracy in both primary and secondary research is essential. The decision maker has to be sure that the methods and calculations used to arrive at the data are technically correct. As we see later, this is easier to do with primary research. Reliability means that if the same or similar research was done, the result would be approximately the same. If research information is unreliable, it is not a good predictor of what will actually happen when an organization tackles a problem or opportunity.

The Marketing Research Process

Before discussing the research process, it is important to realize that each project should be part of a marketing research program. A **marketing research program** is a plan developed by an organization to investigate several opportunities or issues. **Marketing research projects** are different. Programs outline what is to be researched. Projects deal with how the opportunities and issues in the program are to be researched. Programs usually have routine and one-time research project components. For example, a destination marketing organization (DMO) decided it needed to have a profile of the characteristics of visitors and their satisfaction levels with staying in the destination. It decided to conduct a visitor profile study, and this is one marketing research project.

The next decision was to routinely collect the visitor profile information because the DMO needed the data for targeting its marketing. The visitor profile study was set up to gather data each month, so it was a routine research project for the DMO. The DMO also decided to have a feasibility study conducted on the proposed expansion to the local convention center. This represented a one-time research project, since it would be done just once and not repeated in the foreseeable future.

Marketing research projects are most effective if they follow the six sequential steps in the **marketing research process** shown in Figure 6.6.[4]

1. **Define the Research Problem.** Step 1 in the marketing research process is to define the opportunity or issue to be studied. In technical research jargon, this is called the *research problem*, but it does not mean "problem"

Marketing Research Process steps	Detailed Procedures
1. Define the Research Problem	• Gather background information through interviews with marketing executives and other stakeholders • Check internal secondary research data and relevant external secondary research data for preliminary guidance • Articulate the research problem statement in writing
2. Develop an Approach to the Research Problem	• Define the research objectives and related questions based upon the research problem statement • Decide if secondary research data is sufficient or if primary research data will also be needed • Determine which primary research method is most appropriate
3. Formulate the Research Design	• Gather and assess the available secondary research data • If primary research data is required, decide on the sampling process or design (sample frame; sample selection process; sample size) • Select the primary research data collection method(s), e.g., qualitative (focus group; individual depth interviews; human observation; case studies) and/or quantitative (experiment; mechanical observation; survey; simulation)?
4. Conduct the Data Collection or Fieldwork	• Collect the secondary research data from internal and/or external sources • Gather the primary research data through selected quantitative and/or qualitative research methods
5. Prepare the Data and Analysis	• Summarize the secondary research data • Edit and code the primary research data • Tabulate the primary research data and apply statistical tests • Analyze the primary and secondary research data and write up the research results
6. Prepare and Present the Research Report	• Draw conclusions and make recommendations • Finalize the research report in a written format • Design the research report presentation • Present the results of research to stakeholders • Revise the research report based on stakeholder input

FIGURE 6.6   The marketing research process steps and procedures.

in a general sense. You just learned that marketing research projects outline how opportunities or issues in the research program are to be researched. For example, a restaurant chain needed to track customer awareness of its advertising and in-store sales promotions (merchandising). The advertising campaign and supporting merchandising were new and expensive. Its research problem was promotional awareness. This is a broad problem statement and researchers need to get more background information before moving further ahead. The researchers might, in this case, interview marketing executives and other stakeholders about exactly what they want to measure. They might also check internal secondary data on sales history and external secondary research on advertising awareness studies. Once these steps are completed, the research problem statement is articulated and written up.

2. **Develop an Approach to the Research Problem.** More detail is required before a decision can be made on how to tackle the research problem. This is accomplished by specifying one or more research objectives based on the

research problem statement. By specifying research objectives, the researchers then can decide which research method or methods to use and which questions must be asked to achieve the research objectives. For example, they should know if secondary research data will be sufficient to answer the research questions, or alternatively, if primary research data will also be needed and which primary research method is most appropriate.

3. **Formulate the Research Design.** Having specified the research objectives and related questions, the next step is to choose a research design and a method for collecting the data. The first question to be asked is whether to use primary or secondary research data, or both. **Secondary research data** represent previously gathered information available from internal or external sources. **Primary research data** represents information collected for the first time, by a method other than secondary research, to answer specific questions. It is sometimes also referred to as *original* research. Later in this chapter, you will learn about the respective advantages of primary and secondary research data and how to use both of them.

    If secondary research data are judged to be sufficient to answer the research questions, the expected sources of this information should be identified. If primary research data are also needed, a sampling process or design is required. A sample design consists of three elements:

    a. Sample frame
    b. Sample selection process
    c. Sample size

    a. *Sample Frame.* The sample frame determines which groups are to be covered by the research. The DMO mentioned earlier decided to sample only visitors staying overnight in the destination. The restaurant chain decided its sampling frame was adults of ages from 35 to 55.

    b. *Sample Selection Process.* Non-probability and probability sample selection can be used. Non-probability samples are drawn on the basis of convenience or judgment. They are less accurate than probability samples. **Non-probability sampling** is a subjective sample-selection approach where every person in the group does not have a known probability of being in the sample. Probability samples are arrived at using a more scientific and objective approach. **Probability sampling** (where every person in the group to be researched has a known, non-zero probability of being in the sample) techniques are shown in Figure 6.7.

    c. *Sample Size.* Choosing the sample size depends on how precise the information needs to be. The most precise data come from using an established mathematical formula. Describing these formulae is beyond the scope of this book, but you can find a detailed description in most marketing research texts. So we will move right on to the analysis and interpretation of data.

    The final choice of primary research data collection is made. This may be a quantitative or qualitative research method, or a combination of the two. The quantitative methods include experiments, mechanical observations,

1. **SIMPLE RANDOM**: All respondents have an equal chance of being selected. This can be done simply by putting all names into a bowl, mixing them, and then picking out the desired number of names for the sample. Another technique is to use random number tables (a table of numbers randomly generated by computer that correspond to every potential respondent in the sample frame).

2. **SYSTEMATIC**: A system is developed to pick and spread the sample randomly throughout the list of potential respondents. This is common in telephone surveys. A number is selected randomly, let us say seven. The seventh name from the top of each phone book page would be selected for the sample.

3. **STRATIFIED RANDOM**: Here it is recognized that there are distinct subgroupings of respondents (e.g., business versus vacation travelers). The list of respondents is subdivided ("stratified") into these groups and then samples are randomly selected from within each subgroup.

4. **CLUSTER SAMPLING**: Those to be researched are divided into subgroups, and a number of these subgroups (clusters) are randomly selected. *All members* of each cluster are surveyed. For example, a hotel might randomly select days of the year to survey its overnight guests and then survey all the guests on these randomly selected days.

5. **AREA SAMPLING**: This is a type of cluster sampling used when lists of all potential respondents are not available. Areas (e.g., blocks within a city) are randomly selected and all persons or households in the areas are surveyed.

FIGURE 6.7 Probability sampling techniques.

surveys, or simulations. The qualitative methods may involve focus groups, individual depth interviews, human observation, or case studies.

4. **Conduct the Data Collection or Fieldwork.** The fourth step involves collecting the required research data. First, the secondary research data should be gathered and analyzed. These data may come from internal sources within the organization, or from external sources. (Figure 6.8 for a breakdown of these two sources.)

   Based upon the selected research method, the primary research data can be collected online via the Internet, by phone or by mail, by interviewing people, or by having guests or customers self-complete survey questionnaires, or by mechanical observation. Interviewing may be done in-house in a hotel, restaurant, or theme park, or on a plane, cruise ship or other transportation vehicle. Fieldwork data collection means using a trained survey team to collect data via personal interviews outside of the place of business.

5. **Prepare the Data and Analysis.** The raw data that is collected is of limited value. It has to be analyzed and interpreted carefully to be of any use. First, the secondary research data is assembled and summarized.

   For the primary research data, four data preparation and analysis steps are involved:

   a. *Editing.* This step involves checking the primary research data for errors, omissions, and ambiguities. Then the data are "cleaned" to correct for these problems.

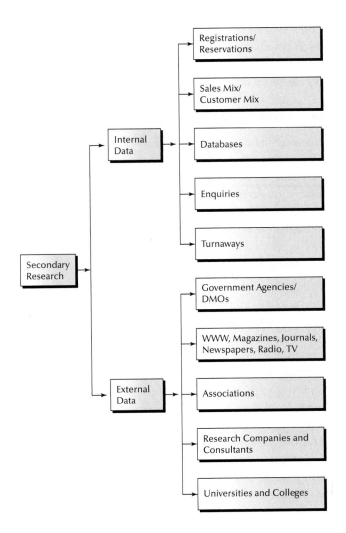

FIGURE 6.8 Sources of secondary research data.

b. *Coding.* This means specifying how responses are to be entered into a computer or on a hard-copy format, e.g., for a "yes-no" question, a "yes" could be entered as a "1" and a "no" as a "0".

c. *Tabulating.* This is calculating and arranging the answers to questions in tabular form. It is often done by a computerized statistical analysis program, but can also be manually recorded in hard-copy format.

d. *Applying statistical analysis tests and procedures.* This is conducting various types of statistical procedures and tests, such as chi-square tests, correlation, regression, and factor-cluster analysis.

6. **Prepare and Present the Research Report.** What does the research mean? This step involves drawing conclusions and recommendations for management and other stakeholders. The final research report is then written and a research report presentation is prepared. The marketing research process is only successful if the research results are effectively communicated to key decision-makers and other stakeholders. Having a research

report is only part of the answer. The researchers must clearly highlight the key research results and communicate them in a way that the audience fully comprehends. After the research is presented, the research report may be revised based on the comments of management and other stakeholders.

Secondary Research Data

Chapter 5 warned against reinventing the wheel in research. Answers may already be available through secondary research (previously gathered information available from internal or external sources). The two broad categories are **internal secondary research data** (information contained within the organization's own records) and **external secondary research data** (information previously published by an outside organization).

Internal Secondary Research Data

Examples of internal secondary data include registration and reservation records, sales-mix and customer-mix information, databases, enquiry records, and turn-away statistics. Most hospitality and travel organizations, including hotels, airlines, car rental firms, restaurants, online travel companies, tour operators and wholesalers, and cruise lines, take reservations. Of course, travel agencies also make reservations for their customers. Some hospitality and travel organizations, such as hotels, are required by law to register guests. This registration information can be an important source of secondary research information. Have you been asked for your zip or postal code lately? Many theme parks and other attractions gather zip/postal code information at their entrances. This not only lets these attractions know where their guests live but, when used along with zip/postal code databases from outside companies, provides demographic and lifestyle information on the attractions' customers.

Sales- and customer-mix records are another important internal secondary research data source, since they are an indicator of business trends and marketing success. As marketing objectives are often expressed in sales or customer volume targets, sales- and customer-mix records are important tools in marketing control and evaluation. Sales-mix figures provide information on sales volume by profit center (e.g., rooms, and food and beverage in a hotel). Some measures of supply capacity usage and customer volumes, such as hotel occupancy percentages, ADRs, and RevPARs, restaurant covers, passenger volumes, and attraction attendance volumes, should be available. Customer-mix figures should include sales revenues and customer counts by target market.

Some hospitality and travel organizations, including casinos, hotels, cruise lines, and airlines, go further than this and maintain large internal **databases** on individual customers. In creating frequent traveler and other club programs, these organizations have developed powerful databases of information on individual customer sales, demographics, and preferences.

Many hospitality and travel organizations receive enquiries directly from customers or from travel trade intermediaries. These enquiries can be from websites or by telephone, mail, fax, e-mail, or in person. Since enquiries are another indicator of marketing success, it is important for an organization to maintain records of them. Much of today's hospitality and travel advertising is **direct-response advertising**, in which the potential customer must call a given telephone number, write to a given address, send back a completed coupon, or complete and submit a Web-based enquiry or site registration form. A good example of measuring the results of direct-response advertising is its use by national, state, provincial, city, and county DMOs. The task of handling these enquiries is often called fulfillment and provides the DMOs with an important database of potential visitors.

Turn-away statistics represent *frustrated demand* or reservations that cannot be accepted or honored because the organization is already at full capacity. It is important that the organization record turn-aways (some of whom are "walks" or "bumps" resulting from the industry's practice of overbooking), since these customers represent another measure of marketing success. The statistics are also useful if the organization is considering an expansion of its capacity.

External Secondary Research Data

Figure 6.9 shows that some of the specific external secondary research data sources include trade or travel associations, government, magazines, journals and newspapers, research companies and consultants. The Web in general, universities, radio and television networks are other sources. Destination marketing organizations (DMOs), including convention and visitor bureaus (CVBs), are

---

Did You Know?

How to Find Out About Where and How Canadians Travel?

- Statistics Canada conducts the *Travel Survey of Residents of Canada* (TSRC) to collect information on where and how Canadians travel within Canada.
- Begun in 2005, results from the survey are reported four times per year by quarter.
- Over 40,000 households respond to the survey.
- The survey is sponsored by Statistics Canada, Canadian Tourism Commission, provincial governments, and two federal organizations.
- TSRC measures the size of domestic travel by Canadians from the demand side.
- The survey's objectives are to provided data on: (1) the volume of trips and expenditures for Canadian residents by trip origin, destination, duration, type of accommodation used, trip reason, mode of travel, etc.; and (2) travel incidence; and (3) socio-demographic profile of travelers and non-travelers.

Sources: Statistics Canada. (2008).

Name of Data Source	Magazines, Journals, and Newspapers	Website Addresses
Auto Rental News Fact Book	• Auto Rental News	• http://www.fleet-central.com/arn/
BTN U.S. Hotel Chain Survey	• Business Travel News Online	• http://www.btnonline.com/businesstravelnews/index.jsp
Business Travel Survey	• Business Travel News Online	• http://www.btnonline.com/businesstravelnews/index.jsp
Consumer Trends	• Travel Weekly	• http://www.travelweekly.com/
Hotels 325	• Hotels	• http://www.hotelsmag.com/
Meetings Market Report	• Meetings & Conventions	• http://www.mcmag.com/
State of the Industry Report	• Successful Meetings	• http://www.mimegasite.com/mimegasite/index.jsp
The NRN Top 100	• Nation's Restaurant News	• http://www.nrn.com/
Traveler Behavior Survey	• T&E Magazine	• http://www.temagazine.com/
Travellers' Pulse Survey	• Lonely Planet	• http://www.lonelyplanet.com/
Travel Weekly U.S. Travel Industry Survey	• Travel Weekly	• http://www.travelweekly.com/
Name of Data Source	**Trade/Travel Associations and Government**	**Website Addresses**
ATA Economic Report	• Air Transport Association	• http://www.airlines.org/economics/review_and_outlook/
CLIA Economic Impact Study	• Cruise Lines International Association	• http://www.cruising.org/
Corporate Air Travel Survey	• International Air Transport Association	• http://www.iata.org/
Cruise Industry Overview	• Cruise Lines International Association	• http://www.cruising.org/
Domestic Travel Market Report	• Travel Industry Association of America	• http://www.tia.org/
Economic Impact of Travel & Tourism	• Travel Industry Association of America	• http://www.tia.org/
Future Watch	• Meeting Professionals International and American Express	• http://www.mpiweb.org/
Market Profile Study	• Cruise Lines International Association	• http://www.cruising.org/
Monthly Traffic Analysis	• International Air Transport Association	• http://www.iata.org/
Motorcoach Census	• American Bus Association	• http://www.buses.org/
Restaurant Industry Operations Report	• National Restaurant Association	• http://www.restaurant.org/
State of the States	• American Gaming Association	• http://www.americangaming.org/
Survey of International Air Travelers	• Office of Travel & Tourism Industries	• http://tinet.ita.doc.gov/research/programs/ifs/index.html
Survey of State & Territory Tourism Office Budgets	• Travel Industry Association of America	• http://www.tia.org/
U.S. Amusement Park Attendance & Revenue History	• International Association of Amusement Parks and Attractions (IAAPA)	• http://www.iaapa.org/
Name of Data Source	**Research Companies and Consultants**	**Website Addresses**
DIRECTIONS® Travel Intelligence System SM	• DK Shifflet & Associates	• http://www.dksa.com/about.html
Trends in the Hotel Industry	• PKF Consulting	• http://www.pkfonline.com/
Leisure TRAK®	• Leisure Trends Group	• http://www.leisuretrends.com/
National Leisure Travel Monitor SM	• Yesawich, Pepperdine, Brown & Russell	• http://www.ypbr.com/
STAR Report	• Smith Travel Research	• http://www.smithtravelresearch.com/
TEA/ERA Theme Park Attendance	• Themed Entertainment Association and Economics Research Associates	• http://www.themeit.com/

FIGURE 6.9 External sources of secondary research data in the hospitality and travel industry.

also major providers of hospitality and travel industry research. These include Tourism Research Australia (TRA), VisitBritain, the Canadian Tourism Commission, and the Office of Travel & Tourism Industries in the United States, as well as the many state, provincial, and territorial tourism offices in these countries.

Magazines, journals, newspapers, radio, and television provide marketers with information on their subscribers, readers, listeners, or viewing audiences. In addition, these organizations may conduct specific surveys or other research studies on customer characteristics and preferences as well as state-of-the-industry studies. Some of the more prominent state-of-the-industry studies conducted periodically by hospitality and travel industry magazines and newspapers are shown in Figure 6.9. Media research information is also available through certain private research firms including AC Nielsen, Arbitron, Mediamark Research (MRI), and Experian Simmons Market Research Bureau (SMRB).

Trade and travel associations sponsor and publish considerable research on the hospitality and travel industry. Some of these research studies are done periodically, whereas others are completed on special topics or issues on a one-time basis. The Cruise Lines International Association (CLIA) conducts a periodic study of cruise ship capacity, passenger volumes, and customer profile and satisfaction levels. The National Restaurant Association (NRA) prepares an annual report of the average operating performance levels of restaurants in the United States. The American Gaming Association (AGA) produces comprehensive annual statistics on gaming in the United States while the American Bus Association (ABA) periodically provides a census of the motorcoach sector.

Research companies and other private consultants are major providers of hospitality and travel industry research. These companies either sell their research reports or restrict their distribution to a specific group of research sponsors who each pay part of the cost of the research. Some companies specialize in specific parts of the hospitality and travel industry, whereas others provide broader statistics on travel volumes and patterns (Figure 6.9). For example, STR Global and PKF Consulting focus on the lodging sector, and ERA produces statistics with TEA on theme parks. D.K. Shifflet and YPartnership provide broader research data on traveler characteristics.

Universities and colleges conduct a large volume of research on the hospitality and travel industry. Much of this is published in major academic journals, such as the *Cornell Hospitality Quarterly*, *Journal of Travel Research*, *Tourism Management*, and *Annals of Tourism Research*, or is presented at major research and educators' conferences.

As you can see, there is a great amount of secondary research information available in the hospitality and travel industry. It is always a good practice to begin a research project by collecting and analyzing secondary data. This may answer some of the research questions or none at all. However, collecting these data means that the organization knows that research dollars are being used in the most effective way. Having done a thorough search, the organization may find that the information needed is not available through internal and external secondary data. When an organization reaches this conclusion, it must conduct primary research if the funds are available to do so. Before looking at primary

Industry Players

Applying Marketing Research in a Top Destination

Las Vegas Convention & Visitors Authority

http://www.lvcva.com

Image copyright Konstantin Sutyagin, 2008. Used under license from Shutterstock.com

The welcome sign to one of the most exciting destinations in the world.

The Las Vegas Convention & Visitors Authority (LVCVA) is one of the largest and best-funded city destination marketing organizations (DMOs) in the world. For LVCVA's fiscal year 2008, the operating funds available to the DMO were around $275 million. Room taxes from all transient lodging establishments in Clark County, Nevada contributed the major portion, at around 80 percent of these funds.

There is no doubt that Las Vegas is one of the top vacation and convention destinations in the United States. As indicated earlier in Figure 6.1, *Vegas FAQ* 39.2 million visitors went to Las Vegas in 2007; among them 6.2 million were convention delegates. The citywide occupancy rate in Las Vegas in 2007 was an amazingly high 90.4 percent. The total gaming revenues in Clark County were $10.9 billion.

These numbers are impressive indeed, but what most people do not see behind them is the LVCVA's long-term commitment to investing in marketing research to guide its programs and activities.

(continues)

(continued)

Marketing Research at the LVCVA

Later in Chapter 9, you will see the organization chart for the LVCVA. Some 534 staff were expected to be employed in fiscal year 2009. However, each year LVCVA spends very large amounts on marketing and advertising; about $36 million on marketing and another $87.6 million on advertising in fiscal 2008. It also invests a large sum of money in marketing research.

The marketing research function is the responsibility of LVCVA's Marketing Division and specifically is administered by its Internet Marketing and Research department. The department has seven staff members. According to LVCVA, "the department's wide range of research projects and programs tracks the dynamics of Las Vegas and Southern Nevada, as well as the nationwide competitive gaming and tourism industries. Among the research programs administered by the department are monthly executive summaries of tourism and convention indicators, annual visitor profile studies that track visitor demographics and behaviors, quarterly marketing bulletins, and a variety of programs to monitor local, national and global travel trends."

Courtesy of Las Vegas News Bureau/LVCVA

Part of the spectacular night skyline in Las Vegas.

The annual *Las Vegas Visitor Profile Study* is the centerpiece of LVCVA's marketing research efforts. Conducted by a private research company,

(continues)

(continued)

300 visitors are personally interviewed each month, or approximately 3,600 each year. The results of the 2007 Visitor Profile Study had some interesting highlights:

- Eighty-eight percent of the visitors were from the USA; 12 percent were from other countries;
- Fifty-two percent of all the visitors were from the Western states; 14 percent were from the Midwest;
- Eighty-one percent were repeat visitors to Las Vegas;
- Average number of visits to Las Vegas in the past five years was 6.3;
- Average age of visitors was 49;
- Seventy-nine percent were married; 80 percent had annual household incomes of $40,000 or more
- Average length of stay was 3.5 nights and 4.5 days;
- The proportion of visitors whose primary purpose was to gamble was just 11 percent; but 84 percent actually gambled while visiting Las Vegas;
- Twenty-five percent used the Internet to book their accommodations;
- The average nightly spending on accommodation was $108.87;
- Visitors who gambled budgeted an average of $555.64 on their trips for gambling;
- The average trip expenditures on food and drinks were $254.49 and shopping expenditures were $114.50.

The LVCVA digs deeper into the data gathered from the annual Las Vegas Visitor Profile Study. For example, a special sub-analysis is prepared that divides all the respondents into four market segments; (1) convention visitors, (2) package purchasers, (3) general tourists, and (4) casino guests. Each of the four market segments are analyzed in detail and all four are compared. Another special sub-analysis is completed on *Internet Travel Planners*; people who used the Internet to plan their trips to Las Vegas. These visitors are analyzed in detail and compared with those who did not rely on the Internet. Other analyses are done on those who arrived by air and by geographic region and by location of lodging.

The LVCVA conducts other studies and analyses. Special visitor profile studies are conducted for the communities of Laughlin and Mesquite, and a *Clark County Resident Survey* is completed biennially. The department also publishes monthly and year-to-date visitor statistics and maintains a *Hotel/Casino Development Construction Bulletin*.

Discussion Questions

1. In such a well-known and popular destination as Las Vegas, do you think it is really that necessary to spend a large amount on marketing research? Why or why not?
2. What can other destinations and DMOs learn most from the LVCVA example and its dedication to doing thorough marketing research?
3. What other types of marketing research might a DMO consider doing?

	SECONDARY RESEARCH	PRIMARY RESEARCH
ADVANTAGES	1. Inexpensive 2. Easily accessible 3. Immediately available	1. Applicable and usable 2. Accurate and reliable 3. Up-to-date
DISADVANTAGES	1. May not be applicable 2. Potentially unreliable 3. Frequently outdated	1. Expensive 2. Not as readily accessible 3. Not available immediately

FIGURE 6.10
Advantages and disadvantages of primary and secondary research.

research, you would probably like to know about the advantages and disadvantages of secondary research, so these are shown in Figure 6.10.

Primary Research Data

Primary (*or original*) research is data collected for the first time, by a method other than secondary research, to answer specific questions. When it is done, this normally happens after some secondary research information has been collected and analyzed. The advantages and disadvantages of primary research are shown in Figure 6.10. So you now want the answer to the question posed earlier: Should we use primary or secondary research, or both? We hope you have already guessed the answer. It is usually both. Although there are some occasions when an organization cannot afford the time and expense required for primary research, secondary research is usually insufficient for making major marketing decisions. It can help shape primary research information collection but cannot take its place.

Choosing the primary research method is the next hurdle to be surmounted. Two broad categories of research design exist: exploratory and conclusive. Secondary research falls into the exploratory category, along with several primary research methods (e.g., focus groups). **Exploratory research** sheds more light on the problem or opportunity. **Conclusive research** helps solve the problem or assess the opportunity.

Dividing primary research methods by the type of data they provide is another common approach. Figure 6.11 shows that the two major divisions of data are quantitative (numerical) and qualitative (non-numerical). Generally, the conclusive research methods produce quantitative data, whereas the exploratory primary research methods provide qualitative information.

Selecting the most appropriate design and method depends on several factors. The selection is based mainly on the research problem and objectives, how much is already known about the problem, and how the results are to be used. Figure 6.11 displays the alternative primary research methods. Four of these methods—(1) experiments, (2) mechanical observation, (3) surveys, and (4) simulation—can be used to produce **quantitative data**. The four other methods—(5) focus groups, (6) individual depth interviews, (7) human observation, and (8) case studies—normally provide researchers with **qualitative data**.

FIGURE 6.11 Primary research methods and techniques.

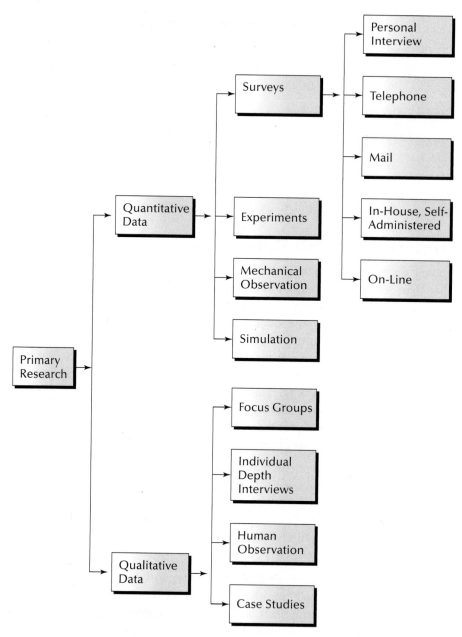

Quantitative Primary Research Methods

1. **Experiments.** You probably associate the word *experiment* with the science classes you had in school. Scientists, in fact, carry out many experiments to test their beliefs. **Experimental research** in our industry usually involves tests of various kinds to determine the likely reactions of customers to new services or products. It is extremely expensive for an organization to introduce a new item and have it fail. By using the experimental method, there is less risk of failure. The experiment can be as simple as a concept test, or as complex and expensive as full-blown **test marketing**.

2. **Mechanical Observation.** Human and mechanical observations are two main forms of **observational research**. People are used to make the first type of observation, whereas mechanical and electronic devices produce the second type.

   Mechanical observation is used in certain parts of the hospitality and travel industry, usually to provide customer counts or sales information. The turnstiles at the entrance to theme parks and other gated attractions are a good example. Cash registers, especially electronic ones backed up by computer systems, are powerful observers of customers' purchasing behaviors. Bar code technology and related scanning devices are widely used in retail shopping situations. Hand counters are used by ships and some attractions, whereas vehicle counts are taken using a counting device stretched across the surface of roads. **Log file analyzer programs** are used to analyze the traffic to websites. Mechanical observation devices are also used in tracking television viewing and in testing advertisements and other promotions.

   While all these devices are capable of producing very accurate, quantitative data, they do not provide the in-depth, qualitative information that human observation gives. They describe rather than explain customer behavior and give little indication of people's motivations, attitudes, opinions, and perceptions.

3. **Survey.** Most of you are already familiar with surveys. Perhaps you have been stopped in the local shopping mall and asked about your favorite brand of shampoo. Or maybe you received a form in the mail from your high school asking for your opinions on various programs offered there. How about that phone call from the life insurance company asking you all kinds of personal questions about your future plans? What about the comment cards you have seen on many restaurant tables or the questionnaire on the website you visited? You have just identified the five principal ways of completing surveys.

   a. Personal interviews (or intercepts)
   b. Mail
   c. Telephone
   d. In-house, self-administered
   e. Online

   Survey research is the most popular research method in the hospitality and travel industry because it is flexible and easy to use. Despite their great popularity, many poor and ineffective surveys are completed every day. Knowing how to implement or "field" a good survey is definitely a science, but also a bit of an art.

   a. *Personal Interviews.* A questionnaire received in the mail can simply be tossed in the garbage. It is also easy to hang up the phone on a researcher. Human nature, however, makes it much more difficult to refuse to give answers in a one-on-one interviewing situation. One of the advantages of personal interviewing, therefore, is the relatively

FIGURE 6.12
Conducting personal interviews usually guarantees the highest response rate.

Image copyright Phil Date, 2008. Used under license from Shutterstock.com

high **response rate**—the percentage of all people surveyed who supply answers to the researcher's questions (Figure 6.12).

Another advantage is its high degree of flexibility. Once committed to paper, the questions in mail and in-house, self-administered surveys cannot be modified. Although telephone researchers can reword questions, they cannot get visual clues from the respondent's behavior and body language. The personal interviewer can show or demonstrate more things. Let us assume we are a hotel company considering a new lifestyle hotel brand. We might write up a description of the new lifestyle hotel (remember concept testing?) and get past guest opinions on it online or via a mail or telephone survey. Much more effective, however, would be a personal interview. We could show the description, along with concept drawings and photos, to some of our current guests and ask them for their reactions.

Interviewers can provide fuller explanations of the meaning of certain questions. They can also gather more complete answers by rephrasing questions and probing further.

Personal interviews can provide very timely data, as can online and telephone surveys. However, there is always a lag time in mail surveys between the mailing date and receipt of completed questionnaires. Thus, if information is required quickly, in-person, online, or telephone surveys are preferable.

Following are some of the disadvantages of personally-administered surveys.

- They are relatively expensive.
- There can be interviewer bias in questioning.
- Respondents may be reluctant to answer personal questions.
- Respondents may not answer in a relaxed way.
- The time of the interview may inconvenience the respondent.

b. *Mail Surveys.* Mail surveys lack the personal touch of one-on-one, personal interviews. Despite this, they offer several distinct advantages.

- They are relatively inexpensive if the response rate is high.
- There is no interviewer bias.
- There is a consistency in the questions and responses.
- They can survey a large number of respondents.
- They can reach every respondent by mail.
- Respondents can remain anonymous.
- Respondents can choose the most convenient time to answer questions.

One of the major drawbacks of mail surveys, apart from their impersonal nature, is the relatively low response rate. Although personal interviewing and telephone surveys usually generate answers from 50 percent or more of the respondents, a response rate of 30 percent to 40 percent is quite good for a mail survey. Response rates below this range are also quite common. In many ways, this survey technique suffers from most of the same disadvantages as direct marketing, particularly the junk mail syndrome (a commonly-held perception that much of one's daily mail is purely commercial solicitation). Like direct marketing, however, there are procedures that help improve the response to mail surveys. These include the following:[5]

- Using highly personalized approaches and avoiding the mass-mailing look (e.g., individually-typed addresses on envelopes, personalized salutations on cover letters, respondents' names in the body of the cover letter, postage stamps rather than metered mail)
- Following up several times after the initial request to remind respondents about completing the questionnaire
- Promising respondents an incentive for completing the questionnaire (e.g., a copy of research findings or a monetary or non-monetary incentive)

- Using accurate and up-to-date mailing lists
- Avoiding lengthy questionnaires
- Including a postage-paid, preaddressed envelope for returning the questionnaire

By following these guidelines carefully, a hospitality and travel organization can increase the response rate so that it approaches that of personal and telephone surveys.

c. *Telephone Surveys.* Telephone surveys share many of the advantages of personal interviews. They are more flexible than mail surveys, since the researcher can reword questions for greater clarification and skip questions that are not applicable. Information can be gathered quickly and inexpensively if only local dialing is required. High response rates can be achieved with good contact lists and trained telephone interviewers (Figure 6.13).

However, like personal interviews, telephone surveys are more obtrusive than mail. Many people regard telephone solicitations and surveys as an invasion of their privacy and quickly hang up the telephone. It is more difficult to build a good rapport with the respondent on the telephone than it is in personal interviews. Telephone surveys also become expensive when long-distance calls have to be made. In this case, the number of questions asked usually has to be kept to a minimum.

As with mail surveys, there are specific telephone survey procedures that help improve response rates and data quality. These procedures are borrowed mainly from the field of telephone selling or telemarketing, which Chapter 17 discusses.

FIGURE 6.13
Telephone surveys are a popular technique, but require great phone skills to be successful.

Image copyright Cecilia Lim H M, 2008. Used under license from Shutterstock.com

d. *In-house, self-administered.* These are surveys that are provided for customers to complete while they are within the premises of hospitality and travel organizations. They include the comment cards often found on restaurant tables as well as the survey forms left in hotel guest rooms and cruise ship staterooms. These surveys can be extremely helpful in determining guest satisfaction with service quality, facilities, and equipment (Figure 6.14).

In-house, self-administered surveys have many of the same disadvantages as mail surveys, the primary one being that they usually generate a low response rate. Response rates to traditional paper **comment cards** are very low. How many comment cards have you filled out in restaurants in the past few months? Your answer is probably "none" or "very few." Unfortunately, many customers feel that nobody is interested in their opinions, and, in most cases, there is really no other incentive for taking the time to express their opinions. Having guests complete comment cards online is now helping to significantly increase response rates.[6]

In the era of relationship marketing in which current and past customers are seen as the key resource for future marketing, this situation is unacceptable. The organization must do all it can to motivate customers to fill out in-house questionnaires. Some hotels have guests enter answers to a computer-based survey at the front desk. Other astute marketers offer incentives for completion such as free desserts or other small rewards.

e. *Online.* The Internet has introduced some exciting new ways of conducting surveys. The two main alternatives are using either e-mail or the Web to deliver and receive questionnaires. For example, many

FIGURE 6.14
Customer satisfaction surveys are essential in hospitality and travel.

INTERNET MARKETING

Using the Internet to Collect Research Data

- The Internet introduced a brand new set of tools for collecting research data and also for building databases.
- The Missouri Division of Tourism (MDT) provides a good example of an online visitor survey for a destination marketing organization. The Clarion Hotel in Stockholm, Sweden gives an appropriate example of a hotel guest satisfaction survey. Chili's provides a good example of an online restaurant satisfaction survey.
- The MDT survey is accessed from its front page; it gathers opinions about the design and contents of the website, and socio-demographic information on site visitors (age, gender, location of residence, household composition, education, household income).
- The MDT survey asks site visitors why they visited the website: (1) to learn about Missouri, (2) to get information about a trip to Missouri you already planned, (3) to decide whether to visit Missouri, (4) to plan a trip to Missouri, (5) just for fun, and (6) other.
- The Clarion Hotel asks guests to rate their service on a five-point scale in five areas of the property: (1) reception (2) conference, (3) restaurant/bar, (4) breakfast, and (5) housekeeping.
- The Clarion also asks a great question about possible guest referrals, "Would you consider recommending our hotel to a friend/colleague who is traveling to the city?" It also asks what the hotel could improve upon to make the guest's stay better.
- Chili's provides another good example of an online survey. Customers complete its *Guest Survey* by entering a personal code on their meal receipts.

Sources: Missouri Division of Tourism. (2008). *Welcome to Missouri Tourism Web Survey*, **http://www.visitmo.com/; Clarion Hotel Stockholm. (2008).** *Guest Survey*. **http://www.clarionstockholm.com/guest_survey.asp**; Chili's. (2008). *Guest Survey*. **http://ww1.empathica.com/sxml/chilisgem1/custsurvey.jsp**

Student Questions

1. What are the major benefits of placing surveys online rather than using other methods to collect the data?
2. What are the key questions that a hotel or restaurant should include in an online survey?
3. What are the key questions that a DMO should incorporate in an online survey?
4. What steps should be taken to get the highest possible response rate for these online surveys?

- Questions that use jargon or technical terms (e.g., check average, occupied room nights, AP/MAP/EP, covers)
- Too many questions
- Questions that are long and wordy
- Questions that are really two questions in one
- Questions that are vague and general
- Failure to tell the respondent how to fill in each question (e.g., how many items to check, how to rank alternatives)
- Questions that are personal and embarrassing
- Questions that do not cover the full range of possible responses (e.g., no "don't know" or "no opinion" responses)
- Questions that give management answers that are too general (e.g., rating broad areas of service as excellent to poor)

FIGURE 6.15 Common faults in questionnaire design.

hospitality and travel organizations have placed questionnaires on their websites to collect information from people visiting their sites.

Researchers are now making much greater use of **online surveys**, and are learning each day how to make the most effective use of **online research**. The relative speed and flexibility of online surveys are two major advantages. Additionally, there is the potential of reaching a large and growing audience of people online, since there are now around 1.5 billion Internet users across the world. The main limitations of online research are that response rates are often low and there often doubts about how representative respondents are of the populations being studied.

All the survey techniques—personal interviews; mail, telephone, in-house, self-administered, and online surveys—normally require a form that lists the questions and provides space for answers. These come in all shapes and sizes and are referred to as **questionnaires**. A good questionnaire is one of the keys to getting quality research information. It is surprising then that many poorly-designed questionnaires are used in our industry. Figure 6.15 lists common faults found in questionnaires and Figure 6.16 presents guidelines for designing effective questionnaires.

4. **Simulation.** The fourth research method involves using computers to simulate marketing situations. A mathematical model is developed that is a **simulation** of the real-life situation. The model can be used to predict sales volumes, customer counts, or other variables important to management.

Qualitative Primary Research Methods

1. **Focus Groups.** A **focus group** is a method in which the researcher directs questions to a small group of people, usually between eight and twelve. The word *focus* means that the researcher draws the group's attention to a specific subject or set of questions and invites a discussion about them. From then on the researcher listens,

FIGURE 6.16
Guidelines for effective questionnaire design.

The following guidelines are suggested for designing effective questionnaires:

LENGTH

1. Keep it as short as possible.
2. Be sure individual questions are short and to the point.

ORGANIZATION

3. Include a date.
4. Place personal questions (e.g., income level, age) at the end.
5. Provide instructions on how the interviewer or respondent should answer each question.
6. If appropriate, always supply "don't know" or "no opinion" options.

WORDING OF QUESTIONS

7. Ask only one question in each question.
8. Be as specific as possible.
9. Avoid technical terms.
10. Use words whose meanings are clear.
11. Make sure there are no overlaps in possible responses (e.g., use $1–$1.99 and $2–$2.99, rather than $1–$2 and $2–$3).

watches people's behavior, refocuses the discussion if necessary, and tries to summarize the group's opinions, comments, and suggestions.

The real strength of focus groups is that they can provide an in-depth understanding of customers' opinions, attitudes, perceptions, and behavior. Researchers can probe even further than they can in one-on-one, personal interviews (Figure 6.17).

The focus group method is widely used in the hospitality and travel industry, especially to explore people's images of specific companies and destination areas. The following are some practical examples of how focus groups have been used in hospitality and travel:

- To pre-test television commercials or other forms of advertising.
- To gather impressions of printed brochures or guides.
- To test out new concepts or products.
- To determine attitudes toward and images of destinations or companies.
- To generate questions for later use in quantitative surveys.
- To explore in greater depth responses received from earlier quantitative surveys.

Despite their great versatility, focus groups produce only qualitative information. The information collected from a focus group session cannot be called representative. It may not accurately represent the opinions, attitudes, perceptions, or behavior of all customers. If an

Image copyright Ragsac, 2008. Used under license from Shutterstock.com

FIGURE 6.17 Focus groups gather qualitative responses from groups of 8-12 people.

organization needs to have numerical data that represent the collective opinions of all its past or potential customers, then the survey method is preferable.

2. **Individual Depth Interviews.** The **individual depth interview (IDI)** has objectives and procedures similar to the focus group, but involves only one interviewee (subject) and one interviewer. These one-on-one sessions usually last for between 30 minutes and more than one hour.[7] It is best to use skilled interviewers to conduct these interviews, as they can uncover more insights than focus groups. Unlike focus groups, the responses can be attributed to an individual.

3. **Human Observation.** Using human observation in research means watching and noting how customers behave. It is a great technique for evaluating competitors. The following are just a few other creative ideas for using human observational research.

   - Count how many times people refill their plates from buffet or salad bars.
   - Tally the number of cars and the license-plate origins in a competitor's parking area.
   - Watch how many people take brochures from a rack.
   - Add up the number of people using a swimming pool during different times of the day.

- Calculate the average amount of time customers spend eating meals in a restaurant.
- Watch how people navigate around a website.

Try to come up with a few more ideas yourself. Is this not a really useful technique? It is surprising then that it often gets overlooked as a source of research information. Whether we watch our own or competitors' customers, the observational method provides a relatively inexpensive and rich supply of data for decision making.

4. **Case Studies.** The purpose of the **case study** method is to get information from one or more situations that are similar to the organization's problem situation.[8] The word *situations* often means other organizations or destinations that are similar to the organization or destination doing the case study and that have had experience in dealing with the same or a similar research problem. Case studies are usually done in the hospitality and travel industry when an organization or destination is investigating the addition of new services or facilities and when potential new target markets and marketing mix approaches are being evaluated. Effective case studies are dependent on obtaining the cooperation of the organizations or destinations being studied and can provide rich and in-depth information on their experiences.

Chapter Conclusion

Properly conducted marketing research helps hospitality and travel organizations make effective decisions. It does not replace the need for managerial experience and judgment, but lessens the risk of poor decisions being made without adequate prior research. Marketing research must be done in every step of the hospitality and travel marketing system.

The two major divisions of research data are primary and secondary. There are many research and statistical techniques available. Selecting from among them should be done using a systematic marketing research process. The steps in this process are to define the research problem, develop an approach to the research problem, formulate the research design, conduct the data collection or fieldwork, prepare the data and analysis, and prepare and present the research report.

**REVIEW
QUESTIONS**

1. How is marketing research defined in this book?
2. What are the reasons for doing marketing research?

3. Sometimes managers do not do marketing research when it seems they should. What are the reasons for not doing marketing research? Are these justifiable?
4. How is research used in each of the steps of the hospitality and travel marketing system?
5. What are the five key requirements for good research information?
6. What are the six steps in the marketing research process?
7. What are the sources of secondary research data?
8. What are the broad categories of primary research data collection methods?
9. What are the advantages and disadvantages of personal interviews; mail, telephone, in-house, self-administered, and online surveys?
10. What are focus groups and how are they used to assist with marketing decisions?
11. What steps can be taken to develop the most effective questionnaires?

CHAPTER ASSIGNMENTS

1. Interview the owner or manager of a local, independent restaurant. What types of ongoing market research does the business carry out? Does it make use of primary or secondary research data? What suggestions do you have for improving or expanding the restaurant's market research program?
2. Gather a selection of comment cards and guest surveys from airlines, hotels, restaurants, and other travel businesses. What common questions or other features do you notice? Can you see any similar faults or weaknesses? Which is the strongest and why? What recommendations would you make to improve these types of in-house, self-administered surveys?
3. You have been approached by a hospitality and travel business to do some research for them. They have been experiencing a growing number of complaints about their service, but cannot pinpoint the specific reasons. Which research method would you use and why? How would you design your research procedures? Draft a questionnaire or questionnaires you would use. How would you suggest that management use your research information?
4. You have just started work in the marketing department of a hospitality and travel organization. To your surprise, you learn that no marketing research has been done because your boss—the director of marketing—thinks research is a waste of time and money. How would you justify a marketing research program to your boss, and what research projects would you include? Can you prove that your

research program and projects may save money and lead to increased sales? If so, how?

WEB RESOURCES

AC Nielsen, http://www.acnielsen.com/
American Marketing Association, http://www.marketingpower.com/
Amtrak, http://www.amtrak.com/
Annals of Tourism Research, http://www.elsevier.com/
Arbitron, http://www.arbitron.com/
Business Travel News, http://btnonline.com/
Club Med, http://www.clubmed.com/
Cornell Hospitality Quarterly, http://www.hotelschool.cornell.edu/
Cruise Lines International Association, http://www.cruising.org/
D.K. Shifflet & Associates, http://www.dksa.com/
Journal of Travel Research, http://jtr.sagepub.com/
Las Vegas Convention & Visitors Authority, http://www.lvcva.com/
Marriott, http://www.marriott.com/
Mediamark Research Inc., http://www.mediamark.com/
Meetings & Conventions, http://www.mcmag.com/
PKF Consulting, http://www.pkfonline.com/
Pizza Hut, http://www.pizzahut.com/
Experian Simmons Market Research Bureau, http://www.smrb.com/
Smith Travel Research, http://www.strglobal.com/
Successful Meetings, http://www.mimegasite.com/
Tourism Management, http://www.elsevier.com/
YPartnership, http://www.ypartnership.com/

REFERENCES

1. Tourism Australia. 2006. *A Uniquely Australian Invitation. The Experience Seeker*. Tourism Australia.

2. Las Vegas Convention and Visitors Authority. 2007. *Survey Says: Vegas Is on a Roll!* http://www.lvcva.com/press/press-releases-2007.jsp?pressId=531, accessed February 13, 2009.

3. American Marketing Association. 2007. *Dictionary of Marketing Terms*, http://www.marketingpower.com/mg-dictionary.php, accessed February 13, 2009.

4. Malhotra, Naresh K. 2007. *Marketing Research. An Applied Orientation*. Pearson Prentice Hall: Upper Saddle River, New Jersey, 10–11.

5. Dillman, Don. 2006. *Mail and Internet Surveys: The Tailored Design Method*. Wiley: New York.

6. Hotel Online Special Report. 2003. *Le Pavillon in New Orleans Reaps 800% Higher Response Rate with New Guest Online Comment Card,*

http://www.hotel-online.com/News/PR2003_2nd/Jun03_LePavillon.
html, accessed February 13, 2009.

7. Malhotra, Naresh K. 2007. *Marketing Research. An Applied Orientation.*
    Pearson Prentice Hall: Upper Saddle River, New Jersey, 152.

8. Zikmund, William G. 2000. *Exploring Marketing Research.* 7th ed. Harcourt College Publishers: Fort Worth, Texas: Harcourt College Publishers.

For additional hospitality and travel marketing resources, visit our Web site at
www.Hospitality-Tourism.delmar.com

PLANNING: MARKETING STRATEGY AND PLANNING

WHERE ARE WE NOW?

WHERE WOULD WE LIKE TO BE?

HOW DO WE GET THERE?

HOW DO WE MAKE SURE WE GET THERE?

HOW DO WE KNOW IF WE GOT THERE?

chapter 7

Marketing Strategy: Market Segmentation and Trends
Where Would We Like to Be?

O V E R V I E W

A wise person once said that you can please some people all of the time and all people some of the time, but you cannot please all people all of the time. This is the basis for one of marketing's core principles—market segmentation.

This chapter explains the role and benefits of market segmentation. It also looks at the characteristics that can be used to segment hospitality and travel markets. It explains the traditional methods used to categorize different customer groups and describes the segmentation practices that are gaining in popularity. Also reviewed are recent customer and industry trends that are re-shaping hospitality and travel and requiring greater emphasis on market segmentation.

O B J E C T I V E S

Having read this chapter, you should be able to:

- Define market segmentation.
- Explain the importance of segmentation to effective marketing.
- Explain the benefits and limitations of market segmentation.
- List and describe the eight criteria used to determine the viability of market segments.
- List and explain the characteristics for segmenting hospitality and travel markets.
- Describe the major demand and supply trends influencing today's hospitality and travel industry.
- Describe the recent trends in the segmentation practices of the hospitality and travel industry.

K E Y   T E R M S

Baby Boomer

behavioral segmentation

benefit segmentation

brand loyalty

brand segmentation

corporate (business) travel
   market

customer mix

database marketing

demographic and socio-
   economic segmentation

distribution channel
   segmentation

frequent travelers

geo-demographic segmentation

geographic segmentation

lifestyle

lifestyle segmentation

market segment

market segmentation

market segmentation analysis

multi-stage segmentation

occasion-based segmentation

pleasure (leisure) and personal
   travel market

positioning

primary segmentation
   characteristic

product-related segmentation

psychographic segmentation

psychographics

purpose-of-trip segmentation

segmentation characteristics

segmentation criteria

segmented marketing strategy

single-stage segmentation

target market

trading area

two-stage segmentation

undifferentiated marketing

use-frequency segmentation

VFR (visiting friends and
   relatives) market

Have you ever considered to how many groups you and other members of your family belong? A good place to start is to list those elements that you and other people have in common. What about your home? Perhaps you share a street address and zip/postal code with several others. You will agree that thousands of people also share your home town, city, county, state, or province. What about your age? You know that many others are the same age as you are, and they may even have the same birthday. How about other things such as your income, educational background, family composition, and religion? Although you like to think of yourself as a one-of-a-kind person, you must admit that other people also have similar characteristics.

Your list of groups is already long! But we are not finished yet. You might not know it, but you have the same culture, subculture, psychographic and lifestyle characteristics, product and service usage rates and patterns, and favorite activities as many other people. You and other people also look for similar benefits from certain products and services.

Your list is probably on a second page by now, and you are wondering about the point of the exercise. It is simple. Although every human being, even an identical twin, is unique, each person can be grouped with others on the basis of shared characteristics. Effective marketing involves identifying those groups to which our services have the greatest appeal, as well as ruling out others that are unlikely to purchase our services.

Market Segmentation

Analyzing market segments is the first step in developing a marketing strategy. This chapter looks at the concept of market segmentation. Chapter 8 discusses the second, third, and fourth steps in the process of developing a marketing strategy and plan: marketing strategy formulation, positioning approach, and marketing objectives.

Market Segmentation Analysis

Market segmentation is the division of the overall market for a service into groups of people with common characteristics. These are usually called market segments or target markets. A **market segment** is an identifiable component group of an overall market whose members have some common characteristics, and to which a specific service appeals. When the term **target market** is used, it means a market segment selected by a hospitality and travel organization for marketing attention.

As you can see, there are two distinct and sequential steps in market segmentation:

1. Dividing the whole market into groups (market segments) with common characteristics (using specific **segmentation characteristics**).
2. Selecting those market segments (target markets) that the organization is best able to serve (using a set of **segmentation criteria**).

This process, known as **market segmentation analysis** (segmenting the market and selecting target markets), requires the types of good primary and secondary research data and analysis that were discussed in Chapters 5 and 6. Before discussing how market segmentation analysis is done, it is important to review the reasons for the increasing importance of market segmentation, as well as segmentation's benefits and limitations.

Reasons for Market Segmentation

Chapter 1 identified market segmentation as one of the core principles of marketing. It contrasted the rifle (targeted) and shotgun (untargeted) approaches to marketing and strongly recommended the first of the two. Why? The basic reason for market segmentation is that trying to appeal to all potential customers—the untargeted approach—is wasteful. There are groups of customers who are just not interested in buying our services.

The essence of good marketing is to pick out the segments that are most interested in specific services and to aim marketing programs at them. In this way, marketing is similar to shuffling and dealing a pack of cards. Many different hands are dealt and played, but only one is a winner. Cards, like customers, can be grouped in several different ways: similar suits or similar values, similar royals or similar faces. Depending on the game, players reorganize their hands in ways that are most likely to win. They know that selecting and grouping their cards is necessary to succeed. Effective marketers recognize the same type of rule. There is, sadly, an end to this analogy. Playing and winning at cards is a gamble. Marketing must not be!

The principal reason for segmentation, therefore, is to focus effort and marketing dollars in the most effective way. There are several choices to be made, and it is helpful to think of the answers to the *who, what, how, where,* and *when* questions:

1. **Who?** Which market segments should we pursue?
2. **What?** What are they looking for in our types of services?
3. **How?** How do we develop our marketing programs to best fit their needs and wants?
4. **Where?** Where do we promote our services?
5. **When?** When do we promote them?

Once target markets have been selected, other decisions and alternatives come into better focus. Through research, we can then identify the needs and wants of these groups. What follows is similar to operating a camera. Once the operator selects the subject, he or she adjusts the environment (lighting, speed, arrangement, and position) and focuses. Clear, sharp photographs require good subjects, proper equipment and accessories, the right environment, careful preplanning, and precise timing. Effective market segmentation is much like photography. The marketer must know how, where, and when to appeal to selected target markets. When the camera operator uses the wrong equipment or environment, or hurriedly snaps a picture, the result is predictable—a blurry photograph. Likewise, the marketer who fails to take adequate time to plan how, where, and when to best appeal to target markets will have an out-of-focus marketing program and will waste precious money.

The need for segmentation has never been greater than it is today. The market trends discussed later in this chapter have caused great fragmentation in hospitality and travel markets.

Benefits of Market Segmentation

The benefits of using market segmentation are:

1. More effective use of marketing dollars
2. Clearer understanding of the needs and wants of selected customer groups
3. More effective **positioning** (developing a service and marketing mix to occupy a specific place in the minds of potential customers within target markets)
4. Greater precision in selecting promotional vehicles and techniques (e.g., website development and navigation, advertising media, sales promotion methods, geographic placement)

The budget hotel concept provides a good example of these benefits. Its developers realized that there are groups of travelers that are not interested in the full range of services provided by the typical roadside hotel, for example. These potential customers wanted inexpensive, clean, and comfortable lodging in limited-service and conveniently located properties. These developers responded by positioning a standardized (same across the nation) service, with few of the frills of a typical motor hotel, at a significantly reduced price. The result is history. A completely new sector of the lodging industry was created. Companies such as Days Inns, Super 8, and Motel 6 are now household names. By selecting economy-minded travelers, these companies concentrated on these customers' needs, chose the best ways to appeal to them, and promoted in the right places at the right times. The no-frills concept has also been used successfully by other hospitality and travel organizations. Examples include Rent-A-Wreck car rentals, last-minute travel clubs, Southwest Airlines, JetBlue, Easy Jet and Ryanair (Europe), WestJet (Western Canada), and a large number of other low-cost airline carriers. Even fast-food chain outlets can be considered a variation on the same theme.

Limitations of Market Segmentation

You may now feel that every hospitality and travel organization should use market segmentation. In more than 95 percent of the cases, you are absolutely correct. Most organizations find that a **segmented marketing strategy** (selecting specific target markets and marketing mixes for each of them) is the most effective. Almost all full-service hotels, table-service restaurants, airlines, cruise lines, gaming operations, and travel trade intermediaries recognize that they have customer groups with different needs and wants to whom specific promotional approaches apply. Convention/meeting planners want the right types of meeting rooms with appropriate audio-visual equipment. Pleasure travelers are not at all interested in this service. Pleasure travelers are more likely to be subscribers to *Travel + Leisure Magazine*. However, convention planners have a greater preference for *Meetings & Conventions* magazine. A segmented marketing strategy makes great sense.

Now turn your attention to fast-food operators. The picture is not as clear, is it? Almost everyone has eaten at least one meal at one their restaurants. When a service's appeal is so broad, does it make any sense to use different approaches for various customer groups, or should the same methods be used for all? We will leave this question for later.

Market segmentation has the following limitations and problems:

1. More expensive than using a non-segmented approach
2. Difficult to select the best customer characteristics to use for segmenting a market
3. Difficult to know how finely or broadly to segment
4. Tendency to appeal to segments that are not viable

1. **More Expensive.** The most obvious limitation of market segmentation is the added expense. Each target market receives individual attention.

This means a wider range of services and price structures must be provided. Websites, advertisements and promotions have to be tailored to the habits and preferences of each segment. Multiple distribution channels may have to be used. Because each additional target market brings an extra cost, each must be examined individually to determine whether pursuing it is worthwhile in terms of return on investment (ROI).

2. **Difficult to Select the Best Segmentation Characteristics.** You will remember that we began this chapter by asking you to list the different groups to which you belong. The problem facing any marketer comes from the size of the list you probably compiled. Many segmentation characteristics can be used. Geographic location, purpose of trip, demographics, lifestyles, benefits sought, and frequency of usage are just a few of the alternatives. The marketer's dilemma is to decide which characteristic or combination of characteristics will produce the best return on the marketing investment. There is no single answer to this question. Each situation requires careful research and planning.

3. **Difficult to Know How Finely or Broadly to Segment.** Market segmentation can be carried too far. It can be as wasteful to have too many as it can be to have too few target markets. Some find that the amount spent to generate business from certain target markets is more than the additional profits generated. However, if a market is divided too broadly, certain segments are not reached effectively. Here, marketing can be compared to panning for gold. If a sieve with a very fine mesh is used, for example, only the very finest sand will pass through. If the perforations are larger, only larger particles are trapped. Marketing to only a few target markets is similar to mining with the large-mesh sieve—some potential customers pass through the marketer's hands. Selecting a large number of target markets can be compared to using the fine-mesh mining implement. In this case, almost all potential customers are netted, but it is difficult to distinguish the value of individual target markets. Just as the miner may not find that much more gold by using this tool, the marketer may find segmentation of limited value if it is carried too far.

4. **Tendency to Appeal to Non-viable Segments.** There are market segments that are not viable. For example, there may be no specific promotional or advertising vehicle to reach them. Some groups may be too small to justify the marketing investment required. Some segments may not be permanent. They may be fad-oriented and exist only for a few years. Other segments may be so dominated by one or more large companies that a newcomer that chooses to pursue these segments will find it both expensive and unrewarding.

Criteria for Effective Segmentation

You now know that there are pitfalls to market segmentation. But how can they be avoided? The answer lies in carefully screening potential target markets to make sure they meet the following eight criteria:

1. Measurable
2. Substantial
3. Accessible
4. Defensible
5. Durable
6. Competitive
7. Homogeneous
8. Compatible

1. **Measurable.** It is inadvisable to pick target markets that cannot be measured without a reasonable degree of accuracy. This book stresses the need to set marketing objectives in numerical (quantitative) terms and to measure the results of marketing plans. If the marketer can only guess the size of a target market, then there is no way of knowing what level of marketing investment is justified, or even if any investment is worthwhile. Similarly, there is an insufficient basis for measuring success against target market objectives.

2. **Substantial.** A target market must be big enough to warrant a separate investment. How big is big? The answer is that it must produce more in added profits than the amount required to pursue it; that is, the benefits must outweigh the investment costs.

3. **Accessible.** The essence of market segmentation is being able to select and reach specific customer groups. However, there are target markets that cannot be reached with the degree of precision the marketer desires. In this case, uninterested people also receive communications, resulting in wasted effort and money.

4. **Defensible.** There are situations in which a similar approach can be used with two or more individual target markets. The marketer must be sure that each group requires individual attention. The marketer must also have confidence that the organization's share of each target market can be defended from competitors.

5. **Durable.** Some market segments are short term or medium term, meaning that they exist for less than five years. Some are fads that enjoy brief popularity. Others result from non-recurrent events. Beanie Babies, Hula hoops, pet rocks, Michael Jackson mania, discos, and roller rinks are examples of fads. Although some ventures are so profitable that they quickly produce a sufficient return on investment, most are not. The prudent marketer should be convinced that each target market has long-term potential.

6. **Competitive.** The sixth criterion is the competitiveness of our service relative to the market segment. Marketers need to take a long, hard look at whether what they offer provides something distinct or unique for these customers. The more precisely the service fits the needs of a particular segment, the more likely it is to succeed. However, if a service does not match the needs well, there is little point in pursuing the segment.

7. **Homogeneous.** In dividing the whole market into its component market segments, the organization should make sure that the segments are as

different from each other, or as heterogeneous, as possible. At the same time, the people within each segment should be as similar, or as homogeneous, as possible.

8. **Compatible.** When an organization selects a target market it must be sure that this market does not conflict in any way with the markets it already serves. Marketers would say that this means ensuring that a new target market is compatible with the existing **customer mix** (the combination of target markets that an organization serves).

The Role of Segmentation in Marketing Strategies

You will remember our earlier discussion of a segmented marketing strategy, and you may also recall the concept of strategic marketing planning from Chapter 3. The terms *strategy* and *strategic* involve long-term planning, or making choices between alternative courses of action for a period of more than two future years. Although Chapter 8 takes a more detailed look at marketing strategy and positioning, you should know about the function of market segmentation in the strategy-selection process.

Market segmentation plays a key role in selecting and detailing a marketing strategy. In fact, deciding on a strategy usually involves choosing a single target market or some combination of target markets, or, alternatively, consciously deciding to ignore segment differences (**undifferentiated marketing**). Selecting target markets for attention is usually a multi-year decision that is subject to annual review using the situation analysis and segment marketing research.

Segmentation Characteristics

What characteristics should be used to divide a market into segments? This is one of the most difficult questions facing all hospitality and travel organizations, yet it is very important in marketing effectiveness. The alternatives are numerous, including the following seven broad characteristics:

1. Geographic
2. Demographic and socio-economic
3. Purpose of trip
4. Psychographic
5. Behavioral
6. Product-related
7. Distribution channel

Each of these seven categories includes several alternative characteristics for dividing the market into segments. For example, a restaurant that uses a geographic segmentation might separate potential customers by zip or postal codes, the first three digits of phone numbers, residential neighborhood, or street addresses. Different combinations of the seven characteristics can be used—for example, geographic, purpose of trip, and demographic—so the alternatives available increase to well over 100. Choosing from among these alternative combinations is a major challenge in market segmentation, as you have already seen.

Segmentation Approaches

Before describing each segmentation characteristic, you should recognize the three different approaches to segmentation described in the following paragraphs:

1. **Single-Stage Segmentation.** Only one of the seven categories of segmentation characteristics is chosen in **single-stage segmentation**. For example, a travel agency might divide groups of potential customers into pleasure and corporate accounts (a purpose-of-trip characteristic). The tour operator, Contiki, uses just age (a demographic characteristic) to identify its target market (18- to 35-year-olds).

2. **Two-Stage Segmentation.** After a **primary segmentation characteristic** (the characteristic most important in determining the customer's choice of a service) is chosen, the market is further subdivided using a second segmentation characteristic. Traditionally, lodging properties use **two-stage segmentation** when they divide their market by purpose of trip and then use geography to pinpoint target markets more finely.

3. **Multi-stage Segmentation.** A primary segmentation characteristic is once again chosen, but then two or more other characteristics are used in **multi-stage segmentation**. For example, a hotel divides its market by purpose of trip. One of the segments it identifies is the convention-meeting market. Because of the limited capacity of its meeting rooms, the hotel narrows its focus further by considering only associations and companies that hold meetings of less than a certain number of people (a product-related characteristic). Finally, it uses geography to pinpoint where these organizations are located.

Which is the best of these three approaches? There is no single, correct answer. Generally, it is more effective to use the two-stage or multi-stage methods, since they provide greater precision in targeting markets. Experts also agree that choosing the first or primary segmentation characteristic is critical to success. This should be the characteristic with the greatest influence on the customer's buying behavior.

Individual Segmentation Characteristics

1. **Geographic Segmentation.** This is the most widely used segmentation characteristic in the hospitality and travel industry. **Geographic segmentation** means dividing the market into groups of customers who share the same geographic location. Areas can be very large (e.g., several countries or even continents) or very small (e.g., residential neighborhoods). Some travel marketing organizations, including the Canadian Tourism Commission, Tourism Australia, VisitBritain, and the Hong Kong Tourism Board use country of origin as their primary segmentation characteristic. However, restaurants need a much finer and more localized approach, such as the zip or postal codes within their cities or towns.

   Why is geographic segmentation so popular? First, it is easy to use. There are universally accepted definitions of geographic areas. This is not the case, as we shall see, with psychographic and benefit segments. Geographic markets can be easily measured, and usually there are numerous demographic and socio-economic, travel, and other statistics available for these markets. The introduction of GIS (geographic information systems) has also made it more convenient to organize and graphically illustrate customer data by geographic area.

The second reason is that most media vehicles (television and radio stations, newspapers, billboards, Yellow Pages, and some magazines) serve specific geographic areas. Aiming promotional messages at target customers inevitably involves the use of geographic segmentation. Organizations with markets in one or more countries feel that cultures and behavior patterns vary with the country or region of residence. Of course, languages also vary across countries and require marketers to develop websites and promotional materials in multiple languages. For example, Tourism Jiangsu in China designed a new Spanish website in 2008 to reach out to all the countries where Spanish is spoken (Figure 7.1).

Figure 7.2 lists the different geographic characteristics used for segmentation. The actual choice of the geographic factor is influenced by **trading area** (the geographic area from which an organization and/or similar organizations tend to attract the majority of its customers). Many hotels, resorts, attractions, airlines, cruise lines, and DMOs have

FIGURE 7.1 Tourism Jiangsu targets the Spanish-speaking countries with its website.

GEOGRAPHIC PERSPECTIVE	LEVELS	EXAMPLES
Global		
	Regions	Africa; Asia; Latin America; Northern America; Oceania (United Nations World Macro Regions)
	Continents	Africa; Antarctica; Asia; Australia/Oceania; Europe; North America; South America
	Hemispheres	Northern Hemisphere; Southern Hemisphere; Eastern Hemisphere; Western Hemishpere
	Time Zones	UTC; GMT
National		
	Countries	Over 190 countries in the world
	Regions	Census regions; economic regions
State/Provincial/Territorial		
	States	Australia; Austria; Brazil; Germany; Malaysia; USA
	Provinces	Belgium; Canada; China; India; Indonesia; Netherlands; Philippines; South Africa; South Korea
	Territories	Australia; Canada; Malaysia; New Zealand
	Prefectures	Japan
	Regions	Denmark; France; Italy; New Zealand
	Autonomous Communities	Spain
	Cantons	Switzerland
	Counties	Ireland; Norway; Sweden
Local		
	Counties	England; Ireland; USA; Wales
	Boroughs	England; Wales
	Districts	England; Northern Ireland; USA
	Councils	Scotland
	Trading areas	MTAs (Major Trading Areas) and BTAs (Basic Trading Areas) in United States (Rand McNally & Company)
	Cities, towns, villages	Defined by population size or by government
	Postal, postcodes, or zip codes	Postal codes (Australia; Canada; Singapore; South Africa); zip codes (USA); postcodes (New Zealand; UK)
	Neighborhoods	
Other		
	Size of city or metropolitan area	By population size; First tier-second tier-third tier
	Population density	Urban; suburban; rural
	Climate	Tropical; dry; temperate; cold; polar

FIGURE 7.2 Factors used in geographic segmentation.

an international trading area covering several foreign countries. Others, such as fast-food and lodging chains, have a predominantly national or domestic market. More locally-oriented businesses, such as independent restaurants and travel agencies, have much narrower trading areas, sometimes consisting of only a few blocks.

2. **Demographic and Socio-economic Segmentation. Demographic and socio-economic segmentation** means dividing markets based on population statistics. These statistics—primarily generated from census information—include age, gender, household and per capita income, family size and composition, occupation, educational level, religion, race/ethnic origin, housing type, and other factors. The Contiki Industry Players Case in this chapter shows an outstanding application of demographic and socio-economic segmentation at an international level. Other variables, such as family life cycle, effective buying incomes, and buying power indices, are based on a combination of demographic and socio-economic statistics.

   Demographic/socio-economic and geographic segmentation are popular for the same reasons. The statistics are readily available, uniformly defined and accepted, and easy to use. It is common for demographic/socio-economic characteristics to be used along with geographic segmentation, giving rise to a technique known as **geo-demographic segmentation** (a two-stage segmentation approach using geographic and demographic/socio-economic characteristics).

3. **Purpose-of-Trip Segmentation.** Chapter 5 introduced the concept of **purpose-of-trip segmentation** (dividing hospitality and travel markets according to the primary purpose of the customer's trip). Use of this segmentation characteristic is widespread. Lodging, restaurant, travel agency, cruise line, airline, and DMOs traditionally apply it as at least part of their segmentation approach.

   The most important consideration in selecting a primary segmentation characteristic should be that it represents the factor with the greatest influence on the customer's behavior. Splitting the hospitality and travel market into two main groups—the **corporate (business) travel market** and the **pleasure (leisure) and personal travel market**—is a widely accepted practice. Within the pleasure and personal travel component, the **VFR (visiting friends and relatives)** segment represents a large proportion. It is generally agreed that the needs and wants of business and pleasure/personal travelers are quite different. For example, businesspersons prefer locations close to their place of business. Pleasure travelers spending their own money are more price-sensitive than businesspersons on expense accounts. While on vacation, these same people look for lodging near attractions. Segmentation in the hospitality and travel industry, therefore, often involves two-stage or multi-stage approaches with purpose of trip as the primary segmentation characteristic.

4. **Psychographic Segmentation. Psychographic segmentation** has grown in popularity and usage in hospitality and travel marketing.

Targeting the 18–35 Year-Old Market

Contiki Holidays

http://www.contiki.com

Company History and Destinations

Contiki Holidays is a tour operator that provides a great example of market segmentation and positioning by user category. Contiki's tours are designed exclusively for 18- to 35-year-olds—a form of segmentation using demographics as a base. Launched originally in Europe in 1961, the company has grown steadily and now has tens of thousands of customers each year on its tours. Contiki's destinations are mainly in Australia, Europe, New Zealand, and North America. The company also offers trips to Egypt, Russia, and Bali, Indonesia. Contiki Holidays is now part of the group TravCorp USA, which also includes Insight Vacations, Trafalgar Tours, and AAT Kings.

Client Profile

On Contiki's tours, everyone is between 18 and 35, and even the Tour Managers and other staff are young. The average age on Contiki tours is about 24. Tour groups usually consist of 20 to 50 young people from a variety of countries. Contiki sells its products in 35 different countries worldwide. Contiki tends to be the most popular with Australians, Americans, Canadians, Germans, British, Swiss, New Zealanders, Japanese, Dutch, South Africans, Italians, Danes, Brazilians, Mexicans, Austrians, Singaporeans, Swedes, and Koreans. There are typically between six and 15 different nationalities on each tour, so it's a great international mixture of people to be traveling with.

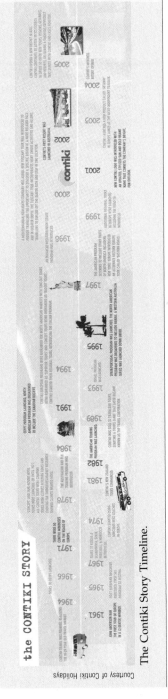

the CONTIKI STORY

The Contiki Story Timeline.

(continues)

(continued)

What makes Contiki Holidays the world leader in travel for 18 to 35's? In the company's own words, it is because:

Don't waste time trying to find the next place to stay or how to get there, with Contiki you can stress less, enjoy more and let our expert staff show you their secrets to a hassle-free holiday. We organize everything from transport and accommodation to sightseeing and meals—helping you make the most of every day.

Tour Details

Once in a destination country, Contiki uses motorcoaches for transportation. Company officials find that they have to counter the misconceptions that motorcoaches are uncomfortable and that motorcoach tours are only for older people. Here's what the Contiki website now says about its coaches:

Our world-wide fleet of luxury, air-conditioned coaches feature widescreen windows to guarantee you the best view from the coach, reclining seats and top-of-the-range audio equipment including DVD and video systems (not available on European tours). We've also fitted most of our coaches with charging units for electronic items like digital cameras and mobile phones. And you'll never have to worry about going cold turkey just because your iPod or MP3 player died minutes after you hit the highway. Just don't forget to bring your country-specific plug adaptors.

While there are many sightseeing and other activities built into Contiki's tours, tour patrons are also able to choose from a list of optional activities and excursions. Contiki offers a variety of different types of tours. The major difference between the styles is in the type of accommodations used and these are best exemplified in the European tours. The *Time Out/Superior* tours use hotel accommodation, while the *Concept/Budget* tours are in cabins and budget hotels. The third option of *Camping* tours is based on tents.

The pricing of Contiki's tours is reasonable. The daily rate includes lodging, as well as almost all breakfasts and about half of the dinners, motorcoach transport, and sightseeing tours and activities. For example, a 15-day tour *Ocean to Outback* tour to Australia was $2,465 (excluding international air fare) departing in January 2009; or about $165 per day. Contiki's tours are packed with sightseeing and activities, but the company has learned that some clients want to add on optional excursions. Here's what they say about these options:

Our clients like the option of deciding for themselves whether to participate in certain activities and excursions. You may choose to go to a Parisian Cabaret, a Gondola ride in Venice, or more adventurous activities such as rafting in Austria, Hot Air Ballooning in Arizona, Scuba Diving on the Great Barrier Reef or Bungy Jumping in Queenstown.

(continues)

(continued)

Contiki's Great Website

Contiki's website—http://www.contiki.com—is very popular with the 18- to 35-year-old niche market. It includes a *Contiki Community* section where past and future customers can talk with each other. There are many different discussion forums within the community. Also included is the *Contikipedia*, which contains extensive travel and destination information. The site also includes video clips and frequently asked questions (FAQs) for people to learn more about Contiki.

Courtesy of Contiki Holidays

Contiki has a great website.

Contiki and Responsible Travel

Contiki is a strong advocate of responsible travel and tourism. You will even find a *Responsible Travel* button on its website. It offers *Responsible Travel Tips* to its customers and others on the website. Contiki contributes to the The Leading Travel Companies of the World Conservation Foundation. Contiki's staff members, on company time, are allowed to spend two days per year volunteering for a charity of their own choice.

Success with Segmentation

Contiki Holidays is an excellent example of a long-standing commitment to serve a specific target market, backed by its slogan of *Holidays for 18–35's*. With a healthy repeat-business rate and a steadily growing

(continues)

(continued)

number of tours and tour patrons, the company clearly demonstrates the success that can result from niche marketing in the highly competitive tour operating business.

Discussion Questions

1. How important is it for a company like Contiki Holidays to use the Web and e-mail to appeal to people in the 18- to 35-year-old age group?
2. What new segments of the 18 to 35 market could Contiki Holidays explore?
3. What can Contiki do to offset this age group's apparent dislike of traveling by motorcoach?

Psychographics is the development of psychological profiles of customers and psychologically-based measures of distinctive modes of living or lifestyles.[1] A **lifestyle** is the manner in which people conduct their lives, including their activities, interests, and opinions—their AIOs.[2] These are all factors used in **lifestyle segmentation**.

People's activities, interests, and opinions are diverse. Just think about yourself for a minute. What you do at college is quite different from what you do at home, on vacation, or during a night out on the town. You probably have many interests. Some revolve around your school life and some are favorite hobbies, sports, or other leisure-time interests. You also hold a variety of beliefs about yourself, the educational system, politics and political events, specific products and services, social issues, and other things in the external environment. The following is a list of activities, interests, and opinions shared by many people.[3]

A	I	O
Activities	**Interests**	**Opinions**
• Work	• Family	• Of oneself
• Hobbies	• Home	• Social issues
• Social events	• Job	• Politics
• Vacation	• Community	• Business
• Entertainment	• Recreation	• Economics
• Clubs	• Fashion	• Education
• Community	• Food	• Products
• Shopping	• Media	• Future
• Sports	• Achievements	• Culture

When we looked at demographic/socio-economic and geographic segmentation, one of the obvious advantages was that everyone uses the same definitions and rules. In the hospitality and travel industry, most people also have a similar understanding of purpose-of-trip segments. This is not the case with psychographic segmentation. There are many alternative ways of defining and describing psychographic or lifestyle segments.

Chapter 4 identified lifestyle as a personal factor that influences customer behavior. It also describes the VALS™ and Claritas PRIZM® NE programs developed by professional research firms as psychographic segmentation techniques that many marketers favor. There are 66 different PRIZM® segments included in the following 14 groupings for the United States:[4]

- Group U1: Urban Uptown
- Group U2: Midtown Mix
- Group U3: Urban Cores
- Group S1: Elite Suburbs
- Group S2: The Affluentials
- Group S3: Middleburbs
- Group S4: Inner Suburbs
- Group C1: 2nd City Society
- Group C2: City Centers
- Group C3: Micro-City Blues
- Group T1: Landed Gentry
- Group T2: Country Comfort
- Group T3: Middle America
- Group T4: Rustic Living

Instead of using a technique such as VALS™ or Claritas PRIZM® NE, an organization can develop its own psychographic segmentation scheme based on marketing research. A battery of questions can be developed that relate to customers' activities, interests, and opinions. Most researchers then use techniques such as factor or cluster analysis to identify specific segments based on the similarity of respondents' answers to certain questions.

Although psychographic segmentation is a more sophisticated method than geographic, demographic/socio-economic, and purpose of trip segmentation and is thought to be a good predictor of customer behavior, one of its major drawbacks is its lack of a uniform approach toward segmentation. Another caution is that it cannot be used on its own. It must be part of a two-stage or multi-stage segmentation approach. Although psychographics can be the primary segmentation characteristic, other factors such as geography and demographics/socio-economics must be used to pinpoint target markets.

5. **Behavioral Segmentation.** **Behavioral segmentation** divides customers by their use occasions, benefits, user status, usage rate, loyalty status, buyer-readiness stage, and attitudes toward the product of service.[5] In other words, it uses some dimension of a customer's past, current, or potential behavior toward a specific product or service category (e.g., restaurants, hotels, airlines, cruise lines, travel agencies) or specific brands (e.g., Carnival, Disney, Princess, or Royal Caribbean).

a. *Use Frequency.* **Use-frequency segmentation** means dividing the overall market based on the number of times a service is purchased. Like psychographic segmentation, this segmentation characteristic is now popular in the hospitality and travel industry. It is based on a very simple concept—there are segments of the population that tend to purchase specific services or products more frequently than others. Because these segments usually account for the major share of an organization's business, it makes sense to devote a large proportion of marketing resources to them.

Until the mid-1970s, the hospitality and travel industry made little use of this type of use-frequency segmentation. However, intensified competition caused by airline deregulation, over-capacity lodging situations, growing emphasis on customer loyalty, and increasing use of **database marketing** dramatically changed this. Organizations started to look more closely at sources of past customers and volumes of repeat business. Research studies showed that there were customers who traveled much more often than average: the **frequent travelers**. All major airlines and hotel companies now have special reward programs for frequent flyers and guests. American Airlines usually receives the credit for originating the concept among the airlines in 1981. Holiday Inn's *Priority Club*, launched in 1983, was the first of its kind among U.S. lodging companies, and it now has around 39 million members. Car rental companies introduced similar programs, and gaming companies, cruise lines, and some destinations have also developed loyalty programs. These programs, now over 25-years-old, have been very successful for the hospitality and travel industry. In the United States, the airline programs award over 20 million free airline tickets per year; and the largest program memberships are 63 million with American Airlines and 52 million with United.[6] In the lodging sector, the *Marriott Rewards* program is the largest with approximately 30 million members.[7] The frequent traveler programs also present some serious challenges to hospitality and travel organizations. Airlines, for example, have to deal with the huge numbers of free trips that program members accumulate.

The objectives of these programs are simple: To encourage repeat use by frequent travelers and to build **brand loyalty** for the airline or hotel chain.

The attractiveness of use-frequency segmentation is clear—money spent on marketing to frequent users should produce a better return on investment than if it is spent on infrequent users and non-users. Although this seems the best logic in the world, a word of caution is necessary. It is not yet known whether frequent travelers have characteristics—apart from their more regular trips—that make them different from other travelers. Additionally, it is clear that not all frequent travelers are alike and that further segmentation is required for maximum effectiveness. Thus, as with psychographic segmentation, use frequency should be chosen as part of a two-stage or multi-stage approach. For example, a multi-stage combination of use frequency, purpose-of-trip, and geographic segmentation might prove effective for many hospitality and travel organizations. Increasing use of computerized databases (database marketing) in our industry is helping marketers pinpoint these lucrative customers.

Another potential drawback is the intense competition for the frequent traveler's business. This approach tends to focus most of the attention on heavy users of services and products and away from medium, light, and non-users. However, some organizations may find great success in targeting one or more of these other segments.

b. *Usage Status and Potential.* Customers can be grouped according to their usage status. Examples of this approach include splitting the market into non-users and former, regular, and potential users. Another application is to divide customers by the number of times they have purchased an organization's services (e.g., first-time customers, two-time customers, and so on). Different marketing programs are often justified for each of these segments.

Much attention in travel research and marketing is given to potential travelers and customers, especially among destination areas, which rely on a high percentage of first-time visitors. Some experts even refer to this as *usage potential segmentation.* Usually, research is done on people who have not visited or used the destination or service before. Based on these people's responses, they are divided into high-, medium-, and low-potential users. Obviously, the high-potential-user segment warrants the greatest attention.

Again, when this approach is used in the hospitality and travel industry, it tends to be part of a two-stage or multi-stage segmentation approach (e.g., a multi-stage combination of geographic, purpose of trip, and usage status or potential).

c. *Brand Loyalty.* Brand loyalty is a segmentation approach that has really caught on in the hospitality and travel industry. Computerized databases and their analysis are helping organizations get much better information on customer loyalty. Customers are divided according to their loyalty to a specific hospitality and travel brand or destination and their use of competitors.

Many approaches to dividing customers into loyalty segments have been proposed. One study by the Cornell Center for Hospitality Research divided past guests into four groups: satisfied switchers (satisfied but patronize a competitor), dissatisfied switchers (dissatisfied and disloyal), satisfied stayers (satisfied and loyal), and dissatisfied stayers (loyal but dissatisfied).[8]

The concept of **brand segmentation** is a hot topic in the hospitality and travel industry, especially among lodging chains, restaurant companies, airlines, and cruise lines. The use of brand-loyalty segmentation will be greater in the future, as more organizations make greater use of customer databases and traffic statistics from websites.

FIGURE 7.3 The Ice Hotel in Canada is an unusual place for a wedding, but an interesting example of use-occasion segmentation.

Courtesy of the Canadian Tourism Commission

d. *Use Occasions.* **Occasion-based segmentation** categorizes customers according to when they buy and the purpose of their purchases. Purpose-of-trip segmentation, discussed earlier in this chapter, is a variant of use-occasion segmentation. Here, the main travel occasions are business; pleasure, leisure, or vacation; and other family or personal reasons. One excellent example of a use-occasion segment is the wedding market where the couples travel to a special destination for the ceremony (Figure 7.3). Special banquets and trips to mark anniversaries, birthdays, retirements, holidays, and awards are another form of use-occasion segmentation in restaurants, lodging properties, cruise lines, and destinations. Another example is splitting the convention-meeting or MICE markets (a purpose-of-trip segment) into annual conventions, chapter meetings, board meetings, educational seminars, sales meetings, and so on (Figure 7.4).

The history of Enterprise Rent-A-Car is perhaps the most outstanding example of a company using occasion-based segmentation to fill a neglected niche in the market. Enterprise supplies vehicles to people who need cars because of accidents, mechanical repairs to their own vehicles, or thefts (the occasions). In the car rental business, this is known as the replacement market segment. The company has grown from 17 vehicles in 1963 and an office in St. Louis, Missouri, to a fleet of about 714,000 automobiles and 6,900 locations in the United States, Canada, U.K., Germany, and Ireland in 2008.

e. *Benefits.* Many marketing experts consider **benefit segmentation** to be the best segmentation characteristic. It groups customers according

FIGURE 7.4
Destinations are placing greater emphasis on attracting the MICE markets.

to similarities in the benefits that they look for in specific hospitality and travel products or services. Why is this form of segmentation thought to be so powerful? The answer is that people do not just buy services; they buy a package of benefits they will get when they buy the service. You will remember also that the essence of a marketing orientation is to provide customers with what they need and want.

Although there have been many studies in the hospitality and travel industry to determine the benefits, attributes, or features that customers look for in certain services, the use of benefit segmentation has been limited. For example, several studies of lodging customers have pinpointed location, cleanliness, and price as three of the top reasons for selecting accommodations. Convention/meeting planners consistently rate the quality of food and foodservice as one of the most important benefits sought. Convenient schedules, lower fares, and on-time departures are very important to business airline travelers. The problem is that, although this type of information exists, few marketers have taken the next step of identifying and pursuing specific benefit segments. It may seem that many are using this approach, but in fact they are simply promoting features corresponding to the benefits that customers typically seek. As with psychographic segmentation, a major drawback of this type of segmentation is the lack of uniform definitions of hospitality and travel benefit segments.

Although the toothpaste market has almost universally accepted benefit segments, our industry has not.

6. *Product-Related Segmentation.* **Product-related segmentation** uses some aspect of the hospitality and travel services to classify customers. It is a popular approach in the hospitality and travel industry. Stop and think about some of the terms that have become commonplace in our business. What about fast-food customers, the MICE and incentive travel markets, the cruise market, the ski market, the budget hotel market, the extended-stay hotel market, the inclusive tour market, the luxury travel market, the motorcoach market, the gaming market, and many others? Common to all of these is the classification of customers according to the degree that specific types of services appeal to them.

Costa Rica in Central America and Sabah in Malaysia provide two great examples of DMOs using product-related segmentation. Costa Rica has very effectively marketed its natural resources to become one of the leading ecotourism destinations in the Americas. Sabah uses a similar product-related approach promoting its "eco treasures from mountain high to ocean deep" (Figure 7.5).

Product-related and brand segmentation have become more popular in the hospitality and travel industry. This is particularly evident among the world's largest lodging chains and is a growing trend among restaurant companies, cruise lines, and car rental firms. Major lodging chains such as the InterContinental Hotels Group, Wyndham Worldwide, Marriott International, Hilton Hotels Corp., Choice International, Accor, Starwood Hotels & Resorts Worldwide, Carlson, and Accor have opened different brands of properties under one corporate umbrella.

FIGURE 7.5   Sabah in Malaysia applies product-related segmentation on its website.

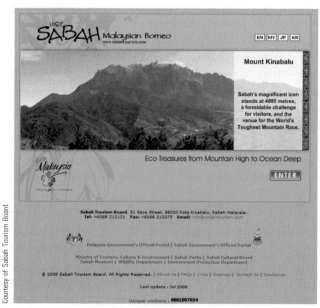

Courtesy of Sabah Tourism Board

You might be thinking that this segmentation characteristic smacks of the very production orientation that was criticized earlier in Chapter 1. Should not the customer's needs, wants, and benefits sought be more important than the service itself? Pat yourself on the back—you are right. Using product-related segmentation on its own is not recommended. In essence, it is a way of describing customer groups with needs and wants that correspond to certain types of hospitality and travel services. For example, the extended-stay hotel concept was created to serve the needs of longer-stay guests, particularly relocated managers and executives. The fast-food restaurant concept emerged to meet the need for inexpensive, quality, standardized, and quick meals.

Product-related segmentation should be used as part of a two-stage or multi-stage approach. It is also useful only when the service's typical users have different characteristics from those of non-users or can be reached directly with some form of promotion. For example, there are many specialized magazines and websites that appeal to people with distinctive interests and hobbies, such as wine, gourmet food, fitness and health, golf, tennis, and even travel itself.

7. *Distribution Channel Segmentation.* Distribution channel segmentation is different from the six previous segmentation characteristics since it involves approaches to divide up travel trade intermediaries rather than customers. Chapter 2 identified distribution channels as a key difference between services and products. Chapter 13 looks at the hospitality and travel industry's distribution channels in detail. The basic concept that both chapters emphasize is that hospitality and travel organizations have the option of (1) marketing directly to customers (consumer marketing or B2C), (2) marketing through intermediary organizations (trade marketing or B2B), or (3) a combination of (1) and (2). Different marketing approaches are required for customers and travel trade intermediaries.

Distribution channel segmentation means dividing travel trade intermediaries by function and by common characteristics shared by sub-groups. As is true with customers in general, all intermediaries or travel trade companies are not alike. There are groups that perform specific functions, such as retailing hospitality and travel services (travel agents), assembling customized incentive trips (incentive travel planners), and developing and coordinating tours and vacation packages (tour wholesalers and operators). Within each group, there are major differences in organization sizes, geographic areas served, degrees of specialization, online vs. offline, policies in dealing with suppliers, carriers and DMOs, and other factors. Other hospitality and travel organizations using their services must decide which of the many available channel segment characteristics match the profile of their target markets. In other words, segmenting customers comes first and is followed by segmenting distribution channels.

An example might further clarify this concept. Suppose that a theme park traditionally has marketed directly to customers, but is exploring the use of travel trade intermediaries to promote new package deals for off-peak periods. By surveying its visitors, the park's management could determine which cities or city districts (geographic segmentation) provide the majority of its business. Management would then identify travel agencies and tour wholesalers in these cities that specialize in the theme park's destination area, have high vacation-travel versus corporate-travel volumes, sufficient total volume, or some combination of the three. The park's managers would then approach these travel trade intermediaries about marketing a special commissionable (pays commissions to travel agents) program of the park's new packages.

Although there are some organizations that deal exclusively with travel intermediaries (e.g., some tour wholesalers), most need to market both to customers and intermediaries. Distribution channel segmentation is a useful method for matching target markets to the most appropriate channel groups. By its very nature, it is always used as part of a two-stage or multi-stage segmentation approach.

Customer and Industry Trends: Impacts on Market Segmentation

The smart marketers are always watching out for trends among customers and trends within the hospitality and travel industry. These trends and changes on both the demand and supply sides are constantly affecting the composition of markets and market segmentation approaches. In Chapter 5, you learned about the steps in doing a situation analysis for an existing hospitality and travel organization. In Chapter 6, you became familiar with methods to do marketing research on market and industry issues and opportunities. Most of these steps and methods involve some identification of trends and an assessment of their impacts.

Many would-be humorists characterize the post-World War II years from 1946 to the early 1960s as the era of mother, father, the two kids, the family car, a dog, and one very large mortgage. The so-called family market was a well-defined target for most marketers. During this time, many of our industry's best-known brands, including Holiday Inns, Disneyland, and McDonald's, got started. You already know that things have changed drastically since then. Now at the end of the first decade of the 21st century, the hospitality and travel market is much more splintered than ever before. Although the family market remains strong, there are multiple target markets that can be pursued. The hospitality and travel industry itself has grown by leaps and bounds, and now there are many more competitors and brands. In such a dynamic environment, it is becoming even more essential that hospitality and travel marketers use the most appropriate market segmentation approaches. Let's now take a look at some of the changes that are occurring on the demand and supply side of the hospitality and travel industry.

In the 1950s, the hospitality and travel industry emphasized standardization, or a "one size fits all" approach. Today the industry's approaches are vastly different and there is a much greater emphasis on customization to fit individual needs. The focus is on providing a diversity of services, facilities, packages, and programs. Changes in customers' needs, wants, and buying behaviors definitely motivated this shift in the industry's approaches. Nowadays, the hospitality and travel industry quickly responds to satisfy new customer needs and service expectations. New trends are occurring on the customer (demand) and the hospitality and travel industry (supply) sides of the marketplace. You will read much more about hospitality and travel industry supply trends later in Chapters 10 and 13. Some of the customer trends by the seven segmentation characteristics you learned about earlier in this chapter are now discussed.

Customer Trends: Changes in Demand

There are so many trends among customers; it's hard to know where to begin. For example, most marketers believe that since the Internet was introduced in the mid-1990s, customers are now in greater control of how they receive information, how they make purchasing decisions, and how they buy. One report says that now the Internet is nearly twice as important as travel agents as an information source.[9] This is certainly true with hospitality and travel, as many people now go to the Web first to get information about our industry. There have also been huge changes in the demographic and socio-economic characteristics of people in many countries. People's lifestyles and interests have diversified greatly. While many customers now have enough money to afford to travel more; they are starved of the time to do it.

Below you will find a short description of some customer trends. There are many others that could be listed, but these will give you a good flavor of what is happening among customers.

1. **Demographic and Socio-economic Trends**
    Significant changes are taking place in the demographic and socio-economic characteristics of the customers in the hospitality and travel market. These include the aging population, increasing importance of ethnic minorities, changing household structures and composition, later marriages, and increasing divorce rates. Below just two of these many trends are highlighted.

    Aging but Engaging: The Baby Boomers
    In most developed countries, particularly in North America, Western Europe and Japan, the population is aging (Figure 7.6). The so-called *Baby Boomers* are now entering the retirement-age category but are staying more active than any previous groups in this age category. A **Baby Boomer** is anyone born between 1946 and 1964. In 2010, the Boomers will all be 46 to 64 years of age. They attract so much marketing

COUNTRY	POPULATION IN MILLIONS (2007)	AGE 0–14 (%)	AGE 15–64 (%)	AGE 65 AND OVER (%)	PER CAPITA GDP (2006)	SERVICE SECTOR PROPORTION (2006)
Developed Countries						
Australia	20.4	19.3%	67.4%	13.2%	$32,900	70.0%
Canada	33.4	17.3%	69.2%	13.5%	$35,200	68.5%
France	63.7	18.6%	65.2%	16.2%	$30,100	77.2%
Germany	82.4	13.9%	66.3%	19.8%	$31,400	70.0%
Italy	58.1	13.8%	66.4%	19.9%	$29,700	69.0%
Japan	127.4	13.8%	65.2%	21.0%	$33,100	73.1%
Russia	141.4	14.6%	71.1%	14.4%	$12,100	58.2%
South Korea	49.0	18.3%	72.1%	9.6%	$24,200	52.0%
UK	60.8	17.2%	67.0%	15.8%	$31,400	73.4%
USA	301.1	20.2%	67.2%	12.6%	$43,500	78.6%
Developing Countries						
Brazil	190.0	25.3%	68.4%	6.3%	$8,600	54.0%
China	1321.8	20.4%	71.7%	7.9%	$7,600	40.0%
India	1129.9	31.8%	63.1%	5.1%	$3,700	60.7%
Indonesia	234.7	28.7%	65.6%	5.7%	$3,800	41.0%

FIGURE 7.6 The aging of the population in the developed world. The over 65 group is more important in the developed nations than in developing countries.

Source: CIA World Factbook 2007.

INTERNET MARKETING

Multicultural and Diversity Marketing on the Internet

- The minority population in the United States topped 100 million for the first time in 2006. The Hispanic population was 44.3 million; African Americans represented 40.2 million; Asian Americans 14.9 million; American Indian and Alaska Native Americans 4.5 million; and Native Hawaiian and Other Pacific Islanders 1 million. The remaining "majority" population was 198.7 million.
- The Atlanta Convention & Visitors Bureau (ACVB) has created a special website to appeal to multicultural markets. It is specifically targeted toward the African American, Latino, and Asian American market segments.
- The site provides these links: (1) calendar of events, (2) festivals and special events, (3) art galleries and museums, (4) attractions (5) shopping, (6) sports scene, (7) colleges and universities, (8) faith and spirit, (9) nightlife, and (10) Atlanta's film industry.
- The dining button leads to information on "some of the best soul food in the nation." The festivals and special events page includes information on events such as the National Black Arts Festival, Martin Luther King Jr. Week, and the Power Networking Conference.
- Diversity marketing goes beyond race. For example, Hyatt Hotels & Resorts has developed an excellent program of marketing to the LGBT (lesbian, gay, bisexual and transgender) segment and has dedicated part of its website to appeal to this growing market.

Sources: U.S. Census Bureau. (2007). *Minority Population Tops 100 Million.* Atlanta Convention & Visitors Bureau. (2008). *The Official Multicultural Website of the Atlanta Convention & Visitors Bureau.* **http://www.atlantaheritage.com/**; Hyatt. (2008). **http://www.hyatt.com/hyatt/resorts/lgbt/index.jsp?icamp=HY_LGBT_BF**

Student Questions

1. What are the advantages of developing a specific program of multicultural and diversity marketing in hospitality and travel?
2. What are the essential elements of an effective multicultural and diversity marketing program?
3. Apart from Atlanta and Hyatt, which destinations and companies demonstrate good examples of these marketing programs?
4. Do you think multicultural marketing will expand in the future and why?

attention from the hospitality and travel industry because of the large size of the market. In the United States there were about 78.2 million Baby Boomers in 2005.[10] By 2020, according to Deloitte Touche

Tohmatsu, there will be 700 million people in the world over 65.[11] The aging population is a positive trend for hospitality and travel, since there are more customers with the independence, desire, and money to travel and dine out.

In a study by AARP in 2005, a sample of Baby Boomers aged 41 to 59 were interviewed about their adventure travel behaviors.[12] More than half of the Baby Boomers (55 percent) considered themselves adventurous and 77 percent thought their travel experiences were more adventurous than their parents. In another AARP survey, 57 percent of respondents aged 60 years old and born in 1946 said they wanted to do more traveling over the next few years (Figure 7.7).[13] So we can say that the older age groups are more willing to travel than previous generations and interested in pursuing more active and adventurous travel experiences.

Break-ationing: Time Poverty

"Cash-rich" but "time-poor" is a good description of many customers in today's high-paced society. There are many more two-income households

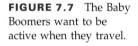

FIGURE 7.7 The Baby Boomers want to be active when they travel.

Courtesy of the Canadian Tourism Commission

FIGURE 7.8
Bloomington, Indiana has cleverly cashed in on the trend to shorter travel trips.

in the marketplace, and time schedules are very hard to juggle to allow for longer holidays or vacations. Hospitality and tourism experts agree that more frequent and shorter-duration trips are a major trend around the world in developed countries.[14] In the United Kingdom these are known as *short-break holidays*, while in North America *mini-vacations* is the preferred terminology. The *Lonely Planet Travellers' Pulse Survey 2006* found that the frequency of short breaks increased 17 percent from the previous year.[15] Bloomington, Indiana has long recognized this trend and has made clever use of the movie, *Breaking Away*, that was shot there. Figure 7.8 shows the Bloomington Convention & Visitors Bureau's website home page, where you will see the slogan of *Breakaway Bloomington Indiana.*

2. **Geographic Trends**
   The landscape of world travel is constantly shifting, as new destinations emerge and sources of travelers shift in relative size. The World Tourism Organization (UNWTO) in its *Tourism 2020 Vision* forecasts that world tourism arrivals will grow to 1 billion by 2010 and 1.6 billion by 2020, up significantly from 903 million in 2007.[16] France has long been the world's leading tourism destination, but China will surpass it during the period of 2010–2020.

   Building with BRIC
   Goldman Sachs has identified the world's fastest-growing country economies as Brazil, Russia, India, and China, or BRIC.[17] The investment company predicts that by 2050 these four countries will be much more powerful than they are now. They will certainly become bigger sources

Did You Know?

What are the Major Trends in Travel for Europe?

1. **External Environment**
   - Demographics (e.g., more but shorter trips)
   - Environmental issues (e.g., rising demand for ecotourism and nature-based holidays)
   - Macroeconomic trends (e.g., more competitive global environment)
   - Political factors (e.g., image of destination countries is increasingly linked to security and health issues)
   - Culture (e.g., cultural tourism is growing in Europe)
   - Safety and security (e.g., growing feeling of insecurity)
2. **Consumer Trends**
   - Travel experience (e.g., experienced travelers will demand higher quality experiences)
   - Lifestyle (e.g., need to develop more niche products)
3. **Travel Products and Marketing**
   - Trends in marketing (e.g., growing investment in Internet strategies for promotion)
   - Information technology and communications (e.g., the Internet will drive the next generation of travel/tourism product distribution methods)
   - Transport (e.g., new destinations are being created through improved accessibility)
   - Second homes–residential tourism (e.g., growth in the self-catering holiday rental markets)

Source: European Travel Commission. (2006). *Tourism Trends for Europe.*

of international travelers in the future, and domestic pleasure, business and MICE travel will also grow within each of these four countries.

3. **Purpose of Trip Trends**

   Hospitality and travel marketers for decades have been putting pleasure, business, visiting friends and relatives (VFR), and trip purpose segments into neat little boxes. Recent experience suggests that many customers cannot be pigeon-holed that way as one trip can involve several purposes and multiple destinations as well.

   Multi-purposing Travel

   Faced with greater time pressures, an increasing number of customers pursue multiple trip purposes when traveling. For example, in 2007 some 56 percent of U.S. residents visiting overseas destinations said their purpose was leisure, recreation, or holidays. However, another 47 percent said it was for VFR and 24 percent had a business purpose. Other responses were study/teaching (6 percent), convention/conference (3 percent), and religion/pilgrimages (3 percent).[18] Don't these add up to more than 100 percent; 139 percent in fact? The answer is "yes" and means that a significant proportion of U.S. residents were "multi-purposing" their overseas travel trips.

4. **Psychographic Trends**

People's lifestyles have greatly changed and diversified. Activities, interests, and opinions (AIOs) are so broad that they are hard to describe in a few words. Changes in customers' interests and activities are affecting what they eat and what they want to do when they travel.

Getting and Staying Healthy

People are increasingly concerned about their health and wellness. In a survey by the National Restaurant Association (NRA) in 2006 in the United States, 71 percent of adults said they were trying to eat more healthfully at restaurants.[19] The popularity of vegetarianism has increased and this has a direct impact on the restaurant and foodservice market. Most estimates indicate that about 3 to 10 percent of the population in developed countries does not eat meat.

More customers are also looking for healthy living and to escape from high-pressure work environments.[20] This trend is leading to the one immediately following, Decompressing in Style.

Decompressing in Style

According to the International Spa Association, 32 million adults in the United States visited a spa in 2007.[21] Figure 7.9 illustrates that people are increasingly looking to be pampered at resort spas to escape from the rigors of their hectic daily lives. A study of the Canadian spa sector in Canada in 2006 indicated that the stress in customers' daily lives was creating a "need for periodic pampering" and spas were regarded "as a means of escaping the pressures and getting re-energized."[22]

Getting Gayer in Travel

The gay, lesbian, bisexual, and transgender (GLBT) market is now a mainstream segment for the hospitality and travel industry and deserves careful attention. In Australia, the gay and lesbian market is recognized throughout the tourism industry as an important niche segment, representing differences in holiday behavior, attitudes, and yield opportunities when compared with the average Australian adult population.[23] In North America, the Travel Industry Association has recognized "the tremendous economic potential of the (GLBT) market to the travel industry.[24]

Orbitz.com, one of the leading online travel companies in North America, has a special section of its website for gay and lesbian travel. The International Gay and Lesbian Travel Association (IGLTA) is an association of travel professionals who specialize in this market segment. Many destinations target this market and most are putting greater emphasis on "gay friendliness."

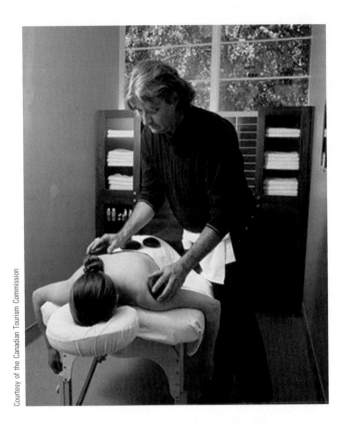

FIGURE 7.9
Decompressing in style. Spa resort visits are increasing in popularity.

Courtesy of the Canadian Tourism Commission

Greening with Meaning

There has been a surge in what some call "green travel" as people continue to show increasing concern for the environment.[25] This type of travel is often called *ecotourism* or nature-based travel for customers who travel to destinations specifically to enjoy nature and/or the local culture and lifestyles (Figure 7.10). However, "greening with meaning" is a wider trend than just these special-interest travelers, and captures customers' overall concerns for the hospitality and travel industry's impact on the environment. For example, this includes things such as how the industry uses energy and disposes of waste products, as well as the materials used for packaging. Global warming, climate change, and alternative energy sources are major world issues that are now of great concern to customers.

Blogging the Memories

Customers are becoming travel writers and critics! A very large and ever-increasing number of customers are blogging about their experiences with hospitality and travel organizations and destinations. Blogging is not only a form of communications, but also a hobby for many customers. In addition, blogs are a good source of (secondary research) information for hospitality and travel marketers. There are no accurate statistics on how many people blog, but one study in the United States

Image copyright Galyna Andrushko, 2008. Used under license from Shutterstock.com

FIGURE 7.10 Healthy vacations and adventure travel are increasing in popularity.

by the Pew Internet & Life Project estimated that 12 million adults keep a blog and about 57 million adults read blogs.[26] The survey also found that most bloggers were younger; 54 percent were between 18 and 29. A collection of websites have developed to help customers post their travel blogs. These include *Virtual Tourist* (http://www.virtualtourist.com), *Trip Advisor* (http://www.tripadvisor.com), *Real Travel* (http://www.realtravel.com), *TravelPod* (http://www.travelpod.com), *Travel Blog* (http://www.travelblog.com), *Travel Blogs* (http://www.travelblogs.com). More blogging areas are also being provided in travel directories such as *Lonely Planet* and *Frommer's*, and in supplier, carrier, travel trade intermediary, and DMO websites.

Podcasting and Downloading

Another technology-enabled trend is the downloading of podcasts, including those made available by the hospitality and travel industry. A survey conducted in May 2008 by the Pew Internet & American Life Project found that 19 percent of Internet users in the United States had downloaded podcasts.[27]

Tourism Australia confirms that customers are taking more control of the information they want. They note that services like YouTube.com and TripAdvisor.com, and other photo- and video-sharing websites are increasingly being used to pass on and to find information about travel destinations."[28]

5.   **Behavioral Trends**

There have been many changes in customers' usage of hospitality and travel organizations and destinations. Some of these have already been highlighted under other segmentation characteristics and so just three more are discussed below.

Going It Alone

The demographic trends toward later marriages and higher divorce rates are leading to increasing travel by singles. One report on travel trends in the United Kingdom divided this market into two parts: independent travelers seeking adventure and new skills and singles looking to find their partners while on holiday.[29] There is a definite trend toward more independent travel, that means traveling alone and not as part of a group. This is especially true in the under-30 age category.

Racking Up the Miles

Many people are obsessed today with accumulating frequent traveler miles. If you don't agree, consider some of the following statistics. Some two-thirds of all Canadian households are members of the AIR MILES Reward Program. This program has 9.5 million active collector accounts.[30] For the United States, one source states that there are over 100 million members of FFPs (frequent flyer programs) with each of the major airline programs having over 20 million members. This estimate, however, includes multiple counting of the same customers, since most frequent flyers are enrolled in 4 to 6 different airline programs.[31]

Decreasing Brand Loyalty

The loyalty to specific brands in the hospitality and travel industry seems to be eroding. There are many more brands to choose from now and each brand is aggressively trying to capture customers. You just learned about the multiple memberships in frequent flyer programs. One source states that corporations in general in the United States lose half of their customers over a span of five years.[32]

6.   **Product-related Trends (Demand Side)**

You might think, what is the term *product-related* doing on the demand side of this trends discussion? As people's needs and wants change, as well as their expectations and interests, this forces the supply or industry side to adapt. Clever entrepreneurs and managers spot these trends and the opportunity to cater to them. For example, the large towers that we see in many cities such as the CN Tower in Toronto and the Seattle Space Needle were built mainly for telecommunications purposes, not for people to jump off for fun. A clever entrepreneur from New Zealand, AJ Hackett, however, saw the opportunity for bungy jumping from the top of the towers (Figure 7.11). Get the point? He did!

Courtesy of Macau Tower Convention & Entertainment Center, 2008.

FIGURE 7.11   Airing it out at the Macau Tower. People's interests are changing; so are the ways they pursue them.

Finding Their Niche

Special-interest or niche travel is one of the hottest customer trends in our industry. For this we need to go back to people's AIOs and specifically the "interests" component of them. Also called *niche travel* or *niche tourism*, this trend involves customer travel to pursue hobbies or interests from other aspects of their daily lives. People's interests today are extremely diverse as shown by the different types of magazines you now can find for sale. To help customers quickly access information on special-interest travel (SIT) trips, online services like the *InfoHub Specialty Travel Guide* (http://www.infohub.com) and *Specialty Travel* (http://www.specialtytravel.com) have been created.

Connoisseuring

Many customers have become or want to become connoisseurs of food, wine, art, architecture, culture, memorabilia, or other things that may involve dining out or travel.[33] This is a branch of special-interest travel that was just discussed, but is of particular interest to a broad range of hospitality and travel organizations. Many wine areas in Australia, New Zealand, United States, Canada, France, Germany, Italy, South Africa, Spain, Chile, and other countries have benefited from the trend to increased interest in wines (Figure 7.12).

7. **Distribution Channel Trends (Demand)**

"Consumers are taking control, and travel marketers are struggling to reach them," according to Travel Weekly's *2006 Consumer Trends* Special Report.[34] There have been monumental shifts in hospitality and travel distribution in the past 10 years, as customers changed how they acquire

FIGURE 7.12 Ice wine has gained in popularity as have visits to wineries.

Courtesy of Inniskillin Wines, 2008.

travel information and make bookings. At the center of this huge shift have been the newer technologies available to customers including the Internet, mobile communication devices (mobile/cell phones and PDAs), and portable entertainment system including iPods and other MP3s, MP4s and MP5s.

Looking and Booking

There were 1.46 billion Internet users in the world in December 2008 and the usage growth rate from 2000 to 2008 was 305 percent.[35] Asia now has the most Internet users in the world, followed by Europe and North America. Many sources indicate that a majority of people are going to the Web to search for information before making hospitality and travel plans and bookings. A 2007 study of United States residents who were planning personal travel trips in the upcoming three months found that 79 percent of respondents would use the Internet for planning trips.[36] Tourism Australia found that 58 percent of its international visitors used the Internet for information before coming to Australia. The highest proportions of Internet use were by visitors from the United States (69%), Germany (68%), Korea (65%), and the United Kingdom (62%).[37]

Hospitality and travel e-commerce is booming as online travel sales around the world have been rapidly growing. For example, booking hotels online is now the second most popular way to make reservations after calling properties directly.[38] In the United States, e-Marketer.com estimated that online travel sales would be $105 billion in 2008, up 12 percent over 2007. This source projected online sales to increase to $116.1 billion by 2009.[39] In Europe, online travel sales were €49.4 billion in 2007 up by 24 percent over 2006.[40] Germany is the second largest online travel sales market in Europe after the United Kingdom; at an estimated €14.81 billion in 2007. These online sales in Germany in 2007 were up 15 percent over 2006.[41]

Virtual Touring

As you learned in Chapter 2, it is difficult for customers to sample hospitality and tourism services and destinations. The intangibility of services limits sampling, but the Internet and other digital technologies are helping to "tangibilize" hospitality and travel like never before. Virtual tours are one of the functions that websites provide and they allow customers to view and experience an environment without having to travel there. A study of United States residents in 2006 by the Pew Internet & American Life Project found that 51 percent of adult Internet users had taken an online virtual tour.[42]

Hospitality and Travel Industry Trends: Changes in Supply

"The industry can no longer expect a 'normal' year for travel and tourism. Terrorism, natural disasters, health crises and other challenges are here to stay" according to *World Travel Trends Report 2006-07*.[43] It is also true to say that today there is no "average customer." Customers' ever-shifting wants, needs, and preferences during the past years have created many new markets, market segments, and marketing opportunities. The hospitality and travel industry has responded with an ever-expanding array of services, facilities, packages, and programs, many of them customized for specific target markets. Later in Chapters 10 and 13, you will learn about the four groups and component sectors of the hospitality and travel industry. You will also learn about the most recent trends within each industry sector.

Figures 7.13a–c provides a summary of these sector trends described in Chapters 10 and 13. Five overall trends are also identified in Chapter 10: (1) more horizontal integration (companies developing or acquiring similar businesses); (2) more vertical integration (expanding up and down the distribution channel); (3) industry's introduction of a wide variety of new services, facilities, and travel alternatives; (4) increased importance of the Internet throughout the industry; and (5) increased level of competition.

Another way of summarizing some of the key trends on the industry side of hospitality and travel marketing is to consider each of the 8 Ps of marketing that you first learned about in Chapter 2:

Product
- Increasing brand segmentation in many sectors of hospitality and travel
- Increasing use of brand extensions as a strategy by major companies, especially hotel chains, e.g., branded beds and bedding
- Growing diversity of special-interest travel (SIT) destinations
- Increasing supply and market popularity of some industry sectors, e.g., cruises (Figure 7.14)

Partnership
- Partnering with other organizations in hospitality and travel is being given a much higher priority
- Partnering with organizations and brands outside of hospitality and travel is now becoming much more common
- The Internet is providing an increasingly convenient and popular platform for "virtual" partnerships

People
- Targeting a broader range of market segments, both globally and by other segmentation characteristics
- Increasing emphasis on improving service quality among hosts
- Increasing importance and use of customer databases

Packaging
- Greater emphasis on customizing packages including the concept of dynamic packaging

SUPPLIER SECTORS	CARRIER SECTORS
Lodging	**Airline**
• Increasing chain domination • Expanding brand segmentation and brand extensions • Growing consolidation and globalization • Increasing importance of frequent-guest and frequent-flyer programs • Growing influence of GDSs and third-party intermediaries • Expanding role of specialized lodging properties	• Increasing concern with safety and security • Growing presence of low-cost carriers (LCCs) • E-ticketing becoming the standard • Aircraft getting bigger and faster • Increasing use of self-service check-in • Maintaining frequent-flyer programs • Expanding global airline strategic alliances
Restaurant and Foodservice	**Railway**
• Globalizing of leading restaurant chain brands • Continuing restaurant sector growth • Growing concern with the nutritional value of restaurant meals • Increasing attention and concern with food safety • Growing demand for a greater variety of food and meals • Increasing co-branding and variety of foodservice locations • Customers demanding greater convenience	• Continuing development of high-speed trains • Privatizing of former state-run railway companies • Upgrading of services, amenities, and programs • Increasing e-ticketing and online bookings
Cruise Line	**Ferry**
• Rapidly growing demand and capacity • Increasing creativity and expansion of target markets • Continuing dependence on travel agents • Changing cruiser demographics • Resort companies entering the cruise business • Increasing cruise line consolidation • Adding innovative amenities and facilities	• Introducing larger and more modern ferry vessels • Increasing involvement of ferry companies in cruise excursions • Upgrading of services and amenities • Increasing e-ticketing and online bookings
Car Rental	**Bus and Motorcoach**
• Globalizing of leading car rental brands • Increasing consolidation and sales concentration among leading brands • Enhancing and expanding customer services • Evolving frequent renter programs • Increasing emphasis on revenue management • Implementing branding and brand segmentation strategies • Experiencing a greater diversity of distribution	• Increasing sophistication of buses and motorcoaches • Upgrading of services and amenities • Increasing e-ticketing and online bookings

FIGURE 7.13A Trends in supplier and carrier sectors.

Attraction and Event

- Continuing growth in theme park demand
- Increasing creativity in use of technology and entertainment programming
- Continuing development of major attractions around the world
- Adding interactivity and attendee participation
- Increasing size and market strength of industry leaders

Casino and Gaming

- Increasing development of casino destinations around the world
- Expanding range of casino locations and concepts
- Increasing economic impact of the casino and gaming sector
- Growing interest in customers in playing poker
- General public maintaining a high level of acceptability of casinos and gaming
- Online gaming growing rapidly

Canal

- Increasing interest in canal tourism, recreation and leisure developments
- Rehabilitating of historic industrial canals and their surrounding environs
- Urban canals becoming more attractive to residents and tourists

Space Tourism Travel

- Increasing number of space tourists, but only the very wealthy
- Offering of more simulated space travel experiences

FIGURE 7.13B   Trends in supplier and carrier sectors.

INTERMEDIARY SECTORS (CHAPTER 13)

Retail Travel Agency

- Reducing airline commissions causing travel agencies to close in several countries
- Increasing competition from online travel companies (OTCs)
- Increasing use of the Web by traditional travel agencies
- Growing number of home-based travel agents
- Leading travel agencies companies growing in market power
- Increasing specialization such as cruise-only agencies
- Diversifying sources of revenues

Tour Wholesaler and Operator

- Increasing use of the Web for marketing and bookings
- Growing interest in dynamic packaging
- Dealing with increased pressure from online travel companies (OTCs)

DESTINATION MARKETING ORGANIZATION (DMO) SECTORS

National Tourism Offices and Administrations (NTOs/NTAs)

State, Province, Territory Tourism Offices (STOs/PTOs/TTOs)

Regional Tourism Offices or Administrations (RTOs/RTAs)

City and County (e.g., CVBs)

- Increasing funding of some; declining funding of others
- Database marketing and destination loyalty programs growing in use and popularity
- Placing greater emphasis on MICE (meetings-incentives-conventions-exhibitions) markets
- Increasing emphasis on destination branding
- Online packaging by DMOs, including dynamic packaging
- Partnering is being given a higher priority
- Growing emphasis on special-interest travel markets
- Increasing importance and use of Internet marketing

FIGURE 7.13C   Trends in travel trade intermediary and DMO sectors.

Corporate Travel

- Increasing use of Internet for finding information and bookings
- Increasing consolidation among mega agencies that specialize in corporate travel
- Growing concern with travel costs among corporations
- Travel policy development becoming a standard procedure
- Increasing use of preferred suppliers and carriers

Incentive Travel Planning (MICE)

- Growing trend toward individual incentives
- Adding business objectives and meetings to incentive trips
- Shortening of incentive trip lengths

Convention/Meeting Planning (MICE)

- Increasing use of Internet for finding information and bookings
- Increasing use of web conferencing

Online Travel Company (OTCs or OTAs)

- Increasing market share
- Experiencing greater competition from supplier and carrier online sites

Global Distribution System (GDS)

- E-tickets becoming the major portion of airline sales
- Increasing global scope of the major systems
- Growing use of dynamic packaging
- Increasing functions for cruise bookings

FIGURE 7.13C *continued*

FIGURE 7.14 The growth in cruises is a major trend in world tourism.

- Greater involvement in packaging (e.g., DMOs) by more parts and sectors of the industry
- Increasing range of short-break and mini-vacation packages being offered

Programming

- Increasing range of entertainment facilities being provided by the hospitality and travel industry (e.g., new theme parks)
- Growing emphasis in providing "hands-on" and participative activities for visitors to many attractions
- Increasing range of educational program opportunities and learning while traveling

Place (Distribution)

- Increasing use of the Internet for online bookings and reservations
- Growing importance of online travel companies
- Greater diversification and activity in more parts and sectors of the industry by GDS companies

Promotion

- Increasing use of the Internet (e-commerce) and mobile technologies (m-commerce) for promotion
- Widening communications channels and approaches, e.g., Web-delivered press/media releases and RSS feeds
- Increasing globalization of communications through the use of multi-lingual approaches

Pricing

- More attention being given to revenue or yield management systems and approaches
- More special prices being offered through the Internet including coupons
- Increasing importance of low-cost and "no frills" carriers, suppliers and travel trade intermediaries, e.g., LCCs (low-cost airlines)

You can see now that customers and the industry is rapidly changing and there are many trends occurring on both the demand and supply sides. (Figure 7.15 provides a summary.) In fact, the situation is so fluid and dynamic that it is very difficult to keep track of all the changes and trends in hospitality and travel around the world. For hospitality and travel marketers, good research data and strong customer databases are essential to staying up-to-date. They must also be constantly reevaluating how they segment markets.

Changing Segmentation Practices

The hospitality and travel industry is becoming increasingly sophisticated in how it develops and applies market segmentation approaches. The industry is now much more aware of the benefits of effective segmentation and the variety of segmentation characteristics available.

CUSTOMER (DEMAND)	INDUSTRY (SUPPLY)
Demographic and Socio-economic • Aging but engaging: The Baby Boomers • Break-ationing: Time poverty **Geographic** • Building with BRIC **Purpose of Trip** • Multi-purposing travel **Psychographic** • Getting and staying healthy • Decompressing in style • Getting gayer in travel • Greening with meaning • Blogging the memories • Podcasting and downloading **Behavioral** • Going it alone • Racking up the miles • Decreasing brand loyalty **Product-related (Demand Side)** • Finding their niche • Connoisseuring **Distribution Channel (Demand Side)** • Looking and booking • Virtual touring	**Product** • Increasing brand segmentation in many sectors of hospitality and travel • Increasing use of brand extensions as a strategy by major companies, especially hotel chains • Growing diversity of special-interest travel destinations, e.g., branded beds and bedding **Partnership** • Partnering with other organizations in hospitality and travel is being given a much higher priority • Partnering with organizations and brands outside of hospitality and travel is now becoming much more common • The Internet is providing an increasingly useful platform for "virtual" partnerships **People** • Targeting a broader range of market segments, both globally and by other segmentation characteristics • Increasing emphasis on improving service quality among hosts • Increasing importance and use of customer databases **Packaging** • Greater emphasis on customizing packages including the concept of dynamic packaging • More parts and sectors of the industry getting involved in packaging (e.g., DMOs) • Increasing range of short-break and mini-vacation packages being offered **Programming** • Increasing range of entertainment facilities being provided by the hospitality and travel industry (e.g., new theme parks) • Growing emphasis in providing "hands-on" and participative activities for visitors to many attractions • Increasing range of educational program opportunities and learning while traveling **Place (distribution)** • Increasing use of the Internet for online bookings and reservations • Growing importance of online travel companies • GDS companies are diversifying and becoming active in more parts and sectors of the industry **Promotion** • Increasing use of the Internet and mobile technologies for promotion • Widening communications channels and approaches, e.g., Web-delivered press/media releases and RSS feeds • Increasing globalizing of communications through the use of multi-lingual approaches **Pricing** • More attention being given to revenue or yield management systems and approaches • More special prices being offered through the Internet including coupons • Increasing importance of low-cost and "no frills" carriers, supplier and travel trade intermediaries, e.g., LCCs

FIGURE 7.15 Summary of customer and industry trends.

Traditionally, hospitality and travel marketers relied upon demographic/socio-economic, geographic, and purpose-of-trip segmentation, but other segmentation characteristics are now being used. With improving customer databases, hospitality and travel organizations are in a better position to identify, record, and analyze customers' characteristics. These databases are particularly helpful in pinpointing frequent and loyal customers and, therefore, in designing and promoting loyalty programs.

The industry is doing more marketing research, including methods that produce research data for psychographic/lifestyle, benefit, and brand-loyalty segmentation. The use of these segmentation characteristics can provide the competitive edge that organizations need.

Chapter Conclusion

The hospitality and travel industry has matured in its use of market segmentation. There is growing recognition of the need to select specific target markets and to aim marketing programs at them. At the same time, the market is becoming increasingly diverse, offering many more possible niches for hospitality and travel marketers. The big winners are most likely to be those organizations that hone in most precisely on their target markets.

Improved marketing research and greater use of computer technology hold great promise for more effective segmentation in the industry. More applications of multi-stage segmentation also hold good potential for more effective marketing.

REVIEW QUESTIONS

1. How is market segmentation defined in this book?
2. Why is market segmentation so important to effective marketing?
3. What are the benefits of using market segmentation?
4. Does market segmentation have any limitations and, if so, what are they?
5. What are the eight criteria used to determine the viability of market segments?
6. What are the differences between the single-stage, two-stage, and multistage segmentation approaches?
7. What are the seven characteristics that can be used to segment hospitality and travel markets?
8. Which of the seven segmentation characteristics have traditionally been used by the industry?
9. Is the hospitality and travel industry becoming more or less segmented? Explain your answer by citing some recent customer and industry trends.
10. Is the industry becoming more or less sophisticated in its use of market segmentation? Justify your answer with a few examples.

CHAPTER ASSIGNMENTS

1. Select an existing hospitality and travel organization and analyze its use of market segmentation. What are the organization's target markets? What segmentation characteristics are being used? Is the organization employing single-stage, two-stage, or multi-stage segmentation? Have new services, facilities, packages, or promotional efforts been introduced to more finely key in on target markets? How could the organization improve its market segmentation practices?
2. You have just been hired as the marketing director of an airline, hotel or restaurant chain, travel agency, convention/visitors bureau, or other hospitality/travel organization. As your first assignment, the chief executive has asked you to report on the major customer and industry trends in your field. You have also been asked to outline how the organization can capitalize on these changes. What specific trends would you mention in your report, and how would you try to benefit from them?

3. Select a part of the hospitality and travel industry (e.g., hotels, airlines, car rental agencies, or restaurants) and examine what companies in this industry are doing to attract the frequent traveler or diner. Are the numbers of programs increasing or decreasing? Do companies follow fairly standardized approaches, or is there a great deal of variation? How are programs promoted, and what incentives are offered? Have the programs been effective in increasing brand loyalty?

4. Select a part of the industry and interview several marketing or general managers about their approaches to market segmentation. What segmentation characteristics are being used? Do the organizations tend to use the same approaches toward segmentation characteristics? Is it common to find single-stage, two-stage, or multi-stage segmentation, and why is this? Have approaches to segmentation changed in recent years? Are organizations experimenting with less frequently used segmentation characteristics (i.e., psychographic, benefit, and behavioral)?

WEB RESOURCES

AAdvantage, http://www.aadvantage.com/
AARP, http://www.aarp.org/
Air Miles, http://www.airmiles.ca/
Canadian Tourism Commission, http://www.corporate.canada.travel/
Contiki, http://www.contiki.com/
Costa Rica, http://www.visitcostarica.com/
Enterprise Rent-A-Car, http://www.enterprise.com/
International Gay and Lesbian Travel Association, http://www.iglta.org/
ITA Office of Travel and Tourism Industries, http://tinet.ita.doc.gov
Pew Internet & American Life Project, http://www.pewinternet.org/
Priority Club, http://www.ichotelsgroup.com/
Sabah Tourism Board, http://www.sabahtourism.com/

REFERENCES

1. Mill, Robert Christie, and Alastair M. Morrison. 2006. *The Tourism System*. 5th ed. Dubuque, Iowa: Kendall/Hunt Publishing Company, 268.

2. American Marketing Association. 2008. *Dictionary of Marketing Terms*, http://www.marketingpower.com/_layouts/Dictionary.aspx, accessed December 13, 2008.

3. Vyncke, Peter. 2002. "Lifestyle Segmentation: From Attitudes, Interests and Opinions, to Values, Aesthetic Styles, Life Visions and Media Preferences." *European Journal of Communication*, 17(4), 448.

4. Claritas. 2008. *PRIZM® NE Lifestyle Segmentation System*, http://www.claritas.com/MyBestSegments/Default.jsp, accessed December 13, 2008.

5. Kotler, Philip, and Kevin Lane Keller. 2006. *Marketing Management*. 12th ed. Pearson Prentice Hall, 238–242.

6. InsideFlyer.com. 2008. *Frequent Flyer Facts & Stats*, http://www.webflyer.com/company/press_room/facts_and_stats/, accessed December 13, 2008.

7. Marriott. (2008). *Happy 25th Anniversary Marriott Rewards!*, http://www.blogs.marriott.com/default.asp?item=2289279, accessed December 13, 2008.

8. Skogland, Iselin, and Judy A. Siguaw. 2004. *Understanding Switchers and Stayers in the Lodging Industry*. The Center for Hospitality Research at Cornell University.

9. ITB Berlin & IPK International. 2007. *World Travel Trends Report 2007-08*, 16.

10. U.S. Census Bureau. 2006. *Oldest Baby Boomers Turn 60!*, http://www.census.gov/Press-Release/www/releases/archives/facts_for_features_special_editions/006105.html, accessed December 13, 2008.

11. Deloitte Touche Tohmatsu. 2007. *Wealth and Wisdom*, 50.

12. AARP. 2005. *2005 Travel & Adventure Report. A Snapshot of Boomers Travel & Adventure Experiences*. Washington, DC: AARP, 1.

13. AARP. 2006. *Boomers Turning 60*. Washington, DC: AARP, 10.

14. ITB Berlin & IPK International. 2007. *World Travel Trends Report 2007–08*, 29.

15. Lonely Planet. 2006. *Lonely Planet Travellers' Pulse Survey 2006*, 4.

16. UN World Tourism Organization. 2008. *Facts & Figures: Tourism 2020 Vision*, http://www.unwto.org/facts/eng/vision.htm, accessed December 13, 2008.

17. Goldman Sachs. 2008. *BRICs*, http://www2.goldmansachs.com/ideas/brics/index.html, accessed December 13, 2008.

18. Office of Travel and Tourism Industries. 2008. *Profile of U.S. Resident Travelers Visiting Overseas Destinations: 2007 Outbound*, http://tinet.ita.doc.gov/outreachpages/download_data_table/2007_Outbound_Profile.pd, accessed December 13, 2008.

19. National Restaurant Association. 2006. *National Restaurant Association 2007 Restaurant Industry Forecast*. Washington, DC: National Restaurant Association, 26.

20. ITB Berlin & IPK International. 2006. *World Travel Trends Report 2006-07*, 26.

21. International Spa Association. 2008. *The U.S. Spa Industry–Fast Facts*, http://www.experienceispa.com/education-resources/facts-and-figures/industry-stats/, accessed December 13, 2008.

22. Canadian Tourism Commission. 2006. *2006 Canadian Spa Sector Profile*, Vancouver, British Columbia: Canadian Tourism Commission, iii.

23. TravelDailyNews.com. 2007. *Gay and lesbian Australians provide a lucrative market*, http://www.traveldailynews.com/new.asp?newid=35255&subcategory_id=99, accessed December 13, 2008.

24. Travel Industry Association. 2006. *Comprehensive Travel and Tourism Study of Gays and Lesbians Highlights Leisure Travel Insights*, http://www.tia.org/pressmedia/pressrec.asp?Item=739, accessed December 13, 2008.

25. Hewitt, Ed. 2007. Travel trends 2007. "What globe-trotters can expect over the next year." *The Independent Traveler*.

26. Lenhart, Amanda, and Susannah Fox. 2006. *Bloggers. A portrait of the Internet's new storytellers*. Washington, DC: Pew Internet & American Life Project, i.

27. Madden, Mary. 2008. *Podcast Downloading 2008*, http://www.pewinternet.org/PPF/r/261/report_display.asp, accessed December 13, 2008.

28. Tourism Australia. 2007. *How the Internet has supercharged word of mouth recommendation*, http://www.tourism.australia.com/Research.asp?sub=0297&al=2424#TargetsMarkets, accessed December 13, 2008.

29. World Travel Market and Euromonitor International. 2006. *World Travel Market 2006 – Global Trends Report*. London, England, 4.

30. LoyaltyOne, Inc. 2008. *Company Facts*, http://www.loyalty.com/WhoWeAre/CompanyFacts.aspx, accessed December 13, 2008.

31. FrequentFlier.com. 2007. *History of Loyalty Programs*, http://www.frequentflier.com/ffp-005.htm, accessed December 13, 2008.

32. Skogland, Iselin, and Judy A. Siguaw. 2004. *Understanding Switchers and Stayers in the Lodging Industry*. The Center for Hospitality Research at Cornell University, 5.

33. Hewitt, Ed. 2007. "Travel trends 2007. What globe-trotters can expect over the next year." *The Independent Traveler*.

34. Miniwatts Marketing Group. 2008. *World Internet Users and Population Statistics*, http://www.internetworldstats.com/stats.htm, accessed December 13, 2008.

35. Del Rosso, Laura. 2006. "Leisure travel study: Power in consumers' hands. Travel Weekly Special Report." *2006 Consumer Trends*, 6.

36. Burst Media Online Insights. 2007. *Online Travel*.

37. Tourism Australia. 2006. "Internet Usage." *Market Insight Facts*, December 2006.

38. Hotel Interactive. 2007. *E-commerce Continues as Sales Goliath*, http://www.hotelinteractive.com/index.asp?page_id=5000&article_id=7676, accessed December 13, 2008.

39. e-Marketer.com. 2008. *US Online Travel: Planning and Booking*, http://www.emarketer.com/Reports/All/Emarketer_2000502.aspx, accessed December 13, 2008.

40. Marcussen, Carl H. 2008. *Trends in European Internet Distribution of Travel and Tourism Services*. Bornholm, Denmark: Centre for Regional and Tourism Research.

41. Web-Tourismus. 2008. *Online tourism on a roll*, http://www.web-tourismus.de/english/intro/intro_studie_wt2008.asp, accessed December 13, 2008.

42. Yuan, Xingpu and Mary Madden. 2006. *Virtual Space is the Place*, http://www.pewinternet.org/PPF/r/195/report display.asp, accessed December 13, 2008

43. ITB Berlin & IPK International. 2006. *World Travel Trends Report 2006–07*, 25.

chapter 8

Marketing Strategy: Strategies, Positioning, and Marketing Objectives
Where Would We Like to Be?

O V E R V I E W

What do you do when the market has been segmented and potential target markets are known? The next steps are rather like planning a journey to some exotic or inaccessible place. Any explorers worth their salt recognize the need for a map and a GPS, a chosen route, the proper types and amount of supplies, a means of access or transportation to their destination, some human (and perhaps animal) help to get there, and day-to-day progress objectives. This chapter begins by describing marketing strategies as the routes to success.

O B J E C T I V E S

Having read this chapter, you should be able to:

- Identify the six components in developing a marketing strategy and plan.

- Define the terms *marketing strategy, positioning,* and *marketing objective.*

- Explain the concept of segmented marketing strategies and describe the alternative strategies by target market focus.

- Describe the alternative strategies by product life cycle (PLC) stage.

- Describe the alternative strategies by industry sector position.

- Explain the concepts of relationship marketing and strategic alliances.

- Identify the reasons that have made positioning essential in today's business climate.

- List and describe the steps required for effective positioning (the five Ds).

- List and describe the six different approaches to positioning.

- Explain the benefits of having marketing objectives and list the four requirements for good marketing objectives.

KEY TERMS

brand segmentation

challengers

combiners

concentrated marketing
   strategy

decline stage

differentiated marketing
   strategies

five Ds of positioning

follower

full-coverage marketing
   strategy

general positioning approach

growth stage

introduction stage

leader

marketing objectives

marketing strategy

maturity stage

nichers

niching

penetration strategies

positioning

positioning statement

preferred suppliers or vendors

product life cycle (PLC)

relationship marketing

segmented marketing
   strategies

segmenters

single-target-market strategy

skimming strategies

strategic alliances

undifferentiated marketing
   strategy

The chapter then looks at the alternative strategies that hospitality and travel organizations can use. It also shows that different strategies work best during the various product life-cycle stages. It describes the strategies that are most effective both for industry leaders, for those trying to catch them, and for smaller organizations. The chapter then examines the technique of positioning and shows how it can be used to obtain the greatest marketing benefits. It ends by looking at marketing objectives and their importance to successful marketing strategies.

Imagine yourself as one of the great explorers of all time—Columbus, Zheng He, Magellan, Raleigh, Scott, Hillary, Marco Polo, Leif Ericson, Livingstone, Baffin, Rasmussen, or even Indiana Jones! All these great men set out to go somewhere and do something that no person had accomplished before. They succeeded. Their great feats took months, sometimes years, of careful planning. In most cases, they had to beg, borrow, and steal to get enough money for their trips. There were many alternate routes to their destinations, but they chose those that involved the least effort and wasted resources. Those who returned alive carefully documented their journeys so that others could retrace their footsteps or find a better route. Of course, they could not blog or have a Facebook page in those days, or we would know much more about what they accomplished.

Now, you are probably wondering what explorations have to do with marketing. Good question! The answer is, as usual, plenty! First, every explorer needs a precise idea of the final destination. For Edmund Hillary, it was the summit of Mount Everest. For Robert Scott, it was the South Pole. All marketers must also know where they want to take their organizations—remember the "Where would we like to be?" question. Both groups need to identify alternate routes and then pick the best ones. Each must also budget for the resources needed along the way and choose those resources that will be most beneficial to reaching the ultimate goal. Explorers and marketers both place a premium on getting the most out of their resources and on having points (or milestones) at which they can check their progress.

The Process of Developing a Marketing Strategy and Plan

When marketers are planning how they will get where they want to be, they look at alternative marketing strategies and pick the ones best suited to their organizations and resources. They put their budgets and human resources into activities (marketing mixes or the 8 Ps) with the greatest expected payoffs or ROI (return on investment). Intermediate progress steps (objectives) are set. If everything works as planned—like explorers who succeed and return alive—marketers will have the privilege of succeeding again.

Before moving ahead, we thought that you would like to know where we are headed. Figure 8.1 is your map, showing how Chapters 6, 7, 8, and 9 link together. Chapter 6 explained how to do marketing research. Chapter 7 described market segmentation analysis, selection of target markets, and customer and industry trends. Chapter 8 describes how a complete marketing strategy is developed and discusses the three concepts of marketing strategy, positioning, and marketing objectives. Chapter 9 talks about developing the marketing plan and the marketing mix (8 Ps).

The leftmost two columns of Figure 8.1 show the six marketing strategy components and where they are discussed in this book. The steps that marketers must complete are listed in the third column. The rightmost column shows the outcomes or choices that result from the completion of the steps. Following are definitions of the three main concepts described in this chapter: marketing strategy (#2 in Figure 8.1), positioning (#3 in Figure 8.1), and marketing objectives (#4 in Figure 8.1):

Marketing Strategy

In this book, as in general practice, **marketing strategy** has a distinct meaning. It is the selection of a course of action from among several alternatives that involves specific customer groups, communication methods, distribution channels, and pricing structures. As most experts would say, it is a combination of the selected target markets, positioning approach, and marketing mixes (the 8 Ps).

Positioning

Positioning is the development of a service and marketing mix to occupy a specific place in the minds of customers within target markets. Usually this

MARKETING STRATEGY COMPONENTS	CHAPTER	STEPS	OUTCOMES AND CHOICES
1. Market Segmentation Analysis	6	• Conduct required secondary (external and internal) and primary research (qualitative and quantitative)	• Research findings and conclusions
	7	• Analyze customer and industry trends	• Identification of key trends and their impacts
	7	• Divide the market into segments by chosen segmentation characteristics (geographic; demographic/socio-economic; purpose of trip; psychographic; behavioral; product-related; distribution channel)	• Market segmentation analysis • Selected approach and target market or markets (single-stage; two-stage; multi-stage)
	7	• Develop selection criteria and then select target markets	• Target market selection criteria • Selected target markets
2. Marketing Strategy Formulation	8	• Choose a target market focus	• Undifferentiated; differentiated (segmented) • Single target market; concentrated; full-coverage
		• Determine industry sector position	• Leader; challenger; follower; nicher
		• Identify the PLC stage of industry sector and organization/destination	• Introduction; growth; maturity; decline
3. Positioning Approach	8	• Select a positioning approach (overall and by target market)	• Selected positioning approach (specific product features; benefits/problem solution/needs; specific usage occasions; user category; against another product; or product class dissociation)
4. Marketing Objectives	8	• Write marketing objectives for each selected target market	• Marketing objectives that are target-market specific, results-oriented, quantitative, and time-specific
5. Marketing Mix (The 8 Ps)	9	• Decide on how the 8 Ps are to be used to achieve the marketing objectives for each selected target market	• Specific activities using product, partnership, people, packaging, programming, place, promotion, and pricing
6. Marketing Plan	9	• Write the marketing plan in three parts (marketing plan rationale; implementation plan; executive summary)	• Written marketing plan
		• Prepare the marketing budget (objective-and-task approach)	• Marketing budget
		• Control and evaluate the success of the marketing plan	• Control and evaluation procedures; measurements of effectiveness

FIGURE 8.1 The process of developing a marketing strategy and plan.

Image copyright Christophe Testi, 2008. Used under license from Shutterstock.com

FIGURE 8.2 Arizona is positioned as the Grand Canyon State.

means having distinctive service features (e.g., Arizona as the *Grand Canyon State*, Figure 8.2) and/or communicating the position in a distinctive way (e.g., Windstar Cruises' *180° degrees from ordinary®*).

Marketing Objectives

A **marketing objective** is a measurable result that a hospitality or travel organization attempts to achieve for a target market within a specific time period, typically one or two years.

Now let us begin discussing the second component in Figure 8.1—marketing strategy formulation.

Marketing Strategy Formulation

Marketing strategy formulation begins by choosing from among alternative strategy options. Three groups of alternatives are discussed in this chapter:

1. Alternative strategies by target market focus
2. Alternative strategies for product life-cycle (PLC) stages
3. Alternative strategies by industry sector position

Every organization is unique and must select the alternatives that best suit its situation.

1. **Alternative Marketing Strategies by Target Market Focus.** There are four target market focus strategies available to hospitality and travel organizations:

   a. Select only one target market from several market segments and market exclusively to it (**single-target-market strategy** or niching).

   b. Select a few target markets from several market segments and concentrate on these (**concentrated marketing strategy** or segmenting).

   c. Appeal to all market segments in the total market with a tailor-made approach for each of them (**full-coverage marketing strategy** or segmenting).

   d. Recognize that there are different market segments, but ignore these differences when marketing (**undifferentiated marketing strategy** or combining).

   Certain names have been coined for organizations that follow these strategies. Groups adopting the single-target-market approach have become known as **nichers**. Organizations using concentrated and full-coverage strategies are often called **segmenters**. The name typically associated with users of the fourth strategy is **combiners**.

   a. *Single-Target-Market Strategy.* As we shall see later, this strategy, known as **niching**, is popular with smaller and low-market-share organizations (those with a minor percentage of total demand for the service).[1] A good example in the travel trade intermediary sector is ElderTreks Adventure Travel Tours Inc. (Figure 8.3). This Canadian tour operator specializes in providing adventure travel trips for people aged 50 and over. You will remember from Chapter 7 that these

FIGURE 8.3 There are tour operators that specialize in adventure travel trips for people of 50 and older.

Image copyright Elli, 2008. Used under license from Shutterstock.com

Baby Boomers want active travel experiences and to be adventuresome. ElderTreks meets this need by providing trips to places such as Mount Everest, Antarctica, Patagonia, and Africa.

There are many other examples of market specialization or market niching in the hospitality and travel industry. For example, Travcoa is a tour operator that specializes in luxury travel to exotic destinations. Panda Express is a North American restaurant chain that specializes in providing high quality Chinese food in a quick-service format, Figure 8.4. The CruiseOutlet.com is a cruise-only travel agency with a strong online presence. Women On a Roll is a company that organizes tours exclusively for lesbians.

The essence of the single-target-market approach is target market specialization and avoiding head-to-head competition with industry sector leaders. The organization selecting this approach chooses one market or product segment, with the goal of serving customer needs more comprehensively than competitive organizations do. In the long term, it is hoped that a strong association with the target market or specific product, as well as a reputation for excellent service, will be developed.

b. *Concentrated Marketing Strategy.* This strategy is similar to the single-target-market one, except that additional market segments are pursued. Most independent hotels and resorts use this approach. Faced with direct competition from global lodging chain brands, they provide uniquely designed properties, added services, or personal touches to attract business and pleasure travelers. They offer a single product that serves the needs of several lodging market segments. As

FIGURE 8.4 Some chains have been highly successful in developing a niche for gourmet Chinese food in North America.

Industry Players

Focusing on Conferences in Scottsdale, Arizona

Scottsdale Resort & Conference Center

http://www.thescottsdaleresort.com

Image copyright Yare Marketing, 2008. Used under license from Shutterstock.com

The golf courses in Scottsdale are a major attraction for conference and meeting delegates.

Chapter 8 introduces the idea of "market focus" strategies and describes the "single-target-market" strategy as one of the alternatives. The Scottsdale Resort & Conference in Scottsdale, Arizona provides a great example of specializing in one target market—conferences and similar meetings. This resort has received numerous accolades and industry recognition since it opened in the 1980s. It has the AAA four-diamond designation, and is the only conference resort in the USA to be recognized by *Successful Meetings* magazines within its Bronze Circle of Hospitality.

It is part of the Benchmark Hospitality International group, which operates 18 conference center resorts in 14 states, plus the Tokyo Conference Center in Japan. With its headquarters at The Woodlands in Texas, the meetings-based philosophy of this group is *Living, Learning and Leisure*™.

(*continues*)

(continued)

Scottsdale Resort & Conference Center's Accommodation Facilities

The accommodation facilities are quite special at this Arizona property. The Scottsdale Resort & Conference Center has 326 guest rooms. It has 12 five-room Casitas, each designed like a private hacienda, and three Executive Suites.

Courtesy of Benchmark Hospitality International

A guest room at the Scottsdale Resort & Conference Center.

The Casitas are set apart from the main building, along the fairway of one of the two adjacent 18-hole golf courses. These Casitas have 60 guest rooms and are a popular choice for smaller, private conferences and retreats. The Casitas have luxurious furnishings and can be set up for various combinations of living and meeting spaces. Each Casita has a ground-floor Executive Suite. These Executive Suites include a master bedroom, living room with fireplace, dining area, and either a wet bar or a boardroom table seating 16. Additionally, each Casita has four other private guest rooms on the second floor that open onto a center hall from a separate entrance foyer. Many of the Casita's guest rooms have great views overlooking the fairways.

There are also three 2,300-square-foot Presidential Suites that are the epitome of luxury Scottsdale accommodation. The Suites feature original artwork, entertainment centers, wet bars, and have balconies overlooking the golf course fairways.

(continues)

(continued)

The Meeting and Conference Facilities

While the accommodations at this property are exceptional, the facilities for meetings are equally outstanding. The Scottsdale Resort & Conference Center has 50,000 square feet (4,645 square meters) of meeting space, divided among 50 versatile meeting rooms. The 10,000-square-foot Grand Coronado is the largest venue, accommodating up to 1,000 participants in a theater-style arrangement. The 6,000 square-foot Arizona and Maricopa rooms can also accommodate larger groups in a wide variety of set-ups. All the meeting rooms are tastefully decorated and supported with state-of-the-art audio-visual technology. The rooms provide ergonomically-designed chairs and the acoustics are almost perfect acoustics.

Courtesy of Benchmark Hospitality International

The Grand Coronado Room set up in a theater-style format.

Media Center

The Scottsdale Resort & Conference Center's Media Center is a crucial element in supporting the focus on conferences and meetings. An investment of around $2 million has been made in its equipment alone. The Media Center has successfully produced meetings for some of the Fortune 1000 companies' most technically-demanding meetings. The conferences and meetings at this property feature sophisticated technology that is supported by an onsite A-V staff team who is experienced in all aspects of media, computer technology, and telecom- munications. The *Media Production Suite* offers video production, PowerPoint presentations, digital photography, 3-D animation

(continues)

(continued)

graphics, and audio productions such as custom voiceovers or soundtracks. Participants can stay connected using the onsite *Videoconferencing Suite* that allows the guests to communicate live with up to four locations anywhere in the world. According to the property's promotional materials, the media services include: theme creation, enhancement, custom set design and special effects; staging and theatrical lighting; corporate group, individual, and candid photography and videography; slide and print processing; meeting and event documentation; pre- and post-production audio, video, PowerPoint; computer rentals and advanced computer support; telecommunications: high-speed lines, equipment, and expertise; videoconferencing; product displays; and state-of-the-art equipment rental.

Benchmark Conference Plan (BCP)

Chapter 12 is dedicated to the topics of packaging and programming; the Scottsdale Resort & Conference Center also excels in the use of these two techniques from the 8 Ps. For example, the Scottsdale Resort & Conference Center makes meetings easier to plan and budget for by offering the Benchmark Conference Plan (BCP). The BCP is a per-person packaged pricing plan that the property's conference professionals can tailor-make to meet a client's specific objectives. It is an all-inclusive package plan that covers guest accommodation and meals, standard A-V equipment usage, refreshment breaks, and the services of a Conference Planner.

In terms of programming, the Scottsdale Resort & Conference Center can arrange a variety of different special events for conference and meeting groups. For example, the resort's Conference Event Planners and Caterers can help guests create unique dining experiences that may include fiestas, western cookouts, poolside barbecues, Caribbean carnivals, and casino nights. These are supported with imaginative décor packages, and staging, costumes, special lighting and effects.

Recreational and Leisure Facilities

The Scottsdale Resort & Conference Center offers an attractive range of recreational and leisure options for conference and meeting delegates. There are two adjacent championship golf courses. The resort has two swimming pools and four outdoor, lighted tennis courts, and a court for either basketball or volleyball. It also features the Amansala Spa/ Salon and a Sports & Fitness Center. There is access to a 7-mile jogging/biking trail. The resort can arrange a variety of other activities in the surrounding areas of Scottsdale and the Arizona desert including bicycle rentals, desert adventures, horseback riding, desert jeep rides, hot air balloons, valley tours, and soaring.

(continues)

(continued)

The Spa/Salon offers a wide variety of spa services and treatments including European skin care treatments, massage therapy, manicures and pedicures, and make-up, hairstyling and salon services.

Discussion Questions

1. What steps has the Scottsdale Resort & Conference Center followed to pursue the single-target-market focus strategy?
2. What are the benefits to a conference and meeting planner in using a property like the Scottsdale Resort & Conference Center?
3. Take a look at the website, http://www.thescottsdaleresort.com. How does the property market and promote itself to this target through the Internet?

you will see in Chapter 10, a majority of the lodging chains have several different brands of properties that they hope as a brand family will appeal to most, if not all, market segments.

c. *Full-Coverage Marketing Strategy.* The most expensive of the four strategies usually is applied by industry sector leaders, those nationally based chains with many branch locations. They provide services for every target market and use a unique marketing mix to promote to each one separately.

The concept of **brand segmentation** in the lodging sector is an application of full-coverage strategy. Marriott International is a prime example. This industry sector leader stole a page from Procter & Gamble's playbook by offering travelers a complete range of lodging services, from its luxury-oriented JW Marriott and Ritz Carlton Hotels to the budget-conscious Fairfield Inns. Recognizing that it is impossible to provide something for everyone under the same roof, Marriott International decided to build properties that appealed strongly to specific market segments.

d. *Undifferentiated Marketing Strategy.* All of the three previous approaches are examples of **segmented marketing** or **differentiated marketing strategies**—methods that recognize differences between target markets by using individualized marketing mixes (Figure 8.5). An undifferentiated marketing strategy is one that overlooks segment differences and uses the same marketing mix for all target markets. You might be thinking that organizations using undifferentiated marketing must have a production orientation because they do not recognize the market segmentation concept. You are both right and wrong. Some start out trying to be all things to all people and end up meaning nothing to anyone. However, some industry sector leaders use undifferentiated marketing very effectively.

TARGET MARKET FOCUS STRATEGIES	ALSO KNOWN AS (AKA)	MAIN CHARACTERISTICS	EXAMPLES
Segmented			
Single-target market	*Nichers*	• Smaller organizations • Specialized expertise or services for one target market • Avoid head-to-head competition with industry sector leaders	• Conference center resorts • Contiki • Couples Resorts • ElderTreks • Spa resorts
Concentrated	*Segmenters (partial)*	• Independents not belonging to a chain or franchise organization • Organizations serving a local market	• Local hotels and restaurants • Organizations classified as *followers* within a specific industry sector
Full-coverage	*Segmenters (full)*	• Industry sector leaders and challengers	• Leading global lodging chains (InterContinental Hotels Group; Wyndham International; Marriott International; Hilton Hotels Corp.; Accor; Choice International; Starwood Hotels & Resorts Worldwide) • Leading cruise lines (Carnival Corporation)
Non-Segmented			
Undifferentiated	*Combiners*	• Organizations with products and services that have a very general appeal	• Leading quick-service/fast-food restaurant chains

FIGURE 8.5 Summary of the characteristics of the four target market focus strategies.

These **combiners** focus on similarities among customers and try to add product options and promotional appeals with one marketing mix.[2] Combiners are aware of differences in the needs of various target markets, but concentrate on the common needs they share. These target markets are then combined into one super target market, and a marketing mix is designed for it.

What are the benefits of the undifferentiated strategy? As mentioned in Chapter 7, market segmentation has drawbacks (added cost, difficulties in choosing the best segmentation base, knowing how finely or broadly to segment, and appealing to nonviable segments). These problems are lessened by combiners, because they aim at several target markets with only one marketing mix.

Are there any combiners in the hospitality and travel industry? If your answer was "yes," please accept a little applause. You might remember that we purposely did not answer one question about fast-food operators in Chapter 7. The question was, "When a service's appeal is so broad, does it make any sense to use different approaches for various customer groups, or should the same methods be used for all?" Most people have eaten at least one meal at McDonald's. McDonald's and other leading fast-food chains use partially undifferentiated marketing strategies. Their national advertising and promotions are designed to appeal to several target markets. Highly standardized, limited-choice menus are provided to meet common away-from-home eating needs. They use heavy television advertising featuring typical customers from all walks of life. We said partially undifferentiated because McDonald's and some of its competitors allow their franchisees to develop local marketing programs. These local advertising, public relations, and sales promotion efforts have a definite geographic target market.

Can you imagine the huge marketing budgets that KFC, Burger King, Starbucks, and McDonald's would need to advertise in all newspapers and magazines and on all radio and television stations to reach each and every market segment? It is much more economical for them to use broad-scale promotions. To keep people coming back, these combiners frequently add new menu items, modified items, or packages of items.

2. **Alternative Marketing Strategies for Product Life-Cycle (PLC) Stages.** Chapter 1 identified the **product life cycle (PLC)** as one of marketing's seven core principles. The basic idea of the PLC is that all products and services pass through the same stages during their histories. They are rather like people—they are born; they go through infancy, childhood, and adolescence; they reach maturity; and finally, they attain old age. Services and products also go through four stages. The effectiveness of different marketing strategies varies with PLC stage. Marketing strategies need to be adapted to meet the new challenges of each stage (Figure 8.6).

   a. Introduction
   b. Growth
   c. Maturity
   d. Decline

   a. *Introduction Stage Strategies.* The **introduction stage** begins when a new service is first offered to the public. Traditionally, this has been considered a period of low profits because of the high promotion and other costs required to establish a firm foothold in the market. Often the service or product is priced high and appeals to more adventurous, higher-

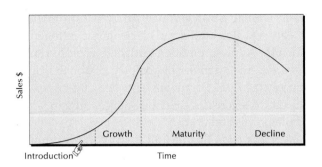

income customers and other innovators. Space tourism is an excellent example of this strategy, with only the world's most wealthy individuals having the money to be being able to join the astronauts in space.

Can you think of any new and revolutionary services recently introduced in the hospitality and travel industry? Yes, of course space tourism is a great example, but it is not accessible yet to most of us. Wi-Fi rooms and areas in hotels, restaurants, airports, cruise ships, and trains is a newer service that fits well in the new online world. Dynamic packaging on the Internet is another recent innovation. The new lifestyle or boutique hotels discussed in Chapter 10 are another good example. One thing you will notice about all of these is that competitors are very quick to copy the originators' services. Remember from Chapter 2 that services can be copied more easily than products. The introduction stage for any new service tends to be quite short.

There are four strategies that companies can use in the introduction stage (Figure 8.7).[3] They are based on two different pricing approaches—**skimming strategies** (using high prices) and **penetration strategies** (using low prices):

- *Rapid-Skimming Strategy* (high price/high promotion). Skim milk is milk from which all the fat has been removed. Market skimming works on exactly the same principle. A high price is charged and the "fat" of the buyers purchase the new service or product. The objective is to earn the highest possible gross profit. A rapid-skimming strategy means the new service is highly promoted when it is first introduced. Although not in hospitality and tourism, the iPhone introduction by Apple in 2007 was a rapid-skimming case.

		Low Promotion	High Promotion	
PRICE	High	**Slow-Skimming Strategy** • Space Tourism	**Rapid-Skimming Strategy** • iPhone	**Skimming Strategies**
	Low	**Slow-Penetration Strategy** • Some low-cost companies	**Rapid-Penetration Strategy** • Low-cost airline carriers (LCCs)	**Penetration Strategies**
		Low	High	

PROMOTION

- *Slow-Skimming Strategy* (high price/low promotion). The difference between slow and rapid skimming is in the amount spent on promotion. A low promotion budget is used in slow skimming. There are a small number of potential customers, but most are aware of the new service. Competitive services are not expected to be introduced for a considerable time. Space tourism is an outstanding example of this strategy.
- *Rapid-Penetration Strategy* (low price/high promotion). The price level is the key difference between penetration and skimming strategies. With a penetration strategy, prices are initially set low to capture as much of the market as possible. The market for the new service is large, but most buyers are price sensitive (they like lower rather than higher prices). Rapid penetration means teaming low introduction prices with a high level of promotion. There is a strong threat that competitors will quickly copy it, so initial promotion is quite intense. Most of the low-cost carriers (LCC) in the airline sector have used a combination of low fares and high levels of promotion.
- *Slow-Penetration Strategy* (low price/low promotion). Here the new service is introduced at a low price with a low level of promotion. Again, the potential market is large and price sensitive. Unlike with rapid penetration, these customers are highly aware of the new service. There are some potential competitors, but the competitive threat is not as great. Some of the airline LCCs used this strategy, and relied almost totally on their websites for promotion.

b. *Growth Stage Strategies.* In the **growth stage**, sales climb rapidly, profit levels improve, and more competitors enter the fray. For the organization pioneering the new service, the following strategies can be used:[4]

- Improving service quality and adding new service features and service elements
- Pursuing new target markets
- Using new channels of distribution
- Lowering prices to attract more price-sensitive customers
- Shifting some advertising emphasis from building awareness to creating desire and action (purchase)

Chapter 10 identifies the growth sectors of the hospitality and travel industry as casinos and gaming, and cruises. The cruise sector provides many good examples of growth stage marketing strategies. New cruise ships are being loaded with new recreation, entertainment, fitness and spa, and dining services. Who ever thought you could go ice skating or rock climbing on a ship? The introduction of "smart cards" by casinos is another good example of a marketing innovation during the growth stage of the PLC.

c. *Maturity Stage Strategies.* You will see later in Chapter 10 that many of the sectors of the hospitality and travel industry are in the **maturity**

stage of the PLC, including lodging, restaurant and foodservice, airlines, and car rental. This stage is characterized by a slow-down in the rate of sales revenue growth. There are overcapacity situations; too much supply is chasing too little demand. An organization can use three strategies if it wants to maintain its sales revenue growth during this stage:[5]

- *Market-Modification Strategy.* The organization goes after its competitors' customers, adds new target markets, or tries to convert non-users into users. Other actions that can be taken include encouraging more frequent use or greater use per purchase, or creating new and more varied uses.

- *Product-Modification Strategy.* The essence of this approach is rejuvenating the organization's physical services or products to make them seem newer and more contemporary. Have you ever watched what airlines do to their equipment? A new paint job now and then, flashy logos one after the other, constant uniform changes for flight attendants, and games of musical chairs with seating layouts are all examples. Hotels also actively try to keep their customers from becoming jaded. The brand segmentation strategies being used by many leading lodging, restaurant, and cruise line companies is another example here.

- *Marketing-Mix-Modification Strategy.* Sales can be stimulated by changing the marketing mix (8 Ps). For example, hotels faced with mature markets can place more emphasis on finding new online distribution channels. Restaurants can use coupons and other sales promotions to increase their volumes. Travel agencies may employ commissioned or outside sales agents to bring in more business.

- *Brand Extension Strategy.* This is a strategy in which a company adds a different type of product line to its existing offerings (Figure 8.8). This allows an organization to appeal to a variety of target markets with differentiated products that carry a single, well-established brand name.[6] For example, Hilton Hospitality, Inc. offers an online store, Hilton to Home®, where customers can buy its *Serenity Bed*, linens, accessories, electronics, and other items. You will learn more about this strategy in Chapter 10.

d. *Decline Stage Strategies.* What do you do when the sales of your service begin to fall in the **decline stage**? There are alternatives to going out of business completely. Most marketing experts recommend reducing costs and milking the company, product, or service as sales decline further. Selling out to someone else is another alternative.

One of the major criticisms of the PLC concept is its assumption that all sales of all products and services eventually decline to zero or to a very low level. Experience has shown that this is not necessarily true. Many old hotel and resort properties have been restored and rejuvenated to recapture former glories. Consider the RMS Queen Mary, which has been transformed

FIGURE 8.8 Lodging chains are applying brand extension strategies in selling bedding and bathroom towels.

Image copyright Lisasaadphotography, 2008. Used under license from Shutterstock.com

from a fabulous ocean liner to a hotel, convention and trade show, and entertainment facility in Long Beach, California (Figure 8.9). Think about the restaurant concepts and menu items that have come and gone, only to be replaced by others. The best answer to the decline-stage dilemma is to rejuvenate the service by finding new uses and customers, picking new channels of distribution, or repositioning (changing perceptions).

3. **Alternative Marketing Strategies by Industry Sector Position.** If you take a look at the hospitality and travel industry, you will find that certain organizations dominate all others. Examples include McDonald's in fast food, Disney in theme parks, Carnival in cruise lines, Paris, France and Las Vegas, Nevada in travel destinations; Enterprise and Hertz in rental cars, American Express in travel agencies, Expedia.com in online travel companies, Sabre in GDS, and so on. You will also recognize that other groups—we will call them challengers and followers—are not as big or successful, but still have a large slice of the business. In this category are organizations such as Burger King, Royal Caribbean, Avis, Universal Studios, Carlson Wagonlit Travel, Travelocity.com, and Amadeus. There are still others—let's use the term *nichers* for them—which are even smaller and target a small number or only one specific target market. To recap, there are four industry sector role or position categories:

   a. Leaders
   b. Challengers
   c. Followers
   d. Nichers[7]

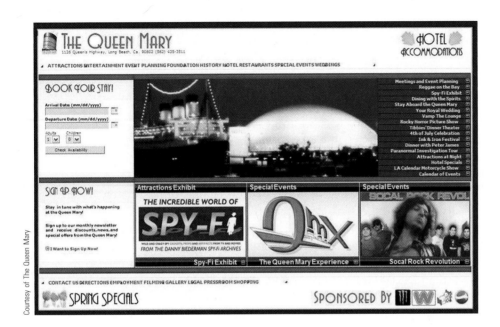

FIGURE 8.9 The Queen Mary in Long Beach, California has enjoyed two different product life cycles (PLCs).

a. *Market Leader Strategies.* Winning is habit-forming. Once an organization becomes the **leader** in its field, it rarely decides to give up the number one position. Many of its competitors, however, would also like to be number one or to grab market share away from the leader. Staying on top is perhaps one of marketing's biggest challenges, but some organizations excel at it. There are three different strategies for market leaders:

- Expanding the size of the total market (or increasing "primary demand")
- Protecting market share
- Expanding market share

Expanding the Size of the Total Market. The total or primary market can be increased in three ways:

1. Finding new target markets.
2. Developing new uses for the services or facilities.
3. Convincing customers to use the services or facilities more frequently.

The market leader has the most to gain if the total demand for the industry sector's services grows. It can identify target markets that are not using these services as frequently as they could be, or are not using them at all.

Another way to build up the primary market is to find and promote new uses for a service. There are several examples of this in the

Did You Know?

Why Is the PLC Not All You See?

- The Queen Mary has had two PLCs.
- The Queen Mary was built in Clydebank, Scotland, by Cunard and launched in 1934. She was 74 years old on September 26, 2008.
- Her maiden voyage was in 1936.
- The Queen Mary was longer and heavier than Titanic (and made many more successful journeys!). The Titanic, unfortunately, carried more passengers.
- The Queen Mary made 1,001 transatlantic crossings and on each trip carried up to 1,957 passengers and 1,200 crew.
- She was put into war service from 1940 until 1946 and carried more than 765,000 military personnel. The Queen Mary was painted all in grey and was known as "The Grey Ghost."
- The Queen Mary was removed from regular passenger service in 1967 and was purchased by the City of Long Beach, California.
- The City of Long Beach had to construct a special landfill, 900-foot pier, parking lot, boarding ramps, and shore protection to accommodate The Queen Mary.
- She was renovated into a hotel and tourist attraction and opened in 1971. The Queen Mary is close to the Long Beach Convention Center.
- The Queen Mary has 365 staterooms, three restaurants and cafés, 85,000 square feet of meeting space in 14 Art Deco salons (including a 50,000 square foot Exhibit Hall), an art gallery, and shops.
- The Queen Mary Seaport also functions as a tourist attraction with a separate admission fee.

Source: **http://www.queenmary.com/**

hospitality and travel industry. Many of the leading cruise lines have been successful in promoting the use of their ships for corporate meetings and conventions, and incentive travel. Traditional summer-only and ski resorts have taken the same tack by marketing to meeting planners for fall and spring events.

Convincing customers to use your service more frequently is the third option. An excellent example of this approach is McDonald's Happy Meal concept, which was introduced in 1979. Children, with their parents in tow, are lured back time and time again to the Golden Arches for the toys and other items in these meals. The frequent-traveler and other loyalty programs discussed in various parts of this book are another example, as are the bounce-back coupons mentioned in Chapter 16.

Image copyright Joseph Caley, 2008. Used under license from Shutterstock.com

FIGURE 8.10 The Burj Al Arab Hotel in Dubai has gained a unique position in the international hotel market as "the best hotel in the world."

Protecting Market Share. Protecting market share is the second main approach available to the market leader. How do leaders hold on to customers when every competitor is eyeing their business? By far the best way is to continue to be innovative, constantly adding new or improved services (Figure 8.10). Again, McDonald's and Holiday Inn (now part of the InterContinental Hotels Group) are two of the industry's brightest stars in this respect. McDonald's introduced the concept of chicken nuggets and was one of the innovators of the drive-through window. Holiday Inn pioneered the frequent-guest award idea (Priority Club) in the lodging sector. Another highly recommended step for the leader is to continually look for diversification opportunities. "Keeping one's eggs in only one basket" is a dangerous business strategy, however. Marriott International and Starwood Hotels & Resorts Worldwide are fine examples of lodging companies that diversified to maintain their market shares. Both introduced several new brands of properties and these include Starwood's lifestyle hotel *aloft*[SM] and element[SM] extended-stay brands introduced in 2006 and 2007.

Expanding Market Share. Leaders can also try to expand their market shares by adding new services, improving service quality, increasing spending on marketing, or acquiring competitive organizations. For example, Carnival Corporation strengthened its position as the world's leading cruise line when it merged with P&O Princess Cruises in 2003. In 2008, Carnival Corporation's brand portfolio had swelled to 11 (Carnival Cruise Lines, Princess Cruises, Holland America Line, Cunard, AIDA (German cruise line), Costa Cruises, P&O Cruises, Ocean Village, Seabourn, Iberocruceros, and P&O Cruises Australia).

b. *Market Challenger Strategies.* Market **challengers** are organizations that decide to take on the leaders in a bid for market share. In the battle of the burgers, Burger King, Wendy's, and Hardee's all have gone after McDonald's commanding market share. Avis and other car rental companies have challenged Hertz. When challengers attack the leader, they usually do it through comparative advertising campaigns. Burger King has compared its menu items several times to McDonald's, including the famous broiled versus fried advertising campaign. Wendy's cleverly put down both McDonald's and Burger King in its celebrated "Where's the Beef?" commercials.

Avis' run at Hertz is well-documented and is often used as one of the best examples of successful positioning. Avis sold the traveling public on the idea that because it was the number two firm, it had to try harder to satisfy its rental customers.

A challenger can mount five different types of attacks on the leader: frontal (head-on), flank, encirclement, bypass, and guerilla.[8] Burger King used the frontal or head-on approach when it questioned McDonald's hamburger cooking methods in broiled versus fried. Attacking the leader's flank means hitting them where they are weak. The challenger can concentrate on geographic areas or market segments that the leader has neglected or sees as a low priority. Encirclement means mounting an attack on all fronts, whereas a bypass attack involves avoiding direct confrontation with the market leader. In the guerilla attack, the challenger makes small, periodic raids on the market leader.

c. *Market Follower Strategies.* Unlike market challengers, **follower** organizations shy away from any direct or indirect attacks on market leaders. To date, the lodging sector has behaved in this fashion. For example, there has been very little comparative advertising among hotel companies. Organizations that take this stance try to copy all or some of what the leader does. They go after the same target markets, choose the same advertising media, or add similar services.

This me-too approach is very evident among lodging chains, fast-food restaurants, airlines, and car rental companies. When the leader pioneers a new concept successfully, most of its competitors are quick to follow suit. American Airlines was first to introduce a frequent-flyer program. Now every major airline has one. The same fate befell Holiday Inn's frequent-guest program. Holiday Inn was one of the first of the major organizations to enter the extended-stay hotel business while Marriott,

Hilton, Sheraton, Radisson, and Choice followed. McDonald's Chicken McNuggets have been emulated by Burger King, KFC, and others.

d. *Market Nicher Strategies.* A market nicher is a smaller organization that also avoids direct confrontation with the major companies but does not necessarily follow them closely. It finds a niche in which it specializes. Regional and commuter airlines service the routes that major companies find unprofitable. They have geographic niches. Doughnut shops specialize in baking doughnuts and refuse to broaden their lines to include more fast-food items.

Relationship Marketing and Strategic Alliances

Many experts believe we are now in an era of relationship marketing in the hospitality and travel industry. They suggest that, in developing marketing strategies, all organizations must place an emphasis on building, maintaining, and enhancing long-term relationships with customers, suppliers, travel trade intermediaries, and perhaps even competitors.[9] There are many examples, including airline frequent-flyer and hotel-frequent guest programs, that try to build greater loyalty among customers. The concept of **preferred suppliers or vendors** is another example. Here, airlines, hotel companies, car rental firms, and cruise lines try to increase their shares of selected travel agencies' business by offering extra commission percentage points (overrides). They hope that, by motivating agents through above-the-industry-average rates of commission, they will become their preferred suppliers.

Whereas there are many short-term partnerships in the hospitality and travel industry—one-time cooperative advertising campaigns or promotions involving two or more organizations—**relationship marketing** is concerned with building long-term loyalty among customers, distribution channels, and complementary organizations. Several hospitality and travel organizations have also tried to build long-term relationships with specific types of customers. For example, some companies have tried to build up loyalty among children, including Hyatt Hotels with its *Camp Hyatt* concept and Pizza Hut's *Book It!* Program (Figure 8.11).

Strategic alliances are special long-term relationships formed between two or more hospitality and travel organizations, or between a hospitality and travel organization and one or more other types of organizations. A good example of these special relationships is the partnering of international air carriers, including the Star, SkyTeam, and **one**world alliances. Strategic alliances are a powerful tool enabling business partners to achieve goals together that they could not achieve alone.[10] They are a fast and flexible way to access complementary resources and skills within other organizations.[11]

Partnerships and strategic alliances are discussed further in Chapter 10, and both Chapters 10 and 11 provide more information about the relationship marketing concept.

FIGURE 8.11 Pizza Hut has developed a special relationship with children through its highly successful Book It! Program.

Image copyright Michael Onisiforou, 2008. Used under license from Shutterstock.com

Positioning Approach

The technique of positioning is attributed to two advertising executives—Al Ries and Jack Trout. After a series of articles in 1972, they wrote a book titled *Positioning: The Battle for Your Mind*, in which they said that "positioning is what you do to the mind of the prospect."[12] Since then, other marketing experts have endorsed their idea and have expanded on the original concept.

As defined earlier, positioning is the development of a service and marketing mix to occupy a specific place in the minds of customers within target markets. In other words, the marketer sets out to create a definite image by offering an appropriate service and communicating to potential customers in a way that is consistent with this image. To clarify this technique, you just need to think about the Holland America Line in the cruise business. It uses the tag line, *A Signature of Excellence*, to position itself as an upscale cruising alternative. The company also describes its *Signature difference* with an online video. (See Figure 8.12 which shows Holland America's Single Partner solo traveler program.)

Reasons for Positioning

There are three main reasons for positioning: human perceptual processes, intensified competition, and the sheer volume of advertising to which most people are exposed every day.

1. **Human Perceptual Processes.** Chapter 4 described perception as a method used by the human brain to sort out people's images of the world around them and dump unnecessary information. The marketer whose advertising messages communicate an unclear or confusing

FIGURE 8.12
Holland America Line has developed a clear position for itself as an upscale cruising experience.

image to customers will find these messages ending up as a pile of mental garbage, screened out by highly sophisticated customers. Research has shown that people forget a very high percentage of the commercial messages to which they are exposed. Clear, concise, and simple messages are the key to slipping past perceptual defenses. This, together with well-positioned service offerings, is the essence of positioning.

2. **Intensified Competition.** This book often refers to the growing competitiveness of the hospitality and travel industry. Positioning is a technique used to give a service an image that is unique and different from that of

competitors. One of the classic cases cited by Ries and Trout is Avis Rent A Car System, Inc. The company, recognizing that Hertz was the established leader in car rentals at that time, successfully positioned itself as the industry's number two company, and it firmly implanted the idea that it had to try harder to satisfy its customers.

3. **Volume of Commercial Messages.** People are exposed to hundreds of commercial messages each day, some from hospitality and travel organizations, but most from other advertisers and promoters. The sheer volume of messages makes it impossible for anyone to absorb all they see, hear, and read. To get a person's attention among what many call the advertising and other online and offline promotional clutter requires effective positioning. Advertisements must stand out from the crowd by being distinctive, while also communicating clear, non-confusing ideas.

Essentials for Effective Positioning

Positioning a service comes after market segments have been identified and target markets chosen. The following information is essential for effective positioning:

1. Target market customers' needs and the benefits they are seeking
2. The organization's industry sector category membership and primary competitors
3. The organization's competitive strengths and weaknesses
4. Primary competitors' strengths and weaknesses
5. Customers' perceptions of the organization relative to primary competitors

As you will probably realize, marketing research must be done to get this five types of vital information. Some of this comes from the situation analysis and the rest from marketing research studies.

Sector category membership means brands of hospitality and travel products and services or groups of destinations with which the organization most closely competes and compares.[13] This may depend on the target market, since sets of primary competitors can vary according to customer groupings.

The Five Ds of Positioning

Effective positioning starts by establishing a clear understanding of target market customers and especially what benefits they are seeking. In other words, the hospitality and travel organization must first find a cogent or salient reason, or proposition for customers to want to purchase.[14] The second step in positioning is to choose an image that the organization will try to place in the minds of customers within the selected target markets. The third step is that the organization or destination must be differentiated from its primary competitors, again from the perspective of the selected target market customers. The fourth step is to design the services or products and communicate with customers in the selected target markets in a way that supports the chosen image. The fifth step is to make sure that the organization or destination delivers on the image that it has created. For example, a company portraying a top-quality image will not succeed if its employees provide poor-quality service. An airline boasting the best-available record for on-time arrivals had better make sure that its planes arrive on time. Positioning can backfire if what is promised is not what is delivered.

An easy way to remember the steps required for effective positioning is to think of them as the **five Ds of positioning**:

1. *Documenting*: Identifying the benefits that are most important to the customers who buy the organization's service and products.
2. *Deciding*: Deciding on the image that the organization wants customers to have within its selected target markets.
3. *Differentiating*: Pinpointing the primary competitors the organization wants to appear different from and the things that makes it different.
4. *Designing*: Creating product or service differences and communicating these in positioning statements and other aspects of the marketing mix (8 Ps).
5. *Delivering*: Making good on the organization's promises!

Positioning Approaches

There are several different ways to create unique images in customers' minds, including specific and general positioning and positioning by information versus imagery.[15] A specific positioning approach is where only one customer benefit is selected and concentrated on. The Belize Tourist Board provides a good example of the specific positioning approach when it puts across the image of the country as *Mother Nature's best kept secret*. The island of Dominica uses a similar theme by calling itself *The Nature Island of Dominica*. These DMO examples specifically position the countries for people interested in nature-based travel or ecotourism. In the lodging business, Courtyard by Marriott specifically appeals to the business travel through the positioning statement, *Multi-Tasking Made Fun*. The **general positioning approach** promises more than one benefit that is not as directly obvious. The customer almost has to read into advertising and service offerings to discover the benefits that are available.

A position can be created at a cognitive level by stating clear, factual and objective information. Earlier in this chapter you learned about Arizona's tourism positioning as the Grand Canyon State (Figure 8.2). No one could argue with this claim by the Arizona Office of Tourism. Positioning can also be done at a more emotional level by using more intangible concepts expressed through images, moods, symbols, or **positioning statements**. Getting a place in the customer's mind through an emotional appeal is shown in the strategy of the Hyatt Corporation. The company's *Hyatt Touch* concept expresses the high level of care that it has for its customers and associates (employees).[16]

There are six possible positioning approaches:[17]

1. Positioning on specific product features
2. Positioning on benefits, problem solution, or needs
3. Positioning for specific usage occasions
4. Positioning for user category
5. Positioning against another product
6. Positioning by product class dissociation

1. **Positioning on Specific Product Features.** This is exactly the same as the concept of specific positioning discussed earlier. A direct link is usually made between some aspect of the service and a customer benefit. It is, of course, possible to position more than one feature. One excellent example of this positioning approach is that used by the increasingly popular resort spas. For example, the Golden Door in Escondido, California is a health spa resort that was "created by a woman for women, Golden Door offers an extraordinary opportunity for catharsis and rejuvenation this renowned haven essentially serves as a women's health spa retreat, offering a highly inviting sanctuary for those in search of a healthier lifestyle and true inner peace."[18] Another example here is the Province of Nova Scotia, which positions itself as *Canada's Seacoast*.

2. **Positioning on Benefits, Problem Solution, or Needs.** The travel literature is loaded with examples of this approach. Most of these positioning statements include the pronoun *you* for close association with the customer's needs or problems. Ontario says it's *Yours to discover*; California suggests that you will *Find Yourself Here* (by visiting the state); and New Hampshire says *You are going to love it here. See yourself in the Nation's Capital, Canberra* is the benefit proposed by Australian Capital Tourism. If you go to Motel 6's website, you will see the statement, *Goin' 6*, a concept that communicates a financial benefit to potential guests.

3. **Positioning for Specific Usage Occasions.** Here the positioning is based on a specific occasion when the customer may find a use for the service. Sandals suggest that *love is all you need* to enjoy the WEDDING-MOONS™ (or destination weddings) at Sandals. This is part of Sandals Resorts positioning approach for the wedding and honeymoon market. Reunion planners and participants are invited to *Discover America's Reunion Resort* at Smuggler's Notch, Vermont.

4. **Positioning for User Category.** The approach here is to identify and associate with a specific group of customers. Couples, a Caribbean resort group, offer vacations for couples. VisitScotland positions itself prominently with golfers as *The Home of Golf*.

5. **Positioning Against Another Product.** As we will see later, another name for this approach is comparative or competitive advertising. We have already talked about the classic examples of Burger King versus McDonald's, and Avis versus Hertz. In 2004, Burger King reinstated its classic positioning statement of *Have It Your Way®*, which underlines its

INTERNET MARKETING

Positioning an Organization on the Internet

- How does an organization put across the intended image about itself through the Internet? That is a very challenging question, but let's takes a look at one well-known hotel brand that is doing a very effective job of online positioning.
- *You don't just stay here—You belong.* This is how you are greeted at the Sheraton Hotels & Resorts website, with a welcome that's warmed by a bright orange background. In fact, this is part of Sheraton's "Warm Welcome" positioning approach that was introduced in April 2006.
- The Sheraton "Belong" positioning is around "warm, comforting, connections."
- The connections element of the positioning is well-demonstrated on Sheraton's website in the *Share Your Story* feature. Past guests share their experiences about staying at Sheraton properties and this helps to build up a feeling of belonging to a group of people with things in common. Some experts call this "social media" or user-generated content.
- The stories and other contents are organized geographically into what Sheraton calls its "our global neighborhood."
- You might think that Sheraton's website approach is a good way of sharing "online word-of-mouth" and their management seems to think so, too.

Sources: Sheraton Hotels & Resorts. (2006). *You Belong at Sheraton. Sheraton launches $20 million ad campaign and signature "Warm Welcome" experience*; Sheraton Hotels & Resorts. (2006). *Sheraton Hotels introduces new website and becomes first in the hotel industry to invite travelers to provide content*; Sheraton Hotels & Resorts. (2008). **http://www.sheraton.com/**

Student Questions

1. Do you think that this approach to getting past guest stories and putting them on its website will benefit Sheraton? Why or why not?
2. Are there any challenges or potential problems that hotels might experience in setting up social exchange networks such as this?
3. What steps could Sheraton follow to make the greatest use of the best stories that it receives apart from just publishing them online?

claim that it individualizes hamburgers for its customers according to their preferences.[19] Another more recent media battle between two industry leaders has been that of the Visa and American Express cards. Visa launched television commercials showing events and attractions at which the American Express card was not accepted. For example, Visa was a major sponsor of the Beijing 2008 Summer Olympic Games and the exclusive payment card for that event. Visa frequently used the statement, "Visa is everywhere."

6. **Positioning by Product Class Dissociation.** What an organization tries to do here is make its services appear different from all competitors. We have already talked about a few examples, including Windstar Cruises. With its *180° degrees from ordinary®* positioning statement, Windstar Cruises sets itself apart from all the other cruise lines.

Marketing Objectives

The next step before developing the marketing plan is to establish marketing objectives for each target market. Earlier **marketing objectives** were defined as the measurable goals that a hospitality and travel organization attempts to achieve within a specific time period for a specific target market.

Benefits of Marketing Objectives

An organization without marketing objectives can be compared to a plane flying without its black box and pilot's flight log. Remember that two of the five key questions in the hospitality and travel marketing system are, "How do we make sure we get there?" and "How do we know if we got there?" With no marketing objectives, you cannot even begin to answer these fundamental questions. The benefits of marketing objectives are as follows:

1. Giving marketing managers a way to measure progress toward their goals and make timely adjustments to marketing programs and activities
2. Providing a yardstick for management to measure the success of marketing programs and activities
3. Representing a benchmark for judging the potential return on alternative marketing-mix activities
4. Providing a frame of reference for all those involved directly in marketing
5. Giving broad directions for the scope and types of marketing programs and activities required in a specific period

Requirements of Marketing Objectives

There are two main dangers to avoid when setting marketing objectives. The first is not to mechanically set them based totally on previous-period results. If there is one thing that can be predicted with 100 percent confidence in the hospitality and travel industry, it is that tomorrow will never be exactly the same as today. The second is that objectives must not be built on guesses, hunches, wishful thinking, or natural intuition. They must always be built on thorough research and analysis, such as that described in Chapters 5 and 6. Additionally, objectives must be consistent with the selected marketing strategy and the relative priorities attached to each selected target market.

All marketing objectives should be:

1. **Target-Market Specific**: Objectives must be set for each target market selected for marketing attention. This is a crucial step to ensure that the investment in individual target markets is justified. When an objective is further detailed into tasks or activities, the costs of pursuing a given target market can be determined. This can then be compared to the revenues and profits generated, giving an indication of each target market's return on investment (ROI).

2. **Results Oriented**: Objectives must be expressed in terms of desired results. In marketing, an objective usually means an improvement over a current situation (e.g., an increase in volume, revenues, or market share). Results should be written using one of these yardsticks. They provide an essential tool for marketing managers as they control, measure, and evaluate the success of marketing plans.

3. **Quantitative**: Objectives must be expressed numerically so that progress and results can be measured. When they are set in qualitative or non-numerical terms, they are almost impossible to measure and subjective judgments enter the picture. By attaching numbers to each objective, the marketing manager is able to set progress points or *milestones* when actual performance can be checked against desired performance. Corrective measures can be taken quickly if required. At the end of a marketing planning period, the manager has a way to gauge success and the amount of variation from desired performance.

4. **Time Specific**: Objectives must be set for specific time periods. They usually span one or two years or the duration of the marketing plan, but they can also be set for a season, weekends or weekdays, a part of the day, or some combination of weeks or months.

A few examples of specific marketing objectives will probably help you grasp these four criteria for effective marketing objectives:

a. *Restaurant*: To increase the average check (result) from business lunches (target market) by 10 percent (quantified) between January 1 and May 31 (time specific).

b. *Hotel*: To increase occupied room nights (result) by 5,000 (quantified) from the corporate meetings market (target market) in the next calendar year (time specific).

c. *Theme Park*: To increase senior citizen (target market) ticket sales (result) by 1,000 (quantified) in the winter season of this year (time specific).

Setting marketing objectives is the last step in answering the question, "Where would we like to be?" Now that the organization knows precisely what it wants to achieve in the upcoming period, it is time to draw up a marketing plan for meeting its objectives.

Chapter Conclusion

Every organization must decide where it wants to be in the future. Following marketing segmentation analysis, choices have to be made between alternative marketing strategies, positioning approaches, and objectives. Making these decisions is part of planning. The service's product life-cycle (PLC) stage and the organization's competitive position influence the selection from among alternative approaches. Marketing research information provides the basis for these decisions.

Having a marketing strategy is similar to having a map to help you get where you want to be. Even with a good map, some people get lost. More careful and detailed planning is necessary to get to the final destination.

REVIEW QUESTIONS

1. How are the terms *marketing strategy, positioning,* and *marketing objective* defined in this book?
2. What is a segmented marketing strategy and what is an undifferentiated strategy?
3. What are the four alternative marketing strategies by target market focus and how do they differ?
4. Should marketing strategies be changed in the four stages of the product life cycle (PLC)? If so, which strategies work best during each stage?
5. Should smaller or lower-share organizations use the same marketing strategies as industry sector leaders? If not, how should their approaches differ?
6. Why has positioning become so important in today's business climate?
7. What information and steps (the five Ds) are required for effective positioning?
8. What are the six positioning approaches?
9. Why are marketing objectives so important in effective marketing?
10. Which four requirements must marketing objectives satisfy?

CHAPTER ASSIGNMENTS

1. Review the recent marketing strategies of three leading hotel chains, restaurant chains, airlines, cruise companies, tourism destinations, travel agency chains, or other hospitality/travel organizations. Which types of marketing strategies are they using? What are their target markets? What image have they tried to create and which positioning approach is used? How have their strategies and positioning changed in the past five years? Use illustrations of advertising or other promotions to back up your points.
2. The product life cycle is a good general guide, but it does not always reflect reality. Discuss this statement by describing companies, destinations, services, or facilities that have extended their life cycles or otherwise not exactly followed the PLC.

3. This chapter notes that each industry sector tends to include market leaders, challengers, followers, and nichers. Select one sector of the hospitality and travel industry and identify the organizations that play these individual roles. What strategies and approaches does each organization use to improve or maintain its competitive position? You can either do this on a national or your local community basis. How successful has each selected organization been with its choice of strategy and related approaches?

4. The owner of a small hospitality and travel business has asked you for some help in developing marketing objectives. What general guidelines would you suggest for objective setting? Detail how you would help the owner develop these objectives. Develop a set of hypothetical (or real) objectives for the business.

WEB RESOURCES

Arizona Office of Tourism, http://www.arizonaguide.com/
Belize Tourist Board, http://www.travelbelize.org/
Burger King, http://www.burgerking.com/
Carnival Corporation, http://www.carnivalcorp.com/
Couples, http://www.couples.com/
ElderTreks, http://www.eldertreks.com/
Dominica, http://www.dominica.dm/
Golden Door, http://www.goldendoor.com/
Holland America Line, http://www.hollandamerica.com/
Global Hyatt, http://www.hyatt.com/
McDonald's, http://www.mcdonalds.com/
Motel 6 Goin'6, http://www.goin6.com/
oneworld Alliance, http://www.oneworldalliance.com/
Panda Express, http://www.pandaexpress.com/
Sandals Resorts, http://www.sandals.com/
SkyTeam Alliance, http://www.skyteam.com/
Star Alliance, http://www.star-alliance.com/
The Queen Mary, http://www.queenmary.com/
Travcoa, http://www.travcoa.com/
Visa, http://www.visa.com/
Windstar Cruises, http://www.windstar.com/

REFERENCES

1. Kotler, Philip, and Kevin Lane Keller. 2006. *Marketing Management*. 12th ed. Upper Saddle River, N.J.: Pearson Prentice Hall, 336–338.

2. Perreault, William D., and E. Jerome McCarthy. 2000. *Essentials of Marketing: A Global-Managerial Approach*. 8th ed. Boston: Irwin McGraw-Hill.

3.   American Marketing Association. 2007. *Dictionary of Marketing Terms*, http://www.marketingpower.com/_layouts/Dictionary.aspx, accessed December 13, 2008.

4.   Kotler, Philip, and Kevin Lane Keller. 2006. *Marketing Management*. 12th ed. Upper Saddle River, N.J.: Pearson Prentice Hall, 303–304.

5.   Kotler, Philip, and Kevin Lane Keller. 2006. Marketing Management. 12th ed. Upper Saddle River, N.J.: Pearson Prentice Hall, 304–307.

6.   Jiang, Weizhong, Chekitan S. Dev, and Vithala R. Rao. 2002. "Brand Extension and Customer Loyalty: Evidence from the Lodging Industry." *Cornell Hotel and Restaurant Administration Quarterly*, 43(4), 5–16.

7.   Kotler, Philip, and Kevin Lane Keller. 2006. *Marketing Management*. 12th ed. Upper Saddle River, N.J.: Pearson Prentice Hall, 323.

8.   Kotler, Philip, and Kevin Lane Keller. 2006. *Marketing Management*. 12th ed. Upper Saddle River, N.J.: Pearson Prentice Hall, 329–333.

9.   McKenna, Regis. 1993. *Relationship Marketing: Successful Strategies for the Age of the Customer*. New York, N.Y.: Basic Books.

10. Foreign Affairs and International Trade Canada. 2002. *Strategic Alliances*, http://www.infoexport.gc.ca/en/DisplayDocument.jsp?did=5273&gid=538, accessed December 13, 2008.

11. Dyer, Jeffrey H., Prashant Kale, and Harbir Singh. 2001. "How to Make Strategic Alliances Work." *MIT Sloan Management Review, Summer 2001*, 37–43.

12. Ries, Al, and Jack Trout. 2001. *Positioning: The Battle for Your Mind*. 2nd ed. Boston: McGraw-Hill.

13. Kotler, Philip, and Kevin Lane Keller. 2006. *Marketing Management*. 12th ed. Upper Saddle River, N.J.: Pearson Prentice Hall, 289.

14. Kotler, Philip, and Kevin Lane Keller. 2006. *Marketing Management*. 12th ed. Upper Saddle River, N.J.: Pearson Prentice Hall, 288.

15. Assael, Henry. 2003. *Consumer Behavior: A Strategic Approach*. Boston, Massachusetts: Houghton Mifflin Company.

16. Hyatt Hotels Corporation. 2008. *About Hyatt Hotels*, http://www.hcareers.com/seeker/employer-profiles/hyatt-hotels-resorts/?feb=true, accessed December 13, 2008.

17. Mahajan, Vijay, and Yoram Wind. 2002. "Got Emotional Product Positioning." *Marketing Management*, May/June, 36–41.

18. Golden Door. 2008. *Women Only*, http://www.goldendoor.com/rates_and_reservations/women_only.cfm, accessed December 13, 2008.

19. Burger King Corporation. 2008. *Marketing and Advertising History*, http://www.bk.com/companyinfo/corporation/history.aspx, accessed December 12, 2008.

chapter 9

The Marketing Plan and the 8 Ps
Where Would We Like To Be?

O V E R V I E W

Where would we like to be? The answer to this question is spelled out in a marketing plan. In Chapter 3, this document was compared to a plane's flight plan that guides its users safely to their final destination. This chapter begins by defining the marketing plan and explaining its role in tactical planning. It lists the contents of a plan and describes the benefits of having one.

The chapter then provides the step-by-step procedure for preparing a plan. It ties in concepts discussed earlier, including market segmentation, marketing strategy, positioning, marketing objectives, and marketing mix (8 Ps). The scene is set for the next ten chapters, as each of the 8 Ps of hospitality and travel marketing is discussed.

O B J E C T I V E S

Having read this chapter, you should be able to:

- Define the term *marketing plan.*
- Explain the difference between tactical and strategic marketing planning.
- Describe eight requirements for an effective marketing plan.
- Explain the benefits of having a marketing plan.
- Describe the contents of a marketing plan.
- Differentiate among the four approaches to developing marketing budgets and recommend one of these approaches.
- Describe the three major steps involved in preparing a marketing plan.
- List and explain each of the 8 Ps of hospitality and travel marketing.

KEY TERMS

competitive budgeting
contingency planning
8 Ps
executive summary
historical budgeting
hospitality and travel
  marketing system
implementation plan
marketing management
marketing mix

marketing plan
marketing plan rationale
metrics
milestones
objective-and-task budgeting
packaging
partnership (cooperative
  marketing)
people
place

pricing
product/service mix
programming
promotion (promotional mix)
rule-of-thumb budgeting
strategic market plan
strategic plans
tactical plans
zero-based budgeting

Would you climb aboard an airliner if you knew that its pilots had no flight plan? Unless you have a great love for danger, you probably answered "no." An organization without a marketing plan is like a plane with no flight plan. Both may know where they are and where they want to be, but everything in between is unknown. A plane can stray off course and end up not reaching its final destination because it burns too much fuel. Similarly, a plan-less organization can find itself going down the wrong paths and using up its marketing budget before it achieves its objectives. As the old saying goes, "Failing to plan is planning to fail."

Marketing Plan Definition

In this book, a **marketing plan** is defined as a written plan that is used to guide an organization's marketing activities for a period of two years or less (Figure 9.1). It is quite detailed and specific, and it helps an organization coordinate the many steps and people that play a role in marketing.

Differences between Strategic and Tactical Planning

Marketing plans are what most experts call **tactical plans** or short-term plans. It is not enough just to have marketing plans, however. Long-term or **strategic plans** are needed. These three-year or more plans are more general and less detailed than tactical plans. They ensure that long-term marketing goals are attained. There must be a close fit between the strategies and objectives in each marketing plan and those in the **strategic market plan** (Figure 9.1). In

particular, the marketing plan must support the organization's vision for the long-term, and be consistent with its mission (Figure 9.2).

Marketing plans take an in-depth look at the organization's marketing mix and contain detailed budgets and timetables. Strategic market plans are more concerned with the external marketing environment and the opportunities and challenges in the medium and long term.

Requirements for an Effective Marketing Plan

Just as every building needs a solid foundation, a marketing plan must be rooted in careful research and analysis. Earlier chapters discussed the situation analysis, marketing research, market segmentation, marketing strategy selection, positioning, and marketing objectives. The marketing plan builds on all of these, giving management a *blueprint* for action (Figure 9.3).

There are a few universal truths about all blueprints, whether they are architectural or the ones we are looking at right now. Every architect and construction manager knows that original blueprints must be modified for unexpected occurrences. They realize that many people are needed to turn an on-paper plan into reality. It is accepted that things must be carefully staged and timed. Walls come before roofs and rough carpentry before fine carpentry, for example. Building professionals also recognize the value of careful construction budgeting, contingency planning, and objective-setting. They are aware that a pre-selected mixture of materials and human skills is essential to meet specifications.

FIGURE 9.2 All successful marketing plans start by describing a vision of the future.

Image copyright Marinini, 2008. Used under license from Shutterstock.com

The requirements of a marketing plan are very similar to those of a construction blueprint. A marketing plan must meet the criteria shown in Figure 9.4 and described below:

1. **Fact-based.** A marketing plan must build on previous research and analysis. A plan established on managerial hunches is like a house of cards; if one key assumption is proven wrong, the whole plan falls apart.

FIGURE 9.3 The marketing plan is the manager's blueprint for action.

Image copyright Mikael Damkier, 2008. Used under license from Shutterstock.com

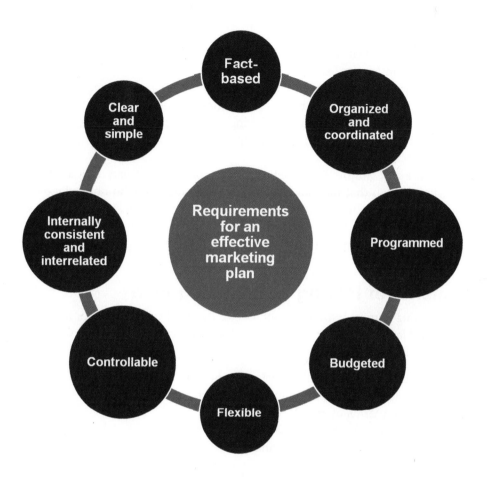

FIGURE 9.4
Requirements for an
effective marketing plan.

2. **Organized and coordinated.** A marketing plan must be as specific and detailed as possible. It needs to clearly identify the departments and people responsible for specific tasks; it must also describe the promotional and other materials that are required. The required level of workmanship should be clarified, including the quality and level of effort and service from all involved.

3. **Programmed.** A marketing plan must be orchestrated so that activities are carefully sequenced. Timing is vitally important in marketing. Thus, a marketing plan must have a detailed, staged timetable.

4. **Budgeted.** Every marketing plan must be budgeted carefully. In fact, several tentative budgets should be prepared before the organization decides on a final figure.

5. **Flexible.** Unforeseen events will happen. Therefore, no plan should be cast in stone. The marketing plan should be adjusted if it appears that objectives will definitely not be achieved, or if there are unexpected competitive moves. **Contingency planning** must be built in. This means allowing some room in the plan and marketing budget to take care of unexpected events.

6. **Controllable.** Making a plan work as it was originally designed is perhaps even more difficult than developing it in the first place. Every plan must contain measurable objectives and ways to determine, during the

planning period, if adequate progress is being made toward satisfying these objectives. The plan must also define who is responsible for measuring progress.

7. **Internally consistent and interrelated.** Most parts of a marketing plan are interrelated and, therefore, need to be consistent. For example, advertising, Internet marketing and other promotions must work together for greatest impact using integrated marketing communication (IMC).

8. **Clear and simple.** Being detailed does not have to mean difficult. It is not enough that the plan's architect is the only one who understands it. The efforts of many go into creating a successful marketing plan. Objectives and tasks must be clearly communicated. Possible areas of overlap, confusion, or misunderstanding need to be eliminated.

Benefits of Having a Marketing Plan

A marketing plan is, without doubt, one of the most useful tools for any organization. Having a written marketing plan as described in this book has the following five key benefits:

1. Activities matched with target markets
2. Consistency of objectives and target-market priorities
3. Common terms of reference
4. Assistance in measuring marketing success
5. Continuity in long-term planning

1. **Activities matched with target markets.** Assuming that a segmented marketing strategy is being used, a plan ensures that activities are focused only on chosen target markets (Figure 9.5). One of the steps involved in writing the plan is detailing the marketing mix (8 Ps) on a market-by-market basis. Budget waste from appealing to unattractive target markets is avoided.

2. **Consistency of objectives and target-market priorities.** How far should the plan go to meet objectives? Should each target market get equal attention? These are two questions that are resolved by a good marketing plan, which ensures that the level of effort is consistent with the marketing objectives for each target market and the relative size of each market. The more ambitious is the objective, the greater the required effort. Usually it does not make sense for an organization to spend 80 percent of its marketing budget on a target market or markets that contribute only 20 percent to its sales or profits, yet this happens frequently. Although an exact, one-to-one ratio is not absolutely essential or possible, the share of budget and a target market's percentage contribution to sales or profits should be quite similar.

3. **Common terms of reference.** A marketing plan details activities for many people both within and outside an organization. A good plan

FIGURE 9.5 A good marketing plan matches activities with the pinpointed target markets.

provides common terms of reference for all. It carefully coordinates their efforts. It improves communication among those responsible for marketing and is a great help in orienting outside advisors such as advertising agency staff and website designers.

4. **Assistance in measuring marketing success.** A marketing plan is a tool of **marketing management**, because it provides the basis for controlling and evaluating marketing activities. In other words, a marketing plan plays a vital role in answering two key questions: How do we make sure we get there? (Control) and How do we know if we got there? (Evaluation).

5. **Continuity in long-term planning.** Marketing plans complement strategic market plans and provide a link between short- and long-term planning. They ensure that an organization's long-term goals are always kept in focus. Because they are carefully rationalized and detailed, marketing plans remain useful even if their originators leave the organization.

Did You Know?

What Are the Marketing Goals for Hawaii's Tourism?

- Hawaii received 7,627,819 million tourists in 2007. These visitor numbers were virtually unchanged from 2006.
- There were just over 503,019 cruise visitors to Hawaii in 2007; up 20.9 percent over 2006.
- The tourism vision for Hawaii is that "by 2015, tourism in Hawaii will:

  - Honor Hawaii's people and heritage;
  - Value and perpetuate Hawaii's natural and cultural resources;
  - Engender mutual respect among all stakeholders;
  - Support a vital and sustainable economy; and
  - Provide a unique, memorable and enriching visitor experience."
  - The marketing goal for Hawaii as stated in the Hawaii Tourism Strategic Plan is "To develop marketing programs that contribute to sustainable economic growth."

- The marketing goals for Hawaii in 2008 are to:

  - Grow Hawaii's share of market by tactically aligning our efforts with key partners to impact grow arrivals, length of stay and per person daily spending.
  - Cultivate the markets through targeting key lifestyle segments.
  - Address historical shoulder periods through HT Partners collaborative co-op plans.
  - Support airline interest in our destination.

Source: Hawaii Tourism Authority. (2008). *Hawaii Tourism Strategic Plan, 2005–2015*; State of Hawaii Department of Business, Economic Development & Tourism.

Contents of a Marketing Plan

There are three parts to a marketing plan: the executive summary, the marketing plan rationale, and the implementation plan. The **executive summary** is a brief summary of the major highlights of the marketing plan; it is for the organization's executives to quickly review. The **marketing plan rationale** explains the facts, analyses, and assumptions upon which the marketing plan is based. It describes the marketing strategies, target markets, positioning approaches, and marketing objectives selected for the planning period. The **implementation plan** (action plan) details the activities, marketing budget, staff responsibilities, timetable, and methods of controlling, measuring and evaluating activities. Figure 9.6 provides a table of contents for the written marketing plan. You will see that a thorough marketing plan addresses all five key questions in the hospitality and travel marketing system.

FIGURE 9.6 The Table of Contents for a marketing plan.

A. Executive Summary

B. Marketing Plan Rationale

    1. Situation Analysis Highlights (Where are we now?)

        a. Environmental Analysis

        b. Location and Community Analysis

        c. Primary Competitor Analysis

        d. Market Potential Analysis

        e. Services Analysis

        f. Marketing Position and Plan Analysis

        g. Major Strengths, Weaknesses, Opportunities, and Constraints

    2. Selected Marketing Strategy (Where would we like to be?)

        a. Market Segmentation and Target Markets

        b. Marketing Strategy

        c. Marketing Mixes

        d. Positioning Approaches

        e. Marketing Objectives

C. Implementation Plan

    1. Activities Plan (How do we get there?)

        a. Activities by Target Market for Each Mix Element

        b. Responsibilities for Activities

        c. Timetable and Activity Schedule

    2. Marketing Budget (How do we get there?)

        a. Budget by Target Market

        b. Budget by Marketing-Mix Element

        c. Contingency Funds

    3. Control Procedures (How do we make sure we get there?)

        a. Results Expected from Each Activity

        b. Progress Reporting and Measures

    4. Evaluation Procedures (How do we know if we got there?)

        a. Measurements

        b. Performance Standards

        c. Evaluation Timetable

Executive Summary

The executive summary should be no more than two to four pages long and should be easy to read. It is called "executive" because executives can peruse it quickly, but still get a good grasp of the main reasons, initiatives, and costs for the marketing plan. A good approach is to sum up the highlights of each of the main sections of the marketing plan rationale and implementation plan. These highlights can be presented in the order in which they appear in the plan, according to the five key questions in the hospitality and travel marketing system.

Marketing Plan Rationale

Although most people remember what is to be done, it is easy to forget why it is being done. The marketing plan rationale draws together on paper all the research and analysis discussed in Chapters 5 and 6. It provides a historic record for those putting together future marketing plans and strategic market plans. The marketing plan rationale is also very helpful to outside advisors, such as advertising agencies and website designers, who are asked to handle only one specific task.

1. **Situation Analysis Highlights** (*Where are we now?*). The situation analysis is a study of an organization's strengths, weaknesses, and opportunities. Chapter 5 pointed out that the situation analysis plays an important role in structuring marketing plans. Why? Because marketing plans must build upon the organization's marketing strengths, address major competitive weaknesses, and capitalize on identified opportunities.

    Some people combine the situation analysis and the marketing plan into one project that is printed in a single document. This book recommends that they be two separate, but closely integrated documents. Only the situation analysis highlights should be written up in the marketing plan, and there is little need to include the detailed worksheets.

    a. *Environmental Analysis.* There are various trends in the external environment that can have a positive or negative effect on hospitality and travel organizations. These trends include competitive and industry-wide, economic, political and legislative, societal and cultural, and technological factors. The marketing plan should list and briefly discuss the major opportunities and threats presented. It should explain what impact is expected during the planning period.

    b. *Location and Community Analysis.* What are the key events predicted for the local community and immediate surrounding area during the planning period? New factory or plant openings, major events to be staged, business closures or workforce reductions, residential development, industrial expansion, and new highway construction or redesign are just a few things that can have a very positive or negative effect on an organization or destination in a short time span. These events should be identified and summarized in the marketing plan, and their impacts reviewed.

    c. *Primary Competitor Analysis.* What new approaches are expected from our most direct competitors during the next 24 months? Will these organizations add to or improve their services? Are new promotional efforts or campaigns expected? These are the main questions that the marketing plan should address. It should also highlight each side's competitive strengths and weaknesses.

    d. *Market Potential Analysis.* What is likely to happen in the near future with past and potential customers? What are the major trends in our target markets? Are new marketing activities required to retain past

INDUSTRY TRENDS

In order to launch any promotion or campaign to encourage visitors to explore the Grand Canyon State, AOT first needs a broad understanding of current industry trends.

In order to launch any promotion or campaign to encourage visitors to explore the Grand Canyon State, AOT first needs a broad understanding of current industry trends. As we prepare for FY 07, several of these trends will help us execute informed, targeted promotions.

SHORTER TRIPS, CLOSER TO HOME

Even more than four years after the events of 9/11, people are still taking shorter trips closer to home, a trend also related to the rising gasoline prices. AOT has responded to this trend by adding instate and regional marketing efforts to our already established long haul marketing program. Audiences in these different markets need to receive different messages, so AOT tailored our advertising to speak to the specific needs of these travelers and encourage them to explore Arizona or visit from a neighboring state.

GEN X AND EXTREME GEN X MARKETS

AOT is also staying ahead of the curve by reaching out to new markets, including the Gen X and Extreme Gen X travelers. Target audiences in these developmental markets are typically coming from short haul destinations or Arizona's neighboring states. While these travelers do not spend as much money and travel as far as our established affluent Baby Boomer market, they have the potential to do so as they grow into their careers and family lives. By establishing Arizona as a premier travel destination with them now, they will continue to consider vacations in Arizona as they grow older and move into a higher income bracket.

EMPTY NESTERS AND AFFLUENT BOOMERS

As the Baby Boomer population begins to turn 60, the leisure time they have available for travel increases. This group is the wealthiest, most educated and most well-traveled generation in U.S. history. AOT is renewing efforts to attract this lucrative segment by aggressively positioning Arizona as a top-of-mind travel destination and entering into new markets that have a high density of affluent boomers.

WELLNESS TRAVEL

In response to this growing domestic trend, AOT has made Arizona's wellness product offerings more visible to consumers, including advertising featuring spas and outdoor recreation. Additionally, AOT's new Web site will include expanded spa and park listings.

INCREASED INTERNATIONAL TRAVEL

Favorable economic conditions in Arizona's top international markets have supported an increase of foreign travel to the United States and Arizona. While AOT has established marketing programs in Canada, Mexico, the UK, Germany and Japan, the increase in international travel opens the door for AOT to enter new foreign markets. Research indicates that France, Belgium and the Netherlands present a viable opportunity for Arizona. In addition to these new markets, China continues to grow in importance as the tourism market of the future. While it is not a primary international market for FY 07, it is on the radar screen for future international marketing development.

FY 07 Marketing Plan and Programs Guide | 4

FIGURE 9.7 A section of the marketing plan rationale on market trends from the Arizona Office of Tourism.

customers? Are there ways to encourage greater use of our services from past or existing customers, or to tap into additional target markets? Answers to these questions, including the highlights of special marketing research studies, should be included. Figure 9.7 shows a section of the marketing plan rationale from the 2007 Marketing Plan of the Arizona Office of Tourism that highlights target market trends.

e. *Services Analysis.* What will be done during the next one to two years to improve or augment our organization's services? What research findings or subsequent analysis motivate these changes? The marketing plan should discuss such development projects and how they will be integrated with other marketing-mix (8 P) activities.

f. *Marketing Position and Plan Analysis.* Have you ever driven in a strange city and gotten lost? What's the best way to refocus and get back on track? You could ask a friendly policeman or gas/petrol station attendant. But another method is to retrace the route that you took to get lost in the first place. The marketing plan and position analysis does just that; it goes over what has been done before so important lessons can be learned for future marketing planning. A synopsis of the organization's current positioning in its target markets and the effectiveness of activities in previous marketing plans is presented.

g. *Major Strengths, Weaknesses, Opportunities, and Constraints.* This part of the plan is similar to a summary. It forces marketers to consolidate all key situation analysis and other research findings. It should involve attaching relative importance weightings and priorities to identified strengths, weaknesses, opportunities, and constraints.

2. **Selected Marketing Strategy (*Where would we like to be?*).** The second part of the marketing plan rationale details the strategy that the organization will follow in the next one to two years. It explains the facts, assumptions, and decisions influencing strategy choices that were discussed in Chapters 7 and 8.

    a. *Market Segmentation and Target Markets.* The plan should briefly review the segmentation approach (single-stage, two-stage, or multi-stage) and characteristics (geography, demographics, purpose of trip, psychographics, behavior, product-related, or channels of distribution) used to divide the market. Some statistics should be presented on the size of the market segments and the organization's penetration or market share of each. The selected target markets should be discussed, along with the reasons for choosing them. It is also useful to briefly review why other market segments are not being targeted and how the chosen target markets will interact with each other.

    b. *Marketing Strategy.* Will a single-target-market, concentrated, full-coverage, or undifferentiated strategy be used? How has the strategy's choice been influenced by product life-cycle stage and the organization's position in the industry sector? The plan should explain the analysis and assumptions that supported these choices.

    c. *Marketing Mixes.* How many sets of the 8 Ps (product, people, packaging, programming, pricing, place, promotion, and partnership) will be used, and why and how will they be employed? The marketing plan should review these individually for each target market. A more detailed list of activities comes later in the implementation plan.

    d. *Positioning Approaches.* Will the organization try to maintain and enhance its image in each target market, or will repositioning be attempted? Which of the six positioning approaches (specific product features, benefits/problem solution/needs, specific usage occasions, user category, against another product, or product class dissociation) will be used, and why? The marketing plan should address these questions and explain how the positioning approaches will be reflected in each marketing-mix element (8 Ps).

    e. *Marketing Objectives.* The objectives for each target market should be clearly stated. They have to be results-oriented, stated in numerical terms, and time specific. A good idea suggested by some experts is to break up each objective into **milestones**.[1] This means dividing each objective into sub-objectives with specific time deadlines (e.g., a 15-percent increase for a year may be divided into a 2-percent gain in the first quarter, a 5-percent gain in the next two quarters, and a 3-percent gain in the final quarter).

Implementation Plan (Action Plan)

There are many detailed arrangements to be made and steps that are involved in creating a successful marketing plan. The function of the implementation plan is to specify all the required activities, responsibilities, costs and budget, time schedules, and control and evaluation procedures. It is sometimes called an action plan. Many marketing plans fail because they are not detailed enough. Too much interpretation of the plan has to be done by those responsible for activities, often resulting in missed deadlines, unproductive spending, and general confusion. It is a far greater mistake to have too little detail rather than too much detail in the implementation plan.

A good way to remember the contents of the implementation plan is to think of them as answers to *what, where, when, who*, and *how* questions.

1.   **What** activities or tasks will be carried out and what will be spent on them? (*Activities by Target Market* and *Marketing Budget*)
2.   **Where** will the activities be carried out? (*Activities by Target Market*)
3.   **When** are activities to commence and be completed? (*Timetable and Activity Schedule*)
4.   **Who** is responsible for each activity? (*Responsibilities for Activities*)
5.   **How** will the plan be controlled and evaluated? (*Control Procedures* and *Evaluation Procedures*)

1.   **Activities Plan (*How do we get there?*).** The Activities Plan details the marketing mixes (8 Ps) for each target market selected. It provides the specifics on all the tasks required for each mix element of each target market.

     a.   *Activities by Target Market.* All planned activities for each target market should be listed and described. It is best to do this separately for each marketing-mix element (8 Ps), and to arrange tasks in a time schedule based on when they will be initiated.

     b.   *Responsibilities for Activities.* In most cases, several departments or divisions, many organization employees, and some outside firms will play a role in implementing the marketing plan. They all must know what is expected of them. A good way to do this is to write a description of major responsibilities into the marketing plan and to identify each responsible party in the timetable and activity schedule.

     c.   *Timetable and Activity Schedule.* This is a key part of the plan that is frequently referred to as the plan is being implemented. It should show each activity's starting and completion dates, where the activity is to be carried out (e.g., in-house or outside the organization or destination), and the persons responsible for the activity. Figure 9.8 is a sample of a form that can be used for this schedule.

2.   **Marketing Budget (*How do we get there?*).** Every marketing plan should include a detailed budget that outlines how much will be spent on each of the 8 Ps or marketing-mix element for each target market. Knowing

FIGURE 9.8 An example of a Timetable and Activity Schedule showing activities by month and responsibilities.

ACTIVITY	ASSIGNED TO	JAN	FEB	MAR	APR	MAY	JUNE	JULY	AUG	SEP	OCT	NOV	DEC

TIMETABLE AND ACTIVITY SCHEDULE: <u>Sales Promotion and Merchandising</u>
Year: 2010
Page: 1

how much money to allocate to marketing is a difficult decision, but a good marketing budget should meet these four criteria:

a. *Comprehensive.* All marketing activities or tasks are identified and estimated.
b. *Coordinated.* Budgeting for all activities or tasks is carefully coordinated to avoid unnecessary duplication of effort and to maximize the synergy among budget items.
c. *Practical.* The budget specifies the sources of the money and human resources for the marketing activities or tasks.
d. *Realistic.* Marketing budgets cannot be set in isolation from other departments' priorities and activities. They have to be related to the organization's resources and position in the industry sector.

There are at least four ways to establish marketing budgets. The most effective is known as the **objective-and-task** or empirical method. This process follows the **zero-based budgeting** idea, which means that every budget starts at zero each year and then builds up activity by activity. A multi-stage budgeting process is used. The advantages and disadvantages of the four budgeting approaches are as follows:

a. *Historical or Arbitrary Budgeting.* This is a very simple and mechanical approach. A certain amount or percentage is added to the last marketing budget. The budget increase is often set close to the economy's rate of inflation. This is not a zero-based approach, because the last budget is considered a given.

Historical budgeting is popular in the hospitality and travel industry because it is easy and requires little time and effort. However, you probably see its dangers. This book emphasizes the need to control and evaluate the results of marketing plans. Such a systematic process always suggests ways to modify and improve marketing activities. This approach pinpoints the organization's marketing successes and failures. Those who use the historical approach, however, tend to perpetuate and continue ineffective marketing activities and fail to identify and enhance their highly successful activities.

The hospitality and travel industry is very dynamic. It is changing quickly and constantly. Every organization should remain as flexible and ready to change as possible. Although it is useful to keep a historic record of marketing spending, past budgets should not provide the main basis for setting future marketing budgets.

b. *Rule-of-Thumb Budgeting.* This approach is also known as the percentage-of-sales or heuristic method. In **rule-of-thumb budgeting**, the marketing budget is calculated using an established industry sector average, and is usually a percentage of total sales revenues. For example, it is common for lodging properties to budget 4 to 6 percent of their total expected sales revenues in the next year for marketing. Why? This is the typical range found in published reports by such firms as PKF Consulting, STR Global, Deloitte, and Ernst & Young. Figure 9.9 shows a section of PKF's report on *Trends in the Hotel Industry USA Edition–2006*. It shows that full-service hotels in the United States spent 5.1 percent of total revenues on marketing. This figure was slightly lower at 4.7 percent in PKF's 2007 edition.[2] The National Restaurant Association in the United States publishes similar benchmarks for marketing in restaurants in its annual *Restaurant Industry Operations Report.*[3]

Like historic budgeting, rule-of-thumb budgeting is not a zero-based approach, because it assumes that the organization will spend some amount close to industry sector norms. Like the historical method, this approach is popular because it does not take very much work and can be done quickly. But it also runs contrary to the principles of the hospitality and travel marketing system. No two organizations and their operations are exactly alike. No two organizations have exactly the same target markets and marketing mixes (8 Ps). Additionally, industry sector marketing spending averages can be very misleading. They are the combination of a wide range of marketing expenditures by different organizations. New businesses trying to build market share normally have to spend above-the-sector average amounts. Established firms with a large core of loyal and repeat customers may not need to spend as much.

The level of competition in different industry sectors and geographic areas varies tremendously. Each sector and geographic area

FIGURE 9.9 PKF Consulting's Trends in the Hotel Industry provides many useful benchmarks for budgeting in hotels.

FULL-SERVICE HOTELS - 2006
Ratios to Total Revenues
Figure Number 10

	All Full-Service Hotels	Average for Top 25%[1]	Rate Groups		
			Under $70.00	$70.00 to $100.00	Over $100.00
Revenues:					
Rooms	65.5 %	65.3 %	69.0 %	69.0 %	64.9 %
Food - including Other Income	24.2	23.3	22.0	22.9	24.4
Beverage	5.1	5.4	5.2	4.6	5.2
Telecommunications	0.9	1.1	0.5	0.6	1.0
Other Operated Departments	3.1	3.5	1.7	2.1	3.2
Rentals and Other Income	1.3	1.4	1.5	0.7	1.3
Total Revenues	100.0 %	100.0 %	100.0 %	100.0 %	100.0 %
Departmental Costs and Expenses:					
Rooms	17.2 %	16.6 %	21.7 %	18.7 %	16.9 %
Food	18.7	17.9	18.2	17.6	18.9
Beverage	2.3	2.4	2.8	2.2	2.4
Telecommunications	0.9	0.8	1.0	1.0	0.9
Other Operated Departments	1.7	2.1	1.7	1.2	1.8
Total Costs and Expenses	40.9 %	39.8 %	45.4 %	40.6 %	40.8 %
Total Operated Departmental Income	59.1 %	60.2 %	54.6 %	59.4 %	59.2 %
Undistributed Operating Expenses:[2]					
Administrative and General	8.4 %	7.4 %	11.3 %	10.1 %	8.2 %
Franchise Fees - including Marketing Fees	3.0	2.4	4.1	3.9	2.9
Marketing	4.7	3.9	6.1	5.8	4.5
Property Operation and Maintenance	4.4	3.8	5.8	5.4	4.2
Utility Costs	3.8	3.0	6.1	5.5	3.6
Other Unallocated Operated Departments	—	—	—	—	—
Total Undistributed Expenses	24.3 %	20.5 %	33.3 %	30.8 %	23.4 %
Income before Fixed Charges	34.8 %	39.7 %	21.3 %	28.7 %	35.8 %
Management Fees, Property Taxes, and Insurance:[2]					
Management Fees	3.3 %	3.5 %	2.9 %	2.9 %	3.3 %
Property Taxes and Other Municipal Charges	3.3	3.3	2.0	3.0	3.3
Insurance	1.3	1.2	1.3	1.6	1.3
Total Management Fees, Property Taxes, and Insurance	7.9 %	7.9 %	6.1 %	7.4 %	8.0 %
Income before Other Fixed Charges[3]	26.9 %	31.7 %	15.2 %	21.3 %	27.8 %
Percentage of Occupancy	71.7 %	78.3 %	67.4 %	66.6 %	73.3 %
Average Daily Rate per Occupied Room	$ 142.74	$ 199.71	$ 64.99	$ 87.34	$ 159.82
Average Size (Rooms)	293	357	217	240	318

[1] Average for top 25% based on Income per Available Room before Other Fixed Charges.
[2] Averages based on total groups, although not all establishments reported data.
[3] Income before deducting Depreciation, Rent, Interest, Amortization, and Income Taxes.
NOTE: Payroll Taxes and Employee Benefits distributed to each department.

(Continued)

40

Courtesy of PKF Consulting

requires marketing budgets tailor-made for the situation. The Las Vegas Convention & Visitors Authority (LVCVA) has a huge budget for marketing at $294 million in fiscal year 2009, and it will spend $88.6 million of that on advertising.[4] The LVCVA has to market an international-class destination and has strong sources of funding through room and gaming taxes. However, most CVBs in the United States have marketing budgets of less than $1 million. In addition, averages or arithmetic means can be very imprecise guides. If you added the LVCVA's marketing budget to all of these, and calculated the average, it would be totally misleading. As Figure 9.10 shows, the LVCVA's marketing department is much larger and more complex than most marketing organizations in hospitality and travel.

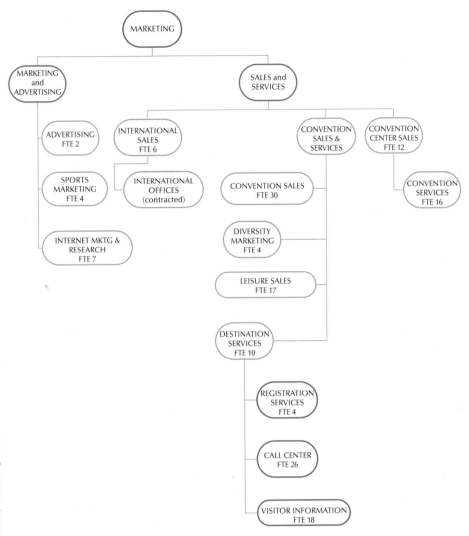

FIGURE 9.10 The Las Vegas Convention & Visitors Authority has a large marketing organization that includes both marketing and advertising and sales and service.

The rule-of-thumb approach is dangerous and should be avoided. It is a rather sloppy practice handed down by past generations of hospitality and travel marketers. Again, although it is interesting to know what the industry sector is spending on average, this should not be the primary basis for setting an individual organization's budget.

c. *Competitive Budgeting.* We looked at the strategies for market followers in Chapter 8. One way that a lower-share firm can mimic the industry leader is to try to match its spending levels and marketing activities. Some call this the competitive-parity approach.[5] Like the previous two methods, this one is easy to use. All that is needed is information on what competitors are budgeting for marketing, which can be found by reading published materials on these organizations or by studying their annual reports. Because this method begins by assuming that some amount will be spent in relation to a specific competitor, it is not a zero-based approach.

Again, the major weakness of **competitive budgeting** is that it overlooks the unique sets of target markets, marketing mixes (8 Ps), objectives, resources, and market positions of individual organizations. Although keeping a close track of competitors' marketing programs is a good marketing practice, it is inadvisable to use only the competitive budgeting approach.

d. *Objective-and-Task Budgeting.* This works exactly the way it sounds; marketing objectives are set first and then the activities (or tasks) to achieve them are detailed. The budget starts at nothing (zero), which implies that it is a zero-based approach. Some call it the build-up method, because an organization establishes the budget from the bottom up, rather than starting with a total amount and then deciding how to spend it.

Using the objective-and-task method takes much more time and effort than the historical, rule-of-thumb, and competitive approaches. All the activities in the previous marketing plan are carefully evaluated. But the primary basis for arriving at the budget is the planned activities (or tasks) to reach the marketing objectives for each target market. Although many marketing budgets are less detailed, the ideal method is to show the amount to be spent for each marketing-mix element (each of the Ps) and for each target market.

a. *Budget by Target Market.* How much of the marketing budget will be devoted to each target market? This is a question that is often skipped over in marketing plans. Nevertheless, it is of great importance. This book suggests that budgets should be apportioned roughly according to each target market's current or expected share of total revenues or profits. Many organizations make the mistake of grossly overspending on small-share target markets at the expense of larger-share customer groups.

b. *Budget by Marketing-Mix Element.* Marketing managers also need to know how much is being spent on each of the 8 Ps. Otherwise, they are unable to measure the effectiveness of each marketing-mix element and to make informed future decisions about how the budget should be allocated.

c. *Contingency Funds.* Always expect the unexpected! The vast majority of budgets end up being exceeded. This is not to say that it is fine to go over budget. It is not! It is essential to make a *reserve fund* available from the beginning to provide for unexpected competitive moves, media production cost overruns, and other unanticipated increases in marketing expenses. Typically, 10 to 15 percent of the total cost of budgeted activities should be set aside as a contingency fund.

3. **Control Procedures** (*How do we make sure we get there?*). Controlling the plan is a marketing management function, which is discussed in greater

detail in Chapter 20. To control effectively, the manager must know what is expected (desired results), when it is expected (progress points or milestones), who it is expected of (responsible parties), and how expectations are to be measured (measures or **metrics**). Financial control of the marketing plan is achieved through budgeting and periodic reports that compare budgeted with actual expenditures. Monitoring progress towards objectives is done by measuring sales volumes (e.g., restaurant covers, occupied room nights, clients served, airline seats sold, or visitor arrivals), revenues, and profits. Sometimes special marketing research studies have to be done. For example, these may be needed if the objective is to increase awareness or improve attitudes toward an organization's services.

   a. *Results Expected from Each Activity.* How is each marketing activity expected to contribute to its related marketing objective? For example, will the new ad in a meeting planning magazine produce 25 percent of the projected 10-percent increase in meeting-room nights? The plan should look at these types of questions on an activity-by-activity basis.

   b. *Progress Reporting and Measures.* Milestones have already been mentioned. Real milestones show how far travelers are from their destinations. The milestones we are interested in are the interim results or sub-objectives that lead toward achieving a marketing objective. A decision should be made on how these will be measured (the metrics), when they will be checked, and how they will be reported.

4. **Evaluation Procedures** (*How do we know if we got there?*). The ultimate test of a marketing plan's success is the extent to which its marketing objectives are achieved. Earlier in the book, Figure 5.12 (marketing position and plan analysis worksheet) showed how the effectiveness of each marketing-mix element (8 Ps) can be evaluated. In addition to this type of analysis, results must be reviewed carefully on an objective-by-objective basis. Effective evaluation requires expected results and measurement techniques, metrics, performance standards, and a timetable for evaluation.

   a. *Measurements or Metrics.* How will success be measured? Will it be measured in sales revenues, customers, number of inquiries, or awareness percentage? Obviously, it is best to tie these directly to marketing objectives.

   b. *Performance Standards.* This is another item that is overlooked in many marketing plans. What deviations from an objective are acceptable and unacceptable? Performance standards should be specified in the marketing plan so that the organization can make an overall judgment on the acceptability of actual results.

   c. *Evaluation Timetable.* Some prior thought should go into the timing of the marketing plan evaluation. To be most useful, evaluation must begin before the planning period ends so it can provide input into the next situation analysis and marketing plan.

INTERNET MARKETING

Putting the Marketing Plan on the Internet: Fancy or Folly?

- Some organizations routinely place their marketing plans on the Internet for everyone to see; others would never consider doing this, considering the plan to be too confidential.
- One organization that regularly puts its marketing plan on the Internet is Tourism Ireland, which is responsible for marketing the island of Ireland overseas.
- Tourism Ireland's *Marketing Plan 2008* contained very clear and measurable marketing objectives: (1) tourism revenues of €4.9 billion; and (2) 9.6 million visitors.
- Tourism Ireland identified four key needs for success in 2008: (1) targeting the most appropriate consumers, (2) communicating the right messages, (3) offering the right products to potential consumers, and (4) increasing the use of innovative marketing channels to deliver the message effectively.
- *Sightseers and Culture Seekers* are identified as Ireland's best prospects and they have an interest in "sightseeing, learning about, visiting, and experiencing the country and its culture—both living and historic."
- Tourism Ireland's three main geographic targets are: (1) Great Britain, (2) Europe, and (3) North America. They also identify India and China as two good prospective markets in the future.
- The destination brand of Ireland is as "the Island of Unique Character and Characters."
- If you visit Tourism Ireland's consumer site, you will see how they are using the Internet to promote internationally.

Source: Tourism Ireland. (2008). *Tourism Ireland Marketing Plan.* **http://www.tourismireland.com/Home/research/marketing-plan.aspx**; *Holidays in Ireland.* (2008). **http://www.discoverireland.com/**

Student Questions

1. What are the benefits to certain types of hospitality, travel and tourism organizations in placing their current marketing plans on the Internet?
2. What are the main reasons that other organizations may not want to have marketing plans on their websites?
3. How does TI's marketing plan compare to what is recommended in Chapter 9?
4. How does TI's consumer website support its marketing plan?

Steps Involved in Preparing a Marketing Plan

You now know what should be included in a marketing plan. What you have read has shown you that a good marketing plan deals with all five key questions in the **hospitality and travel marketing system** (Chapter 3). You have also noticed that the written plan follows the exact same systematic process. In summary, the steps involved in preparing a marketing plan are as follows:

1. **Prepare the Marketing Plan Rationale**
   Review and summarize:

   - Situation analysis
   - Marketing research studies
   - Market segmentation
   - Segmentation approach and characteristics
   - Target-market selection
   - Marketing strategy
   - Positioning approaches
   - Marketing mixes (8 Ps)
   - Marketing objectives

2. **Develop a detailed implementation plan**
   Design and specify:

   - Activities by marketing-mix element (8 Ps) for target markets
   - Responsibilities (internal and external)
   - Timetable and activity schedule
   - Budget and contingency fund
   - Expected results
   - Measurements (metrics)
   - Progress reporting procedures
   - Performance standards
   - Evaluation timetable

3. **Write the Executive Summary**
   Describe highlights of:

   - Marketing Plan Rationale (Where are we now? Where would we like to be?
   - Implementation Plan (How do we get there? How do we make sure we get there? How do we know if we got there?)

FIGURE 9.11 Steps in developing a marketing plan. An organization with three different target markets.

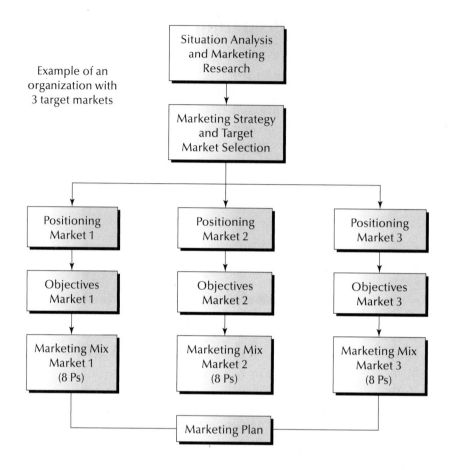

Figure 9.11 shows, in flow-chart format, the steps involved in developing the marketing plan. Figure 9.12 shows the sequence for completing the three main parts of the marketing plan.

FIGURE 9.12
Sequence of completing the three main parts of the marketing plan.

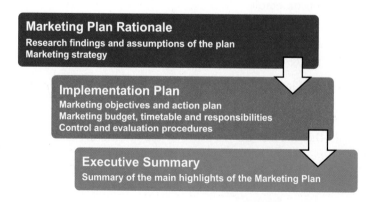

The 8 Ps of Hospitality and Travel Marketing

A large part of a marketing plan concerns how the organization intends to use the **8 Ps** of hospitality and travel marketing (marketing mix). Chapters 10 through 19 review each of the marketing-mix elements, or Ps. Before we get into the details of each element, let us take a brief look at how each is integrated into the marketing plan. The 8 Ps are (Figure 9.13):

1. Product
2. Partnership
3. People
4. Packaging
5. Programming
6. Place
7. Promotion
8. Pricing

1. **Product or Product/Service Mix.** Chapter 10 discusses product development in the hospitality and travel industry. It introduces the term **product/service mix** to describe the range of facilities or products that an individual organization or destination provides to customers. One important point made earlier in this book is that hospitality and travel marketing is a separate branch of marketing, with its own unique requirements. Most traditional marketers lump people, packaging, and programming in with product. Although they are definitely part of the mix of things that hospitality and travel organizations offer, these three factors deserve separate attention.

   How do we define hospitality and travel organizations' products? This is a tough question because, unlike most other products, they are not inanimate objects. People are always involved in the production process. It is doubly difficult to pinpoint because many customers buy more on the basis of their emotions than on hard facts. What they buy is not always what we think we are selling!

2. **People or Host and Guests.** The ways that **people**—employees and managers—are involved in the marketing plan have already been discussed. Let

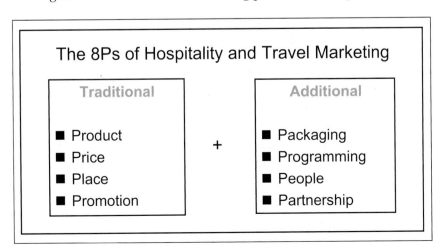

FIGURE 9.13 The 8 Ps of hospitality and travel marketing.

us emphasize, however, that a marketing plan must include programs that have been developed to make use of these vital human resources. Chapter 11 discusses the people aspect of hospitality and travel marketing.

3. **Packaging.** Chapter 12 reviews the related concepts of packaging and programming. In many ways, **packaging** epitomizes a marketing orientation. It results from finding out what people need and want and then assembling and combining destinations, services and facilities to match these needs. The marketing plan should detail the continuing and new packages for the upcoming 12 to 24 months. A financial justification for each package should be included, as well as an explanation about how each package will be tied in with promotional activities and pricing/revenue objectives.

4. **Programming.** The related concept of **programming** is also very customer-oriented. Programs are special events and activities created for customers. For examples, all entertainment and festivals are programming. Programs are normally designed to increase customer spending or length of stay; or to add to the appeal of packages.

5. **Place or Distribution Mix.** How does the organization plan to **place** the product or to work with other complementary groups in the distribution channel? For suppliers, carriers, and DMOs, this means how they will use travel trade intermediaries (both online and offline) to achieve marketing objectives. For the intermediaries, it means the relationships they have with other intermediaries, suppliers, carriers, and DMOs. Chapter 13 introduces the distribution mix concept and describes the travel trade intermediaries.

6. **Promotion or Promotional Mix.** The marketing plan specifies how each technique in the **promotional mix** (advertising, personal selling, sales promotion, merchandising, and public relations and publicity) will be used along with Internet marketing. These techniques must be developed as integrated marketing communications (IMC), and the plan must make sure that each promotional mix element supports the others. **Promotion** usually represents the largest percentage of the marketing budget, and it involves the greatest use of outside advisors and professionals. As such, it must be planned in considerable detail, with great emphasis on costs, responsibilities, and timing. Chapters 14 through 18 provide a detailed discussion of all the promotional mix elements.

7. **Partnership or Cooperative Marketing.** Technically, it would be correct to include **partnership** as part of each of the other 7 Ps. However, to give added emphasis to the value of cooperative advertising and other marketing programs, this book considers it separately in Chapter 10. The marketing plan should discuss the types, costs, and financial returns of proposed cooperative marketing programs.

8. **Pricing.** **Pricing** often gets inadequate consideration in marketing plans. It deserves a much higher priority because it is both a marketing technique and a major profit determinant. What is recommended is a comprehensive revenue management or pricing plan that takes into account all special rates, prices, and discounts projected for the upcoming period. Chapter 19 discusses pricing and price planning in the hospitality and travel industry.

The Global Perspective: The Big Picture

Marketing Planning and Partnerships in Canadian Tourism

Canadian Tourism Commission

http://www.corporate.canada.travel/

The beautiful scenery of the Canadian Rockies is one of Canada's major tourism attractions.

Marketing Goals and Objectives of CTC

The Canadian Tourism Commission (CTC) is widely recognized as one of the best in the world. CTC invests heavily in market research and carefully plans its marketing for each of its key targets. In its document, *Strategy 2008–2012: Transforming vision into reality*, the CTC indentified its major marketing goal as "to grow tourism export revenues for Canada." This goal was articulated into four marketing objectives for 2008–2012:

1. Convert high yield customers;
2. Focus on markets of highest return on investment;
3. Maintain brand consistency; and
4. Research new market opportunities.

The CTC explains its marketing planning approaches to these four objectives as follows:

"The CTC's approach to growing export revenues is based on deepening the relationship with high-yield consumers in an effort to

(continues)

(continued)

influence their travel decisions and establish them as a travel purchaser. Second, the CTC's approach focuses on those global markets or consumer market segments where it is felt there is the highest potential for return on investment."

"Promoting brand consistency is central to marketing Canada as a desirable tourism destination. Over the 2008–2012 planning period, the CTC will work closely with industry to communicate the advantage of a strong global brand for Canada and work collaboratively to leverage the brand. Finally, the Commission's strategy will focus on identifying new niche market opportunities within its core markets and positioning Canada to diversify its marketing strategy."

CTC has developed a new brand visual identity to support all of the marketing of Canadian tourism around the theme of *Canada: Keep Exploring*. To help the industry to implement this approach, CTC developed a very elaborate instructional document in 2007, known as *Experiences: A toolkit for partners of the Canadian Tourism Commission* or the *Canadian Tourism Experiences Resource Guide for Industry*.

Courtesy of the Canadian Tourism Commission

The new marketing strategy of CTC is to put people in these beautiful landscape photos.

(continues)

(continued)

Target Markets

In this publication, the CTC identifies its three highest-yield target markets as being the "Authentic Experiencers," "Cultural Explorers," and "Free Spirits" based upon their Explorer Quotients™ or EQ™. This is a new customer segmentation system based on the Environics 3SC Social Values survey (http://3sc.environics.net). Here's a quick description of CTC's three top segments:

- *Authentic Experiencers* appreciate the understated beauty of both natural and cultural environments, and try to keep a foot in both worlds. They enjoy using all of their senses when they explore their chosen destination and really get to know the places they visit. They quickly adapt to personal challenges and risks, easily figuring out how to make the most of every situation. Authentic Experiencers want to be fully immersed in their travel experience and tend to stay away from group tours and rigid plans.
- *Cultural Explorers* seek constant opportunities to embrace, discover, and immerse themselves in the entire experience of the culture, people, and settings of the places they visit. Not content to just visit historic sites and watch from the sidelines, they want to participate in the modern-day culture as well. They often attempt to converse with locals, attend cultural festivals or go off the beaten track to discover how locals truly live.
- Travel satisfies *Free Spirits'* insatiable need for the exciting and the exotic. They like the best of everything and want to be with others

Image copyright Helen Filatova, 2008. Used under license from Shutterstock.com

Niagara Falls is another of Canada's spectacular attractions that must be experienced.

(continues)

(continued)

who feel the same way. They have a lot of energy and want to see and do everything. It all adds up to fun! Young, or young-at-heart, they travel for the thrill and emotional charge of doing things. Carpe diem (seize the day) is their motto.

Canada's nine best geographic origin markets are pinpointed as being the UK, France, Germany, USA, Mexico, South Korea, Japan, China, and Australia. CTC identifies seven overall trends that are happening in these markets:

- Experiential travel
- Fully independent travel (FIT)
- Responsible/sustainable tourism
- The aging traveler
- Internet usage
- Luxury travel
- Multigenerational travel

CTC offers its potential industry partners the use of its brand's visual identity (VI), which includes the key phrase of "Canada. Keep Exploring" ™. The logo includes a contemporary version of the Canadian maple leaf.

Niagara Falls provides the second shower of the day.

(continues)

(continued)

Discussion Questions
1. What can other destinations and DMOs learn from the great example set by CTC in marketing planning and partnership-building?
2. As one of the 8 Ps of hospitality and travel marketing, how important are partnerships to the marketing success of a country?
3. The CTC has moved away from showing spectacular landscapes in its promotions to depicting people having fun and enjoying themselves. Do you think this is a good change in today's marketplace? Why or why not?

Chapter Conclusion

The marketing plan is a blueprint for action. It shows how the organization proposes to attain its marketing objectives. The plan details all the marketing activities to be carried out in the next year or two. It is really a series of plans, one for each of the eight marketing-mix elements (Ps), carefully coordinated within one overall plan.

A plan should be written in ink, but not cast in stone. An organization must monitor implementation of the plan and make adjustments when necessary. Like any airline flight, no organization is guaranteed perfect flying weather. Plans take weeks and sometimes months to draft, but it may take even more time and effort to make them work as effectively as possible.

REVIEW QUESTIONS

1. Is a marketing plan tactical or strategic? What is the difference between the two types of plans?
2. How is the term *marketing plan* defined in this book?
3. What are the eight requirements for an effective marketing plan?
4. What are the benefits of having a marketing plan?
5. What are the three parts of the marketing plan?
6. Should a marketing plan always be written down? Why?
7. Does the marketing plan address all five questions in the hospitality and travel marketing system? If so, how is this done?
8. What are the 8 Ps of hospitality and travel marketing? Are they the same as the marketing mix?
9. What are the four approaches to preparing marketing budgets? Which is the best and why is it superior to the other three?

CHAPTER ASSIGNMENTS

1. You have just joined a non-profit organization that has never had a marketing plan. The board of directors is very skeptical of the time and money required to complete a plan. How would you sell your idea to prepare the organization's first marketing plan? How would you justify the time and expense needed to prepare the plan? What would you include in the plan?

2. You have just been promoted as the new director of marketing. Using the objective-and-task budgeting approach, you have just calculated the upcoming year's marketing budget to be 30 percent higher than the previous year's. Your company has always used the historic approach in the past, adding 5 to 10 percent each year to the previous year's spending. How would you justify your position? What drawbacks would you highlight in the historic approach?

3. The owner of a small hospitality and travel business in your community has just asked you to help her prepare a marketing plan. What would you include in the plan? Who would you consult in preparing the plan and what sources of information would you use? Using Figure 9.6 as a guide, develop a more detailed table of contents for the plan. How long would your plan be? To whom would you give copies?

4. Choose a hospitality and travel organization. How has it made use of the 8 Ps of hospitality and travel marketing? Are all the Ps given equal emphasis, or are some emphasized more than others? Have any of the Ps been overlooked? What recommendations would you make to the organization about improving its use of these eight marketing-mix elements? Use examples from other organizations to back up your recommendations.

WEB RESOURCES

Arizona Office of Tourism, http://www.azot.com/
Canadian Tourism Commission, http://www.corporate.canada.travel/
Hawaii Tourism Authority, http://www.hawaiitourismauthority.org/
Las Vegas Convention and Visitors Authority, http://www.lvcva.com/
National Restaurant Association, http://www.restaurant.org/
PKF Consulting, http://www.pkfonline.com/
STR Global (Smith Travel Research), http://www.strglobal.com/
Tourism Ireland, http://www.tourismireland.com/

REFERENCES

1. Palo Alto Software. 2008. *Marketing Plan Pro.* http://www.paloalto.com/ps/mp/features.cfm, accessed December 13, 2008.

2. PKF Consulting, *Annual Trends*, http://www.pkfc.com/store/Download_Samples.aspx, accessed December 13, 2008.

3. National Restaurant Association. 2008. *Restaurant Industry Operations Report 2007/2008*, http://www.restaurant.org/research/operations/report.cfm, accessed December 13, 2008.

4. Las Vegas Convention and Visitors Authority. 2008. *Las Vegas Convention and Visitors Authority: Annual Budget Fiscal Year 2008–09*.

5. American Marketing Association. 2008. *Dictionary*, http://www.marketingpower.com/_layouts/Dictionary.aspx, accessed December 13, 2008.

IMPLEMENTING THE MARKETING PLAN

WHERE ARE WE NOW?

WHERE WOULD WE LIKE TO BE?

HOW DO WE GET THERE?

HOW DO WE MAKE SURE WE GET THERE?

HOW DO WE KNOW IF WE GOT THERE?

chapter 10

Product Development and Partnership
How Do We Get There?

O V E R V I E W

What are the products that the hospitality and travel industry markets to customers? To start with, you already know that we should replace the word products with services. The services provided by the industry are many and varied, ranging from 1,000-plus-room hotels and cruise ships with over 3,000 passenger capacity to two- or three-person travel agencies and owner-operated bed & breakfasts.

Understanding the structure of the industry is fundamental for marketing managers. This chapter begins by describing the four groups of the hospitality and travel organizations and their component sectors. The major trends among suppliers and carriers are explained.

O B J E C T I V E S

Having read this chapter, you should be able to:

- Describe the four major groups of hospitality and travel organizations and the roles played by each of them.

- Describe the sectors that comprise each of the four groups of organizations.

- Identify some of the major recent trends in the supplier and carrier sectors.

- Identify five overall trends and industry realities.

- Define the product/service mix.

- Identify and describe the six components of an organization's product/service mix.

- Explain the types of product development decisions that an organization must make.

- Define the term *partnership* and list the potential benefits of marketing partnerships to hospitality and travel organizations.

- Identify the types of partners available to hospitality and travel organizations.

K E Y   T E R M S

brand extension
branding
brand segmentation
carriers
co-branding
convention and visitors
　　bureaus (CVBs)
database marketing
destination marketing
　　organizations (DMOs)

gaming
horizontal integration
lifestyle hotel
low-cost carriers
loyalty programs
multi-branding
partnerships
product/service mix

product/service-mix length
product/service-mix width
relationship marketing
strategic alliances
suppliers
third-party intermediaries
travel trade intermediaries
vertical integration

The product/service mix concept is introduced and each of its components is described. The chapter shows how decisions are made to modify an organization's product/service mix. Chapter 10 ends by discussing partnership—another of the 8 Ps—and the boundless opportunities for cooperative marketing in the hospitality and travel industry.

Have you ever tried to put your finger on a blob of mercury? What happens is quite predictable, right? Whenever you think you have got the mercury pinned down, it squeezes away from you. Describing the hospitality and travel industry is very similar. It is a fast-changing business. If you take a snapshot of it today, the picture is sure to become outdated in a few months. When putting this book together, we gathered the latest statistics, but there probably will be many changes after the book is published. That's also probably why you are in this business, because it's so exciting and international in scope.

Some of you are probably most interested in hotel and restaurant careers—others in the airlines and the travel trade. Some may be pursuing other fields such as cruise-line operations, theme parks and attractions, convention and meeting planning, country club management, government or association travel promotion, or ski area management. Whatever your favorite area, you will find this chapter both interesting and informative. You may even see new career opportunities opening up.

Before discussing product development decisions, we will take a look at the overall industry structure. Taking this broader perspective first will help you better understand the role played by the groups of organizations and sectors in our industry.

Types and Roles of Hospitality and Travel Industry Organizations

This book identifies and describes four groups of organizations in the industry based on the functions they perform. **Suppliers** provide the services that travel trade intermediaries wholesale (or package) and retail, and that customers can also buy directly. **Carriers** provide transportation from the customers' origins to their destinations. **Travel trade intermediaries** package and retail supplier and carrier services to travelers, both offline and online. **Destination marketing organizations (DMOs)** promote their cities, counties, regions, states, and countries to travel trade intermediaries and individual travelers. One of the major messages in this book is that all these businesses and organizations are interrelated. You may remember from Chapter 3 that we called the industry the macro-system and the individual organizations were micro-systems. Using these expressions was one way of showing that many hospitality and travel organizations are interdependent. Figure 10.1 identifies all four groups and their component sectors. You now will learn about each of the industry groups and sectors, and some of the major trends in the hospitality and travel industry.

Suppliers

The suppliers in the hospitality and travel industry both are located and provide services and facilities within and between destinations. Many of them exclusively serve out-of-town visitors, but others cater to both visitors and local residents.

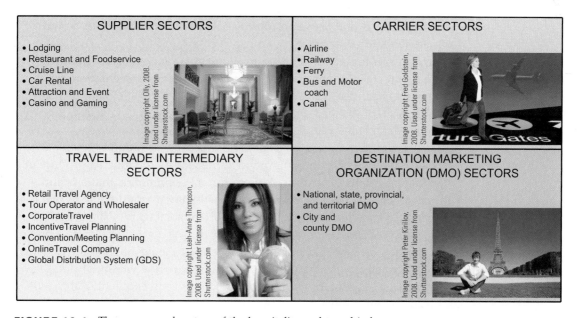

SUPPLIER SECTORS

- Lodging
- Restaurant and Foodservice
- Cruise Line
- Car Rental
- Attraction and Event
- Casino and Gaming

Image copyright Olly, 2008. Used under license from Shutterstock.com

CARRIER SECTORS

- Airline
- Railway
- Ferry
- Bus and Motor coach
- Canal

Image copyright Fred Goldstein, 2008. Used under license from Shutterstock.com

TRAVEL TRADE INTERMEDIARY SECTORS

- Retail Travel Agency
- Tour Operator and Wholesaler
- Corporate Travel
- Incentive Travel Planning
- Convention/Meeting Planning
- Online Travel Company
- Global Distribution System (GDS)

Image copyright Leah-Anne Thompson, 2008. Used under license from Shutterstock.com

DESTINATION MARKETING ORGANIZATION (DMO) SECTORS

- National, state, provincial, and territorial DMO
- City and county DMO

Image copyright Peter Kirillov, 2008. Used under license from Shutterstock.com

FIGURE 10.1 The groups and sectors of the hospitality and travel industry.

Lodging Sector

This huge sector of the industry contains a diverse variety of property types. According to Smith Travel Research's *2008 STR Chain Scales*, lodging chains in North America can be divided into seven groups: luxury, upper upscale, upscale, midscale with food and beverage, midscale without food and beverage, economy, and unaffiliated.[1] Chain brands such as Four Seasons, Sofitel, Mandarin Oriental, Peninsula, St. Regis, Ritz-Carlton, and W Hotels are in the luxury group. STR places Hyatt, Marriott, Sheraton, and Westin in the upper upscale category; while Days Inns and Red Roof Inns are two of the well-known brands in the economy group. Additionally, there are many non-chain, unaffiliated or "independent" lodging properties. At the smaller end of the spectrum, the Professional Association of Innkeepers International (PAII) identifies bed and breakfasts (B&B) and country inns.[2] Another grouping of lodging properties is resorts, which generally means a lodging property in a non-urban environment.

a. *Increasing Chain Domination.* Although a large proportion of lodging establishments still have fewer than 50 rooms, larger chain-owned properties predominate from a marketing standpoint. For 2007, *Hotels* magazine in its *Hotels' Corporate 300 Ranking* found the top 10 lodging chains in the world, in terms of total available rooms, to be InterContinental Hotels Group (IHG), Wyndham Hotels & Resorts, Marriott International, Hilton Hotels Corp., Accor, Choice Hotels International, Best Western International, Starwood Hotels & Resorts Worldwide, Carlson Hotels Worldwide, and Global Hyatt Corp.[3] Each of these chains had more than 135,000 rooms in 2007. Appendices 11a and 11b provide more detailed information on these leading lodging chains.

b. *Expanding Brand Segmentation and Brand Extensions.* Hotel **brand segmentation** is a concept that has been around for many years now, and means broad types or brand segments of hotels that are aimed at different customer profiles.[4] This type of lodging segmentation has greatly expanded the range of property types available. Figure 10.2 shows six of the leading lodging chains along with their brands of properties and some examples of brand extensions.

   The brand extension concept is not the same as brand segmentation; it is when an existing lodging brand name is used to launch a product in a different product category. A more formal definition is that a **brand extension** is using the leverage of a well-known brand name in one category to launch a new product in a different category.[5] The introduction of Westin's *Heavenly Bed* in the late 1990s was a great example of brand extension by a hotel chain brand. Several of the leading lodging chains have online stores where they merchandise a wide variety of different products. The W Store offered by W Hotels is an excellent example of using brand extensions in lodging.

c. *Growing Consolidation and Globalization.* The lodging sector is now more consolidated with the leading chains having a larger proportion

InterContinental Hotels Group	Wyndham Worldwide	Marriott International	Hilton Hotels Corp.	Choice International	Accor
	**BRAND SEGMENTS**				
• Candlewood Suites	• AmeriHost Inn	• Courtyard	• Conrad	• Cambria Suites	• Etap Hotel
• Crowne Plaza	• Baymont Inn	• Fairfield Inn	• Bouble Tree	• Clarion	• Formule 1
• Hotel Indico	• Days Inn	• JW Marriott Hotels & Resorts	• Embassy Suites	• Comfort Inn	• Ibis
• Hotel Inn	• Howard Johnson	• Marriott Conference Centers	• Hampton	• Comfort Suites	• Mercure
• Holiday Inn Express	• Knights Inn	• Marriott ExecuStay	• Hilton Garden Inn	• Econo Lodge	• Motel 6
• InterContinental	• Ramada	• Marriott Executive Apartments	• Hilton Hotels	• MainStay Suites	• Novotel
• Staybridge Suites	• Super 8	• Marriott Hotels & Resorts	• Homewood Suites	• Quality	• Red Roof Inn
	• Travelodge	• Marriott Vacation Club International	• Scandic	• Rodeway Inn	• Sofitel
	• Wingate Inn	• Renaissance Hotels & Resorts	• Waldorf-Astoria	• Sleep Inn	• Studio 6
	• Wyndham	• Residence Inn		• Suburban	• Suite hotel
		• The Ritz-Carlton			
		• Spring Hill Suites			
		• Towne Place Suites			
	**BRAND EXTENSIONS** (EXAMPLES)				
• Simply Smart Bedding Collection	• Wyndham at Home store	• The Revive Collection	• Serenity Bed		• SO Bed
	•	• The Marriott Bed	• Hilton to Home store		

FIGURE 10.2 Brand segmentation and brand extension examples of leading lodging chains.

of the available rooms. Companies increasingly move across national borders, with the French-based Accor group having a solid foothold in North America, and the British-based InterContinental Hotels Group (IHG) now being the leading global lodging company.

d. ***Increasing Importance of Frequent-Guest and Frequent-Flyer Programs.*** Another significant lodging trend is the increasing importance of frequent-guest programs and lodging chain participation in airline frequent flyer programs. These are also sometimes called **loyalty programs**. There are several reasons for these programs: (1) to identify and build databases of frequent guests, (2) to promote directly to frequent guests, (3) to reward and provide special services frequent guests, and (4) to build loyalty to the chain among frequent guests. IHG's Priority Club is the longest-established frequent guest programs, originally introduced by Holiday Inns.

e. ***Growing Influence of GDSs and Third-Party Intermediaries.*** The Internet has changed the way lodging chains receive bookings and also how they sell rooms. A significant proportion of bookings now come through the major Global Distribution Systems (GDSs) including Sabre, Amadeus, Galileo and Worldspan (the Galileo and Worldspan brands are now part of Travelport), and **third-party intermediaries** (Internet travel companies) such as Expedia.com, Hotels.com, Travelocity.com, and Orbitz.com.

f. ***Expanding Role for Specialized Lodging Properties.*** The splintering of the markets for lodging has opened up opportunities for specialized types of lodging. These include B&Bs, boutique hotels and inns, all-inclusive resorts, ecotourism lodges, dude ranches, just to name a few. Sandals is a good example in the all-inclusive resort category (Figure 10.3).

Another category that has emerged recently is the lifestyle hotel. The term **lifestyle hotel** is an umbrella for town house, boutique, designer, and themed hotels and these are usually small, specialized properties that fill a niche within the luxury hotel segment. The main features of these lifestyle hotels tend to be: individual and contemporary character, smaller properties, high levels of personal service, reflective of the personality/style of their designers or owners/operators, and stylish, carefully designed buildings and interiors.[6] The Malmaison group has a collection of these unique properties in key British cities. Some lodging chains have brands that can also be included in the lifestyle category, including Starwood's W Hotels and IHG's Indigo Hotels.

FIGURE 10.3 Sandals Resorts, the all-inclusive resort company in the Caribbean, is a good example of the growth in specialized lodging.

Restaurant and Foodservice Sector

This is another huge and complex sector of the hospitality and tourism industry. As with lodging, it is dominated by the large chains. Appendix 10.2a shows the top foodservice chains in the United States by total system-wide sales. According to *Nation's Restaurant News*, the top 100 chains had combined sales of $191.6 billion in 2006–2007.[7] The top five of the top 10 foodservice chains were sandwich restaurants (McDonald's, Burger King, Wendy's, Subway, and Taco Bell). Together the 17-chain sandwich segment accounted for approximately 40 percent of the total sales of the top 100 chains. Figure 10.4 shows a classification of foodservice facilities as suggested by *Nation's Restaurant News*.

a. *Globalizing of Leading Restaurant Chain Brands.* The leading restaurant and foodservice chain brands are becoming increasingly global, just as is in the lodging sector. Starbucks and Yum! Brands Inc. clearly reflect this trend. Starbucks opened its first two stores outside of Seattle in 1987; these were located in Chicago and Vancouver. At the end of 2008, it had more than 15,000 locations in 47 countries around the world.[8] Yum! Brands Inc.—the parent company of KFC, Pizza Hut, Taco Bell, Long John Silver's, and A&W Restaurants—is even larger and more global, with 34,000 restaurants in 100 countries and territories.[9] Of course, McDonald's have long been a leader in global expansion, and its restaurants are now in approximately 120 countries.[10]

Foodservice Segments	Examples
•Bagel	▪Einstein Bros. Bagels
•Bakery-Café	▪Panera Bread Co.
•Buffet	▪HomeTown Buffet
•Cafeteria	▪Luby's Cafeteria; Piccadilly Cafeteria; MCL Cafeteria
•Chicken	▪KFC; Chick-fil-A; Popeye's Chicken & Biscuits
•Chinese QSR	▪Panda Express
•Coffee/Beverages	▪Starbucks Coffee
•Contract	▪Aramark Global Food & Support Services; Canteen Services; Sodexho
•C-Store	▪7-Eleven; Wawa
•Dinner house	▪Applebee's Neighborhood Grill & Bar; Outback Steakhouse; Olive Garden
•Family	▪Denny's; International House of Pancakes; Cracker Barrel Old Country Store
•Fish QSR	▪Long John Silver's; Captain D's Seafood
•Grill-buffet	▪Golden Corral; Ryan's Family Steak House; Ponderosa Steakhouse
•Hotel	▪Marriott Hotels, Resorts & Suites; Hilton Hotels; Sheraton Hotels
•Italian QSR	▪Sbarro, The Italian Eatery; Fazoli's
•Pizza	▪Pizza Hut; Domino's Pizza; Papa John's Pizza
•Sandwich	▪McDonald's; Burger King; Wendy's
•Snack	▪Dunkin' Donuts; Krispy Kreme Doughnuts; Baskin Robbins
•Theme park	▪Disney Theme Parks, Hotels & Resorts

Source: 2008 Nation's Restaurant News' Annual Top 100 Report.

FIGURE 10.4 Restaurant classification by Nation's Restaurant News.

   b. *Continuing Restaurant Sector Growth.* According to the National Restaurant Association (NRA) in the United States, the restaurant sector in 2008 would record its 17th consecutive year of real sales growth. Sales in 2008 were forecast to reach a record of $558.3 billion.[11] The NRA also estimates that there were approximately 945,000 restaurants in the United States in 2008.[12] *Restaurant & Institutions'* 2007 New American Diner Survey found that 94 percent of US residents had patronized a foodservice operation in the previous 12 months.[13]

   c. *Growing Concern with the Nutritional Value of Restaurant Meals.* The book, *Fast Food Nation*, and the movie with the same name that followed in 2006 caused a "big stir" in the restaurant and foodservice sector and especially among the sandwich or QSR (quick-service restaurant) chains in North America.[14] Another movie, *Super Size Me* (2003), the classic book by George Ritzer, *The McDonaldization of Society*, and *The Omnivore's Dilemma* by Michael Pollan also stimulated more debate about the value of "fast food" to the world and people's nutrition.[15] Restaurant and foodservice customers are putting an increasing emphasis on eating healthfully, and are demanding more healthful options on menus.[16,17] The restaurant and foodservice sector has responded by providing healthful options and nutritional information on menus.

   d. *Increasing Attention and Concern with Food Safety.* There have been several recent outbreaks of food-borne illnesses traced to food served in restaurants and cruise ships. This has raised the public's concern about the safety of food served in restaurants and other foodservice facilities. The NRA has identified the need for more training in food safety for managers and hourly employees among its long-term trend forecast or "7 Sure Things in 2015."[18]

   e. *Growing Demand for Greater Variety of Food and Meals.* Customers are becoming more experienced and sophisticated in dining. They are exploring more national cuisines, and constantly challenging restaurants to develop new concepts and introduce novel menu items (Figure 10.5). Restaurant companies are following a brand segmentation trend similar to lodging in adding new brands as a growth strategy. Darden Restaurants is one of the world's leading restaurant companies, and one that has been especially innovative in introducing new concepts.

   f. *Increasing Co-branding and Variety of Foodservice Locations.* Another strong trend is the movement toward **co-branding** or putting two or more branded restaurant and foodservice concepts together in one business location. **Multi-branding** is another name for co-branding, as is brand bundling and brand alliances. It is a strategy in which a firm puts more than one of its brands into the same restaurant in hopes of raising sales and improving operating efficiency.[19] Keller suggests that this strategy has seven distinct advantages: (1) borrowing expertise from sibling brands, (2) leveraging combined brand equity, (3) reducing production costs, (4) reducing marketing costs, (5) expanding brand meaning, (6) increasing customer access points and (7) increasing unit

FIGURE 10.5
Customers today are more interested in exploring different national and ethnic cuisines.

revenues.[20] Yum! Brands, Inc. has used this strategy extensively with all of its branded restaurants.

Restaurant chains are also finding new locations for their units, and this has been a trend allied with co-branding. To sustain their growth, the leading chains now have units or kiosks in airports, gas and convenience stores (C-stores), stadiums, theme and amusement parks, and universities and colleges.

g. ***Customers Demanding Greater Convenience.*** Another major trend in this sector is that customers continually seek greater convenience in the foods they consume at home, and in restaurants and foodservice establishments. This convenience trend sprouted many restaurant concepts such as home delivery, drive-through restaurants, restaurant kiosks, many "to-go" containers, and many "grab-and-go" concepts such as Pret a Manger, Panera Bread, Delifrance, Starbucks, and a host of others. Time-pressed consumers increasingly want not only to eat more healthily, but seem to want to do it more quickly.

Cruise Line Sector

Although cruise ships are a mode of transportation, cruise line companies are suppliers rather than carriers. The only real difference between cruises and resorts today is that the cruise resort hotel moves. Appendix 1.3 lists the major cruise lines that cater to North Americans and other customers around the world.

a. ***Rapidly Growing Demand and Capacity.*** Cruising is one of the fastest growing segments of the hospitality and travel industry. The Cruise Lines International Association (CLIA) estimated that 12.56 million people took cruise vacations originating from North America in 2007, almost 25 times as many as in 1970.[21] It is expected that 16.5 million people worldwide will take cruises in 2009.[22] In the late 1950s, scheduled transatlantic ocean liners carried more than 1 million persons between Europe and North America. Today scheduled liner services are almost nonexistent, and major vessels are built for the cruise business (Figure 10.6). Unlike most parts of the North American hospitality and travel industry, cruising is controlled by foreign companies. The Scandinavians have an especially large share of the North American cruise business.

Along with the rapid growth in demand for cruises, there has been a major increase in cruise ship capacity. *The ISL Cruise Fleet Register 2007/2008* included 284 cruise ships operating worldwide in 2008.[23] The Cruise Lines International Association estimated that 185 cruise ships with a combined capacity of 263,936 lower berths were serving the North American market (see Appendix 1.3). CLIA estimated that 34 new ships would be added from 2008 to 2012 to the fleet positioned to serve North Americans.[24]

b. ***Increasing Creativity and Expansion of Target Markets.*** The key to the success of cruising has been its repositioning as a viable alternative to traditional resort vacations. Cruise ships are now perceived as floating resorts with a full range of accommodations and dining, recreation, and entertainment services. Cruise line companies have been among the most creative in the industry in developing a broad spectrum of cruise packages and programs. In addition to traditional packages, a variety of specialized shipboard packages are now available. For example, the Crystal Cruises Creative Learning Institute (CLI) offers a variety of learning and self-enrichment programs from piano playing to a collegiate

FIGURE 10.6 Cruises have grown in popularity partly because of their purchase convenience and all-inclusiveness.

Image copyright Ocuio, 2008. Used under license from Shutterstock.com

Did You Know?

What Is the Fastest-growing Part of the Hospitality, Travel and Tourism Business?

- Many would say it is cruising and the cruise lines.
- The Cruise Lines International Association (CLIA) states that in the 1980s, 40 new cruise ships were built; in the 1990s, there were 80 new ships; and from 2000–2007, 100 new cruise ships were added.
- The number of North Americans taking cruises grew by 2100 percent from 1970 to 2007.
- An estimated 12.5 million North Americans cruised in 2007.
- Cruise ships are also getting bigger with more passenger capacity. They can now accommodate 5,000 or more passengers.
- Cruising is also booming in Europe and Asia. The European Cruise Council estimates that in 2005, 2.8 million passengers embarked on cruise ships from European ports and 3.3 million Europeans booked cruises that year.
- In 2005, Asia had 1.07 million cruise passengers, but that was projected to grow to 1.5 million by 2010.

Sources: CLIA. 2007. *Cruise Industry Source Book.* 2007 Mid-year Update, page 9; European Cruise Council. (2007). "Seatrade Europe 2007 rides the wave of the buoyant European cruise market"; Ministry of Culture and Tourism, Republic of Indonesia. (2007). *Cruise ASEAN.*

course in computers.[25] Cruise line companies have also been quick to spot new target markets and emerging trends. Most now have a significant volume of group business, both in shipboard conventions and meetings, and in incentive trips. Innovative companies have introduced fly-cruise and cruise-land packages. Mini-cruises, often for weekends, have also become more popular. The family cruise marketing is also continuing to grow, and is getting more attention from the cruise lines.[26]

Cruise market demand and ship capacity are becoming more global, as other parts of the world far from the Caribbean enjoy rapid growth. The Asia-Pacific region is one of the fastest-growing cruise destinations and markets. It is expected that 1.5 million people per year will be cruising in the Asia-Pacific region by 2010. The two largest cruise ship companies, Carnival and Royal Caribbean, are now positioning some of their ships to serve Asian markets. Star Cruises is the leading cruise line in the Asia-Pacific market, and is the parent company of Norwegian Cruise Line. It has 21 ships and 33,300 lower berths.[27,28]

c. ***Continuing Dependence on Travel Agents.*** One of the best examples of industry interdependency is the cruise line-travel agent relationship. Ninety percent of North Americans who reserve cruise vacations do so through retail travel agents.[29] Individual cruise lines are highly dependent on the positive recommendations of agents.

d. *Changing Cruiser Demographics.* For some time, cruises had a reputation of only being for wealthy, elderly people. More recently, the average age and income of North American cruise passengers have decreased dramatically since the early 1970s. However, the average cruise passenger is 49 years-old, has a higher median household income of around $84,000, and has more education, 57% having graduated from college.[30]

e. *Resort Companies Entering the Cruise Business.* If you can manage a land-based resort hotel successfully, then why not a floating resort hotel? The Disney Cruise Line operates two ships in the Caribbean, and plans to add two more ships, each with 4000-passenger capacities, in 2011 and 2012.

f. *Increasing Cruise Line Consolidation.* As was true in the lodging, restaurant and foodservice sectors, the leading cruise lines are getting bigger and more powerful in the cruise sector. The two leading cruise brands, Carnival and Royal Caribbean International, had 50,882 and 52,838 total passenger capacity respectively in 2007 representing 39.3 percent of the total for the North American market. Seven brands (Carnival, Royal Caribbean International, Princess Cruises, Norwegian Cruise Line, Costa Cruise Lines, Holland America Line, and Celebrity Cruises) have around 83 percent of this total capacity.[31]

g. *Adding Innovative Amenities and Facilities.* Cruise ships are increasingly allowing passengers to stay connected with the onshore world by providing cell phone access, Internet cafés, and Wi-Fi zones. New recreational facilities such as rock-climbing walls, water parks, and ice-skating rinks are being incorporated in the newer and larger ships. Additional spa, health, and fitness facilities are also being incorporated and themed restaurants and bars are being added.[32]

Car Rental Sector

The car rental sector has also enjoyed steady growth in the past five years, and especially since the repercussions of 9–11 wore off. According to *Auto Rental News*, the total revenues of the auto rental market in the United States in 2007 was $21.54 billion, and there were more than 1.851 million cars in the fleet.[33] The six largest companies (Enterprise Rent-A-Car, Hertz, National Car Rental/Alamo Rent A Car, Avis Rent A Car, Budget Rent A Car, and Dollar Thrifty Automotive Group) each had 140,000 or more cars. Appendix 1.4 lists the major car rental firms in the United States.

a. *Globalizing of Leading Car Rental Brands.* The major car rental operations are becoming truly global brand names and their distinctive logos and color schemes are popping up all over the world. Enterprise Rent-A-Car had a global fleet of 714,000 vehicles, more than 6,900 branches, and revenues of $10.1 billion in 2008. As well as being the sector's leading brand in the United States, Enterprise has approximately 500 branches and 40,000 rental vehicles in the United Kingdom, Ireland, and Germany. It has

400 branches and 40,000 vehicles in Canada.[34] Hertz remains the global leading brand group in the car rental sector with 8,100 branches in 147 countries. It is the leading brand in the United States in terms of airport branches, and has many branches at major European airports.[35]

b. *Increasing Consolidation and Sales Concentration among Leading Brands.* Although there are many car rental firms around the world, the majority are small businesses. The bulk of the sales are made by a small group of the leading brands. According to *Auto Rental News*, the top six rental car companies had approximately 92 percent of the total 2007 car rental market revenues in the United States. The car rental sector is becoming more consolidated, as in most of the other hospitality and tourism industry sectors. Two of the leading brands, National and Alamo, are owned by Vanguard Car Rental USA. Avis and Budget are now one company consisting of two car rental brands under the Avis Budget Group, Inc. Two other leading brands, Dollar and Thrifty, are also part of one corporation, the Dollar Thrifty Automotive Group, Inc.

c. *Enhancing and Expanding Customer Services.* The car rental is increasingly competitive and the leading brands are continuously adding new and improved customer services. These include express services for frequent renters, self-booking online, more in-car amenities such as mobile phones and GPS (Figure 10.7), and a larger selection of automobile types.[36] For example, Hertz offers the NeverLost® navigation system and Avis the Where2™ portable GPS system by Garmin. Hertz also offers SIRIUS satellite radio in cars, and a unique collection of cars and SUVs that include Corvettes and Hummers in the Hertz Fun Collection®.

d. *Evolving Frequent Renter Programs.* All the major car rental brands have introduced frequent renter or loyalty programs. Most of these programs offer members benefits such as counter-bypass service, awards such as

FIGURE 10.7 GPS devices in rental cars are now becoming more popular.

free rental days, and guarantees of certain vehicles when making reservations. These programs are also linked with selected airline frequent flier programs and hotel chain frequent guest programs.

e.   *Increasing Emphasis on Revenue Management.* Car rental companies face many of the same problems as airlines and hotels in ensuring high capacity usage throughout the week and satisfactory levels of profitability. "No-shows" are particularly high for car rental companies, and demand peaks in midweek due to high corporate usage.[37] The solution to these problems was for the car rental sector to introduce revenue management systems that are similar to the airlines and hotel chains.

f.   *Implementing Branding and Brand Segmentation Strategies.* The car rental companies are increasingly relying upon branding strategies for growth, much like the lodging and restaurant and foodservice sectors. Many of the companies are adding new brands, for example, in the replacement market and through truck rentals. Hertz Local Edition® (HLE) is an example of a new brand introduced for insurance replacement and local car rentals. Hertz also divides its vehicles into the Prestige, Fun, and Green (fuel efficient and environmentally friendly) Collections. Enterprise also has a truck rental brand, and a car sales unit.

g.   *Experiencing a Greater Diversity of Distribution.* The car rental sector, much like lodging, is experiencing changes in its channels of distribution. Car rental brands are now more dependent of GDS and online travel companies, and receive more reservations through direct online bookings by customers. Many brands have contracts with major corporations, and therefore rely heavily on business through corporate travel departments. Travel agents still provide a significant share of bookings.

Attraction and Event Sector

Attractions and events usually play a key role in luring visitors to destinations, as well as entertaining local residents. Some attractions are both physical and fixed, such as the Eiffel Tower, the Great Wall of China, Canada's Wonderland in Toronto, Hong Kong Disneyland, the Grand Canyon, the Taj Mahal, and Niagara Falls. Others are event-oriented, are less permanent, and have locations that, in some cases, frequently change (e.g., mega-events such the Summer and Winter Olympic Games, the Pan American Games, World Expo, and soccer's World Cup). A wide variety of private-sector, government, and nonprofit organizations operate attractions. They range in size from corporations as big as Disney and Universal Studios to small, local museum boards.

a.   *Continuing Growth in Theme Park Demand.* Disney pioneered the theme park concept by opening Disneyland in 1955. Fifty years later in 2005, it started operating Hong Kong Disneyland. In that half century and to this day, new theme parks were built all around the world, making them another of the fast-growing elements of the hospitality and travel industry. The combined attendance at the top 20 theme parks in the United States in 2007 was 122.8 million. The top 20 European theme parks had a combined attendance of 60.9 million in 2007; while 65.8 million attended the top 10 theme parks in the Asia-Pacific region.[38] PricewaterhouseCoopers estimated the worldwide spending at theme parks and amusement parks would grow at a compound annual rate of 4.6 percent from 2007 to 2011.[39] Additional information on theme park attendance is provided in Appendix 1.5A and Appendix 1.5B.

b. *Increasing Creativity in Use of Technology and Entertainment Programming.* Theme parks and other attractions continue to thrive because they continually update and add to the mix of entertainment they provide. New "rides" have been added in theme and amusement parks such as pneumatic tower rides, interactive dark and 4-D rides, LIM and hydraulic launch coasters, and "giant" rides. Park guests are also being given specialized personal assistant devices that help them keep in touch with their friends and family, and maximize their time in a park. They are also adding more live entertainment, animal shows, family rides, interactive experiences, and nightlife activities.[40] Another trend has been for theme parks to add full-scale waterparks, which add to the mix of attractions while helping with crowding at other rides and providing guest "relief" on hot days.[41]

c. *Continuing Development of Major Attractions around the World.* Although the development of theme parks is slowing down in North America, major theme parks and attractions are being added and built worldwide. Hong Kong Disneyland opened in September 2005, and new theme parks have also started operations in India and the People's Republic of China. A theme park based on Charles Dickens' stories, Dickens World, opened in Kent, England in May 2007 (Figure 10.8). A new

FIGURE 10.8 Dickens World is a new theme park concept in England.

Courtesy of Dickens World Chatham Maritime England

park with a rock-and-roll theme, the Hard Rock Park, opened in 2008 in the United States at Myrtle Beach, South Carolina.

d. *Adding Interactivity and Attendee Participation.* The modern theme parks are highly interactive and offer many opportunities for audience participation. Other attractions, especially museums, have traditionally been very static and one-dimensional. This is changing as museums and science centers add more interactive exhibits and programming for attendees.

e. *Increasing Size and Market Strength of Industry Leaders.* As in most of the previous sectors, the leading attraction companies are becoming bigger and stronger. Disney remains the undisputed world leader in the theme park business while Universal Studios, Paramount Parks, and Six Flags Theme Parks are other leading companies in North America. Merlin Entertainments of the United Kingdom is now among the world's leaders with attractions and theme parks across Europe and the Legoland California theme park.

Casino and Gaming Sector

Gaming is not gambling, according to the American Gaming Association (AGA). **Gaming** is defined by the AGA as the action or habit of playing at games of chance for stakes.[42] Whatever you call it, the rapid growth of casino destinations around the world is a major trend in the hospitality and travel industry. In the United States, this sector includes the casino destinations in Nevada and Atlantic City, New Jersey; tribal casinos; and regional casinos (Colorado, Illinois, Indiana, Iowa, Louisiana, Michigan, Mississippi, Missouri, and South Dakota). Canada has casinos in Ontario, British Columbia, Alberta, and Nova Scotia. There are many casinos in Europe, especially in the United Kingdom, France, Germany, Spain, and the Netherlands. South Africa is also a major casino destination on the African continent. Macau is the major casino destination in the Asia-Pacific region, followed by Australia, South Korea, Malaysia, Philippines, and New Zealand.[43] Casinos are illegal in Mainland China.

a. *Increasing Development of Casino Destinations.* The relaxation of government policies and the general public's attitudes toward gaming has fueled the casino destination growth trend in many parts of the world (Figure 10.9). The excellent profitability levels of casino operations have attracted developers, and these entrepreneurs have designed highly attractive and imaginative facilities that draw guests. Additionally, casino destinations create numerous economic benefits for their surrounding communities. In 2007, there were 467 commercial casinos in 12 states of the United States, employing 361,000 people. The total commercial casino gaming revenues in 2007 were $34.1 billion.[44,45] The six leading casino markets in the United States in terms of gross revenues were the Las Vegas Strip, Atlantic City, Chicagoland (Illinois-Indiana), Connecticut, Detroit, and Tunica/Lula in Mississippi.

The fastest growing casino destination area in the world is the Asia-Pacific region; by 2010 it is projected to be the second largest in gross casino

Image copyright Yuri Arcurs, 2008. Used under license from Shutterstock.com

FIGURE 10.9 Casinos have enjoyed a rapid and steady growth rate in North America, Macau, and other parts of the world.

destination revenues behind only North America. Macau is the main casino destination with more than half of the total revenues in the region. With the development of several large new casino resorts, Macau will garner an even larger market share and has surpassed Las Vegas in gaming revenues.[46] The Venetian is one of the newer casino resort hotels in Macau.

b. ***Expanding Range of Casino Locations and Concepts.*** Casinos can be found in a wide variety of locations. These include traditional casino resorts destinations such as Las Vegas, Atlantic City, and Macau. There are also many casinos on the water (riverboats and cruise ships) or at water-side (ocean, lakes, and rivers), and on native people's lands in the United States and Canada. For example, Foxwoods in Connecticut is one of the largest casinos in the world, with 340,000 square feet of gaming space and 1,416 guest rooms. It is operated by the Mashantucket Pequot Tribal Nation.

Carriers

The carriers, including airlines, railways, ferries, buses or motorcoaches, and canals, provide transportation from the customers' origins to their destinations. Airlines are the most powerful sector within the carriers and they influence most of the other groups of organizations.

Airline Sector

Although airlines are classified as carriers, many have diversified into other parts of hospitality and tourism, including tour operations. Meanwhile, the world's major airlines have become truly global brands, such as Lufthansa, British Airways, Air France, KLM, American Airlines, United, and Singapore

Airlines. The airlines sector is one of the largest in hospitality and tourism, with the International Air Transport Association (IATA) estimating total worldwide commercial aviation passenger revenues at $384 billion in 2007.[47]

a. *Increasing Concern with Safety and Security.* The tragic events of 9–11 dramatically increased the world's concern with airline safety and security. This has resulted in additional security procedures at airports and on aircraft, as well as more documentation and screening at international entry points.

b. *Growing Presence of Low-Cost Carriers.* The greatest recent growth in airline passenger transportation in all parts of the world has been with the low-cost carriers. The low-cost carriers (LCC) include companies such as Southwest Airlines and JetBlue Airways in the United States; WestJet in Canada; EasyJet and Ryanair in the UK and Europe; AirAsia, Air Deccan, and Tiger Airways in Asia; and Virgin Blue in Australia. These airlines had captured significant market shares in North America, Europe, and Asia-Pacific by 2008. **Low-cost carriers** operate only one class of service, with a single type of short-haul aircraft, and take reservations mainly through the Internet and by telephone. Another LCC definition from the United States is that these are airlines which operate a point-to-point network, pay employees below the industry average, and offer no frills service.[48,49]

c. *E-ticketing Becoming the Standard.* The need for "hard copies" of airline tickets is fast vanishing, as the airline sector pushes toward its goal of ticketless travel. On June 1, 2008, IATA announced that the international airlines had achieved its goal of 100 percent e-ticketing. E-tickets save the airlines, since the cost of processing a paper ticket is 10 times higher than an e-ticket. E-tickets are also much more convenient for passengers, and give retail travel agents greater flexibility in serving clients.[50]

d. *Aircraft Getting Bigger and Faster.* In March 2007, the Airbus A380 made its first flight across the Atlantic Ocean (Figure 10.10). This is the largest aircraft in operation carrying 525 passengers. Technological innovations are also helping to increase the speed and range of new aircraft.

e. *Increasing Use of Self-Service Check-in.* Common-use self-service (CUSS) is now common in most major airports. These are self-service kiosks that allow passengers to check-in without going to the counter. This allows passengers to check-in more quickly and saves money for the airlines.

f. *Maintaining Frequent-Flier Programs (FFPs).* The airlines introduced the concept of frequent-traveler award or loyalty programs to the industry in the early 1980s. FFPs now have millions of members; for example, United's *Mileage Plus* program had around 52 million members in 2008.[51] These programs bring many benefits but also create significant challenges for the airlines. They create greater passenger loyalty and allow the airlines to build extensive customer databases. FFPs, however, create significant future "liabilities" for airlines in miles to be redeemed in the future by members.

FIGURE 10.10 The Airbus 380 is the largest passenger aircraft in the world.

g. *Expanding Global Airline Strategic Alliances.* Strategic alliances are very important to the world's larger airlines. The three major airline **strategic alliances** in the world are the Star Alliance, oneworld, and SkyTeam. According to Lufthansa, these alliances allow the airlines achieve higher revenues and reduce costs by exploiting synergy effects. These effects range from joint use of ground facilities, such as check-in counters, a city office, and airport terminals.[52] However, these are primarily marketing alliances, using common branding strategies to promote them.[53]

Railway Sector

In many parts of the world, railways are a major carrier linking countries, major cities, and tourism destination areas. This is especially true in Europe and Japan, where a highly advanced passenger railway system has been developed. Railway systems are also of great importance to large developing countries such as the People's Republic of China and India. The passenger rail systems in these countries are much more important to the hospitality and travel industry than railways are in North America. However, Amtrak and Via Rail Canada, the two major passenger rail companies in the United States and Canada, still play a significant role.

The continuing development of high-speed trains is one of the major trends in passenger railways (Figure 10.11). These include the *Eurostar* that links Paris, London, Brussels, and Disneyland ResortParis; the *TGV* (*train à grande vitesse*) in France; *ICE* (InterCity Express) and *ICE T* (ICE trains with tilting technology) in Germany and Switzerland; and the *Shinkansen* (bullet train) in Japan. High-speed trains are also in operation in other countries such as the

FIGURE 10.11 Many countries in the world have introduced high-speed passenger trains.

Image copyright Holger Mette, 2008. Used under license from Shutterstock.com

United States and China. These trains now reach speeds up to 300 kilometers per hour, but are capable of higher speeds; a TGV train reached 575 KMPH in early April 2007.[54] The introduction of trains with magnetic levitation technology (MAGLEV) will significantly increase the speed of trains. There is one MAGLEV train in operation from Shanghai's Pudong International Airport to the Pudong area of Shanghai in China.

The privatization of railways is a second major trend among passenger railway systems. This has resulted in several new private railway companies being established in the United Kingdom, including Virgin Trains, the sister company of Virgin Atlantic. The railways have also been privatized in Australia and New Zealand, and other parts of the world.

The services, amenities, and programs provided on passenger trains around the world are constantly being upgraded, especially on the newer, high-speed trains. The seats in rail coaches are increasingly becoming like those in modern airplanes. VIA Rail Canada introduced Wi-Fi wireless Internet services for *VIA 1* customers in the Quebec City-Windsor corridor. VIA has also introduced some programming in the *Easterly* class service between Montreal and Halifax in the summer. A complete Maritime learning experience involving regional culture, history, and geography is offered, and customers actively participate in a variety of on-board activities.[55]

Passenger railway companies are experiencing many of the same technological changes brought about by the Internet, as well an increasing concern with safety and security in response to global terrorism. E-ticketing and online booking at the railway's websites and through Internet travel companies are other strong trends. Many of the railways have their own frequent passenger clubs and partner with other frequent traveler programs in the hospitality and travel industry.

Ferry Sector

Ferries are an especially important carrier for sea passage between countries and among islands and mainland areas. In most cases, they carry local commuters as well as visitors. In Western Europe, ferry services are particularly important for crossing the Irish Sea, English Channel, North Sea, and Baltic Sea. Some of the major operators are P&O Ferries, Irish Ferries, Stena Line, and SeaFrance. There are also major ferry services in Australia, Canada, and the United States. For example, in Canada, The British Columbia Ferry Corporation carried more than 21 million passengers and 8.5 million vehicles in 2008.[56] Ferries are also of great importance to hospitality and tourism in the Pearl River Delta of China, carrying passengers between Hong Kong, Macau, and multiple cities in Guangdong Province.

The major trends in the ferry sector include the introduction of larger, more modern, and faster ferries. Ferry companies are also becoming more involved in offering cruise excursions, and in carrying freight. There is also an increasing emphasis in cooperative marketing among ferry companies, as they seek to counter more competition from other carriers. These partnerships include the Sail and Drive campaign (http://www.sailanddrive.com) among the major ferry operator companies operating between the United Kingdom and Europe. Like the railways, ferry companies are constantly trying to improve and add to the onboard experiences of passengers.

Bus and Motorcoach Sector

Buses and motorcoaches play a very important role in destinations around the world, both within cities and for inter-city and long-distance travel, and are vital to escorted and sightseeing tours. Bus and motorcoach companies offer both scheduled and charter services and many provide tour programs. Scheduled services offer a lower-cost alternative to air and rail transport, and are important for budget and youth travel. The American Bus Association (ABA) defines a motorcoach as a bus designed for the long-distance transportation of passengers, that has integral construction with an elevated passenger deck located over a baggage compartment, and that is at least 35 feet in length with a capacity of more than 30 passengers. So not all buses are motorcoaches.[57]

The bus and motorcoach sector is made up of thousands of companies, ranging in size from the small companies with less than 25 buses to the larger bus companies with 100 or more vehicles. Some of the larger companies are very well known, such as Greyhound in the United States and Canada, National Express and Stagecoach in the United Kingdom, and Greyhound Australia. Recent research suggests that bus and motorcoach passenger travel is on the upswing. A study conducted by DePaul University in 2008 showed that intercity scheduled bus travel increased by 9.8 percent from the fourth quarter in 2007 to the fourth quarter in 2008.[58] The American Bus Association (ABA) believes that partly this is due to the increase in non-traditional bus riders in their 20s who prefer "traveling green" in buses than in their own or others' cars.[59]

As with the railway and ferry sectors, buses and motorcoaches are becoming bigger, faster, and more comfortable. The services provided on the vehicles are also continuously improving.

Canal Sector

You might not immediately think of canals as a part of the hospitality and travel industry, but in fact they play a significant role in transportation, as tourism attractions, and as places for leisure and recreation. For example, the Panama Canal in Central America is not only a vital shipping route, but is also a major cruising destination. The canals of Venice, Italy are another major tourism attraction, as is sailing and barging on the canals in France and the Netherlands. The United Kingdom is crisscrossed with many canal systems and canals are important sites for tourism, recreation, and leisure. In North America, the New York State Canal system in the United States and the Rideau Canal system in Canada are two good examples of important tourism and recreation destinations.

Travel Trade Intermediaries

The travel trade intermediaries are so important to distribution in the hospitality and travel industry that Chapter 13 is devoted entirely to them. In this chapter, there is just a brief description of the major travel trade intermediaries and the roles they play.

Retail Travel Agent Sector

Travel agencies in many countries are experiencing turbulent times, especially in the United States and Canada. A period of rapid growth ended as agencies confronted reduced airline commissions, new competition from Internet travel companies, and more online self-booking by customers. Historically, travel agencies were almost totally dependent on carriers, suppliers, and other intermediaries for revenues through commissions. Today, most travel agencies have diversified revenue sources and most in North America and Europe now charge clients with service fees. Many hospitality and travel organizations still depend heavily on the travel agent's positive recommendations, including the cruise lines and tour operators. This two-way relationship and interdependence is a unique feature of hospitality and travel marketing, and is a good example of the partnership concept discussed later in this chapter.

Travel agents are a key target market for suppliers, carriers, DMOs, and other travel trade intermediaries. Many have set up preferred supplier or vendor relationships with individual travel agencies in order to secure a larger share of the agencies' bookings. Usually these relationships offer agencies higher commission rates on the preferred supplier's/vendor's services.

Tour Wholesaler and Operator Sector

Chapter 12 takes an in-depth look at the seemingly endless selection of packages and programs developed by the industry. Many are put together and operated by this second group of intermediaries. Wholesalers and operators negotiate and block space and prices with suppliers and carriers and then add a markup to all the elements to determine an all-inclusive price. They prepare brochures about tours and packages, which they distribute mainly through travel agencies and on the web. There are thousands of companies that assemble tours. Most suppliers and carriers assemble their own tours and packages and, at the same time, participate in those of tour operators and wholesalers.

Corporate Travel Sector

Corporations, governments, and non-profit organizations are increasingly sensitive to the escalating costs of travel. The traditional approach allowed individual departments, divisions, or even managers to book their own flights, rooms, and rental cars. However, an increasing number of organizations now recognize the inefficiencies of this approach and the financial benefits of negotiating rates and prices based on the combined purchasing power of an entire group. Corporate travel managers are a key target for many suppliers and carriers, including hotels, airlines, rental car firms, and convention/meeting destinations and facilities.

Incentive Travel Planning Sector

Although what usually happens on incentive travel trips is definitely pleasurable, the buyers of these specialized vacation-like packages are businesses. More corporations are realizing the increasing value of using travel to reward employees, dealers, and others for outstanding performance. Consequently, the incentive travel business has grown from a very small part of the industry to a multibillion-dollar trade. There are now many specialized incentive travel-planning firms. Incentive travel planners are really specialized tour wholesalers who provide services directly to sponsoring organizations. They are compensated by a markup on the various elements of the incentive package. Many lodging chains, airlines, resorts, DMOs, cruise lines, and others have noticed the trend, and have added in-house incentive specialists or complete incentive departments.

Convention/Meeting Planning Sector

The fifth main travel trade group is made up of convention/meeting planners. Some are employed by major national associations, large non-profit groups, government agencies, educational institutions, and large corporations. There are also many independent meeting planners. The convention/meeting business is a multibillion-dollar market that has shown continually high growth rates. As a result, it has attracted greater attention from various suppliers (hotels, resorts, cruise lines, car rental firms, and conference and convention centers), carriers (airlines), other intermediaries (travel agents), and DMOs (national and state/provincial tourism offices and convention and visitors bureaus).

Convention/meeting planners organize events ranging from international conventions with hundreds of thousands of attendees to small board meetings with ten or fewer persons. They select meeting destinations, lodging and convention/meeting facilities, delegate/spouse tours and programs, and official airline carriers. A significant proportion of these planners are also responsible for arranging incentive travel trips.

Online Travel Company Sector

These include companies such as Expedia.com, Travelocity.com, Orbitz.com, Priceline.com, Hotels.com, and many others. They have grown in number and importance since the Internet began.

Global Distribution Systems (GDSs)

There are four major global distribution systems in the world (Amadeus, Galileo, Sabre, and Worldspan). These systems are very important for booking and reservations to travel agencies, airlines, hotels, car rentals, and others.

Destination Marketing Organizations (DMOs)

Hospitality and travel industry growth is luring many government agencies and other groups into marketing their destinations to pleasure and business travelers. Every state, province, and territory now has a destination marketing organization (DMO). Nationally, organizations such as Tourism Australia, VisitBritain, Canadian Tourism Commission, Hong Kong Tourism Board, and Singapore Tourism Board are investing millions of dollars in tourism marketing and development. More cities, regions, and areas are creating convention and visitors bureaus (CVBs) or tourism boards to handle this specialized type of marketing.

National, State, Provincial, and Territorial DMO Sector

Most countries, states, provinces, and territories have an official DMO, although surprisingly the United States is an exception. The marketing of the United States as a destination is done by the private sector and by the Travel Industry Association (TIA), a non-profit trade association. Other countries are spending significant amounts on their national DMOs, including Tourism Australia with AU$161.5 million of funding for the operating year of 2007–08; in 2008, the Canadian Tourism Commission used C$84.4 in its operations and VisitBritain received an appropriation of €47.9 million from government for its operating year of 2008–09.[59] The UN World Tourism Organization in Madrid, Spain is the official agency that coordinates and assists all of these national tourism administrations.

Many of these organizations have offices in other countries to market their countries. They are now placing much greater emphasis on Internet marketing, and several have multilingual websites. Their marketing programs target both individual travelers and travel trade intermediaries. Often they enter into cooperative marketing with suppliers, carriers, travel trade intermediaries, and other destination marketing organizations. Many also provide seed money—in cooperative marketing programs—to other DMOs in their countries.

INTERNET MARKETING

Marketing the USA and Canada Abroad: International Tourism Marketing on the Internet

- Countries and companies around the world are placing more emphasis on international tourism and marketing to foreign visitors.
- The Travel Industry Association (TIA) in 2008 introduced new *Discover America* websites for five of the USA's top international markets (Canada–English and French, Mexico, U.K., Japan, and Germany). These five markets represent 75 percent of the foreign travel to the U.S.
- Although world travel is growing, research by TIA showed a decline in international travel to the U.S. since 2000.
- The U.S. received *Approved Destination Status* from China in late 2007 and is hoping that this will further boost its international tourism. However, it has no Chinese-language website.
- Canada seems to be well ahead of the USA in its international tourism marketing and has had a strong presence on the Internet for many years.
- The *Canada Keep Exploring* websites are available for nine countries (Australia, China, France, Germany, Japan, Korea, Mexico, U.K., and the USA).
- Some of the interesting features on these Canadian Tourism Commission websites are the "Pure Canada" magazine and the "Blogs" page. Pure Canada looks like an online magazine, with sections on different topics (arts, books, drink, feature destination, feature trends, food, lodging, "out" travel, shopping, sports, and wellness). The Blogs page shows short stories by travelers on their trips to Canada.

Sources: Travel Industry Association. (2007). **http:/www.tia.org/pressmedia/current_news.html;** Travel Industry Association of America. (2008). **http:/www.DiscoverAmerica.com/;** Canadian Tourism Commission. (2008). **http:/www.explore.canada.travel/ctc/ke/homepage.jsp?localeId=16**

Student Questions

1. Why do you think that Canada is so far ahead of the United States in its international tourism marketing, including online promotion?
2. What should the U.S. do to attract more international tourists?
3. What are the most essential features and types of information to include in websites aimed at international tourists?
4. How can a destination put across a sense of safety and security though its website?

City and County DMO Sector

Most communities around the world with a resident population of more than 50,000 now have some form of local DMO. In North America, these tend to be called convention and visitors bureaus (CVBs); other parts of the world often use different names such as tourism boards or tourism administrations. More than 625 of the larger DMOs in 25 countries belong to Destination Marketing Association International (DMAI). These local DMOs try to bring more conventions, meetings, and pleasure travelers to their communities. They represent a broad group of suppliers and travel trade intermediaries in their destination areas. Like the previous group, these DMOs divide their attention between the travel trade, particularly convention/meeting planners and tour operators/wholesalers, and individual travelers.

In North America, these local DMOs are often called **convention and visitors bureaus (CVBs)**. A CVB is a not-for-profit organization supported by transient room tax, government budget allocations, private membership, or a combination of any or all three. The bureau in each city, county, or region has three prime responsibilities: (1) to encourage groups to hold meetings, conventions, and tradeshows in the city or area it represents; (2) to assist those groups with meeting preparations and while their meeting is in progress; and (3) to encourage tourists to visit and enjoy the historic, cultural, and recreational opportunities the destination offers.[60]

Overall Trends and Industry Realities

You have now had a detailed look at the hospitality and travel industry and the diversity of roles played by the four groups and 20 sectors. You should have noticed five main points in reviewing this material:

1. There has been a trend toward organizations increasing the scope of their operations within their specific field (e.g., lodging, restaurant and foodservice, cruise line, and car rental brand segmentation). The technical term for these moves is **horizontal integration** which is developing or acquiring similar businesses.

2. More organizations in the industry are expanding up and down the distribution channel. The name for these combinations is **vertical integration**. Carlson is one of the best examples in North America. Its companies include Carlson Hotels Worldwide, Carlson Restaurants Worldwide (including T.G.I. Friday's), Carlson Marketing Group, Regent Seven Seas Cruises, and Carlson Wagonlit Travel.

3. The hospitality and travel industry has steadily introduced a wide variety of new services, facilities, and travel alternatives. Although demand growth is tapering off in some industry groups and sectors, there are still great opportunities for new services, facilities, and travel services.

4. The Internet has had a major impact on all groups and sectors of the industry.

5. The industry is becoming increasingly competitive, forcing all participants to constantly improve, or at least maintain, service levels.

Industry Players

Vertical Integration in Hospitality and Travel

Carlson

http://www.carlson.com

Founded in 1938 by Curtis L. Carlson, Carlson has become one of North America's largest and perhaps, the most vertically integrated hospitality and travel organization. In 2008, the company's brands, all of which are in the service industries, included a travel management company (Carlson Wagonlit Travel), hotels and cruises (Radisson Hotels & Resorts, Regent Hotels & Resorts, Country Inns & Suites by Carlson, Park Plaza Hotels & Resorts, Park Inn, and Regent Seven Seas Cruises), restaurants (T.G.I. Friday's®, Pick Up Stix), and a full-service marketing agency (Carlson Marketing Worldwide). The company is, therefore, both on the supplier (hotels, restaurants, cruises) and travel trade intermediary (travel agencies, incentive travel, tour wholesaling and operations) sides of hospitality and travel.

Begun in Minneapolis in 1962, Carlson Hotels Worldwide had more than 995 hotels with 148,500 rooms in 73 countries at the end of July 2008. It has continued to climb the ranks of North America's largest lodging chains and is one of the leaders in brand segmentation with the following types of properties:

- Radisson Hotels & Resorts
- Radisson SAS Hotels & Resorts
- Country Inns & Suites By Carlson
- Park Plaza Hotels & Resorts
- Park Inn

Carlson Hotels Worldwide is a firm believer in the value of marketing research as a tool for marketing decisions, and in the importance of friendly service. Radisson's primary research of frequent business travelers showed that they disliked the typical reactions of hotel employees when asked by a guest for an out-of-the ordinary service. Backed by media advertising, the "Yes I Can" employee-training program was introduced. The program is one of the most extensive in the industry and features training sessions, skill-building sessions, and monthly team meetings. The program now has a 20-year history, showing Radisson's strong commitment. Radisson clearly recognizes the importance of quality service—the people side of its product.

Radisson Hotels & Resorts has introduced several other innovative marketing programs and has followed the trend of brand extensions. These include its "Express Yourself^{SM}" program that allows guests to

(continues)

(continued)

check-in online before they arrive at the hotel. If the guests like their beds, called the *Sleep Number bed by Select Comfort*™, they can be purchased.

Carlson Wagonlit Travel (CWT) attained worldwide sales of $25.5 billion in 2007. It now has four lines of business: (1) traveler and transaction services, (2) program optimization, (3) safety and security, and (4) meetings and events. CWT says it "is the leading travel management company. Specialized in business travel management, CWT is dedicated to helping companies of all sizes, as well as government institutions and non-governmental organizations, optimize their travel program and provide best-in-class service and assistance to travelers."

T.G.I. Friday's® has also enjoyed strong growth as a restaurant brand. It now has 1,019 units in 60 different countries around the world. The first T.G.I. Friday's® was opened in 1965 in New York City. Since then, the brand has expanded rapidly in the USA and abroad. For example, it opened its 300th restaurant outside of the USA in 2007.

Apart from Carlson, there are other examples of vertical integration in our industry around the world. These include TUI AG, which has its headquarters in Hanover, Germany. TUI Travel PLC was formed in September 2007 and has its main office in the UK. However, its travel agency and tour operating units are represented in 180 countries worldwide. TUI's second major brand grouping is TUI Hotels & Resorts, which it claims to be the biggest leisure hotel operator in Europe. TUI's third major operating unit is Hapag-Lloyd, which encompasses Hapag-Lloyd AG in container shipping, and Hapag-Lloyd Cruises.

The Virgin group is a second company originating from Europe that has an extensive vertical integration strategy. Its portfolio of travel companies includes several airlines and a passenger railway company.

Discussion Questions

1. How has Carlson used the vertical integration concept to stimulate its growth in the hospitality and travel industry?
2. What can other major hospitality and travel organizations learn from the approaches that Carlson employed to increase its power and influence in the industry? Which specific companies might be able to follow these same approaches?
3. How should Carlson use its various brands to increase its market share in each of the parts of the hospitality and travel industry in which they operate (i.e., hotels, restaurants, travel agencies, incentive travel, and cruising)?

Carlson Brand Websites:

http://www.radisson.com/
http://www.carlsonwagonlit.com/en/
http://www.tgifridays.com/home/welcome.aspx
http://www.rssc.com/

TUI AG

http://www.tui-group.com/en/

The Product/Service Mix

The products of the hospitality and travel industry are many and varied. Each organization within the industry has its own **product/service mix**, the assortment of services and products that are provided to customers. This mix consists of every visible element in the organization, including the following:

1. Staff behavior, appearance, and uniforms
2. Building exteriors
3. Equipment
4. Furniture and fixtures
5. Signage
6. Communications with customers and other publics

The many behind-the-scenes facilities, equipment, and staff members cannot be forgotten. Although not outwardly visible, they contribute directly to customer satisfaction and are part of the product/service mix. Technically, the mix includes all services, facilities, and packages and programs provided by the organization. This book separates the last two items (packaging and programming) from the first two because of their unique role in the hospitality and travel industry.

1. **Staff Behavior, Appearance, and Uniforms.** Chapter 11 is devoted to the people part of the marketing mix. Here, it is sufficient to mention that the physical aspects of staff appearance must be carefully considered in the marketing plan.
2. **Building Exteriors.** Many hospitality and travel organizations serve their guests in one or more buildings. The overall physical condition and cleanliness of these structures greatly influence the customer's image of the organization and their own satisfaction. A run-down building does not fit well with a luxury positioning. The marketing plan should mention any steps that organizations envisage for the period that will enhance the exterior appearance of their buildings.
3. **Equipment.** Customers evaluate several types of hospitality and travel businesses partly on the upkeep and cleanliness of their equipment. Airline, cruise line, car rental, bus and motorcoach, train, ferry, and attraction companies are a few examples of the relevancy of this element. Many hotels and some restaurants also use shuttle transportation equipment and should be concerned about maintaining it and keeping it clean. A marketing plan should address scheduled improvements and other changes in such equipment.
4. **Furniture and Fixtures.** Customers are sensitive to the quality of the furniture and fixtures within buildings and transportation equipment. Many hospitality and travel companies back up their high-quality images with high-quality furniture and fixtures. A section of the marketing plan should be devoted to improvements and changes in furniture and fixtures.

5. **Signage.** This is another part of the product/service mix that is often forgotten. Most organizations have a variety of signs, including billboards, directional signs, and exterior building signs. Customers often equate a broken or poorly maintained sign with low quality and a non-caring management attitude. The marketing plan should address not only advertising-oriented outdoor signs, but all signs used by customers. New signs can also be used to reflect a new positioning approach by an organization or to signal that a company has remodeled or modernized its facilities and equipment.

6. **Communications with Customers and Other Publics.** Advertising, personal selling, sales promotion, merchandising, public relations and publicity activities, and Internet marketing are often considered only as ways to influence customers to buy. They do, however, play a more subtle role in influencing customers' images of organizations. Negative publicity can detract from an organization's image. Positive publicity can enhance that image. The quality and size of an advertisement, as well as its media placement choice, give customers mental clues to the organization's stature. Promotional giveaways and premiums must be consistent with the organization's image of quality. The organization's website is another important element of these communications.

   If there is one single requirement for all hospitality and travel organization product/service mixes, it is that it must be consistent. Customers notice inconsistencies. By considering all aspects, the marketing plan ensures continuity among the various components.

Product Development Decisions

Most organizations must make product development decisions at two different levels: (1) organization-wide and (2) for individual facilities or services.

1. **Organization-Wide Decisions.**

   a. *Width and Length of Product/Service Mix.* When Disney established the Disney Cruise Line, it expanded its **product/service-mix width** (the number of different services provided by an organization) (Figure 10.12). In marketing jargon, it added a product line. In developing Hong Kong Disneyland, it increased its **product/service-mix length** (the number of similar services provided by an organization). Figure 10.12 shows other examples of these types of decisions. For example, when Richard Branson's company, Virgin, expanded into the passenger rail business in the United Kingdom it was diversifying and adding to its product/service-mix width. When Accor acquired Motel 6 and Red Roof Inn, it increased the length of its product/ service mix, as did Marriott International when it acquired a part ownership of Ritz-Carlton Hotels.

   b. *Improving or Modernizing the Product/Service Mix.* Sometimes a company determines, usually through a situation analysis or

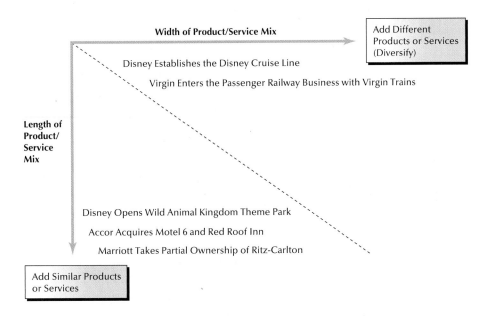

FIGURE 10.12 Width and length of the product/service mix.

marketing research that the time has come to upgrade all or part of its product/service mix. Airlines do this frequently, often repainting their entire fleets or changing their interior finishes, seating layouts, and cabin crew uniforms. Theme parks are constantly updating and adding to their entertainment mix. They do this to encourage repeat visitation. Cruise lines temporarily remove ships from service in order to undertake necessary maintenance and onboard improvements.

c. *Branding.* There was a time when **branding** was relatively unimportant in the hospitality and travel industry; the company's name was all that was attached to the service. Branding is becoming more important as many companies expand the width and length of their product service mixes. Some of the advantages of branding include the following:

- Helps the company segment markets
- Gives the company the potential to attract loyal and profitable customers
- Improves the company's image if their brands are successful
- Helps track reservations, sales, problems, and complaints

Increasing brand segmentation and brand extension in the hospitality and travel industry has already been highlighted in this chapter. It has been occurring in several sectors of the industry including lodging, restaurant and foodservice, rental car, and cruise lines. This approach offers companies the chance to attract larger shares of specific target markets by giving customers facilities and services that better match their needs. In essence, it broadens the customer base from which each branding company draws.

Most of the major lodging and restaurant chains now use a multi-brand approach. Although the advantages are obvious, there are also potential drawbacks. One brand may cannibalize another, or take customers away from the other company brand.

2. *Individual Facility/Service Decisions.* Product/service-mix decisions also have to be made by the individual hotel, restaurant, agency, cruise ship, or other hospitality/travel outlet. These decisions concern the quality, range, and design of the facilities and services provided. Again, the situation analysis and other marketing research studies should provide the impetus for changing these elements.

Partnership

Marketing partnerships of all types are popular in the hospitality and travel industry as more organizations realize the advantages of **relationship marketing** (building, maintaining, and enhancing long-term relationships with customers, suppliers, and travel trade intermediaries). **Partnerships** are cooperative promotions and other cooperative marketing efforts by hospitality and travel organizations. They range from "one-shot" (short-term) cooperative promotions to strategic (long-term) joint marketing agreements that may involve some combination of the products or services of two or more organizations, such as the airline strategic alliances.

Types of Partners

This chapter has described 20 sectors of the hospitality and travel industry organized into four main functional groups. Many of the industry sectors are highly interdependent and share similar goals and target markets. Additionally, the hospitality and travel industry is becoming more globalized, and the major companies and organizations operate across the world. These circumstances create almost limitless opportunities for partnerships in hospitality and tourism.

1. **Customers.** Frequent traveler programs are a good example of a partnership program with customers. These were introduced to build customer loyalty to the companies, but now some go much further than this. Some hospitality and travel companies form advisory groups from among their frequent travelers, and others employ them as advocates of the company to help attract new customers.

   An interesting variation on this theme is the *Brown County Valued Visitors Discount Program* developed by the Brown County Convention & Visitors Bureau in southern Indiana. For a small sign-up fee of $10, people join the program and receive a *Valued Visitors* card and an attractive shopping bag with the *Valued Visitors* logo printed on it. Meanwhile, local shops, restaurants, and lodging places were also recruited to join the program. These businesspeople agreed to post the *Valued Visitors* decal on their premises and to provide either a gift or a discount to anyone presenting a *Valued Visitors* card. The bureau mails a *Valued Visitors* newsletter to members to keep in touch and to promote what is going on in Brown County. The program has been very successful.

2. **Organizations in the Same Business.** You have already heard about the concept of strategic alliances in the airline business. Another good example is the *BestCities.net* alliance comprising the convention and visitors bureaus in Cape Town, Dubai, Copenhagen, Edinburgh, Melbourne, San Juan, Singapore, and Vancouver. The mission of the BestCities Global Alliance is to deliver the world's best service experience for the meetings sector and to help its partners earn more business as a result. The Alliance maintains a website and has set up a unique Global Client Service Charter.

   Some countries' national tourism organizations have joined forces either for website promotions or other cooperative marketing. For example, the Alpine Tourist Commission represents the five Alpine countries of Austria, France, Germany, Italy, and Switzerland, and has a website, *AlpsEurope.com.* The Scandinavia Tourist Boards represents the five Scandinavian countries in North America (*GoScandinavia.com*). Another concept that was discussed earlier is that of co-branding or multi-branding. In this situation, two brands of a similar type of operation (e.g., a Taco Bell and a KFC) are located together.

3. **Organizations in Related Businesses.** Frequent-traveler programs are a good example here as they bring together airlines, lodging chains, car rental firms, and others in the hospitality and travel industry. Industry organizations are also working with credit card companies including MasterCard and Visa, both in joint promotions and in the issuance of specially designed credit cards bearing the hospitality and travel organizations' names.

4. **Organizations in Non-Related Businesses.** It is also possible for hospitality and travel organizations to work with businesses outside of the industry. An excellent example of this is the relationship between Park West Gallery®, a fine art dealer, and several cruise lines. Park West at Sea® stages art auctions during the cruises, which provides another form of activity and entertainment for the guests. It is truly a win-win proposition for both sides. Park West gets increased sales of its artwork, while the cruise lines are able to offer more to their guests.

5. **Online Alliances.** The introduction of Internet technology brought with it new forms of potential partnerships among organizations. The *BestCities.net* and *AlpsEurope.com* cases cited earlier in this chapter are prime examples of these online alliances that are increasing found in hospitality and tourism. Another example of online partnership is reciprocal hyperlinking of partners' websites.

Benefits of Partnership

Partnerships such as these offer many possible benefits to the organizations involved:

1. **Access to New Markets.** A partnership may provide new geographic markets or other new target markets for the organizations involved. For example, a code-share alliance between American Airlines and China Eastern gives each brand visibility in the United States and China.

2. **Expansion of Product/Service Mixes.** By teaming up with other organizations, an organization may be able to expand its product/service mix at little or lesser cost. The airlines, in a code-sharing agreement, are able to use each others' check-in counters and check-in staff. Frequent flyer program members and those seating in business and first class cabins are able to use the airport lounges of their airline's strategic alliances.

3. **Increased Ability to Serve Customer Needs.** When hospitality and travel organizations or destination areas pool their facilities, services, and other resources, they usually can better serve customer needs. For example, the code-sharing agreements between partnered airlines are helping to make international air travel simpler and more convenient for travelers.

4. **Increased Marketing Budgets.** When hospitality and travel organizations agree to cooperate, they increase the total budget amount available for marketing for each individual partner. The Scandinavian Tourist Boards and the Alpine Tourist Commission cases provided earlier in this chapter are good examples of this benefit. Most DMOs are able to leverage their own funding through in-kind and other contributions of their partners and members.

5. **Sharing of Facilities and Facility Costs.** Teaming up with other organizations may help each partner to provide and afford certain physical facilities. Food courts in many shopping malls make operations more economical for restaurant and foodservice companies. DMOs that share office space in foreign countries find this arrangement more affordable than having their own stand-alone offices.

6. **Enhanced Image or Positioning.** Associating with other hospitality and travel organizations or famous non-industry brands may improve the image or enhance an organization's positioning. Just think about the marketing partnership between Ritz-Carlton Hotels and Mercedes-Benz, and the benefits the coupling of these two luxury brands create for each other. Similarly, Ritz-Carlton partnering with La Prairiein its spa facilities enhances its position as a luxury hotel brand.

7. **Access to Partners' Customer Databases.** You have already heard about the increasing importance of **database marketing**. This sharing of the partners' proprietary customer databases can be a powerful advantage of cooperation. For example, the tie-ins between airlines, credit card firms, long-distance telephone companies, and hotel chains in frequent traveler programs give each partner the potential to access databases with records on millions of individual customers. The partnership between

American Express and the Small Luxury Hotels of the World group is a good example.

8. **Access to Partners' Expertise.** A partnership may be formed because each of the partners has experience or expertise that the other partners want. This experience or expertise may be well-recognized by customers. For example, some car rental firms are providing GPS systems in their vehicles that are produced by Garmin International, a company known for its leading technological expertise in global positioning system equipment.

Chapter Conclusion

The hospitality and travel industry is a complex mixture of interrelated companies, government agencies, and non-profit organizations. The four main groups are suppliers, carriers, travel trade intermediaries, and destination marketing organizations. There are multiple sectors within each group, and many interdependencies among them.

Each industry organization has a unique product/service mix that periodically must be upgraded, augmented, and pruned. Product/service-mix decisions have to be made at two levels: (1) organization-wide and (2) for individual facilities or services.

---

1. What are the four major groups of organizations within the hospitality and travel industry and what roles does each group play?
2. What are the sectors that comprise each of the four groups of hospitality and travel organizations?
3. What are some of the major trends in the supplier sectors and among carriers?
4. How is the term *product/service mix* defined in this book?
5. What are the six components of the product/service mix and what does each component include?
6. What are the steps involved in product development?
7. What is the meaning of the term *partnership*?
8. What are the potential benefits of marketing partnerships for hospitality and travel organizations?
9. What are the types of partnerships available to hospitality and travel organizations?

---

1. You have been hired by a hotel, airline, attraction, cruise line, or travel trade organization that is interested in expanding both its domestic and international operations. You have been given a project to analyze the benefits and possible disadvantages of marketing partnerships in

achieving these growth objectives. What advantages and disadvantages of potential partnerships would you present to the organization's senior executives? Draw upon actual cases of successful and unsuccessful marketing partnerships in our industry to justify your conclusions.

2. Choose a specific part or sector of the hospitality and travel industry. How has the structure of this industry group changed over the past 10 years? Which organizations have made the greatest changes or improvements to their product/service mixes? Who are the leaders in terms of quality of service provided? What techniques have they followed to earn this reputation?

3. This chapter identifies four distinct parts of the hospitality and travel industry (suppliers, carriers, travel trade intermediaries, and destination marketing organizations). Write a paper describing how each part is related to the others. How important is it for someone involved in hospitality and travel marketing to keep up to date on developments in each of these industry parts and sectors?

4. The owners of a small hospitality and travel business have asked you to help them review their facilities and services. They are interested in exploring ways to improve and perhaps also add to their existing facilities and services. Prepare a proposal outlining the steps you would take to review this organization's product/service mix. Be specific about the possible techniques you would use to evaluate facilities and levels of service.

WEB RESOURCES

Air Transport Association, http://www.airlines.org/

Alpine Tourist Commission, http://www.alpseurope.org/

American Bus Association (ABA), http://www.buses.org/

BestCities Alliance, http://www.bestcities.net/

BC Ferries, http://www.bcferries.com/

Brown County Convention & Visitors Bureau, http://www.browncounty.com/

Cruise Lines International Association (CLIA), http://www.cruising.org/

Darden Restaurants, http://www.darden.com/

Destination Marketing Association International (DMAI), http://www.destinationmarketing.org/

Foxwoods Resort Casino, http://www.foxwoods.com/

International Air Transport Association (IATA), http://www.iata.org/

Irish Ferries, http://www.irishferries.ie/

Nation's Restaurant News, http://www.nrn.com/

P&O Ferries, http://www.poferries.com/

Priority Club, http://www.ichotelsgroup.com/

Rail Europe, http://www.raileurope.com/

Regent Seven Seas Cruises, http://www.rssc.com/

Sail and Drive, http://www.sailanddrive.com
Scandinavian Tourist Boards, http://www.goscandinavia.com/
Shanghai Maglev, http://www.smtdc.com/en/
Small Luxury Hotels of the World, http://www.slh.com/
Virgin Trains, http://www.virgintrains.co.uk/

REFERENCES

1. Smith Travel Research. 2008. *Glossary*. http://www.strglobal.com/ Resources/Glossary.aspx, accessed December 8, 2008.
2. Professional Association of Innkeepers International. 2008. *About PAII*, http://www.paii.org/about_paii.asp, accessed December 8, 2008.
3. Hotels. 2008. *Hotels' Corporate 300 Ranking, 40*.
4. Lynn, Michael. 2007. " Brand Segmentation in the Hotel and Cruise Industries: Fact or Fiction?" *Cornell Hospitality Report*, Vol. 7 No. 4, 7.
5. Tauber, Edward M. 2004. *Understanding Brand Extension*, http://www. brandextension.org/definition.html, accessed April 21, 2007.
6. PricewaterhouseCoopers. 2005. "The secret of lifestyle hotels' popularity is simple: They are in tune with the needs of the new, complex consumer." *Hospitality Directions Europe Edition*, Issue 12, 4.
7. Nation's Restaurant News. 2008. "Top 100 Chains Ranked by U.S. Systemwide Foodservice Sales." *Nation's Restaurant News*, 70.
8. Starbucks. 2008. *Company Fact Sheet*, http://www.starbucks.com/ aboutus/, accessed December 8, 2008.
9. Yum! Brands, Inc. 2007. *Yum! Brands Fact Sheet*.
10. McDonald's Corporation. 2008. *About McDonald's*, http://www. mcdonalds.com/content/corp/about.html, accessed December 8, 2008.
11. National Restaurant Association. 2008. *National Restaurant Association 2008 Restaurant Industry Pocket Factbook*, http://www.restaurant.org/ pdfs/research/2008forecast_factbook.pdf, accessed December 8, 2008.
12. National Restaurant Association. 2007. *National Restaurant Association 2008 Restaurant Industry Pocket Factbook*, http://www.restaurant.org/ pdfs/research/2008forecast_factbook.pdf, accessed December 8, 2008.
13. Restaurants & Institutions. 2007. *Special Report: Consuming Passions*.
14. Schlosser, Eric. 2001. *Fast Food Nation: The Dark Side of the All-American Meal*. New York: Houghton Mifflin Company; *Fast Food Nation*, 2006. DVD.
15. Ritzer, George. 2004. *The McDonaldization of Society: Revised New Century Edition*. Thousand Oaks, California: Sage Publications, Inc.; Pollan, Michael. 2006. *The Omnivore's Dilemma: A Natural History of Four Meals*. New York: Penguin Group; *Super Size Me*, 2003. DVD.
16. Folkes, Gillian, and Allen Wysocki. 2001. *Current Trends in Foodservice and How They Affect the Marketing Mix of American Restaurants*. Institute of Food and Agricultural Sciences, University of Florida Extension, 2.

17. National Restaurant Association. 2006. *2007 Restaurant Industry Forecast*. Washington, DC: National Restaurant Association, 21.

18. National Restaurant Association. 2006. *2007 Restaurant Industry Forecast*. Washington, DC: National Restaurant Association, 4.

19. Enz, Cathy A. 2005. "Multi-branding Strategy: The Case of Yum! Brands." *Cornell Hotel and Restaurant Administration Quarterly*, 46, 86.

20. Keller, Kevin L. 2003. *Strategic Brand Management: Building, Measuring and Managing Brand Equity*. Upper Saddle River, New Jersey: Prentice-Hall; Muller, Christopher. 2005. "The Case for Co-branding in Restaurant Segments." *Cornell Hotel and Restaurant Administration Quarterly*, 46, 93.

21. Cruise Lines International Association. 2008. *2008 CLIA Cruise Market Overview*, http://www.cruising.org/press/overview2008/, accessed December 8, 2008.

22. European Cruise Council. 2008. *Press Room, ECC Presentations*, http://www.europeancruisecouncil.com, accessed December 8, 2008.

23. Institute of Shipping Economics and Logistics. 2008. *ISL Shipping Statistics and Market Review (SSMR) August 2008*, http://www.seabase.isl.org, accessed December 8, 2008.

24. Cruise Lines International Association. 2008. *2008 CLIA Cruise Market Overview*, http://www.cruising.org/press/overview2008/, accessed December 8, 2008.

25. World Cruise Network. 2007. *Artful Learning and Enriching Discoveries*, http://www.worldcruise-network.com/features/feature952/, accessed April 24, 2007.

26. Cruise Lines International Association. 2006. *Cruise Industry Trends for 2006*.

27. USA Today. 2007. *Asian nations begin push for more exposure in the cruise market*, http://www.usatoday.com/travel/destinations/2007-03-15-asia-cruises_N.htm, accessed April 24, 2007.

28. Star Cruises. 2008. *Development of Star Cruises: A Vision Fulfilled*, http://www.starcruises.com/About/index.html, accessed December 7, 2008.

29. Cruise Lines International Association. 2007. *Profile of the U.S. Cruise Industry*, http://www.cruising.org/press/sourcebook2007/profile_cruise_industry.cfm, accessed April 24, 2007.

30. Cruise Lines International Association. 2006. *The 2006 Overview*. New York: CLIA, 12.

31. Cruise Lines International Association. 2008. *2008 CLIA Cruise Market Overview*, http://www.cruising.org/press/overview2008/, accessed December 8, 2008.

32. Cruise Lines International Association. 2007. *Profile of the U.S. Cruise Industry*, http://www.cruising.org/press/sourcebook2007/profile_cruise_industry.cfm, accessed April 24, 2007.

33. Auto Rental News. 2008. *2007 U.S. Car Rental Market*, http://www.fleet-central.com/resources, accessed December 8, 2008.

34. Enterprise Rent-A-Car. 2008. *Company Fact Sheets*, http://aboutus. enterprise.com/press_room.asp, accessed December 8, 2008.

35. The Hertz Corporation. 2008. *Hertz Corporate Profile. Hertz History*, https://www.hertz.com/rentacar/abouthertz/, accessed December 8, 2008.

36. TACSnet. *Car Rental Industry "Point of View"*, http://www.tacsnet. com/scripts/car_rental.cfm, accessed April 24, 2007.

37. Geraghty, M. K., and Ernest Johnson. 1997. "Revenue Management Saves National Car Rental." *Interfaces*, 27, 1, 107–127.

38. TEA and ERA. 2008. *TEA/ERA Attraction Attendance Report*. The TEA, 6–7.

39. International Association of Amusement Parks and Attractions. 2008. *Amusement and Theme Park Industry Poised for Worldwide Growth*, http://www.iaapa.org/pressroom/pressreleases/GrowthinAsia.asp, accessed December 7, 2008.

40. Robinson, J. Clark. 2007. *Innovative Trends in the Global Amusement Industry*. Recreation Management.

41. PricewaterhouseCoopers LLP. 2006. "Global Entertainment and Media Outlook: 2006–2010." *Theme Parks and Amusement Parks*, 542.

42. American Gaming Association. 2003. *Gaming vs. Gambling*, http://www.americangaming.org/Industry/factsheets/general_info_detail.cfv?id=9, accessed April 28, 2007.

43. PricewaterhouseCoopers LLP. 2006. "Global Entertainment and Media Outlook: 2006–2010." *Casino and Other Regulated Gaming*.

44. American Gaming Association. 2006. "State of the States." *The AGA Survey of Casino Entertainment*, 2.

45. American Gaming Association. 2008. *2008 State of the States: The AGA Survey of Casino Entertainment*, http://www.americangaming.org/, accessed December 7, 2008.

46. PricewaterhouseCoopers LLP. 2006. "Global Entertainment and Media Outlook: 2006–2010." *Casino and Other Regulated Gaming*, 582.

47. International Air Transport Association. 2008. *Fact Sheet: Industry Statistics*.

48. Shameen, Assif. 2006. "Asia takes flight on low-cost carriers." *Business Week online*.

49. Najda, Charles. 2003. *Low-cost carriers and low fares: Competition and concentration in the U.S. airline industry*, 8.

50. International Air Transport Association. 2007. *Why ET?* http://www.iata.org/stbsupportportal/et/ETBackground.htm, accessed April 28, 2007.

51. United Airlines, 2008. *United Mileage Plus*, http://www.united.com, accessed December 8, 2008.

52. Deutsche Lufthansa AG, 2007. *Star Alliance: Economic effects for the airlines*. http://konzern.lufthansa.com/en/html/allianzen/star_alliance/vorteile/index.html, accessed April 28, 2007.

53. Kleymann, Birgit, and Hannu Seristo. 2004. *Managing strategic airline alliances.* London: Ashgate.

54. Cable News Network. 2007. "French train breaks speed record." *CNN.com International,* http://edition.cnn.com/2007/WORLD/europe/04/03/TGVspeedrecord.ap/index.html, accessed April 30, 2007.

55. Via Rail Canada. 2006. *Annual Report 2005,* 23–24, 29.

56. British Columbia Ferry Services Inc., 2008. *Investor Fact Sheet (November 2008),* http://www.bcferries.com, accessed December 8, 2008.

57. Chaddick Institute of Metropolitan Study. 2008. *2008 Update on Intercity Bus Service: Summary of Annual Change.* Chicago, IL: DePaul University.

58. American Bus Association. 2008. *The Outlook for the Motorcoach Industry in 2009,* http://www.buses.org/mediacenter, accessed December 8, 2008.

59. Department of Industry, Tourism and Resources. 2008. *Tourism Budget Facts 07/08*; VisitBritain. 2008. *VisitBritain's role, structure, funding and performance*; Canadian Tourism Commission. 2008. *2007 Annual Report.*

60. Destination Marketing Association International. 2008. *About DMAI.* http://www.destinationmarketing.org/, accessed December 8, 2008.

chapter 11

People: Services and Service Quality
How Do We Get There?

OVERVIEW

People represent one of the 8 Ps of hospitality and travel marketing, and this chapter emphasizes the key role played by people in creating satisfied customers. Guest-host relationships are discussed within the context of quality management programs such as total quality management (TQM) concept and ISO 9000-9001. Methods for improving service quality levels as well as employees' customer-orientation and guest-relations skills are presented. Techniques for measuring service quality are reviewed. This chapter also describes the relationship marketing concept—how organizations can build and maintain long-term relationships with individual customers. It ends with an examination of the customer mix and how this mix affects an organization's image and the quality of the customer's service quality experience.

OBJECTIVES

Having read this chapter, you should be able to:

- Identify the two main groups of people involved in hospitality and travel marketing and explain how they interact.
- Explain the key role played by people in the marketing mix.
- Describe the concepts of service orientation and service culture, providing examples for the hospitality and travel industry.
- Explain the difference between customer satisfaction and customer delight.
- Describe quality management programs including the total quality management (TQM) and ISO 9000-9001 program concepts.
- Identify the benefits of customer codes, guarantees, and promises.
- Explain the importance of employee recruitment, selection, orientation, training, and motivation programs in delivering service quality.
- Describe the concept of empowering employees and how important this is to customer satisfaction.
- Explain the five dimensions of the SERVQUAL model and how this technique is used to measure service quality.
- Explain why the relationship marketing concept is so important in the hospitality and travel industry and how it is done successfully.
- Describe the customer mix and explain why organizations must manage it.

KEY TERMS

customer codes, guarantees, or promises

customer delight

customer mix

customer satisfaction

empowerment

external customers

guests

hosts

internal customers

internal marketing

ISO 9000-9001 certification

lifetime value (CLV or LTV)

mystery shopper programs

people

quality

relationship marketing

service culture

service encounter

service orientation

SERVQUAL

total quality management (TQM)

word-of-mouth information

The Two Main Groups of People: Guests and Hosts

What do you like about the hospitality and travel industry? What attracted you to this industry rather than to another? Some might say "the opportunity to travel" or "to work in nice places," but is it because you like to work with other people? Many of us are attracted to this industry because of the desire to meet and to serve a wide variety of people, sometimes from many different cultures and countries.

There are two groups of people in hospitality and travel marketing—the **guests** (customers) and the **hosts** (those who work within hospitality and travel organizations). Managing this guest-host relationship is one of the key functions in our industry; in fact, some say it is the most important. In this chapter the focus is mainly on the hosts and the quality of service they provide. However, you will also read about managing long-term relationships with individual guests (relationship marketing) and about the importance of considering how guests interact with each other in hospitality and travel businesses and destinations (customer mix).

Key Role of People in the Marketing Mix (8 Ps)

In Chapter 2 you learned about the generic and contextual differences between the marketing of services and products. That chapter highlighted the greater difficulties with standardizing services, as well as the relationship of the quality of services to those providing the services. It is much more difficult with services to give the customer an error-free experience because of the human factor involved in service transactions. Services are not mass-produced on a factory line but are delivered one customer at a time. Services involve person-to-person interactions, both employees (hosts) with customers (guests) and customers with other customers (guest to guest).

To say that people make the main difference in services marketing is perhaps both obvious and an understatement of the real truth. Services marketing is all about people! To borrow a quote from a famous U.S. stock brokerage firm, success in services marketing needs to be measured "one customer at a time." While you will read much about communications and promotion in later in Chapters 14–18, the real foundations of a hospitality and travel organization's success and survival are the people it employs and the people it serves. How the organization selects and treats both of these two groups of people has perhaps the greatest impact on its ultimate marketing effectiveness.

The front-line people who provide the services in the hospitality and travel industry play a key role. They alone can make or break a guest's experience. An otherwise ordinary occasion can be made extra special by above-average courtesy and attention. However, a superior environment and facilities can be spoiled by indifferent, curt, or unfriendly service. People—the service providers—play the pivotal role in hospitality and travel marketing. No amount of jazzy websites, slick advertising, and catchy promotions can compensate for below-average service. Hospitality and travel organizations must not only satisfy customers by providing good and reliable physical products, but must match or surpass this through quality personal service. The human dimension of hospitality and travel services, although harder to control and standardize, deserves at least equal attention. Most marketing textbooks ignore this human element in marketing, but not this one!

Although much of what the hospitality and travel industry provides involves physical facilities and equipment, most experts believe that it is the level of service provided that separates the successful from the unsuccessful; this is the **people** element of the marketing mix (8 Ps). Traditional thinking separates marketing and human resources management (HRM) into two distinct management functions. However, the two are very closely linked in the service industries. Organizations with superior human resources policies and practices are usually the most successful marketers.

Organizations such as The Ritz-Carlton Company, Disney, Peninsula Hotels, Four Seasons Hotels and Resorts, Shangri-La Hotels and Resorts, Mandarin Oriental Hotel Group, Singapore Airlines, and Marriott know the rich payoffs that come from positive host-guest service encounters. They learned years ago that only satisfied customers come back and that positive **word-of-mouth information** is the most powerful force in attracting new customers. These organizations have a very strong **service orientation**, which is an organizational predisposition and strategic organizational affinity or preference for service excellence.[1] They have consciously developed a service culture to make sure that this service orientation percolates to all employees within the organization. A **service culture** is defined as a well-documented, shared understanding among all staff that defines how the organization interacts with the customer.[2]

- **The Ritz-Carlton Company**, *The Ritz-Carlton Leadership Center.* This is a training resource for organizations that want to benchmark the business practices that led to The Ritz-Carlton Hotel Company, L.L.C. becoming a two-time recipient of the Malcolm Baldrige National Quality Award.

- **Disney**, *The Disney Institute.* Disney is known for its mastery in providing a high level of consistent customer service. The Disney Institute was established to provide training for other organizations in Disney's *Approach to Service Quality.*[3]
- **The Peninsula Hotels**, *Portraits of Peninsula.* Annie Leibovitz, the famous photographer, captured the legendary service culture and quality at Peninsula Hotels in the *Portraits of Peninsula.*
- **Four Seasons Hotels and Resorts**, *Our Goals, Our Beliefs, Our Principles.* These company guidelines are well documented and indicate that the hotel company's people are its greatest asset and a key to its success.
- **Shangri-La Hotels and Resorts**, *Shangri-La Care.* Shangri-La's philosophy is "hospitality from caring people." The company's mission is "delighting customers each and every time." *Shangri-La Care* is a four-module, customer service training program for all staff (Figure 11.1).

FIGURE 11.1 Training in Shangri-La Care makes this hotel company one of the best in the business.

- **Mandarin Oriental Hotel Group**, *Our Guiding Principles.* These carefully documented principles express the hotel company's emphasis on "delighting our guests" (Figure 11.2).
- **Singapore Airlines, the** *Singapore Girl* is used as the airline's symbol of quality customer care and service.[4,5]
- **Marriott**, *The Marriott Way* **and** *Spirit to Serve.* Marriott has very carefully documented and communicated its *Core Values & Culture.* These include *The Marriott Way* that incorporates its *Spirit to Serve*, which explains how the company serves guests, associates (Marriott employees), and communities.[6]

One concept we hope you notice from these case studies is "customer delight." **Customer satisfaction** is a positive post-consumption evaluation that customers make when the consumption experience either meets or exceeds expectations.[7] Customer delight is not the same as customer satisfaction! Just satisfying customers is not enough today, as even satisfied customers will not be loyal and use competitors.[8] **Customer delight** happens when guests feel their expectations of a hospitality and travel organization have been exceeded, not just met.[9]

If there is one universal truth about the hospitality and travel industry, it is that nothing can make up for poor service. Excellent food, exquisitely decorated hotel lobbies and guest rooms, or on-time arrival cannot swing the pendulum far enough to make up for unfriendly or inadequate employee service. According to Mill and Morrison, although excellent service cannot totally make up for a hard bed, tough steak, bumpy bus ride, or rainy weather, poor service can certainly spoil an otherwise excellent vacation.[10] Many people do

Courtesy of Mandarin Oriental Hotel Group

FIGURE 11.2
Mandarin Oriental clearly communicates its service orientation and service culture through its Guiding Principles.

not fully understand the bond between the quality of the physical product (destination, hotel, restaurant, plane, ship, motor coach, menu items, etc.) and the quality of the service experienced by guests. Customers form their overall evaluations based on a combined assessment of these two factors (the physical product and service quality).

Books such as *Service America in the New Economy*, suggest that there is a crisis in the service industries and this has deepened since the arrival of the Web.[11] Poor or indifferent service is the rule, rather than the exception. In this era of mediocre service, those who devote above-average attention to hiring, orienting, training, empowering, and keeping service-oriented employees will have a wonderful marketing advantage.

Marketers must be concerned about service quality! Poor service quality places a hospitality and travel organization at a competitive disadvantage, potentially driving away dissatisfied customers.[12] Therefore, hospitality and travel marketers must be concerned with service quality and make sure that their organizations have a process in place for managing the quality of service provided to customers.

Before we start talking about service quality, you might want to know what we mean by quality. According to the American Society for Quality (ASQ), quality is a subjective term for which each person or (industry) sector has its own definition. In technical usage, **quality** can have two meanings: (1) the characteristics of a product or service that bear on its ability to satisfy stated or implied needs, and (2) a product or service free of deficiencies. According to Joseph Juran, quality means "fitness for use;" according to Philip Crosby, it means "conformance to requirements."[13]

Quality Management Programs

Total quality management, or **TQM** as it is sometimes called, is a quality management concept that has gained widespread recognition. The impetus for the TQM concept is largely attributed to Japanese manufacturing companies and to quality experts including W. Edward Deming, Joseph M. Juran, and Philip Crosby. A TQM program is designed to cut down on an organization's defects, to determine its customers' requirements, and to satisfy these requirements. There have been many descriptions of TQM. One of these is through the five sides of the *TQM Pyramid*: (1) management commitment, (2) focus on the customer and the employee, (3) continuous improvements, (4) focus on facts, and (5) everybody's participation.[14] A second description, based on Deming's work, is that there are seven focus concepts in TQM: (1) forward-looking leadership, (2) internal and external cooperation, (3) learning, (4) administrative processes, (5) continuous improvement, (6) employees' performance, and (7) customer satisfaction.[15]

There have been many and varied applications of TQM with and outside of the services industries. A TQS (Total Quality Service) approach has also been suggested for service organizations incorporating the critical principles of TQM:[16]

- **Top Management Commitment and Visionary Leadership.** Organizations' leaders must be committed to improving service quality and must propagate an appropriate vision.
- **Human Resource Management.** Organizations must focus on human resources management (HRM) and see HRM as a source of competitive advantage.
- **Technical System.** Organizations must design service delivery processes so that customers can receive the service without any hassles.
- **Information and Analysis System.** Employees must be given adequate information on processes and customers, especially in handling peak and rush periods. This is partly done through internal marketing.
- **Benchmarking.** Organizations must continually gather data on customer and employee satisfaction, as well as comparing service delivery processes with peers in the same industry sector.
- **Continuous Improvement.** Organizations must continually search for ways to improve levels of service quality to customers.
- **Customer Focus.** Organizations must operate on the belief that customer satisfaction is the ultimate measure of service quality.
- **Employee Satisfaction.** Organizations must continually satisfy employees' needs.
- **Union Intervention.** Organizations must work together with unions (if appropriate) to implement TQM programs.
- **Social Responsibility.** Organizations must continuously meet their social and community obligations.
- **Servicescapes.** Organizations must be concerned about the physical settings for service experiences and these must fully support personal service quality delivery.
- **Service Culture.** Organizations must develop and maintain effective service cultures.

Below, you will read about The Ritz-Carlton Hotel Company and how it adapted the TQM concept to hotel operations. This example shows how the key concepts and principles of TQM can be used by a hospitality and travel organization. The Baldrige National Quality Award (BNQA) in the United States was developed by the National Institute of Standards and Technology (NIST). The Ritz-Carlton Company has won this award on two different occasions.

There are other approaches to quality management programs for services apart from TQM.[17,18] These include **ISO 9000-9001 Certification** (International Organization for Standards). ISO 9000 provides requirements, definitions, guidelines, and related standards to provide an independent assessment and

Industry Players

Service Quality at its Best

THE RITZ-CARLTON COMPANY, L.L.C.

http://www.ritzcarlton.com
http://corporate.ritzcarlton.com/en/Default.htm

In 1992, The Ritz-Carlton Company, L.L.C. did something that no U.S. hotel chain had done before—it won the highly coveted Malcolm Baldrige National Quality Award. Named after the late Secretary of Commerce, Malcolm Baldrige, the award was created in 1987 by the U.S. Congress to recognize companies that achieve excellence in their products or services through the use of quality improvement programs. The Chevy Chase, Maryland-based company achieved this enviable position after only 10 years of operation. In 1999, Ritz-Carlton went one step further by winning the Malcolm Baldrige National Quality Award for the second time. This was an unprecedented event, since no service company has ever earned the award more than once.

W. B. Johnson Properties founded the company when it bought the U.S. rights to the Ritz-Carlton name. W. B. Johnson acquired the rights to the famous hotel name when it bought the Boston Ritz-Carlton. In 2008, the company had 70 hotels in 23 countries (Bahrain, Canada, Chile, China, Egypt, Germany, Grand Cayman, Indonesia, Italy, Jamaica, Japan, Korea, Malaysia, Mexico, Portugal, Qatar, Russia, Singapore, Spain, Turkey, the United Arab Emirates, and the United States). In August 2008, sixteen new hotels are under development and expected to be completed by 2010.

Ritz-Carlton has adopted many of the principles of total quality management (TQM). It began its efforts toward winning the Baldrige award in 1989. However, Ritz-Carlton's great concern for service quality began when it started operations in 1983 with its self-expressed born at birth insistence on high-quality service. The company's "Gold Standards" concept has been in place since the very start, but has been added to and modified over the years. It is Ritz-Carlton's quality training and assurance program and has six elements: (1) The Credo, (2) The Motto, (3) The Three Steps of Service, (4) Service Values, (5) The 6th Diamond, and (6) The Employee Promise.

The Credo: This stresses that the company's topmost mission is to make guests comfortable and to make them really feel cared for.

The Motto: This puts across the high standards of professionalism in the company's hotels in providing quality service.

(continues)

(continued)

The Three Steps of Service: Emphasizes addressing the guest by his or her name; anticipating what each guest needs; and saying a sincere goodbye to guests using their names.

Service Values: I Am Proud To Be Ritz-Carlton: These are 12 statements that specify the values and responsibilities of company employees in delivering quality service to hotel guests. Employees are encouraged to help fellow employees, even if they work in different departments of the hotel, if it means that a higher quality customer service is delivered.

The "lateral service" concept means that employees are encouraged to help fellow employees, even if they work in different departments of the hotel, if it means that a higher quality customer service is delivered.

The 6th Diamond: This communicates to hotel staff what it takes to deliver service beyond a 5-star level, and the type of service that exclusively associated with Ritz-Carlton.

The Employee Promise: This indicates that Ritz-Carlton's hotel employees are its greatest asset. The company also emphasizes its commitment to developing its staff members and providing a diverse work environment in which all can prosper.

The company says that it empowers all employees to make a positive difference in providing high quality service to guests. They can break away from their own duties to help a guest. In addition, a variety of tools are used to improve customer service, including "nine-step quality improvement teams" and guest surveys. The result is that Ritz-Carlton hotels provide consistent and reliable service quality levels.

However you measure it, Ritz-Carlton is a success story in service quality because of its unique approaches. Since winning the Malcolm Baldrige Awards in 1992 and 1999, it was flooded with requests to share its secrets of success with others. In 2000, the company established The Leadership Center where it shares its service quality practices with senior executives, managers, and staff of other industries.

Ritz-Carlton is now an independently-operated division of Marriott International. It has now extended its brand name by developing spas, a private club management division, The Ritz-Carlton Club (fractional home ownership concept), The Residences at The Ritz-Carlton (luxury residential condominiums), and The Ritz-Carlton Leadership Center (educational division).

Discussion Questions

1. How has The Ritz-Carlton Company adapted the five key principles of total quality management in its operations?

(continues)

(continued)

2. What can other hospitality and travel organizations learn from what Ritz-Carlton has done?
3. How important has employee empowerment been in producing quality service at The Ritz-Carlton Company?

Sources: The author acknowledges the use of information from the corporate website of The Ritz-Carlton Company, L.L.C. on its Gold Standards.

certification of a service organization's quality management system. There are eight principles underlying the ISO 9000 standards:[19]

1. **Customer focus.** Organizations depend on their customers and therefore should understand current and future customer needs, should meet customer requirements and strive to exceed customer expectations.
2. **Leadership.** Leaders establish unity of purpose and direction of the organization. They should create and maintain the internal environment in which people can become fully involved in achieving the organization's objectives.
3. **Involvement of people.** People at all levels are the essence of an organization and their full involvement enables their abilities to be used for the organization's benefit.
4. **Process approach.** A desired result is achieved more efficiently when activities and related resources are managed as a process.
5. **Systems approach to management.** Identifying, understanding, and managing interrelated processes as a system contributes to the organization's effectiveness and efficiency in achieving its objectives.
6. **Continual improvement.** Continual improvement of the organization's overall performance should be a permanent objective of the organization.
7. **Factual approach to decision making.** Effective decisions are based on the analysis of data and information.
8. **Mutually beneficial supplier relationships.** An organization and its suppliers are interdependent and a mutually beneficial relationship enhances the ability of both to create value.

ISO 9001-2008 sets the specific standards and requirements that an organization's quality management system must meet to the criteria in the ISO 9000 system.

Customer Codes, Guarantees, or Promises

You now have seen how some organizations have strived for service excellence and succeeded. But how can other organizations emulate what a company like Ritz-Carlton has done in managing its host-guest relationships? One clear lesson that you have no doubt learned from the Ritz-Carlton Industry Players Case is that it is important for an organization to articulate its service culture and standards in writing. Some hospitality and travel organizations have done this

FIGURE 11.3 Delta Hotels' Meeting Maestros: Our Promise offers an assurance of service quality to meeting planners.

through **customer codes, guarantees, or promises**. A few good examples of these will help you get the picture and understand their value:

- **Delta Hotels**, Canada. Delta Hotels has a special program for meetings called *Meeting Maestros: Our Promise*. Figure 11.3 provides the details of this *Promise*, which includes a written proposal within 24 hours.[20]
- **Hampton Inn, USA.** The *100% Hampton Guarantee*™ states that "If you're not 100% satisfied, we don't expect you to pay. That's our promise and your guarantee. That's 100% Hampton.™"[21]
- **Southwest Airlines, USA.** Southwest has developed the *Southwest Airlines Customer Service Commitment*, which can be accessed online. Southwest's mission statement even underlines the importance of customer satisfaction to the airline.
- **Swiss Tourism Quality Label, Switzerland.** The Swiss Tourism Federation manages the *Swiss Tourism Quality Label* program. The *Q-Label* as it is called can be earned at three levels.[22,23] Level 1 has a focus on the quality of service, Level 2 is based on management quality, and Level 3 is the most advanced where an organization introduces a Quality Management System (QMS) (Figure 11.4).
- **Hong Kong Tourism Board** *Quality Tourism Services (QTS) Scheme*, **Hong Kong SAR, China.** This quality scheme operated by HKTB covers restaurants, visitor accommodation, and retail shops. According to HKTB, "QTS-accredited establishments must pass stringent annual assessments showing they meet high quality standards of product quality and service."[24]

FIGURE 11.4
Switzerland has developed a very complete quality management program for the hospitality and travel industry.

Quality Label for Swiss Tourism

What is behind the Quality Label for Swiss Tourism?
The "Quality Label for Swiss Tourism" programme is supported by all major Swiss tourism associations. Its purpose is to encourage establishments like ours to enhance and safeguard the quality of service in Switzerland.

How do you benefit as a guest?
In the establishments that have reached the Quality Label for Swiss Tourism, as a guest, you have the assurance that the staff and management are continuously giving serious thought to quality. They are striving to take steps so that you as their guest feel good.

Level I of the Quality Label certifies ongoing attention to a high quality of service.

Level II of the Quality Label also refers to the quality of management. This level is awarded to companies and providers that have been assessed by external inspectors.

The Level III award is given to those companies and providers who have compiled and successfully implemented a comprehensive and internationally recognised Quality Management System (QMS).

For detailed information and the list of quality companies and providers, please visit www.swisstourfed.ch.

Media Corner	Newsletter	Privacy Statement	Contact
Trade / Partners	Swiss Quality	RSS	© Switzerland Tourism: Impressum

Customer codes, guarantees, or promises benefit both the organization and its customers. Putting the organization's service commitments in writing is important in communicating to guests what to expect in the service delivery. Additionally, it gives the organization's employees a clear idea of what is expected of them in serving guests. In a way, this becomes a service contract between hosts and guests.

Now you may be a bit skeptical about these codes, guarantees, or promises. Why? No guarantee is foolproof, you might be thinking. We tend to agree with you, because it takes people to deliver on all of these promises, and people's behaviors tend to be variable. An organization must recruit, select, orient, train, motivate, retain, and empower the best customer-oriented people. So those are the next topics.

Did You Know?

How do you know that you will get quality tourism services when in Hong Kong?

- The Hong Kong Tourism Board operates the Quality Tourism Services (QTS) Scheme. Only businesses accredited by the Quality Tourism Services (QTS) Scheme are listed, meaning they have passed stringent annual assessments showing that they:

  Shops and restaurants
- Provide clearly displayed prices;
- Display clear information; and
- Ensure superb customer service.

  Visitor Accommodation
- Provide clear and sufficient information on the type of accommodation available with clearly displayed prices for rooms and other services;
- Provide a comfortable and pleasant environment with good standards of cleanliness and hygiene; and
- Offer warm and efficient customer service with front-line staff possessing extensive product and service knowledge.

Sources: Hong Kong Tourism Board. (2008). **http://www.discoverhongkong.com/eng/mustknow/qts/index.jhtml**

Employees: Managing Internal Customers for Service Quality

The main focus of any hospitality and travel organization wishing to improve its service quality must be its employees through effective human resources management (HRM) programs and special communications about marketing (called **internal marketing** and discussed later). It must develop HRM programs that recruit, select, orient, train, motivate, reward, retain, and empower the best people for the organization's unique service culture, positioning approach, and distinctive style of operations. Tanke defines HRM as the implementation of the strategies, plans, and programs required to attract, motivate, develop, reward, and retain the best people to meet the organizational goals and operational objectives of the hospitality enterprise.[25] An organization must also consistently require all employees to adhere to policies regarding behavior and personal grooming (Figure 11.5).

Staff Recruitment, Selection, Orientation, and Training

All hospitality and travel employees contribute to the quality of service provided to customers. Therefore, if an organization wants to maintain or

FIGURE 11.5 Staff may be trained to provide a consistent and distinctive greeting for customers.

Image copyright Paulaphoto, 2008. Used under license from Shutterstock.com

improve its service quality, the place to start is when recruiting and hiring new employees (Figure 11.6). A book on marketing such as this one cannot do justice to all of the details and procedures about employee recruitment and selection. However, successful service organizations recognize the need to employ people with good interpersonal skills, communication abilities, and empathy; these are very important in the host-guest relationship. Previous

FIGURE 11.6 Recruiting and hiring great employees is the key to successful service in hospitality and travel.

Image copyright Stephen Coburn, 2008. Used under license from Shutterstock.com

work experience is another key to selecting the right people for the job, but it may not be the most important criterion.

People's personalities and attitudes are also fundamental in determining their success in the hospitality and travel industry, and especially in serving customers. A study conducted in Scotland found that 65 percent of employers rated the right personality as critical for front-line employees in hospitality and retail businesses.[26] Some organizations use instruments such as those based on the *Myers-Briggs* four preferences (extroversion and introversion, sensing and intuition, thinking and feeling, and judging and perceiving) and resulting 16 personality types (the MBTI® instrument).[27] Another way of evaluating personality is through an assessment of *The Big Five* (extraversion, agreeableness, conscientiousness, emotional stability, and intellect/imagination) personality characteristics.[28]

There are many alternative approaches to recruiting and selecting employees for hospitality and travel organizations. While traditional recruiting practices still are popular, the Internet is now playing a much greater role in finding, testing, and selecting staff. Standard practices include an application, screening, reference-checking, and interviewing process. Whatever route they choose, the successful service companies really sweat the details in recruiting the best people. The Ritz-Carlton Company uses "character trait recruiting" based on an instrument that predicts whether a potential employee has the right characteristics or attributes. Existing employees are also involved in the interviewing process.[29]

Service-oriented behavior is innate in some people but must be sharpened through good orientation (or induction) programs after they are hired. Orientation programs provide an introduction to the organization and its service culture and standards. An effective orientation program should include the following eight steps:[30]

1. Prepare all the paperwork, handbooks, workbooks, and other details in advance.
2. Provide an agenda/itinerary for the orientation program.
3. Inform co-workers by e-mail about the new employees.
4. Send essential details to new employees' residences before the orientation program.
5. Use a variety of presenters and audio-visual materials in the orientation program.
6. Spread the orientation program over 2 to 3 days to avoid "information overload."
7. Give new employees "take-home" materials to review after completion of the orientation program.
8. Have the new employees complete an evaluation of the orientation program.

Effective orientation programs lead to improved guest service, increased employee satisfaction, and higher rates of employee retention.[31]

Training is the next cornerstone, after recruitment, selection, and orientation, for preparing service-oriented employees. Most experts agree that several days or weeks of supervised, on-the-job training are best. However, this does not mean sink-or-swim training where new employees are thrown in at the deep end and learn the job by themselves. At The Ritz-Carlton Company, new employee receives at least 310 hours of training within their first year of employment.[32]

Motivating and Retaining Staff

Keeping highly motivated, service-oriented employees is the next major challenge. These techniques seem to work for several companies:

1. Maintaining regular communications with employees. For example, most major firms have an internal newsletter.
2. Complimenting or rewarding employees frequently. Employees should be made to feel important. Many companies have employee-of-the-month awards.
3. Setting clear objectives and performance standards for employees.
4. Making sure that there are advancement opportunities. Many successful companies have strong promotion-from-within policies and clear, mapped-out career paths.
5. Using management and supervisory staff who are honest, open, and willing to listen to employees.
6. Giving service employees an accurate description of what the typical customer expects from the services that the organization provides.

Motivating and retaining good staff also involves having effective compensation programs. Starbucks Coffee was ranked 7th among the 100 Best Companies to Work for 2008 by Fortune. One of the reasons for this high ranking is the excellent *Starbucks Total Pay* program of compensation, benefits, savings, stock, and "partner perks."[33]

Many experts believe that organizations need to treat their employees as **internal customers** with guests being the **external customers**. Just like the guests or external customers, internal customers need their own dedicated internal marketing program.

Empowering Staff to Deliver Guest Satisfaction

How much is a dissatisfied guest worth to a hospitality and travel organization? Too much is probably the best answer to this difficult question. Dissatisfied customers are customers who usually do not return and who share their negative experiences, through word of mouth information, with friends, relatives and other acquaintances. Therefore, converting potentially dissatisfied guests into satisfied guests—known as service recovery—is a major challenge for hospitality and travel organizations. Empowering employees to go the extra mile to satisfy guests is recognized as one of the most powerful tools available to a service organization. The potential benefits of empowering staff in hospitality and travel organizations are:[34]

- More responsive service
- Guests' complaints dealt with quickly
- Greater customer satisfaction
- More repeat guests
- Well-motivated staff

Empowerment means giving employees the authority to identify and solve guest problems or complaints on the spot, and to make improvements in work processes when necessary.[35] How many times have you heard the words "I'm sorry, that's not my job," "I'm sorry, it's company policy," or "I'm sorry, that's the way we always do it" from employees of service organizations? You will not hear these excuses in a service business that effectively empowers its employees.

Empowerment gives more control to employees and requires their commitment to follow through and deliver quality service to customers.[36] Since employees are given more power to satisfy customers, they are asked to take ownership of guest problems or complaints. This means that if a guest tells an employee about a problem that he or she has experienced, then that employee owns the problem and must take action to correct it to the customer's satisfaction, even if the problem occurred in another department or division within the employee's organization.

Staff Behavior, Appearance, and Uniforms

Can you think of one feature that stands out about the employees of the hospitality travel industry's leaders, such as Disney and McDonald's? You are correct if you mentioned employees, attitudes, behavior, appearance, or uniforms. These and other corporations stay on top of the group because of the time and effort they invest in their people. Disney even has a concept known as *The Disney Look*, which is provided for all new employees to study and comply with.

There is no place in companies like Disney for soiled uniforms, outlandish hairstyles, or ad lib dressing. There are dress codes, rules of conduct, and sometimes even a unique language that everyone knows and uses. Such companies recognize that their people can greatly enhance the customer's image of the company.

What about managers and people who work behind the scenes? Are dishwashers, cooks, mechanics, cleaners, accountants, and other back-of-the-house personnel not part of the product because they are not visible to customers? The answer is that managers and non-front-line staff are definitely part of the service-quality team. Front-line, customer-contact staff members rely heavily on these people. Effective managers do not spend the majority of their time sequestered in their offices. They recognize the need to be part of the service-quality team—meeting, greeting, and making sure customers get what they expect and want.

Many marketing plans make no reference to staff and management programs but concentrate entirely on promotional, pricing, and distribution activities. A take-it-for-granted attitude seems to prevail about how employees will perform. This is a serious mistake because it ignores the powerful positive (or negative) impacts that people have on an organization's sales and profits. At a minimum, the marketing plan should specify the following:

1. Staff uniform improvements and changes
2. Employee and management recognition and award programs
3. Employee and management incentive and reward programs
4. Sales and guest relations training programs
5. Orientation programs on marketing plan objectives and activities
6. Communication mechanisms on marketing progress and results
7. Other internal marketing programs and activities

All hospitality and travel organizations have to be concerned about the quality of their people. This is a particularly difficult challenge for destination marketing organizations (DMOs) that employ only limited numbers of people themselves but rely on quality service from the employees of many other organizations (e.g., hotels and resorts, restaurants, attractions, etc.). Several DMOs have developed hospitality and service training programs for their members and other local organizations.

Internal Marketing Programs

The American Marketing Association defines internal marketing as marketing to employees of an organization to ensure that they are effectively carrying out desired programs and policies.[37] Effective communications with employees about marketing programs and activities is a key to building excellent relationships with customers and delivering on all that a hospitality and travel organization promises.[38] The following are six characteristics of highly effective internal marketing programs:[39]

1. Senior management participation
2. Integrated organizational structure
3. Strategic marketing approach
4. Human resources partnership
5. Focus on employee engagement (Figure 11.7)
6. Internal brand communication

Measuring Service Quality

As you now know, quality personal service is important in creating positive guest experiences. You have also learned about some of the programs for improving service quality. The measurement of service quality is required as part of the process in applying these service quality programs. Several techniques have been suggested for measuring service quality. One of these is the **SERVQUAL** instrument that was developed based upon research conducted by

Image copyright Andresr, 2008. Used under license from Shutterstock.com

FIGURE 11.7
Employees should all be engaged in marketing through training and team presentations.

Parasuraman, Zeithaml, and Berry.[40] These three authors and others have defined a series of "service gaps" that should be measured and closed.[41,42]

SERVQUAL measures the gap between what customers expect from a service and what they perceive they receive. The SERVQUAL instrument is based on the following five individual dimensions that measure this gap between customers' expectations and perceptions:

1. **Tangibles**: The hospitality and travel organization's physical facilities, equipment, and appearance of staff.
2. **Reliability**: The hospitality and travel organization's ability to perform the service dependably and accurately (Figure 11.8).
3. **Responsiveness**: The willingness of staff to help customers and provide prompt service.
4. **Assurance**: The knowledge and courtesy of staff and their ability to convey trust and confidence.
5. **Empathy**: The degree of caring, individualized attention that the hospitality and travel organization's staff provides to its customers.

Service quality is measured by SERVQUAL through the use of a special questionnaire, which is usually filled out by the customers themselves (self-administered). The questionnaire contains 22 statements, reflecting the five service dimensions. Customers rate both their expectations and perceptions for each of these 22 statements using a seven-point scale, with one being labeled strongly disagree. For example, in the tangibles dimension, one of the expectation statements is "employees should be well dressed and neat" and the parallel perception statement is "employees are well dressed and appear neat."

FIGURE 11.8
Reliability means the ability to accurately and dependably perform the service.

Image copyright Eric Limon, 2008. Used under license from Shutterstock.com

The scores for all of the statements under each of the five service dimensions are averaged and then a perceived quality score is calculated by subtracting the expectation average scores from the perceived average scores. More simply stated, this means that perceived service quality is the difference between the quality of service provided by a specific hospitality and travel organization and the quality of service customers expect to receive from similar hospitality and travel organizations (PERCEPTIONS – EXPECTATIONS = QUALITY).

Many hospitality and travel organizations now make use of **mystery shopper programs** to periodically check on service quality. Also called secret shopper programs, these involve the use of pre-recruited and qualified consumers (typically independent contractors) or professional staff trained to evaluate a business anonymously using a prescribed evaluation form. The evaluation may take place in person at the business establishment or through other public media such as telephone or Internet.[43]

Relationship Marketing: Treating Guests as People with Long-term Value

In the past, there has been a tendency for hospitality and travel marketers to place most emphasis on attracting new customers. Present and past customers were taken for granted and not given such a high priority. This has all changed in the highly competitive hospitality and travel global marketplace. Recently, the idea of nurturing the individual relationships with present and past customers has received much greater attention. Most marketers now accept that it is less expensive to attract repeat customers than to create new customers. This is the basic concept behind **relationship marketing**, or marketing with the conscious aim to develop and manage long-term and/or trusting relationships with customers, distributors, suppliers, or other parties in the marketing environment.[44] You might look at it as treating the individual guest as a person, rather than as a statistic. It means having a long-term interest in an individual customer, which some refer to as customer **lifetime value (CLV or LTV)** (Figure 11.9). The CLV/LTV is the future value, expressed in revenues and profits, of a customer during a given tracking window.[45] It examines customer value over time by comparing acquisition and retention costs to revenues and profits.[46]

The ultimate goal of relationship marketing programs for customers is to make individual guests loyal to the organization. This is particularly important in the hospitality and travel industry where there are many frequent travelers and where word-of-mouth information has such a great influence. For example, a *Travel Weekly study* in 2006 using data from the National Leisure Travel Monitor found that 82 percent of people were either extremely or very confident in information from friends or family members when considering travel destinations.[47] The comparable figures for websites and travel

Image copyright Galina Barskaya, 2008. Used under license from Shutterstock.com

FIGURE 11.9
Rewarding frequent business travelers is a popular way of recognizing customers' lifetime value (LTV).

INTERNET MARKETING

At Your Service on the Internet: The Online FAQ

- A major limitation of the Internet is that it is not human and therefore cannot provide true personal service as Chapter 11 discusses.
- Hospitality and travel organizations can use a number of techniques to combat the impersonal nature of the Internet, such as a live dialog, email-in and email-back responses, or FAQs (frequently asked questions). FAQs are perhaps the most pervasive and function like an "online concierge desk."
- The websites of some of the leading cruise lines provide a good example of FAQs since people often have many questions about cruising.

  - Carnival Cruise Lines: Supplies a list of Top FAQs plus a "laundry list" of other questions.
  - Costa Cruise Lines: Provides a list of about 20 questions in alphabetical order.
  - Norwegian Cruise Lines: Provides a very long list of answers to "most common questions about cruising."
  - Princess Cruises: Supplies a well-organized set of FAQs in five categories: (1) pre-cruise, (2) post-cruise, (3) travel agent information, (4) the onboard experience, and (5) technical problems.
  - Royal Caribbean International: Gives a nicely-organized group of FAQs in five types with photo illustrations: (1) planning, (2) reserving, (3) preparing, (4) onboard, and (5) afterward.

- While there is no perfect substitute for the "real thing," these FAQs are very helpful and a reflection of the overall service concept of an organization.

Sources: Company websites. (2008). **http:/www.carnival.com/, http:/www. costacruise. com/, http:/www.ncl.com/, http:/www.princess.com/, http:/www.royalcaribbean.com/**

Student Questions

1. Which of these five leading cruise lines has the best approach to FAQs and why?
2. Is it important to constantly review and update FAQs? Why or why not?
3. Which customers are the most likely to use FAQs and what are the reasons for your answer?
4. What do you think is the most effective approach for organizations to "deliver service" on the Internet, and what are the major difficulties or challenges involved with implementing this approach?

advertising were 33 percent and 13 percent respectively in the 2008 version of this study.[48] Retaining loyal, repeat customers is also crucial because it is easy for people to switch among carriers, suppliers, travel trade intermediaries, and destinations. The key outcome of all relationship marketing efforts is to make individual customers feel special so they believe that the organization has singled them out for extraordinary attention.

This individualization or customization can be achieved through the following procedures:

1. **Managing service encounters.** Training hospitality and travel organization staff members to treat customers as individuals, e.g., by using their names, knowing their preferences and interests, etc.
2. **Providing customer incentives.** Giving customers incentives or inducements to make repeat use of the organization or destination, e.g., frequent-flyer and frequent-guest programs, preferred supplier arrangements, destination loyalty programs, etc.
3. **Providing special service options.** Giving enhanced services or special extras to repeat or club customers, including, for example, upgrades to executive or concierge floors in hotels, airline club lounge memberships, and personalized baggage tags.
4. **Developing pricing strategies to encourage long-term use.** Offering repeat customers special prices or rates, e.g., annual memberships to theme parks, museums, zoos, and other gated attractions; VIP club programs, etc.
5. **Maintaining a customer database.** Keeping an up-to-date database on individual customers, including purchase history, preferences, likes and dislikes, demographics, etc.
6. **Communicating with customers through direct or specialized media.** Using non-mass media approaches to communicate directly with individual customers, e.g., e-mail, online newsletters or e-newsletters, direct mail, etc.

The Customer Mix

Another important people-related decision for a hospitality and travel organization is its customer mix. The **customer mix** is the combination of customers (or target markets) that use or are attracted to a specific hospitality and travel organization. The term *mix* is most appropriate for the hospitality and travel industry, since our guests do mix and often interact with one another. Of course, this concept is closely related to market segmentation and marketing strategy that were discussed in Chapters 7 and 8. In actual practice, the customer mix requires the careful management of the interactions among customers, mostly when they are in the process of using hospitality and travel organizations' services. The types of customers who use hospitality and travel organizations definitely influence the images among other present and potential customers. In some cases, certain types of customers attract other similar customers, and the reverse may be true as well. Customers also directly influence other customers' quality of service experiences. The actions and behavior of individual customers (e.g., guests who are loud or rude, who smoke, who are drunk, or who push or shove) may also be annoying or offensive to other customers and lead to lowered customer satisfaction levels. Conversely, very considerate or friendly customers may enhance other customers' service experiences.

Some hospitality and travel organizations in their positioning approaches make it quite clear which groups of customers they wish to attract and serve. They may have a niche marketing strategy, for example. Contiki Holidays explicitly indicates in all of its advertising and other promotions that it is a tour company for persons aged 18 to 35 years. Their communications carry photographs of men and women in this age group to emphasize the appropriate youthful image of Contiki.

Some exclusive and expensive resorts have no children policies or do not allow children under a certain age to stay with them. The reason is that they believe that their typical guests do not like to be bothered by children, who can be noisy and boisterous if not properly supervised by adults. Other resorts

FIGURE 11.10 Private resources such as rental companies can provide valuable equipment.

advertised as being for couples only, have chosen to target only adult guests as part of their marketing strategies. In contrast, a growing number of hospitality and travel organizations, such as Westin and their Westin Kids Club®, are actively trying to recruit children into their customer mixes. Other examples include the Hyatt Corporation with its Camp Hyatt program, and Carnival's Camp Carnival.

For guests who like to vacation in places without all or most of their clothes, some companies offer special tours, resorts, or beach areas. These include a very appropriately named tour company whose site on the Web is bare-necessities.com. Another example of a specific customer mix is the growing number of hospitality and travel organizations that are targeting the gay and lesbian market. Montreal is one of the most popular destinations in Canada for this market and Figure 11.10 shows the excellent website information provided for these customers.

Chapter Conclusion

The interaction of customers (guests) and employees (hosts) has a great influence on marketing success. In particular, the quality of service provided plays the pivotal role in the success of a hospitality and travel organization. Organizations that devote above-average attention to their employees usually prosper the most. Successful organizations train their employees to do things right the first time and empower employees to quickly resolve customer problems and complaints. Service quality must constantly be measured by a hospitality and travel organization, and a variety of techniques can be used to accomplish this.

All hospitality and travel organizations should apply the relationship marketing concept. This means building long-term customer loyalty among individual customers through customized programs that make guests feel extra-special.

An organization's customer mix may affect both its image and the service quality that individual customers experience. Efforts are needed to manage the customer mix, not only for profitability reasons, but also to maximize guest satisfaction.

REVIEW QUESTIONS

1. Who are the two major groups of people involved in hospitality and travel marketing, and what are the most important interactions between these two groups?
2. How important are a hospitality and travel organization's staff members to its marketing success and effectiveness?
3. What is the total quality management (TQM) concept and what are its key principles?
4. Which techniques can be used to make employees provide more consistent and higher quality service to customers?

5. What is empowerment and how does it contribute to increasing service quality?
6. What is SERVQUAL and how is it used in evaluating service quality?
7. What other techniques can be used to measure service quality?
8. What is relationship marketing and what steps should a hospitality and travel organization take to build long-term relationships with individual customers?
9. How does the customer mix affect an organization's image and the quality of its customers' service experiences?

CHAPTER ASSIGNMENTS

1. You have been hired by a hotel, restaurant, travel agency, airline, or other hospitality and travel organization with a reputation for below-average service. Your task is to significantly upgrade the service orientation and service quality of supervisors and other staff members. What steps would you follow in satisfying this objective? Draw on examples of successful organizations in the hospitality and travel industry. Try to come up with two or more creative ideas of your own.

2. You have been asked by your boss to develop a program for measuring service quality in your hospitality and travel organization. What technique or techniques would you recommend be used for this measurement? Write a report to your boss explaining your plan and how it should be implemented.

3. Choose a specific hospitality and travel organization and describe how you would develop a relationship marketing program for it. How would you attract and recognize repeat customers? What special options or services would you offer repeat customers? What type of database would be developed and how would it be maintained? How would you communicate with past guests?

4. Describe the importance of the customer mix concept to a particular hospitality and travel organization. Explain how the types of customers it attracts affects its image, and how customers' service experiences are either enhanced or made less satisfactory. Make constructive suggestions to the organization's management on how they could manage their customer mix more effectively.

WEB RESOURCES

American Society for Quality (ASQ), http://www.asq.org/
Bare Necessities, http://www.bare-necessities.com/
Delta Hotels, http://www.deltahotels.com/
Disney Institute, http://www.disneyinstitute.com/
Four Seasons Hotels and Resorts, http://www.fourseasons.com/
Hampton Inn, http://hamptoninn1.hilton.com/en_US/hp/index.do
Mandarin Oriental Hotel Group, http://www.mandarinoriental.com/
National Institute for Quality Standards, http://www.quality.nist.gov/

The Peninsula Hotels, http://www.peninsula.com/
The Ritz-Carlton Company, http://www.ritzcarlton.com/
The Ritz-Carlton Leadership Centre, http://corporate.ritzcarlton.com/
Shangri-La Hotels and Resorts, http://www.shangri-la.com/
Singapore Airlines, http://www.singaporeair.com/
Southwest Airlines, http://www.southwest.com/
Tourisme Montréal, http://www.tourisme-montreal.org/

REFERENCES

1. Lytle, Richard S., and John E. Timmerman. 2006. "Service orientation and performance: an organizational perspective." *Journal of Services Marketing*, 20(2), 136–147.
2. Younger Jay, and Wes Trochill. 2004. *Customers at the Core*. Association Management, accessed June 25, 2007.
3. Disney. 2007. *The Disney Institute*, http://www.disneyinstitute.com/quality/quality-service-brief.cfm, accessed June 24, 2007.
4. Singapore Airlines. 2007. *Celebrating 60 years in 2007*, https://60years.singaporeair.com/global_icon.asp, accessed June 27, 2007.
5. Chan, Daniel. 2000. "The story of Singapore Airlines and the Singapore Girl." *Journal of Management Development*, 19(6), 456–472.
6. Marriott International. 2007. *Core Values*, http://www.marriott.com/corporateinfo/culture/coreValues.mi, accessed June 27, 2007.
7. Blackwell, Roger D., Paul W. Miniard, and James F. Engel. 2006. *Consumer Behavior*, 10th ed. Mason, Ohio: Thomson South-Western, 742.
8. Schneider, Benjamin, and David E. Bowen. 1999. "Understanding Customer Delight and Outrage." *MIT Sloan Management Review*, 41(1), 35–45.
9. Torres, Edwin N., and Sheryl Kline. 2006. "From satisfaction to delight: a model for the hotel industry." *International Journal of Contemporary Hospitality Management*, 18(4), 290–301.
10. Mill, Robert Christie, and Alastair M. Morrison. 2006. *The Tourism System*. Dubuque, Iowa: Kendall/Hunt Publishing Company, 30.
11. Albrecht, Karl, and Ron Zemke. 2001. 2nd ed. *Service America in the New Economy*. Columbus, Ohio: McGraw-Hill Companies.
12. Lovelock, Christopher, and Jochen Wirtz. 2007. *Services Marketing. People, Technology, Strategy*. 6th edition. Upper Saddle River, N.J.: Pearson Prentice Hall, 417.
13. American Society for Quality. 2007. *Glossary*, http://www.asq.org/glossary/index.html, accessed June 22, 2007.
14. Dahlgaard, Jens J., Kai Kristensen, and Ghopal K. Khanji. 2005. *Fundamentals of Total Quality Management*. Cheltenham, England: Nelson Thornes Ltd.
15. Tari, Juan Jose. 2005. "Components of Successful Total Quality Management." *The TQM Magazine*, 17(2), 182–194.

16. Sureshchandar, G.S., Chandrasekharan Rajendran, and R. N. Anantha-raman. 2001. "A Holistic Model of Total Quality Service." *International Journal of Service Industry Management*, 12 (3/4), 378–412.

17. Andersson, Roy, Henrik Eriksson, and Hakan Torstensson. 2006. "Similarities and Differences between TQM, Six Sigma, and Lean." *The TQM Magazine*, 18(3), 282–296.

18. Lovelock, Christopher, and Jochen Wirtz. 2007. *Services Marketing. People, Technology, Strategy.* 6th edition. Upper Saddle River, N.J.: Pearson Prentice Hall, 442–444.

19. International Organization for Standardization (ISO). 2007. *Quality management principles*, http://www.iso.org/iso/en/iso9000-14000/understand/qmp.html, accessed June 17, 2007.

20. Delta Hotels & Resorts. 2007. *Meetings & Groups*, http://www.deltahotels.com/en/meetings/ourpromise.html, accessed June 24, 2007.

21. Hilton Hospitality, Inc. 2007. *About Hampton*®, http://hamptoninn.hilton.com/en/hp/brand/about.jhtml, accessed June 23, 2007.

22. Swiss Tourism Federation. 2007. *The Q-Label*, http://www.quality-our-passion.ch/index.cfm/fuseaction/show/path/1-430-646.htm, accessed June 23, 2007.

23. Koch, Karl. 2004. *Quality Offensive in Swiss Tourism.* Vilnius, Lithuania: World Tourism Organization.

24. Hong Kong Tourism Board. 2007. *Quality Tourism Services Scheme*, http://www.discoverhongkong.com/eng/mustknow/qts/index.jhtml, accessed June 23, 2007.

25. Tanke, Mary L. 2001. *Human Resources Management for the Hospitality Industry.* 2nd ed. Albany, New York: Delmar Thomson Learning, 4.

26. Nickson, D., Chris Warhurst, and Eli Dutton. 2005. "The importance of attitude and appearance in the service encounter in retail and hospitality." *Managing Service Quality*, 15(2), 195–208.

27. The Myers & Briggs Foundation. 2007. *The MBTI Instrument*® *for Life*, http://www.myersbriggs.org/, accessed June 22, 2007.

28. Silva, Paula. 2006. "Effects of disposition on hospitality employee job satisfaction and commitment." *International Journal of Contemporary Hospitality Management*, 18(4), 317–328.

29. Anonymous. 2004. "Delighted, returning customers: service the Ritz-Carlton way." *Strategic Direction*, 20(11), 7–9.

30. Moretti, Denise. 2006. *Corporate Orientation Programs: Retaining Great People Begins Before Day One*, http://www.hospitalitynet.org/news/4028387.print, accessed June 22, 2007.

31. Nobles, Harry, and Cheryl Thompson Griggs. 2003. *New Employee Orientation: Necessity or Luxury?* http://www.hotel-online.com/News/PR2003_3rd/Jul03_Orientation.html, accessed June 22, 2007.

32. The Ritz-Carlton Company. 2007. *Career FAQs*, http://corporate.ritzcarlton.com/en/Careers/FAQs.htm, accessed June 23, 2007.

33. Starbucks Coffee. 2006. *Career Center*, http://www.starbucks.com/aboutus/jobcenter.asp, accessed June 26, 2007.

34. Lashley, Conrad. 1995. "Towards an understanding of employee empowerment in hospitality services." *International Journal of Contemporary Hospitality Management*, 7(1), 27–32.

35. Partlow, Charles G. 1993. "How Ritz-Carlton applies TQM." *Cornell Hotel and Restaurant Administration Quarterly*, 34 (4), 23.

36. Lashley, Conrad. 1995. "Towards an understanding of employee empowerment in hospitality services." *International Journal of Contemporary Hospitality Management*, 7(1), 27–32.

37. American Marketing Association. 2007. *Dictionary of Marketing Terms*, http://www.marketingpower.com/mg-dictionary.php, accessed June 22, 2007.

38. Drake, Susan M., Michelle J. Gulman, and Sarah M. Roberts. 2005. *Light Their Fire. Using Internal Marketing to Ignite Employee Performance and Wow Your Customers*. Chicago, Illinois: Dearborn Trade Publishing.

39. Forum for People Performance Management and Measurement. 2007. *The Six Characteristics of Highly Effective Internal Marketing Programs*, http://www.performanceforum.org/fileadmin/pdf/internal_marketing_best_practice_study.pdf, accessed June 24, 2007.

40. Lovelock, Christopher, and Jochen Wirtz. 2007. *Services Marketing. People, Technology, Strategy*. 6th edition. Upper Saddle River, N.J.: Pearson Prentice Hall, 402–422.

41. Kotler, Philip, and Kevin Lane Keller. 2006. *Marketing Management*. 12th ed. Upper Saddle River, N.J.: Pearson Prentice Hall, 382–383.

42. Lovelock, Christopher, and Jochen Wirtz. 2007. *Services Marketing. People, Technology, Strategy*. 6th edition. Upper Saddle River, N.J.: Pearson Prentice Hall, 424–425.

43. Mystery Shopping Providers Association. 2007. *Types and terminology of mystery shopping*, http://www.mysteryshop.org/searchmspa/#2, accessed June 23, 2007.

44. American Marketing Association. 2007. *Dictionary of Marketing Terms*, http://www.marketingpower.com/mg-dictionary.php, accessed June 26, 2007.

45. Yang, Amoy X. 2005. "Using lifetime value to gain long-term profitability." *Database Marketing & Customer Strategy Management*, 12(2), 142–152.

46. Lee, Jonathan, Janghyuk Lee, and Lawrence Feick. 2006. "Incorporating word-of-mouth effects in estimating customer lifetime value." *Database Marketing & Customer Strategy Management*, 14(1), 29–39.

47. Travel Weekly. 2006. *2006 Consumer Trends*, 7.

48. Travel Weekly. 2008. *2008 Consumer Trends*, 7.

chapter 12

Packaging and Programming
How Do We Get There?

O V E R V I E W

Hospitality and travel services are perishable. A sale not made today is lost forever. Packaging and programming play a key role in selling services when demand for them is lowest. Packages are popular with customers because they make travel easier and more convenient. In addition, they usually offer added value through a price break on regular rates and fares. Packages and programs are the epitome of the marketing concept. They are tailor-made offerings to meet specific customer needs and wants.

The packaging of hospitality and travel services is unique. It is very different from the packaging of consumer products found in supermarkets; they cannot be placed on shelves for sale. Our industry's packages usually involve some combination of services from suppliers, carriers, travel trade intermediaries, and destination marketing organizations (DMOs). They are an excellent example of partnership, because they require the cooperative efforts of several industry groups.

O B J E C T I V E S

Having read this chapter, you should be able to:

- Define the terms *packaging* and *programming*.

- Explain the relationship between packaging and programming.

- List the reasons for the popularity of packages and programs in the hospitality and travel industry.

- Explain the five key roles of packaging and programming in marketing hospitality and travel services.

- Explain the difference between packages developed by intermediaries and packages developed by others.

- List and explain four ways of classifying packages.

- Describe the concept of dynamic packaging and its advantages.

- Describe the steps that should be followed in developing effective packages.

- Describe the procedures used to price packages.

KEY TERMS

affinity group packages
all-inclusive package
American Plan (AP)
Bed & Breakfast (B&B)
blocking space
break-even analysis
charter tour
commissionable
Continental Plan (CP)
convention/meeting packages
destination management
    companies (DMCs)
destination package
double-occupancy basis

dynamic packaging
escorted tours
European Plan (EP)
event packages
family vacation or holiday
    packages
fixed costs
fly-cruise packages
fly-drive packages
fly-rail packages
foreign independent tour (FIT)
group inclusive tour (GIT)
incentive packages

Modified American Plan
    (MAP)
packaging
partnership
programming
rail-drive packages
shared-room basis
single supplement
special-interest travel (SIT)
    packages
synergism
travel demand generators
variable or direct costs

When you walk into a supermarket, you are confronted by thousands of products on the shelves in a myriad of packages. If you select a box of cereal, you know that it is packaged exactly the same as the other boxes of the same brand on the shelf. Unless the product is visibly damaged, you will not spend even an instant thinking about which box or package of your selected brand to choose. Consumer-goods manufacturers, however, spend millions of dollars designing packages to catch your eye. The hospitality and travel industry's version of packaging is very different, however. Packaging is not physical, but involves blending several services into appealing, convenient customer offerings.

Programming is a related concept that is vitally important to the industry. These are special events and activities with drawing power that give a service an added dimension and appeal. Programming is very helpful in creating interest in off-peak times and in maintaining customer interest in the service.

Definition of Packaging and Programming

You have heard the expression *package deal*, which means that the seller throws in a variety of products at a total price that is usually less than the sum of all individual items. Most packages offered by the hospitality and travel industry are of the package-deal type. In our industry, **packaging** is the combination of related and complementary services into a single-price offering. **Programming** is a technique closely related to packaging. It involves developing special activities, events, or programs to increase customer spending, or to give added appeal to a package or other hospitality/travel service.

Packaging and programming are related concepts, since a large number of packages include some programming. For example, many golf and tennis packages include some instruction. The instruction portions of these packages are a special activity (program) arranged by the host resort. Gourmet cooking classes at resorts and on cruise ships are another example, in which skilled chefs provide expert demonstrations and instruction (the program) to participants. Of course, not all programming occurs within packages; parades and holiday celebrations at theme parks and most tourism festivals are examples.

Relationship of Packaging and Programming

Packaging and programming are related concepts. Many packages include some programming, and often the program is the package's principal travel demand generator. The once-every-ten-years staging of the Oberammergau Passion Play in Germany is an excellent example. It is also possible to have packages with no programming and to program without packaging. Packages do not have to incorporate programming. For example, they can simply be accommodation and meal packages, as shown on the left of Figure 12.1. Wyndham Hotels and Resorts *Weekender* packages are a good example. This package offers a room for two adults plus two full breakfasts, plus a 50 percent discount on the next day's stay. What is the core appeal and travel demand generator? It is simply a price reduction with no added frills.

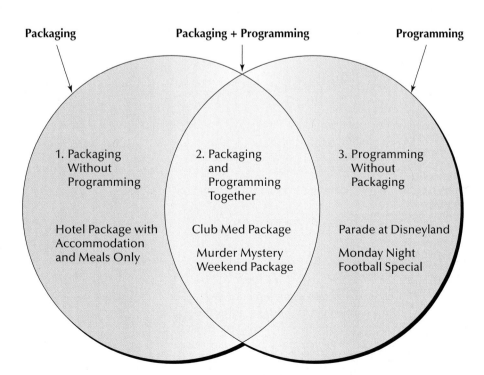

FIGURE 12.1
Relationship of packaging and programming.

Packaging | Packaging + Programming | Programming

1. Packaging Without Programming

Hotel Package with Accommodation and Meals Only

2. Packaging and Programming Together

Club Med Package

Murder Mystery Weekend Package

3. Programming Without Packaging

Parade at Disneyland

Monday Night Football Special

Packaging and programming are related techniques. They can be done together or separately.

Sometimes a reduced price is enough to sell the package, and no programming is needed.

But programming can be a powerful ally of packaging, especially when a lower price alone cannot generate enough customer interest. Programming can be the travel demand generator, as in a murder-mystery weekend, or it can be an integral part of the package. As Figure 12.1 shows, the murder-mystery weekend and program-based vacations such as Club Med's are examples of situations where programming and packaging overlap. Programming can also be done on its own, and not in conjunction with packaging. The two examples of this in Figure 12.1 are a parade at Disneyland and the live entertainment bars, lounges, and restaurants.

Reasons for the Popularity of Packages and Programming

The travel package probably ranks among the concepts that have had the greatest influence on the industry in the past 50 or 60 years. The range of packages available today seems limitless. Why has there been such growth in their popularity? The reasons can be divided into two categories: customer-related and participant-related. (Figure 12.2).

1. **Customer-Related Reasons.** Packages and programs are very user-friendly concepts. They respond to various customer needs, including more convenient holiday/vacation planning, added value in travel, and

FIGURE 12.2 Reasons for the increased popularity of packaging and programming.

1. **CUSTOMER-RELATED REASONS**
   a. Greater convenience
   b. Greater economy
   c. Ability to budget for trips
   d. Implicit assurance of consistent quality
   e. Satisfaction of special interests
   f. Added dimension to traveling and dining out

2. **PARTICIPANT-RELATED REASONS**
   a. Increased business in off-peak periods
   b. Enhanced appeal to specific target markets
   c. Attraction of new target markets
   d. Easier business forecasting and improved efficiency
   e. Use of complementary facilities, attractions, and events
   f. Flexibility to capitalize on new market trends
   g. Stimulation of repeat and more frequent usage
   h. Increased per capita spending and lengths of stay
   i. Public relations and publicity value of unique packages
   j. Increased customer satisfaction

a greater desire for specialized experiences. The main customer benefits of travel packages are as follows:

a. *Greater Convenience.* Although some people experience great joy from assembling the different pieces of their holidays/vacations, meetings, or incentive trips, many others prefer the convenience of buying packages (Figure 12.3). Why? The travel package requires less planning time and effort. For an increasing number of people, time is becoming an even more precious resource than money. This trend toward greater demand for time-saving convenience was highlighted in Chapter 7. The popularity of packages should continue to increase with the growth of two-income families in many countries around the world.

b. *Added Value.* Packages not only make travel and travel planning easier and less time consuming, but also they offer added value and are more affordable. For many packages involving air travel, the total package price might be less than the regular, return-trip airfare. You might wonder how this can be. Do the carriers and suppliers involved not lose money? Sometimes they do, but usually they do not. As you will see later, packages are also financially attractive for the industry.

Packages offer value in three ways. First, if travel intermediaries put them together, they buy in bulk and receive discounts from suppliers and carriers. They pass on part of these discounts to customers. Second, many packages are offered by suppliers and carriers at off-peak periods. The weekend package at a city hotel is a prime example.

Image copyright Sgame, 2008. Used under license from Shutterstock.com

FIGURE 12.3
Packaging = the world in a box? Not quite! But a good metaphor all the same.

Did You Know?

What are the advantages of packages and tours?

- The United States Tour Operator Association (USTOA) suggests that there is great variety in vacation packages available to customers. What are the major customer advantages according to USTOA?
- **Savings:** Tour operators buy in bulk from hotels, accommodations, ground transportation, sightseeing tours, restaurants, and other services, and get better prices. They pass these savings along to travelers.
- **Volume purchasing:** Often tour operators can secure prices from hotels and airlines that are impossible for customers to get from other sources.
- **Peace of mind:** Buying packages or tours or package gives customers greater "peace of mind." Customers pre-pay for their travel, so costs are known in advance and they can budget for vacations with greater certainty.
- **Professional planning:** Customers have the assurance that their vacations have been planned by professionals.

Source: United States Tour Operators Association. (2008). *Advantages of Tours & Packages,* **http://www.ustoa.com/advantagesoftours.cfm**

Most urban hotels that are busy serving business travelers on weekday nights have a sharp drop in occupancies on Friday and Saturday nights. Specially-priced weekend packages help fill the void. Third, the industry realizes that customers buy packages partly because of their desire for greater value.

c. *Ability to Budget for Trips.* Many packages are fully or partially inclusive, meaning that customers know how much they will have to spend weeks or months in advance. This is part of the reason why cruises and all-inclusive resort concepts such as Club Med and Sandals have become so popular. Club Med offers, for one price, everything from return-trip airfare to unlimited free wine, beer, and soft drinks at mealtime. Participation in a wide variety of sports is also included. The only elements not covered in *The Club Med Package* are *a la carte* items such as scuba diving instruction and spa packages. The tremendous growth in the popularity of cruises is another great example of all-inclusive holidays/vacations. The Cruise Line Industry Association (CLIA) in its *Top Ten Reasons to Choose to Cruise* lists value as the first reason, since one price covers the guests' cabin, dining, and entertainment (Figure 12.4).[1] The inclusive nature of packages

Image copyright Rob Marmion, 2008. Used under license from Shutterstock.com

removes much customer anxiety about how much they will have to spend, and what they will get for their money.

d. *Assurance of Consistent Quality.* Consider the alternative to purchasing a package: customers have to put all the pieces together themselves. Often, they have to buy hospitality and travel services sight unseen. The results can be disastrous if expectations of quality and service are not met.

The travel intermediaries, suppliers, and carriers that assemble packages have more experience and a wider knowledge base. They are professionals in this line of work. Customers can usually rely on this professionalism, in-depth knowledge and experience, and the participants' stake in delivering what is expected. Most organizations recognize the vast power of word-of-mouth recommendations (positive and negative) and the importance of repeat customers. It is in their best long-term interests to provide consistent quality in all package elements. Customers notice inconsistencies and are apt to judge their entire experiences on the weakest elements. Packages, therefore, offer greater assurance of consistent quality among hospitality and travel elements.

e. *Satisfaction of Special Interests.* Along with the numerous, more general packages, there is an ever-expanding menu of **special interest travel (SIT)** offerings, ranging from weekends for chocoholics to guided tour packages featuring the art of China and Tibet. The Specialty Travel Index and SpecialtyTravel.com provide an excellent online guide to packages ranging alphabetically from academic/educational tours to zoology.[2] Another good online source of information on SIT packages is InfoHub.com (InfoHub Specialty Travel Guide). Chapter 7 mentioned the trend toward using holiday or vacation time to brush up on or otherwise pursue special interests.

Many of these special-interest packages require considerable prior research, careful programming, and expert instructors or guides. Normally, customers do not have the experience, time, or resources to put these elements together. The packages offer a customized alternative to satisfying their needs.

f. *Added Dimension to Traveling and Dining Out.* Programming adds an extra dimension, and sometimes a fresh appeal, to hospitality and travel services. Theme parks are masters of the art of programming. Many of them are highly dependent on repeat use from local residents. How can you get customers to come back if what you have to sell remains essentially the same? The answer lies in programming— constantly offering new entertainment, special events, and activities that renew and heighten customer interest (Figure 12.5). Parks such as Walt Disney World and Hong Kong Disneyland hold special parades, and holiday and other celebrations, to bring back past guests who otherwise would not return. Many restaurants also use programming successfully to induce customers to return more frequently (the dinner theatre is one good example, as are restaurants offering special-theme meals). Medieval Times is a chain of restaurants in the United States and Canada in which customers are treated to an

FIGURE 12.5   Live entertainment is a popular type of programming at theme parks.

Image copyright Brian Chase, 2008. Used under license from Shutterstock.com

exciting program of jousting, sword fights, and horse riding among knights while they eat dinner. This is an excellent example of turning a meal into a memorable experience through programming.

Programming adds excitement to the customer's experience and planning. It gives an added dimension to services that they find very appealing. The themed dinners or parties staged at conventions and other meetings are good examples. A specialized group of organizations in the hospitality and travel industry called **destination management companies (DMCs)** arrange these themed dinners or parties. The Association of Destination Management Executives (ADME) defines a DMC as "a professional services company possessing extensive local knowledge, expertise and resources, specializing in the design and implementation of events, activities, tours, transportation and program logistics."[3] They should not be confused with DMOs (destination marketing organizations), as the functions of the two are quite different.

2. **Participant-Related Reasons.** The real beauty of packaging and programming is that they benefit both the customer and the package/program participants. These participants can include travel trade intermediaries (tour operators, travel agents, incentive travel planners), suppliers (lodging, restaurant, car rental, cruise line, and attraction organizations), carriers (airlines, bus, train, and ferry companies), and destination marketing organizations. Whatever the mixture of participants, well-conceived and marketed packages and programs help build customer volumes and improve profitability.

   a. *Increased Business in Off-Peak Periods.* One of the major reasons for organizing or participating in packages or programs is their ability to create demand at off-peak times. For many restaurants and bars, Mondays and Tuesdays are the lowest-volume days. Most city lodging properties have their poorest occupancies on weekends. The Hilton *Bed & Breakfast* package runs from Thursday night through Sunday, and includes a room for two and two full breakfasts each morning.[4] Airlines experience their lowest load factors on weekends and outside the early-morning and late-afternoon rush times. Most resorts have great swings in business volumes by season. Good packages and programs help even out otherwise cyclical business patterns by creating new reasons for customers to use services.

   b. *Enhanced Appeal to Specific Target Markets.* Packages and programs help participants hone in on selected target markets. Most of these packages and programs are tailor-made to fit the needs and desires of specific customer groups. There are numerous examples in the resort business, such as skiing packages for alpine and cross-country enthusiasts, golf and tennis packages, spa packages, offerings for scuba divers, sailors, the health- and fitness-conscious, and many others. Many resorts also put together special package deals for organizations with conventions/meetings and incentive trips (or the so-called MICE markets).

Two specific examples will help clarify this benefit of specific target markets. The Scottsdale Resort & Conference Center in Arizona offers a *Benchmark Conference Plan* that includes the services of a Professional Conference Planner. Its Media Center offers state-of-the-art audio-visual equipment and the services of several in-house skilled technicians and support personnel to help meeting planners stage even the most sophisticated productions.

Sandals, the all-inclusive Caribbean resort group, have developed an outstanding combination of packaging and programming for the wedding market, and honeymoons. As the website page in Figure 12.6 shows, all the details for planning and holding a wedding are covered by Sandals, and the resort company. Even a streaming video can be prepared for the couple to be shared online with family and friends. By "sweating the details" of programming and packaging, Sandals offers a highly attractive offering and set of destinations for this special-occasion market.

c. *Attraction of New Target Markets.* As well as solidifying its appeal to existing target markets, a hospitality and travel business can use packages and programs to pursue new target markets. A good example of this is in the cruise line business. Cruises traditionally were only taken by people on holiday or vacation. Now cruise ships are

FIGURE 12.6 Sandals has a highly impressive packaging and programming approach for the wedding market.

Courtesy of Sandals

being used by more organizations for shipboard meetings, conventions, and incentive trips. Cruise line companies have developed a new target market by preparing and promoting packages to these MICE groups.

d. *Easier Business Forecasting and Improved Efficiency.* Many packages are booked and paid for well in advance of the customer's visit. Therefore, the hospitality and travel organization is in a better position to predict customer volumes and to schedule staff, supplies, and other resources with greater efficiency. However, there is also a related danger if a large number of cancellations are received close to arrival dates. In recent years, the hospitality and travel industry has done much to encourage advance bookings by their customers. Many of the cruise lines offer special incentives to customers that book early.

e. *Use of Complementary Facilities, Attractions, and Events.* This book makes frequent mention of the **partnership** concept (cooperative marketing of related hospitality and travel services). Many packages and programs provide excellent examples of this approach, as various groups meld their services into more marketable customer offerings.

Packaging and programming offer a great opportunity to use **travel demand generators** (primary reasons for travel) creatively. For example, many hotels and restaurants combine their services with visits to key local attractions, events, and other activities. Many hotels in cities with major sports events offer packages that include game tickets. Some lodging properties close to vineyards incorporate wine tours into their packages; whereas hotels close the theatre districts include shows along with guest rooms. Many restaurants offer dining-entertainment packages featuring the performing arts.

Carriers and travel trade intermediaries also benefit from these arrangements, as do other categories of suppliers and DMOs. Many airlines, passenger rail, and bus companies themselves offer packages built around special events or attractions in the cities they serve. The Greater Pittsburgh Convention & Visitors Bureau offers packages combining lodging with tickets to Pittsburgh Pirates baseball games that can be booked online at VisitPittsburgh.com (Figure 12.7).

f. *Flexibility to Capitalize on New Market Trends.* The physical facilities and equipment of many hospitality and travel organizations are fixed and cannot be altered significantly in the short term. Packaging and programming give these organizations the flexibility to capitalize on new market trends, often without having to make expensive physical changes. The *Theme Programs* offered by the Mohonk Mountain House in New Paltz, New York, provide an excellent example. The resort hotel, built in 1869, has focused on the trend toward people using vacation time to learn or otherwise enhance their education. It offers several such opportunities, including packages featuring gardening, birding, and ballroom dancing.

FIGURE 12.7 Visit Pittsburgh offers online packages featuring Pittsburgh Pirates' games.

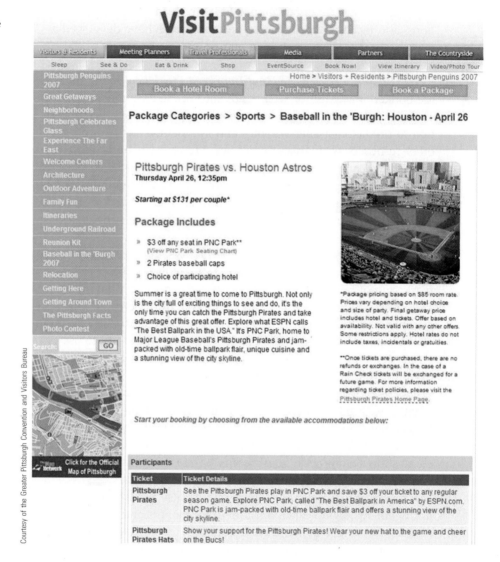

Courtesy of the Greater Pittsburgh Convention and Visitors Bureau

g. *Stimulation of Repeat and More Frequent Usage.* This is the flip side of the previously mentioned customer benefit. New packaging and programming can rekindle and increase customers' interest in the service. Theme parks have already been mentioned as strong believers in keeping their entertainment offerings fresh by holding numerous special events. Several restaurants offer themed meals, gourmet dining and wine-tasting nights, and other events partly to bring customers back more regularly. Food festivals are a good example of this, and appeal to both local residents and visitors. The added dimension given to the service through programming and packaging benefits both the customer and the organization.

h. *Increased Per Capita Spending and Lengths of Stay.* Used correctly, packages and programs help hospitality and travel organizations increase both the average amount spent by customers and their lengths of stay. Again, many theme parks have perfected this technique. By adding live shows, holiday celebrations, fireworks, or parades, they encourage guests to remain longer, and the customer who stays longer spends more (Figure 12.8). Pre- and post-convention tours at hotels and resorts are another excellent example. By offering side trips to local attractions or events, these packages extend convention/meeting guests' lengths of stay.

i. *Public Relations and Publicity Value of Unique Packages.* Chapter 18 takes a detailed look at public relations and publicity and their great long-term value to hospitality and travel organizations. Often businesses find that they have a limited variety of newsworthy items for the media to cover. Unique and creative packages grab the attention of newspapers, magazines, television and radio stations. Packages that latch on to popular issues and trends (e.g., health/fitness packages, lifestyle and stress management, and personal financial management) frequently attract widespread media attention. Others, such as *Chocoholic Packages*, are so different that they appeal to the public's curiosity. The Royal Windsor Hotel in Brussels, Belgium,

Image copyright Gilmanshin, 2008. Used under license from Shutterstock.com

FIGURE 12.8
Fireworks bring color to an evening sky and are a good example of programming in hospitality and travel.

offers a Chocoholic Package that includes among other items a box of Belgian chocolates, and entrance tickets to the Museum of Cocoa and Chocolate. Used correctly, packages can be very effective in generating greater publicity.

j. *Increased Customer Satisfaction.* The bottom line on packaging and programming is their contribution to greater customer satisfaction. Both concepts are true reflections of the marketing concept. They are tailor-made to fit specific customer needs and provide many useful benefits to travelers.

Roles of Packaging and Programming in Marketing

What roles do packaging and programming play in the marketing of hospitality and travel services? You already know from previous chapters that they can be part of an organization's marketing mix (8 Ps) and, therefore, should figure in its marketing plan. (Remember the "How do we get there?" question?) You may also have a good idea about their roles from the previous discussion on reasons for their popularity.

Packages and programs perform the following five key roles in hospitality and travel marketing:

1. Smoothing patterns of business
2. Improving profitability
3. Assisting in use of segmented marketing strategies
4. Complementing other product/service-mix elements
5. Bringing together related hospitality and travel organizations

1. **Smoothing Patterns of Business.** Chapter 2 compared unsold inventories of services to water running down a drain. In fact, the pipe for unused services is eternal. The sale of such services is lost forever. One of the principal roles of packages and programs is to plug the drain and to even out the peaks and valleys in this often-cyclical business.

2. **Improving Profitability.** By smoothing out the kinks in business, packages and programs improve profitability. They also add to profits by doing the following:

   a. Increasing per capita spending
   b. Extending lengths of stay
   c. Generating new business
   d. Encouraging more frequent use and repeat use
   e. Improving efficiency through more accurate sales forecasting

3. **Assisting in Use of Segmented Marketing Strategies.** Chapter 8 highlighted the various marketing strategies, including the segmented approach. Packages and programs are a useful tool for segmenters who

are trying to match their offerings to the needs of specific customer groups.

4. **Complementing Other Product/Service-Mix Elements.** Packages and programs are part of an organization's product/service mix. They are an important complement to the other elements, including facilities, equipment, and other services. In a way, they are much like product and gift packages—they make hospitality and travel services more attractive to customers. They wrap up the other product/mix elements into more appealing and marketable offerings.

5. **Bringing Together Related Hospitality and Travel Organizations.** When you think about the overall impact of packages and programs, you might come up with the word *synergy*. **Synergism** is the combined action of two or more hospitality and travel organizations that produces a result that individually would not have been possible. A well-conceived, professionally promoted, and well-executed package does this for all its participants. It produces results that they could not match on their own. Packages bring together travel trade intermediaries, carriers, suppliers, and DMOs. They are an excellent example of cooperative marketing (or partnership) in the industry.

Packaging Concepts Offered By Industry

Two major categories of packages are available from the hospitality and travel industry.

Packages Developed by Intermediaries

Many travel trade intermediaries, including tour wholesalers and operators, incentive travel planners, some travel agents, and convention/meeting planners, put together packages.

Packages Developed by Others

Other packages are developed by suppliers, carriers, DMOs, clubs, and special-interest groups. These packages can usually be purchased directly from the source (e.g., a hotel weekend package) and may or may not also be booked through a travel agent (e.g., a tour package). In some instances, like many cruise packages, booking can only be done through travel agencies.

Packages can also be classified in four different ways by their:

1. Package elements
2. Target markets
3. Package duration or timing
4. Travel arrangements or destinations

1. **Package Elements.**

    a. *All-Inclusive Packages.* The **all-inclusive package** is a generic term for packages that include all or nearly all the elements that travelers require for their trips, including airfare, lodging, ground transportation, meals, recreation activities and entertainment, taxes, and gratuities. The packages offered by cruise lines, Club Med, and Sandals are of this type, as are those provided by many other resorts and destinations.

b. *Escorted Tours.* The key word here is *tour.* **Escorted tours** follow a predetermined itinerary, and tour managers or guides accompany travelers. These packages are usually all inclusive, but may have some optional (e.g., special side trips) or on-your-own (e.g., arrange your own meals or activities) elements. Most motorcoach packages fit into this category and include motorcoach transportation, lodging, meals, and admissions to various attractions and entertainment facilities. Even prestigious organizations such as the National Geographic Society, the Smithsonian, and the American Museum of Natural History are in the escorted tour business. For example, National Geographic Expeditions offers more than 100 trips per year and provide professional tour managers, accommodations, meals, excursions, and expert lectures.

c. *Fly-Drive Packages.* **Fly-drive packages** are single-price packages that include return-trip airfare and a rental car at destinations. For example, Lufthansa and United provide air travel from the United States to Europe, plus a rental car. These packages appeal to independent travelers who like to put together their own travel plans within a destination area.

d. *Fly-Cruise Packages.* **Fly-cruise packages** include return airfare to a port of departure, plus a cruise. Many cruise lines advertise free or low-cost airfares from gateway airports to departure ports. Free air travel is seldom a reality, however. Although it is discounted, the airfare is usually buried in the total package price.

e. *Fly-Rail Packages.* **Fly-rail packages** are a combination of air and railway travel.

f. *Rail-Drive Packages.* **Rail-drive packages** involve transportation by train combined with a rental car at the destination.

g. *Accommodation and Meal Packages.* Most resorts and certain other lodging properties promote packages that incorporate one or more nights of accommodation, plus a specified number of meals. For example, **American Plan (AP)** rates include three meals each day—typically breakfast, lunch, and dinner. **Modified American Plan (MAP)** packages provide two meals daily, normally allowing guests to arrange their own lunches.

    Bed and Breakfast (B&B) rates combine a night's accommodation with breakfast the following day (Figure 12.9). A variant of B&B packages is the **Continental Plan (CP)**, which includes a continental (cold) breakfast. Finally, the term **European Plan (EP)** rate implies that no meals are provided with the accommodations.

Image copyright Iofoto, 2008. Used under license from Shutterstock.com

FIGURE 12.9 Bed & breakfast packages are very popular and especially in Europe.

h. *Event Packages.* Every year, special one-time events, festivals, entertainment and cultural performances, or other occurrences take place throughout the world. They present the industry with a considerable store of packaging and programming opportunities. These include major sports championships such as the Olympic, Pan American, and Commonwealth Games; the World Cup, the Super Bowl, and the World Series. There are also numerous large festivals and celebrations such as the Oberammergau Passion Play, New Orleans' Mardi Gras, the Rio Carnival, and the Edinburgh Festival (Figure 12.10). **Event packages** may be simple transportation-plus-admission offerings, but may also provide on-site lodging and meals.

i. *Packages with Programming for Special Interests.* The primary attractions of these packages are the special activities, programs, and events arranged by one or more of the participants. This can be sports and sports instruction (tennis, golf, sailing, boardsailing, scuba diving, mountaineering, etc.), hobbies or other pastimes (gourmet cooking, wine appreciation, photography, fine arts, crafts, etc.), and continuing and self-education topics (e.g., money management, coping with stress, literature, foreign languages, cultural history, medicine, etc.). special-interest travel (SIT) packages are normally offered by lodging properties as an extension of basic accommodation and meals packages.

j. *Local Attraction or Entertainment Packages.* These typically do not include a lodging component and are aimed at local area residents.

FIGURE 12.10 Mardi Gras and major cultural festivals like the one in Venice, Italy are often incorporated into event packages.

Image copyright Dwight Smith, 2008. Used under license from Shutterstock.com

Examples are restaurant/theatre, theme park/meal, and tour/meal packages.

2. **Target Markets.** These are packages specifically developed to meet the needs of certain target markets. They include the following:

   a. *Incentive Packages or Tours.* Chapter 7 pinpointed incentive travel as a major growth market. **Incentive packages** are assembled by a variety of groups and individuals, including travel trade intermediaries (full-service incentive companies, specialized incentive travel-planning firms, travel agents, corporate travel managers, convention/meeting planners), suppliers (lodging chains, cruise lines, and some theme parks), airlines, and DMOs (government tourism agencies and CVBs). The packages are all inclusive, and all expenses are paid for the groups or individuals who travel. Companies, associations, and other groups buy the packages, usually as a reward for outstanding sales achievements, new product introductions, or fund raising.

INTERNET MARKETING

Finding Out What's Going on in Canada? The Use of Events Calendars on the Internet

- The Internet is a great tool for giving up-to-date information to customers and they in turn expect to find the most current information online.
- Events and festivals comprise an important element of the programming in destinations and the Internet is a fantastic venue for posting "what's going on."
- The Ontario Tourism Marketing Partnership (OTMP) has developed and an *Events Calendar* on its website. The site visitor enters the city and region and the event type (aboriginal events, agricultural fairs, exhibitions and shows, festivals, carnivals, celebrations, holiday related, outdoor, performing arts, sporting events).
- The events can be displayed by specific week or month.
- Tourism British Columbia also provides an events calendar with some other useful features.
- Site visitors choose "Festivals & Events" from a drop-down search menu and then specify the starting and ending dates in which they are interested. With the next click, the website produces a Google map of British Columbia with the festivals and events pinpointed on it. The site visitor can then click on the "map pins" for further information.

Sources: Ontario Tourism Marketing Partnership. (2008). **http://www.ontariotravel. net**; *Tourism British Columbia. (2008).* **http://www.hellobc.com/en-CA/default.htm**

Student Questions

1. What are the benefits of a destination having *Events Calendars* like these for Ontario and British Columbia?
2. What are the customer advantages of having this information readily available online?
3. What are the potential problems and challenges in maintaining such online *Events Calendars*?
4. How can other businesses such as hotels and restaurants take advantage of these types of online features?

b. *Convention/Meeting Packages.* Almost all resorts, hotels, and conference centers provide packages to attract conventions and other meetings. Normally, **convention/meeting packages** include accommodations and meals, but they may also include some local tours or attraction admissions, or special events or programs. Programming is often a key feature of meetings and conventions. Earlier, you heard about the special theme parties staged at events. The programs are often recreational—the resort or hotel arranges golf or tennis tournaments for the group.

c. *Affinity Group Packages or Tours.* **Affinity group packages** are arranged for groups that share some form of affinity, usually a close social, religious, or ethnic bond. Examples include packages developed for university alumni associations, church groups, the physically challenged, racial and ethnic minorities, service clubs, and other social and recreation clubs or associations.

d. *Family Vacation or Holiday Packages.* **Family vacation or holiday packages** provide something for everyone in parent-child households. Frequently, they incorporate special programming for the children (Figure 12.11). For example, several cruise lines including Disney and Carnival have developed specially supervised programs within packages for children. Similarly, Hyatt Hotels' Camp Hyatt concept offers special activities and amenities for children.

e. *Packages for Special-Interest Groups.* These were discussed earlier under the first classification scheme. Refer to that section for more information on these types of packages.

3. **Package Duration or Timing.** A third way to categorize packages is by their length or timing. Some examples follow:

a. *Weekend and mini-vacation packages* (packages for weekends or for a period of less than six nights)

FIGURE 12.11
Programs for children are important to attract the family market at resorts and on cruise ships.

The Global Perspective: The Big Picture

Programming on a Grand Scale: The 2005 and 2010 World Expos

Expo 2005 Aichi, Japan and Expo 2010 Shanghai, China

http://www.expo2005.or.jp/en/index.html
http://www.expo2005.com/
http://www.expo2010china.com/expo/expoenglish/oe/es/index.html
http://www.bie-paris.org/

Courtesy of the Department of Canadian Heritage

愛知万博カナダ・パビリオン
WWW.EXPO2005CANADA.GC.CA
EXPO 2005 AICHI
25|03|05 » 25|09|05

The 2005 World Expo in Aichi, Japan attracted 22 million people

The 2005 World Exposition was held in Aichi, Japan (March 25 to September 25); the 2010 World Exposition will be held in Shanghai, PR China from May 1 to October 31. Expo 2005 in Japan emphasized the close links between human beings and nature in the 21st century through the theme of "Nature's Wisdom." Just over 22 million people attended the event, which ended in September 2005. One of the key objectives of Expo 2010 Shanghai is to attract 70 million visitors from China and all over the world. By anyone's standards, these are what experts call "mega events" that provide a huge boost to the hospitality and travel industry in host cities over several months. The sites for these events are selected by BIE (Bureau International des Expositions), which is located in Paris, France.

Expo 2005 Aichi, Japan

Expo 2005 Aichi (near Nagoya) gave visitors a chance to experience first-hand leading-edge technologies, new social systems, and future lifestyles that may provide solutions to the many serious issues facing the world. It was also an opportunity for people from all nations to share different insights and unique approaches, and to set the foundations for working together on a global scale. There were 121 official participating countries and four participating international organizations. The expected number of visitors was 15 million, but actually 22 million attended. The average number of visitors per day was 119,186, ranging from a daily low of 43,023 to a daily high of 281,441. A total of 17.1 million tickets were sold for the event, and 439,000 full-season passes were bought. Expo 2005 Aichi attracted around 1,800 foreign reporters representing 380 media organizations from 75 countries.

(continues)

(continued)

A study of the visitors to Expo 2005 Aichi produced the following highlight results:

- Visitors' average time at the Expo was 6 hours and 55 minutes
- 53 percent of the visitors were local area residents (Tokai three prefectures)
- 38.1 percent were repeat visitors (visited twice or more)
- 4.6 percent were foreign visitors
- Major sources of foreign visitors were Taiwan (18.2%), Korea (15.7%), USA (13%), Mainland China (11%), Hong Kong (9.2%), and Australia (4.1%).
- 80 percent were satisfied with their visits
- Season-pass holders on average made 11 visits

The numbers of visitors to the major pavilions were as follows:

• Global House	6.96 million
• JR Central Pavilion	6.90 million
• Mountain of Dreams	6.00 million
• Aichi Pavilion, Nagakute	3.75 million
• Wonder Circus-Electric Power Pavilion	3.74 million
• Japan Pavilion, Nagakute	3.08 million
• Earth Tower, Nagoya City	3.03 million
• Mitsubishi Pavilion @ Earth	3.03 million
• Wanpaku Treasure Island	2.70 million
• Toyota Group Pavilion	2.65 million
• Gas Pavilion	2.47 million
• NGO Global Village	2.12 million
• JAMA Wonder Wheel Pavilion	1.48 million
• Hitachi Group Pavilion	1.70 million
• MITSUI-TOSHIBA Pavilion	1.63 million
• Aichi Pavilion, Seto	930,000
• Japan Pavilion, Seto	690,000

One of the major marketing tools used was the official website of the Expo 2005 Aichi, which was developed in seven language options (Japanese, Simplified Chinese, Traditional Chinese, Korean, English, French, and Spanish). A number of special events and tours were also organized. The Great Tea Gathering introduced the way of tea to the world and enabled visitors to have a hands-on experience of the tea ceremony. The Art Program introduced works by young artists representing today's world and served a bridge to the innovative culture of the 21st century. The Japan Association for the 2005 World Exposition developed special tour packages centering on the theme "Nature's Wisdom" in order to raise the awareness of environmental protection among visitors. They prepared three different kinds of free eco-tours for specific visitor groups.

(continues)

(continued)

Courtesy of the Bureau of Shanghai World Expo Coordination

The China Pavilion will be the centerpiece of the 2010 Shanghai World Expo

Expo 2010 Shanghai, China

The theme for Expo 2010 Shanghai is "Better City, Better Life." The location of Expo is in downtown Shanghai on the Huangpu River. It hopes to attract 200 participating countries and international organizations. By December 2008, some 183 countries and 45 international organizations had confirmed that they would participate. Of the targeted 70 million visits, around 66.5 million (95%) are expected to be from China and the remaining 3.5 million from other countries.

To date, Expo 2010 Shanghai has attracted 12 Official Partners, which include Coca Cola, Siemens, Shanghai Automotive Industry Corporation/GM, and China Eastern Airlines. The following is a general description of Expo 2010 Shanghai:

> "Expo 2010 Shanghai China will be a great event to explore the full potential of urban life in the 21st century and a significant period in urban evolution. Fifty-five percent of the world population is expected to live in cities by the year 2010. The prospect of future urban life, a subject of global interest, concerns all nations, developed or less developed, and their people. Being the first World Exposition on the theme of city, Exposition 2010 will attract governments and people from across the world, focusing on the theme "Better City, Better Life." For its 184 days, participants will display urban civilization to the full extent, exchange their experiences of urban development, disseminate advanced notions on cities and explore new approaches to human habitat, lifestyle and working conditions in the new century. They will learn how to

(continues)

(continued)

create an eco-friendly society and maintain the sustainable development of human beings."

Discussion Questions

1. How should the hospitality and travel industry in the host cities of mega events like these two World Expos take full advantage of the events?
2. What special programs can hotels, restaurants, and other businesses design to coincide with these Expos to increase their own revenues?
3. How should hotels and DMOs develop new packages around very special occasions such as these?

    b. *Holiday packages* (packages at public and other holidays. e.g., Christmas, New Year, Memorial Day, Labor Day)

    c. *Seasonal packages* (winter, spring, summer, and fall/autumn packages)

    d. *Pre- and post-convention packages and tours* (packages tagged on, before or at the end of conventions or meetings)

    e. *Other specific-length packages or tours* (e.g., a one- or two-week package)

    f. *Off-peak specials* (packages advertised as travel bargains because they occur in off-peak periods)

4. **Travel Arrangements or Destination.** Packages can also be classified by the manner in which they are arranged. Examples include:

    a. **Foreign Independent Tour (FIT).** A special package arranged by travel agents or other foreign independent travel specialists that fits individual clients' needs while they are traveling in foreign countries. You should note that there are some other uses of the acronym FIT, including "fully inclusive tour" and "free independent travel" but we prefer our own definition!

    b. **Group Inclusive Tour (GIT).** An all-inclusive package with a specified minimum size involving one or more groups traveling on scheduled or chartered air service.

    c. **Charter Tour.** A trip or package where the aircraft or other equipment is chartered by a tour wholesaler, tour operator, other individual, or group.

    d. **Destination Package.** A package can be categorized by the destination areas it features. Magazines for travel agents often have special inserts on packages to Hawaii, Florida, California, the Caribbean, Bermuda, Europe, South America, Asia, Australia/New Zealand, and other destinations.

Dynamic Packaging

Dynamic packaging is a concept that emerged with the development of hospitality and travel websites and the databases of information supporting them. This is an interactive online feature that allows customers or travel trade intermediaries to assemble packages by selecting those elements that meet their own or clients' needs. There is still not full agreement in the industry on the exact definition of dynamic packaging, but the following three characteristics are often cited:[5]

- Based on an individual customer search request.
- Technology includes the ability to combine multiple travel elements (e.g., air, lodging, car, etc.) in real time.
- Provides a single, fully priced package within 5 to 15 seconds.

The advantages of dynamic packaging are that it gives the customer greater choice and flexibility in planning travel, and more control over what is included in their packages. The customer's online search taps into two or more databases, and they are not limited by the scope of just one company's offerings. Of course, it is more convenient for the customer to assemble a package on their own computers, and much faster to get the results of their searches.

Much of this chapter has been devoted to describing how suppliers and travel intermediaries put together packages, and the benefits of using these industry-developed packages. The United States Tour Operator Association (USTOA) suggests that savings, volume purchasing, and peace of mind are the major advantages of tours and packages created by its tour operators.[6]

Steps in Developing Effective Packages

You now have a good idea of why packages are so popular, the roles they play, and the types of packages available. The next item on our agenda is to look at the mechanics of developing packages. What makes a package successful? The simple answer, just as for any good recipe, is the right ingredients, combined and prepared in the best way possible and served in an attractive, appealing manner. Before we look at this step by step, we should address some preliminary questions and concerns.

Potential Packaging Problems and Concerns

Some packages prove to be unprofitable or below customer expectations. Two major concerns are financial viability (will the package produce a profit?) and the loss of total control over the customer's experience (will the other participants deliver a level of service consistent with ours?). Because most packages involve price discounts, suppliers and carriers must also worry about displacing those customers who pay regular rates or fares in favor of lower-paying customers.

There is the risk of **blocking space** (groups of rooms or seats) and then having cancellations or below-expected bookings or sales. This often happens and there is insufficient time to get more confirmed bookings and reservations, and to resell the space set aside. Convention/meeting planners especially encounter this problem when organizing major events and the issue is usually referred to as "attrition." The Convention Industry Council in the U.S. has established *Project Attrition* to help convention/meeting planners and hotels to find ways to deal with the issue.

Another worry is that the package customers will be incompatible with our other target markets. Mixing a planeload of delegates to a Christian conference in with customers on a gambling spree or en route to a major football game may not be the best idea. Simultaneously housing a hunting convention and an animal rights conference also seems to be a combination riddled with problems.

Will the packaging support or detract from our chosen positioning approach? This is a very real problem for companies that choose to provide luxury hospitality and travel services. Will they turn off their regular customers who pay high prices by offering cut-rate packages? Alternatively, can a budget-oriented company modify its image sufficiently to market higher-priced packages successfully?

Although we will leave you to ponder these tricky questions, they do bring us to the main point of this discussion. Packaging and programming must be consistent with and support the chosen marketing strategy, target markets, positioning approach, and marketing objectives. Of course, they must also meet the basic goal of marketing—to satisfy customers' needs and wants at a profit.

Ingredients of Successful Packages

A package is a mixture of hospitality and travel elements, often provided by more than one participant organization. Putting together a successful package is similar to cooking, in that a lower-quality ingredient often spoils the flavor and taste of the overall experience. These ingredients are the hallmarks of successful packages, and they must do the following:

1. **Include Attractions or Demand-Generators.** Every package needs one or more core attractions or other demand-generators, whether it is tickets to a major sporting event or a visit to Paris. The simplest core appeal is reduced prices, an approach used in many hotel weekend packages. Some packages, such as escorted tours, include several attractions or destinations.

2. **Provide Value to the Customer.** Customers buy packages because they perceive that they will receive greater value for the travel dollars they spend. For many, value translates into a total package that costs less than the sum of the regular prices of its individual elements. Others measure value by the caliber and variety of the package elements. For example, wine lovers put a high value on hearing lectures from recognized wine experts and having complimentary wine tastings built into the package price. Murder-mystery fanatics attach added value to the presence of a famous author, whereas chocoholics swoon when quantities of their favorite substance is made available.

   Almost all of us can be hooked by the words *specials, value offer, free* or *complimentary.* We are intrigued by the prospect of getting something for nothing or a great bargain. Packages with free or complimentary elements have added value and appeal.

3. **Offer Consistent Quality and Compatibility among Elements.** Successful packages provide consistent quality and compatibility in their elements. Earlier, we pointed out that customers buy packages partly because they expect this consistency. If inconsistencies are found in the levels of service or in the quality of facilities, customers are very likely to notice them. They are apt to judge the entire package experience on the quality of an inconsistent element or service. Here is an example to prove the point. A young couple bought a one-week package in the Caribbean from a company that offered a high-quality experience on a small sailing ship. They had a fabulous time on the ship. However, service on the airline that carried them to the departure port was below par. Flights were delayed en route, and no one on the airline's staff made a special effort to compensate them for their long waiting time in the airport. Their

entire vacation experience was spoiled because the airline's service did not match the personal attention and quality service that they received from the sailing-boat operator.

4. **Be Well Planned and Coordinated.** An excellent package is carefully planned and coordinated to fit the customer's needs as closely as possible. The Club Med concept again provides a great example. Their underlying concept, and packages, are planned to allow vacationers to relax completely and to escape from their humdrum or high-stress everyday lives. Sports activities, instruction, and entertainment are very well planned and coordinated. These items are, in fact, programmed for the maximum enjoyment of GMs (*Gentils Membres*—the Club's name for its guests). From the opening welcome ceremony staged by the GOs (*Gentils Organisateurs*—the Club's employees) to the seating arrangements that ensure that GMs get to know each other, the Club Med vacation package is planned and coordinated to provide the most enjoyable experience possible.

5. **Provide a Distinctive Customer Benefit.** The best packages give customers something they would not get if they purchased the hospitality and travel elements separately. Often this distinctive benefit is the offer of value for money as shown earlier in the Wyndham *Weekender* and Hilton *Bed & Breakfast* packages. A lower-than-normal price is not always the benefit that appeals to customers the most. It can be a ticket to see a famous entertainer or a major sports event, a lecture by a famous author or historian, or a gift certificate to a plush department store. The key appeal here is that these features or programs are not readily available to individual customers. The package provides a unique and convenient way for customers to gain access to these programs or services.

6. **Cover All the Details.** In many cases, it is simple to throw together a package, but it is the attention to minute and sometimes seemingly trivial details that make excellent packages stand out. What happens if customers have to cancel because of unexpected circumstances? What if there is no snow when you arrive for your ski vacation? What if you or your companions do not want to visit one of the attractions on the itinerary? What if it rains every day during your tropical vacation? These are just a few of the problems that can happen and that must be anticipated by the package planner.

Making sure that all the details are covered is almost like assuming that *Murphy's Law* ("if anything can go wrong, it will") will prevail, a too-gloomy perspective for many people. However, it is the attention to these details that often produces the most satisfied customers and positive word-of-mouth advertising. Another example proves this point. An elderly couple booked an escorted package tour offered by a leading tour operator to the Galapagos Islands and Peru. While on the trip, the woman was advised by a doctor that the side trip to Machu Picchu in the Peruvian Andes might adversely affect her health. The tour wholesaler had anticipated this possibility, and refunded the cost of the

Machu Picchu trip. The couple was greatly impressed by the wholesaler's forethought and fairness, and has told many acquaintances about the company's professionalism and high regard for its individual customers. What this travel story illustrates is that it is often the little things that a business does for customers that matter the most. There are several key factors to be considered in covering all the details:

a. Having a clear policy on deposits, cancellations, and refunds
b. Offering customers the maximum amount of flexibility in booking dates and optional activities
c. Providing complete information on all package elements included in the price, items not included, clothing or equipment needed, substitutions allowed and options available, reservation procedures, minimum group sizes (if applicable), single room supplements (additional charges for a single room), policy and charges regarding children and pets accompanying adults, contingency arrangements in case of weather or other problems, and other specific data

7. **Generate a Profit.** Although packages are a marvelous way to satisfy a customer's needs and wants, they must also generate a profit. Many packages offered by the industry have turned into financial disasters. In most cases, packages really represent a type of price discounting and must follow the same rules. A more detailed look at pricing comes later, but for now it is enough to say that services generally should not be included in packages if they are priced below their variable (direct) costs. The ideal times to offer packages are when other demand sources are at their minimum or are non-existent, and when they do not displace higher-revenue-generating customers.

Pricing Packages

How do you give the customer the right amount of value, yet still make an acceptable profit? The answer lies in a careful, step-by-step approach to package pricing employing the **break-even analysis** technique (making pricing decisions based upon the consideration of fixed and variable costs, customer volumes, and profit margins):

1. **Identify and Quantify Fixed Costs. Fixed costs** will be the same no matter how many customers buy the package. They include the costs of developing specific websites or pages, other Internet marketing, printing and mailing special brochures, media advertisements, and certain package elements (e.g., tour manager salary and travel expenses, chartered transportation equipment, speakers' fees, and so on). If the package is unescorted and includes no transportation to the destination (e.g., the typical hotel weekend package), the fixed costs are usually only those for producing and mailing brochures, Internet marketing, advertising, and fixed-payment or lump-sum elements such as entertainers and blocks of

tickets. The real beauty of weekend packages for hotels is that, except for these items, packages add only a very minimal amount to other fixed costs. The hotel only needs to worry about covering variable costs once the up-front expenses are matched. The hotel may want to add a small amount of overhead expenses to the other fixed costs to cover such items as administrative and maintenance costs.

2. **Identify and Quantify Variable Costs. Variable or direct costs** vary directly with the number of customers who buy the package. For the hotel weekend package, these costs are primarily for the housekeeping of rooms, meals included, giveaways (e.g., bottles of wine or champagne, gift certificates, fruit baskets, chocolates or other sweets, tote bags), and other items that will be expensed per person or per room. Some hotel weekend packages are **commissionable** (pay commissions to travel agents who reserve them for their clients) and commission expenses vary directly with the number of travel agent bookings.

    The range of variable costs is more extensive for wholesalers, travel agents, and others who assemble packages and tours. Typically, these costs include the following:

    a. Air ticket fares
    b. Hotel or resort guest room rates
    c. Dining charges
    d. Services charges or tips
    e. Entrance fees to attractions and sites
    f. Costs of local tours charged on a per-person basis
    g. Local taxes
    h. Baggage handling charges on a per-person basis

3. **Calculate Total Package Costs Per Person.** You now have two cost estimates: (1) the total fixed costs that will have to be paid no matter how many packages are sold and (2) the total variable costs per person, which change directly with the number of guests. Because your goal is to come up with a package price per person, you must express the fixed costs on this basis as well. Doing this means estimating the number of customers who are expected to buy the package. But how do you do this? Should you use the maximum, the minimum, or a middle-range figure? The least risky and recommended route is to use the minimum expected. Once you have calculated the expected number of buyers, divide the total fixed costs (plus any allocation of overhead) by that number.

4. **Add a Markup for Profit.** Many different types of organizations in the hospitality and travel industry put together packages. They do so with one common thought in mind—to make a profit. How this profit is made varies by type of organization:

    a. Packages Developed by Intermediaries

        • If the package planner is a tour wholesaler or incentive travel company, then none of the package elements has provided a profit thus far. A "markup" must be added, either as a percentage or a fixed amount. Normally, the markup is made on the "land portion" only, meaning that airfares are not marked up.

- Travel agents who assemble packages are compensated through the commissions earned on various package elements.

b. Packages Developed by Others

- Suppliers and carriers that develop packages make their money from the elements they supply (e.g., rooms, meals, airfare, car rental, cruises). Their profits are built into the costs they have calculated for these package elements.

In tour wholesaler and incentive travel-company packages, the markup is usually from 10 percent to 30 percent. The company, therefore, adds an amount equal to this percentage of the variable and fixed costs per person (excluding, if appropriate, the airfare) to arrive at the final per-person package price.

5. **Calculate the Single Supplement.** Most packages and tours are sold on a **shared-room** or **double-occupancy basis**, and prices are quoted this way. To give customers maximum flexibility, packages can normally be booked, with an added charge, on a single-occupancy basis. In the travel trade, this additional amount is known as the **single supplement**. It is equal to the difference between the single- and double-room rate on a per-person basis times the number of nights, plus taxes, service charges/gratuities, and markup (if appropriate).

6. **Calculate the Break-Even Point.** The last step in pricing a package is to calculate the break-even point. This is the point at which the total revenues earned from the package exactly equal the sum of the total costs (fixed and variable) and the desired profits. The exact formula for calculation is discussed in Chapter 19.

Chapter Conclusion

The hospitality and travel industry's version of packaging is unique, and the increased popularity of packaging has been one of the major industry trends over the past few decades. Part of the reason is that packages provide benefits to both customers and participating organizations. They make for a better fit between customers' needs and available services. At the same time, packages help the industry deal with the problem of perishability by creating business at otherwise low-volume periods.

Programming is related to packaging, and it also adds to the appeal of hospitality and travel services. Programming often occurs within packages, but it can also be done on its own.

REVIEW QUESTIONS

1. What do the terms *packaging* and *programming* mean? Are they related and, if so, how?
2. Why have packages and programs increased in popularity in the past 40 years?
3. What five key roles do packaging and programming play in marketing hospitality and travel services?
4. What are the two main categories of packages found in the industry?
5. Which three additional factors can be used to classify packages? What types of packages are included in these three groups?
6. What is dynamic packaging and what are its customer advantages?
7. What are the seven steps to be followed in developing effective packages?
8. What procedures must be followed to establish the price of a package?
9. Does programming always occur within packages and, if not, what are some examples of stand-alone programs?

CHAPTER ASSIGNMENTS

1. You are the marketing director of a small resort. The resort does very well in the summer and winter, but business drops off significantly in the spring and fall. Develop five or six creative packages that you would introduce to boost fall and spring business. What elements would you include in these packages? What prices would you charge, and how would you market the packages? What would be the target markets? How would you measure the success of each package?
2. Visit a travel agency and collect the brochures for five or six competitive packages (e.g., cruise vacations, resort packages, hotel weekend packages). Compare the elements in each package. Are they exactly the same or, if not, how do they differ? How do the prices compare? Do any of the packages include programming? Which package do you think is the best? Why? How could you improve these packages?
3. The owner of a restaurant or attraction in your community has asked you to suggest some potential programs to increase sales. What steps would you follow in developing these programming ideas? Suggest five or six programs that could be used. Try to prove that the added costs of the programs will be justified by increased profits. How would the restaurant or attraction benefit from offering the programs?
4. This chapter explains that packages can be categorized by package elements, target market, duration or timing, or travel arrangements or destination. Do some research and find at least three examples of each of the four categories of packages (other than those mentioned in the chapter). You may select examples from your local region, or you may want to pick a specific part of our industry (e.g., resorts or airlines). Provide a description of each of the packages you find.

WEB RESOURCES

AMNH Expeditions, http://www.amnhexpeditions.org/
Camp Hyatt, http://www.hyatt.com/
Club Med, http://www.clubmed.com/
Convention Industry Council *Project Attrition*,
    http://www.conventionindustry.org/
Cruise Line Industry Association, http://www.cruising.org/
Hilton Hospitality, http://www1.hilton.com/en_US/hi/index.do
Holland America Line, http://www.hollandamerica.com/
InfoHub, http://www.infohub.com/
Medieval Times, http://www.medievaltimes.com/
Mohonk Mountain House, http://www.mohonk.com/
National Geographic Expeditions,
    http://www.nationalgeographicexpeditions.com/
Royal Windsor Hotel, Brussels, http://www.royalwindsorbrussels.com/
Scottsdale Resort & Conference Center,
    http://www.thescottsdaleresort.com/
Smithsonian Journeys, http://www.smithsonianjourneys.org/
Specialty Travel Index, http://www.specialtytravel.com/
United States Tour Operators Association (USTOA),
    http://www.ustoa.com/
Wyndham Hotels and Resorts, http://www.wyndham.com/

REFERENCES

1. Cruise Lines International Association. 2008. *Top Ten Reasons to Choose to Cruise, 2008*, http://www.cruising.org/planyourcruise/faqs/topten.cfm, accessed December 26, 2008.
2. Specialty Travel Index. 2008. *Adventure & Special Interest Travel*, http://www.specialtytravel.com/, accessed December 26, 2008.
3. Definition is from the Association of Destination Management Executives. 2009.
4. Convention Industry Council. 2004. *Project Attrition*, http://www.conventionindustry.org/projects/project_attrition.htm, accessed December 26, 2008.
5. Helsel, Caryl, and Kathleen Cullen. 2005. "Executive Summary: Dynamic Publishing." *Hotel Electronic Distribution Network Association*, 3.
6. United States Tour Operators Association. 2008. *Advantages of Tours & Packages*, http://www.ustoa.com/advantagesoftours.cfm, accessed December 26, 2008.

chapter 13

The Distribution Mix and the Travel Trade
How Do We Get There?

O V E R V I E W

What is the best way to deliver hospitality and travel services to customers? As you already know from Chapter 2, except for home delivery of certain foods, there is no physical distribution system in this industry. Services are intangible. They cannot be shipped from point A to point B. Companies and other organizations either provide their services directly to customers or indirectly through one or more travel trade intermediaries, online and offline.

The industry's distribution system is both complex and unique. It is unique because of the influence that travel intermediaries and the Internet have on customers' choices. It is complex because of the diversity of organizations involved and their relationships with each other. This chapter takes an in-depth look at the industry's distribution channels and the roles played by the key organizations involved. The newer distribution tools via the Internet and mobile technologies are discussed. They have changed how distribution is accomplished in the hospitality and travel industry.

O B J E C T I V E S

Having read this chapter, you should be able to:

- **Define the terms** *distribution mix* **and** *travel trade.*

- **Explain why the distribution mixes in the hospitality and travel industry are different from those in other industries.**

- **List the major travel trade intermediaries.**

- **Explain the roles played by each of the major travel trade intermediaries.**

- **Identify the major online travel services and the customer benefits in using them.**

- **List the steps involved in marketing to the travel trade.**

KEY TERMS

accreditation

B2B

channel of distribution

convention/meeting planners

corporate travel agency

corporate travel managers

cruise-only agents

destination management
companies (DMCs)

direct distribution

disintermediation

distribution mix

dynamic packaging

e-commerce

GDS (global distribution
systems)

home-based agents

inbound tour operators

incentive travel

incentive travel planners

indirect distribution

in-plant

MICE

m-commerce

online travel companies

preferred supplier or vendor

rebating

retail travel agents

service fees

third-party intermediaries

tour operator

tour wholesaler

trade advertising

travel management

travel trade

travel trade intermediaries

Drive along any major highway and you will see many trucks delivering products to retail stores, to wholesale warehouses, or to other locations for further processing and manufacturing. Check any good-sized airport and you will notice that several cargo planes are taking off and landing. If a railway passes through your town, you might be acutely aware of the seemingly endless freight trains lumbering by. What you are witnessing is the physical distribution of products from many large companies. The hospitality and travel industry's distribution system is not as visible, however, because many of our products are intangible. The only outward sign of a distribution system may be one or more travel agencies in your area.

Although our industry's distribution system is largely invisible, it is every bit as important as the one for manufacturing and agriculture. The travel trade intermediaries in the distribution system provide many benefits, both for customers and other industry groups. Their knowledge and expertise make the customer's travel experience more satisfying and enjoyable. Their services, retail outlets, and promotions greatly increase sales and awareness for carriers, suppliers, and destinations. The online distribution channels make it easier for customers to search for information and to make bookings.

Definitions of the Distribution Mix and the Travel Trade

This book describes the marketing mix (8 Ps, Chapter 9), the promotional mix (Chapters 14-19), and the product/service mix (Chapter 10). The **distribution mix** is similar to these concepts. It is the combination of the direct and indirect distribution channels that a hospitality and travel organization uses to make customers aware of its services and to reserve and deliver them. **Direct distribution** occurs when the organization assumes total responsibility for promoting, reserving, and providing services to customers. Generally, this applies to suppliers and carriers when they do not work with any **travel trade intermediaries** collectively known as the **travel trade**. For example, some hotel weekend packages can only be booked directly through the hotel itself. **Indirect distribution** occurs when part of the responsibility for promoting, reserving, and providing services is given to one or more other hospitality and travel organizations, or to an online travel company. Often, these other groups are travel trade intermediaries. **Third-party intermediaries** are often mentioned in hotel and resort distribution. These together represent an indirect online distribution channel; they re-sell hotel rooms and other travel services mainly through the Internet.[1] They include companies such as Hotels.com, Expedia.com, and Travelocity.com. For the sake of simplicity, they are called online travel companies in this book. A **channel of distribution** is a particular direct or indirect distribution arrangement used by a supplier, carrier, or destination marketing organization (DMO).

Figure 13.1 visually displays the concepts of direct and indirect distribution. It also highlights the following six major travel trade intermediaries:

1. Retail travel agents
2. Tour wholesalers and operators
3. Corporate travel managers and agencies
4. Incentive travel planners
5. Convention/meeting planners
6. Online travel companies

Let us take a more detailed look at these intermediaries to clarify the distribution-mix concept further. As Figure 13.1 illustrates, carriers and suppliers are the foundation of the hospitality and travel distribution system, because they provide the transportation and destination services that customers require. Individual carriers and suppliers normally work through more than one channel of distribution in their distribution mixes, and they use both direct and indirect distribution. For example, most major airlines promote directly to individual pleasure and business travelers, as well as to corporate and other group customers. They take reservations and issue tickets directly to customers, if customers so desire. Now, of course, they also make extensive use of their websites to generate online bookings.

Travelers can also choose to make reservations through retail travel agents and to have their airline tickets issued by the agencies (an indirect distribution channel for airlines). In November 2008 in the U.S., 98.98 percent of the airline bookings were in the form of e-tickets.[2] As you will see later, travel agency revenues (commissions earned) from airlines have been on a steady decline in the past 10 to 15 years. Airlines also frequently work through the other travel

FIGURE 13.1 The hospitality and travel distribution system.

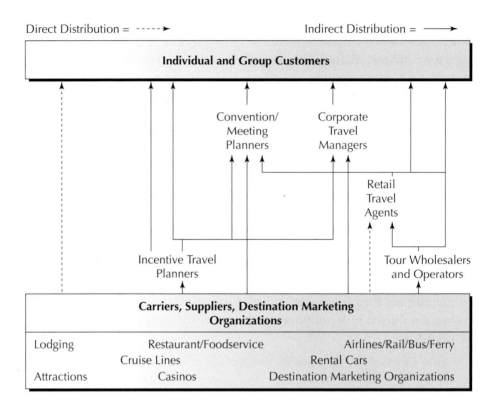

Direct Distribution = ----▶   Indirect Distribution = ———▶

Individual and Group Customers

Convention/
Meeting
Planners

Corporate
Travel
Managers

Retail
Travel
Agents

Incentive Travel
Planners

Tour Wholesalers
and Operators

**Carriers, Suppliers, Destination Marketing
Organizations**

Lodging   Restaurant/Foodservice   Airlines/Rail/Bus/Ferry
               Cruise Lines   Rental Cars
Attractions   Casinos   Destination Marketing Organizations

trade intermediaries, promoting directly in their specialized trade journals and participating in packages created by tour wholesalers/operators, incentive travel planners, corporate travel managers/agencies, convention/meeting planners, and online travel companies. Again, these are indirect distribution channels for airlines.

Lodging chains can also be used to illustrate this concept. If you choose, you can make a hotel reservation directly with your destination hotel or you can use the chain's website or central reservation system (CRS). You can also book indirectly through a travel agency, airline or third-party intermediary (online travel company). Finally, you may get a reservation indirectly through the efforts of a tour wholesaler/operator, incentive travel planner, corporate travel planner, or convention/meeting planner. Why is it that suppliers and carriers do not use direct distribution all the time? The simple answer is that using several distribution channels and intermediaries generally broadens the impact and effectiveness of in-house marketing plans. Intermediaries function almost like an external reservations and sales staff. Their specific roles and benefits include the following:

1. **Retailing the services of suppliers, carriers, DMOs, and other intermediaries at locations convenient for travelers.** No supplier,

carrier, DMO, or other intermediary could afford to have thousands of retail sales outlets such as there are in many developed countries. Independent and chain travel agencies, and many online travel companies, perform this important function, and thus provide a major benefit to other industry groups.

2. **Expanding the distribution network for suppliers, carriers, DMOs, and other intermediaries.** The net effect of the activities of all intermediaries is to provide more channels for distributing the services of carriers, suppliers, DMOs, and, in some cases, other intermediaries. This creates greater awareness of their services, while it expands their internal reservations/booking capacity.

3. **Providing specialized, knowledgeable advice to travelers on destinations, prices, facilities, schedules, and services.** Travel trade intermediaries are specialists and experts at their work. Customers view them as being one step removed from carriers, suppliers, DMOs, and other intermediaries. Travel agents especially are perceived as having large quantities of information and knowledge on hospitality and travel services (Figure 13.2). In some countries, traditional "brick-and-mortar" travel agencies are trusted more than online travel company booking websites, and preferred because of the personal touch and interpersonal interaction. Their professional advice and recommendations influence customer choices of suppliers, carriers, destinations, and other intermediaries. Positive relationships with agencies often have rich paybacks for other industry groups.

4. **Coordinating corporate travel arrangements to maximize the efficiency of corporations' travel expenditures.** Corporate travel departments and travel agents who coordinate corporate clients' accounts produce rich benefits for the organizations they serve. They are in-house advisors to business travelers and perform a function similar to the one that retail travel agents perform for pleasure travelers.

5. **Assembling vacation/holiday packages by bringing together an array of destinations and the services of suppliers and carriers at all-inclusive prices.** Chapter 12 highlighted the benefits of packaging for customers and various groups within the hospitality and travel industry. Some travel intermediaries, especially tour wholesalers and operators, are experts at doing this type of thing. They make supplier and carrier services more attractive to customers by tailor-making vacations to fit these customers' needs. Travel agents often assist individual and group travelers by putting together foreign independent tours (FITs) and packages for them.

6. **Tailor-making incentive travel trips for corporations and others.** Incentive travel planners are professionals at developing these special trips. They fill a need for corporations and other groups by creating experiences that are lucrative to potential travel award recipients. Again, the

FIGURE 13.2 Travel trade intermediaries have great knowledge about destinations around the world.

Image copyright Leah-Anne Thompson, 2008. Used under license from Shutterstock.com

suppliers and carriers that participate in incentive packages find that, by using the expertise of an incentive travel planner, their services are better molded to fit client needs.

7. **Organizing and coordinating conventions, conferences, and meetings for associations, corporations, and other organizations.** Corporate, association, government, and other convention/meeting planners package supplier and carrier services for their organizations. Like other professionals who assemble vacation/holiday and incentive packages, these experts provide for a better fit between their organizations' needs and the available hospitality and travel services.

8. **Operating and guiding group tours.** Certain travel intermediaries offer guide and escort services. In doing so, they enrich and enhance travelers' experiences.

Although one of the six types of travel trade intermediaries takes the lead in performing each one of these eight roles, many organizations take on more than one role. For example, whereas tour wholesalers play the lead role in assembling vacation/holiday packages, many travel agents also perform the tour wholesaling function. Another example of multiple role-playing is the corporate travel manager who also acts as the firm's meeting planner. You might now be getting the idea that the hospitality and travel distribution system is very complex. This complexity is quite evident from the structure of some of the industry's giants. Companies such as American Express, Carlson, and Maritz each have several divisions that perform different travel trade intermediary roles, including travel agencies, incentive travel planning, tour wholesaling, and online travel reservations.

Individual Travel Trade Intermediaries

As the end of the first decade in the 21st century, the distribution of hospitality and travel services is vastly different than it was in 1990 and 2000. The Internet emerged as a viable distribution channel during the mid-1990s and, along with the increasing popularity of online travel companies and other online booking options, caused a trend that some call **disintermediation** (the decreasing importance of traditional travel trade intermediaries, especially travel agents). Now electronic commerce or **e-commerce** (buying and selling of goods and services on the Internet) and **m-commerce** (buying and selling goods and services using mobile technologies) are booming, and travel is one of the most popular items to buy electronically (Figure 13.3). As you read through the following descriptions of individual travel intermediaries, be aware that the Internet and mobile technologies have significantly changed the whole distribution channel system in hospitality and travel.

Retail Travel Agents

Chapter 10 highlighted the spectacular growth in the North American travel agency business up until the mid-1990s, which was followed by a slowdown caused by reductions in airline commissions. The 10-year period from 1995 to 2005 was challenging for travel agencies as they had to cope with the declining airline commissions, new competition from the online travel companies (the so-called, third-party intermediaries), and the overall impacts of the Internet and mobile technologies on travel distribution. Despite the adversity, travel agencies have survived all around the world, and still play a major role in travel distribution in many countries. The Airlines Reporting Corporation (ARC) found that airline tickets sales through U.S. travel agencies and corporate travel departments were 2.8 percent higher in 2007 than in 2006, and reached a level not seen since 2000 (however, total airline fare sales dropped by 1.4 percent in the 12 months from December 2007 to November 2008).[3]

FIGURE 13.3 More families and other travelers are using the Internet to search for travel information and making bookings.

Image copyright Rob Marmion, 2008. Used under license from Shutterstock.com

When combined with the increasing hospitality and travel sales online, these figures show that the hospitality and travel industry is a strong retail market, both online and offline.

Faced with new competition from online travel companies, the traditional travel agencies put the latest technologies to work for themselves. Most traditional "brick-and-mortar" travel agencies have set up shop on the Internet and are using websites and e-mail to sell their services both in the local market and far beyond their local areas. Of course, there are also many online travel companies, including online travel agencies that deal with clients exclusively through the Internet.

Global distribution systems (GDSs) have existed for around 50 years and have had a major impact on travel agencies, hotels, and other organizations. The proportion of U.S. travel agencies making reservations through GDSs dropped in 2007, but 83 percent still used them.[4] One source also estimates that hotels in the U.S. receive almost one-third of their room reservation business through the GDSs.[5] The four major systems are Sabre, Travelport (Galileo and Worldspan), and Amadeus (Figure 13.4). Sabre is the largest GDS in the world, serving an estimated 50,000 travel agencies in 113 countries. Sabre reported that in 2005 more than $80 billion of travel-related products and services were sold through its GDS.[6]

Preferred supplier or vendor relationships are special arrangements established by suppliers (hotels, rental car firms, cruise lines) and other travel trade

Courtesy of Sabre Holdings

intermediaries in which above-average commission rates (overrides) are paid to particular agencies, usually in recognition of booking certain volumes of business. Most travel agencies have these types of relationships, especially with cruise lines and tour operators.[7] Other programs include those used by several destinations, including Australia and New Zealand, that offer a specialist or preferred status to individual travel agencies who meet certain criteria.

Retail travel agents receive most of their revenues from suppliers, carriers, and other travel trade intermediaries in the form of commissions. Normally, customers are not charged for the agent's services. In the U.S. in 2006, commissions represented 73 percent of travel agencies' total revenues.[8] **Service fees** have become common among U.S. travel agencies as a result of airline commission cuts. The sources of revenues of travel agencies have changed. According to the *2008 Travel Industry Survey* by Travel Weekly, only 25 percent of U.S. travel agencies' revenues in 2007 were from airlines. Thirty-two percent of their revenues were from cruises, 15 percent from inclusive resorts, 11 percent from tours, 10 percent from hotels, 5 percent from car rentals, 2 percent from rail and other sources.[9]

Did You Know?

What are the Trends in Travel Agency Numbers and Airline Sales?

- The number of travel agency retail locations and satellite ticket printers (STPs) in the United States is declining.
- The following table shows this trend. The second column represents the agency retail locations. The figures in the third column show the number of satellite ticket printer locations.

Year	Agency Retail Locations	STPs	Total	Airline Fare Sales: Domestic and International ($ billions)	E-ticket Percent
2001	27,719	6,352	34,071	$63.72	na.
2002	24,797	4,725	29,522	$57.39	78.45%
2003	22,381	3,239	25,620	$55.32	84.01%
2004	20,876	2,448	23,324	$58.63	87.34%
2005	20,033	2,010	22,043	$62.48	89.47%
2006	19,026	1,764	20,790	$68.72	95.43%
2007	18,261	1,454	19,715	$69.35	97.45%
2008	17,834	1,218	18,952	$64.64*	98.98%

*For 11 months of 2008 up to and including November 2008.
Source: Airlines Reporting Corporation, 2002–2008.

- After a setback in airline sales in 2002, accredited travel agency airline fare sales improved and reached a new high of $69.35 billion in 2007. Fare sales in 2008 were down slightly; by 1.41% in the 12 months up to and including November 2008.
- The percentage of E-ticket sales rose steadily since 2002, and now almost all tickets (98.98%) are sold in the paperless way.

To receive commissions from certain carriers and suppliers, agencies must be accredited by specific associations or other groups. For commissions on U.S. domestic air flights and from Amtrak, **accreditation** is needed from the Airlines Reporting Corporation (ARC). International flight commissions require an IATAN (International Airlines Travel Agent Network) accreditation. If travel agencies meet the membership requirements of the Cruise Lines International Association (CLIA) and join CLIA, they can more easily earn cruise travel commissions. There is no requirement for appointments in making hotel, rental car, or other supplier reservations.

Although most travel agencies employ five or less full-time staff,[10] there are now a number of mega-agencies that employ thousands of agents. The leader of these agency superpowers in terms of total revenues is American Express Business Travel, with 2007 gross sales of $26.4 billion. Carlson Wagonlit Travel, the sister company of Radisson, is the second largest U.S. mega-agency, with 2005 sales of $24.9 billion. Expedia, Inc. was the third largest, with 2007 sales of $20 billion. Other large agencies with 2007 sales of more than $4 billion were HRG (Hogg Robinson Group), BCD Travel, Orbitz World-wide, Travelocity, Priceline.com, and AAA Travel.[11]

There are several major trade associations representing travel agents in North America. They include the American Society of Travel Agents (ASTA), Association of Retail Travel Agents (ARTA), and the Association of Canadian Travel Agencies (ACTA). The equivalent association in the U.K. is the Association of British Travel Agents (ABTA), while Australia has the Australian Federation of Travel Agents (AFTA). North America also has several smaller travel agency associations including the Society of Government Travel Professionals (SGTP) and the National Association of Commissioned Travel Agents (NACTA).

There are some important crossovers between the retail travel agency and corporate travel management. One of these is the **in-plant**, a retail travel agency office that is located on the premises of a corporate client. Another option for corporations and government agencies is to pass along or "outsource" total responsibility for their travel arrangements to a **corporate travel agency** (a company specializing partly or wholly in corporate and government travel accounts). A few of these, for example, Sato Travel (a branch of Carlson Wagonlit Travel), concentrate almost exclusively on military and government travel.

Another example of greater specialization in the agency field are **cruise-only agents** (retail travel agents involved exclusively in selling and booking cruises) (Figure 13.5). **Home-based agents** are another group of travel agents,

FIGURE 13.5 There are now retail travel agents that specialize in selling cruises, known as cruise-only agents.

and these have emerged due to the ability to use the Internet from the agent's home. A survey of more than 1,000 home-based agents based in the U.S. and reported in Travel Weekly in 2007, found that 57 percent worked full-time for an average of 43 hours per person. These full-time home-based agents booked $310,000 in travel on average.[12]

It is becoming increasingly difficult these days to draw the line between retail travel agents and online travel companies. Many of the mega-agencies have very strong online booking and reservation sites, especially American Express and Carlson. Additionally, authoritative sources such as Travel Weekly's *Travel Industry Survey* include the online travel companies in the same group as traditional retail travel agencies. In fact, as you saw earlier, the top 10 travel agency companies in the U.S. included Expedia.com, Travelocity.com, and Priceline.com, which most experts would classify as online travel companies.

Industry Players

Riding the Wave of a Strong Market Growth Trend: Cruise Lines and Travel Agencies

Cruise Lines International Association (CLIA)

http://www.cruising.org

Courtesy of Norwegian Cruise Line

The *Norwegian Gem* off the coast of Dover, England.

One of the most rapidly-increasing sectors of hospitality and travel in the world is cruising. The growth has been created by the strong popularity of the type of all-inclusive vacations that cruise lines offer

(continues)

(continued)

as well as the cruise lines' innovative marketing and ship development approaches. Another major reason has been the excellent partnership between the cruise lines and retail travel agents, particularly the way cruise lines have developed mutually beneficial relationships with agencies.

Formed in 1975 and now located in Fort Lauderdale, Florida, the Cruise Lines International Association (CLIA), with 24 member cruise lines and 97 percent of the current capacity, estimated that the number of North American passengers on cruise ships increased to 10.25 million in 2007. CLIA estimates that 59.1 million residents of the United States have taken a cruise. CLIA's *2008 Cruise Market Profile Study* research indicated that 43 percent of all adults over 25 with incomes above $40,000 (128.6 million people) are the "prime candidates" for future cruises. This study also estimates that about 33.7 million people definitely or probably will cruise within the next three years. The assistance of retail travel agencies will be crucial in the cruise lines realizing this potential. With more than 16,000 travel agency affiliates, the CLIA cruise lines seem well positioned to meet this increasing demand.

Travel Weekly's *2008 Travel Industry Survey* indicated that cruise sales represented 32 percent of all the revenues of U.S. travel agencies. In 1998, the figure was only 18 percent. A significant portion of the cruises booked in North America are booked through retail travel agents. The Travel Weekly survey also found that 72 percent of travel agencies emphasize cruises among the travel products available. In fact, cruise lines are the only type of hospitality and travel organization that depends almost exclusively on travel agent bookings (indirect distribution).

The appeal of selling cruises to travel agents is based both on the total amount of commissions earned and the rate of commission. The fully inclusive nature of cruise prices means that the agent can earn commissions on all elements of the package, including the airfare, lodging, meals and entertainment, and optional shore excursions. Agent commission rates begin at a standard 10 percent on the cruise package price but may go as high as about 15 percent for preferred agencies. Thus, if a preferred agency sells a couple a seven-night Caribbean cruise at $3,000 at a commission rate of 15 percent, this one sale is worth $450 to the agency. According to Travel Weekly's *2007 Travel Industry Survey*, U.S. travel agents sell 50 percent of their cruise packages through preferred supplier (cruise lines).

CLIA offers training programs for retail travel agents under its *Certified Cruise Counsellor* program and the *CLIA Cruise Academy*. There are four levels of qualifications that can be attained by individuals: (1) CLIA Accredited Cruise Counsellor (ACC), (2) CLIA Master Cruise Counsellor (MCC), (3) CLIA Elite Cruise Counsellor (ECC), and

(continues)

(continued)

(4) CLIA Elite Scholar. The requirements are that agents successfully complete some compulsory training courses, attend cruise conferences, and conduct ship inspections.

The cruise lines offer a great diversity of ships and itineraries, and thus cruise package prices vary widely. Per diems (daily cost per passenger) typically include round-trip airfare to the port of embarkation. Each ship contains a variety of inside and outside staterooms and decks, and prices can vary quite significantly, even on the same ship, depending on the stateroom or suite selected. Cruise lines have positioned themselves differently based on their ship designs, types of passengers served, cruise themes, and types of itineraries.

The utilization rate of cruise ship capacity is exceptionally high by our industry's standards. CLIA believes that it is around 100 percent, which is approximately 30 percentage points above the average occupancy rates for hotels and resorts in most regions of North America. This pinnacle of performance has been reached through a combination of excellent travel trade and consumer promotions and the provision of exciting and often highly programmed vacation/holiday experiences. In fact, the cruise lines have been among the most innovative users of packaging and programming within the hospitality and travel industry.

Courtesy of Norwegian Cruise Line

The climbing wall on the *Norwegian Gem*.

The media advertising by the cruise lines is supported by a wide range of sales promotion, merchandising, and personal selling efforts aimed at the travel agent. Most of the major cruise lines use regional sales teams to liaise with individual agencies and to assist agencies in their advertising and sales promotion programs to their clients. These

(continues)

(continued)

sales representatives often help individual agencies with special promotions such as cruise nights where potential cruisers are invited to open houses to find out more about cruises. Cruise lines also frequently ask agencies to sample their ships through agent familiarization trips or in-port ship tours.

Websites have become extremely important to the cruise lines, and all of the major cruise lines have established an excellent presence on the Internet. Additionally, brochures are still an important merchandising tool of the cruise lines and are prominently displayed in most agencies. These are usually of a very high quality, and most agents agree that they make cruises easier to sell. As well as presenting colorful images of their ships and cruise destinations, these brochures normally show deck-by-deck layouts indicating the location of every room and facility on each ship.

Other reasons for the popularity of cruises among travel agents are the very high rate of customer satisfaction with cruises and the relatively high rate of repeat cruising. The cruise lines themselves do a marvelous job of relationship and database marketing with their past passengers. Passengers are often asked to provide their mailing addresses and to complete questionnaires prior to disembarkation. With this, they join the loyalty programs of the cruise line and receive its periodic newsletters and special offers. For example, NCL has a program called *Latitudes* and periodically makes its *Latitudes Magazine* available to members.

Courtesy of Norwegian Cruise Line

Norwegian Gem's fabulous Stardust Theater.

Another travel trade intermediary now being targeted by the cruise lines is the convention/meeting planner. Cruises are becoming increasingly popular destinations for the MICE markets and new ships

(continues)

(continued)

are being equipped to handle the unique requirements of these customers. The meeting and function rooms in the Norwegian Gem are a great example of this trend of attracting MICE groups onto cruise ships.

Courtesy of Norwegian Cruise Line

The Rialto Room set up in boardroom meeting style aboard the *Norwegian Gem.*

In summary, the relationship of cruise lines and travel agencies is one of mutual benefit and dependence. It is a shining example for the rest of the hospitality and travel industry of within-industry relationship marketing. As more mega-cruise ships in the 3,000- to 5,000-passenger capacity range leave the shipyards in 2009–2012, the linkage between agencies and cruise lines is likely to become even stronger. Certainly, retail travel agencies will be one of the keys to absorbing the major increase in cruise-ship capacity expected in the future.

Discussion Questions
1. How have travel agencies helped cruise lines achieve high rates of passenger growth and ship utilization?
2. What unique approaches have the cruise lines used in travel trade marketing?
3. What can other hospitality and travel organizations learn from the cruise lines in terms of marketing to the travel trade?

Tour Wholesalers and Operators

As highlighted in Chapters 10 and 12, tour wholesalers and operators are one of the two main sources of vacation and holiday packages. A **tour wholesaler** is a company or individual who plans, prepares, markets, and administers travel packages, usually combining the services of several suppliers and carriers. Traditionally, tour wholesalers normally did not sell packages directly to customers, and used retail travel agencies to handle bookings. Like wholesalers of retail products, they bought in bulk from carriers and suppliers and re-sold through retail agency outlets. Nowadays, however, the Internet has provided tour wholesalers with a convenient direct channel to potential customers.

The wholesaler's administration function may or may not include operating the package or tour, meaning that it provides ground transportation, guides, and escort services. A **tour operator** is a tour wholesaler, other company, or individual who operates packages or tours (i.e., provides the necessary ground transportation and guide services). As you can see, the tour wholesaler performs a broader set of functions than the operator does, although it is common in the industry for the terms *tour operator* and *tour wholesaler* to be used interchangeably.

Although there are thousands of tour wholesalers and operators in the world, the business is becoming more highly concentrated and specialized. For example in the U.S., fewer than 100 firms control most of the revenue volume. Many of these high-volume firms are members of the United States Tour Operators Association (USTOA). To belong to USTOA, the active tour company members—who numbered 46 in 2008—must have been in business for at least three years under the same ownership and/or management, must meet specific minimums in terms of passenger volumes or dollar tour volume, and must carry $1 million in Travel Agent/Tour Operator liability insurance with worldwide coverage.[13] In Europe, the European Tour Operators Association (EOTA) has 133 members who are either incoming tour operators or online intermediaries.[14] Incoming or **inbound tour operators** specialize in providing local services to other tour operators in specific countries or destinations. These tour operators also have their specialized trade associations, such as the Inbound Tour Operators Council in New Zealand. Some of these companies call themselves **destination management companies** (DMCs).

Tour wholesalers start developing tours and packages by doing careful marketing research, usually more than a year before the first tour departs.[15] About 12 to 18 months in advance, they negotiate bookings, fares, and rates with carriers and suppliers. They then establish tour or package prices, prepare brochures to distribute to travel agencies, and develop updated itinerary information on their websites. Printed and online materials may be developed by the wholesaler itself or in conjunction with a carrier, supplier, other intermediary, or DMO. Wholesalers' other promotional approaches include having sales representatives call on key agencies, advertising in consumer travel magazines, and **trade advertising** (print advertising in magazines and journals serving the travel trade). Figure 13.6 shows an example of trade advertising to retail travel agencies by Trafalgar Tours.

FIGURE 13.6
Trafalgar Tours
advertises to retail travel
agencies in *Travel Weekly*.

Corporate Travel Managers and Agencies

Travel management, according to the National Business Travel Association (NBTA), is the practice of approaching corporate travel strategically. Pointing out that travel is a corporation's second or third largest controllable expense, NBTA suggested that corporate travel management must embrace the following best practices:[16]

1. Monitor and analyze travel expenditures at a company-wide level
2. Set, communicate, enforce, and adjust travel policy
3. Put a payment platform in place
4. Negotiate corporate travel contracts and discounts
5. Globalize
6. Create strategic meetings management programs (SMMPs)
7. Mandate an online booking system

The traditional way of handling corporate travel was to have each department, division, or even individual manager make their own plans and reservations. Some of the problems of this approach were that the travelers may not necessarily come up with the most convenient travel schedules, the appropriate quality of services, or the most economical fares and rates. From the organization's standpoint, potential negotiation and bargaining power

Image copyright Dmitriy Shironosov, 2008. Used under license from Shutterstock.com

FIGURE 13.7
Corporate travel managers save their companies money by negotiating with suppliers and carriers.

with carriers and suppliers was lost (Figure 13.7). However, the challenging economic conditions and increasing globalization of business caused many corporations, government agencies, and large, nonprofit organizations to institute travel management programs.

Runzheimer's 2007 Travel Management Professional Profile Survey found that the most common responsibilities of **corporate travel managers** were: (1) travel policy development (90%), (2) responding to traveler concerns and questions (90%), (3) recommending and implementing cost-saving initiatives (87%), (4) travel vendor negotiations (84%), (5) policy enforcement (81%), and (6) all company travel (81%).[17] The global corporate travel market is enormous and the largest corporations have huge travel and entertainment (T&E) expenses. Competition for the corporate market is fierce among travel trade intermediaries, carriers, and suppliers. Corporate travel managers collectively wield a tremendous amount of bargaining power. The concept of rebating also demonstrates companies' market power. **Rebating** occurs when an agency pays back a certain percentage of the commissions it earns to the corporation.

The trend toward centralizing corporate travel arrangements was instrumental in creating other hospitality and travel industry changes. For example, it spurred the development of mega-travel agencies, corporate travel agencies, agency cooperatives and consortia, and franchised agency groups. It also motivated large travel agencies, airlines, hotel chains, rental car firms, and others to mount national advertising campaigns aimed specifically at corporate travel managers.

The two major associations for corporate travel managers in North America are the National Business Travel Association (NBTA) and the Association of

Corporate Travel Managers (ACTE). With more than 7,500 members between them, NBTA and ACTE hold annual conferences and trade shows that provide an excellent opportunity for hotels, airlines, rental car firms, travel agency chains, DMOs, and others to promote to the most influential travel managers.

Global distribution systems (GDSs) have also had a great impact on corporate travel departments. A majority of the larger organizations have these on-line capabilities. Again, this highlights the importance of these systems and the desirability for suppliers, especially airlines, hotels, and rental car companies, to have their information listed on one or more of these global networks.

Incentive Travel Planners

Chapter 7 characterized incentive travel as a business travel segment that is experiencing significant growth. **Incentive travel** is used by an increasing number of companies and other organizations as a motivational tool, by rewarding employees, dealers, and others who meet or exceed objectives.

What are the reasons for this trend? The bottom line is that the promise of travel as a reward is becoming increasingly lucrative to potential recipients. Traditionally, incentive travel has been used to recognize outstanding sales performances by company employees, dealers, or distributors, but the variety of applications is expanding. These other reasons include increasing production, encouraging better customer service, improving plant safety, introducing new products, selling new accounts, and enhancing morale and goodwill. According to Maritz, 38 percent of companies that initiate incentive travel award programs want to increase sales. The same source says that research indicates that $1,000 in a non-cash award is as effective in influencing employee behavior as a $4,000 cash award.[18]

Many different organizations get involved in planning incentive trips. Some companies do all the work themselves, using their corporate travel departments, convention/meeting planners, or other management personnel. It is more common, however, for the incentive trip packages to be developed by outside experts, either by full-service incentive houses, specialized incentive travel-planning firms, or travel agencies or tour wholesalers dabbling in this field. There are now hundreds of incentive travel planning companies around the world, many of which belong to the major trade association, SITE (Society of Incentive & Travel Executives). Two of the major incentive travel planning companies in the world are Carlson Marketing and Maritz.

Incentive travel planners are really specialized tour wholesalers. The only difference is that they deal directly with their corporate clients. They assemble tailor-made packages that include transportation, accommodations, meals, special functions, theme parties, and tours. Like tour wholesalers, they negotiate with carriers and suppliers for the best prices and blocks of space. They also add a mark-up commission, which represents their fees for the

Image copyright Nick Stubbs, 2008. Used under license from Shutterstock.com

FIGURE 13.8
Individual incentive trips are growing in popularity.

planning service. Normally, the sponsoring corporate client pays all the costs of promoting the incentive trips to potential recipients.

Incentive travel is growing steadily in all parts of the world. The original concept of incentive planning—sending only the top performers (usually salespersons) in large groups to exotic destinations—has been expanded to include non-sales personnel, individual incentives (Figure 13.8), cruise incentives, and multi-destination trips. The growth in incentive travel has attracted the attention of many suppliers, carriers, and DMOs.

Convention/Meeting Planners

Conventions and meetings—also widely known as part of the **MICE** (meetings, incentives, conventions, and exhibitions) business—are a major part of global business travel. According to a survey conducted by Meetings & Conventions magazine, total meeting expenditures in the U.S. reached a record high of $103 billion in 2007.[19] **Convention/meeting planners** plan and coordinate their organizations' external meeting events (Figure 13.9). They work for associations, corporations, large non-profit organizations, government agencies, and educational institutions. Some combine the task of convention/meeting planning with that of corporate travel management, whereas other organizations split up the tasks.

These planners attract the attention of many suppliers, carriers, other travel trade intermediaries, and DMOs. Promotion to them is usually split among advertising in special meeting planners' journals (e.g., *Meetings & Conventions*,

FIGURE 13.9
Convention/meeting planners are skilled professionals in arranging events of all sizes.

Successful Meetings, Meeting News), exhibiting at major MICE shows and exhibitions, and personal selling to individual planners. In the Internet era, many hospitality and travel websites provide dedicated pages specifically designed to provide information and helpful tools, such as RFPs (requests for proposals), to assist these planners in selecting sites and facilities.

Online Travel Companies

You have already heard in this chapter about online travel companies, and perhaps, like most of us, you have used them. There are now so many of these services, it is hard to keep track of them. In North America, the leading online travel companies include Expedia.com, Travelocity.com, Priceline.com, and Orbitz.com (Travelport.com). There are other major online travel companies in Europe including Opodo, Lastminute.com, ebookers.com, and Cheapflights.com.

The **online travel companies** provide several benefits for customers, the major of which are as follows:

1. Ability to self-book travel online
2. Assistance in planning travel trips
3. Availability of online pricing comparisons for hospitality and travel services
4. Convenience of accessing travel information at home or work

5. Immediate confirmation of travel bookings
6. Instant access to travel information
7. Potential of securing lower prices on hospitality and travel services

Several of the major online travel companies and GDSs belong to the Interactive Travel Services Association (ITSA). The ITSA's mission is "to promote consumer choice, access, confidence, protection and information in the rapidly growing world of online travel."[20] According to eMarketer, online consumer travel sales in the U.S. reached $105 billion in 2008, and were forecast to grow by 12 percent per year to reach $128.9 billion in 2010.[21] Online travel sales are also growing rapidly in other parts of the world. For 2007, online travel sales in Europe were estimated at EUR 49.4 billion, representing 19.4 percent of all travel sales.[22]

The websites of airlines, suppliers (particularly hotels and car rentals), and tour operators have also become popular for finding travel information and booking. Several of these sites offer "lowest Internet price" guarantees to encourage web users to purchase directly. According to an estimate at the end of 2008, 39 percent of online travel sales were through online travel company sites, and 61 percent through suppliers and carriers sites.[23]

The presence of these online travel companies in the distribution channel has also contributed to the emergence of the **dynamic packaging** concept. This is an interactive online feature that allows customers or travel trade intermediaries to assemble their own packages. Dynamic packaging is like an electronic *a la carte* menu of package elements that the website users select from to meet their own or clients' needs. An example of this is TripTailor™ introduced in 2006 by Sabre Holdings for use by travel agencies (Figure 13.10). This allows travel agents to create customized packages for clients to more than 1,500 destinations around the world.[24]

Marketing to the Travel Trade

Travel trade intermediaries play a major role in generating business for suppliers, carriers, and DMOs. Their influence on customers is so great that they deserve separate attention in the marketing plan. This is an example of what now is called **B2B** (business to business) marketing. Suppliers, carriers, and DMOs must treat them as a separate target market or markets.

Should you promote to all trade intermediaries or only to selected ones? The answer is no different than for customers in general—it is usually more effective to use a segmented strategy. Not all travel agents, tour wholesalers, corporate travel managers, incentive travel planners, convention/meeting planners, and online travel companies are alike. They vary by their geographic locations, sales or booking volumes, types and volumes of clients served, areas of specialization, existing affiliations through preferred supplier or vendor relationships, and many other ways. A supplier, carrier, and DMO must research each trade segment carefully to determine which companies are most likely to use its services.

INTERNET MARKETING

Giving the Traveler More Choices Online: Dynamic Packaging on the Internet

- The Internet has given customers more control over their travel purchases along with many planning and purchasing tools and options. They can now do things online that before only travel agents could accomplish with CRS or GDS systems.
- Dynamic packaging is one of the technological advances in software that allows travelers to pick and choose preferred travel arrangements within their budget ranges. As one vendor, GoQuo, states, their software "gives the traveler the ability to create and customize travel that is most suitable to his/her requirements—checking multiple flights, multiple types of fares, multiple suppliers, hotel, car, insurance, and cruise availabilities."
- Dynamic packaging is in essence a "self-booking" system for customers, offering the benefits of greater convenience, time savings, and potentially lower-priced packages. However, dynamic packaging is also a great marketing tool for travel agencies, tour operators, airlines, car rental firms, and other suppliers. By incorporating a dynamic packaging feature in their websites, they may be more likely to get business from site visitors. A travel agency journal in the U.K. stated that, "giving our customers the tools by which they can put together their own tailor-made holidays is a highly powerful marketing tool."

Sources: Travel Weekly U.K. (2006). *Dynamic Packaging.* **http:/www.travelweekly. co.uk**; GoQuo. (2008). *GQDynamic.* **http:/www.traveldynamicpackaging.com/**

Student Questions

1. What are the major advantages of dynamic packaging for customers and do see any limitations to this concept?
2. What are the major benefits to travel agencies and tour operators in incorporating dynamic packaging on their websites?
3. What are the major challenges that suppliers face in adapting to this relatively new concept of dynamic packaging? For example, how can hotels and resorts control their room inventory in this more customer-controlled situation?
4. Do you foresee that dynamic packaging will become more popular and decrease the use of traditional packages and tours? Why or why not?

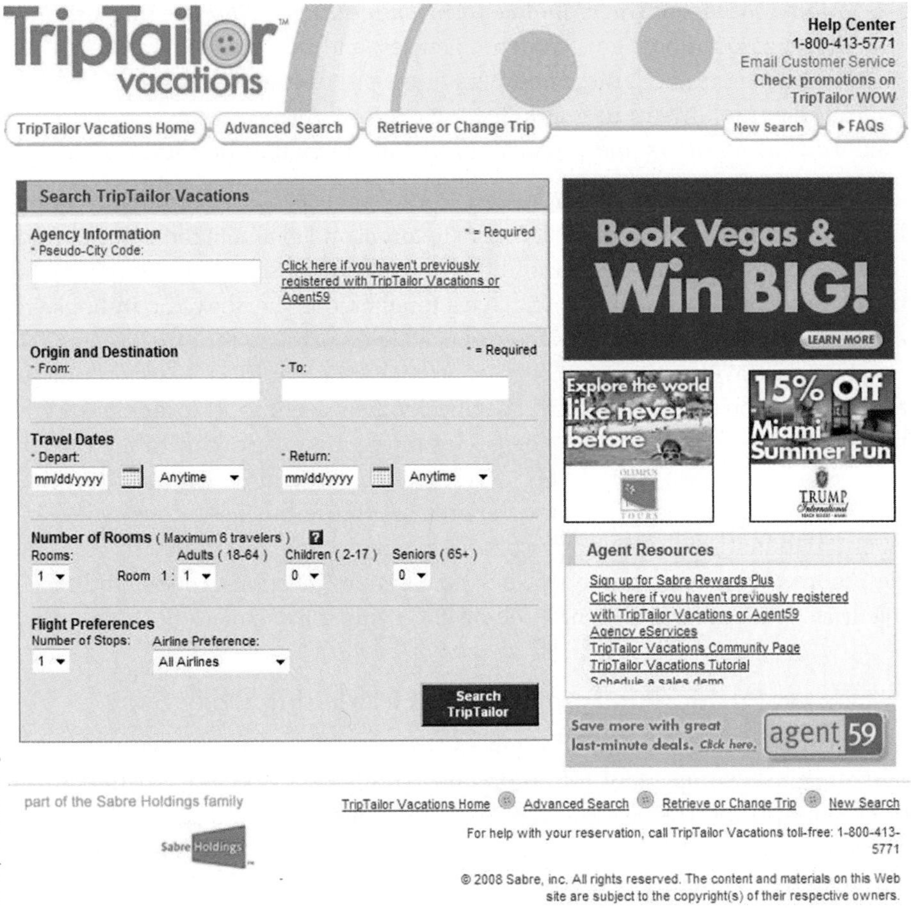

Courtesy of Sabre Holdings

FIGURE 13.10
TripTailor™ is a dynamic packaging program for travel agencies offered by Sabre Holdings.

A three-step process should be used in marketing to intermediaries: (1) research and select trade segments, (2) decide on the positioning approach and marketing objectives, and (3) establish a promotional mix for travel intermediaries.

Research and Select Trade Segments

Internal reservation and registration records and other computerized databases are often the best source of information for trade marketing. For lodging facilities, registration data indicate where customers live and work, as well as the names of travel trade companies that have made reservations for guests. Registration data should be analyzed frequently (or automatically through updating a computerized guest and travel agent database) to determine the following:

1. *Key feeder market areas*—cities or regions that provide the highest numbers of guests. There is a high probability that the most important trade intermediaries are located in these cities or regions.

2. *Major corporate travel and convention/meeting accounts*—the corporations, associations, government agencies, and non-profit organizations that generate the largest numbers of guests. These organizations require constant follow-up to guarantee their future business.
3. *Tour wholesalers and incentive travel planners* that provide business.

Computerized databases and reservation systems provide suppliers, carriers, DMOs, and others with an excellent tool to target and evaluate the value of trade intermediaries. New hospitality and travel organizations, and ones targeting the travel trade for the very first time, have a tougher job. They have no in-house records upon which to base decisions and need to do primary (original) research to find the best travel trade prospects. The starting point for this research should be the organization's target markets, specifically their geographic locations and demographics. With key geographic markets pinpointed, the organization can survey travel agencies, corporate travel managers, and convention/meeting planners to determine which has the greatest future business potential. Other clues are found in what existing competitors are doing and which travel agencies, tour wholesalers, tour operators, convention/meeting groups, and incentive travel planners are currently selling and using the destination.

Decide on Positioning Approach and Marketing Objectives

Every supplier, carrier, and DMO faces stiff competition for travel trade business. It is just as important for an organization to establish a distinctive image or position in the travel trade as it is to establish one with other customers. The specific product features positioning approach tends to be the most popular in trade marketing, because it is commonly assumed that travel trade intermediaries make decisions based more on factual information than on the recommendations of other customers. For example, the InterContinental Hotels Group (IHG) offers the *IHG Commission Guarantee* and has a special website for travel trade professionals.

It is important to set marketing objectives for each travel trade segment targeted. Only by doing this can an organization plan trade promotions realistically and evaluate the success of these efforts. This can be done by apportioning some share of previously established objectives (discussed in Chapter 8) to specific travel trade segments. For example, a hotel may set an overall objective of a 5-percent increase in the number of pleasure travelers it attracts. It may project that 40 percent of this total will come through travel agents, thus apportioning 2 percent of the gain to agents.

Establish a Promotional Mix for Travel Trade Intermediaries

The promotional mix is a combination of advertising, sales promotion, merchandising, personal selling, public relations/publicity, plus Internet marketing. Chapter 14 explores this concept in detail. It is essential that suppliers, carriers, and DMOs develop a separate promotional mix for the travel trade.

1. **Trade Advertising.** Trade advertising is paid advertising by suppliers, carriers, DMOs, and other intermediaries in specialized travel trade magazines, journals, and newspapers. Appendix 2–1 is a partial list of some of the principal publications oriented toward the trade. E-mail and direct mail is also used in communicating with the travel trade. Advertising in these media should follow the guidelines and steps discussed in Chapter 15.

   One very important consideration in placing trade advertising is its timing. If travel agents are the audience, they need advance knowledge of the services so that they can provide their clients with accurate and complete information. In this case, trade advertising should precede consumer advertising.

2. **Directories and Computerized Databases.** Because of the sheer volume of travel alternatives, travel agents and other intermediaries are forced to rely on specialized directories and computerized databases including the GDSs. They cannot possibly be personally familiar with all the facilities, services, and destinations available. Some of these directories allow advertising in addition to lists of facilities and services. Appendix 2–2 lists major directories that are used by the travel trade.

   There are a growing number of computerized and online databases that cover hospitality and travel facilities and services. The major ones are associated with the global distribution systems (GDSs). Because travel agents are increasingly relying on online information rather than on printed facts, it is becoming more important for suppliers, carriers, and DMOs to have their data on these systems.

3. **Trade Sales Promotions.** Other items to be considered are special sales promotion activities aimed at travel trade intermediaries. These include the following:

   a. *Familiarization Trips or Fams.* These are free or reduced-price trips given to travel agents and other intermediaries by suppliers, carriers, and DMOs. They are an excellent promotion for giving intermediaries a first-hand appreciation of the facilities and services being offered.

   b. *Contests, Sweepstakes, and Incentive Programs.* Contests and sweepstakes are frequently used in the industry to obtain travel trade business, especially from travel agents.

   c. *Specialty Advertising Giveaways.* These are items bearing the sponsor's name that are given away to travel trade intermediaries.

   d. *Trade Shows.* Several travel trade associations hold annual trade shows where suppliers, carriers, DMOs, and intermediaries can exhibit. Some are marketplaces where participants arrange interviews or discussions with each other. In the field of incentive travel, The Motivation Show (IT&ME) held annually in Chicago, Illinois is the largest in the world (Figure 13.11). There are also many privately sponsored travel shows, where agents and others become more familiar with other organizations' services.

FIGURE 13.11 The Motivation Show is the world's largest trade show for incentive travel.

Courtesy of The Motivation Show

4. **Personal and Telephone Selling.** One of the most effective promotional techniques involves personal sales calls to selected travel trade intermediaries. Chapter 17 takes a detailed look at personal selling, and you will see that much of the personal selling in the industry is directed at the travel trade. There are two aspects of selling to the trade—field sales and telephone sales and service. Many suppliers, carriers, DMOs, and other intermediaries employ full-time salespersons, who devote all or part of their time to calling on travel agents. Included are most airlines, cruise ship companies, hotel/resort chains, tour wholesalers, car rental firms, and passenger rail services. These salespersons often call on other intermediaries as well, including corporate travel managers, convention/meeting planners, and tour wholesalers.

An increasingly important part of travel trade sales and service is via telecommunications and electronics. Today it is essential for those dealing with the travel trade to provide online information and toll-free telephone numbers and dedicated website for travel agent information and reservations.

5. **Merchandising and Brochures.** Travel agencies are retail outlets, where the services and facilities of various suppliers, carriers, DMOs, and tour wholesalers are merchandised. Each agency contains an extensive range of travel brochures, posters, and window and other merchandising displays. It is definitely in the best interests of other organizations to keep their key agencies well stocked with attractive brochures, posters and displays, and other sales tools that agents can use.

6. **Public Relations and Publicity.** Other companies in the hospitality and travel industry have a vested interest in maintaining open and cordial relationships with the travel trade. Activities designed to develop and maintain these positive relationships should not be haphazard, but should be part of a carefully conceived public relations plan. Public relations and publicity are discussed in detail in Chapter 18. Typical trade public relations activities include periodic news releases to travel trade magazines, participation in various travel trade association conferences and seminars, and development of press kits and stock photography for media and individual company use.

7. **Cooperative Marketing (Partnership).** Another element of the travel trade promotional mix should be marketing activities jointly funded with selected intermediaries. For example, airlines, hotels and resorts, and DMOs often share the costs of developing brochures to distribute to travel agents and customers. Expenses of familiarization trips are frequently split by non-agent organizations, as are the costs of joint sales blitzes to travel generating areas. Jointly sponsored consumer travel shows are another excellent example of cooperative marketing.

8. **Website Access.** Most organizations have created special sections of their websites for travel trade intermediaries. CVBs, for example, often have a meeting planner section, or information for tour operators. Hotel, cruise, and tour company sites have dedicated pages for travel agents. As the importance of online travel distribution increases, it is essential that websites be designed with these intermediaries in mind.

Chapter Conclusion

The distribution system in the hospitality and travel industry is very different from the one used by all other industries. The intermediaries are usually referred to as the travel trade. They include retail travel agents, tour wholesalers and tour operators, corporate travel managers and agencies, incentive travel planners, convention/meeting planners, and online travel companies. The travel trade performs several key roles, including widely disseminating information on available services and facilities. They also help other organizations by making hospitality and travel services more accessible and appealing to customers.

Marketing to the travel trade deserves separate attention in the marketing plan. In essence, travel trade intermediaries should be regarded as separate target markets, with their own strategies, positioning approaches, objectives, and promotional mix.

1. What is the meaning of the terms *distribution mix* and *travel trade*?
2. What is the difference between direct and indirect distribution in the hospitality and travel industry?

REVIEW QUESTIONS

3. How does the hospitality and travel industry's distribution system differ from that in other industries?
4. What are the eight roles that travel trade intermediaries play in the industry?
5. What are the roles of the six major travel intermediaries?
6. What are the three steps that other organizations should follow in marketing to the travel trade?
7. Which elements are normally included in the promotional mix used for the travel trade?

CHAPTER ASSIGNMENTS

1. Select a major carrier, supplier, or DMO and examine its distribution system. Does it use both direct and indirect distribution? Which trade intermediaries does it target? What positioning approach or approaches does it employ? What promotional activities are used for the travel trade? How could it expand or improve its travel trade marketing?
2. You are the marketing director for a new hotel chain, theme park, cruise line, rental car company, tour wholesaler, or airline. Which travel trade intermediaries would you target? How would you identify the specific travel trade companies to concentrate on? Would you use a segmented strategy? What positioning approach or approaches would you adopt? How would you promote to the travel trade?
3. A small, local area hotel, resort, or attraction has asked you for some specialized advice on marketing to the travel trade. Very little business has been received from travel trade intermediaries in the past, but the owners feel that there is good potential to develop additional revenues from this source. What steps would you recommend they follow? How would you describe the advantages and disadvantages of dealing with intermediaries? Which specific intermediaries would you suggest be targeted, and why? What promotional mix elements and activities would you recommend?
4. This chapter outlines eight roles played by travel intermediaries. Describe these roles, citing at least two actual examples of organizations that perform these roles. How important is cooperation with other organizations in providing services to customers? Are the organizations you selected performing their role effectively?

WEB RESOURCES

Airlines Reporting Corporation, http://www.arccorp.com/
Association of Canadian Travel Agencies, http://www.acta.ca/
Amadeus, http://www.amadeus.com/amadeus/amadeus.html
AAA Travel, http://www.aaa.com/
American Express, http://corp.americanexpress.com/
American Society of Travel Agents (ASTA), http://www.astanet.com/
Association of British Travel Agents, http://www.abta.com/home

Association of Corporate Travel Executives, http://www.acte.org/
Association Retail Travel Agents, http://www.artaonline.com/
Australian Federation of Travel Agents, http://www.afta.com.au/
BCD Travel, http://www.bcdtravel.com/
Carlson Wagonlit Travel, http://www.carlsonwagonlit.com/
Cruise Lines International Association, http://www.cruising.org/
European Tour Operators Association, http://www.etoa.org/
Expedia.com, http://www.expedia.com/
Galileo, http://www.galileo.com/
Hotels.com, http://www.hotels.com/
HRG Worldwide, http://www.hrgworldwide.com/
Inbound Tour Operators Council, http://www.itoc.org.nz/
Interactive Travel Services Association, http://www.interactivetravel.org/
International Airlines Travel Agent Network, http://www.iatan.org/
Maritz, http://www.maritz.com/
Meetings & Conventions Magazine,
    http://www.meetings-conventions.com/
Motivation Show, http://www.motivationshow.com/
National Association of Commissioned Travel Agents,
    http://www.nacta.org/
National Business Travel Association, http://www.nbta.org/
Opodo, http://www.opodo.co.uk/
Priceline, http://www.priceline.com/
Runzheimer International, http://www.runzheimer.com/
Sabre, http://www.sabre.com/
Sato Travel, http://www.satotravel.com/
Society of Government Travel Professionals,
    http://www.government-travel.org/
Society of Incentive & Travel Executives, http://www.site-intl.org/
Travel Weekly, http://www.travelweekly.com/
Travelocity, http://www.travelocity.com/
Travelport, http://www.travelport.com/en/
TripTailor, https://www.triptailor.com/
Worldspan, http://www.worldspan.com/

REFERENCES

1. Hotel Sales Online. 2004. *How to Use Third Party Intermediaries Profitably.* http://www.hotelsalesonline.com/intermedia.htm, accessed December 27, 2008.
2. ARC. 2008. *ARC Processing Data November 2008.* Airlines Reporting Corporation.
3. ARC. 2008. *ARC Processing Data November 2008.* Airlines Reporting Corporation.
4. Travel Weekly. 2008. *2008 Travel Industry Survey*, 50.

5. Green, Cindy Estis. 2006. "Disappearing act: Are global distribution systems going away? Hardly." *Lodging*, 53.

6. Sabre. 2008. *Fact Sheet*. http://www.sabretravelnetwork.com/news/factsheet.htm, accessed December 27, 2008.

7. Travel Weekly. 2008. *2008 Travel Industry Survey*, 15.

8. Travel Weekly. 2006. *2006 Travel Industry Survey*, 12.

9. Travel Weekly. 2008. *2008 Travel Industry Survey*, 12.

10. Travel Weekly, 2006. *2006 Travel Industry Survey*, 8.

11. Travel Weekly. 2008. *Travel Weekly's 2008 Power List*, 6–10.

12. Luzadder, Dan, and Bill Poling. 2007. "Home Alone." *Travel Weekly*, 3.

13. United States Tour Operator Association. 2008. *Membership FastFacts*, http://www.ustoa.com/fastfacts.cfm, accessed December 27, 2008.

14. European Tour Operators Association. 2008. *About EOTA*, http://www.etoa.org/AboutUs.aspx, accessed December 27, 2008.

15. Mill, Robert Christie, and Alastair M. Morrison. 2006. *The Tourism System*. 5th ed. Dubuque, Iowa: Kendall/Hunt Publishing Company, 230.

16. Business Week. 2005. *NBTA's Corporate Travel Management 2005*.

17. Runzheimer International. 2007. *Runzheimer's 2007 Travel Management Professional Profile Survey*.

18. Maritz. 2005. *Is Everybody Happy?*, 1–2.

19. Meetings & Conventions Magazine. 2008. *2008 Meetings Market Report*, http://www.mcmag.com, accessed December 27, 2008.

20. Interactive Travel Services Association. 2008. *Our Mission*. http://www.interactivetravel.org/, accessed December 27, 2008.

21. eMarketer. 2008. *US Online Travel: Planning and Booking*, http://www.emarketer.com/Reports/All/Emarketer_2000502.aspx, accessed December 27, 2008.

22. Marcussen, Carl H. 2008. *Trends in European Internet Distribution of Travel and Tourism Services*, http://www.crt.dk/uk/staff/chm/trends.htm, accessed December 27, 2008.

23. HotelMarketing.com. 2006. *Sabre launches TripTailor*, http://www.hotelmarketing.com/index.php/article/060809_sabre_launches_triptailor/, accessed December 27, 2008.

24. eMarketer. 2008. *Online Travel Companies Choose Their Targets*, http://www.emarketer.com/Article.aspx?id=1006835, accessed December 27, 2008.

chapter 14

Communications and the Promotional Mix
How Do We Get There?

OVERVIEW

How does a hospitality and travel organization communicate its unique appeals and benefits to customers? The answer is through promotion and the combination of techniques known as the promotional mix. This chapter begins by explaining the relationship of promotion to communications and looks at the objectives of promotion. The five elements of the promotional mix are defined, and their individual advantages and disadvantages are discussed.

OBJECTIVES

Having read this chapter, you should be able to:

- Define the term *promotional mix*.

- List the five elements of the promotional mix.

- List and explain the nine elements of the communications process.

- Explain the difference between explicit and implicit communications.

- List the three principal goals of promotion.

- Explain the relationship of the promotional mix and the marketing mix.

- Define the terms *advertising, personal selling, sales promotion, merchandising, public relations,* and *publicity.*

- List the advantages and disadvantages of each of the five promotional mix elements.

- Identify four factors that affect the promotional mix.

KEY TERMS

advertising

commercial sources

communications process

decode

direct marketing

direct-response advertising

e-commerce

encode

explicit communications

feedback

implicit communications

integrated marketing
   communications (IMC)

interactive media

m-commerce

medium

merchandising

message

noise

permission marketing

personal selling

promotional mix

public relations

publicity

receivers

response

sales promotions

social sources

source

surrogate cues

word-of-mouth

As a consumer of products and services, you are exposed to hundreds, perhaps even thousands, of promotions every week of your life. These include television and radio commercials, newspaper and magazine advertisements, billboards, coupon deals, ads received through the mail, store merchandising displays, various pieces of publicity covered by the media, the Internet, your cell phone, and others. The human brain cannot possibly absorb all these messages, and it actually sifts out and retains few of them. This is a very perplexing problem for hospitality and travel organizations. They are faced with two known facts—there are a multitude of promotional alternatives available, but no matter which ones are chosen, the chances of being noticed are slim. The challenge, therefore, is to select the promotional technique that works best in the given situation and to use it in the way most likely to get the customer's attention and result in a purchase.

Promotion and Communications

Promotion is the communications part of marketing. In many ways, it is the culmination of all the research, analysis, and decisions we reviewed in Chapters 5 to 13. It is the way we tell the world our story, now that we know it ourselves! Promotion provides customers with information and knowledge in an informative and persuasive manner. This, we hope, will sooner or later result in sales of our services. The information and knowledge can be communicated using one or more of the five promotional techniques—advertising, personal selling, sales promotion, merchandising, and public relations and publicity. Taken together, these techniques are referred to as the **promotional mix** (the combination of advertising, personal selling, sales promotion, merchandising, and public relations and publicity approaches used for a specific time period).

The Communications Process

How many times have you noticed that what you intended to say was not what the other person or persons heard? Sure, they heard exactly what you said, but they interpreted it incorrectly. This occurs because communication is a two-way interaction between a sender and a receiver. To design effective promotional messages, hospitality and travel marketers (the sources) must first understand the target market (the receivers) and the **communications process**.

The communications process in the hospitality and travel industry has nine key elements (Figure 14.1). They are as follows:

1. Source
2. Encoding
3. Message
4. Medium
5. Decoding
6. Noise
7. Receiver
8. Response
9. Feedback

1. **Source.** The **source** is the person or organization (e.g., hotel chain, airline, travel agency, restaurant, DMO) that transmits the information to customers. There are two main sources—commercial and social. **Commercial sources** are advertising and other promotions that are

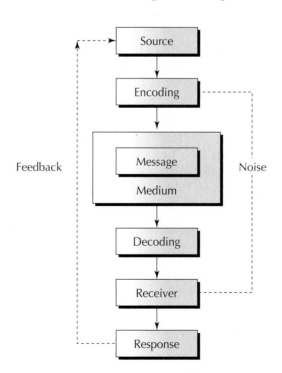

FIGURE 14.1 The communications process.
Source: KOTLER, PHILIP; ARMSTRONG, GARY, MARKETING MANAGEMENT: MILLENNIUM EDITION, 10th Edition, © 2000; pg. 551. Adapted by permission of Pearson Education, Inc., Upper Saddle River, NJ.

designed by hospitality and travel organizations. **Social sources** (also known as word-of-mouth) are interpersonal channels of information, including friends, relatives, business associates, and opinion leaders.

2. **Encoding.** Sources know exactly what they want to communicate, but they must translate or **encode** the information into an arrangement of words, pictures, colors, sounds, movements, or even body language. For example, the Mandarin Oriental Hotel Group has an international advertising campaign with the title of *Fans of Mandarin Oriental*. The company's logo symbol is an oriental fan, but this is cleverly encoded through a play on words in the advertising campaign to show famous celebrities who are "fans" of Mandarin Oriental Hotels, including Whoopi Goldberg, Maggie Cheung, Helen Mirren, Liam Neeson, and Jane Seymour.[1] Travel Michigan uses a similar approach with famous comedian and actor, Tim Allen, in its *Pure Michigan* radio and television commercials.[2]

3. **Message.** The **message** is what the source wants to communicate and hopes that the receivers understand. You probably recognize the famous *got milk?* or *National Milk Mustache* advertising campaign that was first launched in 1996 by the Milk Processor Education Program (MilkPEP).[3] The basic message communicated in this highly memorable campaign is that milk is highly nutritional.

4. **Medium.** The **medium** or media are the communications channels that sources select to pass their messages to receivers. The mass (broadcast and print) media—television, radio, newspapers, and magazines—are commonly used by commercial sources (Figure 14.2). Now the interactive media—mainly the Internet and mobile technologies—have become very popular for communications by hospitality and travel organizations. However, the medium can simply be two-way communications between a salesperson and a potential customer. Therefore, the medium is either impersonal (mass media) or interpersonal (e.g., a presentation from a travel agent or hotel or airline salesperson, or a recommendation from a friend, relative, associate, or opinion leader).

5. **Decoding.** When you see or hear a promotional message, you **decode** it—you interpret it in such a way that it has real meaning for you. Of course, the source hopes that you hear or notice the encoded message and do not screen it out. (Remember perceptual screens and selective retention from Chapter 4?) It also hopes that you interpret the message in the way the source intended. (Remember perceptual biases from Chapter 4?)

6. **Noise.** Have you ever tried to tune into a radio station and given up because there was too much static or distortion? You could not hear the station's program because of the noise. In communications, **noise** can be a physical distraction such as the one you experience when you try to tune your radio. The background noise level may be so high that the source and receiver perceive different messages in a person-to-person or

Image copyright Monkey Business Images, 2008. Used under license from Shutterstock.com

FIGURE 14.2
Newspapers are a
traditional medium
for communications
in hospitality and
travel promotion.

telephone conversation. In the mass media, the noise is different. The source's message is competing for the receiver's attention with messages from competitors and promotions of unrelated services and products (Figure 14.3).

7. **Receiver.** **Receivers** are the people who notice or hear the source's message. It is hoped that receivers will also accurately decode the message's encoding.

8. **Response.** The ultimate objective of all promotion is to affect customer buying behaviors—to get a **response**. Many hospitality and travel marketers do this by using a technique called direct-response promotion. Customers are asked to respond either by calling a toll-free number or sending back a completed coupon. The Singapore Tourism Board (STB) includes on its website a link to a request for brochures (Figure 14.4). By filling out the online form and submitting it to the STB, potential travelers receive a variety of brochures on the Southeast Asian nation. This

FIGURE 14.3 Noise can stop the message from getting to the receiver from the sender.

Image copyright Magdalena Szachowska, 2008. Used under license from Shutterstock.com

type of promotion tends to motivate customers to take action. In this case, it also helps the promoters (STB) evaluate the effectiveness of their website and provides them with a valuable database of information on potential travelers.

9. **Feedback.** **Feedback** is the response message that the receiver transmits back to the source. In communications between two persons, feedback is relatively easy to judge. The receiver gives the source verbal and non-verbal (body language) feedback. When mass communications are used, feedback is much more difficult to evaluate. Obviously, feedback ultimately is expressed in the promotion's impact on sales. Special marketing research studies must usually be undertaken to determine the effect of mass-media promotions, especially advertising campaigns. There has been a definite trend in recent years for hospitality and travel promoters to place more emphasis on direct-response promotions, often referred to collectively as **direct marketing**. These are promotional techniques (including interactive Web and e-mail marketing, direct mail, telemarketing, direct-response advertising, and personal selling) that require customers to provide feedback by responding by phone, e-mail, mail, or in person. **Direct-response advertising** is a form of direct marketing that includes a method of response such as a mailing address, telephone number, website address, or e-mail address whereby members of the audience can respond directly to the advertiser in order to purchase a product or service offered in the advertising message.[4]

Figure 14.1 depicts the communications process.[5] It illustrates that promotion—a form of communications—is a system that begins with a

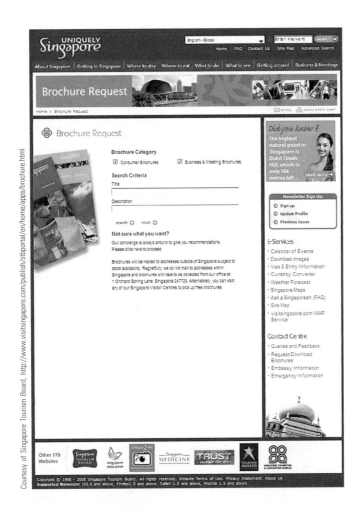

FIGURE 14.4

Singapore Tourism Board's Brochure Request website page encourages potential travelers to respond and gives an excellent database.

Courtesy of Singapore Tourism Board, http://www.visitsingapore.com/publish/stbportal/en/home/apps/brochure.html

source and ends with feedback from the receiver to the source. It also shows that the intended message (what we say) is often not the message that is actually received (what is heard and understood). The actual messages that receivers get result from their perceptual biases and decoding. The intended message, encoded for maximum impact, is what the promoter is trying to express through an advertisement, sales call, coupon promotion, press release, website, or other promotional tool.

In reviewing the model shown in Figure 14.1, it is also important to realize the social impact on the communications process. Research has shown that **word-of-mouth** (information relayed verbally between customers) further disseminates and reinforces messages. When customers buy hospitality and travel services, they are influenced more by interpersonal information from within their social network (friends, relatives, associates, opinion leaders) than by direct exposure to messages from the mass media. This is why so much attention is paid to developing promotions that generate widespread public interest and conversation, particularly among opinion leaders.

Another important point about the model is that, before customers can begin decoding, they must first pay attention to the messages. Hospitality and travel promoters go to great lengths to capture customers' attention by using the stimulus factors discussed in Chapter 4. These factors are used to encode messages and are expressed either through the service itself or in a symbolic way through words and pictures. Take for example the photograph and text on the webpage from the Peninsula Hotel Hong Kong in Figure 14.5. By showing its fleet of 14 Rolls-Royce Phantoms, this famous hotel is clearly, although symbolically, communicating its luxury services.

Other effective techniques for capturing customers' attention include novelty (the gnome you see all the time on Travelocity.com's website), contrast (the casual clothing worn by flight attendants of Southwest Airlines, and motion (the electronic billboards that constantly change displays). Marketers must use just the right amount of stimulation. If promotional messages have too strong an impact or too many stimuli, internal noise (a psychological state that inhibits customers from absorbing the message) can result. If customers are over-stimulated, they may ignore or forget the main point of the message. The credibility of the promotion may also be lost.

FIGURE 14.5 The Rolls-Royce Fleet at The Peninsula Hong Kong symbolically communicates luxury and outstanding service levels at the property.

Courtesy of The Peninsula Hong Kong, http://hongkong.peninsula.com/phk/information08.html

The concept of noise needs further explanation. There are four principal sources of noise:

a. Directly competitive promotions
b. Non-competitive promotions
c. Level of stimulation in the promotional message
d. Customer's state of readiness

When potential customers watch an evening's worth of television or read a travel magazine, they may be exposed to so many competitive advertisements that they do not notice the ad of one specific hotel company, destination, or airline. There is just too much competitive noise. The clutter of other non-competitive promotions (e.g., for cars, clothes, watches, perfumes, etc.) also severely taxes customers' patience and ability to notice and absorb messages. There are many examples that prove that customers have been oversaturated with commercial promotions. Many people make a point of visiting the refrigerator or bathroom during TV commercials: others automatically throw direct mail ads into the waste-paper basket. Another noise source is a customer's physical state at the time of exposure to the promotion. For instance, hungry customers are much more likely to notice fast-food billboards than are those who have just finished eating. As mentioned previously, some promotions are so complicated (over-stimulating) that they create internal noise. Keeping promotions very simple, yet informative, is one of the key challenges.

Explicit and Implicit Communications

Explicit and implicit communications are the two basic ways that promotional messages are conveyed to customers. **Explicit communications** are definite messages that are given to customers through the use of language, either oral (e.g., website, television, radio, telephone, or personal sales) or written (e.g., the web, e-mail, ad copy, or sales proposals). Language is used to promote a common understanding between the seller and potential buyer (or source and receiver). Advertising, personal selling, sales promotion, merchandising, public relations and publicity (the promotional mix elements), and websites are used to transmit explicit communications to customers.

Implicit communications are cues or messages conveyed through body language (e.g., facial expressions, gestures, other body movements) (Figure 14.6). They can also be conveyed by other non-verbal means, including the following:

1. The inherent nature of the product/service mix (e.g., quality and variety of facilities and service, decor, staff uniforms, color schemes)
2. The prices, rates, or fares
3. The channels of distribution
4. The medium chosen for promotion

FIGURE 14.6 Body language is a form of implicit communication; this woman is in a contemplative pose.

Image copyright Robert Studio, 2008. Used under license from Shutterstock.com

5. The media vehicle that carries the promotion (e.g., name of magazine or newspaper, television or radio station and type of program)
6. The partners chosen for cooperative promotions
7. The quality of packages and programs offered
8. The people managing and providing the service

   With implicit communications or promotions, the salesperson, product/ service, price, and distribution channels carry connotations for customers. These are the experience clues mentioned in Chapter 2 as being so important to service businesses. Customers often make up their minds about services by looking at the clues they get from the facilities, services, prices, and distribution channels available. High prices usually connote high quality and are often used to communicate this level of service or facility. Spectacular atrium lobbies (such as those in many Hyatt Hotels), Oriental carpets, and the use of marble, glass, copper, and brass are also clues to high-quality hotels, restaurants, and other hospitality/travel businesses. A hotel, restaurant, travel agency, or retail store in a trendy downtown location generates a different message than one in a low-income neighborhood. The packages, tours, cruises, and suppliers in which a travel agency specializes all carry a definite connotation. If the agency has many clients who buy Seabourn Cruises and Abercrombie & Kent tours, for example, this gives the impression that it serves primarily upper-income, more luxury-oriented customers.

Surrogate cues are product/service features that provide no direct use benefits, but convey a message about what is being offered. The name and size of an individual business or chain often convey a definite image. In the lodging industry, the names Econo Lodge and Budgetel (*Unbelievable Comfort. . . . Unbelievable Rates!*) transmit an impression of relatively low-cost accommodations. Thrifty conveys a similar image in the car rental field.

Size is another important surrogate cue. Lodging customers expect more and different facilities in a 1,000-room hotel than they do in a 20-room motel. Generally, the larger the chain or company, the more services customers expect to be available. For example, most travelers would anticipate finding a frequent-guest awards program at a national hotel chain, but would not expect the same in a smaller regional company or independent hotel.

What else did you notice about the list of non-verbal, implicit communications shown earlier? You are doing well if you realized that it includes all the other seven marketing-mix elements (8 Ps), excluding promotion. What do you think this means? Again, you are on the right track if you said that all eight marketing-mix elements must communicate the same message consistently; we call this integrated marketing communications or IMC. If the implicit communications do not support explicit promotions, these promotions will lack credibility. For example, the McDonald's Express restaurant concept was introduced at gas stations and other non-traditional McDonald's locations. The menu selections are more limited and customers can be served more rapidly. If these units offered a broad menu that took several minutes to prepare and serve, it would be guilty of creating a dramatic conflict between its explicit (promotional) and implicit communications. The reverse is also true—advertising and other promotions must support and be consistent with the other seven marketing-mix elements.

Goals of Promotion

The ultimate purpose of promotion is to modify behavior through communication. This requires helping customers through the various buying process stages so they eventually purchase or repurchase a particular service. As Figure 14.7 shows, promotion accomplishes this by informing, persuading, and reminding—the three principal goals of promotion.[6]

Informative promotions work best with new services or products (early product-life-cycle stages) and with customers in early buying process stages (need recognition and search for information). These types of promotions tend to communicate data or ideas about the key features of services. Persuasive promotions are harder hitting. They are aimed at getting customers to select one particular company or brand over those of competitors, and to actually make

FIGURE 14.7 Goals of promotion and consumer decision process stages. *Source*: Adapted from Mill, Robert Christie, and Alastair M. Morrison, 2006. The Tourism System, 5th ed. Dubuque, Iowa; Kendall Hunt Publishing. Used with permission.

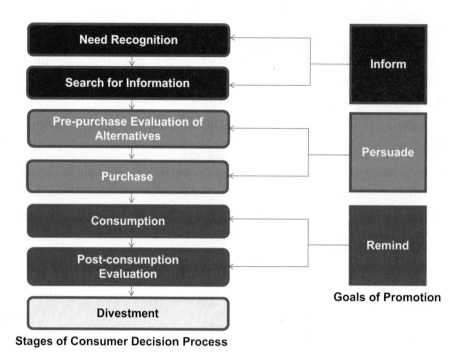

the purchase. Advertisements that compare one company's services to another, and most sales promotions, fit into this category. Persuasive promotions work best in intermediate/late stages of the product life cycle (growth and maturity) and the buying process (pre-purchase evaluation of alternatives and purchase). Reminder promotions are used to jog customers' memories about advertising they may have seen, and to stimulate repurchases. They are most effective in the late product-life-cycle (maturity and decline) and buying process stages (consumption and post-consumption evaluation).

The Promotional Mix

The marketing mix or the 8 Ps (product, promotion, place, price, packaging, programming, partnership, and people) contains the elements that an organization must work with when it develops a marketing plan. Therefore, the promotional mix is only one element of the marketing mix. You already know that the promotional mix must complement the other seven parts of the marketing mix. We have also seen that these seven other Ps themselves implicitly promote services, communicating definite messages to customers. The five promotional mix elements are as follows:

1. Advertising
2. Personal selling
3. Sales promotion
4. Merchandising
5. Public relations and publicity

Advertising

Advertising is the most widely visible and well-recognized element of the promotional mix. It is also the item on which significant promotional funds are spent.

1. **Definition. Advertising** is "the placement of announcements and persuasive messages in time or space purchased in any of the mass media by business firms, non-profit organizations, government agencies, and individuals who seek to inform and/or persuade members of a particular target market or audience about their products, services, organizations, or ideas."[7] Advertising is usually paid for, while publicity (Chapter 18) is free. The communications medium is non-personal—neither the sponsors nor their representatives are physically present to give the message to customers.

   Advertising messages do not always have to be aimed directly at creating a sale. Sometimes it is the sponsor's goal simply to convey a positive idea or a favorable image of the organization (often called institutional advertising). Coca Cola has sponsored ads during the children's Special Olympics, and McDonald's has advertisements centering on their Ronald McDonald House Charities (discussed in Chapter 18).

2. **Advantages.** There are several principal advantages of advertising, including the following:

   a. *Low Cost Per Contact.* Although the total costs of advertising campaigns often run into the millions, the cost per contact is relatively low when advertising is compared to alternative promotional approaches. The average cost of placing a 30-second advertisement on Super Bowl XLII on CBS in 2008 was $2.7 million.[8] The cost of producing these ads probably raised the average total investment per ad to over $4 million.[9] However, with the viewing audience estimated at around 90 million,[10] the cost per viewer was a matter of cents. Of course, most of the advertising by hospitality and travel organizations is not on the Super Bowl!

   b. *Ability to Reach Customers Where and When Salespersons Cannot.* The salesperson usually cannot drive home with customers, spend an evening with them in their television room, or be on their doorstep every morning. They cannot successfully pass through the mail slot either. However, advertisements can confront customers in almost every facet of their lives. They reach people in places and at times when salespeople cannot.

   c. *Great Scope for Creative Versatility and Dramatization of Messages.* Advertising provides limitless opportunities for creative approaches and for the dramatization of the promoter's message. This can be done through the brilliant colors of a magazine ad showing a destination's breathtaking scenery or through the reprise of an old ballad or rock-'n-roll song, such as the State of Georgia's "Georgia on My Mind" and Jamaica's "One Love." Since there is so much advertising today, ads must stand out in the crowd. The ads from Tourism Australia with the tag line, "Come Walkabout" demonstrate this. The uniquely Australian tag line and unmistakable Australian scenery help this advertising campaign stand out from other destinations' promotions.

d. *Ability to Create Images that Salespersons Cannot.* Advertising is great at creating images in customers' minds. Television, with its use of sounds, colors, and movements, is especially effective at this. The TV commercials that put across Tourism Australia's "Come Walkabout" campaign in 2008 communicated much more than even hundreds or thousands of salespersons could possibly have said.

e. *Non-threatening Nature of Non-personal Presentation.* Have you ever entered a store and been immediately confronted by an aggressive salesperson obviously eager to make a commission on your purchase? "Can I help you find what you want?" usually follows on the heels of a curt greeting. Many of us are threatened, or at least put on the defensive, by this type of approach. It is a face-to-face communication that forces us to come up with an answer or to make a decision quickly. Advertising, however, is a non-personal form of communications. Customers are not forced to respond, evaluate, or decide immediately. Because customers do not have their guards up, sponsors' messages often slip through consciously or unconsciously when other promotions would be resisted (Figure 14.8).

f. *Potential to Repeat Message Several Times.* Some promotional messages work best if customers are exposed to them several times. For

FIGURE 14.8
Advertising in magazines is colorful and impressive while often being read at leisure.

Image copyright Kurhan, 2008. Used under license from Shutterstock.com

example, if you are driving to a vacation or holiday destination and have not made previous plans, you are definitely in the market for a hotel room, meals, and perhaps a few quick side trips to attractions. The chances that you are aware of and choose a particular hotel, fast-food restaurant, or attraction increases with the number of their billboards you see en route.

g. *Prestige and Impressiveness of Mass-Media Advertising.* Advertising, and the specific advertising medium selected, can enhance the prestige and credibility of hospitality and travel organizations. An emerging hotel company that launches a national television advertising campaign signals that it has arrived in the big leagues. A tour wholesaler that places a full-page, four-color ad in *Travel + Leisure*, *Condé Nast Traveler*, or *National Geographic Traveler*, gets almost instant credibility.

3. **Disadvantages.** The powerful, persuasive, and pervasive nature of advertising cannot be denied. It does, however, have its limitations and drawbacks.

a. *Inability to Close Sales.* Advertising is strong in creating awareness, improving understanding (comprehension), changing attitudes, and creating purchase intentions, but it can seldom get the whole job done on its own. It rarely closes the sale (finally convincing customers to make reservations, buy tickets, make deposits, and take other actions that clinch the sale). Personal selling is far more effective than advertising in closing sales. This is especially true with high-involvement (extensive problem solving) decisions. In other words, advertising usually cannot, without the help of other promotional mix elements, guide customers through all their buying process stages.

b. *Advertising Clutter.* The opportunities for advertising are limitless. This is both an advantage and disadvantage. As many as 3,000 advertisements compete for your attention each day, but you remember few of them. Why? The human brain has a very limited memory and storage capacity. There are so many ads in so many places that they appear as a clutter of commercial messages. There are too many to notice and assimilate. Other promotional mix elements, particularly personal selling, allow a more individualized, personal presentation of the message.

c. *Customer's Ability to Ignore Advertising Messages.* Although advertisers can be guaranteed of reaching their target audiences, there is no iron-clad assurance that everyone will notice them. Many of us automatically throw unopened direct mail ads into the waste-paper basket. People find other things to do during the commercial breaks in TV and radio programs. Many avoid the advertising pages in the front of magazines with a quick flip to the lead article. Pop-up ads are automatically blocked or quickly deleted by most website visitors. Potential customers develop these advertising avoidance habits because they are oversaturated with commercial messages (advertising clutter). They know that advertising is biased toward the sponsor, and they do not even let messages pass through the attention filter.

d. *Difficulty Getting Immediate Response or Action.* Advertising often does not require the customer to respond quickly or to take immediate action. Other promotional mix elements, specifically sales promotions and personal selling, are usually more effective. As stated earlier, the increased emphasis on direct market and on the Internet by hospitality and travel promoters is helping the industry to overcome this problem.

e. *Inability to Get Quick Feedback and to Adjust Message.* Without careful marketing research, it is very difficult to determine customer reactions to advertising. Ineffective ads may continue to run while research information is gathered. Personal selling gives the organization immediate feedback and great flexibility in adjusting the message to suit the prospect. Advertising is powerful in its ability to influence the earlier stages of customers' buying processes, but not as effective as other promotional mix elements in later stages. The increasing use of direct marketing techniques and the interactive media with **e-commerce** and **m-commerce** is providing advertisers with more timely feedback from customers (Figure 14.9). **Interactive media**

FIGURE 14.9 The Web provides global reach and 24-hour availability year-round

Courtesy of Jiangsu Provincial Tourism Bureau

involve some combination of electronic (e.g., laptop and desktop PCs) and communication devices (e.g., cell phones, PDAs) that permit the customers to interact with the sponsors' information or reservation services.

The Global Perspective: The Big Picture

Online Promotion by International Theme Parks

Chapter 13 discussed the promotional mix and its elements, which includes online marketing and promotion. Theme parks are especially dependent on promotion because they must generate high volumes of use and since they often change the entertainment offerings available. Online marketing and promotion is an exceptionally valuable tool for theme parks given their interactive and highly visual characteristics. In this *Global Perspective* case, several international theme park websites are analyzed to show their strengths and advantages in promotion according to eight specific criteria.

Tangibilizing the Experiences

What do people do at theme parks? They are entertained and have a fun time by interacting with rides and other people. An effective theme park website should make the experiences feel very real and tangible for the potential visitor. Showing people on the rides or providing a virtual park tour are two ways to do this.

Courtesy of Legoland Billund, © 2008 The LEGO Group.

A great way to tangibilize the experience of a theme park.

(continues)

(continued)

Positioning and Branding

Themes are central to these types of tourism operations, so positioning is essential. Huis Ten Bosch is a residential-style resort in Sasebo, Japan, which includes a theme park, built after a medieval 17th-century Dutch town. Legoland in Billund, Denmark is build around Lego products and therefore is strongly positioned toward families with children.

Market Segmentation

An effective theme park website provides specific information for each of its target markets. Alton Towers in England does an especially good job of market segmentation. It has separate navigation buttons for these markets: (1) coming with toddlers, (2) coming with older children, (3) thrill seekers, (4) special occasions, and (5) groups and schools. It also has another special button leading to information for corporate events.

Courtesy of Europa-Park

Thrill seekers are an important market segment for theme parks with major roller-coasters like Europa-Park in Germany.

Globalization

Having different language versions of the website is a great way for international theme parks to promote to foreign visitors. Huis Ten Bosch provides its website in Japanese, English, Korean, and simplified and traditional Chinese Mandarin. Futuroscope distributes brochures in French, German, Italian, Spanish, and Dutch through its website.

(continues)

(continued)

Appealing to Organizational Buyers

The market for most theme parks is not just families, couples, and singles; it also includes groups of various types including corporations. Europa-Park, for example, has a section of its website called *Confertainment*, which is the combining of conferences at the park with entertaining dinners. Futuroscope offers a team-building program for organizations with a theme built around sustainable development.

Relationship Marketing

An effective theme park website should include features that allow it to build ongoing relationships with site visitors. For example, Europa-Park has developed a category of "EP Insider" on its website where people can register to get updated information on the park and its special offers. Alton Towers has an area on its website where site visitors can register with the chance of winning tickets up to the value of £100.

Pricing and Value Adding

A theme park's website should not only be used to distribute information about prices, but also to add value for people to visit the site. For example, Ocean Park in Hong Kong offers an Online Ticket Purchase system that adds value for the website user. Gardaland in Italy offers a 9 percent discount for those who buy multi-visit tickets online. Alton Towers in England supplies a 35 percent discount for online bookings of a theme park family ticket.

Managing Capacity and Demand

Chapter 2 pointed out that perishability of inventory is a constant challenge in hospitality and travel. Managing capacity and demand means trying to better match demand with the available capacity. For example, last-minute offers are made by Alton Towers on its website. PortAventura in Spain very effectively promotes its special events at Christmas and around Halloween on its website.

Discussion Questions

1. How important is a website as a promotional tool for a theme park?
2. Which other criteria could be used to evaluate the effectiveness of a theme park's website?
3. What are the advantages of a theme park website over each of the traditional five promotional mix elements?

Websites of International Theme Parks

Alton Towers Resort, Staffordshire, England,
   http://www.altontowers.com/pages/home

(continues)

(continued)

Europa-Park, Rust, Germany,
  http://www.europapark.de/lang-en/c51/default.html
Futuroscope, Poitiers, France,
  http://www.futuroscope.com/eng/index.php
Gardaland, Italy,
  http://www.gardaland.it/en/home.php
Huis Ten Bosch, Sasebo, Japan,
  http://english.huistenbosch.co.jp/index.html
Legoland, Billund, Denmark,
  http://www.legoland.dk/?lc=en
Ocean Park, Hong Kong,
  http://www.oceanpark.com.hk
Port Aventura, Salou, Spain,
  http://www.portaventura.co.uk/

f. ***Difficulty Measuring Advertising Effectiveness.*** So many variables influence customer purchases that it is usually difficult to separate the impact of advertising. The most troublesome issue is usually whether advertising led directly to a sale or whether it only assisted.

g. ***Relatively High Waste Factor.*** Waste means having people who are not part of the target market see, hear, or read advertisements. Most forms of advertising involve significant waste. Newspapers, for example, have the advantage of broad coverage (they are read by many), but as a result they are not effective in appealing to specific target markets (except geographic ones). Direct marketing and magazine advertising are two of the best advertising vehicles for reaching specific markets.

Personal Selling

1. **Definition.** **Personal selling** involves oral conversations. These are held, either by telephone or face-to-face, between salespersons and prospective customers.

2. **Advantages.**

   a. ***Ability to Close Sales.*** The most powerful feature of personal selling is its ability to close sales. As you will see in Chapter 17, one of the keys to a successful sales call is for the salesperson to ask for the sale. Experts refer to this as using a close or just closing the sale. The customer (or prospect) is persuaded to make a decision one way or the other. Other promotional mix elements allow customers to ignore the sales message completely or to postpone the purchase decision indefinitely.

   b. ***Ability to Hold the Customer's Attention.*** There is no better way to hold the customer's attention than in a face-to-face conversation (Figure 14.10). Customers, however, are completely free to ignore the

Image copyright Visi.stock, 2008. Used under license from Shutterstock.com

FIGURE 14.10 A major advantage of personal selling is the two-way communications.

messages carried by the four other promotional mix elements (advertising, sales promotion, merchandising, and public relations and publicity) and Internet marketing.

c. *Immediate Feedback and Two-Way Communications.* The relative success in closing sales using personal selling results partly from the two-way communications involved and the ability to get quick customer feedback. All four other promotional mix elements use impersonal means of getting their messages across. A personal sales message can be adjusted based on the customer's reactions. The other four promotional mix elements are not as flexible.

d. *Presentations Tailored to Individual Needs.* Personal sales presentations are tailor-made to fit the prospect's needs and requirements. Customers can ask questions and get answers. If customers have objections (problems or concerns about the service or product), the salesperson can address these directly.

e. *Ability to Target Customers Precisely.* If an effective prospecting (choosing potential customers for sales presentations) job is done, there is very little waste in personal selling. In fact, good salespersons carefully screen and qualify customers (verify that the prospect is a potential buyer) before they arrange face-to-face meetings. The other promotional mix elements usually result in higher levels of waste.

f. *Ability to Cultivate Relationships.* With personal selling, the salesperson can develop an ongoing relationship with prospects. This does not mean that it is advisable for the salesperson to become best friends with all prospects—this is generally not recommended. What it does imply is that prospects can establish a more personal link with a company or a destination through a salesperson. Having this personal communications channel often is a more powerful inducement to customers to make repeat purchases than are the company's advertising and other promotions.

g. *Ability to Get Immediate Action.* As you saw earlier, advertising leads only indirectly to sales or it delays the purchase response. Personal selling always has the potential of producing immediate action from the prospect.

3. **Disadvantages**

a. *High Cost per Contact.* The major drawback to personal selling is its high cost per contact compared to the four other promotional mix elements. Whereas most other promotions usually cost no more than a few dollars per person reached, a field sales presentation often means salary and travel costs that exceed several hundred per day. Although personalizing the sales message is a powerful inducement for the customer to purchase, it involves a great deal of added expense. Some forms of personal selling are more efficient. For example, in-house and telephone selling do not require the travel costs necessary for field sales presentations. Also, using online messenger services such as MSN *Live*, Yahoo Messenger, and Skype are proving cheaper ways to communicate with sales clients.

b. *Inability to Reach Some Customers as Effectively.* Customers may refuse a salesperson's help or presentation. As noted earlier, some people are put on their guard by personal selling approaches. They are less defensive when it comes to impersonal communications such as advertising, sales promotion, merchandising, public relations and publicity, and Internet marketing. Prospects may also be "inaccessible" for other reasons, such as their geographic locations and schedules.

Sales Promotion

1. **Definition. Sales promotions** are approaches other than advertising, personal selling, and public relations and publicity where customers are given a short-term inducement to make an immediate purchase

FIGURE 14.11 Many sales promotions offer short-term inducements for customers to buy.

(Figure 14.11). Like advertising, the sponsor is clearly identified and the communication is non-personal. Examples include discount coupons, contests and sweepstakes, samples, and premiums.

2. **Advantages**

   a. *Combination of Some Advantages of Advertising and Personal Selling.* In their ability to generate immediate purchases, sales promotions share this key advantage of personal selling. However, they have an added advantage over personal selling—they can be mass-communicated and distributed. For example, coupons can be sent through the mail, or customers can clip them out of magazines or newspapers. They can also be rapidly distributed through the Web.

   b. *Ability to Provide Quick Feedback.* Many sales promotions offer incentives that must be claimed within a short time period. Most coupons must be redeemed before a specified date. Usually, there is also a deadline with contests, sweepstakes, and premiums. Customers must react quickly—thus, the sponsor gets rapid feedback on the offer.

   c. *Ability to Add Excitement to a Service or Product.* An imaginative sales promotion can add excitement to a hospitality and travel service. For example, Red Lobster each year stages its mouth-watering Lobsterfest® that adds excitement to visits to their restaurants.

   d. *Additional Ways to Communicate with Customers.* Sales promotions provide an added assortment of communications channels to customers. Bounce-back coupons can be attached to take-out and home-delivered food. Menus and coupon offers can be designed as doorknob hangers.

   e. *Flexible Timing.* Another example of the flexibility of sales promotions is that they can be used on short notice and at almost any time.

They are particularly helpful in building sales during off-peak times (e.g., two-for-one restaurant meals on Monday and Tuesday nights). If other promotional mix elements are unsuccessful in attracting forecasted sales volumes, a last-minute sales promotion may be used to fill the slack. Again, you can see that it is the ability of sales promotion to generate increased revenues in the short term that is its key advantage.

f. *Efficiency.* Sales promotions can be very efficient or low-cost. Both advertising and personal selling involve significant, up-front fixed costs. However, sales promotions can be launched with modest initial investments (e.g., printing coupons). Additional costs may vary directly with the number of customers taking advantage of the promotion (e.g., coupon redemptions, guests claiming frequent-flyer or frequent-guest awards).

3. **Disadvantages**

a. *Short-Term Benefits.* The beauty of sales promotions is their quick payback in increased sales. It is paradoxical, but this is also their major shortcoming—sales promotions usually do not lead to long-term sales increases. A sales promotion tends to increase short-term revenues, but when the promotion is over, sales return to normal or below-normal levels. Furthermore, a company that offers too many deals runs the risk of having customers permanently undervalue its services.

b. *Ineffective in Building Long-Term Loyalty for Company or Brand.* Sales promotions are very appealing to brand switchers, who flip between competitive services based on which company offers the best deal at the time. They are not effective in developing true company, brand or destination loyalty. Because most organizations are more concerned with building a long-term customer base, sales promotions are not as effective for them as other explicit and implicit promotions.

c. *Inability to Be Used on Its Own in the Long Term without Other Promotional Mix Elements.* In the long-term, sales promotions are most effective if they dovetail with, and are supported by, the other promotional techniques. Frequent-guest programs must be advertised, sold to corporate accounts, and described in a brochure or brochures. For example, Red Lobster's Lobsterfest® is supported with a significant amount of media advertising.

d. *Often Misused.* Sales promotions are often used as quick-fix solutions for long-term marketing problems. Some national restaurant chains seem to offer a constant stream of sales promotion deals, seemingly buying customers away from competitors. They should, however, be concentrating on attracting loyal, long-term customers by improving menu selections, redesigning restaurants or re-concepting, repositioning, or upgrading service or food quality.

Image copyright Christopher DeLaura, 2008. Used under license from Shutterstock.com

FIGURE 14.12
Merchandising involves in-house techniques used to encourage customers to make purchases, such as this wine display.

Merchandising (Point-of-Purchase Advertising)

It is a common practice to categorize merchandising as a sales promotion technique, because it does not involve media advertising, personal selling, or public relations and publicity. In this text, merchandising is separated from other sales promotion techniques because of its uniqueness and its importance to the industry.

1. **Definition.** Merchandising, or point-of-purchase advertising, includes materials used in-house to stimulate sales (Figure 14.12). These include menus, wine lists, tent cards, signs, posters, displays, and other point-of-sale promotional items.

2. **Advantages.** The advantages of merchandising are very similar to those for sales promotions:

   a. Combining some of the advantages of advertising and personal selling
   b. Producing quick feedback
   c. Adding excitement to a service or product
   d. Providing additional ways to communicate to customers
   e. Allowing flexible timing

   Think of some of your recent trips to the supermarket or clothing store. You may have bought one or more grocery items on impulse because of a special aisle-end or other display. You may also have spent a few more dollars than you planned to on clothes, because of an attractive window display or arrangement inside the clothing store. Or perhaps you have visited a restaurant recently, and because of its unique menu or mouth-watering menu descriptions, significantly departed from your diet. Merchandising excites the visual senses at the point of purchase and often results in increased sales.

There are two additional advantages of merchandising.

   a. *Stimulation of Impulse Purchases and Higher Per Capita Spending.* What we have just talked about is the ability of merchandising to get you to make purchases you had not intended to make. You may be drawn into a travel agency by an attractive display for a cruise line or resort company. Once you are on the hospitality or travel business' premises, other visual merchandising may lead you to spend more than you planned.

   b. *Support for Advertising Campaigns.* Advertising campaign effectiveness can be greatly increased if customers receive a visual reminder at the point of purchase. Fast-food chains are masters of this technique. Through television advertising they promote children's meal packages that include certain toys or toy premiums with any purchases that customers make. Attractive, in-house displays are quick to remind children of this merchandise and to rivet their attention.

3. **Disadvantages.** The key difference between merchandising and other sales promotion techniques is that merchandising does not necessarily involve giving the customer a financial incentive. The impact of certain merchandising items can also be longer-term. A good menu can last for several years. In-store displays may be suitable for several months, as may posters, tent cards, and brochure displays.

   Merchandising may have a longer-lasting positive impact, but it is still not effective in building long-term loyalty for the company or brand. Although it can be used without support from other promotional mix elements, again it is much more effective if it is coordinated with personal selling and advertising.

   Another disadvantage of some merchandising is its contribution to visual clutter. Some people are so annoyed by the number of tent cards on restaurant tables that they consciously or subconsciously ignore all of them.

Public Relations and Publicity

1. **Definition. Public relations** include all the activities that a hospitality and travel organization engages in to maintain or improve its relationship with other organizations and individuals. **Publicity** is one public relations technique that involves non-paid communication of information about an organization's services.

2. **Advantages**

   a. *Low Cost.* Compared to other promotional mix elements, public relations and publicity costs relatively little. However, there is a common misconception that it is totally free. Effective public relations and publicity requires careful planning and considerable management and staff time.

b. *Effective Because They Are Not Seen as Commercial Messages.* You saw earlier that media advertising is recognized as a biased form of communications. People do not treat public relations messages on radio and television, and in newspaper and magazine articles, with the same skepticism, because the services are being described by an independent party. Customers do not turn off as readily to this information as they do to media advertisements. Publicity has a way of slipping past perceptual defenses.

c. *Credibility and Implied Endorsements.* If a travel critic writes favorably about a destination, hotel, or restaurant, this carries greater credibility than sponsors' paid advertisements. Customers also feel that they are receiving the reporter's endorsement.

d. *Prestige and Impressiveness of Mass-Media Coverage.* Both publicity and advertising are carried by the mass media (Figure 14.13). Thus, publicity shares the advantage of prestige and impressiveness with advertising.

e. *Added Excitement and Dramatization.* A writer's use of the English language, or the skills of a reporter or camera crew, can accentuate the benefits and unique features of a hospitality or travel organization or destination. Dramatic opening ceremonies for hotels or restaurants, inaugural departures of ships, or new airline routes are other examples of heightening the excitement of services.

f. *Maintenance of a Public Presence.* Public relations activities ensure that an organization maintains a continued, positive presence in its

FIGURE 14.13 Public relations and publicity includes working with the media to get coverage on television, and in newspapers and magazines.

INTERNET MARKETING

Maintaining Ongoing Customer Communications Via Email and E-newsletters

- Before the Internet, keeping in touch with customers was quite difficult, and mostly made use of the postal services. This was fraught with problems as people moved their homes and had a tendency to quickly "toss out" non-essential mail.
- The Internet now has introduced a set of new ways of "keeping in touch" or maintaining communications with customers. This must be founded on the principle of **permission marketing**; that is, customers must give their permission before receiving these online communications.
- The restaurant and foodservice sector has implemented a variety of different online programs to stay in contact with customers including: (1) sign-ups to receive emails; (2) invitations to club memberships; and (3) sign-ups to receive e-newsletters. Here's a few examples from leading dinner-house restaurants in North America:
- Applebee's, *Receive Our Emails*. To receive updates from Applebee's, a customer must submit name, email address, zip code, and date of birth.
- Chili's Grill & Bar, *Email Club*. To join, a customer must submit name, email address, zip code, and date of birth.
- Olive Garden, *Newsletter Sign-up*. This newsletter requires name, email address, zip code, and date of birth. Customers use their email address as a login and choose their own password. They receive *"The Family Table"* newsletter by email.
- Outback Steakhouse, *Keep in Touch*. Customers must supply email address and zip code.
- Red Lobster, *Join the Fresh Catch Club*. Name, street address, email address, date of birth, telephone number, and a password must be supplied by the customer.

Source: Company websites. (2008). **http://www.applebees.com/, http://www.chilis. com/, http://www.olivegarden.com/, http://www.outbacksteakhouse.com/, http:// www.redlobster.com/**

Student Questions

1. What are the benefits to these restaurant chains in maintaining customer email lists?
2. What are the potential advantages to customers of belonging to these lists?
3. What are the likely drawbacks, if any, of joining?
4. Which of these approaches do you think are the most effective, and why?

various publics. These include local, media, financial, employees, and trade/industry segments.

3. **Disadvantages**

   a. *Difficult to Arrange Consistently.* Receiving positive publicity is often a hit-and-miss proposition. Coverage is totally at the discretion of media people. Its timing cannot be controlled with the same degree of accuracy as other promotional techniques.

   b. *Lack of Control.* Another aspect of this lack of control is the inability to ensure that what is covered and said are exactly what you want. Reporters may fail to include key facts or selling ideas, or they may distort words and ideas.

   Figure 14.14 provides a summary of the advantages and disadvantages of the five promotional mix elements.

   Because these five promotional mix elements have unique strengths and weaknesses, they should be combined together in an **integrated marketing communications (IMC)** framework. Thus, the strengths of one element can compensate for the weaknesses of another. In addition, these five traditional promotional mix elements should be blended together with Internet marketing (Figure 14.15).

Factors Affecting the Promotional Mix

You now understand the advantages and disadvantages of each promotional mix element. However, there are other factors that affect promotional mix decisions.

Target Markets

The effectiveness of the five promotional mix elements varies according to the target market. On the one hand, in promoting its convention/meeting facilities, a lodging property might find that personal selling to key meeting planners is much more effective than advertising. On the other hand, using personal selling to attract individual pleasure travelers would not be feasible. Generally, the more complex is the service, the greater the value of personal selling.

The geographic location of potential customers also has an impact. Where they are widely dispersed, advertising may be the most efficient and effective way to reach them.

Marketing Objectives

The promotional mix selected should flow directly from the objectives for each target market. For example, on the one hand, if the objective is to build awareness by a certain percentage, the emphasis may be placed on media advertising. If, on the other hand, it is to build sales significantly in a short time period, the focus may be put on sales promotion.

	ADVERTISING	PERSONAL SELLING	SALES PROMOTION	MERCHANDISING	PUBLIC RELATIONS AND PUBLICITY
ADVANTAGES	• Low cost per contact • Ability to reach customers where salespersons cannot • Great scope for creative versatility and dramatization • Ability to create images that salespersons cannot • Nonthreatening nature of nonpersonal presentation • Potential to repeat message several times • Prestige and impressiveness of mass-media advertising	• Ability to close sales • Ability to hold the customer's attention • Immediate feedback and two-way communications • Presentations tailored to individual needs • Ability to target customers precisely • Ability to cultivate relationships • Ability to get immediate action	• Combination of some advantages of advertising and personal selling • Ability to provide quick feedback • Ability to add excitement to a service or product • Additional ways to communicate with customers • Flexible timing • Efficiency	• Ability to provide quick feedback • Ability to add excitement to a service or product • Additional ways to communicate with customers • Flexible timing • Stimulation of impulse purchases and higher per capita spending	• Low cost • Effective because they are not seen as commercial messages • Credibility and implied endorsements • Prestige and impressiveness of mass-media coverage • Added excitement and dramatization • Maintenance of a public presence
DISADVANTAGES	• Inability to close sales • Advertising clutter • Customer's ability to ignore advertising messages • Difficulty getting immediate response or action • Inability to get quick feedback and to adjust message • Difficulty measuring advertising effectiveness • Relatively high waste factor	• High cost per contact • Inability to reach some customers as effectively	• Short-term benefits • Ineffective in building long-term loyalty for company or brand • Inability to be used on its own in the long term without other promotional mix elements • Often misused	• Does not necessarily give the customer a financial incentive • Ineffective in building long-term loyalty for company or brand • Contributes to visual clutter	• Difficult to arrange consistently • Lack of control

FIGURE 14.14 Summary of the advantages and disadvantages of the five promotional mix elements.

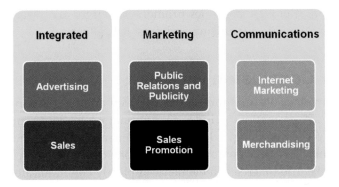

FIGURE 14.15 The components of integrated marketing communications.

Competition and Promotional Practices

There is a distinct tendency in certain parts of the hospitality and travel industry for most competitive organizations to use the same lead element in promotional mixes. Fast-food chains focus on heavy television advertising, hotels and airlines are locked in a battle of frequent-traveler award programs, and cruise lines put a heavy emphasis on personal selling to travel agents. It is difficult and extremely risky for one competitor to break from the pack in this respect.

Promotional Budget Available

Obviously the funds available for promotion have a direct impact on choosing promotional mix elements. Smaller organizations with more limited budgets usually have to place greater emphasis on lower-cost promotions, including

Did You Know?

Where Does the Advertising Spending go?

- According to the *100 Leading National Advertisers* results for 2006, airlines, hotels, car rental and travel companies in the USA spent 1.3 percent less on measured media advertising than they did in 2005.
- The same report showed that restaurants increased their measured media advertising by 4.5 percent.
- Airlines, hotels, car rental and travel companies spent $1.484 billion on magazine advertising and $1.413 billion on newspaper advertising. Restaurants spent only $134.9 million and $183.8 million respectively on magazine and newspaper advertising.
- Restaurants spent $3.339 billion on TV advertising while airlines, hotels, car rental and travel companies spent a much lower $876.1 million.

Source: Advertising Age. (2007). **http://www.adage.com**

public relations, publicity and sales promotions. Larger organizations can better afford to use media advertising and personal selling.

Chapter Conclusion

Promotion involves all communications between an organization and its customers. Explicit promotion includes five techniques in the promotional mix: advertising, personal selling, sales promotion, merchandising, and public relations and publicity. The promotional mix is one of the eight elements of the marketing mix. The other seven elements implicitly communicate information about an organization to its customers.

Choosing a promotional program for an upcoming period requires very careful research and planning. Although target markets and marketing objectives provide the foundation for promotion selections, other factors must be considered. These include product-life-cycle stages, competitors and their promotional practices, and the available promotional budget.

REVIEW QUESTIONS

1. What are the five elements of the promotional mix?
2. Is the marketing mix an element of the promotional mix, or vice versa? Explain your answer.
3. Are the five promotional mix elements related, or is it better to develop them separately? Why do you think one approach is better than the other?
4. What are the nine elements of the communications process?
5. What is the difference between explicit and implicit communications? Is the promotional mix implicit or explicit? Are implicit and explicit promotions related?
6. What are the three principal goals of promotion? What is the ultimate purpose of promotion?
7. What are the advantages and disadvantages of each of the five promotional mix elements?
8. What factors influence the choice of promotional mix elements?

CHAPTER ASSIGNMENTS

1. Consider the following four purchases of hospitality and travel services:

   a. Participating in clown face-painting at a theme park
   b. Selecting a place to eat during a 30-minute lunch break
   c. Selecting a restaurant for a 25th anniversary celebration
   d. Deciding which country club or fitness club to join

   Which of the four are usually high-involvement (extensive problem solving) and which are low-involvement (routine problem solving) decisions? Would the promotional techniques best suited for each decision type be the same? If not, how would they differ?

2. Select a part of the hospitality and travel industry in which you are most interested (e.g., hotel, airline, restaurant, travel agency, theme park, resort, tour operations, destination). Assume you have just been hired as the marketing vice president. Your organization is not very satisfied with its past promotional activities, and you have been asked to recommend more effective promotional approaches. How would you present this information, making sure that you mention the advantages and disadvantages of each of the five promotional mix elements?

3. This chapter emphasizes the importance of keeping promotional messages simple. Review hospitality and travel promotions either at the local or national level. Find and describe at least five examples of promotions that use simple communications, and five examples of ones you feel are overly complicated. How could each of the latter messages be improved to communicate more effectively?

4. Both explicit and implicit communications influence how customers perceive an organization's services. Choose three organizations in your local community, or three national firms, and analyze their use of these two factors. How consistent are explicit and implicit communications in each case? Which of the three has the greatest consistency? What could each organization do to create greater consistency? Why do you think consistency or the lack of it has influenced the success of these organizations?

WEB RESOURCES

Abercrombie & Kent, http://www.abercrombiekent.com/
Budgetel, http://www.budgetel.com/
Econo Lodge, http://www.econolodge.com/
Georgia Travel, http://www.georgia.org/travel/
Jamaica Tourist Board, http://www.visitjamaica.com/
Mandarin Oriental Hotel Group, http://www.mandarinoriental.com/
Peninsula Hotel Hong Kong, http://hongkong.peninsula.com/
Seabourn Cruise Line, http://www.seabourn.com/
Singapore Tourism Board, http://www.visitsingapore.com/
Southwest Airlines, http://www.southwest.com/
Tourism Australia, http://www.australia.com/

REFERENCES

1. *Fans of Mandarin Oriental*. 2008. http://www.mandarinoriental.com/our_fans/, December 27, 2008.
2. Travel Michigan. 2008. *Award-Winning Pure Michigan Campaign Launches Winter Campaign First Michigan winter advertising campaign in more than 15 years*, http://www.michigan.org/PressReleases/Detail.aspx?ContentId=3a2dfd55-3a2b-466e-8621-36932a557303, accessed December 27, 2008.

3. *got milk? campaign*. 2008. http://www.milkdelivers.org/gotmilk/index. cfm, accessed December 27, 2008.

4. American Marketing Association. 2008. *Dictionary*. http://www. marketingpower.com/_layouts/Dictionary.aspx, accessed December 27, 2008.

5. Kotler, Philip. 2000. *Marketing Management: Millennium Edition*. 10th ed. Upper Saddle River, N.J: Prentice-Hall, Inc.

6. Mill, Robert Christie, and Alastair M. Morrison. 2009. *The Tourism System*. 6th ed. Dubuque, Iowa: Kendall/Hunt Publishing Company.

7. American Marketing Association. 2008. *Dictionary*. http://www. marketingpower.com/_layouts/Dictionary.aspx, accessed December 27, 2008.

8. Reuters. 2008. *Super Bowl 30-second ads to cost $3 million in 2009: report*, http://www.reuters.com/article/rbssTechMediaTelecomNews/idUSN06 44484220 080506, accessed December 27, 2008.

9. eMediaWire. 2007. *Super Bowl XLI: Do the ROI numbers add up for advertisers? Analysis suggests that 75% of expenditure is wasted*. http://www. emediawire.com/releases/2007/3/emw512828.htm, accessed December 27, 2008.

10. Reuters. 2007. *Advertisers go for Super Bowl laughs*. http://www.reuters. com/article/ousiv/idUSN0217724920070205, accessed December 27, 2008.

chapter 15

Advertising
How Do We Get There?

OVERVIEW

Advertising is perhaps the most pervasive and powerful promotional mix element. This chapter begins by emphasizing the need to integrate the planning of all promotional mix elements, and then provides a step-by-step approach for developing the advertising plan. The chapter also takes a detailed look at various media alternatives. The use of advertising in the hospitality and travel industry is explored. The role of advertising agencies is explained at the end of the chapter.

OBJECTIVES

Having read this chapter, you should be able to:

- Describe the steps involved in planning the advertising effort.

- List the three categories into which advertising objectives can be divided.

- Explain the difference between consumer and trade advertising.

- Explain the three components of advertising message strategy and list the alternative creative formats.

- Explain the seven factors considered when selecting advertising media.

- Identify and describe the five major advertising media alternatives.

- Describe the advantages and disadvantages of various advertising media alternatives.

- Explain how the hospitality and travel industry uses different advertising media.

- Describe the role of advertising agencies and the advantages of using them.

KEY TERMS

advertising	direct marketing	message idea
advertising agencies	direct-response advertising	message strategy
banners	dominance	mood
broadcast media	fear appeal	partnership
celebrity testimonials	freestanding inserts (FSI)	pass-along rate
circulation	frequency	permanence
click-through rates	gross rating points (GRP)	persuasive impact
clutter	honestTwist	post-testing
comparative advertising	infomercials	pre-testing
consumer advertising	integrated marketing	print media
cookie	communications (IMC)	reach
cooperative advertising	interactive advertising	slice-of-life
copy platform	interactive media	spots
cost-per-thousand (CPM)	Internet	testimonial
database marketing	lead time	tone
designated market	log file	trade advertising
areas (DMA)	media vehicles	waste
direct mail	message format	Web

In 2007, total advertising expenditures in the United States were $283.9 billion.[1] Total worldwide advertising spending in 2008 was expected to be $653.9 billion; and total U.S. advertising to be $294.4 billion.[2] Most of you are probably not surprised by these figures. After all, you are exposed to some form of advertising all the time. Advertising is the most pervasive promotional mix element. You see it on the Internet, television, billboards, buses, and buildings—and now even on your mobile phone! It comes in your mailbox at least once a day. You hear it on the radio and see it in newspapers, magazines, journals, flyers, posters, and other printed formats. People are so infatuated with advertising that they even pay money to carry advertising messages on their clothes! You only have to look at the popularity of *Nike*, *Adidas*, and *Umbro* sportswear to see this.

The choices of advertising media and vehicles are almost limitless. Selecting the most effective ways to advertise is a complex and often perplexing process. As with all aspects of marketing, careful planning is the key to effective advertising. Some of the advertising expenditures spent by the hospitality and travel industry are wasted because of a lack of preplanning and clear advertising objectives.

Global Perspective: The Big Picture

Integrated Marketing Communications in the Hotel Business

The Hong Kong and Shanghai Hotels, Limited

http://www.peninsula.com
http://www.peninsulaboutique.com/

The Rolls Royce fleet outside The Peninsula Hong Kong.

Integrated Marketing Communications

Integrated marketing communications (IMC) is the use of advertising in combination with the other four traditional promotional mix elements and Internet marketing. Some of IMC's benefits are:

- Greater consistency in communicating messages
- Added impact since messages are repeated
- Reflects different customer buying stages (need recognition/search for information/pre-purchase evaluation of alternatives/purchase/consumption/post-consumption evaluation)
- More effectively puts across positioning and branding
- Reflects better consumers' different learning styles
- The elements complement and support each other (strengths of one compensate for the weaknesses of others)

The Peninsula Hotels (Hong Kong and Shanghai Hotels, Limited)

The Peninsula Hotels provides a good case study in the application of IMC in the hotel business. There are eight Peninsula Hotels in the world (Hong Kong, New York, Chicago, Beverly Hills, Tokyo, Bangkok, Beijing, and Manila), and the ninth will be in Shanghai, China. The original Peninsula Hotel is located in Hong Kong close to

(continues)

(continued)

the waterfront in Kowloon, and was opened in 1928. This is a group of luxury hotels operated by Hong Kong and Shanghai Hotels, Limited, which has its headquarters in Hong Kong.

The company has communicated very consistent messages for years through its advertising, website, and other promotional elements. Many of the visual components are drawn from the original hotel in Hong Kong. These range from the traditional porter uniforms with the pillbox hats to the wall/ceiling décor, and have been extended into a range of retail merchandise items sold through Peninsula Boutiques.

The distinctive ceiling and wall décor in the original Peninsula Hong Kong.

There are now 18 Peninsula Boutiques around the world and selected items can also be purchased on Cathay Pacific flights. Now these delicious items can be bought online through Peninsula Boutiques' website.

This box of chocolates available in Peninsula Boutiques reflects the décor and other symbols in The Peninsula Hong Kong.

(continues)

(continued)

The Peninsula Boutiques merchandise- some of the items from the famous afternoon tea served at The Peninsula Hong Kong.

These symbols were also carried through into an award-winning advertising campaign, *Portraits of Peninsula*, which can be viewed on the company's website. The *Portraits* were based on black-and-white photographs taken by the famous American photographer, Annie Leibovitz. They showed various poses of staff and hotel guests, and clearly reflected the high quality personal service levels and unique services provided at The Peninsula Hong Kong and The Peninsula New York. They contained strong visual images of the distinctive porter and housekeeper uniforms, the Rolls Royce fleet, and the scones from afternoon tea, thus reinforcing these symbols in customers' minds.

This is an exquisite and tasteful example of how to apply IMC to a group of hotels. As well as spreading the 80-year history of the famous Peninsula Hong Kong around the globe, these linked promotions produce a greater impact on current and potential hotel guests. They visually reinforce one another, and communicate strong and consistent messages to the market.

Discussion Questions

1. How does Peninsula Hotels make effective use of integrated marketing communications (IMC)?
2. Which other hotel companies have used similar approaches in IMC and how have they implemented these approaches?
3. The Peninsula Boutiques concept of retail merchandise stores is a unique concept in the hotel business. How does this concept help to reinforce the luxury positioning of Peninsula Hotels and promote the hotel group to a larger audience of people?

Advertising and the Promotional Mix

Advertising is one of five promotional mix elements and can be defined as "the placement of announcements and persuasive messages in time or space purchased in any of the mass media by business firms, non-profit organizations, government agencies, and individuals who seek to inform and/or persuade members of a particular target market or audience about their products, services, organizations, or ideas."[3] This highly varied promotional tool is probably the first one that comes to mind when most people think of promotion.

In many cases, other promotional mix elements have a greater impact on sales than advertising. Chapter 14 indicated that these choices must be based on careful consideration of target markets, marketing objectives, customer buying process stages, buying decision classifications, competitors and their promotional practices, and the total budget available for promotion.

Plan Integrated Marketing Communications First

Once marketing objectives are set, there is a tendency to look at each promotional mix element and Internet marketing separately. This is not the ideal or recommended approach. Promotion is much more effective if each of the five promotional mix elements and Internet marketing are developed to support and complement the others (e.g., making sure that similar colors, graphics, and positioning statements are included in all written promotional materials). Another example is using advertising to create awareness and remind people about short-term sales promotions. Closely coordinated planning of the promotional mix through integrated marketing communications must come before the detailed planning for each of its elements.

Integrated marketing communications (IMC) is a planning process designed to assure that all brand contacts received by a customer or prospect for a product, service, or organization are relevant to that person and consistent over time.[4] It is also used to refer to the closer coordination among a company's promotional consultants and advisors, including advertising agencies, sales promotion firms, and public relations consultants. Broader IMC objectives should be established before advertising objectives are written, and a tentative promotional budget should be developed before a final advertising budget is set.

Planning the Advertising Effort

An organization should draw up a written plan for each promotional mix element, including advertising. The 10 steps involved in developing and implementing an advertising plan are shown in Figure 15.1 and described below.

Planning the Advertising Effort

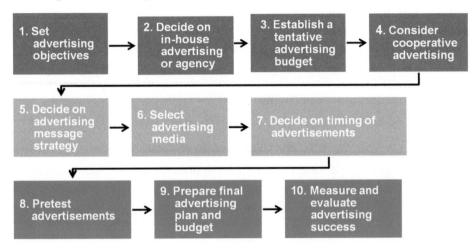

FIGURE 15.1   Steps in preparing and evaluating an advertising plan.

Set Advertising Objectives (Step 1)

As with all plans, the best way to start the advertising plan is by setting advertising objectives. These must meet the same types of criteria as overall marketing objectives, which were discussed in Chapter 8. Like marketing objectives, advertising objectives serve a dual purpose: they are guidelines for planning, but they are also a way to measure and evaluate success in advertising implementation. The three principal goals of promotion are to inform, persuade, and remind customers. Advertising objectives also can usually be divided into these three categories.

Most hospitality and travel organizations, with the exception of retail-only travel agencies, engage in the following two distinct branches of advertising:

- **Consumer Advertising**—Advertising to the customers who will actually use the services being promoted.
- **Trade Advertising**—Advertising to travel trade intermediaries who will influence customers' buying decisions.

Objectives should be defined for each of these two broad categories of advertising. A good example of a consumer advertising objective is from Tourism Australia's "Come Walkabout" campaign. Tourism Australia's objective in this advertising was to "ensure Australia reaches its forecast growth rate of 3.2 per cent in international arrivals in 2009 and halts the predicted decline in domestic travel within Australia.[5] Visit Mississippi had the trade advertising objective in 2009 of increasing *awareness* of Mississippi as a vacation destination to domestic our operators, travel planners and the group trade industry.[6]

Decide on In-House Advertising or Agency (Step 2)

Most medium-sized and large hospitality and travel organizations use outside agencies to develop and place their advertising. The services of these agencies are discussed later in this chapter. Obviously, this tends to be an infrequent, rather than an annual, decision. However, an organization's retention of a particular advertising agency is based on the success or failure of the agency's most recent advertising campaigns.

Establish a Tentative Advertising Budget (Step 3)

Chapters 9 and 20 provide detailed descriptions of the available budgeting methods. As you know from Chapter 9, the objective-and-task approach is the one that this book recommends. This method involves building the budget on objectives and the specific activities needed to attain them. It would be nice, but unrealistic, if marketers felt that they would always get the promotion funds they need. Every organization has priorities other than marketing, and the funds available for marketing and promotion are greatly influenced by other activities and initiatives.

The realistic time to start budgeting for advertising is after setting a tentative total marketing budget. A portion of this total budget will be designated for the promotional mix and IMC. When all the detailed plans for each promotional mix element have been developed—as you will read about in Chapters 15 to 18—their costs should be estimated and compared to the tentative budget allocations. Individual plans may then have to be adjusted and recalculated to better align the tentative allocation with the plan's costs. In essence, this recommends a multi- rather than a single-stage budgeting process for the promotional mix and each of its elements.

Consider Cooperative Advertising (Partnerships) (Step 4)

This book clearly emphasizes the close relationship between many hospitality and travel organizations in delivering satisfying customer experiences. In a sense, they are partners in satisfying customer needs and wants. This **partnership** (cooperative marketing) opportunity is considered so vital that it has been singled out as one of the special Ps of the hospitality and travel marketing mix. Cooperation is possible for all elements of the promotional mix, including advertising. In **cooperative advertising**, two or more organizations share the costs of an advertisement or an advertising campaign.

There are many good examples of cooperative advertising in the hospitality and travel industry. The key is to find target markets and advertising objectives in which the partners share a mutual interest. The American Express Card shares a common goal with almost all airlines and hotel chains—encouraging more people to travel and, incidentally, to use their green, gold, platinum, and blue cards to reserve and pay for trips. For this reason, you will notice the American Express Card prominently displayed within the ads of many hotel chains, car rental firms, airlines, and some cruise lines. In October 2006, Starwood Hotels & Resorts and American Express introduced the enhanced *Starwood Preferred Guest*® credit card, backed by considerable advertising. A close competitor, Visa, has formed an exclusive partnership with the Olympic Games, and will continue to be the exclusive payment card and official payment service of the Olympic Games through 2012, including the Beijing 2008 Olympic Games, the Vancouver 2010 Olympic Winter Games, and the London 2012 Olympic Games.[7]

There are several advantages of cooperative advertising. This form of advertising:

1. **Increases the total budget available for advertising.** This can result in more ad placements, using a more expensive medium, or increasing the ad size or its persuasive impact.
2. **May enhance the image or positioning of the sponsor.** For example, a hotel chain like Starwood Hotels & Resorts that associates with the American Express Card can augment its image by appealing to more affluent business and pleasure travelers.
3. **Can communicate a better match between the customer's needs and the partners' services.** Ads may be more convincing because of the convenient packaging of the partners' services or destinations.

Although these advantages are powerful, there are certain limitations with cooperative advertising.

1. More time is needed to plan advertisements so that all partners are satisfied with the arrangements.
2. Each partner has to give up absolute control over the advertising message strategy (how the ads will be developed and used).
3. Each partner loses the opportunity to showcase only its services or destinations.
4. Other compromises may also be required that need to be weighed carefully against the promotional goals and advertising objectives.

Decide on the Advertising Message Strategy (Step 5)

The fifth step in developing the advertising plan is to decide on the message strategy. Although writers use varying names for the components of the message strategy, the key ones are (1) message idea, (2) copy platform, and (3) message format.

1. **Message Idea.** The **message idea** is the main theme, appeal, or benefit to be communicated in the advertisement. The "Come Walkabout" advertising campaign in 2008–2009 by Tourism Australia had the following message idea:

   "'Walkabout' involves a person returning to the bush for a short period of time to re-connect to their traditional way of life and the land. For the majority of us, our 'walkabout' takes the form of a holiday—a time to refresh and rebalance. By encouraging people to 'walkabout' in Australia, the tradition set by Tourism Australia of issuing a warm invitation is maintained in an authentic and unique way" (Tourism Australia. 2008. *Tourism Australia's destination campaign by Baz Luhrmann*).

2. **Copy Platform**. The **copy platform** is a statement that fully describes the message (creative) strategy and idea. The message idea serves as the basis for the copy (or text) within an advertising campaign. An outline of what message should be conveyed, to whom, and with what tone. This provides the guiding principles for copywriters and art directors who actually design the advertisement. The written statement describing the message strategy and idea is called the copy platform.[8] It may fill as much as one page, and it is usually prepared by the advertising agency. The copy platform should cover the following seven items:[9,10]

   a. Target market or markets (Which customer or travel-trade market segments are the target?)
   b. The key appeal or benefit (What is the message idea?)
   c. Supporting information (Which statistics or other information will be used to support the sponsor's claims?)
   d. Positioning approach and statement (How does the sponsoring organization want to be perceived relative to competitors?)
   e. Tone (Will the key appeal or benefit be expressed emotionally or rationally? Will competitors be mentioned? How strongly should the message be delivered?)
   f. Rationale (How should these first five items work together to achieve advertising objectives?)
   g. Tie-in with other promotional mix elements and Internet marketing (How should the ad mesh with other elements of the promotional mix? This is in support of integrated marketing communications.)

   Although you have already been exposed to most of these concepts, some elaboration is necessary. Chapter 8 outlined six alternative positioning approaches based on (1) specific product features, (2) benefits/problem solution/needs, (3) specific usage occasions, (4) user category, (5) going against another competitive service, and (6) product class dissociation. The copy platform provides the first step in articulating the selected positioning approach so that it can be communicated to customers. The positioning statement is a short, memorable phrase or sentence that summarizes the chosen positioning.

   The **tone** of an advertisement is the basic way that the message idea will be communicated. It is based on choosing between rational and emotional appeals, dealing with competitors' services versus not mentioning them, and the strength of the message. For example, in the Tourism Australia campaign mentioned earlier, the tone of the invitation is uniquely Australian (Walkabout), as well being authentic and credible.

Rational appeals or benefits are fact-based and are keyed to people's rational, physiological, and safety needs. (Remember Maslow's needs hierarchy from Chapter 4?) Emotional appeals play on psychological needs (e.g., belonging/social, esteem, self-actualization). There is much argument about which type of appeal is more effective, but the consensus seems to be that most hospitality and travel services are communicated more effectively with an emotional tone. There are exceptions, however. Trade advertising is thought to be communicated more effectively using rational appeals and information. The choice between a rational or an emotional tone ultimately depends on the organization's individual situation, including its audience (consumer vs. trade), product life-cycle stage, and the type of service provided. Rational appeals are thought to work best in early product-life-cycle stages, whereas emotional ones are more effective at later stages.

A heated debate also exists about the relative merits of a competitive tone, such as the one used in **comparative advertising** (ads that specifically mention competitors). In our industry, this approach is often common with fast-food, airline, credit card, and car rental companies. Positioning is by its very nature competitive, but its competitive tone varies with the approach that is selected. The fifth positioning approach—against a specific competitor or competitors—is the most direct and extreme. Usually this is used by the number two or a lower-level company against the market leader or leaders (e.g., Visa vs. American Express).

Another component of tone is the strength of the message: How extreme or believable should the message be? You might think that the stronger the message, the more likely it will get people's attention and persuade them of the sponsor's arguments. This, however, is not always the case, depending on the positioning approach selected. The strength of an ad must be tempered with its believability.

3. **Message Format**. The next stage in developing the message idea is to select a **message format**. This is a broad creative approach that is used to communicate the message idea to the target audiences. Some of these approaches have become associated with certain major advertising agencies and key agency executives. A description of several better-recognized formats follows.

    a. *Testimonial*. A **testimonial** is an advertisement that uses people to endorse a product or service, either satisfied customers or celebrities.[11] This technique is used frequently in the hospitality and travel industry. Examples of **celebrity testimonials** include actors, Tim Allen for Travel Michigan and Liam Neeson for the Mandarin Oriental Hotel Group. Celebrities attract attention to the ads and make them stand out from competitive promotions. They also support the advertiser's claim if they are in some way associated with the service, e.g., Tiger Woods, the famous golfer, travels the world so he is highly believable when endorsing the American Express card. If the same celebrity appears in the ads of several organizations, however, each ad's effectiveness may be decreased.

Authority figures, such as presidents of the companies that sponsor the ads, often deliver very effective testimonials. This approach has been used several times in the hospitality and travel industry, e.g., Richard Branson for Virgin Atlantic, and Donald Trump and Steve Wynn for their hotels and casinos.

The third variety of testimonials uses actual customers, travel trade staff members, or actors who play the part of customers. Continuing characters are the final type of testimonials. Applications in our industry include Ronald McDonald for McDonald's, the gnome for Travelocity.com, and the Peabody Hotel ducks.

b. *Slice of Life*. The **slice-of-life** format is a type of commercial consisting of a dramatization of a real-life situation in which the product is tried and becomes the solution to a problem.[12] Some of the best examples in our industry are many of McDonald's commercials. The slice-of-life format is very popular because of its believability and close correlation to typical customer problems and concerns.

c. *Analogy, Association, and Symbolism*. This format uses analogies, association, or symbolism to communicate benefits to customers.

d. *Trick Photography or Exaggerated Situations*. This approach is most often used in television commercials and print advertisements. It employs photographic tricks, special effects, or exaggerated situations to emphasize or clarify the advertiser's message.

e. *Word Plays and Made-Up Phrases*. This format is used primarily with print (magazine and newspaper) media. The sponsor's approach is to get your attention and interest by using intriguing or humorous made-up phrases or word plays. Often these words or phrases appear in the ad headline, and they usually play against a photographic or other graphic element. Chick-fil-A had a great idea to convince more people to choose chicken over beef, when it introduced the *Eat Mor Chikin* cows. While the cows obviously could not spell very well, what they did manage to scrawl caught the attention of many people.

f. *HonestTwist*. The **honesttwist** format is where the sponsor first communicates its problem honestly (e.g., Avis' "When you're only No. 2"), and then twists (turns) the problem into an advantage (e.g., "You try harder. Or else."). Figure 15.2 shows Avis using this theme in advertising how its cars are designed for the physically challenged.

g. *Fear*. The **fear appeal** uses a negative emotional appeal to arouse or shock the customer into making a purchase or changing their attitude. This format is often used to sell insurance, traveler's checks, and socially acceptable causes (e.g., AIDS prevention, non-smoking,

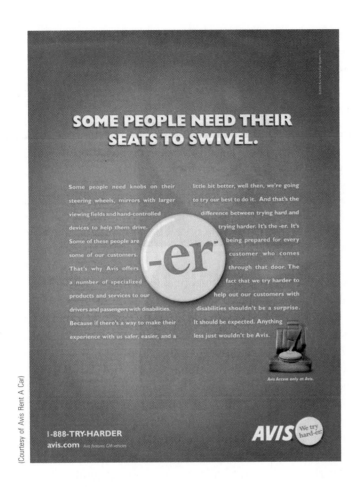

FIGURE 15.2 Avis tries harder to make its cars accessible for all.

anti-drug, and anti-drunk-driving messages). Experts have mixed feelings about the application of fear appeals. If the message is too strong, target customers may ignore it.

h. *Comparisons*. You have already read about this format. It involves direct comparisons between the sponsor and its competitors.

You should realize that some of these formats can be combined. The effectiveness of ads can also be heightened by using humor and emotional appeals.

Select Advertising Media (Step 6)

Selecting the medium or media for the advertisement is the next step in drawing up the plan. This is often an extremely difficult choice to make, because of the variety of media and **media vehicles** (specific newspapers, magazines, journals, directories, television and radio stations, websites) available. There are two main categories of media—print and broadcast. The **print media** contains all advertisements that appear in print, including those in newspapers, magazines, direct mail, and out-of-home advertising. **Broadcast media** are advertisements displayed by means of electronics; they encompass television (including cable), radio, video, and computer-generated graphic presentations. The **interactive media** include all the features of the Internet and mobile technologies.

Media Selection Procedure

Choosing the best media for advertisements is one of the most critical elements in the advertising plan. These selections must be based on the following seven considerations:

1. **Target Markets and Their Reading, Viewing, and Listening Habits**. Through marketing research, an organization should have established the media habits of chosen target markets. If potential customers live in defined metropolitan areas, then geographically specific media such as local newspapers, radio, television, direct marketing, and out-of-home media advertising may be preferable. In contrast, specialized travel trade journals may be the optimum mode of communications if the targets are travel trade intermediaries (trade advertising). Customers with special interests, such as golf, tennis, or scuba diving, might be reached most effectively through special-interest magazines.

2. **Positioning Approach, Promotional Goals, and Advertising Objectives**. The media and media vehicles selected must support the image that the organization wants to convey, its promotional goals, and its advertising objectives. For example, if an organization wants a luxury-oriented position, then upscale magazine advertising in publications such as *Travel + Leisure* may be the most appropriate. The promotional goal and associated advertising objective will determine the general suitability of each advertising media alternative. For example, television, considered the most persuasive of the media, may be selected if the goal is persuasion and the objective is to increase customer preference for the organization's services. Direct marketing may work better with an informative promotional goal and the objective of explaining the characteristics of a newly introduced service.

3. **Media Evaluation Criteria**. An organization should use a battery of criteria to judge the appropriateness of each media alternative relative to the promotional goal and advertising objective. These criteria may include one or more of the following eight factors:

    a. *Costs*. This represents the total campaign costs and the average cost per reader, viewer, or listener. Often the latter is measured on a **cost-per-thousand** (or **CPM**) basis.

    b. *Reach*. The **reach** of a medium is the number of potential customers who are exposed to a given advertisement at least once. The **circulation** of a newspaper or magazine (number of households or others who subscribe) is one measure of reach. Some of the print media have primary and secondary audiences (**pass-along rate** of circulation).

Most magazines, for example, are passed from the original subscriber or buyer to other persons, which results in additional reach.

c. *Frequency*. **Frequency** refers to the average number of times that potential customers are exposed to a given advertisement or advertising campaign. Some authors also use the word frequency to describe the number of times a specific medium can be used in a given time period.[13]

d. *Waste*. The **waste** factor represents the number of customers exposed to an advertisement who are not part of an organization's target markets. Newspapers, for example, are read by so many different types of people that significant waste circulation is often encountered.

e. *Lead Time and Flexibility*. **Lead time** refers to the space of time between the design of an ad and its actual appearance in the selected medium. Some media have long lead times (particularly magazines), whereas others have short ones (especially newspapers). The shorter is the lead time, the greater the media's flexibility (i.e., the ability to adjust the campaign if necessary to better appeal to customers' needs).

f. *Clutter and Dominance*. **Clutter** represents the number of ads in one newspaper or magazine issue, or one radio or television program.[14] In a more generic sense, the word is used to describe the large number of ads that customers are exposed to each day. **Dominance** means a sponsor's ability to dominate a particular medium at a specific time period. In a highly cluttered medium, this is usually not possible.

g. *Message Permanence*. The **permanence** of a message refers to its life span and its potential for repeated exposures to the same customers.[15] A billboard on a busy commuter route has a relatively long life span, and it may be noticed many times by the same commuters. Radio and television ads, on the other hand, have very short life spans—15 to 60 seconds.

h. *Persuasive Impact and Mood*. Some media and media vehicles have a greater **persuasive impact** than others (ability of advertisement to convince customers in accordance with the advertiser's objectives). Television, for example, with its use of many stimuli (audio and visual), often has a high persuasive impact. **Mood** is the added enhancement or feeling of excitement that a particular medium or vehicle gives to an ad.[16] Again, television, with the availability of sound, movement, and other visual stimuli, tends to create the most added excitement or mood.

4. **Relative Strengths and Weaknesses of Each Media Alternative**. Once an organization has selected the criteria from this list of eight, it should evaluate the relative merits of each media alternative. For example, an ad placed in a special-interest magazine (e.g., *Golf Digest*, *Gourmet*, or *Ski Magazine*) may have a smaller reach than if it appears in a major daily newspaper (e.g., *USA Today*, *Globe & Mail*, *Daily Telegraph* or *The Australian*).

5. **Creative Requirements**. The creative format selected and the specific way it will be used also influence the choice of media and vehicles. For example, most travel destination ads placed by DMOs require color and a visual presentation to have the greatest impact. Magazines, television, and brochures work best, whereas radio and newspaper ads do not generate the same excitement or mood.

6. **Competitive Media Placements**. Every organization must constantly keep one eye on its own marketing plan and the other eye on what its competitors are doing. Often the market leader has the largest advertising budget available and may try to dominate certain media. Other organizations are forced to respond with some level of presence in these media.

7. **Approximate Total Advertising Budget Available**. The tentative promotional budget allocated to advertising places a practical limit on the number of ads that can be run and the media that can be selected. Many small hospitality and travel organizations have limited budgets and must use the least expensive media and vehicles (e.g., newspapers and radio). Making the jump into television advertising is often one of the most difficult decisions for small- to medium-sized organizations.

Decide on Timing of Advertisements (Step 7)

At this point in planning advertising, both the media and media vehicles have been chosen. Another difficult decision must be made about when and how often to place the ads. Different scheduling approaches are available, and the choice among them is based primarily on customers' decision processes and the sponsor's advertising objectives. Before looking at the alternative approaches, it is important to realize that there are really two decisions—macro-scheduling and micro-scheduling.[17] Macro-scheduling means in which seasons or months to advertise, whereas micro-scheduling refers to specific times of the week and day. The three major scheduling approaches available are:[18,19]

1. **Intermittent**. Here ads are placed intermittently over a certain time period. The number of ads placed in each flight or wave may be level or uneven. Cruise lines might use this approach because they emphasize different cruising areas at certain times during the year (e.g., the Caribbean and Alaska).

2. **Concentrated**. Using this approach, ads are concentrated in a specific part of the planning period and are not run at other times. Resorts open for only one season and downhill ski areas tend to use this approach by concentrating their ads in the months leading up to their peak operating periods.

3. **Continuous**. With the third scheduling method, ads are spread continuously throughout the planning period. Hospitality and travel organizations that need a steady, year-round and week-to-week flow of customers, including hotels and restaurants, tend to use this approach.

Pre-test Advertisements (Step 8)

How does an organization know whether its advertising campaign will meet the advertising objectives? The answer is that it can never be 100-percent certain that ads will deliver the intended results, but there is a way of cutting the risk. **Pre-testing** uses marketing research techniques to find out whether advertisements communicate information to customers in the manner the sponsor intends. Although pre-testing can be put to many uses, it is most valuable in determining the effectiveness of the creative format and media selected.

Pre-tests serve three specific purposes: (1) testing *rough* ads before developing the finished versions, (2) testing *finished* ads before placing them in the media, and (3) deciding how often to use the individual ads initially in a campaign that has several different ones.[20] Many marketing research alternatives exist for pre-testing, including direct ratings or rankings (customers are shown an ad or ads and are asked to rate or rank them), and portfolio tests (customers are shown an ad or ads including others not from the sponsor and are asked to indicate which ads they remember). Another alternative is theater/laboratory tests (e.g., customers in a theatre are shown TV commercials and use electronic hand dials to express their emotions).[21] The choice of test should be based on the advertising objectives, which themselves are related to customers' buying decision process stages and the buying decision classification.

Prepare Final Advertising Plan and Budget (Step 9)

The pre-tests clear the way for preparing finished advertisements and finalizing the advertising plan and budget. Like the marketing plan itself, the written advertising plan must clearly state the objectives, research results, and assumptions that lead to choices, budget, and the implementation timetable. It must also outline the message strategy comprehensively. Detailed advertising costs will now be available and must be compared to the tentative advertising budget. This comparison may result in further modifications to the plan and to those for the other promotional mix elements.

Measure and Evaluate Advertising Success (Step 10)

Advertising planning does not end when the last page of the plan is written. It continues through the year. The success of individual ads and campaigns is carefully monitored and measured. Because campaigns often cost millions of dollars, they must be tracked carefully and continuously. Companies often pull campaigns, because of negative research findings and sales results, before their planned ending dates. Again, marketing research helps with these types of decisions.

Post-testing is a term commonly used for a variety of marketing research approaches to determine the effectiveness of ads after they have run. The choice of a post-test method is again based on the advertising objectives and the media used. The following criteria and measurements can be used, however:[22]

1. *Exposure Measures*—How many potential customers were exposed to the advertising?
2. *Processing Measures*—How did customers respond to the advertising?
3. *Communication Effects Measures*—Did customers react in the way intended by the advertising objectives?
4. *Target-Audience-Action Measures*—Did target customers take the actions that the spnsor wanted?
5. *Sales or Market-Share Measures*—Did the sponsor achieve the sales or market share that we desired?
6. *Profit Measures*—Did the sponsor make the profit it wanted to?

There are also many specific marketing research and other measurement techniques that can be used for each of these six measurements. **Gross rating points (GRP)** is one useful exposure measure. It is a measure of the total amount of the advertising exposures produced by a specific media vehicle or a media schedule during a specific period of time. It is expressed in terms of the rating of a specific media vehicle (if only one is being used) or the sum of all the ratings of the vehicles included in a media schedule. It includes any audience duplication and is equal to the reach of a media schedule multiplied by the average frequency of the schedule.[23] Recall tests are an example of a processing measure in which customers' ability to remember advertising is evaluated.

Advertising Media Alternatives

You already know about the criteria for selecting media, but we still must take a detailed look at each option. The five major media alternatives are:

- Print media
- Broadcast media
- Out-of-home media
- Direct marketing media
- Interactive media

Print Media

Newspapers

Newspapers are the most popular medium for advertising, based on the total volume of spending. Some organizations in the hospitality and travel industry, particularly airlines, make heavy use of newspaper advertising. In 2007, U.S. advertisers spent $42.1 billion on newspaper advertising; this was around 18 percent of total advertising expenditures.[24] This is not surprising since 77 percent of Americans read a newspaper over the course of one week.[25]

Advantages

a. *High Reach*. Newspapers reach a very high percentage of the population. For example, the Newspaper Association of America estimates that 77 percent of all adults in the U.S. are reached in a given week by newspapers in print and website formats. Three-quarters of Canadians aged 18+ read a printed copy of a daily newspaper once a week. They are read by people both sexes, all ages, all income and occupational groups, and all ethnic segments. Some major dailies are read by more than a million persons each day (Figure 15.3). The total paid circulation of daily newspapers in the U.S. in 2007 was 50.7 million, and Sunday newspapers had total circulation of 51.2 million.[26] There are 99 daily newspapers in Canada, with an average total daily paid circulation of 4.674 million in 2007.[27]

b. *High Geographic Concentration*. Newspapers allow advertisers to be highly selective concerning the geographic markets they reach. Most major cities are served by at least one major daily. In 2008, the Newspaper Association of America (NAA) stated that it represented 2,000 newspapers in the United States and Canada. There were 1,349 daily newspapers in the United States in 2005 with circulations of 100,000 or less, most of which served specific local areas. There were 103 daily newspapers with circulations of 100,001 and more. Only 34 newspapers had circulation rates of over 250,000 per day.[28] For organizations that use geography as part of their segmentation approach, newspapers should be considered for media placements. Most restaurants, for

Image copyright Pedro Tavares, 2008. Used under license from Shutterstock.com

FIGURE 15.3
Newspapers have high reach and good frequency for advertisers.

example, draw customers mainly from local markets, and they often find newspapers to be a very effective medium.

c. *Good Frequency*. Most newspapers are issued daily, with many Sunday newspapers as well. Therefore, newspapers are a good medium for messages that must be repeated several times to achieve the highest impact (e.g., an airline announcing a new route from a particular city).

d. *Tangibility*. Newspapers are tangible. They allow readers to clip and save advertisements, coupons, or other offers and can also be easily shown or given to other people. They are useful when customers are being offered a sales promotion coupon, or in cases where they must provide further information by completing an address coupon.

e. *Short Lead Times*. Finished ads can be placed in newspapers on very short notice. Although a great deal depends on the ad itself and the amount of original artwork needed, a newspaper ad can be produced and published in as little as a few days. They are good, therefore, in announcing specials, price changes, or other updated information.

f. *Relatively Low Cost*. Compared with many of the other major media alternatives, newspapers are a relatively low-cost medium. For this reason, newspaper advertising is popular among small- and medium-sized organizations.

g. *Ability to Communicate Detailed Information*. Newspaper advertisements can convey more detailed information to potential customers than can many of the other media alternatives (i.e., television, radio, and billboards). Some larger advertisers convey even more information, either themselves or in cooperation with selected partners, by using **freestanding inserts (FSIs)**. These are separate, preprinted, and multi-page sections that fit into a daily or Sunday edition.

h. *Ability to Place in Most Appropriate Location*. Most newspapers contain several specialized sections, which allow advertisers to choose the one that is most appropriate to their target markets. Many Sunday editions have travel sections—excellent locations for the ads of many organizations in our industry. Some newspapers have daily or once-a-week dining and entertainment sections, which are ideal for restaurant and attraction advertisers. Companies targeting the business traveler usually find the business section the most appropriate.

i. *Ability to Schedule to Exploit Day-of-Week Factors*. Advertising some hospitality and travel services is more effective on certain days of the week than on others. For example, advertising attractions, events, and dining-out facilities tends to produce more results on Thursdays and Fridays than it does on Mondays and Tuesdays. Advertisers have complete flexibility to choose the best days to run their ads.

Disadvantages

a. *High Waste Factor and Inability to Target*. Newspapers reach so many people that an organization using a segmented strategy will encounter a high waste factor. Organizations that use segmentation criteria other than geographic (e.g., demographic or psychographic) find that newspapers are a poor medium for pinpointing target markets.

b. *Limitations on Creative Format*. Other media, especially television, allow the advertiser greater flexibility in choice of format. For example, newspapers do not allow for the most effective use of the slice-of-life format, nor can humor or other emotions be used as effectively. The lack of audio communications and the inability to show movement are shortcomings that newspapers share with magazines. There is no way to talk person-to-person in either of these two print media.

c. *Relatively Poor Reproduction Quality*. Newspapers have relatively poor reproduction qualities when compared to other (visual) media alternatives. They lack the sharpness and range of color found in magazine, television, and even billboard advertising, although newspaper printing technology is advancing rapidly.

d. *Clutter*. Newspaper advertising is so popular that a single advertiser faces stiff competition for the reader's attention each day. Many ads fill every newspaper issue, and only the largest ones stand out. Small advertisements tend to get lost.

e. *Short Life Span*. Newspapers are usually read quickly, and they are tossed away just as quickly. Thus, the ads that they contain have a very short time to get the reader's attention. Given the creative limitations, this places an even greater premium on concepts that really stand out from those of competitors. Newspapers also do not have as high a (life-extending) pass-along rate as do magazines.

f. *High Cost of National Coverage*. Running a national advertising campaign in newspapers can cost more than network television commercials. Although the per-newspaper expense is quite reasonable, there are so many newspapers that the total bill is very high.

Now many newspapers have special editions on the Web and millions of people are exposed to these each day. In the U.S. in the third quarter of 2008, an average of 68.3 million people per month visited online newspaper websites.[29]

Magazines

According to the National Directory of Magazines, 19,532 different magazines (mainly consumer) were published in 2007 in the U.S.[30] In 2007, the annual combined paid circulation of all magazines in the U.S. was 369.8 million.[31] A total of $13.8 billion was spent on magazine advertising in 2007 in the U.S., representing 4.8 percent of all advertising expenditures.[32]

Many hospitality and travel organizations, especially destination areas, hotels and resorts, and airlines, invest heavily in magazine advertising. Some of its key attractions are its specialized readership groups, high reproduction qualities, and general prestige. The number of magazines being published has increased rapidly in recent decades. Magazines run the gamut from major national consumer publications such as *National Geographic*, with a worldwide monthly circulation of 8.5 million copies,[33] to specialized travel trade intermediary periodicals such as *Travel Weekly* and *Travel Trade*, with circulations of less than 100,000.

Because they are a print medium, magazines have some of the same advantages and disadvantages as newspapers. In some respects, such as in higher reproduction quality and greater targeting ability, they are superior to newspapers. However, they have lower reach and frequency, and longer lead times, than newspapers.

Advantages

a. *Tangibility*. Like newspapers, magazines are tangible and can be saved easily. Ads and coupons can be clipped and kept, or they can be passed along to others.

b. *High Audience Selectivity*. Magazines lack the high reach and frequency of newspapers, but they offer the advertiser more selective audiences. They have less waste circulation and are very appropriate for organizations with segmented marketing strategies. Many magazines provide extensive demographic profiles of their subscribers, which gives advertisers the ability to select the magazines with reader characteristics most similar to their target markets.

   Magazines are also specialized by interest area. For example, there are several business-oriented magazines, such as *Business Week*, *Fortune*, and *Forbes*, for organizations that want to reach business travelers. There are consumer travel publications, including *Travel + Leisure*, *Endless Vacation*, *National Geographic Traveler*, and *Condé Nast Traveler*, that supply information to audiences primed for vacations. Many magazines appeal to enthusiasts of specific sports, hobbies, and other leisure-time pursuits, such as *Field & Stream*, *Golf Digest*, *Golf Magazine*, *Ski*, and *Tennis*. These are popular with organizations that cater specifically to these interest groups. There are also lifestyle and food and wine magazine that relate to hospitality and tourism, including *Southern Living*, *Bon Appétit*, *Gourmet*, and *Food & Wine*. Finally, there are many trade magazines that serve travel trade intermediaries.

c. *Good Reproduction Quality*. The reproduction quality of magazines is much better than it is with newspapers. Many magazine ads are extremely attractive, with sharp and varied colors. Colors are a very important stimulus factor to most hospitality and travel advertisers. Whether it is the deep blues of the Caribbean water, the stark grays of an impressive mountain range, or the deep browns of a well-seared steak, color is an especially effective communicator in our industry.

It has a great impact on creating the intended perception of the destination or service.

d.   *Long Life Span and Good Pass-Along Rate.* Magazines are read in a much more leisurely way than newspapers are. They are kept around the home or office longer, and they tend to be read intermittently over a period of days, rather than in a few minutes. You probably are like many others of us who are reluctant to throw them out because of their relatively high initial purchase price. Magazines are also passed along more frequently than newspapers to relatives, friends, and associates, giving them a secondary circulation. This added readership extends a magazine's life span and its reach. For example, *Travel Weekly UK* estimates that every copy is read by five people.[34]

The result of these factors is that a magazine ad has more time to be noticed, read, and absorbed. If the magazine is reread, more than one exposure may result.

e.   *Prestige and Credibility.* Unlike newspapers, magazines offer prestige because of their higher initial purchase price, reproduction quality, and, in some cases, the nature of their contents and editorial coverage. Customers also view their contents as being more believable than those communicated by other media, especially television. Advertisers that want to create a prestigious image, and to appeal to upscale or affluent customers, find that magazines are a particularly effective medium. For example, *Travel + Leisure* has been published for many years and its contents are highly respected and credible. It is considered an authority in the travel field. In addition to a large circulation of just under one million, the magazine's subscribers have high household incomes at $103,182 in 2008.[35] Advertisers in *Travel + Leisure* find that this prestige and credibility rubs off on their messages.

f.   *Ability to Communicate Detailed Information.* Like newspapers, magazines are good at transmitting more detailed information about the service. They are, therefore, more effective than certain other media (e.g., television, radio, out-of-home advertising) in situations where customers require more data (e.g., in extensive problem-solving, high-involvement purchases) (Figure 15.4).

Although magazines have these six compelling strengths, they are not the best medium for all hospitality and travel organizations. They are better suited for high-ticket items and extensive problem solvers—in situations where the purchase decision is protracted. Magazine advertising is not as persuasive nor does it have the same sense of urgency as certain other media, especially television. For these reasons, magazines are seldom used by fast-food companies, who prefer the greater persuasive impact and urgency of television.

As with newspapers, many magazines now have online versions. Figure 15.5 shows the website for *Travel + Leisure.* Since this magazine is published by the American Express company, it has the added advantage of having access to its 17 million card members.

FIGURE 15.4
Magazines are often read at leisure, so they can communicate detailed information.

Image copyright Galina Barskaya, 2008. Used under license from Shutterstock.com

FIGURE 15.5 *The online version of* Travel + Leisure *shows how the Internet is expanding the reach and appeal of travel magazines.*

Courtesy of Travel + Leisure magazine, www.travelandleisure.com

Disadvantages

a. *Limitations on Creative Format.* Although magazines can communicate emotionally oriented messages better than newspapers can, they do the same relatively poor job with the slice-of-life format and the use of humor. Again, the lack of an audio message and movement definitely limits the creative approaches that are feasible.

b. *Clutter*. Magazines suffer from the same clutter problem as do newspapers, although the problem is perhaps not quite as severe. Advertising in this medium is so popular that smaller ads may not be noticed.

c. *Low Reach*. Magazines have much more specialized audiences than do newspapers, and they lack their broad reach. Advertisers whose services and products have very widespread appeal, such as fast-food companies, find that the appeal of magazines is too fragmented for their purposes.

d. *Low Frequency*. Most magazines are published monthly, therefore, magazine advertisements have much lower frequencies than television, radio, and newspaper ads. These other media are more appropriate for messages that require greater repetition (e.g., special offers) and in cases where the customer's decision process is short (e.g., routine problem-solving choices such as which fast-food outlet to visit).

e. *Long Lead Times*. Newspapers ads can be developed and placed in a matter of days. For magazine ads, it is often several months. It takes much longer to prepare magazine ads, and the closing dates for placement are often two or more months before the magazine is published. Again, this means that magazine ads are better suited for higher-ticket purchases (e.g., cruises and other vacation/holiday packages) and for services with distinct seasonal business patterns.

f. *Relatively Expensive*. Magazine advertising is significantly more expensive than newspaper ads. In a few instances, the cost can even exceed that of prime-time television commercials. For example, according to the rate card for *Travel + Leisure* in early 2009, a full-page, four-color advertisement cost $106,395 for a one-time insertion.[36]

g. *Difficulties in Geographic Targeting*. Magazine readers are geographically dispersed, and this creates problems for organizations that want to target specific regions and cities. Other media alternatives offer the advertiser a greater ability to use geographic segmentation.

h. **Inability to Schedule to Exploit Day-of-Week Factors**. Although some magazines are published weekly, most are issued monthly. Because they are not available daily—like newspapers, radio, and television are—their advertisements cannot take advantage of day-of-week opportunities.

Yellow Pages, Directories, and Other Printed Media

Several other printed media can also be used, including the Yellow Pages and specialized directories (e.g., AAA tour books and the *Hotel & Travel Index*). Yellow Pages advertising in the U.S. is significant at $12.3 billion in local Yellow Pages advertising in 2007. According to the Yellow Pages Association, 49 percent of U.S. adults refer to the Yellow Pages at least one per week.[37] The specialized directories include automobile club member books (such as the American Automobile Association), the *Hotel & Travel Index*, the *Official Hotel Guide Worldwide*, *M&C Official Meeting Facilities Guide*, *Specialty Travel Index*, and others. Like newspapers and magazines, these traditionally printed materials all now have online versions, and offer advertisers the opportunity to promote through them on the Web.

Broadcast Media

Radio

As is true with television, radio advertising can be placed nationally with a network or with local stations. However, unlike television, most radio advertising is carried on local rather than network stations. Radio advertisers also have the option of buying **spots**, or programs broadcast by the networks and local stations. Spot advertising is done between programs, whereas program sponsorship means that ads are aired on a specific program.

In 2007, advertisers in the U.S. spent just over $19 billion on radio advertising, representing 6.8 percent of total advertising expenditures.[38] Arbitron estimated that in late 2008, 234 million people in the U.S. of 12 and older listened to the radio over the course of a typical week. They found that 92 percent of people listened to the radio at least once per week.[39]

One of the major strengths of radio advertising, besides its reasonable cost, is its ability to target specific listening audiences based on the program format. Each format attracts certain specific groups of people. Following are the most popular radio formats based on station counts in the United States:[40]

1. Country
2. News, talk, information
3. Adult contemporary (AC)
4. Pop contemporary hit radio
5. Classic rock
6. Rhythmic contemporary hit radio
7. Urban contemporary
8. Oldies
9. Hot AC (adult contemporary)
10. Urban AC (adult contemporary)
11. Mexican regional
12. Alternative
13. Active rock
14. Contemporary Christian
15. All sports
16. Classical
17. Album oriented rock (AOR)
18. Talk personality
19. Spanish contemporary
20. New AC/smooth jazz

Advantages

a. *Relatively Low Cost.* Radio is one of the most affordable mediums for all sizes of organizations. It has one of the lowest cost-per-thousand (CPM) ratios among all the media alternatives.

b. *Audience Selectivity.* Radio offers a segmented audience for advertisers, according to program format. It is especially effective for organizations that target teenagers and young adults, because they make up most of the listeners of contemporary programs (Figure 15.6). Because radio stations serve distinct local areas, geographic segmentation is also possible. Most radio stations cover smaller geographic areas than their counterparts in television, which allows even greater precision in geographic targeting.

c. *High Frequency.* Advertisements on radio can be repeated more frequently than they can in almost any of the other media alternatives. Therefore, although radio ads do not have as high a reach as television ads, this is compensated for by the larger number of exposures per listener.

d. *Short Lead Times.* Radio advertisements can be produced on very short notice, often in a few days. The advertiser simply gives the radio station a script for the commercial or a prerecorded message.

e. *Ability to Schedule to Exploit Day-of-Week and Time-of-Day Factors.* Radio advertising has great timing flexibility, which allows sponsors to take full advantage of both day-of-week and time-of-day factors. For example, restaurants can air commercials just before major meal periods and whet listeners' appetites. Attractions can push special weekend admission discounts, and car rental firms can hype weekend rate deals.

Radio advertising seems best suited for advertisers of services and products that require low-involvement decisions (i.e., routine

FIGURE 15.6 Podcasts are now another way to get audio messages out to the markets.

problem solving). These items seem to benefit most from the repetition that radio provides. Radio is not the ideal medium for communicating detailed information, or for services and destinations that benefit from a visual presentation.

Disadvantages

a. *No Visual Communications*. All other media alternatives provide visual information to potential customers. Radio does not. This is a major shortcoming for marketing certain hospitality and travel services, including destination areas and many types of attractions. Some of the important stimuli, such as color and movement, are not present on radio, which makes it more difficult to create a desired image.

b. *Inability to Transmit Complex Messages and Detailed Information*. Radio is not a good medium for communicating complex messages and detailed information. Therefore, it is not very effective in advertising relatively expensive (high-involvement) services, such as cruise and vacation/holiday packages.

c. *Short Life Span*. The life span of a radio commercial is one minute or less. If only heard once, a radio ad can easily be forgotten. To be noticed, radio ads usually require considerable repetition.

d. *Clutter*. Although the number of commercials varies from station to station, and by program format, radio is generally a fairly cluttered medium. Therefore, it shares this disadvantage with both newspapers and magazines.

e. *Shared Attention*. Another hazard of radio advertising is that the radio often is not the main focus of the listener's attention. It may share the attention with some other activity (e.g., driving, doing homework, or cooking). Because of this, an advertiser's message can easily go unnoticed.

Television

There is no doubt today that television is the most persuasive media alternative. The TV Advertising Bureau reported that in 2006, 66.5 percent of U.S. adults considered television to be the most persuasive of the major advertising media.[41] It appeals to all the senses, except smell. Television also allows advertisers to use all possible creative formats, including slice of life. For companies such as fast-food chains that are trying to reach national markets, television advertising seems the favored alternative.

As is true with radio, television advertisers can buy commercial time from local stations or, in the United States, from the English-language broadcast networks (including ABC, CBS, NBC, FOX, and PBS). Each network has a stable of local station affiliates to which they supply programs. These affiliates give the network almost complete national coverage. Ads placed with the networks appear within their programs and are, therefore, broadcast throughout the country. Again, sponsors can purchase spots (between programs) or advertise within programs.

In the United States, television viewing audiences are divided geographically into 210 **designated market areas (DMAs)**. The three largest of these DMAs are New York (7,366,950 TV households), Los Angeles (5,611,110), and Chicago (3,455,020).[42] These local viewing areas are larger than those served by radio stations, and they do not allow for the same precision in geographic targeting.

Advantages

a. *Potentially High Reach*. According to the Television Bureau of Advertising, 98.9 percent of U.S. households—115.76 million households—owned at least one television set in 2009.[43] In March 2007, Nielsen Media Research announced that U.S. households were reached by a record high number of 118.6 TV channels, and on average each TV household had 2.8 television sets.[44] Network commercials have the potential of very high reach, to the millions of households and viewers. Although North Americans spend many hours watching TV every week, the likelihood of everyone seeing a one-time spot commercial is low. Therefore, reach is maximized by selecting many top-viewing market areas and repeating commercials several times in prime time over a number of weeks. In 2007, 85 percent of TV households in the U.S. had cable.[45] Advertising on cable television was at $20.6 billion and represented 7.4 percent of the total media advertising in the United States in 2005. Broadcast television advertising spending totaled $44.5 billion or 15.9 percent of total advertising expenditures. Together, broadcast and cable television advertising accounted for 23.3 per cent of all media advertising in 2005.[46]

b. *High Persuasive Impact*. Television commercials can be highly persuasive because of their ability to employ all the creative formats and to make full use of emotions and humor to get viewers' attention and give added mood. Television is also an excellent medium to demonstrate services and products (Figure 15.7).

c. *Availability of Uniform National Coverage*. Television is very popular with major national companies, such as McDonald's, Subway, and Applebee's, because they can conveniently purchase national coverage. They are almost guaranteed that commercials will be uniformly broadcast at the same time (according to time zone) throughout the country. This is definitely a lucrative feature for organizations with fairly standardized services and broad public appeal (the combiners you learned about in Chapter 8).

d. *Ability to Schedule to Exploit Day-of-Week and Time-of-Day Factors*. Television advertisements can be scheduled for different parts of the day and for certain days of the week. They share this advantage with radio ads.

FIGURE 15.7
Television has a high persuasive impact on people.

Image copyright Milevski Petar, 2008. Used under license from Shutterstock.com

e. *Some Geographic and Demographic Selectivity.* Television allows the segmenter some possibility of geographic and demographic targeting based on their choice of local stations and DMAs, and the program format. Other media, however, generally offer equivalent or even superior targeting possibilities.

Disadvantages

a. *High Total Cost.* Although the cost-per-thousand ratio for television advertising can be quite reasonable, the absolute minimum that must be spent precludes many small and medium-sized businesses from using it. There are two significant cost items to be considered in television advertising—the cost of producing commercials and the cost of buying the time from the networks or local stations. Although production costs vary widely, they can be very significant. According to the *2007 Television Production Cost Survey* conducted by the Association of American Advertising Agencies (AAAA), the average cost of a 30-second national television spot was $361,000 in 2007.[47] To this must be added the cost of placing them on a TV station.

b. *Short Life Span.* Television commercials, like those on radio, are very impermanent—they last only 60 seconds or less. They must be repeated several times to be effective, which increases the advertiser's costs significantly.

c. *Inability to Transmit Detailed Information.* Because of their short duration, television advertisements are not effective in communicating detailed information to potential customers. Other media alternatives, especially direct marketing, magazines, and newspapers, do a much better job.

d. *Clutter*. Television is a highly cluttered medium, with dozens of ads each hour competing for the viewer's attention. Many people are so inundated with TV commercials that they use commercial breaks to switch channels or leave the room to do something else. A television commercial must be very, very good to break through the high clutter level.

e. *Relatively High Waste Factor*. Television is not a highly precise medium for segmenters. Therefore, it leads to relatively high waste.

Out-of-Home Media

There are four major product categories within out-of-home advertising: (1) billboards (64%), (2) alternative outdoor (17%), (3) transit (12%), and (4) street furniture (7%). The street furniture category includes bus shelters, convenience stores, shopping malls, urban furniture, and kiosks. Transit advertising consists of buses, airports, subway and rail, truck sides, taxi displays, and wrapped vehicles. The alternative outdoor includes arenas and stadiums, digital media, and various interior and exterior places not included in the street and transit categories.[48] In 2007, advertisers in the United States spent $7.2 billion on out-of-home advertising, which was 2.6 percent of the total advertising expenditures that year.[49]

Outdoor advertising plays an important role in the hospitality and travel industry partly because of the need to inform and direct travelers to unfamiliar places. In the United States in 2007, airlines, hotels, car rentals, and travel was the fifth and restaurants were the seventh among the top 10 outdoor advertiser groups. McDonald's Restaurants was the leading brand in terms of total outdoor advertising expenditures that year.[50]

Advantages

a. *High Reach and Good Frequency*. Although the average person's exposure to an out-of-home ad is usually very short, there is the potential of high reach and frequency. Everyone who drives past a billboard is exposed to it (reach). If the billboard is located on a route that a person uses once a day, for example, several exposures occur in a month (frequency).

b. *Geographic Selectivity*. The locations of out-of-home advertising can be matched almost exactly to the sponsor's geographic target markets. For example, restaurants that serve a local market can place billboards and other signs within that area. Business travelers can be targeted with advertising at airports.

c. *Relatively Uncluttered*. Compared with other media alternatives, especially television and radio, an out-of-home ad does not usually suffer from as high a clutter level. Although it seems that certain stretches of highway are littered with billboards and other signs, the number of advertising messages is generally fewer than the customer is exposed to in other media.

FIGURE 15.8 The large size of outdoor advertisements can give added impact to the message.

d. *Long Life Span*. Out-of-home advertising is more permanent than most of the alternative media. Many signs are indeed permanent, or are at least intended to last for several years. Poster panels (billboards) are reserved by the month. Painted bulletins are either permanent, or are moved to other locations periodically.

e. *Large Size*. One visual stimuli that can have a positive impact on potential customers is the size of the advertisement. For example, full-page newspaper and magazine ads have a greater impact than smaller ones do. Outdoor signs can be very large, and their imposing size can be enough to catch the passerby's attention (Figure 15.8).

The real power of most out-of-home advertising is its ability to communicate short, but memorable messages. This advertising is especially effective with services that involve routine and limited problem solving, such as fast food, other restaurant, and hotel selection decisions.

Disadvantages

a. *High Waste Factor and Inability to Target*. Although out-of-home advertising can be geographically targeted, it does not permit any other form of segmentation. Like those in newspapers, outdoor messages are seen by all types of people, and a high waste factor results for segmenters that use criteria other than geography. Out-of-home advertising is not as highly targeted a medium as others, particularly magazines, direct marketing, and radio.

b. *Relatively Long Lead Times*. Most billboards and signs take a relatively long time to design, print or paint, and place. This may be several weeks or months. In addition, there is an undersupply of locations for billboards and painted bulletins, which means that advertisers may have to wait to rent their chosen locations.

c. *Inability to Transmit Complex Messages or Detailed Information.* Only a handful of words can be communicated effectively through an out-of-home advertisement. Symbols often have to take the place of words, and messages must be short and to the point. Artwork must have strong visual appeal and be eye-catching. Therefore, it is not a suitable medium for high-involvement (extensive problem solving) purchases.

d. *Not Prestigious.* Billboards and bulletins are not as prestigious a form of advertising as magazines and television. Many people consider highway and transit advertising to be unaesthetic and feel that it spoils the natural character of the surroundings. In fact, certain forms of outdoor advertising are highly restricted or even illegal in some areas.

e. *Limitations on Creative Format.* Out-of-home advertising does not allow the advertiser to use all the creative formats available. It is not particularly effective for humor or other emotional appeals or for the slice-of-life format. Many outdoor ads are, in fact, purely informative, rather than persuasive (i.e., they support other media advertising). However, this medium is becoming increasing innovative and creative.

f. *Inability to Schedule to Exploit Day-of-Week and Time-of-Day Factors.* With the exception of some signs that can be changed frequently, out-of-home advertisements usually cannot take advantage of day-of-week and time-of-day opportunities. They share this limitation with magazine advertising.

Direct Marketing Media

Direct mail advertising is one element of a broader category of techniques commonly referred to as **direct marketing** or **direct-response marketing**. The *direct* part of direct marketing means that no intermediaries are used. The producer of the services or products promotes directly to customers, takes their orders or reservations, and distributes the services or products directly. The major elements of direct marketing are direct mail and telemarketing (sales made over the telephone). Other forms of direct marketing include responses generated by television (via **infomercials** and cable programs), radio, and the Web. The effectiveness of direct marketing is increasing through a greater emphasis on **database marketing**. The American Marketing Association defines database marketing as an approach by which computer database technologies are harnessed to design, create, and manage customer data lists containing information about each customer's characteristics and history of interactions with the company. The lists are used as needed for locating, selecting, targeting, servicing, and establishing relationships with customers in order to enhance the long-term value of these customers to the company.[51] The growing sophistication of database marketing, principally through computer technology, is enhancing the advantages of direct mail advertising.

Direct mail represents a large portion of the advertising expenditures of marketers in the United States. In 2007, $60.2 billion was spent on direct-mail advertising, which was 21.5 percent of the total advertising expenditures.[52] This was more than was spent on newspaper and broadcast television advertising.

The major direct marketing technique used in the hospitality and travel industry is direct mail advertising. Direct mail shares many of the same characteristics as newspapers and magazines, as it is usually in print format.

Advantages

a. *Audience Selectivity*. Direct mail advertising is the most selective medium of all, because it allows segmenters to pinpoint their target markets with the smallest amount of waste. This is one of the reasons for its great popularity in the hospitality and travel industry. It is especially effective with geographic segmentation and in cases where potential customers can be divided into distinctive groups such as travel agents, convention/meeting planners, or skiers, for example. The most powerful source of direct-mail mailing lists is an organization's own in-house records of past customers and inquirers. Many specialized lists can also be acquired from other organizations (e.g., membership directories) or from commercial mailing list brokers. These companies' lists can be rented for a fee and can be found in a directory published by Standard Rate & Data Service Inc.[53]

b. *Highly Flexible*. All the other media alternatives involve physical and time constraints that are not as severe in direct mail advertising. All ad placements must be made before media companies' deadlines, for example. Print and outdoor advertisements have to conform to size restrictions, and broadcast ads have very definite time limitations. Although physically controlled by postal regulations, direct mail ads give the advertiser greater freedom and flexibility in designing and placing them (Figure 15.9).

c. *Relatively Uncluttered*. Direct mail is a relatively uncluttered medium when compared to the other advertising alternatives. Each direct mail piece is physically separated and thus isolated from others, whereas there are many ads within most newspapers and magazines. Clutter does occur, however, when customers receive excessively large quantities of direct mail ads.

d. *High Level of Personalization*. All other media, with the exception of interactive media, are impersonal and do not communicate with customers effectively on a one-on-one basis. However, direct mail gives advertisers a great opportunity for more personalized communication. This is a trademark of the most effective direct mailing pieces (as it is of good mail questionnaire surveys). The more personalized the direct mail piece (e.g., postage stamp on envelope, hand-signed letter, and use of person's name in salutation—"Dear Ms. Brown," for example), the more likely it is to be opened and read.

FIGURE 15.9 Direct mail comes in all shapes and sizes.

e. *Ability to Measure Response*. It is easy to measure the impact of direct mail advertising. The sender knows exactly how many pieces were mailed (thus, the number of exposures) and can monitor the responses in a variety of ways (e.g., number of response/request cards mailed back, number of coupons redeemed). With other media, especially television and radio, it is more difficult to evaluate advertising response.

A growing portion of the advertising in the hospitality and travel industry is of the direct-response variety. The objective of these direct-response advertisements is usually to develop databases or mailing lists of inquiries. Once these inquiries have been generated—through devices such as toll-free numbers or mail-in coupon cards—the promoter fulfills the inquiry, often by mailing out collateral materials such as visitor guides, brochures, maps, or videos.

f. *Tangibility*. Direct mail gives customers something tangible to touch, feel, save, or pass on to others. In this sense, it is similar to newspaper and magazine ads.

g. *Low Minimum Cost*. Although direct mail is generally considered to be a relatively high-cost medium on a cost-per-thousand (CPM) basis, it has a relatively low minimum cost. There are certain minimum charges associated with newspaper, magazine, television, radio, and out-of-home advertising. Sometimes these minimum rates are too high for smaller organizations. Direct mailing is affordable for organizations of all sizes.

h. *Short Lead Times*. Direct mail ads reach potential customers a few days after they are mailed. The lead time is short once the sender has assembled the mailing list and prepared the mailing.

INTERNET MARKETING

Saving on Snail Mail with Digital Brochures

- Many destination marketing organizations, hotels, and tour operators have traditionally printed color brochures each year. Printing and mailing costs were high, and it was impossible to update these materials once they were sent out.
- Having the brochures available for downloading in PDF format is one of the solutions that the Internet has brought. This gives the customer "instant delivery" by downloading the materials they want, and saves on mailing costs too.
- Digital publishing is another possibility for saving on expensive mailing and printing costs. One of the companies providing this service is Nxtbook Media and they have developed digital visitor guides for several destinations in the United States, including California, Chicago, Omaha, New Orleans, and Scottsdale.
- Another company providing these services is EBXP, based in the United Kingdom. They have a long list of clients including Contiki, French Tourism, German Tourist Board, Norwegian Tourist Board, Star Alliance, Thai Airways, Thomson Worldwide (TUI), Tourism Ireland, and VisitBritain.
- On the website, the visitor just clicks and the pages flip over just as with a normal leaflet or magazine.
- For the customer, one of the benefits is the instant availability of the brochures or visitor guides; there is no need to order and wait for the materials in the mail. The interactivity involved is another customer benefit.

Sources: Nxtbook Media, EBXP, and destination websites. (2008). **http://www. nxtbook.com/, http://www.ebxp.com/, http://www.visitcalifornia.com/, http://www. choosechicago.com/, http://www.visitomaha.com/, http://www.scottsdalecvb.com/, http://www.neworleanscvb.com/**

Student Questions

1. What are the benefits to destinations, hotels and resorts, and tour operators in using digital brochures compared to traditional printed brochures?
2. What are the advantages to customers in having (1) PDFs of brochures or visitor guides, and (2) digital brochures or visitor guides?
3. Do you think this trend toward Internet distribution of these materials will grow in the future? Why or why not?
4. Do you think that some people will still want to get printed copies of brochures and visitor guides? Why or why not? What types of people or in what situations do you feel customers may want to have the printed copies?

Disadvantages

a. *Junk Mail Syndrome and High Discard Rate*. *Junk mail* is a term we tend to use for mass-produced direct mail advertisements, the type that arrive addressed to "Dear Occupant" or "Resident." People are often irritated by the amount of this type of mail they receive and junk (discard) it without opening or reading it. Unfortunately, this negativism spills over to all direct mail advertisements, meaning that ads must be highly personalized or unique to avoid being thrown away immediately. The response rates of direct mail are typically 5 percent or lower.

b. *Relatively High Total Cost*. Although the minimum cost can be low, direct mail is a relatively expensive medium on a cost-per-thousand (CPM) basis. To avoid the look of junk mail, it is often necessary to use first-class postage. At current postal rates in the United States, this means that, to mail 1,000 pieces, a company must incur a minimum CPM of $420 (C$520 by Canada Post) plus the cost of the mailing piece, list rental (if appropriate), and other expenses associated with the mailing. Even at bulk mail rates, the CPM is significantly higher than it is in the mass media, especially television.

c. *Limitations on Creative Format*. Although direct mail has fewer physical limitations than newspaper and magazine advertising, it is still only a visual medium. The slice-of-life format cannot be used, nor can emotional or humorous approaches be employed effectively.

Interactive Media (Online Marketing)

The interactive media are mainly those provided through the **Internet** and mobile technologies. They include the **Web**, e-mail, interactive television, mobile phones, PDAs, and other mobile technologies. Most of these media use some combination of computers, wireless technologies, telephone/cable lines, and televisions. They are a component of **interactive advertising**, which includes all forms of online, wireless, and interactive television advertising including **banners**, sponsorships, e-mail, keyword searches, referrals, slotting fees, classified ads, and interactive television commercials.[54]

The interactive media is one of the most rapidly growing types of advertising. Estimates of the total amount spent vary. One source estimated that U.S. advertisers spent $10.5 billion on Internet advertising in 2007,[55] while another placed it at $11.3 billion.[56]

Advantages

a. *Cost Effectiveness*. These media are relatively inexpensive when compared with the other traditional advertising media.

b. *Global Reach*. By having a presence on the Web, a hospitality and travel organization has the potential of instantly reaching around the world. In June 2008, Asia had 578.5 million Internet users, Europe had 384.6 million, and North America had an Internet user population of 248.2 million.[57]

c. *24-Hour Availability*. The Web is available 24 hours per day and 7 days a week.

d. *Rapidly Growing Market*. The number of people using the Internet is growing rapidly. In June 2008, there were an estimated 1.463 billion Internet users in the world. This was 305 per cent more than in 2000.[58]

e. *Interactivity*. The Internet allows a customer to communicate directly with hospitality and travel organizations; there is instant, two-way communications. Customers can search databases online, and can request information and make travel reservations. Figure 15.10 provides a good example of useful interactive content from the Singapore Tourism Board's website. This online *Itinerary Planner* allows people to plan their trips to Singapore based upon travel dates, type of trip, and preferred activities.

f. *Instant Feedback for Customers*. Through interactive features on Web pages or by e-mail, travelers can be given instant feedback such as immediate on-screen or e-mail confirmation of a reservation or booking, finding relevant information on a website by using a "search" function, connecting successfully to a plug-in for video or sound, and printing out pages, maps, photos, etc. on the travelers' printers.

FIGURE 15.10 The interactive power of the Internet is well demonstrated in this Itinerary Planner of the Singapore Tourism Board website.

Courtesy of Singapore Tourism Board, http://www.visitsingapore.com/publish/stbportal/en/home/apps/brochure.html

Did You Know?

What Is the Size of the World's Internet Population?

- In mid-2008, the world's Internet population increased to just over 1.46 billion.
- There are some interesting contrasts in usage statistics around the world. The highest percentage of Internet use is among North Americans, at 73.6%.
- The world's largest Internet market is in Asia at just over 578.5 million. However, only 15.3% of the Asian population is classified as Internet users.
- Europe is the second largest Internet market in the world at around 384.6 million. However, Internet penetration is still much lower than in North America.

Regions	Internet Usage	Usage Percent (World)	Usage Growth Rate (2000–2007)	Internet Usage as Percent of Population
Asia	578,538,257	39.5%	406.1%	15.3%
Europe	384,633,765	26.3%	266.0%	48.1%
North America	248,241,969	17.0%	129.6%	73.6%
Latin America/ Caribbean	139,009,209	9.5%	669.3%	24.1%
Africa	51,065,630	5.3%	1,031.2%	3.5%
Middle East	41,939,200	2.9%	1,176.8%	21.3%
Oceania/ Australia	20,204,331	1.4%	165.1%	59.5%
World Total	1,463,632,361	100.0%	305.5%	21.9%

Source: Miniwatts Marketing Group. (2008). *Internet Usage Statistics. The Internet Big Picture. World Internet Users and Population Stats.*

g. *Ability to Customize Information by Market Segment.* The interactive media are a great venue for using market segmentation. For example, Web pages can be designed for different target markets.

h. *Increased Speed of Transactions.* Travelers can make immediate reservations and bookings on the Internet, and have these confirmed instantly (Figure 15.11). Hospitality and travel organizations can constantly update the information on their websites. This is much superior to traditional brochure materials that had to be reprinted when updated information (e.g., new prices) needed to be added. The Web can also maintain an automatic inventory and deny bookings/reservations when a sell-out is reached.

i. *Capacity to Instantly Update.* Unlike most advertising that cannot be modified once it is placed, the interactive media can be modified

FIGURE 15.11
Customers can book online and get instant confirmation of purchases.

Image copyright Lein de Leán Yong, 2008. Used under license from Shutterstock.com

almost instantly. Messages can be changed frequently and content can be kept current.

j. *Ability to Tangibilize*. Chapter 2 highlighted the intangibility of services as an important generic difference between products and services. It also talked about the difficulties potential customers have in assessing hospitality and travel services before buying them. The interactive media helps to partly overcome these challenge by making the industry's offerings seem more tangible. This is done in a variety of ways such as using music or sounds to give people an enhanced experience, including interactive maps, providing virtual tours, showing live videos of places, allowing people to look at videos and TV commercials online, showing great photographs of the destination or property, and posting customer testimonials.

k. *Ability to Gather Research and Build Databases*. Hospitality and travel marketers can use the interactive media to conduct customer surveys. Important databases can be developed in a variety of ways. These include data collected when customers request brochures and other information and when they "opt in" to receive future e-mail communications or e-newsletters.

l. *Ease of Forming Virtual Partnerships*. By building websites together, hospitality and travel organizations can easily form virtual partnerships. For example, the BestCities Global Alliance has a website that showcases the meeting and exhibition facilities in its member cities.

m. *Ease of Traffic Measurement*. In contrast to most other media, Internet technology allows marketers to know exactly how many customers see their messages. Through the use of access **log file** analyzer software programs, marketers can get very accurate traffic measurements for every page on their websites. **Cookie** technology also enables marketers to recognize return visitors to sites. **Click-through rates** are measured by tracking the number of people that follow a hyperlink within an advertisement or editorial content to another website or frame within a website.[59]

Disadvantages

a. *Security and Privacy Concerns*. Some customers are concerned that their security and privacy may be breached on the Internet, especially with respect to credit card transactions. Identity theft has become a major problem in e-commerce.

b. *Spamming*. There are also major problems with spamming in e-mail marketing, with customers receiving many unsolicited e-mail advertising messages.

c. *Partial Market Coverage*. While use of the Internet is growing rapidly, it does not yet provide the same level of market penetration as traditional media such as television, radio, and newspapers. There are uneven adoption rates of the Internet internationally. Internet use is highest in North America at 73.6 percent in June 2008, but adoption rates in Europe (48.1%) and Asia (15.3%) are significantly lower.[60]

d. *Navigation Problems*. There is so much information available on the Internet that it is often time-consuming and tedious for customers to find exactly what they want. Added to this is the fact that many consumers have slow modems and some websites are slow to download.

e. *Loss of Control*. The marketer gives up control to the customer in the interactive media. The customer chooses what to look at, as well as the time and place to view the information.

f. *Dependency on the Abilities and Equipment of Users*. No matter how sophisticated the messages communicated, marketers are dependent on customers' abilities to view the information and the capabilities of their computer or mobile technology equipment. If equipment is not updated or if the users' skills are limited, the messages may not be received in the way the marketer intended.

g. *Volume of Information and Difficulties in Establishing Credibility of Information*. There are oceans of information available on the Internet and via mobile technologies. It is difficult for customers to find exactly what they are seeking, and also to establish the credibility of the information they download. To give an example of the volume of information downloaded, comScore, Inc. estimated that in November 2008 there were 12.3 billion online searches conducted in the United States, with 63.5 and 20.4 percent of these being on *Google* and *Yahoo!* sites.[61]

h. *Lack of the Human Touch*. Of course, this media uses technology and lacks the human touch in communications. If individual customers have unique problems to resolve, it can be difficult to do this without human intervention.

Advertising by the Hospitality and Travel Industry

Now that you are familiar with the strengths and weaknesses of each of the media alternatives, you probably are interested in knowing more about how our industry uses these media. You will see that there are some distinct patterns to the industry's advertising, including the airlines' heavy emphasis on newspapers and the fast-food companies' focus on television commercials. You will also notice, however, that companies within the same part of the industry have quite different media use patterns.

Several hospitality and travel companies are among the 100 leading national advertisers in the United States (Appendix 1.7). They include McDonald's (#32 in 2007), American Express (#40), Yum Brands (#41), Wendy's International (#89), and Burger King (#95). In 2007, McDonald's had the highest advertising expenditures in the industry at $1.15 billion.[62] Other companies that are divisions of larger parents would be among the leading advertisers if their advertising budgets were viewed separately. These companies include Walt Disney Co. (cruise line, resorts, and theme parks).

Appendix 1.8 provides a more detailed breakdown of the 2007 advertising expenditures of our industry's leaders. The figures are for measured media only. That is, they are media statistics that are measured by various associations and service companies. Unmeasured spending occurs in media that are not measured by outside firms and associations. The data come from the sponsoring companies themselves. This latter category includes direct marketing, other forms of advertising (e.g., Yellow Pages), and some sales promotion spending.

The total measured media spending in 2007 for airlines, hotels, car rental and travel (including cruise lines) was approximately $5.414 billion, while restaurants and fast food spent an additional $5.349.8 billion. Note that these are measured-media-spending figures only, and they did not include Yellow Pages, spot cable, FSIs, and direct mail. The two industry groups had very different media spending patterns. Airlines, hotels, car rental and travel spent the most on print media (53.2 percent), while restaurants spent only 6.4 percent on print advertising. However, restaurants allocated 87.2 percent to broadcast advertising, compared to 31.1 percent for airlines, hotels, car rental and travel. The airlines, hotels, car rental and travel group had 9.5 percent in Internet advertising, while restaurants allocated only 2.0 percent to online advertising.[63]

Role of Advertising Agencies

Most medium-sized and large hospitality and travel organizations use the services of advertising agencies to develop and place their advertisements. The top full-service advertising agencies in the world in 2007 included the Omnicom Group (New York), WPP Group (London), Interpublic Group of Cos. (New York), Publicis Group (Paris), and Dentsu (Tokyo).[64]

Advertising agencies provide five distinct types of services:[65]

1. **Advertising Planning**. Most full-service advertising agencies can put together the entire advertising plan for an organization, including all ten steps described earlier. Although this service exists, the sponsor should generally perform steps 1 to 4, and give the agency an indication of the message idea.

2. **Creative Services**. Creating effective advertisements is definitely an art, and ad agencies employ the most talented people to do this. Agencies develop the copy platform, decide on the message format, and select the advertising media and media vehicles. They are most often asked to do this for television, radio, newspaper, and magazine advertising, but they can assist with all forms of advertising and sales promotion. Advertising agencies do not actually develop advertisements, but contract this function out to other specialized firms.

3. **Media Services**. Advertising agencies select the media and buy the time or space. In fact, agencies earn most of their money in commissions from the media companies with which they place advertisements. Agencies also monitor and control campaigns as they progress.

4. **Research Services**. All but the smallest agencies also offer marketing research services, particularly related to pre-testing and post-testing advertisements. Again, the research is usually done under subcontract by specialized research firms, with the agency's supervision.

5. **Sales Promotion and Merchandising Services**. Many agencies provide creative services related to sales promotion and merchandising materials. Because these promotions are often supported by special advertising campaigns, this arrangement can be convenient.

A hospitality and travel organization has at least four options in creating and placing its advertising: (1) do it in-house, (2) use one advertising agency for all its advertising, (3) do some work in-house and some with an agency or agencies, and (4) use more than one agency or other specialists.

It is advisable for all hospitality and travel organizations, except those that are very small, to use advertising agencies. The principal advantages of using an agency are as follows:

a. Agencies employ the best creative minds in advertising and, because of their large client base, are able to compensate these individuals well.

b. Agencies have accumulated experience from working with diverse clients and, therefore, have a broader perspective than the client. They are an independent party and are more objective about the client's opportunities and problems.

c. Contracting an advertising agency may actually save the sponsor money. Hiring full-time advertising specialists for in-house positions normally is more expensive than using agency personnel.

d. Agencies are likely to be more familiar with the media and media vehicles than the sponsor.

Chapter Conclusion

Advertising is the most pervasive promotional mix element and is used by organizations of all types and sizes. It can be extremely powerful if it is well researched, carefully planned, and creatively implemented. Most advertising media are cluttered, and developing attention-getting, memorable advertisements is the key challenge.

Advertising is a mini-system in itself, beginning by establishing advertising objectives and ending by measuring results. Effective advertising is based on the research, analysis, and decisions from the situation analysis, marketing research results, marketing strategy, positioning approach, and marketing objectives. The advertising plan is one component of the overall marketing plan.

REVIEW QUESTIONS

1. What are the ten steps that should be followed when developing an advertising plan?
2. What are the three main categories of advertising objectives? When should each category be used?
3. What is the difference between consumer and trade advertising? Which media vehicles would be most appropriate for each of these?
4. What are the components of a message strategy?
5. What are the most popular creative formats used in advertising? Are all the media alternatives equally effective in using these formats? Why or why not?
6. Which seven factors should be considered when selecting an advertising medium?
7. What are the characteristics of the five main advertising media alternatives?
8. What are the advantages and disadvantages of the major advertising media alternatives?
9. Does the hospitality and travel industry make uniform use of the media alternatives? Explain your answer.
10. Which five services do advertising agencies usually provide, and what are the advantages of using an agency?

CHAPTER ASSIGNMENTS

1. Select a part of the hospitality and travel industry in which you are most interested. Choose five or six of the leading companies or organizations in the field. Watch, listen to, or gather recent advertisements from each organization. Study the advertisements carefully and determine the message ideas and creative formats being used by the sponsors. Are the approaches similar and, if not, how do they differ? Which do you think are most effective, and why? Do all organizations tend to use the same types of media and media vehicles?

2. You are an executive with an advertising agency specializing in hospitality and travel company accounts. A new potential client (hotel or restaurant chain, airline, theme park, DMO, or other) has asked for your recommendations on which media it should use. What selection criteria would you suggest, and how would you assess each media alternative against these criteria? Which specific media and media vehicles would you recommend?

3. The owner of a small hospitality and travel business in the local community has asked you to develop an advertising plan. What steps would you follow in developing this plan? Who would you involve in the preparation of the plan? Prepare a detailed outline for the plan and, where possible, make specific recommendations on particular steps (e.g., media to use, message strategy, timing, amount of cooperative advertising).

4. This chapter emphasizes the importance of cooperative advertising. Either at the national, regional, or local level, find five good examples of cooperative advertising. Interview the participants in the cooperative programs to determine their feelings about joint promotional efforts. How beneficial have they found this type of advertising to be? What are its limitations or problems? Describe each of the ads or advertising campaigns. Based on your analysis, do you believe that more organizations in our industry should get involved in cooperative advertising? Why or why not?

WEB RESOURCES

ABC, http://abc.go.com/
American Association of Advertising Agencies, http://www.aaaa.org/
American Express, http://www.americanexpress.com/
Advertising Age, http://adage.com/
Arbitron, http://www.arbiton.com/
Avis Rent A Car, http://www.avis.com/
Best Cities Global Alliance, http://www.bestcities.net/
Business Week, http://www.businessweek.com/
Canadian Newspaper Association, http://www.cna-acj.ca/
CBS, http://www.cbs.com/
Chick-fil-A, http://www.chick-fil-a.com/
Condé Nast Traveler, http://www.cntraveler.com/
Direct Marketing Association, http://www.the-dma.org/
Field & Stream, http://www.fieldandstream.com/
Forbes, http://www.forbes.com/
Fortune Magazine, http://www.fortune.com/
Fox, http://www.fox.com/
Golf Digest, http://www.golfdigest.com/
Interactive Advertising Bureau, http://www.iab.net/
Magazine Publishers of America, http://www.magazine.org/
Marriott International Hotels, http://www.marriott.com/

Visit Mississippi, http://www.visitmississippi.org/
NBC, http://www.nbc.com/
National Geographic Traveler, http://www.nationalgeographic.com/
Newspaper Association of America, http://www.naa.org/
Outdoor Advertising Association of America, http://www.oaaa.org/
Nielsen Media. Research, http://www.nielsen.com/
Radio Advertising Bureau, http://www.rab.com/
Singapore Tourism Board, http://www.visitsingapore.com/
Standard Rate & Data Service (SRDS), http://www.srds.com/
Starwood Hotels & Resorts, http://www.starwood.com/
Television Bureau of Advertising, http://www.tvb.org/
Travel + Leisure, http://www.travelandleisure.com/
Virgin Atlantic Airways, http://www.virgin-atlantic.com/
Wynn Resorts, http://www.wynnresorts.com/

REFERENCES

1. Advertising Age. 2008. 100 Leading National Advertisers, http://adage.com/images/random/datacenter/2008/spendtrends08.pdf, accessed December 28, 2008.

2. Universal McCann. 2007. *Insider's Report. Robert Coen Presentation on Advertising Expenditures*, December 2007, http://www.universalmccann.com/, accessed December 28, 2008.

3. American Marketing Association. 2008. *Dictionary*. http://www.marketingpower.com/_layouts/Dictionary.aspx, accessed December 28, 2008.

4. American Marketing Association. 2008. *Dictionary*. http://www.marketingpower.com/_layouts/Dictionary.aspx, accessed December 28, 2008.

5. Tourism Australia. 2008. *Campaign Facts*. http://www.tourism.australia.com/Marketing.asp?sub=0413&al=3017, accessed December 27, 2008.

6. Mississippi Development Authority. 2008. *Domestic & Group Trade FY 2009 Marketing Plan*.

7. Visa. 2008. *The Olympic Promise*, http://sponsorships.visa.com/olympic/olympic_spirit.jsp, accessed December 28, 2008.

8. Texas Advertising & Public Relations. 2007. *Glossary*. http://advertising.utexas.edu/resources/terms/index.htm, accessed December 28, 2008.

9. Ray, Michael L. 1982. *Advertising & Communication Management*. Englewood Cliffs, N.J.: Prentice-Hall, Inc., 209–210.

10. Nylen, David W. 1993. *Advertising: Planning, Implementation, & Control*. 4th ed. Cincinnati, Ohio: South-Western Publishing Co., 459–461.

11. McGraw-Hill Irwin. 2006. *McGraw-Hill Contemporary Advertising Glossary*. http://highered.mcgraw-hill.com/sites/0072964723/student_view0/glossary.html, accessed December 28, 2008.

12. McGraw-Hill Irwin. 2006. *McGraw-Hill Contemporary Advertising Glossary*. http://highered.mcgraw-hill.com/sites/0072964723/student_view0/glossary.html, accessed December 28, 2008.

13. Evans, Joel R., and Barry Berman. 2000. *Marketing*. 7th ed. Upper Saddle River, N.J.: Prentice-Hall, Inc.

14. Evans, Joel R., and Barry Berman. 2000. *Marketing*. 7th ed. Upper Saddle River, N.J.: Prentice-Hall, Inc.

15. Evans, Joel R., and Barry Berman. 2000. *Marketing*. 7th ed. Upper Saddle River, N.J.: Prentice-Hall, Inc.

16. Ray, Michael L. 1982. *Advertising & Communication Management*. Englewood Cliffs, N.J.: Prentice-Hall, Inc., 365.

17. Kotler, Philip. 2000. *Marketing Management: Millennium Edition*. Upper Saddle River, N.J.: Prentice-Hall, Inc.

18. Kotler, Philip. 2000. *Marketing Management: Millennium Edition*. Upper Saddle River, N.J.: Prentice-Hall, Inc.

19. Belch, George E., and Michael A. Belch. 1993. *Introduction to Advertising & Promotion: An Integrated Communications Perspective*. 2nd ed. Homewood, Ill.: Irwin, 402–403.

20. Rossiter, John R., and Larry Percy. 2000. *Advertising Communications & Promotions Management*. 2nd ed. Boston: McGraw-Hill.

21. Derived from various sources including Dommermuth, William P. 1989. *Promotion: Analysis, Creativity, and Strategy*. 2nd ed. Boston: PWS-Kent Publishing Company, 537–538; Kotler, 594–597; Rossiter and Percy, 523–551; Ray, 327–331; Nylen, 629–659.

22. Rossiter, John R., and Larry Percy. 2000. *Advertising Communications & Promotions Management*. 2nd ed. Boston: McGraw-Hill.

23. American Marketing Association. 2008. *Dictionary*. http://www.marketingpower.com/_layouts/Dictionary.aspx, accessed December 28, 2008.

24. Advertising Age. 2008. *Ad spending totals by medium*, http://adage.com/datacenter/article?article_id=127791, accessed December 28, 2008.

25. Newspaper Association of America. 2007. *The Newspaper Footprint*, http://www.naa.org/docs/TrendsandNumbers/NAANewspaperFootprint.pdf, accessed December 28, 2008.

26. Newspaper Association of America. 2008. *Total Paid Circulation*, http://www.naa.org/docs/Research/Total-Paid-Circulation.xls, accessed December 28, 2008.

27. Canadian Newspaper Association. 2008. *2007 Daily Newspaper Paid Circulation Data*, http://www.cna-acj.ca/en/aboutnewspapers/circulation, accessed December 28, 2008.

28. Newspaper Association of America. 2006. *The Source: Newspapers by the Numbers*, 24.

29. Newspaper Association of America. 2008. *Newspaper web site audience increases sixteen percent in third quarter to 68.3 million visitors*, http://www.naa.org/PressCenter/SearchPressReleases/2008/NEWSPAPER-WEB-SITE-AUDIENCE-INCREASES-SIXTEEN-PERCENT-IN-THIRD-QUARTER.aspx, accessed December 28, 2008.

30. Oxbridge Communications, Inc. 2008. *National Directory of Magazines*.

31. Magazine Publishers of America. 2008. *The Magazine Handbook: A Comprehensive Guide 2008-09*, 13.

32. Advertising Age. 2008. *Ad spending totals by medium*, http://adage.com/datacenter/article?article_id=127791, accessed December 28, 2008.

33. National Geographic. 2007. *National Geographic expands its world*, http://press.nationalgeographic.com/pressroom/index.jsp?pageID=factSheets_detail&siteID=1&cid=1058466231550, accessed December 28, 2008.

34. Travel Weekly. 2008. *Advertise with TW Group.* http://www.travelweekly.co.uk/Articles/2008/02/18/26702/advertise-with-tw-group.html, accessed December 28, 2008.

35. Travel + Leisure. 2008. *T + L MRI Reader Profile .08*, http://www.tlmediakit.com/reader_profile.cfm, accessed December 28, 2008.

36. Travel + Leisure. 2008. *Rate Card. 2009 National Edition*, http://www.tlmediakit.com/national_rates.cfm, accessed December 28, 2008.

37. Yellow Pages Association. 2008. *Yellow Pages Basics. Who Uses the Yellow Pages?*, http://www.buyyellow.com/basics/who.html, accessed December 28, 2008.

38. Advertising Age. 2008. *Ad spending totals by medium*, http://adage.com/datacenter/article?article_id=127791, accessed December 28, 2008.

39. Radio Online. 2008. http://news.radio-online.com/cgi-bin/$rol.exe/headline_id=b11300, accessed December 28, 2008..

40. Arbitron. 2006. Radio Today. *How America Listens to Radio*. 2006 Edition, 14–79.

41. TV Advertising Bureau. 2008. *2008 Media Comparison Study: Television Advertising Has the Best Perception among adults: Most persuasive*, http://www.tvb.org/nav/build_frameset.asp, accessed December 28, 2008.

42. Nielsen Media Research, Inc. 2006. *Nielsen Station Index (NSI)*.

43. TV Advertising Bureau. 2008. *Media Trends Track. Trends in Television*, http://www.tvb.org/nav/build_frameset.asp, accessed December 28, 2008

44. Nielsen Media Research, Inc. 2008. *Average U.S. home now receives a record 118.6 TV channels*, http://www.nielsenmedia.com/nc/portal/site/Public/menuitem.55dc65b4a7d5adff3f65936147a062a0/?vgnextoid=48839bc66a961110VgnVCM100000ac0a260aRCRD, accessed December 28, 2008.

45. Cable Television Advertising Bureau. 2007. *2007 TV Facts User Guide*, http://www.onetvworld.org/main/cab/downloads/2007_Fact_Book_User_Guide2.doc, accessed April 1, 2007.

46. Advertising Age. 2008. *Ad spending totals by medium*, http://adage.com/datacenter/article?article_id=127791, accessed December 28, 2008.

47. American Association of Advertising Agencies. 2007. *AAAA Television Production Cost Survey*.

48. Outdoor Advertising Association of America. 2008. *Facts and Figures,* http://www.oaaa.org/marketingresources/factsandfigures.aspx, accessed December 28, 2008.

49. Advertising Age. 2008. *Ad spending totals by medium,* http://adage.com/datacenter/article?article_id=127791, accessed December 28, 2008.

50. Outdoor Advertising Association of America. 2008. *Facts and Figures,* Advertising Age. 2008. *Ad spending totals by medium,* http://adage.com/datacenter/article?article_id=127791, accessed December 28, 2008.

51. American Marketing Association. 2008. *Dictionary.* http://www.marketingpower.com/_layouts/Dictionary.aspx, accessed December 28, 2008.

52. Advertising Age. 2008. *Ad spending totals by medium,* http://adage.com/datacenter/article?article_id=127791, accessed December 28, 2008.

53. Standard Rate & Data Service, Inc. *Subscription & Product Information,* http://www.srds.com/portal/main?action=LinkHit&frameset=yes&link=ips, accessed December 28, 2008.

54. Interactive Advertising Bureau. 2008. *Glossary of Interactive Advertising Terms.* http://www.iab.net/insights_research/530422/1494, accessed December 28, 2008.

55. Advertising Age. 2008. *Ad spending totals by medium,* http://adage.com/datacenter/article?article_id=127791, accessed December 28, 2008.

56. PricewaterhouseCoopers/Interactive Advertising Bureau. 2006. *IAB Internet Advertising Revenue Report,* 3.

57. Miniwatts Marketing Group. 2008. *Internet World Stats.* http://www.internetworldstats.com/stats.htm, accessed December 28, 2008.

58. Miniwatts Marketing Group. 2008. *Internet World Stats.* http://www.internetworldstats.com/stats.htm, accessed December 28, 2008.

59. Interactive Advertising Bureau. 2008. *Glossary of Interactive Advertising Terms.* http://www.iab.net/insights_research/530422/1494, accessed December 28, 2008.

60. Miniwatts Marketing Group. 2008. *Internet World Stats.* http://www.internetworldstats.com/stats.htm, accessed December 28, 2008.

61. comScore, Inc. 2008. *comScore releases November 2008 U.S. search engine rankings.* http://www.comscore.com/press/release.asp?press=2652, accessed December 28, 2008.

62. Advertising Age. 2008. *World's Top 50 Agency Companies.*

63. Advertising Age. 2008. *100 Leading National Advertisers,* http://adage.com/datacenter/article?article_id=127791, accessed December 28, 2008.

64. Advertising Age. 2008. *100 Leading National Advertisers,* http://adage.com/datacenter/article?article_id=127791, accessed December 28, 2008.

65. Nylen, David W. 1993. *Advertising: Planning, Implementation, & Control.* 4th ed. Cincinnati, Ohio: South-Western Publishing Co., 71–74.

chapter 16

Sales Promotion and Merchandising
How Do We Get There?

O V E R V I E W

Sales promotion and merchandising are two related promotional mix elements that can have a powerful influence on sales. This chapter begins by defining the two terms and explaining the roles they play. Again, it is emphasized that these two activities should be carefully planned in advance and should be coordinated with other promotional mix elements in integrated marketing communications (IMC).

The chapter then describes the specific sales promotion and merchandising techniques available and their roles and advantages are reviewed. The chapter concludes with an outline of a step-by-step process that can be used to plan and implement sales promotions and merchandising activities.

O B J E C T I V E S

Having read this chapter, you should be able to:

- Define the terms *sales promotion* and *merchandising*.

- Explain the six roles of sales promotion and merchandising.

- Describe the steps involved in developing a sales promotion and merchandising plan.

- Explain the difference between special communication methods and special-offer promotions.

- List the various sales promotion and merchandising techniques available.

- Explain the roles and advantages of each sales promotion and merchandising technique.

KEY TERMS

affinity cards

brand extensions

contests

continuity programs

coupon redemption rates

coupons

familiarization (fam) trips
   (or tours)

freestanding inserts (FSIs)

frequent-flyer programs

frequent-guest award
   programs

games

gift certificates

merchandising

premiums

price-offs

pull strategy

push strategy

recognition program

sales promotions

sampling

site inspections

special communication methods

special offers

specialty advertising

sponsorships

sweepstakes

travel trade promotions

travel trade shows

As a consumer of many goods and services, you are probably more aware of sales promotion and merchandising than you think. As you stroll around the local shopping mall, you are surrounded by retail merchandising. There are mannequins in store windows, end-of-aisle displays, eye-catching posters, and even moving objects designed to get your attention. When you pick up the newspaper or mail, or go to a website, you will find many coupons offering special prices on items ranging from pizza to Pisa. Many products you purchase come with a mail-in rebate offer. You can substantially add to your collection of glassware, dishware, or toys if you go to fast-food stores often enough. If you want a better sleep, just log onto a hotel chain's website, and use your credit card to purchase one of their specially branded beds. These are all examples of sales promotion and merchandising—visual and material inducements to get you to make purchases.

It is quite difficult to find accurate measurements of the total spending on sales promotions in any country, since this is not measured in the same way as is advertising. However, it appears that the recent emphasis has shifted away from media advertising toward sales promotion and merchandising, and of course also to the Internet. A study by Northwestern University on behalf of the Promotion Marketing Association found that 20 to 35 percent of all consumer purchases in the United States involved some kind of sales promotion.[1] You will learn some of the reasons for this trend as you read about the advantages of sales promotion and merchandising.

Sales Promotion, Merchandising, and the Promotional Mix

Definitions

Sales promotions are approaches other than advertising, personal selling, and public relations and publicity where the customer is given a short-term inducement to make an immediate purchase. Included are such items as coupons, free samples, and games. **Merchandising** or point-of-purchase promotion includes materials used in-house to stimulate sales (e.g., menus, wine lists, tent cards, signs, posters, displays, and other point-of-purchase promotional items). Nowadays, it also includes the online merchandising or *e-tailing* of various products offered by hospitality and travel companies such as beds, toiletries, food, and other branded items.

The two techniques are closely related, and some authors consider merchandising to be a sales promotion technique. Because of the great importance of merchandising in retailing hospitality and travel services, this book separates these two promotional mix elements.

FIGURE 16.1
Beautiful posters of destinations can be very striking merchandising tools.

Courtesy of the Canadian Tourism Commission

INTERNET MARKETING

Searching Online to Find a Bed That's Heavenly: Internet Retailing by Westin

- Westin was the pioneer of the modern era of brand extensions by hotel chains in introducing its heavenly® bed.
- Now through the Westin® at home section of the hotel chain's website, customers can order this bed and many other items online.
- Clicking on the "bed" button on the site reveals these product lines: (1) heavenly® bed, blankets & bedding, mattress/box spring, ensembles, roll-a-way bed, pillows & cases, and sheets. You will find out that the heavenly® bed is very comfortable, but not cheap! To buy a queen-size bed with all bedding, and including shipping charges, you will pay around $4,500 to $5,000.
- Under the "bath" category can be found: (1) bath & body amenities, (2) bathrobes and towels, (3) shower hardware, and (4) slippers.
- You can also order up a "Heavenly Dog Bed" and dog collar and leash for your favorite pet.
- Finally, there are various white tea products available (candles, potpourri, scent, diffuser oil), as well as necklaces, eye masks, a shoe tree, posters, and a lavender sachet.
- Westin has been a true trendsetter among hotel brands. Now several of the other brands within Starwood have their own online merchandise stores including W Hotels, Sheraton, and Four Points.

Source: Starwood Hotels & Resorts Worldwide. (2008). *Westin® at home.* **http://www.westin-hotelsathome.com/**

Student Questions

1. What do you feel are the major benefits to hotel brands like Westin in having online stores like this?
2. Do you think this gives Westin and Starwood a competitive advantage over other hotel chains and hotels that do not have online stores? Why or why not?
3. What steps should the hotel chain take to merchandise and cross-promote the online store within its hotel properties?
4. How could a hotel brand like Westin get greater distribution of its products, for example, by partnering with specialized bedding stores?

Plan Integrated Marketing Communications First

It is again important to think about integrated marketing communications (IMC) and to realize that organizations do not always look at sales promotion and merchandising as alternatives to advertising, personal selling, public relations and publicity, and Internet marketing. Often all five promotional mix elements and Internet marketing are part of a carefully coordinated IMC approach. They can work together in a powerful six-punch combination. Advertising, PR/publicity, and Internet marketing create the awareness, in-store merchandising jogs the customer's memory, sales promotion induces the sale, and the salesperson upsells and closes the sale. The leading fast-food chains have perfected this six-level approach. Television commercials and websites make customers aware of the sales promotion (e.g., a child's toy in a McDonald's *Happy Meal*, two-for-one or other price offer), press releases describe them in detail, exterior signs and interior displays and posters remind customers about the ads and publicity, and the availability of the offer in the restaurant creates the sale. In-house (personal) selling of the offer by servers further increases the promotion's effectiveness and closes the sale.

What this adds up to is that there can be great synergy among the five promotional mix elements and Internet marketing if they are consistent and carefully coordinated. This takes careful preplanning and timing. Again, it also means that all promotional mix elements and Internet marketing should not be planned independently, but should complement each other as much as possible in an IMC approach.

Roles of Sales Promotion and Merchandising

Spending on sales promotions and merchandising are increasing as a percentage of total marketing budgets when compared to media advertising. This is especially true for consumer packaged goods (CPG) manufacturers, but also seems to be a trend in the hospitality and travel industry. This trend has been caused by growing competitive intensity, rising costs of advertising, and mounting pressure on marketing managers to increase sales.[2]

There is a danger in employing sales promotions and particularly price promotions as a *quick fix* for situations that need longer-term solutions. For example, an organization can have serious marketing problems, such as an inappropriate marketing strategy, wrong positioning approach or poor reputation, ineffective advertising, or inadequate service or variety. Sales promotions produce quick, positive results that mask these longer-term problems. Promotions can be introduced quickly and whenever management decides to do so. They make managers look good in the short term when sales expand. If each sales promotion is immediately followed by another, management may not even be aware that serious problems exist. When they find out that this is the case, it may be too late to correct the situation. If price promotions are used too often,

FIGURE 16.2 Roles of sales promotion and merchandising.

Getting customers to try a new service or menu item

Increasing off-peak sales

Increasing sales in periods that coincide with major events, vacations, or special occasions

Encouraging travel trade intermediaries to make a special effort to sell services

Helping sales representatives get business from prospects

Facilitating travel trade intermediary sales

customers may always look from them from a particular hospitality and travel organization or brand. They may only buy when price deals are offered.

What then is the most appropriate role for sales promotion and merchandising? The simplest answer is that they should be used to take advantage of their principal strengths (listed in Chapter 14), particularly in meeting tactical and short-term objectives (Figure 16.2). Sales promotions generally should not be used to satisfy objectives relative to which they are known to have weaknesses, such as building long-term company or brand loyalty. Research studies have indicated that sales promotions produce faster and more measurable impacts on sales; but do not attract long-term customers in industry sectors that are mature.[3]

There are exceptions to these rules, because not all sales promotions are alike. Coupons and other price offers usually do not change customers' basic attitudes toward a company or its brands. They do not encourage long-term use of the organization's services or products. However, giving customers free samples (e.g., a taste of a new menu item or wine, a free upgrade to a new level of service) may change their attitudes and they may eventually become loyal, long-term customers.

Sales promotions and merchandising should be used on an as-needed or tactical rather than a continuous basis. In this respect, they are unlike advertising, personal selling, and public relations, which require continuous, long-term use. They should be introduced periodically to meet short-term objectives such as the following:

1. **Getting Customers to Try a New Service or Menu Item.** This is frequently an objective of hospitality and travel companies when they introduce new services or menu items. The Olive Garden introduced new

menu items, *Chicken Carbonara or Shrimp Carbonara*, for a short time period in October 2008. Guests could go online and get free recipes for these dishes.

2. **Increasing Off-Peak Sales.** This is a second key role of sales promotion, and it is applied frequently in the hospitality and travel industry. For example, the Rail Europe Group offers reduced prices on BritRail passes for travel in off-peak periods. Many destinations in the Caribbean feature off-peak price deals in the spring and summer months.[4] The Harrison Hot Springs Resort & Spa in British Columbia, Canada offers special package rates to people who travel mid-week (Sunday through Thursday). Nowadays, many hospitality and travel websites have a "specials" page or section that features off-peak bargains.

3. **Increasing Sales in Periods that Coincide with Major Events, Vacations, or Special Occasions.** Each year there are several events and vacation periods when companies can use creative sales promotions and merchandising to boost sales well above their normal levels. Think about the Christmas season for a minute. (If you're in Asia, your example might be the Lunar New Year.) You will quickly recognize that stores make a special effort to get your business during these festive times. Fast-food restaurants also intensify their sales promotions during certain seasons and holidays. Increasingly, hospitality and travel companies are featuring sales promotions to coincide with the release of new movies. Holiday Inns & Resorts in the U.K. offered special package rates in March-April 2007 at the time of the release of Disney's *Meet the Robinsons.*

   Sometimes an important sporting event or a company's anniversary is the occasion. Mega-events such as the Summer and Winter Olympics, and the World Cup™ often tied in with sales promotions. This may be done through paying for **sponsorships** of the events. McDonald's has been a sponsor for many years of the Olympic Games. For the Beijing 2008 Summer Olympics, it was one of the *Worldwide Olympic Partners*. China Eastern Airlines is an Official Partner of the Expo 2010 Shanghai. Emirates Airlines, VISA, and McDonald's are FIFA Partners or FIFA World Cup™ Sponsors for the 2010 World Cup in South Africa.

4. **Encouraging Travel Trade Intermediaries to Make a Special Effort to Sell Services.** Trade promotions frequently have this as their objective. Airlines, car rental firms, cruise lines, and others dangle extra commission points, free familiarization or "fam" trips, and other prizes in front of travel agents and tour wholesalers/operators if they supply business or client leads to the promotion's sponsors. In 2008, Hyatt offered an incentive program to travel agents to book clients into its hotels and resorts. The *Hyatt Resorts' Slice of Paradise* program gave the travel agent one free night at a Hyatt resort for every three paid client nights in the Continental U.S. or for four paid client nights in Hawaii or the Caribbean.[5] You also know about preferred supplier relationships from

Chapters 10 and 13, in which travel agents are given extra commission rate points for their clients' business.

5. **Helping Sales Representatives Get Business from Prospects.** Certain types of sales promotions can be used to help sales representatives close sales (get a commitment for future business). Often companies provide giveaway items that are handed or mailed to prospects. These free gifts are called *specialty advertising* (various types of items carrying the sponsor's name) items.

6. **Facilitating Travel Trade Intermediary Sales.** Carriers, suppliers, tour wholesalers/operators and DMOs supply a variety of in-store merchandising materials to travel agents to help them sell their services. These include DVDs, PowerPoint presentations, brochures and other printed materials, posters, displays of all types, and specialty advertising items (e.g., wearables, calendars, pens, bags, etc.).

Planning Sales Promotion and Merchandising Efforts

As is true with all of the promotional mix elements, a written sales promotion and merchandising plan should be prepared and included in the marketing plan. The basic procedures for preparing this plan are quite similar to those used to draw up the advertising plan that you learned about in the Chapter 15 (Figure 16.3).

FIGURE 16.3 Steps in preparing and evaluating a sales promotion and merchandising plan.

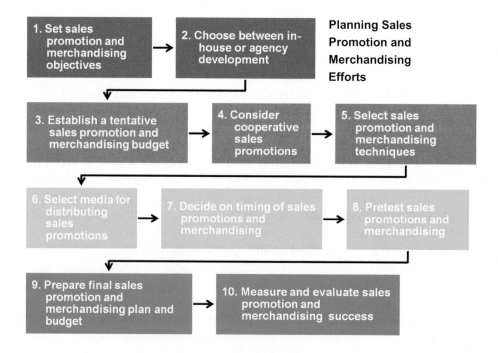

Set Sales Promotion and Merchandising Objectives (Step 1)

Every sales promotion and merchandising activity should be based on a clear objective or objectives. As you should realize from previous discussions, these objectives are usually more tactical or short-term than for advertising objectives. Sales promotion and merchandising must also meet the four basic criteria for all marketing objectives: target-market specific, results oriented, quantitative, and time specific. Sales promotion and merchandising objectives are generally in the persuasive communications category. Many sales promotions are tactical and designed to generate sales in the short term by:

- Incenting new customers to sample hospitality and travel services, facilities, or destinations
- Generating increased sales from existing customers by increasing frequency of purchases or per capita spending
- Convincing more travel trade intermediaries to book or recommend the hospitality and travel organization or destination
- Encouraging travel trade intermediaries to increase booking volumes

Hospitality and travel marketers must also consider the desired behavioral response from the customers in the markets being targeted. Among others, these may include:[6]

- Switching from another brand or destination to ours
- Purchasing more quickly or earlier than intended
- Stockpiling, e.g., accumulating frequent flyer or frequent guest program points
- Trying out services or products
- Increasing spending

You should realize that advertising, sales promotion, merchandising, personal selling, PR/publicity, and Internet marketing objectives should be closely meshed within carefully integrated marketing communication (IMC) programs. In fact, sales promotion and merchandising objectives should not be set independently of other promotional mix elements, as they are normally supportive of these other elements. They should be closely related to longer-term advertising, personal selling, PR/publicity, and Internet marketing objectives.

Choose between In-House or Agency Development (Step 2)

Every hospitality and travel organization must decide whether it is better to produce sales promotion and merchandising materials internally or to use outside companies to design and produce them. Most medium-sized and large companies choose the external or outsourcing route, contracting with advertising agencies, sales promotion specialists, creative designers, or website developers. The advantages and disadvantages of the two alternatives are exactly the same as they are in making decisions about hiring an advertising agency.

> ### Did You Know?
>
> ### *Where to buy hotel merchandise online?*
>
> - Many of the major hotel chains now sell merchandise online. Here are some links and the product selections available at some of these companies' websites:
> - **Hilton to Home**, bedding, bath, accessories, electronics, pets, http://www.hiltontohome.com/
> - **Hyatt at Home**, Hyatt Grand Bed, Signature Collections, bath accessories, eShave®, Eton radios, Park Hyatt exclusive, Portico & Hyatt Pure™, room furnishings, stay fit equipment, http://www.hyattathome.com/?icamp=HY_HyattAtHome_HPGS
> - **Shop Marriott**, The Marriott Bed, bed basics, bed linens, bath, spa, home décor, The Marriott Bear™, holiday gifts, http://www.shopmarriott.com/index.aspx
> - **Peninsula Boutique**, chocolatier, coffee, cookies, connoisseur, gift sets, tea, lifestyle, seasonal, Naturally Peninsula, http://www.peninsulaboutique.com/
> - **Westin at Home**, bed, bath, dog, white tea & gifts, http://www.westin-hotelsathome.com/
> - **Wyndham at Home**, bedding, bath, exclusives, http://www.wyndham-hotelsathome.com/
>
> *Source:* Hotel chain websites, accessed December 28, 2008.

Establish Tentative Sales Promotion and Merchandising Budget (Step 3)

An approximate allocation from the total tentative promotional budget should be made for sales promotion and merchandising. This preliminary amount is used as a guide to select and design sales promotion and merchandising activities. The tentative budget can be reassessed once the actual costs of these activities are known. As you learned in Chapter 9, the objective-and-task method is the best way to put together such a budget.

Consider Cooperative Sales Promotions (Step 4)

The next step is to consider potential partnership approaches for sales promotion and merchandising. There are many opportunities for cooperative sales promotions or "co-ops" in the hospitality and travel industry, just as there are for advertising promotions. For example, **familiarization** or **fam trips or tours** (fams) are free or reduced-price trips for travel agents and tour wholesalers/operators to encourage them to recommend or use the sponsoring organizations' or destinations' services. Frequently, the costs of these trips are shared among carriers, suppliers, and DMOs.

Cross-promotional efforts are also possible with companies outside the hospitality and travel industry. You heard earlier in the chapter about Holiday Inns & Resorts' joint promotion in the U.K. with Disney.

Select Sales Promotion and Merchandising Techniques (Step 5)

The next question to consider is which sales promotion or merchandising techniques will be the most effective in achieving objectives. There are many alternatives available. Although not a direct parallel, choosing the right technique is similar to selecting the best message format in advertising.

Most hospitality and travel organizations are involved both in consumer and travel trade sales promotions. Some sales promotion programs and merchandising materials are geared directly toward customers, whereas others are aimed at travel trade intermediaries. Travel trade promotions are often referred to as a **push strategy**, which means pushing sales by promoting to travel trade intermediaries who, in turn, promote to customers. A **pull strategy** aims promotions at customers, whose demands pull services and products through the travel trade distribution channels. Most parts of the hospitality and travel industry favor the push strategy, primarily because there are far fewer travel trade intermediaries than potential customers, so money can be saved. In certain cases, such as with restaurants, travel trade intermediaries are not used and a push strategy is, therefore, inappropriate. Before leaving this subject, you should realize that this is not simply an either/or situation. An organization may employ a combination of travel trade (push) and customer (pull) promotions.

Some hospitality and travel organizations use promotions to intensify the personal selling efforts of their own salespeople. These are categorized as sales-force promotions.

Another way to divide sales promotion and merchandising techniques is by trial and usage promotions. For example, coupons and sampling are considered quite effective in getting new customers to try a service or product. Contests, sweepstakes, and games are good at convincing present customers or travel trade intermediaries to use a hospitality and travel organization or destination more often. Once again, an organization may decide to use a combination of trial and usage promotions.

In this book, sales promotion and merchandising techniques are categorized by their functional characteristics. This route was selected because, as you will come to understand, the same techniques can be used for travel trade intermediary, customer, and sales-force promotions.

Sales promotion and merchandising techniques can be divided into two functional groups: (1) **special communication methods** and (2) **special offers**[7] (Figure 16.4). The first group gives the promoter additional options for communicating with present and potential customers, and travel trade intermediaries.

FIGURE 16.4 Types of sales promotion and merchandising techniques.

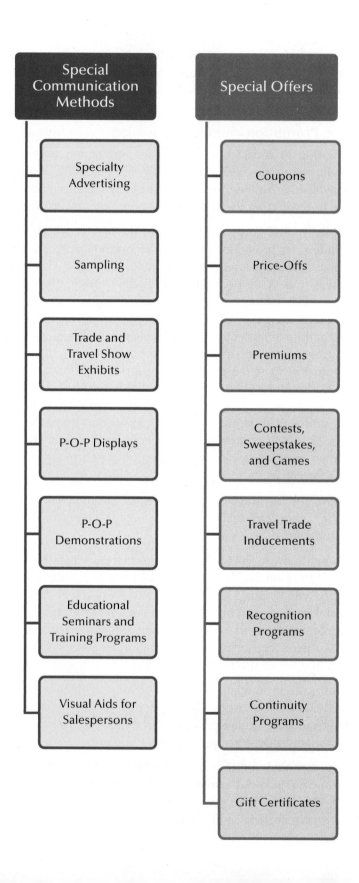

Special offers are short-term inducements given to customers, travel trade intermediaries, and sales representatives to take action. Customers and intermediaries who use special offers are generally required to make a purchase or reservation. If not, they at least have to take some definite action (e.g., enter and submit information online). Offers come in many forms, including sales or price reductions, gifts, free trips and meals, and extra commissions for travel trade intermediaries and sales representatives.

The choice from among the many sales promotion and merchandising techniques should be based on several factors. The first selection criterion must be the specific sales promotion and merchandising objectives. The second should be the characteristics of the customers within the markets being targeted. This includes the demographic/socio-economic and geographic profiles of customers. For example, customers in the United States respond well to coupons; however Spanish customers and marketers prefer immediate price reductions.[8]

Special Communication Methods

This group of techniques includes external promotions and various methods of in-house merchandising by hospitality and travel organizations. Nowadays it also includes the online merchandising or e-tailing of **brand extensions** by lodging, restaurants, attractions, DMOs, and other organizations. They also include techniques that some experts call *added-value promotions.*[9]

a. *Specialty Advertising.* **Specialty advertising** (also sometimes referred to as *advertising specialties* or *promotional products*) includes free items given to present or potential customers, or travel trade intermediaries. The five main strengths of specialty advertising items are: (1) targetability (can be sent or given directly to customers), (2) lasting ability (stay around, and be viewed again and again), (3) creative impact (can be especially themed and creatively designed), (4) goodwill (people like to receive gifts), and (5) applications flexibility.[10] Applications flexibility means they can be given to present or potential customers, or to travel trade intermediaries or sales representatives. They can be handed out at trade or travel shows, mailed, or passed on by sales representatives in the field.

   Often displaying the sponsor's name, logo, website address, or advertising message, these items normally are either office products or unique or unusual gifts. They include pens, pencils, cups, glasses, paperweights, calendars, mouse pads, stationery, key rings, tote bags, balloons, T-shirts, and many other items. The in-room guest amenities found in many hotel rooms (soaps, shampoo, skin conditioners, toothpaste, sewing kits, shower caps) also belong in this category, as do the amenity packs given out by airlines in first and business class cabins. According to the Promotional Products Association International, the most popular product categories in 2007 were wearables (30.71%), writing instruments (10.39%), bags (7.05%), drinkware (6.32%), desk/office/business accessories (6.19%), and calendars (5.51%).[11]

To be most effective, these items should be chosen and used according to the following steps:[12,13]

- Have a specific objective, e.g., to increase traffic to a booth or exhibit at a travel trade show or exhibition.
- Have a specific target market and are products that are highly desirable for these people, e.g., business people.
- Represent items that are useful, different or interesting. They should also relate to the type of hospitality and travel organization or destination.
- Are simple but not cheap.
- Have central themes that tie in with the items and, recognizable logos and/or color schemes.
- Have an effective distribution plan to get the items to the target market.
- Are integrated with advertising and other promotional mix elements, and are supported with a distinctive message.
- Are given to present customers first and also to employees.

Figure 16.5 shows an exquisite cookbook titled *Jinling Hotel Recipe 88*, which is given away to special guests and prospects. The Jinling

FIGURE 16.5 The Jinling Hotel's *Jinling Recipe Book 88* is an exquisite example of specialty advertising.

Courtesy of Jinling Hotel Corporation

Hotel Corporation in Nanjing, China, designed the book for the five-star hotel in Jiangsu Province. Eighty-eight different dishes and their recipes are included in this excellent specialty advertising piece.

There are also some limitations of weaknesses associated with specialty advertising items. They may have relatively high unit costs, require a plan for distribution, and the receiver must find somewhere to place or store the items, and may face space limitations in so doing. With approximately 500,000 potential items to select from, making a choice can be very difficult.[14] It is also true that many of these items are useless to customers, or look ugly or are in poor taste. They can quickly find an exit door!

b. *Sampling.* **Sampling** means giving away free samples of items to encourage sales, or arranging in some way for people to try all or part of a service. This is much easier for manufacturers of products to do, because what they have to sell is tangible and can be mailed or handed out. As you will recall from Chapter 2, most hospitality and travel services are intangible. Therefore, they cannot be mailed or handed out; or sampled in part. To sample them, the customer or travel trade intermediary must be invited to try services on a complimentary or no-additional-charge basis.

There are exceptions in the hospitality and travel industry including within some parts of the restaurant and foodservice, and lodging sectors. Restaurants, bars, and lounges can, subject to certain legal restrictions, give customers free samples of menu items or beverages. Often this is done with new items or in an effort to boost sales in certain meal periods or food and beverage categories (e.g., breakfasts, desserts, appetizers, wines, mixed cocktails). Starbucks is a good example of a company that regularly gives free samples of coffees and other items to customers. Restaurants in shopping malls also give away free tidbits to people passing by. Hotels can give tours of their properties to local companies or even free nights' of stay to local corporate travel managers. In January 2007, KFC gave away free samples in its United States' restaurants of its signature *Crispy Strips.* The company did this "sampling blitz" to boost sales of this popular menu item.[15]

Familiarization (or fam) trips (or tours) for travel agents, tour wholesalers/operators or travel writers are a second good example of sampling. **Site inspections** by convention/meeting planners are a third case in which potential MICE customers of destinations can have a first-hand experience of attractions, facilities and services. A fourth sampling technique is the free upgrade, where an airline, car rental firm, or hotel company allows travelers to enjoy a higher level of service than the one they paid for.

c. *Travel Trade Shows and Exhibitions.* Many hospitality and travel organizations exhibit at **travel trade shows**, exhibitions, fairs, or conventions

FIGURE 16.6 The China International Travel Mart (CITM) is a major annual travel show.

Photo by author

(Figure 16.6). Generally, these events bring all parts of the industry (suppliers, carriers, travel trade intermediaries, and DMOs) together. Some of the major shows held in the world each year are listed in Figure 16.7.

FIGURE 16.7 Major travel trade shows and exhibitions around the world.

Australian Tourism Exchange	Australia	http://www.tradeevents.australia.com/
BIT (Borsa Internazaionale del Turismo)	Milan, Italy	http://bit.expocts.it
EIBTM	Barcelona, Spain	http://www.eibtm.com/
International Pow Wow	United States	http://www.tia.org/powwow/
ITB	Berlin, Germany	http://www.itb-berlin.com
ITE HK	Hong Kong, China	http://www.itehk.com/ITEHK/
IT&ME (The Motivation Show)	Chicago	http://www.motivationshow.com
NTA Convention (National Tour Association)	United States	http://www.ntaonline.com
PATA Travel Mart	Asia-Pacific	http://www.pata.org
Rendez-vous Canada	Canada	http://www.rendezvouscanada.travel/
Salon Mondial du Tourisme	France	http://www.mondialtourisme.com/
World Travel Market	London, England	http://www.wtmlondon.com

There are several potential objectives in deciding to exhibit and have a booth at a travel trade show:[16]

- Developing an interest in the company, organization, or destination.
- Developing an interest in a brand or product.
- Increasing awareness.
- Generating qualified sales leads.
- Maintaining an image.
- Establishing a presence.
- Introducing a new product or service.
- Securing requests for proposals (RFPs) or other bids.

There are many advantages to trade show and exhibition participation. These include (relatively) inexpensive person-to-person contact, information exchange between buyers and sellers, and a shorter sales cycle (time compression in purchasing). There is considered to be real value in face-to-face meetings of sellers and buyers that cannot be matched by using e-mail, telephone, or mail. They provide an opportunity to build sound business relationships or points of negotiation. More information and answers can be gathered in a short period of time.[17]

Exhibiting at a travel trade show is similar to putting together a mini-promotional mix or IMC activity. Some exhibitors send out e-mails or direct mail pieces in advance (advertising) to travel trade intermediaries, inviting them to visit their booths. They may have written materials about show participation on their website (public relations and publicity). The booth displays (merchandising) attractively portray the available services and may be closely tied in with recent advertising campaigns. Representatives working the booth hand out brochures and other printed or digital materials, and try to develop sales leads (personal selling). They may also give away specialty advertising items (sales promotion). When the travel trade show is over, exhibitors often follow up with personalized mailings (e-mail or direct marketing), telephone or personal sales calls, or communications via an online messengers service (MSN, Yahoo, or Skype). A variety of sales promotion and merchandising techniques are often combined with good effect at a travel trade show. In fact, the travel trade show exhibit booth is a great example of the combination of sales promotion and merchandising. The booth merchandises, while the sales promotions include the specialty advertising items (e.g., bags) and brochures handed out.[18]

Travel trade shows are relatively expensive, because they involve travel costs, registration fees, exhibit booth display design and production, and other costs. To be the most effective, they require considerable planning before the events and careful follow-up and evaluation after the show is concluded. However, they offer the exhibitor a highly specialized target audience and an efficient alternative to making sales calls to thousands of prospects.

There are also many privately operated trade shows not listed in Figure 16.7 that are held in major cities and that move across the world. Additionally, hospitality and travel organizations can exhibit at numerous consumer travel, recreation, leisure, sports, and hobby shows. Here, they promote directly to customers rather than to intermediaries. These range from small shows in local shopping malls (sometimes called "road shows") to privately organized sports and recreation shows with hundreds of exhibitors.

INTERNET MARKETING

Travel Trade Show Promotion

The Charterhouse Hotel, Hong Kong

http://www.charterhouse.com/

Courtesy of Hong Kong Tourism Board

Hong Kong Island skyline at night.

Most hospitality, travel and tourism organizations put significant investments into the advertising and promotion of their brands, services, and products. Although online and offline advertising serve the purposes of creating awareness, image building and reinforcement, they are not sufficient for creating an interactive platform for both sellers and buyers.

To meet travel trade partners from different places means substantial travel and spending on transportation and accommodation. Moreover, the sales and marketing managers in travel trade companies have to invest much time to fly to different countries and cities to identify and find the right supplier and destination partners.

The Charterhouse is a privately-owned hotel with 294 rooms, conveniently located between Causeway Bay and Wan Chai in Hong Kong. It is not affiliated with any hotel chain; it's considered to be an "independent" hotel. Therefore, its marketing team needs to work harder to promote the hotel's brand.

(continues)

(continued)

Description of The Charterhouse Hotel on its website.

The Executive Assistant Manager of The Charterhouse Hotel in Hong Kong finds exhibiting at quality travel trade shows an effective tool to promote his hotel in the travel trade. He sees the return on investment in terms of exposure, business deals, client contacts, and incremental business. He feels the main benefits are as follows:

Benefits of Exhibiting at Quality Travel Trade Shows

Reaching Target Markets

Developing business from new markets means heavy investment in terms of time and travel. One has to fly to different cities to meet many contacts to find the right buyer. Marketers should know the target markets they are pursuing. So, it is more cost-effective to attend a travel trade show targeting a particular region or market like China,

(continues)

(continued)

India, Europe, or the U.S.A., where buyers such as travel managers of corporations, product managers of tour wholesalers, and travel media representatives gather. For example, exhibitors such as tour operators, hotels, and DMOs can meet many incentive and wholesale agents from China at the China International Travel Mart (CITM) that takes place in Shanghai or Kunming on alternative years.

Promoting New Services or Products

Throughout each year, international hotel chains launch new properties, airlines start new schedules and routes, and DMOs introduce different attractions and events. Having a booth at a travel trade show is effective in introducing new products and services, since sales and marketing executives can give a face-to-face introduction to buyers and the media. Promotional materials such as brochures, videos, and PowerPoint slides can be shown. Enquiries can be efficiently answered and in sufficient detail.

Cost-effective in Communications

A successful travel trade show draws a large number of visitors/buyers and exhibitors from different industry parts who share common objectives: buying, selling or promoting. Additionally, it offers a perfect opportunity for exhibitors to reinforce their corporate images. The show organizers invite qualified buyers or visitors to attend, according to the specific market segments and objectives of the shows. In most cases, successful travel trade shows bring quality buyers and sellers together. To target these buyers or visitors, different tourism suppliers such as hotels, attractions, DMOs, media companies, airlines and land tour operators pay participation fees (depending on the size and location of booths) to attend shows as exhibitors. Some of the shows such as PATA Travel Mart in Asia have a pre-show matching scheme to enable sellers and buyers to pre-schedule meetings before the show.

The exhibition fee varies according to the budget, number of participants, company scale, market potential and objectives of exhibitors. International hotel chains such as Marriott, Starwood, and InterContinental Hotel Group spend significant amounts each year when they have their Sales Directors from different hotel properties participating at various travel trade shows.

Some Popular Industry Trade Shows

European Incentive & Business Travel & Meetings Exhibition (EIBTM)
One of the world's leading incentive, business travel and meetings exhibitions, targeting major corporate and incentive agents, meeting planners and corporate end-users from European markets; www.eibtm.com

China International Travel Mart (CITM)
An annual event and the largest trade and consumer travel show in China. Wholesalers and tour operators in China participate in this

(continues)

(continued)

show. Many overseas buyers also join to meet suppliers in China; www.citm.com.cn/en/index.php

Incentive Travel & Meeting Executives Show (IT&ME)
(The Motivation Show)
It is one of the world's largest trade shows targeting incentive travel buyers, meeting planners, conventions and exhibitions organizers in the Americas; www.motivationshow.com

International Tourismus Boerse (ITB)
One of the world's most important international travel shows held in Berlin, Germany. Many European buyers participate in this show due to its proximity; http://www1.messe-berlin.de/vip8_1/website/Internet/Internet/www.itb-berlin/englisch/index.html

Arabian Travel Market (ATM)
A travel trade show held in Dubai, United Arab Emirates. It is a leading business platform for inbound, outbound, and intra-regional tourism in the Middle East and the only one to serve the whole Pan-Arab region; www.arabiantravelmarket.com

Seatrade Cruise Shipping Convention
A convention and exhibition held in Miami. It is a show covering the cruise and shipping industry; www.cruiseshipping.net

World Travel Market (WTM)
The World Travel Market is held annually in London. This is a mega travel trade platform for buyers and sellers to meet; www.wtmlondon.com

Tips for Effective Exhibition Participation

There are some important steps to enable exhibitors to differentiate themselves from competitors, including:

Exhibit Booth Design

To attract visitors or buyers and enhance corporate image, exhibitors must build booths with creative and impressive designs, according to their budgets, scale of operations, and corporate images. They should secure a booth location that is able to attract the right group of people. For example, a hotel in Singapore should choose a site close to the Singapore Tourism Board or in its pavilion. An Internet travel portal should select a booth location in the e-commerce business pavilion.

Pre-show Promotion

Before the trade show, exhibitors should promote their participation and booth locations. They can inform existing buyers or visitors by e-mail or regular mail. Some exhibitors advertise in the travel trade media in order to get more booth traffic. In addition, it is very important to produce sufficient marketing collateral materials (e.g., brochures, DVDs, etc.) to be distributed during a show.

(continues)

(continued)

Selling in the Booth

Exhibitors should send professionally trained sales executives to meet with buyers. They should be prepared to meet buyers, media representatives, and other visitors, and to introduce services or products. For those buyers who show a keen interest, they should be ready to negotiate and close deals. Some hotel chains and DMOs have hospitality areas or meeting rooms where chain executives and buyers can meet in greater comfort. This is also an effective way to enhance corporate image.

Courtesy of Belle Tourism International Consulting

Giving away bags for collecting information is popular at travel trade shows.

Timely Follow Up

After the show, the sales executives must take prompt action such as organizing familiarization tours, site visit invitations, quotations, submissions of contracts, or mailing of promotional materials. Most exhibitors want to see a return on investment from travel trade shows in terms of incremental business and revenue, and following up is a key to securing that ROI.

(continues)

(continued)

Discussion Questions

1. How can all of the promotional mix elements and Internet marketing be used in planning and exhibiting at travel trade shows?
2. What steps should be followed to determine the return on investment (ROI) of exhibiting at a travel trade show?
3. Which techniques can a hospitality and travel organization use to make its exhibit booth stand out from its competitors?

Source: The author acknowledges the contribution of Raymond Siu in his preparing this case study. Raymond is the Executive Assistant Manager—Sales & Marketing, The Charterhouse Hotel, 209-219 Wanchai Road, Wanchai, Hong Kong SAR.

---

d. *Point-of-Sale (P-O-S) Displays and Other Merchandising Materials.*
You already know about the importance of merchandising in the hospitality and travel industry. This promotional technique is used most effectively at the point of sale or purchase, hence its frequent abbreviation to point-of-sale advertising. An enormous variety of display items and configurations is available. In the restaurant and foodservice sector, menus, wine and drink lists, and tent cards are the key tools (Figure 16.8). Some restaurants and bars also attach banners to building exteriors, or use signs that can be updated frequently, to announce special promotions. Others post menus online, give away mini-menus, or place their full menus near front entrances. Brochures, posters, and window and stand-up displays are common in retail travel agencies. Hotels use a wide range of merchandising techniques, including in-room guest

FIGURE 16.8 Menus are a primary merchandising tool in restaurants.

directories, room-service menus, elevator and lobby displays, and brochure racks (Figure 16.9).

e. *Point-of-Purchase Demonstrations.* Again because of the intangibility of services, it is more difficult to demonstrate their use at the point of purchase. It is much easier to do this with products. You have probably seen many salespeople demonstrate the cleaning capabilities of vacuum cleaners or the chopping features of vegetable cutters. So how do you tangibly demonstrate the seemingly intangible? One method being used by an increasing number of travel agencies is to show travel promotion DVDs on in-store TV or computer monitors. Other possibilities include demonstrating cooking methods or mixing cocktails in restaurants and bars. Cinnabon offers a wonderful example of this in making its cinnamon rolls in front of customers.

f. *Educational Seminars and Training Programs.* The hospitality and travel industry invests heavily in this type of sales promotion to inform and educate travel trade intermediaries. Airlines, cruise lines, tour wholesalers, and DMOs frequently arrange these seminars, workshops, receptions, and training programs for travel agents and tour wholesalers. The primary objective is to pass on more detailed information and to help travel agents sell services to clients and to assist tour wholesalers with tour product development. Like travel trade shows, these events, often staged throughout the country, are relatively expensive, but they offer the sponsor a highly targeted and influential audience. A good example is the *Aussie Specialist* program offered by Tourism Australia. This training program for retail travel agents is offered in an online format. Celebrity Cruises offers *Celebrity's 5 Star Academy*, a five-part online training program for travel agents. Cancun Visitors and Convention Bureau in

FIGURE 16.9 Colorful merchandising at a club.

Mexico has the *Cancun Tourism Institute*, in which travel agents can study to become an *Official Cancun Counselor*.

g. ***Audio-visual Materials for Sales Representatives.*** The intangibility of hospitality and travel services also poses a problem for field sales representatives. They cannot, like most salespeople representing products, demonstrate the service in the prospect's place of business. Audio-visual materials such as DVDs and PowerPoint presentations play a key role in helping them give prospects an understanding of the quality and variety of their organizations' services. Other materials used include binders containing high-quality color photographs and stand-up displays.

Special Offers

The second main category of sales promotion techniques is special offers— short-term inducements to get people to take action, frequently to make purchases. These offers are usually run in conjunction with Internet marketing programs or media advertising campaigns and are often supported by point-of-sale merchandising, personal selling, and publicity. Many of these can be categorized as *price promotions* including coupons, price offs, and premiums.[19]

a. *Coupons.* **Coupons** are one of the most popular sales promotion techniques. They are used extensively in the hospitality and travel industry, especially among restaurants. You will be interested to know that they are also the most misused. Coupons are vouchers or certificates that entitle customers or intermediaries to a reduced price on the couponed service or services. They can be handed, sent to customers, or included in newspaper or magazine ("hard copy"); or downloaded from a website or sent by e-mail ("soft copy"). Customers make heavy use of coupons. For example, the Promotional Marketing Association estimates that 76 percent of U.S. consumers use coupons.[20]

People around the world are inundated by coupons. They are offered online and through the mail, newspapers, and magazines; on bulletin boards; and even with your pizza. According to NCH Marketing Services, Inc. a staggering 285 billion coupons were distributed in the United States in 2007. Customers used coupons worth approximately $2.6 billion. The average face value of a redeemed coupon was 99 cents in 2007.[21]

Coupon redemption rates (percentage of total issued coupons used by customers) vary according to how the coupons are distributed. The coupons used by the hospitality and travel industry are mainly manufacturer coupons. They are developed and distributed directly to customers, not through travel trade intermediaries. The main methods of distributing these coupons are:[22]

- Distribution in the print media. For example, a large proportion (88 percent in the U.S. in 2007) of coupons are distributed as **FSIs (freestanding inserts)**
- Handouts to consumers
- Direct mail

- Magazines and other newspapers
- In or on packaging

Why have coupons so popular? There are two sides to the story. The first reason is that customers are more concerned with prices and value for money than ever before. Coupons deliver greater value in the form of a price reduction. The second reason is the increased competitiveness among manufacturers and service organizations. Advertising alone often cannot provide enough of a competitive edge.

There are different types of coupons used in the hospitality and travel industry. A *time-fused coupon* offer includes several individual coupons that can be used during specified days, weeks, or months during the offer period. Coupons should all have a clearly indicated expiry date. A *bounce-back coupon* is an offer that attempts to get the customer to use a restaurant or other service again. These are handed to customers or glued, stapled, or inserted in packages. Most pizza chains use this approach by gluing bounce-backs to the outside of pizza delivery boxes.

b. *Price-Offs.* **Price-offs** are simply an advertised price reduction that does not involve using a coupon (Figure 16.10). These discounts are often limited to certain services (menu items, air fares, and cruise excursions), target markets (business travelers, senior citizens, or children), geographic areas, or time periods. They are really a form of price

FIGURE 16.10 Sales and price-offs are a common type of special-offer sales promotion.

Image copyright Petr Vaclavek, 2008. Used under license from Shutterstock.com

discounting supported by promotion. Price-offs are popular because they can be introduced almost immediately.

Price-offs should not be used on their own, but as part of carefully developed IMC programs. They work best when offered only for a short time. For example, the Malaysia Savings Sales 2008 offered large shopping discounts over the period of November 29, 2008 to January 4, 2009. These sales also included a special *Tourist Privilege Card* offering further deals for foreign visitors to Malaysia.

c. *Premiums.* **Premiums** are merchandise items that are offered at a reduced price with the purchase of services or products. They differ from specialty advertising because there is a definite obligation to purchase. The most successful premiums require multiple-item purchases or multiple purchase occasions. In other words, they are *frequency* or *continuity* devices. Customers have to visit more than once to collect the whole set or must show several proofs of purchase. Another important guideline for premiums is that they must be consistent with the sponsor's image (position) and target market. This again is the experience clues concept discussed in Chapter 2. An inexpensive, low-quality toy that falls apart after only a few minutes' use does not reflect the quality of food that most fast-food restaurants claim to serve. Conversely, it does not make much sense for a budget-oriented organization to promote top-of-the-line premiums.

Premiums should be thought of as another way to communicate the positioning approach and association with the selected target markets, e.g., children and families with McDonald's *Happy Meals.* The use of children's toys is very consistent with fast-food chains' appeal to and reliance on children. For example, in late 2008 Burger King was including Wii™ toys in its BK® Kids Meals in the U.S.

d. *Contests, Sweepstakes, and Games.* You, like everybody else, love to win prizes or games. Entering contests, sweepstakes, or other forms of games is exciting. It elevates your interest in a subject, product, or service.

Contests are sales promotions where entrants win prizes based on some required skill that they are asked to demonstrate. For example, the Bermuda Department of Tourism and JetBlue offered the "Feel the Love" contest in April-May 2008. Entrants were required to submit a short essay about how they fell in love with Bermuda.[23]

Sweepstakes are sales promotions that require entrants to submit their names and addresses. Winners are chosen on the basis of chance, not skill. In some countries these are called "lucky draws." In late 2008, Starwood Hotels & Resorts Worldwide introduced a clever online training program for travel agents, which was combined with a sweepstakes. If agents completed module one of the program by January 31, 2009, they were eligible to enter the sweepstakes to win a 4-night stay at a Starwood property.[24]

Games are sales promotion events similar to sweepstakes, but they involve using game pieces, such as scratch-and-win and match-and-win cards. McDonald's combined with Monopoly in a *Money Monopoly* game in 2006 and earlier years. This match-and-win game was offered in

McDonald's restaurants using game pieces, but there was also an online version of the game.[25] Scratch-and-win games are used in restaurants throughout China, where rub off sections in their receipts to win instant discounts on their dining bills.

Contests, sweepstakes, and games are helpful in communicating key benefits, unique selling points (USPs), and other information. They are also good at elevating awareness and reminding people about the sponsor's services. Contests, sweepstakes, and games can be directed at customers, travel trade intermediaries, or sales representatives.

Hyatt introduced an interesting variation of this technique in 2007 with its *Hyatt Resorts Recommend Reward Program* for travel agents. Travel agents were eligible to win a $500 prize if they recommended a Hyatt Resort on the telephone in response to an enquiry from a member of the Hyatt resorts' team.[26]

e. *Travel Trade Intermediary Inducements.* As you have seen throughout this book, travel trade intermediaries can be a powerful ally to suppliers, carriers, and DMOs. Because of this, they are aggressively pursued by many organizations and are sometimes offered inducements of various kinds for reservations and confirmed bookings.

Travel agents, convention/meeting planners, and corporate travel managers are among the most hotly pursued travel trade intermediaries. Preferred supplier relationships and the offering of above-average commissions are becoming popular ways for carriers and suppliers to get more business from particular travel agencies. Convention/meeting planners and corporate travel managers often have enough bargaining power to convince suppliers, carriers, and DMOs to provide price discounts or other extras in order to secure their business.

You already know that other forms of inducements are used in travel trade promotions. They include specialty advertising items, familiarization trips, sweepstakes, and educational seminars.

f. *Recognition Programs.* A **recognition program** offers awards to travel trade intermediaries, sales representatives, or customers for achieving or providing certain levels of sales or business. The award may or may not involve cash. The Unlimited Budget program for travel agents is a cash award program operated by Budget Rent A Car System. For every qualified booking, Budget pays points in a stored value MasterCard account (http://www.unlimitedbudget.com). Non-cash awards such as free travel, trophies, wall plaques, or photographs in prominent journals are sometimes better at getting people to use the sponsor's services more often or to reach sales volume goals.

Frequent-flyer and **frequent-guest award programs** are examples of recognition programs for customers. A good example of a customer recognition program is "Priority Club," InterContinental Hotels Group's frequent guest program and the first of its type in the lodging sector. In the PerksPlus® program operated by United and Lufthansa, small and medium-sized companies earn mileage points for their employees when they fly. To qualify, companies must spend at least $20,000 on a yearly basis on flights with United, Lufthansa, United Express, and Ted.[27]

g. *Continuity Programs.* **Continuity programs** are sales promotions that require people to make several purchases, sometimes over a long period of time. Frequent-flyer and frequent-guest programs are *continuity recognition programs.* Travelers must stay at a hotel chain several times, or log a certain number of air miles, to earn rewards. Usually, the objective of a continuity program is either to stimulate more frequent purchases or to build long-term loyalty for a company or brand. They are considered one of the best sales promotions for building a long-term business. For example, American Airlines has an 18-month *AAdvantage*® *Mileage Retention Policy.* This requires that members must have mileage earning or redemption activity once every 18 months to be active and retain their miles.[28]

Continuity programs are not really a different technique, but an approach that can be used with any of the sales promotions already described. For example, a continuity premium is a program where customers must make several purchases to collect a set of items (e.g., a set of four glasses, one available each week in a four-week period).

Credit-card companies have become heavily involved with the hospitality and travel industry's continuity recognition programs. For example, by charging any purchases to a special Citibank Visa card, members of American Airlines' AAdvantage program receive additional miles. As well as being a type of sales promotion, these **affinity cards** are also a good example of partnerships in marketing hospitality and travel along with other industries' services. While the airlines set the initial trend toward these affinity cards, others in hospitality and tourism were quick to emulate them, including the hotel chains and some DMOs.

h. *Gift Certificates.* **Gift certificates** are vouchers or checks that are either selectively given away by the sponsor or sold to customers who, in turn, give them to others as gifts. The first type of certificate functions much like coupons encouraging recipients to try the services. Again, these are frequently used by restaurants. For example, Hardee's sells "gift cards" through its website (http://www.hardees.com/giftcards/). Gift certificates are also extensively promoted by hotel chains. Hyatt makes "Hyatt Gift Cards and Gift Certificates" available online at its website.[29] A gift certificate pack may or may not feature a discount on its face value.

Select Media for Distributing Sales Promotions (Step 6)

Now that you know there are a great variety of sales promotion techniques to choose from, it is time to consider how your selected promotion will be distributed. The distribution method you selected is extremely important, because it influences the percentage of targeted persons who take advantage of a sales promotion.

Decide on Timing of Sales Promotions and Merchandising (Step 7)

As you already know, sales promotions and merchandising programs should be tactical or short term. They are often used to attack traditionally slow business periods, and this seems to be their most effective application. But there are really two parts to the timing question: (1) When is the best time to use sales promotions? and (2) How often should they be used? Overusing sales promotions can erode profitability and give an organization an unfavorable image. Some of the major dangers in using them too often include the following:

1. They may lead to temporary sales increases, masking longer-term problems in other marketing and promotional mix elements. Stated another way, they treat the symptoms, not the illness.
2. Sales promotions that promote special offers (e.g., coupons and premiums) are, in essence, a form of price competition (as you will see in Chapter 19). There are two basic problems with price competition: (1) it is an approach that competitors can easily imitate and (2) it loses its impact over the long term.
3. Sales promotions can be introduced quickly, and they produce almost immediate results. For this reason, they are often used hurriedly without sufficient consideration of their impact on other promotional and marketing-mix elements.

It is best to consider sales promotions as a supportive, tactical tool for advertising, personal selling, public relations, and Internet marketing as part of integrated marketing communications (IMC) programs. The timing of promotions, therefore, should be dictated by the schedules for advertising, personal selling activities, and public relations. Sales promotions should be used when the marketer is confident that they can complement and increase the probability of achieving selling and advertising objectives.

Pre-test Sales Promotions and Merchandising (Step 8)

Again, it is important to pre-test sales promotions and merchandising materials before introducing them. This should be done by using marketing research techniques similar to those described for advertising in Chapter 15.

Prepare Final Sales Promotion and Merchandising Plan and Budget (Step 9)

With the pre-testing completed, the final sales promotion plan and budget can be written. The sales promotion plan should describe the sales promotion objectives, research results, and assumptions leading to decisions, budget, and implementation timetable. Detailed sales promotion costs should then be compared with the tentative sales promotion budget and modifications made where necessary.

Measure and Evaluate Sales Promotion and Merchandising Success (Step 10)

Because sales promotion results are more immediate and short term, it is even more important to monitor their implementation closely. Marketing research techniques, including post-testing, should be used to determine if sales promotion and merchandising objectives have been achieved.

Chapter Conclusion

Sales promotions and merchandising can be powerful elements in the promotional mix. The potential power of sales promotions is in creating almost immediate sales increases, which are especially helpful during off-peak periods. Overuse of sales promotions, however, carries serious dangers, including erosion of customer loyalty and reduced profitability.

Sales promotions should be used tactically and be carefully planned to coincide with and complement advertising, personal selling, public relations, and Internet marketing efforts. It is in a supportive role to these other promotional mix elements that the greatest benefits of sales promotion and merchandising can be realized.

REVIEW QUESTIONS

1. How are the terms *sales promotion* and *merchandising* defined in this chapter?
2. What six roles do sales promotions and merchandising play in the marketing of hospitality and travel services?
3. Sales promotions are best used to support advertising, personal selling, public relations, and Internet marketing. Is this an accurate statement? Explain your answer.
4. How are special communication methods and special-offer promotions different?
5. Which sales promotion techniques are available to hospitality and travel marketers?
6. What are the advantages and disadvantages of each sales promotion and merchandising technique?
7. What are the 10 steps that should be followed when developing the sales promotion and merchandising plan?

CHAPTER ASSIGNMENTS

1. Select the part of the hospitality and travel industry in which you are most interested. Over a period of several weeks or months, track the sales promotion and merchandising activities of five or six leaders in the field. Collect items such as coupons, premiums, and contest/ sweepstake/game materials. Are the techniques that are used similar

and, if not, how do they differ? Do you feel that any of your selected companies are overusing sales promotions? Are sales promotions tied in with advertising, personal selling, public relations, and Internet marketing? Who has the most effective sales promotion program and why?

2. You are in charge of the marketing program for a travel agency, hotel, resort, airline, cruise line, restaurant, DMO, or other hospitality and travel organization. A period of traditionally low sales is approaching, and you have decided to use a sales promotion or promotions to boost sales. What technique(s) would you choose, and why? What steps would you follow in planning, implementing, and evaluating these activities? How would you tie the sales promotions and merchandising in with advertising, personal selling, public relations, and Internet marketing for maximum impact?

3. The owners of a small hospitality and travel business are considering using coupon promotions, and they have come to you for advice. What advantages and disadvantages of coupons would you discuss with them? What types of coupons would you recommend that they use? When and how should they be used? How should the success of these promotions be measured and evaluated?

4. Sales promotions can be divided into two distinct categories: (1) special communication methods and (2) special offers. Write a paper outlining the advantages and disadvantages of both approaches. Which of the approaches and specific techniques would you recommend to a hospitality and travel organization that has never used them before? How would you suggest these approaches and techniques be used for maximum effectiveness?

WEB RESOURCES

Cancun Tourism Institute, http://www.cancun-cti.com/cti_intro_en.html
Celebrity Cruises Celebrity's 5 Star Academy,
    http://www. celebrity5staracademy.com/
Harrison Hot Springs Resort & Spa, http://www.harrisonresort.com/
Hyatt, http://www.hyatt.com/
Malaysia Savings Sale, http://www.malaysiamegasale.com.my/
NCH Marketing Services, Inc., http://www.nchmarketing.com/
Olive Garden, http://www.olivegarden.com/
PerksPlus®, http://www.perkspluspartners.com/
Promotional Marketing Association, http://www.pmalink.org/
Promo, http://promomagazine.com/
Promotional Products Association International, http://www.ppa.org/
Rail Europe, http://www.raileurope.com/
Tourism Australia, http://www.specialist.australia.com/

REFERENCES

1. Promotion Marketing Association. 2002. *Four-year Research Study Concludes: Sales Promotion Benefit to Consumers and Businesses*, http://www.pmalink.org/press_releases/default.asp?p=pr_06112002, accessed December 28, 2008.

2. Kotler, Philip, and Kevin Lane Keller. 2006. *Marketing Management*. 12th ed. Upper Saddle River, N.J.: Pearson Prentice Hall, 544.

3. Kotler, Philip, and Kevin Lane Keller. 2006. *Marketing Management*. 12th ed. Upper Saddle River, N.J.: Pearson Prentice Hall, 545.

4. ShermansTravel.com. 2008. *Caribbean & Mexico Vacation Deals*, http://www.shermanstravel.com/deals/vacations/mexico/, accessed December 28, 2008.

5. Hyatt Corporation. 2008. *Hyatt Resorts' Slice of Paradise*, https://www.hyatt.com/hyatt/travelagents/paradise/index.jsp?icamp=HY_SliceOfParadise_BF, accessed December 28, 2008.

6. Shi, Yi-Zheng, Ka-Man Cheung, and Gerard Prendergast. 2005. "Behavioral response to sales promotion tools." A Hong Kong study. *International Journal of Advertising*, 24(4), 467–486.

7. Dommermuth, William P. 1989. *Promotion: Analysis, Creativity, and Strategy*. 2nd ed. Boston: PWS-Kent Publishing Company, 47–48.

8. Alverez, Begona Alverez, and Rodolfo Vazquez Casielles. 2005. "Consumer evaluations of sales promotion: the effect on brand choice." *European Journal of Marketing*, 39 (1/2), 54–70.

9. Kotler, Philip, and Kevin Lane Keller. 2006. *Marketing Management*. 12th ed. Upper Saddle River, N.J.: Pearson Prentice Hall, 544.

10. Nelson, Richard Alan, and Ali Kanso. 2002. "Today's Promotional Products Industry: The Rise of a Powerful Marketing Communication Medium." *Journal of Promotion Management*, 8(1), 3–24.

11. Promotional Products Association International. 2007. "PPAI: The 2007 Estimate of Promotional Products Distributor Sales." Irving, Texas: Promotional Products Association International.

12. Council of Better Business Bureaus, Inc. 2002. *Ordering Specialty Advertising Items Can Be Good for Business*, http://www.bbb.org/Alerts/article.asp?ID=383, accessed December 29, 2008.

13. Promotional Products Association International. 2008. *Seven Steps to a Successful Promotional Campaign*, http://www.ppa.org/Media/Industry%20Information/Seven%20Steps%20to%20a%20Successful%20Promotional%20Campaign/, accessed December 28, 2008.

14. Nelson, Richard Alan, and Ali Kanso. 2002. "Today's Promotional Products Industry: The Rise of a Powerful Marketing Communication Medium." *Journal of Promotion Management*, 8(1), 16–17.

15. Johannes, Amy. 2007. "KFC takes a shot at Wendy's with free chicken strips." *Promo Magazine*, January 29, 2007.

16. Tanner, Jr., John F., and Lawrence B. Chonko. 2002. "Using Trade Shows Throughout the Product Life Cycle." *Journal of Promotion Management*, 8(1), 109–125.

17. Palumbo, Fred, and Paul A. Herbig. 2002. "Trade Shows and Fairs: An Important Part of the International Promotion Mix." *Journal of Promotion Management*, 8(1), 93–108.

18. Horn, Lisa. 2002. "Making Trade Shows Pay Off: Utilizing Promotional Gifts Rather Than Giveaways." *Journal of Promotion Management*, 8(1), 127–136.

19. Kotler, Philip, and Kevin Lane Keller. 2006. *Marketing Management*. 12th ed. Upper Saddle River, N.J.: Pearson Prentice Hall, 544.

20. Promotion Marketing Association. 2005. *For the Love of the Deal: Consumers Rave about Deal Enjoyment of Using Coupons, As Well As Cost Savings*, http://www.pmalink.org/press_releases/default.asp?p=pr_09012005, accessed December 28, 2008.

21. NCH Marketing Services. 2008. *Overview of U.S. Coupon Distribution and Redemption Trends*, https://www.nchmarketing.com/Resource Center/couponknowledgestream2_ektid2941.aspx, accessed December 29, 2008.

22. NCH Marketing Services. 2008. *2008 Coupon Facts*, http://www.nchcouponfacts.com/Main/d1.aspx, accessed December 29, 2008.

23. Johannes, Amy. 2008. "Bermuda Tourism Department, JetBlue Team for Sweeps." *Promo Magazine*, April 8, 2008.

24. Starwood Hotels & Resorts Worldwide. 2008. *Introducing ProLearning*. http://www.starwoodhotels.com/pro/index.html?EM=VTY_CORP_pro, accessed December 29, 2008.

25. Jaffee, Larry. 2007. "Burger Blast." *Promo Magazine*, May 2007, 48.

26. Hyatt Corporation. 2008. *Hyatt Resorts Recommend Reward Program*, https://www.hyatt.com/hyatt/travelagents/paradise/recommend.jsp?icamp=HY_ComplimentaryAmenity_BF, accessed December 29, 2008.

27. PerksPlus. 2008. *Making business travel more fruitful*, http://www.perkspluspartners.com/, accessed December 29, 2008.

28. American Airlines. 2008. *AAdvantage Mileage Retention Policy*. http://www.aa.com/aa/i18nForward.do?p=/utility/mileageExpiration.jsp, accessed December 29, 2008.

29. Hyatt Corporation. 2008. *Create a lasting impression with Hyatt Gift Cards and Gift Certificates*. https://www.certificates.hyatt.com/ConsumerCerts.aspx?icamp=HY_GiftCards_HPGS, accessed December 29, 2008.

chapter 17

Personal Selling and Sales Management
How Do We Get There?

O V E R V I E W

Many consider personal selling to be the most powerful promotional mix element in generating sales. In October 2005, this was confirmed in a survey of US lodging sales and marketing managers conducted by Hospitality Sales and Marketing Association International (HSMAI) and PKF Hospitality Research.[1] The results showed personal selling was considered to have the best return on investment (ROI), followed by the hotel's website, public relations, e-mail marketing, national/corporate advertising, and local advertising. However, personal selling is also one of the most expensive promotional mix elements. For example, in 2005 it was estimated that the salaries, wages, and benefits paid to sales department staff in lodging properties represented 55.6 percent of total marketing department expenses.[2]

O B J E C T I V E S

Having read this chapter, you should be able to:

- Define personal selling.
- Explain the roles of personal selling.
- List the three categories of personal selling.
- Describe five major personal selling strategies.
- Explain the steps in the sales process.
- Describe the seven possible strategies for closing sales.
- Define sales management and explain its functions.
- Describe the characteristics of the successful salesperson.
- Describe the contents and role of the sales plan.
- Explain four characteristics of personal selling in the hospitality and travel industry.

KEY TERMS

AIDA formula	lead prospecting	sales management
approach	MICE market	sales management audit
blind prospecting	online prospecting	sales mission
call centers	outlined presentation	sales plan
canned sales presentation	outside sales	sales presentation
closing	personal selling	sales process
cold calling (canvassing)	pre-approach	sales prospects
consultative selling	prospecting	sales quotas
customer relationship management (CRM)	qualifying	sales territories
	relationship selling	stimulus response
Directors of Sales (DOS)	RFP	suggestive selling (up-selling)
field sales	sales blitz	telemarketing
handling objections	sales calls	telephone sales
inside sales	sales lead	

This chapter begins by defining personal selling and then discusses the role played by personal selling in the promotional mix. Personal selling varies in importance in different parts of the hospitality and travel industry. The chapter explains the reasons for these differences and the role of selling in specific industry parts and sectors. The steps involved in the personal sales process are also reviewed. The chapter ends by looking at the sales plan and sales management.

Have you ever gone into a store and bought much more than you thought you would? Have you recently consumed a calorie-laden dessert on the recommendation of a waitperson? How often have you heard the question, "Do you want fries with that?" and succumbed to the temptation? Was your new car, stereo, or outfit just a little more expensive than you thought it would be? If you answered "yes" to any of these questions, then you know how effective personal selling can be.

Advertising, sales promotion, and merchandising are impersonal and mass forms of communications. No matter how hard the companies that use them try, they are not dealing with you as an individual. You can turn the volume down on your radio, MP3, or television when commercials are playing. Commercial time can easily become a convenient time for a trip to the refrigerator or bathroom. You can toss coupons in the waste-paper basket, along with direct mail flyers. You can even completely ignore gimmicky in-store merchandising. But if you are like most of us, you cannot turn off another human being quite as easily. People buy many of those extra desserts and French fries because they find it hard to say "no" to others presenting them with sales arguments. No matter how much you might come to resent the questions, "Can I help you with something?" or "Do you want _____ with that?" you cannot really ignore the messages because of the person who is delivering them. This is the real power of personal selling—the ability to deal one-on-one with customers and to develop rapport and personal relationships.

Personal Selling and the Promotional Mix

Definition

Personal selling involves oral conversations, either by telephone or face-to-face, between salespersons and prospective customers. These days it also includes two-way communications through online messenger services like MSN, Yahoo, and Skype to name a few. Unlike advertising, sales promotion, merchandising, and Internet marketing, this promotional mix element is a form of personal communication, which introduces some unique advantages and potential problems.

The high degree of personalization that personal selling involves usually comes at a much greater cost per contact than does mass communications techniques. Marketers must decide whether this added expense can be justified, or whether marketing objectives can be achieved by communicating with potential customers as groups. As you will see later, some hospitality and travel organizations favor personal selling far more than others. For them, the potential benefits greatly outweigh the extra costs. In other words, the strengths of personal selling are more important to some hospitality and travel organizations than to others. Other organizations are turning more to the Internet, finding it to be more efficient and cost-saving than having a large professional sales staff.

Plan Integrated Marketing Communications First

Again, you should know up-front that it is incorrect to think of personal selling as an alternative to advertising, sales promotion, merchandising, public relations and publicity, and Internet marketing. Rather, they should all be viewed as the ingredients of a good recipe. Each ingredient in a recipe adds something special to the dish. Varying the quantities of ingredients can change the dish's flavor, taste, color, and texture. Forgetting to include an important ingredient can spoil the entire dish. Choosing a promotional mix in this way is similar to cooking. An organization can select its own combination of promotional mix elements and Internet marketing. Like a garnish, personal selling tends to add the finishing touch to the promotional mix and Internet marketing. An organization's sales representatives draw upon what has been communicated through mass communications channels.

Chapter 16 mentioned the five-punch combination of advertising, Internet marketing, sales promotion, merchandising, and public relations/publicity. Each of these builds on the other. This approach can be even more powerful in generating sales when it is finished off with personal selling. For example, many cruise lines use a combination of magazine and television advertising and the Web to make potential passengers aware of their departures. This media and online effort is supported by various forms of sales promotion and merchandising, including brochures, travel trade show exhibits, educational seminars and familiarization trips for travel agents, and retail travel agency displays. The final ingredient, and the one that really closes cruise sales, is personal selling by the retail travel agent. These knowledgeable professionals can fully explain the advantages of cruises over other forms of vacations, and they can excite clients about an individual cruise line's format. For example, Figure 17.1 shows the *How to Book* web page of Carnival Cruise Lines that leads customers to travel agents who will complete the sales. To make sure that travel agents stay well informed and enthusiastic, cruise lines have their own sales representatives who call on travel agencies throughout the country. Whether it is a cruise line or a small, independent restaurant trying to increase its wine sales, the greatest success comes from the well-orchestrated and carefully preplanned use of personal selling in combination with advertising, sales promotion, merchandising, public relations and publicity, and Internet marketing.

FIGURE 17.1 Carnival Cruise Lines' website refers customers to travel agents for bookings.

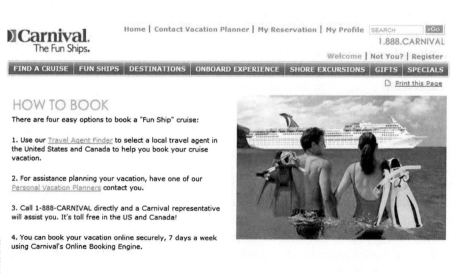

Roles of Personal Selling

What are the roles of personal selling in marketing and the promotional mix? Let us start by saying that there is a role for personal selling in every hospitality and travel organization, although its relative importance varies. Why? The answer is that our business is service, and it is very difficult to separate good service from effective personal selling. When a desk clerk, waitperson, reservationist, or travel agent says the right things and pleases customers, this constitutes both good service and good personal selling. Customers return primarily because of good service.

There are several important roles of personal selling in the hospitality and travel industry. The six that follow are the most important:

1. **Identifying Decision Makers, Decision Processes, and Qualified Buyers.** When targeting corporations, associations, and other groups, it is often very difficult to identify qualified buyers (the most likely purchasers of travel services), key decision makers (the person or persons who have the final say in travel decisions), and the decision processes used (the steps involved in making travel decisions). This important information can be gathered effectively through online searches, telephone inquiries by sales representatives and sales calls on organizations. In this way, costly mistakes can be avoided, such as communicating with the wrong people (non-decision-makers) at an inappropriate time (e.g., too late in the decision process), or addressing irrelevant needs or requirements in sales presentations.

2. **Promoting to Corporate, Travel Trade, and Other Groups.** Many organizations find personal selling to be most effective in promoting to key travel decision makers and influencers, such as corporate travel managers, convention/meeting planners, tour wholesalers/operators, and retail travel agents. These people's decisions affect the trip plans of many individual travelers. Their purchasing power is impressive and there are relatively few of them; this justifies the added expense of personal selling. The **MICE market** (Meeting-Incentive-Conference/Convention-Event/Exhibition) is an especially important target for personal selling in the hospitality and travel industry, and particularly for hotels, DMOs, and convention/exhibition centers.

3. **Generating Increased Sales at the Point of Purchase.** Used effectively at the point of purchase, personal selling can significantly increase the likelihood of a purchase and the amount spent by customers. Where are the points of purchase in the hospitality and travel industry? They include the hotel reservation (e.g., selling upgraded guest accommodations) and car rental desk (e.g., selling more expensive car models), the restaurant floor (e.g., selling more expensive or additional menu items and beverages), and the travel agency office (e.g., booking hotels and cars along with airline reservations). Another important place is where telephone

The Global Perspective: The Big Picture

Selling Cities to Mice Markets on the World Stage

BestCities Global Alliance

http://www.bestcities.net

Image copyright July Flower, 2008. Used under license from Shutterstock.com

Vancouver Harbour and the Vancouver Convention & Exhibition Centre.

The BestCities Global Alliance links together eight major cities and their convention bureaus. The cities are Vancouver (British Columbia, Canada), Cape Town (South Africa), Copenhagen (Denmark), Edinburgh (Scotland), Singapore, Dubai (UAE), San Juan (Puerto Rico), and Melbourne (Australia). It is a great example of a partnership among DMOs, as was discussed in Chapter 10. However, it's also an outstanding example of sales and service for the MICE markets at a worldwide level.

In terms of service to MICE clients, the BestCities Global Alliance has developed a *global client service charter*. This guarantees that its members' service levels are built around reliability, assurance, innovation, empathy and responsiveness. The Service Charter is as follows:

> *As members of BestCities Global Alliance we commit ourselves to the principles of the Service Charter in all dealings with our clients thus setting new standards of service excellence for Convention & Visitor Bureaux. The Service Charter sets out measures of success in five key areas. Our clients can expect the following from all BestCities members:*

Measures of Success Our Commitment

- *Reliability*—To deliver consistency in our service standards to audit our service standards by an independent organization

(continues)

(continued)

- *Assurance*—To deliver destination expertise in an honest and professional manner that meets or exceeds our client's expectations to ask our clients for their evaluation and satisfactions
- *Innovation*—To explore new ideas and opportunities with our clients that enhance the meeting experience and value to embrace a global perspective
- *Empathy*—We are client driven we will engage our global network to enhance client relationships that promote a better understanding of their needs
- *Responsiveness*—We will provide accurate, relevant and timely responses to client requests

The Alliance achieved a third party certification of their convention service standards by Lloyd's Register Quality Assurance in 2008 as part of establishing a global quality management system and 33 service standards. BestCities Global Alliance partners also undertake joint sales & PR activities and share conference leads to increase sales opportunities.

Image copyright Sculpies, 2008. Used under license from Shutterstock.com

Table Mountain in Cape Town, South Africa.

The RFP for a Convention or Meeting

From the sales perspective, all of the destinations in the BestCities Alliance have developed RFPs as a basis for their personal selling efforts in the MICE markets. Completed RFPs provide the foundation for more detailed follow-up by the sales staff at DMOs, hotels and resorts, and convention/exhibition venues. The typical RFP will ask MICE planners for the following information:

(continues)

(continued)

- Contact details (name of organization, business type, name of contact, title of contact, postal address, telephone and fax numbers, e-mail and website addresses)
- Name or title of the convention, exhibition or meeting
- Expected total attendance
- Total number of hotel guestrooms expected on the peak night of the event
- Range of acceptable hotel room rates
- Anticipated dates for the event
- Date when site selection will be made
- Preferred location and venue type for the event
- Set-up and capacity of largest meeting room required. Requirement for breakout rooms
- If exhibits included, number and size of exhibits

All of the DMOs include RFPs on their websites, while still distributing them in the traditional ways by handing them out and by faxing. Of course, RFPs are of little value in personal selling without quick and appropriate follow-up by sales representatives.

Dubai Creek Golf Course.

Discussion Questions

1. Overall, how do think the members of BestCities Global Alliance will benefit from this unique partnership?
2. Do you believe that being a member of the BestCities Global Alliance helps these destinations become more competitive in selling to the MICE markets. Why or why not?

(continues)

(continued)

3. What steps can hotels, DMOs, and convention/exhibition venues ensure the maximum distribution of their RFPs? How can the Internet help in this respect?

Website Addresses of Selected BestCities DMOs
www.bestcities.net
Cape Town, South Africa, http://www.tourismcapetown.co.za
Copenhagen, Denmark, http://www.meetincopenhagen.com/
San Juan, Puerto Rico, http://www.meetpuertorico.com/
Dubai Convention Bureau, http://www.dcb.ae
Tourism Vancouver, http://www.tourismvancouver.com

Edinburgh's website
http://conventionedinburgh.com
Singapore, http://www.visitsingapore.com/businessevents
Melbourne, http://www.mcvb.com.au

inquiries are answered and reservations are accepted. Increased sales result from the proper training of service and reservations staff in personal selling techniques. To prove this point, think back to the unwanted desserts and French fries we talked about earlier.

The Internet has become important virtual point-of-purchase for most hospitality and travel companies. In addition to selling flights and rooms online, several leading companies are now selling brand-extended products online. Many hotel chains have online stores selling a variety of products from beds and blankets to cookies and chocolates. The Peninsula Boutique (Figure 17.2) provides an outstanding example of this growing trend to online product sales by hotels. The UnitedShop.com is United Air Lines' online store for a variety of its logo merchandise. This trend among hotel chains was triggered by the introduction of *The Heavenly Bed* by Westin in 1999, and led to "the Bed Race" as one author has called it.[3] According to PricewaterhouseCoopers, U.S. hotels purchased 1.4 million beds in 2005, many of which were bought to support this brand extension strategy.

4. **Providing Detailed and Up-to-Date Information to the Travel Trade.** Most forms of advertising and sales promotion can transmit only limited quantities of information. Direct marketing and the Web are the best in this respect. Personal selling not only allows an organization to pass on more detailed information, but it also provides the opportunity to deal immediately with a prospect's concerns and questions. This is especially important for an organization that relies on convention/meeting planners and other travel trade intermediaries for part or all of its business. It is

FIGURE 17.2 A delicious example of a brand extension sales strategy by a hotel company.

Courtesy of Peninsula Merchandising Limited

very important for these professionals to fully comprehend an organization's services in order to communicate effectively with their clients and customers.

5. **Maintaining a Personal Relationship with Key Clients.** The key word in the term personal selling is undoubtedly *personal*, not *selling*. This promotional mix element, communicated through an organization's sales representatives and reservationists, gives it a personality that cannot be created as effectively through the mass media or the Web. These people are a human reflection of an otherwise impersonal corporation or government agency. As such, they must mirror the quality levels and positioning of their organizations.

   Most of us react more favorably if we are approached as individuals rather than as just one person in a group of people. Careful attention to individual needs and requirements is perhaps the most powerful form of marketing in the hospitality and travel industry. Key customers really appreciate the personal attention they receive from professional sales representatives and reservationists. This normally pays off in increased sales and repeat use.

6. **Gathering Information on Competitors' Promotions.** Salespeople constantly rub shoulders with potential customers who are also the targets

of competitors. Many sales prospects voluntarily pass on information about competitive promotional efforts. Thus, the sales force can be an important source of competitive intelligence.

Categories of Personal Selling

Personal selling within the hospitality and travel industry has changed dramatically in the past 25 years, especially due to the impact of technological advances including the industry's use of the Internet since the mid-1990s. Communication technologies have changed how customers search for information and purchase products and services. For example, online bookings of hospitality and travel services have mushroomed, especially in North America and Europe. These technologies have also changed how sales people do their jobs.

There are three principal categories of personal selling in the hospitality and travel industry: field, telephone, and internal. Some organizations use all three, whereas almost everyone is involved in internal and telephone selling.

1. **Field Sales. Field sales** (external selling) are selling efforts that take place in person outside the hospitality and travel organization's place of business. Often referred to as **sales calls**, these involve face-to-face presentations to prospective customers (or **sales prospects**). Examples include outside sales agents of travel agencies and hotel sales representatives who call on corporations and convention/meeting planners and sales representatives from airlines, cruise lines, tour wholesalers, and car rental firms who visit travel agencies. This is the most expensive type of personal selling because it involves employing a sales force and adding travel costs when they are away from the home office. Additional funds also have to be invested in sales support materials, such as PowerPoint slide presentations, CDs/DVDs, and presentation manuals with photographs.

   Another term that is found in the hospitality and travel industry is **outside sales** (Figure 17.3). For example, an outside sales person in a retail travel agency is someone who works outside the agency office to generate sales and leads for the agency. Faced with decreasing airline commissions and increasing competition from major online travel websites, many travel agencies in North America have decided to outsource their sales functions to home-based agents or other independent contactors. The Outside Sales Support Network (OSSN) is a trade association that represents these outside sales professionals.

FIGURE 17.3 Sales calls are an important technique in hospitality and travel.

Image copyright Stephen Coburn, 2008. Used under license from Shutterstock.com

2. **Telephone Sales.** **Telephone sales** are any communications via the phone that lead directly or indirectly to sales (Figure 17.4). Communications by telephone are playing an increasingly important role in

FIGURE 17.4 Telephone sales are now more important in today's mobile technology era.

Image copyright hfng, 2008. Used under license from Shutterstock.com

many aspects of personal selling. Generally, this is now referred to as **telemarketing**. The phone is an efficient way of **prospecting** (identifying prospective customers) and **qualifying** (determining the potential value and ranking of) sales prospects. It is used to arrange appointments for sales calls, to gather important background information before making a field sales call, to follow up with promised information, and to confirm the details of a sales prospect's requirements. In some cases, especially where an organization cannot justify the travel and salary costs of a field visit, it substitutes for an in-person sales call.

Another important role of the telephone in our industry is accepting telephone reservations and handling inquiries. Although not as well recognized as a sales tool, the telephone, along with e-mail and messenger services, plays a huge role in distributing business among hospitality and travel organizations. Training employees who handle telephone calls to be an extension of the sales force rather than just order takers pays off handsomely, as does providing easy telephone access to information and reservations via toll-free numbers. Several large airline and lodging companies operate **call centers** at which trained telephone reservationists provide information and accept bookings.

3. **Inside Sales. Inside sales** (internal selling) are efforts made within an organization's place of business to either increase the likelihood of a sale or to add to customers' average spending levels. You saw earlier that it is very difficult to draw a line between good service and effective inside sales. However, one readily discernible form of inside sales is **suggestive selling** or **up-selling**, where employees suggest or recommend additional or higher-priced items. Every retail situation at the point of purchase provides an opportunity for this form of selling.

   Another type of selling that has emerged more recently is **relationship selling**, or the practice of building ties to customers based on a salesperson's attention and commitment to customer needs over time.[4] The focus here is not on just getting one sale or transaction, but on creating and keeping long-term customers. This is just one part of a process that has become known as **customer relationship management (CRM)**.

Personal Selling Strategies

A sales representative or other staff member can select from several sales strategies when involved in field, telephone, or inside sales. The major ones are (1) stimulus response or canned sales presentations, (2) mental states, (3) formula, (4) need satisfaction, and (5) problem solving.

1. **Stimulus Response or Canned Sales Presentations.** These approaches are most often used with inside and telephone sales. **Stimulus response** is a sales presentation method that emphasizes the importance of saying the right things at the right time by means of a well-prepared sales

presentation (stimulus) in order to elicit the desired response (sale).

A **canned sales presentation** is standardized sales presentation that includes all the key selling points arranged in the order designed to elicit the best response from the customer.[5] In the stimulus response approach, staff members are asked to memorize certain questions or phrases or consistently to behave in a specific fashion. By giving customers a stimulus (question, phrase, or behavior pattern), a predictable response is expected. For example, restaurants that train servers to ask patrons, "Can I interest you in one of our desserts?" or "Would you like _____ with that?" expect that the power of suggestion will stimulate customers to respond by ordering additional menu items. Likewise, travel agents who ask "Do you need a car or hotel room as well?" are likely to earn increased commissions.

Canned sales presentations are used in field sales to guarantee that every sales representative communicates the same key messages to prospective customers. However, there is a greater need for a flexible approach in field sales that adapts to the needs and requirements of individual customers. These two personal selling strategies ignore individual differences among customers, but they still work well in our industry.

2. **Mental States Strategy.** The sales representative who uses this approach assumes that customers must go through sequential mental states before they make a purchase.[6] Chapter 4 referred to these as buying process stages. Sales calls and follow-ups are planned and timed to correspond with the buying process stages (need recognition, search for information, pre-purchase evaluation of alternatives, purchase, consumption, and post-consumption evaluation). This approach is used primarily for field sales and in cases where the purchase amount is large or very important to customers (i.e., high-involvement, extensive problem-solving decisions). Examples of these situations include travel agents who assist clients with plans for foreign vacations/holidays and hotel sales representatives who attempt to land an annual convention from a major association or a major corporate account.

3. **Formula Selling.** This is a variation of the mental states approach. It is a selling strategy in which the sales presentation is designed to move the customer through the stages in the decision-making process.[7] Based on these stages, sales representatives use a formula (preplanned sales process).

The sales process model focuses on the steps that the sales representative must follow. Normally, there are four major steps: (1) the approach, (2) a sales presentation or demonstration, (3) handling customer questions and objections, and (4) closing the sale. This model is discussed in detail later. You should note at this point that this is an approach best suited for field sales and high-involvement purchase decisions.

The **AIDA formula** is an example that assumes that the sales representative must do four things: (1) get the prospect's attention (the first A),

(2) stimulate interest in the organization's services (I), (3) create a desire for these services (D) and (4) get the prospect to take action by reserving or buying the services (the last A).

AIDA FORMULA

$$\text{Attention} \rightarrow \text{Interest} \rightarrow \text{Desire} \rightarrow \text{Action}$$

The AIDA formula is another approach that is best suited to field sales and high-involvement decisions. Sales representatives can make the best use of AIDA by doing the following:

a. Doing careful approach work before making sales calls (e.g., doing their homework on a prospective organization)
b. Stimulating interest (e.g., through the presentations used in sales calls)
c. Creating and holding desire by handling objections and demonstrating their services (e.g., complimentary trips for prospects)
d. Using one of several methods to close the sale (e.g., asking the prospect to make some form of action-oriented decision).

4. **Need-Satisfaction Approach.** The three previous strategies are based on the assumption that all sales prospects are more or less alike. The need-satisfaction approach is more sophisticated. It is a customized sales presentation in which the sales person first determines the prospective customer's needs and then tries to offer a solution that satisfies those needs.[8] It is particularly well suited for hospitality and travel organizations that act as advisors to their customers, such as travel agents and incentive travel planners. The need-satisfaction approach also works well in other situations where the customer is involved in significant amounts of pre-trip planning (e.g., an association planning a major national or international convention). There are four steps in this approach:

a. Determining customer needs through discussion and questioning—summarizing the needs discovered
b. Presenting tailor-made services to satisfy the needs that have been mutually discovered
c. Obtaining customers' agreement that services meet their needs—addressing any remaining concerns or questions
d. Closing the sale—making sure customers' needs are satisfied

You should instantly recognize this as a mini-model of the marketing concept itself. It is a highly effective sales strategy, but one that requires considerable time and effort, as well as attention to individual details.

5. **Problem-Solving Approach.** The problem-solving approach, like need satisfaction, begins with the assumption that every customer's needs are unique. It is also known as consultative selling or collaborative selling. **Consultative selling** is a customized sales presentation approach in which the salesperson is viewed as an expert and serves as a consultant to the customer (Figure 17.5). The salesperson identifies the prospects'needs

FIGURE 17.5
Consultative selling
often involves group
discussions such as this.

Photo by author

and recommends the best solution even if the best solution does not require the salesperson's products or services.[9] Even more time and effort are necessary to make this approach work, however. The sales representative begins by proving that the sales prospect has a problem. Let us assume that the prospect is a corporation. The problem could be that the company is spending an unnecessary amount of money on employee travel or on one specific travel element, such as lodging, airfares, car rentals, or other ground transportation. The sales representative could compare the prospect's expenses to typical situations to prove this point. Identifying such client problems often involves background research and several meetings with the client.

This strategy differs from need satisfaction because prospects are usually unaware of the problems before they are contacted by sales representatives. In other cases, prospects are generally aware of the problem, but they have not defined or researched it. This approach requires considerable cooperation from prospects, as sales representatives research and define the problems.

You are probably now wondering which of the five personal selling strategies is the best. The answer is that it all depends on the individual situation; there is no universal approach to personal selling that fits every situation. An organization and its sales representatives must evaluate each selling opportunity and sales prospect carefully before deciding which strategy to use.

The factors that most influence the choice of selling strategy are the type of hospitality and travel service, the target market, and the size and complexity of the purchase. For example, fast-food and other restaurants are likely to use the least expensive and sophisticated stimulus-response approach. Their menu items have broad market appeal, are relatively inexpensive, and are purchased routinely. At the other end of the spectrum, corporate travel managers often coordinate travel budgets in millions. The decisions they make about which hospitality and travel services to use are complex and involve large sums of money. Here, the more expensive and time-consuming approaches of need satisfaction or problem solving are more justified. Similarly, carriers, suppliers, and other travel intermediaries may find these two more individualized strategies most appropriate for selling to travel agencies.

The Sales Process

Now that you know the specific approaches used in personal selling, it is time to look at the common steps followed in field sales, and some types of telephone selling. The step-by-step sales process described is usually more elaborate than the one required for inside sales. The **sales process** consists of the six steps shown in Figure 17.6.

1. **Prospecting and Qualifying Prospective Customers.** What is another word for digging for gold and other precious metals or stones? Congratulations if you answered *prospecting*. The first step in the sales process is very similar to digging for gold—the sales representative has to explore and do research to find the most likely sources of business. *Prospecting*, or identifying sales prospects, includes a variety of techniques that sales

1	Prospecting and Qualifying Prospective Customers
2	Preplanning Prior to Sales Calls
3	Presenting and Demonstrating Services
4	Handling Objectives and Questions
5	Closing the Sale
6	Following Up After Closing the Sale

FIGURE 17.6 The sales process.

representatives use to pinpoint potential customers. To be a sales prospect (often called a **sales lead**), a potential customer must meet three criteria.[10]

a. Have an existing or potential need for the services
b. Be able to afford the purchase or purchases involved
c. Be authorized to purchase the services

Whereas many pleasure-travel sales prospects walk into travel agency offices, it is much more common for hospitality and travel organizations to have to do prospecting outside their own places of business (field sales), by telephone, or through the Internet. There are several different types of prospecting. **Online prospecting** or searching for sales leads through the Internet has become very popular in the past 10 to 15 years. **Blind prospecting** involves using telephone directories and other published lists to find sales prospects.[11] The use of the adjective *blind* means that the sales representative has no prior knowledge of the groups or individuals on these lists and no idea if they are true sales prospects. This type of approach might be used by a new hotel that is trying to generate business from local industries, a travel agency that is attempting to attract group tour business from local clubs and organizations, or an incentive travel planner who is looking for companies interested in setting up incentive trips.

A closely related technique is **cold calling** or **canvassing**. You already know what cold calling is if you frequently answer the door only to find someone trying to sell you something. Cold calling is really blind prospecting in the field. It is not a very systematic approach, but it often works. Sales representatives have no idea whether the individuals or organizations they visit will turn out to be sales prospects. The basic assumption here is that if the sales representative visits enough people with potentially similar requirements or needs, some of them will be prospects. A **sales blitz** involves contacting potential customers in a specific geographic area over a relatively short time period. A blitz is usually only a one-time activity or is repeated infrequently. Blitzing is either done by a team of people or done via the telephone. In November 2006 the Jacksonville & the Beaches Convention and Visitors Bureau sales team and 20 volunteers from local hotels contacted 2,000 meeting planners by phone over a two-day period from a call center in Jacksonville, Florida.[12]

Another related technique is the **sales mission** that is most often used by destination marketing organizations (DMOs), and when doing personal selling abroad or at a long distance from the destination. In September 2006, a tourism delegation from the United Kingdom, led by Visit Britain and Virgin Atlantic Airways, staged a 4-day sales mission to the United Arab Emirates. The sales mission was designed to strengthen the relationships with UAE-based travel trade intermediaries.[13] Unlike sales blitzes, these sales missions usually include many prearranged sales calls and presentations.

INTERNET MARKETING

Using the Internet to Appeal to Convention-meeting Planners: The Online RFP for Cape Town

- The Internet has been a great help to hospitality, travel and tourism marketers in selling to organizational buyers including meeting and convention planners. One of the most popular tools in this respect is the online request for proposals (**RFP**). The completed RFPs are a great source of leads for hotels, DMOs, and other marketers.
- Cape Town Tourism in South Africa has an extensive online RFP. The following are some of the items to be entered for submission:
  - Name of organization and business category (academic, association, corporate, government, incentive, travel agency/airline, meeting, professional conference organizer, exhibition organizer, or other).
  - Contact details for person completing the RFP.
  - Name of meeting/event and event type (meeting, conference, exhibition, incentive, or other).
  - Date of event and estimated total attendance.
  - Number, price range, and preferred location of hotel rooms.
  - Type of venue (venue with accommodation, venue without accommodation, convention hotel, venue with a difference, or exhibition venue).
  - Largest meeting room set up type and number of people.
  - Exhibit space and breakout room requirements.

Source: Cape Town Tourism. (2008). *Request for proposal.*
http://www.tourismcapetown.co.za/index.php?requestProposal

Student Questions

1. What are the main advantages to hotels and DMOs in posting online RFPs on the Internet?
2. In what ways should an organization respond when it receives a completed online RFP?
3. How can the organization use the sales process and other promotional techniques to increase the probability of securing this event?
4. What are the limitations of online RFPs when compared to traditional sales methods?

You are probably wondering why a systematic book such as this one is recommending such an unsystematic approach as blind prospecting. Is this not just a mini version of the undifferentiated marketing strategy discussed in Chapter 8? Are we not taking a shotgun approach to marketing? The answer to your dilemma is that there are better ways to prospect, but certain specific situations justify blind prospecting and cold calling. These include cases where the hospitality and travel business or service is new—the organization and potential customers are unfamiliar with each other. These prospecting approaches also are better justified if the potential purchase amounts are large relative to the organization's or business' current revenues (i.e., a very large potential sale). Another situation is where the organization is trying to get sales from a completely new geographic area or sales territory.

The most desirable way to do prospecting is to have leads to begin with. Some call this **lead prospecting**, or contacting individuals and organizations that have a high probability of being sales prospects.[14] There are many sources of leads in hospitality and travel sales. Some come from the cold calling, sales blitzes, and sales missions discussed earlier. Other leads come through online prospecting, searching print and computerized databases, printed directories, and through telemarketing. Interpersonal sources of leads are also very important, including referrals from current and past clients, and business associates and friends. In addition, advertising and sales promotion efforts should also be designed to generate sales leads.

Not all sales prospects are worth pursuing, and the next step— qualifying—is used to narrow the list down to the most likely purchasers. Because the normal field sales call costs approximately $380 in 2006, this procedure makes great financial as well as marketing sense.[15] Qualifying means using pre-selected criteria to identify the best sales prospects. Following are typical criteria and questions used to qualify sales prospects:

a. If prospects are past customers, what volume of business did they provide?
b. Do prospects have needs or problems that the sales representative's services can satisfy?
c. Do prospects have the authority to make purchases?
d. Do prospects have the financial capabilities to pay for purchases?
e. Have the prospects entered into a long-term contract or arrangement with a competitor?
f. What volume of sales will prospects generate, and how profitable will their business be?

A fairly common approach is to divide prospects and past customers into account types. For example, an A account might be a person or organization that generates the highest levels of sales or profits. A B account would include those on the next level, and so on. The designation attached to each account usually determines the frequency of sales follow-ups and whether field or telephone sales are used.

You should think of qualifying as a smaller-scale version of market segmentation. Sales representatives use a continuous program of research to identify their target markets for future selling efforts. Obviously, internal records of sales volumes by customer are important here. For prospects other than past customers, a combination of secondary research mainly on the Web and personal inquiries via the telephone or in person is often used. There are many excellent published sources of information on corporations, associations, and nonprofit organizations. For associations, one these includes the *Encyclopedia of Associations* published by Thomson Gale. Now available in a searchable online version, *Associations Unlimited*, this contains a database on 456,000 associations. Data gathered on leads through secondary and primary research should be recorded and continually updated in individual sales prospect files.

Several software programs have been specifically developed to help hospitality and travel sales representatives track and manage leads and prospects. Destinations CVBreeze automates this process for CVBs in North America. Hotel SalesPro automates the sales process for hotel sales representatives by recording and storing all of the information for key clients and prospects (Figure 17.7).

2. **Preplanning Prior to Sales Calls.** A successful sales call, made either by telephone or in the field, requires careful preplanning and preparation. In this respect, it is very similar to a successful job interview in that the interviewee must think ahead about what he or she wants to say. There are two elements to preplanning a sales call: (1) the **pre-approach**, and (2) the **approach**.[16] In the pre-approach stage, sales representatives carefully review each sales prospect's files and other relevant information. If no file exists, the representative must use the information-gathering process discussed in the previous section. The objective is to develop enough familiarity with the prospect's situation to be able to establish a

Courtesy of hotel SalesPro, LLC

FIGURE 17.7 Hotel SalesPro is a software program that automates the sales process for hotel sales representatives.

rapport during the sales call and to have the foundation on which to build the sales presentation itself.

The approach stage follows and involves all the activities that lead to the sales presentation. These include making appointments with prospects or their administrative assistants, building smooth communications when the sales call starts and verifying important details before beginning the sales presentation. Sales representatives have three principal objectives in their approaches.[17] You will see that the last two objectives are the first two steps in the AIDA formula (attention-interest-desire-action) mentioned earlier.

a. To build rapport with the prospect
b. To capture a person's full attention
c. To generate interest in the product or service

It is important to recognize that some hospitality and travel organizations have no opportunity to do prospecting, qualifying, or preplanning. The first time they encounter customers is when they walk through the company's doors or when the customer calls or sends an e-mail. Most travel agents face this problem with walk-in, phone-in, and Internet customers. Careful questioning and probing determine the inquirer's needs and their probability of making reservations. Other inside sales opportunities in the hospitality and travel industry require much less preplanning than field or telephone sales calls. Here, the stimulus-response, suggestive selling strategy is usually sufficient.

3. **Presenting and Demonstrating Services.** After the approach, the next step in the sales call is the **sales presentation** and **demonstration**. In the sales presentation, sales representatives present facts and other information proving that their services can satisfy prospects' needs or solve their problems. In the sales demonstration, the ability of services to meet prospects' needs or problems is demonstrated. Because of the intangibility of hospitality and travel services, the opportunity to demonstrate them is much more limited. Visual aids, familiarization trips, and other on-site inspection visits play a major role in overcoming the intangibility problem.

During the sales presentation, sales representatives provide information about their organizations and services. Prospects' needs and problems are discussed and confirmed. Careful listening by the sales representative is as important as talking. Prospects are verbally shown how the services can satisfy their needs. The objective of the sales presentation is to be persuasive, creating a desire in the prospect to buy or reserve the services offered (the D and the A in the AIDA model). One of the experts in doing sales presentations has suggested the following "10 Laws of Sales Success":[18]

1. Keep your mouth shut and your ears open.
2. Sell with questions, not answers.
3. Pretend you're on your first date with your prospect.

4. Speak to your prospect just as you speak to your family and friends.
5. Pay close attention to what your prospect *isn't* saying.
6. If you're asked a question, answer it briefly and move on.
7. Only after you've correctly assessed the needs of your prospect do you mention anything about what you're offering.
8. Refrain from delivering a three-hour product seminar.
9. Ask the prospect if there are any barriers to them taking the next logical step.
10. Invite your prospect to take some kind of action.

The careful preplanning of sales presentations is most important. Many hospitality and travel sales representatives develop **outlined presentations**, which are systematic sales presentations that list the most important sales points that the salesperson needs to make.[19] Audiovisuals such as PowerPoint slides or DVDs may be shown to structure the presentation, or to add excitement and appeal to the salesperson's oral communications. The presentation may involve several sales calls, especially if the need satisfaction or problem-solving approaches are being used.

4. **Handling Objections and Questions.** When most sales presentations are completed, prospects ask questions and raise one or more objections. Objections come in all forms, even through body language. Of course, the best thing is for sales representatives to anticipate typical objections in preplanning and address them in the sales presentation. Otherwise, sales representatives must spot and tackle objections, not ignore them. Prospects may voice a variety of concerns ranging from the price, characteristics, or timing of services to current economic constraints to purchasing them.

There are several effective ways for **handling objections**. One is to restate the objection and to prove diplomatically that it is not as important as it seems. Another is the "agree and neutralize" tactic or the "yes, but" approach. Here, sales representatives initially agree with the problem, but go on to show that the objection is not relevant or accurate. No matter which approach is used, objections must be met head-to-head. If they are not, an otherwise interested prospect may slip through the salesperson's hands. Listening is a key skill here, both in carefully hearing what is said and observing body movements.

5. **Closing the Sale.** If objections and questions have been handled effectively, sales representatives should then try to close sales. **Closing** means getting a sales prospect to agree with the objectives of the sales call, which normally implies making a definite purchase or reservation. In a multi-staged presentation, it may involve getting a commitment for a follow-up visit or other additional discussions. A sales call without a close is definitely unsuccessful. Every sales representative must ask for the business or at least some commitment to continue the dialogue. Failing to close sales is a common problem in all types of personal selling, and may cause some anxiety among sales representatives. Overcoming this psychological barrier is essential to effective personal selling.

Knowing when and how to close are the keys to success. As with objections, this again takes careful attention to the prospect's words and body language. Sales representatives must watch for verbal and non-verbal clues indicating that prospects have almost made up their minds. These include the following:[20]

a. *Verbal Closing Clues*

- Questions ("When will the balance be due?" "How soon can we receive a written proposal from you?" "When can you give us confirmation of this reservation?").
- Recognitions ("That really sounds good." "We've always dreamed of taking this type of trip." "Your organization's services definitely fit our needs." "Your price is certainly in our ball park.").
- Requirements ("We'll need to get your lowest possible corporate rate." "This will have to be okayed by our finance department." "The departure will have to fit our vacation dates.").

b. *Non-verbal Closing Clues*

- Signs of acceptance and agreement indicated by nodding of head.
- Posture changes indicating greater interest in services being offered (e.g., leaning forward and listening more attentively, hands on chin, other signs of increased relaxation such as uncrossing legs and opening up hands and examining sales literature more thoroughly).

As soon as they notice any of these signals, sales representatives should use one of seven closing strategies:

a. *Trial Closes.* The sales representative who uses this strategy tests the water by asking questions that either determine a prospect's intentions to purchase or help them make a definite decision. The trial close also helps get a prospect to voice any remaining objections. For example, a travel agent could ask, "Shall I check on space availability for you?" A hotel representative might say, "Do you want one of our staff members to arrange the spouse's program?"

b. *Assumptive Close.* This is very similar to the trial close. The sales representative asks a question that assumes the prospect's willingness to buy. Examples include "Will you be paying for this in cash, by check, or with a credit card?" or "Would you like us to direct bill you?"

c. *Summary or Summary-of-the-Benefits Close.* The sales representative recapitulates the main points of the presentation or the major benefits to the prospect. The whole picture is put together, making an even more convincing argument for the purchase. This summarizing is immediately followed by a request for the reservation or purchase.

d. *Special Concession Close.* The sales representative offers a special inducement to the prospect if the reservation or sale is made.[21] The inducement is usually a further discount or a limited-time price or rate. For example, a travel agent in late 2008 might say, "If I book you on the *Princess* before February 14, 2009, you can save up to $600 on the cruise."

e. *Eliminating-the-Single-Objection or Final-Concern Close.* Despite the sale representatives' efforts, one important objection stands in the way of closing. One way to use this strategy is to say, "Assuming that we can solve this one problem, can we count on your reservation?" Another method is to point out that only one problem remains and to make another attempt to eliminate the objection.

f. *Limited-Choice Close.* The sales representative may have presented a prospect with a large number of alternatives (e.g., vacation/holiday packages, departure dates, banquet meals). When the prospect shows signs of nearing some type of commitment, the sales representative narrows the selection to a more limited number of alternatives, thereby making the prospect's decision easier.

g. *Direct-Appeal Close.* There is no mystery to this one: The sales representative flat-out asks for the sale or booking.

6. **Following Up After Closing the Sale.** The sales process does not end with a successful closing. On the contrary, this is the beginning of another cycle that leads up to additional sales to the prospect. Sales representatives' work is not done until they ensure that all the required steps and arrangements are made to deliver the promised services. In some cases, such as organizing major association conventions or planning incentive travel trips, this "delivery" work is extensive.

It is also advisable for sales representatives to give prospects some form of reassurance, to remove the cognitive dissonance discussed in Chapter 4. A simple letter or e-mail complimenting the prospect on the decision is enough in most cases.

A third aspect of post-sale activities involves immediate follow-up after prospects or their clients have actually used the services. Many travel agents employ this effectively by telephoning or e-mailing clients soon after their trips to find out what they liked and did not like. Some hotel companies touch base with key corporate clients monthly to ensure that these customers are pleased with the lodging services. In addition to being essential in maintaining a customer base, this is another form of prospecting. It might help if you think of the following analogy. Once prospectors find a trace of gold, they follow certain steps to mine it to its full potential. Maintaining close contact with past customers is very similar—the more effort that goes in, the more rewards that come out.

The Sales Plan and Sales Management

You have already seen the importance of having individual plans for advertising and sales promotion (Chapters 15 and 16). It is also essential to have a **personal selling** or **sales plan**. The sales plan is a detailed description of personal selling objectives, sales forecasts, sales-force responsibilities, activities, and budgets. Besides being an important part of the overall marketing plan, the sales plan is a key tool in **sales management** (the management of the sales force and personal selling efforts to achieve desired sales objectives).

The task of preparing sales plans normally is assigned to sales managers, also sometimes known as **Directors of Sales (DOS)** or sales coordinators. The sales management functions for which these individuals are responsible include (1) sales-force staffing and operations, (2) sales planning, and (3) sales performance evaluation.[22] As you can see, there is much more to sales management than preparing sales plans.

Sales-Force Staffing and Operations

1. **Recruitment, Selection, and Training.** The sales director's first job is to hire competent people to fill available positions. In all industries, there are basically three categories of sales positions.[23]

    a. *Order Getters.* These are the sales representatives that you have heard about in this chapter. They are the ones who are responsible for the sales process that was just discussed. They prospect and qualify customers, preplan sales calls, present and demonstrate services, handle objections and questions, close sales, and perform after-sales follow-up. One of their key jobs is to promote their organizations' services persuasively. In the hospitality and travel industry, these sales representatives spend most of their time on field sales, along with some telemarketing.

    b. *Order Takers.* Order takers are inside salespeople, who in our industry may or may not work within the sales department itself. Examples include waitpersons in restaurants, servers in fast-food outlets, front desk clerks in hotels, airline ticket agents; and travel agency, hotel, car rental, cruise line, tour wholesaler, and airline reservationists. Their primary function is to accept reservations, orders, or enquiries and to process reservations or provide the services purchased.

       Although these people do not have the same level of persuasive responsibilities as sales representatives do, they should be well trained in inside sales techniques such as suggestive or up-selling. It is also important to repeat a key point mentioned earlier—the quality of service that is provided by these people, even if their only contact with customers is on the telephone, sells future, repeat business.

    c. *Support Staff.* The third category includes sales staff commonly referred to as *missionary salespersons* or *sales engineers.* They are employed directly by the sales department. The missionary salesperson's job is to distribute information about, and to describe the features of, new services. They do not, like sales representatives, make sales presentations. Sales engineers are resource people with specific technical knowledge who, when required, accompany sales representatives on sales calls.

       The hospitality and travel industry makes much less use of these support people than do other industries, including manufacturers of highly technical products (e.g., pharmaceuticals). The closest thing to missionary salespersons in our industry are the sales representatives who call on travel agencies, trying to get agents to convince more clients to use their airline, car rental firm, hotel or resort, cruise line, packages or tours, attraction, or other travel services. Convention service staff members in CVBs are another example of the support staff who back up convention sales people. These sales representatives do not normally close sales, although they often help in making sales presentations. It is the sales representative's function to close sales with their clients.

Where does an organization find these staff members? Sources of new sales staff include in-house employees, other related organizations (competitors, customers, other supplier, carrier, travel trade, or DMOs), hospitality and travel schools, executive placement consultants and employment agencies, and voluntary applications. In the hospitality and travel industry, it is uncommon for field sales representatives to be hired directly from college without prior sales experience. The more established practice is for entry-level people to be order-takers, with eventual in-house promotion to sales representative. Hiring sales personnel from competitors and related outside organizations is also common. For example, many sales representatives who call on travel agents are former agents themselves. Given the more recent, increased emphasis on marketing and sales, many hospitality and travel organizations hire people

Did You Know?

How do CVBs help meeting planners "sell the city"?

- CVBs can assist planners in all areas of meeting preparation and provide planners with detailed reference material.
- CVBs can establish room blocks at local hotels.
- CVBs will market the destination to attendees via promotional material, thereby encouraging attendance.
- CVBs can act as a liaison between the planner and community officials, thus clearing the way for special permits, street closures, etc.
- CVBs can obtain special letters of welcome from high-ranking government officials and in some cases, can bring officials to speak at a meeting.
- CVBs can offer suggestions about ways meeting attendees can maximize free time, along with helping to develop spouse programs and pre- and post-convention tours.

Source: Destination Marketing Association International. (2008). *How do CVBs help meeting planners?* **http:/www.destinationmarketing.org/**

with sales experience in other industries. A survey conducted in 2002 by Hospitality Sales and Marketing Association International (HSMAI) indicated that the turnover rates of sales people in hospitality businesses were very high. Money, leadership, and training were the main reasons why sales professionals left their jobs.[24]

What are the characteristics of the successful salesperson? For many years, people thought that you had to be born with the gift of sales and could not learn the skills required. This has changed. Many people have written on how to determine success in personal selling, but the following three characteristics seem to be key:[25]

- Sales aptitude—the extent of an individual's ability to perform a given sales job, consisting of the following:
  i. Mental abilities (overall intelligence, oral communications skills, mental reasoning, mathematical abilities)
  ii. Personality traits (empathy, ego drive, sociability)
- Skill levels—skills obtained in personal communications and knowledge of services, obtained through the following:
  i. Sales training
  ii. Previous sales and operational experience
- Personal characteristics:
  i. Demographic profile, including educational background
  ii. Psychographic and lifestyle characteristics
  iii. Physical appearance and traits

Although these factors generally provide a good guide to an individual's potential success in personal selling, they are not foolproof. Research shows that there is no one set of physical characteristics, mental abilities, and personality traits that predict success in every situation. Salespersons' success depends more on the actual tasks assigned to them and the industrial environment in which they operate.[26] For example, a person given order-taking responsibilities may perform very well, but may not succeed as a field sales representative. The same can be true when a field sales representative is moved to inside sales. Research also shows that it is not particularly effective to recruit sales representatives who have characteristics that match those of customers.

Sales training programs are extremely important to continuing success in personal selling (Figure 17.8). Following are typical objectives of programs for new and existing sales staff:[27]

- Reduce turnover rates of sales staff
- Improve relations with customers and prospects
- Enhance morale
- Generate more effective time management skills
- Improve control of sales staff

FIGURE 17.8 Sales training is needed to develop and polish selling skills.

Because of the high cost of field sales, the last two objectives play a key role in controlling sales costs.

The topics covered in sales training programs for new staff usually include an orientation to the organization, its industry and target markets, a detailed description of the services offered, and territory management (if appropriate). Training may include lectures, discussions, demonstrations, role playing, videos, on-the-job instruction, use of an Intranet site, or some combination of these six approaches.[28]

There are several educational and training programs available to people in sales positions. In the hospitality and travel field, these include the certification programs provided by Hospitality Sales and Marketing Association International (the Certified Hospitality Marketing Executive or CHME), and the Educational Institute of the American Hotel & Lodging Association (the Certified Hospitality Sales Professional or CHSP) (Figure 17.9). The Sales & Marketing Executive International Association also offers certification programs for sales people in general, including the Certified Marketing Executive (CME), Certified Sales Executive (CSE), and SME Certified Professional Salesperson (SCPS). Destination Marketing Association International (DMAI) offers the Certified Destination Management Executive (CDME) program, which includes course modules in marketing and sales. As mentioned in Chapter 16, many DMOs provide specific training programs to assist travel agents in selling their destinations.

2. **Leading, Motivating, and Compensating.** Just like any other manager, the sales manager must be an effective leader and have the respect and confidence of the sales staff. Sales managers must understand motivation

FIGURE 17.9 The Certified Hospitality Sales Professional Program.

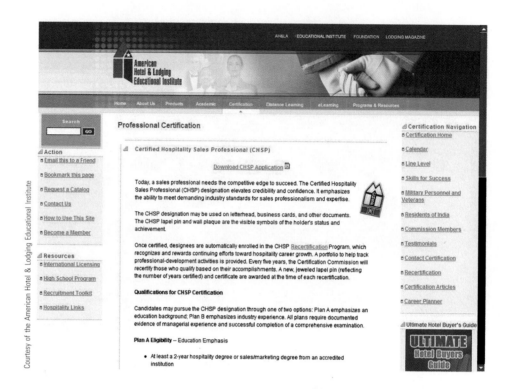

theories (such as those discussed in Chapter 4), and provide financial and non-monetary incentives to keep sales-force motivation at its peak. Enthusiasm among salespeople quickly rubs off on customers and prospects.

Financial incentives include salary and commissions, and fringe benefits such as paid vacations, insurance programs, and medical/dental programs. In our industry, free travel is also a very important fringe, especially with travel agency and airline staff. Non-monetary compensation and motivators are award/recognition programs and job advancement opportunities (usually to a sales coordinator or director).

Several choices of financial compensation are available. The first choice is straight salary which involves fixed salary payments with no commissions. Research shows that service organizations, including those in the hospitality and travel industry, like this approach the most.[29] Because a great deal of the field selling in our industry is to the travel trade and not to final customers, straight-salary compensation seems justified. It is also the approach best suited for inside sales. The second choice is straight commission, payment based totally on the person's sales results. There are very few examples of this in the hospitality and travel industry. However, one is travel agencies that use outside salespeople and pay them a portion of the commissions earned on the reservations they generate. Straight-commission plans work best with smaller companies that cannot afford a sales department, and in cases where very little missionary selling is required.[30]

The third and most prevalent choice of compensation is a combination approach—a base salary plus commission and/or bonuses. Commissions are tied directly to the volumes of sales or profits generated by each salesperson. Bonuses are payments made when predetermined volumes of sales and profits, or sales quotas, are achieved. This third choice is most appropriate with field sales, when selling is being done to prospective final customers and in cases where sales result primarily from the sales representative's persuasive efforts.

Another motivator that can be used is the sales promotion that is aimed at the sales force. Chapter 16 pointed out that promotions tend to work best to achieve short-term objectives and are not advisable for the long term. Various forms of contests are popular in motivating sales representatives to intensify their efforts. They are most frequently used when an organization is attempting to (1) secure new customers or travel trade outlets, (2) promote the sale of specific services, (3) generate larger sales volumes per sales call, (4) counteract lower volumes in off-seasons, and (5) introduce new facilities or services.[31] Chapters 7 and 13 mentioned the growing role of incentive travel trips as rewards for outstanding sales performances. These can be used for sales contest winners. RoadTrips® (Exclusive Group Experiences) of Winnipeg, Manitoba, Canada offers a fantastic set of incentive trips that can be used for top sales staff. They have teamed up with Porsche Travel Club Germany and one of the trips is the *"Porsche 911 Experience in the Black Forest"* where winners drive their own sports car through this beautiful part of Bavaria.[32]

Non-monetary compensation also plays a large role in motivating salespeople, as it does with most employees. Normally, these are certificates, plaques, or cups that are awarded by sales managers at formal sales-force meetings or conventions.

3. **Supervising and Controlling.** Supervision and control of salespeople, especially those in the field, is more difficult for sales managers than it is for most other managers. Distance from home offices, extensive travel away from home, high levels of independence, and the continuous stress of peak performance complicate the supervisory function. Salespersons' abuse of expense accounts and above-average alcoholism rates are two fairly common supervisory problems.

The sales manager's supervisory methods and techniques include periodic, face-to-face meetings with individual staff members, telephone and e-mail conversations, sales-call reports and other written correspondence, compensation plan (especially with plans involving commissions and bonuses), sales territories, quotas, expense accounts, and sales management audit.[33] Sales meetings, conventions, or rallies provide another excellent opportunity for training and other communication with the sales force. A significant percentage of all meetings and conventions held in North America are of this type.

You should know something about sales territories and quotas before we leave this section on sales-force staffing and operations. **Sales territories** are specific areas of responsibility, usually geographic, that are assigned to individual sales representatives or branch offices. Territories can be based on geography, customers, services or products, or some combination of these three.[34] Small organizations that serve local markets, such as most restaurants and travel agencies, usually do not need to set up territories. Larger companies that serve regional or national markets, however, can often justify this move because of the following benefits of sales territories:[35]

b. Reduced selling costs
c. Improved supervision, control, and evaluation of sales representatives
d. Adequate coverage of potential markets
e. Improved relations with individual customers
f. Increased sales-force morale and effectiveness
g. Enhanced research and analysis of sales results

If you will recall the benefits of personal selling mentioned earlier, you will quickly realize the strength of territorial sales management. Two of the benefits were to target precisely and to cultivate relationships with potential customers. Effective sales representatives who remain in their territories for sufficient time develop strong relationships with customers and travel trade partners. Most national airlines organize sales personnel in this way. Regional sales managers supervise teams of sales representatives, with the regional headquarters based at or near a "hub" or other major airport.

Another major advantage you will see immediately is achieving greater efficiency in salespersons' travel expenses. It is obviously less expensive to send one person to a specific geographic area than it is to send two or more.

Sales quotas are performance targets periodically set for individual sales representatives, branch offices, or regions. They help sales managers motivate, supervise, control, and evaluate sales staff. Quotas can be based on sales volumes, activities (e.g., total sales calls in a period, calls on new sales prospects), financial results (e.g., gross or net profit generated), travel-expenses-to-sales ratios, or some combination of these. Besides the obvious benefits from a human resources standpoint, quotas also reflect the fact that not all territories are alike, and that all offices or sales representatives cannot be expected to perform at exactly the same levels.

Sales Planning

The heart of sales planning is the sales plan, prepared periodically (usually annually) by the sales manager with information from the sales force. Its contents are quite similar to those of the advertising, sales promotion/merchandising, and public relations plans. The sales plan contains a detailed description of personal selling objectives, sales activities, and the sales budget. It differs from the other promotional plans in its sections on sales-force responsibilities, territories, and quotas. This is certainly the case with larger organizations that farm out all their advertising, sales promotion, and public relations work to outside agencies and consultants. The only in-house, promotional staff members they have to consider are in the sales department.

1. **Preparing Sales Forecasts.** Personal selling objectives are frequently set as forecasts of unit or sales volumes or some other financial target (e.g., gross or net profits) derived from expected sales levels. However, sales forecasts are not the only type of personal selling objectives. Non-financial ones may be equally important. These may include levels-of-activity objectives, such as numbers of sales calls, new sales prospects converted to customers, or volumes of enquiries answered successfully.

   You probably already realize that the sales forecast is very useful to others outside the sales department. In fact, it is a key planning tool for the entire organization. Expected sales levels influence the allocation of staff and financial resources in many other departments.

2. **Developing Sales Department Budgets.** Given the relatively high costs of personal selling, this budget plays a key role in planning and controlling the sales effort. Typically, the sales budget has the following components:

   a. Sales forecast—the total revenues and/or unit sales volumes expected in an upcoming period.
   b. Selling-expenses budget—the salaries, fringe benefits, commissions, bonuses, and travel expenses projected for the sales force.
   c. Sales administration budget—the salaries, fringe benefits, and administrative costs of regional and head offices of the sales department.
   d. Advertising and sales promotion budget—the amount to be spent on sales-force promotions (e.g., contests, recognition and award programs) and advertising that directly supports selling efforts. These amounts are also usually identified in the advertising and sales promotion budgets.

3. **Assigning Sales Territories and Quotas.** You have already been introduced to these concepts, but you should realize that they have an important function in sales planning. Sales managers normally derive financially based quotas from the overall sales forecast. They use a combination of past territory performance and market indices (a percentage or other numerical factor based on two or more factors related to a market) to allocate quotas for each territory.

Evaluating Sales Performance

The third and final function of sales management is measuring and evaluating sales performance. Instead of being viewed as the final step in a series of many, the sales management audit should be considered the first step in improving the effectiveness of an organization's personal selling efforts.

A **sales management audit** is a periodic analysis of the sales department's policies, objectives, activities, staff, and performance. Sales analysis is a term most frequently used for the evaluation of performance. This can be done by considering total sales volumes or sales by territory, service or facility category, or customer groups.[36] One of the most important bases of evaluation is to judge actual results against sales forecasts and budgets.

Personal Selling in the Hospitality and Travel Industry

You have seen frequent references in this chapter to personal selling within the hospitality and travel industry. In this final discussion, we will summarize a few key points.

1. **Importance of Personal Selling Varies.** Personal selling is not equally important to all hospitality and travel organizations. Smaller, more localized operations tend to limit their sales activities to inside sales. In this category are most restaurants and many travel agencies—the retail side of the industry.

   The importance of personal selling within the promotional mix increases with the size of the organization, the geographical scope of its target markets, and its dependence on the travel trade and other decision-makers who influence the travel behavior of groups of people. The types of organizations that are most likely to have teams of field sales representatives are the following:

   a. Hotels, resorts, conference centers, and other lodging businesses
   b. Convention and visitors bureaus (CVBs) and convention/exhibition centers
   c. Airlines, cruise lines, passenger rail companies (e.g., Amtrak and Via Rail Canada)
   d. Car rental firms
   e. Incentive travel-planning companies
   f. National and state government tourism-promotion agencies

   Other organizations also use sales forces. They include some travel agencies, tour wholesalers, and motorcoach tour operators.

2. **Inside Selling Closely Related to Service Levels.** In our industry, it is extremely difficult to draw the line between quality service to customers and internal selling. As Chapter 11 pointed out, the quality of service usually determines customer satisfaction. Although you can easily see that suggestive selling is part of personal selling, quality service is probably much more important in creating customer satisfaction and repeat patronage.

3. **No Generally Accepted Qualifications for Industry Sales Positions.** Sales does not tend to be an entry-level position in the hospitality and travel industry. It is normally mandatory that you learn the ropes in operations or reservations before you become a sales representative. The rationale is that you know your product, customers, and sales prospects better after a stint in the actual workings of the organization.

One serious problem that our industry has is the absence of generally accepted qualifications or criteria for hiring marketing and sales people. At the same time, there are few educational programs that specialize exclusively in hospitality and travel sales and marketing. The industry and its trade associations must establish standard criteria.

4. **Importance of Missionary Sales Work.** Chapter 13 highlighted the vital role played by travel trade intermediaries. You should realize that some intermediaries are themselves decision-makers, whereas others are decision-influencers. For example, decision-makers include corporate travel managers and convention/meeting planners. Decision-influencers include retail travel agents, tour wholesalers, and incentive travel planners. Selling approaches to these two categories of intermediaries are different. Keeping them informed and up to date—performing missionary sales work—is most important with decision-influencers, whereas persuasive selling is more appropriate with decision-makers. With the rapid pace of change in services, fares, prices, and facilities, missionary sales is very important in the hospitality and travel industry.

Chapter Conclusion

Nothing is as effective in getting sales as well-executed personal selling. It is much harder to say "no" to a personal presentation than to an impersonally communicated message in an advertisement, sales promotion, or website. However, personal selling, especially the field sales element, is relatively expensive. Careful management of personal selling activities (sales management) is crucial. The heart of an effective sales program and sales management is the sales plan.

Following the step-by-step approach in the sales process usually produces the best results. This requires preplanning, effective presentation skills and methods, and follow-up. It is now believed that these skills can be learned. They are not necessarily inherent only in certain natural salespeople.

---

1. How are the terms *personal selling* and *sales management* defined in this chapter?
2. What roles does personal selling play in the marketing of hospitality and travel services?
3. What are the three categories of personal selling?
4. Which five strategies can be used in personal selling, and how are they different?
5. What are the steps in the sales process, and what does each entail?
6. Which seven strategies can be used in closing sales, and what does each involve?
7. What are the functions of sales management?

REVIEW QUESTIONS

8. To be effective in sales, one must be born with certain talents. Is this an accurate statement? Explain your answer, citing the characteristics of the successful salesperson.
9. What is the role of the sales plan, and what does it include?
10. Is personal selling in the hospitality and travel industry any different from that in other industries? Explain your answer, mentioning four distinct characteristics of selling in our industry.

CHAPTER ASSIGNMENTS

1. Arrange to spend a day accompanying a field salesperson in your favorite part of the hospitality and travel industry. At the end of the day, evaluate this person's performance. Did the sales representative follow the steps in the sales process? How successful was the person in achieving his or her objectives? Did you observe any closes, and what closing strategies were used? What did you like about the person's approaches? What did you dislike? Could you improve upon this salesperson's approaches and techniques? How?
2. Arrange to spend a day in a travel agency, hotel, or restaurant to observe its inside and telephone selling procedures. At the end of the day, evaluate the organization's sales techniques in these two areas. Were opportunities for inside and telephone sales used to their fullest potential, or do staff members need further training in these areas? Did you see any evidence of suggestive or up-selling? What recommendations would you make to management to upgrade selling in these two categories?
3. You have been hired as the new sales manager of a hospitality and travel organization (real or hypothetical). Write your own job description for the position. What responsibilities would you have? What procedures would you use for (1) sales-force staffing and operations, (2) sales planning, and (3) evaluating sales performance? Be as specific as you can.
4. You are the sales manager of a hospitality and travel organization. Prepare a written set of instructions for field sales representatives, being as specific as possible. What steps would you outline for prospecting and qualifying sales prospects? What advertising and sales promotions would you use to support sales representatives?

WEB RESOURCES

Destination Marketing Association International (DMAI), http://www.destinationmarketing.org/
Direct Marketing Association (DMA), http://www.the-dma.org/
Educational Institute of the American Hotel & Lodging Association, http://www.ei-ahla.org/
Hospitality Sales & Marketing Association International (HSMAI), http://www.hsmai.org/
Outside Sales Support Network (OSSN), http://www.ossn.com/
Roadtrips Inc., http://www.roadtripsinc.com/

Sales & Marketing Executives (SME) International, http://www.smei.org/
Sales & Marketing Management Magazine, http://www.salesandmarketing.com/
Selling Power, http://www.sellingpower.com/
Thomson Gale, http://www.gale.com/

REFERENCES

1. Hospitality Net. 2005. *Hotels yield best results from person-to-person sales.* http://www.hospitalitynet.org/news/154000320/4024926.search? query= hotels+yield+best+results+from+person, accessed December 29, 2008.
2. Mandelbaum, Robert. 2005. *Hotel marketing: An investment in people.* PKF Consulting Corporation.
3. Bauman, Gabi. 2006. *The bed race–hotel companies' everlasting pursuit of differentiation.* HVS International.
4. Cathcart, Jim. 2002. *The Eight Competencies of Relationship Selling. How to Reach the Top 15% in Just 15 Extra Minutes a Day.* New York: Leading Authorities Press.
5. American Marketing Association. 2007. *Dictionary of Marketing Terms.* http://www.marketingpower.com, accessed March 1, 2007.
6. Hite, Robert E., and Johnston, Wesley J. (1997). *Managing Salespeople: A Relationship Approach.* Cincinnati: South-Western College Publishing.
7. American Marketing Association. 2008. *Dictionary.* http://www. marketingpower.com/_layouts/Dictionary.aspx, accessed December 29, 2008.
8. American Marketing Association. 2008. *Dictionary.* http://www. marketingpower.com/_layouts/Dictionary.aspx, accessed December 29, 2008.
9. American Marketing Association. 2008. *Dictionary.* http://www. marketingpower.com/_layouts/Dictionary.aspx, accessed December 29, 2008.
10. Manning, Gerald L., and Barry L. Reece. 2000. *Selling Today: Building Quality Partnerships.* 8th ed. Upper Saddle River, N.J.: Prentice-Hall, Inc.
11. Evans, Joel R., and Barry Berman. 2000. *Marketing.* 7th ed. Upper Saddle River, N.J.: Prentice-Hall, Inc.
12. "CVB sales blitz targets late summer meetings." November 16, 2006. *Jacksonville Business Journal.*
13. AME Info. *British tourism delegation on a sales mission to the UAE.* http://www.ameinfo.com/95864.htm, December 29, 2008.
14. Evans, Joel R., and Barry Berman. 2000. *Marketing.* 7th ed. Upper Saddle River, N.J.: Prentice-Hall, Inc.
15. "How to convert prospects to sales faster with pre-call planning." 2007. *Hoover's White Paper Series.* Hoover's, Inc.

16. Manning, Gerald L., and Barry L. Reece. 2000. *Selling Today: Building Quality Partnerships*. 8th ed. Upper Saddle River, N.J.: Prentice-Hall, Inc.

17. Manning, Gerald L., and Barry L. Reece. 2000. *Selling Today: Building Quality Partnerships*. 8th ed. Upper Saddle River, N.J.: Prentice-Hall, Inc.

18. Foley, Len. 2005. *The 10 laws of sales success*. http://www.entrepreneur. com. Accessed March 1, 2007.

19. American Marketing Association. 2008. *Dictionary*. http://www. marketingpower.com/_layouts/Dictionary.aspx, accessed December 29, 2008.

20. Manning, Gerald L., and Barry L. Reece. 2000. *Selling Today: Building Quality Partnerships*. 8th ed. Upper Saddle River, N.J.: Prentice-Hall, Inc.

21. Manning, Gerald L., and Barry L. Reece. 2000. *Selling Today: Building Quality Partnerships*. 8th ed. Upper Saddle River, N.J.: Prentice-Hall, Inc.

22. Stanton, William J., Rosann Spiro, and Richard H. Buskirk. 1998. *Management of a Sales Force*. 10th ed. Boston: McGraw-Hill.

23. Evans, Joel R., and Barry Berman. 2000. *Marketing*. 7th ed. Upper Saddle River, N.J.: Prentice-Hall, Inc.

24. Amarante, Kristin. 2002. *New survey shows high turnover in sales and marketing. Hotel Interactive*, accessed March 1, 2007.

25. Churchill, Gilbert A., Neil M. Ford, Orville C. Walker, et al. 1999. *Sales Force Management*. 6th ed. Boston: McGraw-Hill.

26. Churchill, Gilbert A., Neil M. Ford, Orville C. Walker, et al. 1999. *Sales Force Management*. 6th ed. Boston: McGraw-Hill.

27. Stanton, William J., Rosann Spiro, and Richard H. Buskirk. 1998. *Management of a Sales Force*. 10th ed. Boston: McGraw-Hill.

28. Stanton, William J., Rosann Spiro, and Richard H. Buskirk. 1998. *Management of a Sales Force*. 10th ed. Boston: McGraw-Hill.

29. Stanton, William J., Rosann Spiro, and Richard H. Buskirk. 1998. *Management of a Sales Force*. 10th ed. Boston: McGraw-Hill.

30. Stanton, William J., Rosann Spiro, and Richard H. Buskirk. 1998. *Management of a Sales Force*. 10th ed. Boston: McGraw-Hill.

31. Churchill, Gilbert A., Neil M. Ford, Orville C. Walker, et al. 1999. *Sales Force Management*. 6th ed. Boston: McGraw-Hill.

32. Casison, Jeanie. 2008. "Incentives Get Revved Up." *Sales and Marketing Management*, December 23, 2008; Roadtrips Inc. 2008. Unforgettable Exclusive Group Experiences, http://www.roadtripsinc.com/case-studies.aspx, accessed December 29, 2008.

33. Stanton, William J., Rosann Spiro, and Richard H. Buskirk. 1998. *Management of a Sales Force*. 10th ed. Boston: McGraw-Hill.

34. Robertson, Dan H., and Danny N. Bellenger. 1980. *Sales Management*. New York: Macmillan Publishing Company, 296–299.

35. Stanton, William J., Rosann Spiro, and Richard H. Buskirk. 1998. *Management of a Sales Force*. 10th ed. Boston: McGraw-Hill.

36. Stanton, William J., Rosann Spiro, and Richard H. Buskirk. 1998. *Management of a Sales Force*. 10th ed. Boston: McGraw-Hill.

chapter 18

Public Relations and Publicity
How Do We Get There?

OVERVIEW

Hospitality and travel organizations deal with a wide variety of groups and individuals in a typical year. Because they provide intangible services and rely heavily on word-of-mouth advertising, maintaining positive relationships with all these external people is of paramount importance. This chapter begins by defining public relations and publicity. It then explains their importance in the hospitality and travel industry and identifies the targets of public relations and publicity efforts—known as publics.

A step-by-step procedure for preparing a public relations plan is outlined, and the techniques and media vehicles available for public relations and publicity are explained. The chapter also looks at the structure of media organizations and how good relationships are built with key individuals within these organizations. The chapter concludes with a review of the role and advantages of specialized public relations consultants.

OBJECTIVES

Having read this chapter, you should be able to:

- Define the terms *public relations* and *publicity*.

- Explain the roles of public relations and publicity in hospitality and travel marketing.

- List the publics served by a hospitality and travel organization.

- Describe the steps involved in developing a public relations plan.

- Identify and describe the techniques and vehicles used for public relations and publicity.

- Explain the steps involved in developing good relationships with the media.

- Describe the roles and benefits of using public relations consultants.

KEY TERMS

blogs

co-opetition

community involvement

crisis management plan

FAQs (frequently-asked
  questions)

feature stories

integrated marketing
  communications (IMC)

media (press) kits

media vehicles

news (press) conference

news (press) release

newsworthy

podcasts

pre-opening public relations

public relations

public relations consultants

public relations plan

publicity

publics

RSS

webcasting

Have you ever been nice to someone you did not know, or to anyone you do not particularly like? Why on earth did you do this? Why bother to take the time? Could it be that you saw some long-term advantages to maintaining good relationships with these people? Maybe you realized that burning bridges behind you is not a good idea if you want to return to the same point some time in the future. Although you may not know it, you have used your own brand of public relations. When you think of it, you are your own personal diplomat.

Taking a business perspective, have you ever heard the expressions "that's only PR" or "that's just a publicity stunt"? What you have listened to are uncomplimentary statements about the activities of organizational diplomats, those persons who coordinate public relations and publicity efforts. It seems that most non-marketing people misunderstand or misinterpret the role of public relations. It is almost as if they see public relations and publicity as a smokescreen to hide company secrets or the inferior quality of products and services—promotion to manipulate the media and the general public.

Although this perception is quite widespread, it is a myopic and misguided view of this, the last promotional mix element. Public relations and publicity are valuable and important activities that help ensure the long-term survival of hospitality and travel organizations.

Public Relations, Publicity, and the Promotional Mix

Definitions

Public relations include all the activities that a hospitality and travel organization uses to maintain or improve its relationship with other organizations and individuals. **Publicity** is just one public relations technique, which involves non-paid communication of information about an organization's services (e.g., news releases and press conferences).

Public relations and publicity are different from the other four promotional mix elements and Internet marketing because with this element, the organization gives up total control of the promotion. Despite this drawback, public relations and publicity is a relatively low-cost and affordable promotional tool for organizations of all sizes. Another primary advantage of public relations and publicity is their persuasive impact, because they are not usually perceived as commercial messages.

Plan Integrated Marketing Communications First

You should understand from the beginning that public relations and publicity are not substitutes for advertising, sales promotion, merchandising, personal selling, and Internet marketing. The modern view of public relations is also that it is not an optional marketing activity, but one in which every organization, no matter how small, must engage. Public relations and publicity are affected by the four other promotional mix elements and Internet marketing, and vice versa. Although this relationship initially is not as obvious as the one between advertising and sales promotion, for example, good public relations makes advertising, sales promotion, merchandising, personal selling, and Internet marketing even more effective in **integrated marketing communications (IMC)**. Poor management of public relations usually has the opposite effect. Again, the objective of this short introduction is to show you that all five promotional mix elements along with Internet marketing must be planned together, not independently of one another.

Roles of Public Relations and Publicity

What roles do public relations and publicity play in marketing and the promotional mix? Let us start by returning to Chapter 2. You will remember that three of the differences between marketing services and products are the intangibility of services, more emotional buying appeals with services, and greater emphasis on stature and imagery with services. In Chapter 4, you learned about the great importance to hospitality and travel organizations of word-of-mouth information from social sources. What does this review add up to? It shows that personal opinions have an above-average impact on customers who are choosing hospitality and travel services. Customers cannot try them out before buying them; there are limited opportunities to sample. Friends, relatives, business associates, opinion leaders, and knowledgeable counselors such as travel agents are the social and professional opinion sources that customers rely on heavily. Public relations activities try to ensure that these opinions are favorable. Therefore, the three most important roles of public relations and publicity in the hospitality and travel industry are illustrated in Figure 18.1 and described below.

FIGURE 18.1 Roles of public relations and publicity.

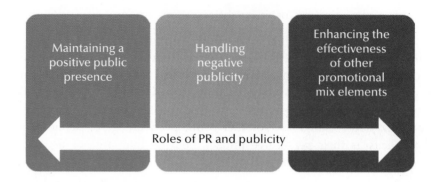

1. **Maintaining a Positive Public Presence.** The major function of public relations is to guarantee a continuing, positive relationship with individuals and groups with which an organization deals directly (e.g., customers, employees, other hospitality and travel organizations) and indirectly (e.g., the media, educational institutions, local communities and citizens in general). Included are all individuals and groups who now, or in the future, can have an impact on the organization's marketing success.

2. **Handling Negative Publicity.** No matter how hard an organization tries to emphasize the positive aspects of its operations, it will encounter negative publicity once, if not many times, in its history. Examples are allegations of food poisoning in a restaurant, an outbreak of a disease within a destination, a fire in a hotel, travel agents whose passengers are left stranded by carriers, an airplane crash, a natural disaster, or media stories that rate an organization's quality levels as substandard. Service organizations are especially vulnerable to the side effects of negative publicity because of the importance of word-of-mouth information sources. One leading public relations consulting company says that there are two sides to public relations—proactive and reactive.[1] On the proactive side, steps are taken to generate positive public relations (PR). Reactive PR or vulnerability relations are how negative publicity is handled. The key to reactive PR is to have a system for dealing with these undesirable situations and to have thought through in advance some potential ways of handling them.

3. **Enhancing the Effectiveness of Other Promotional Mix Elements.** Chapter 17 compared the promotional mix to a good recipe, one with the right ingredients in the correct proportions. In many ways, good public relations management makes the other four promotional mix elements and Internet marketing more palatable. Effective public relations paves the way for advertising, sales promotion, merchandising, personal selling, and Internet marketing by making customers more receptive to persuasive messages. It increases the likelihood that persuasive promotions will make it past customers' perceptual defenses.

Hospitality and Travel Industry Publics

What does the *public* in public relations mean? Does it imply the general public and, if so, what does this elusive term mean? The answer to these questions is that public relations and publicity involves communications and other relationships with various groups and individuals, both external and internal. **Publics** are a convenient name for all those with whom an organization interacts. Managing the relationships and communications with each and every public is essential to effective public relations. The hospitality and travel industry's publics include the 14 identified in Figure 18.2.

Internal Publics

1. **Employees.** Imagine the great impact of having organizations paint or otherwise attach an advertisement to all its managers and other staff members. Maintaining good relationships with employees and their families is just like having walking-talking billboards. They pass on their enthusiasm about the organization to everyone else. Good human resources management results not only in more satisfied employees, but also in increased marketing effectiveness.

2. **Employees' Families.** Hospitality and travel organizations must also consider employees' families as an internal public. Arranging special events and parties involving family members is a good idea, and they show that the organization cares for employees and their families.

3. **Unions.** Several sectors of the hospitality and travel industry are unionized, and management must always strive to maintain a harmonious relationship with these employee groups. To demonstrate this point, think about the union-management disagreements that have grounded air carriers, or the picketing of hotels by labor groups. Such cases can have a disastrous short-term impact on a company's performance and on customer confidence levels. In November 2008, Alitalia was faced with a

IN-HOUSE	OUT-OF-HOUSE
❏ Employees	❏ Customers and potential customers
❏ Employees' families	❏ Other complementary hospitality and travel organizations
❏ Unions	❏ Competitors
❏ Shareholders	❏ Industry community
❏ Owner	❏ Local community
	❏ Government
	❏ Media
	❏ Financial community
	❏ Hospitality and travel schools

FIGURE 18.2
The hospitality and travel industry's publics.

series of strikes and had to cancel 124 flights on one day, mainly in Rome and Milan. With the impending sale of the Italian airline at the same time, this adversely affected the public's confidence in the airline carrier.[2]

4. **Shareholders.** Corporations must be very concerned about their relationships with shareholders or other equity participants. These people primarily look to the company for a return on their investment (ROI), but they must also have pride in their association with the company. The situation is slightly different for non-profit organizations and government agencies. Non-profits, such as associations and boards, need to maintain good relations with members, contributors, or benefactors. Government agencies must be concerned with their image among individual citizens and elected politicians.

5. **Owners.** Many hospitality and travel organizations are small- or medium-sized enterprises (SMEs) that are privately owned. Just as with shareholders of larger public companies, it is essential that these owners are kept informed about their companies and operations.

External Publics

6. **Customers and Potential Customers.** If you have not gotten the message already, customers and potential customers are the reason for marketing. Keeping on the right terms with them is not just advisable, it is essential.

7. **Other Complementary Hospitality and Travel Organizations.** In Chapter 13, you learned about the importance of travel trade intermediaries to suppliers, carriers, and DMOs. Besides linking supplier, carriers, and DMOs to customers, travel trade intermediaries are also an important promotional target of most other hospitality and travel organizations. Looking at it from the opposite perspective, you should realize that influencer intermediaries such as travel agents, incentive travel planning companies, and tour wholesalers must maintain good relationships with suppliers, carriers, and DMOs. Therefore, public relations and publicity within the industry itself is a two-way process.

8. **Competitors.** Why worry about competitors? Are they not the opponents you are trying to beat in the first place? Yes, this is generally true, but there are times when cooperation is better in the long run than head-to-head, no-holds-barred competition. Sometimes competitive organizations must get together to satisfy the needs of certain clients (e.g., a large city-wide convention group that will need rooms in several hotels). Joint effort and planning may be needed to resolve issues that have a potentially negative impact on all competitors (e.g., an airport closing, the planned demolition of an important historic building, or the proposed imposition of a new, local tax). In other words, an antagonistic relationship with competitors should be avoided. Communication channels with competitors should be left open to allow for the exploration of areas of mutual interest in the future. Some experts have referred to this as **co-opetition** or cooperation among competitive organizations.[3]

9. **Industry Community.** The hospitality and travel industry includes a large number of trade associations, most of which were mentioned in Chapter 10. These associations provide many important member services—lobbying against adverse legislation, education and upgrading professional skills, informing others about the importance of the industry, and holding periodic conventions and trade shows. At a minimum, an organization should belong to one key trade association. From a public relations standpoint, it is even better if an organization is more active. For example, managers may serve as association officers or as seminar and convention speakers.

10. **Local Community.** Many hospitality and travel organizations, including most travel agencies and restaurants, and many hotels, are highly dependent on their immediate local communities for customers. Others, such as CVBs and other DMOs, must have strong citizen and political support to be successful. Being an active and concerned local community member is a must for most organizations in our industry. Normally, this means that management should participate in local clubs and associations such as the chamber of commerce, CVB or other DMO, and service clubs such as Rotary, Lions, and Kiwanis.

11. **Government.** Various levels of government, including municipal, county, state or provincial, and national agencies, affect hospitality and travel organizations. Compliance with the many pieces of legislation and regulatory measures is essential. It is also important to maintain good relations with key elected officials by keeping them informed of developments within the organization.

12. **The Media (or the press).** The media—newspapers, magazines, television and radio stations, and Internet news services—are the primary target of publicity efforts. Building open and cordial communications with them is one of the most important public relations functions. The topic of media relations is discussed in detail later in this chapter.

13. **Financial Community.** Banks, trust companies, and other lending agencies are important sources of short- and long-term capital for most corporations and many non-profit organizations. It is very important to have a positive relationship with current lenders and others who might provide additional financing in the future.

14. **Hospitality and Tourism Schools.** North America now has more than 500 colleges, universities, and private schools that offer specialized hospitality and tourism education programs. The International Council on Hotel, Restaurant, and Institutional Education (I-CHRIE) and EuroCHRIE are the major associations of these educators. These range from proprietary schools that train travel agency reservationists to doctorate programs at major universities. Each year, hospitality and travel organizations are placing more emphasis on hiring people with formal training and education in the field. It is beneficial for these organizations to be seen in the most positive light by the students and faculty in these programs.

Planning Public Relations Efforts

Every hospitality and travel organization, no matter how small, should have a public relations plan. Like advertising, sales promotion, and sales plans, new public relations plans should be prepared periodically, at least once a year. There is a greater-than-average tendency to let this slip, however, because of the lack of deadlines for placing materials (as in advertising) and the fact that public relations often is not a responsibility of specific staff members. Many organizations mistakenly assign it a low priority and only engage in sporadic public relations efforts, often to counter negative publicity (reactive PR). One of the major points made in this chapter is that public relations must be a continuous activity, regardless of whether an organization has an in-house public relations specialist, uses an outside consultant, or does neither of the two.

There are nine steps involved in preparing the **public relations plan** (Figure 18.3).

Set Public Relations Objectives (Step 1)

The place to start any plan is with a clear set of objectives. You already know from Chapter 8 that overall marketing objectives are set by target market. Similarly, with public relations it is best to set objectives for each of the organization's publics. This ensures that all publics are continually kept in focus.

Public relations objectives are generally informative. They provide oral, written, or visual information about an organization to one or more of its publics. It is a soft-sell form of promotion that is aimed mainly at enhancing the

FIGURE 18.3 Steps in preparing and evaluating a public relations plan.

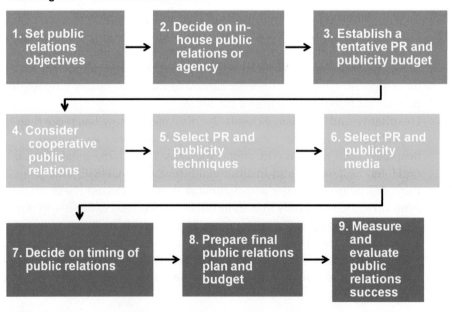

Planning the Public Relations Effort

1. Set public relations objectives → 2. Decide on in-house public relations or agency → 3. Establish a tentative PR and publicity budget

4. Consider cooperative public relations → 5. Select PR and publicity techniques → 6. Select PR and publicity media

7. Decide on timing of public relations → 8. Prepare final public relations plan and budget → 9. Measure and evaluate public relations success

organization's image. An example of setting a public relations objective is a restaurant that decides to improve its image in the local community. Again, although quite difficult to do with public relations, it is best to set measurable objectives. This requires taking measurements before and after implementing the public relations plan. In our restaurant example, this might involve conducting local surveys to measure the restaurant's image before and after the new public relations activities.

Decide on In-House Public Relations or Agency (Step 2)

The next decision concerns assigning responsibility for implementing the public relations plan. Many alternative approaches are used in the hospitality and travel industry:

1. Managers or owners assuming sole responsibility
2. Assigning public relations responsibilities to a multi-department committee
3. Adding the public relations function to the responsibilities of one of the marketing department managers or directors (e.g., the director of marketing or the sales manager)
4. Appointing a full-time public relations director or manager to the marketing department
5. Hiring an outside public relations consultant or agency
6. Combining 2, 3, 4, and/or 5

The approach chosen depends primarily on the size of the organization. The larger the organization, the more likely it is to have a full-time public relations director and to use outside specialists. Smaller organizations generally use one of the first three approaches.

Establish Tentative Public Relations and Publicity Budget (Step 3)

There is a fairly common misconception that public relations and publicity are entirely free. However, staff costs are involved if there is a full-time public relations director and support staff. Outside public relations specialists charge consulting fees for their services. Even if public relations activities are guided by an in-house committee, the general manager, or another manager, there are some charges for the time they devote to these activities. There are also definite costs incurred when an organization hosts the media, stages public relations events, and prepares press releases. For example, pre-opening public relations for new hotels often involve large budgets.

Again, it is best to use a two-step process to set the public relations and publicity budget. First, a portion of the total promotional budget is tentatively allocated. Second, this is followed by mapping out all the public relations activities for the upcoming period, based on the objectives for each public. Once the plan has been set, the costs of each activity are estimated and the final budget is determined.

Consider Cooperative Public Relations (Step 4)

Many opportunities for promotional partnerships exist with public relations and publicity that should be considered before going it alone. A good example is various suppliers and DMOs from a specific area that jointly fund a media reception or "road show" in a large city. Complementary hospitality and travel organizations may also get together to prepare press releases about new services they are offering jointly.

Select Public Relations and Publicity Techniques (Step 5)

A wide variety of public relations and publicity techniques are available to hospitality and travel organizations. They can be divided into three distinct categories: (1) continuous activities, (2) preplanned, short-term activities, and (3) unpredictable, short-term activities (Figure 18.4).

FIGURE 18.4 Public relations and publicity techniques.

CONTINUOUS PUBLIC RELATIONS ACTIVITIES

---

1. Local community involvement
2. Industry community involvement
3. Newsletters, newspapers, and company magazines
4. Employee relations
5. Media relations
6. Media kits and photography
7. Shareholder, owner, and financial community relations
8. Relations with hospitality and travel schools
9. Relationships with complementary and competitive organizations
10. Government relations
11. Customer relations
12. Advertising

PREPLANNED, SHORT-TERM ACTIVITIES

---

1. News (press) releases (traditional and on–line)
2. News (press) conferences
3. Ceremonies, openings, and events
4. Announcements
5. Feature stories
6. Press and travel trade seminars
7. Marketing research

UNPREDICTABLE, SHORT-TERM ACTIVITIES

---

1. Handling negative publicity
2. Media interviews

1. **Continuous Public Relations Activities.** One important point about public relations is that it must be done continuously, not just when emergency situations or newsworthy stories arise. A hospitality and travel organization must maintain ongoing relationships with each of its publics. It must have a continuous public presence. For example, it is not enough to call the media only when a good story idea comes up. An organization must use an ongoing program of media contact.

    Dealing with publics is similar to operating a savings account. If you put no money into the account, you cannot make a withdrawal. Likewise, if an organization does not establish and continuously maintain a relationship with each of its publics, it cannot expect to draw on the goodwill that has been accumulated. When you deposit money into your savings account periodically, you know that you not only can make future withdrawals, but you will also earn interest. An organization must continuously and frequently communicate with each of its publics to build goodwill and to be able to ask for special favors when they are needed. For example, a hotel should get to know all the key people (editors, reporters, publishers) at local newspapers and television and radio stations, perhaps by hosting lunches or dinners for them periodically. Each of these people should always be sent announcements and stories (and perhaps even holiday and birthday cards) so that they are constantly up-to-date on what is happening at the hotel. By building these open and continuous channels of communication with media people, the hotel has a much greater likelihood that its news releases and announcements will be covered. Of course, paid advertising with each of the media also helps get additional free publicity.

    What types of activities can a hospitality and travel organization conduct continuously? The major ones follow.

    a. *Local Community Involvement.* Every hospitality and travel organization should constantly strive to be an exemplary citizen in the local community or communities that it serves. Local **community involvement** can mean making financial or in-kind (e.g., free services) donations to worthy local causes or charities, becoming a member and actively serving in local clubs and associations (e.g., chamber of commerce, DMO/CVB, historical or museum board), and advocating support of community interests (e.g., economic development, social or environmental issues).

    b. *Industry Community Involvement.* Membership and active participation in key trade associations is another must. The payoffs are perhaps less immediate, but they are nonetheless significant. They help improve the industry for all its component organizations. An organization can participate by attending annual conventions, serving on boards of directors or committees, attending and supporting professional development and educational programs, speaking at conventions and seminars, and being spokespersons on important industry issues. Appendix 2–3 identifies many of the industry's key trade associations.

c. *Newsletters, Newspapers, and Company Magazines.* Newsletters are an excellent way to maintain a steady flow of communications with employees and other publics. Many hospitality and travel organizations have in-house newsletters or newspapers that are distributed to employees. Some periodically publish newsletters or magazines that are given to customers and other external publics. The Cunard Line and its *World Club* provides a good example of the customer-directed newsletter, which the company calls its *Cunarder* newsletter. Details of this magazine and the entire *World Club* membership program are provided on Cunard's website at www.cunard.com. In-flight magazines are another good example. These provide their sponsoring airlines with both a public relations and an advertising vehicle.

The distribution of newsletters and company magazines through e-mail is gaining popularity in the hospitality and travel industry. The Peninsula Hotels provides an excellent example of this. Its company magazine, *The Peninsula*, can be viewed through its website and the pages turned just as in a real publication. This is a cost-effective alternative to distributing a company magazine when compared with the traditional methods of producing and distributing these publications.

d. *Employee Relations.* In-house newsletters and newspapers are just one technique among several that are used in human resources management. Others with definite public relations value are employee recognition programs (e.g., employee-of-the-month awards), cards or gifts that mark important dates such as birthdays and anniversaries, incentive programs (e.g., incentive travel trips, bonuses, other special awards), and promotions. Happy employees tend to provide better service, which leads to more satisfied customers and word-of-mouth recommendations.

e. *Media Relations.* You have already read about the importance of continuous contacts with key media people. This should be similar to an organization's system of staying in contact with important past customers and sales prospects. Follow-up should be made at predetermined intervals, which may involve face-to-face meetings either at media offices or at the organization's place of business.

f. *Media Kits and Photography.* It is much better for an organization to anticipate media requests for information and photographs than it is to have to assemble these at the last minute. This is accomplished by preassembling **media (press) kits**. The Internet now provides a convenient way for organizations to distribute these materials to the media. These are usually found in the company background or "About Us" pages, but they often are accessed simply by clicking the news releases or media/press buttons on the home page. In some cases, the news releases are supplemented with an online photo gallery, which allows media professionals to download individual photos with the click of a mouse. Company histories and **frequently-asked questions (FAQs)** provide other useful information for the press.

Figure 18.5 shows an outstanding example of the use of the Internet to distribute information to the media about a tourism destination. The Las Vegas Convention & Visitors Authority, in the Press & Research section of its website, provides comprehensive destination information for the press and other readers. Included on these website pages are a Press Kit, Media Resources, and Stats & Facts about tourism in Las Vegas.

g. *Shareholder, Owner, and Financial Community Relations.* For legal, tax, and financial management reasons, hospitality and travel organizations must prepare annual reports and other financial statements. These reports and statements also have definite public relations value. In addition, periodic meetings with key shareholders, owners, and current and potential lenders are important in building positive relationships and open communications channels. Again, these are now often found on a company's website.

h. *Relations with Hospitality and Travel Schools.* Many hospitality and travel organizations recognize the value of staying in continuous contact with these educational institutions. Maintaining a positive image at these universities and colleges has both immediate payoffs (recruiting new staff members) and long-term benefits (faculty and former students spreading positive, word-of-mouth information on the organization). Because of their industry expertise, graduates and faculty members often are opinion leaders or are more influential in convincing others to use services than most people not associated with the schools. Serving as guest speakers in

FIGURE 18.5 Media relations are no gamble in Las Vegas. An excellent example of online information distribution by a destination.

classes at these schools is a great way to get the word out about an organization.

i. *Relationships with Complementary and Competitive Organizations.* It is essential for suppliers, carriers, and DMOs to stay on good terms with travel trade intermediaries. As you have seen in recent chapters, this involves placing advertisements in travel trade magazines, exhibiting at travel trade fairs and exhibitions, implementing other trade-oriented sales promotions, and conducting personal selling. However, building a good and lasting relationship means doing more than this. It includes such techniques as joining travel trade associations as associate members, speaking at travel trade conventions, mailing newsletters to individual travel trade organizations, and being advocates of travel trade groups.

j. *Government Relations.* Every hospitality and travel organization must comply with the laws and regulations that affect it; often failing to do so results in bad publicity. Dealing with government should go further than mere compliance, however. There are many government agencies that are now involved in promoting and developing the hospitality and travel industry. Every state, province, and territory in the United States, Canada, United Kingdom, and Australia has a tourism or travel marketing department (DMO). Supporting the efforts of these agencies definitely benefits hospitality and travel organizations directly. An organization can serve on tourism advisory boards, help agencies publicize the economic importance of the hospitality and travel industry, and give moral support when agencies request increased budgets.

k. *Customer Relations.* Customers are the lifeblood of every organization, and techniques that improve relationships with them are very important to an organization's long-term survival. However, it is very difficult to draw a clear line between a public relations activity and advertising, sales promotion, and personal selling. For example, if a sales representative sends holiday cards to past customers and prospects are these public relations or a part of personal selling? Is a company-published magazine, such as *The Peninsula*, a form of advertising or a form of public relations? Was the McDonald's advertising campaign highlighting the nutritional contents of its menu items pure advertising, or did it have a public relations purpose? The answer is not simple, but it implies that persuasive promotions alone do not guarantee long-term success. It is equally important to do the little things for customers, such as remembering their birthdays—things that do not have immediate payoffs.

One of the newer ways to communicate with customers is through **blogs** (web logs) written by corporate executives or marketing/public relations officers. A wonderful example of this is to be found on the Marriott International website, where a variety of blogs by CEO Bill Marriott are to be found. This is an excellent

INTERNET MARKETING

Keeping Up-to-Date with Vegas: Using the Internet for Press and Media Communications

- The Las Vegas Convention & Visitors Authority (LVCVA) has developed one of the best online sources of information for the press and media.
- On these pages, the following categories of information are provided:

  - Press releases
  - Press kit
  - Media resources
  - Stats & facts
  - When in Vegas

- The Press Kit leads to a variety of interesting themes of information about Las Vegas including "A Global Culinary Crossroads," "Attractions for All Ages," "Diversity in the Desert," "Gaming: 75 Years and Counting," "Las Vegas Nightlife" and several others.
- The Media Resources provided include: (1) a Monthly News Brief from LVCVA, (2) Vegas Images, (3) Vegas Links (links to related websites), (4) The Authority (a monthly newsletter from LVCVA), and (5) a Contact Us button.
- The Stats & Facts section gives information on: (1) visitor statistics, (2) statistical publications, (3) history of Las Vegas, (4) population, and (5) additional sources.
- The When in Vegas button leads to an image gallery of selected photographs and information provided for press and media use.

Source: Las Vegas Convention & Visitors Authority. (2008). *For Press & Research.* **http://www.lvcva.com/press/index.jsp**

Student Questions

1. What are the major advantages for hospitality and travel organizations of using the Internet for ongoing communications with the media and press?
2. The LVCVA provides a comprehensive set of visitor statistics on its website. Why is it a good idea for a DMO to share its research data online?
3. What do you think are the major challenges for an organization in keeping this portion of its website completely updated?
4. How can an organization use the Internet to see if its public relations and publicity activities are effective?

way for a senior officer to communicate with thousands of existing and potential customers.

l. *Advertising.* How do you make sure that the media covers your public relations message exactly the way you want? The answer is to make it a paid advertisement. In 2003, the City of Toronto launched the *Toronto: You Belong Here* campaign to encourage its residents to stay in town that summer and use local business in the post-SARS period.[4] This book has mentioned McDonald's nutrition-oriented advertisements several times. The same company in Canada used paid advertising to communicate the career success of its former employees.

2. **Preplanned, Short-Term Activities.** These public relations and publicity activities are also planned in advance, but they are short term rather than continuous. A grand opening of a new restaurant, hotel, or theme park is a good example, as are the activities publicizing an airline's inaugural flight on a new route. Another example is the news release. Although organizations should be producing these continuously, preparing each individual release is a short-term activity.

   a. **News or Press Releases.** A **news** or **press release** is a short article about an organization that is written in an attempt to attract media attention, which will then lead to media coverage of the materials contained within the news release. It is a publicity-generating tool that is used to communicate with publics without paid sponsorship. Preparing news releases is probably the most popular and widespread public relations activity.

      The contents of an effective news release are summarized in the following verse from a Rudyard Kipling poem.[5]

      I keep six honest serving-men
      (They taught me all I know);
      Their names are What and Why and When
      And How and Where and Who.

      The news release should open with a paragraph that summarizes the main points of the news story by stating who did what, when, why, and where. Other important contents and details for news releases follow. They

      - Must be **newsworthy**, containing recent information with news value
      - Must have a date
      - Must list a contact person, telephone number, and e-mail
      - Are usually marked "for immediate release"
      - Are typed in double-space format
      - Should have a headline (e.g., *Travel Industry Association Forecasts Stable Leisure Travel Market Despite Rough Economy*[6])
      - Should be printed on a specially-designed, news-release paper, with a consistent heading on each release
      - Should be as brief as possible, generally not more than two pages
      - Should contain no grammatical or typographical errors

- Should be very factual, avoiding unnecessary hype and flowery language
- Must have the approval of all persons quoted in the release
- Normally end with a signature (e.g., -30-, ###, -0-, or END)

Industry Players

Helping Children at McDonald's

McDonald's Corporation: Ronald McDonald House Charities

http://www.rmhc.org

Courtesy of Ronald McDonald House Charities

Ronald McDonald House Charities is an independent charitable organization.

(continues)

(continued)

Ronald McDonald House Charities, Inc. (RMHC®) programs are one of the best examples in our industry of a continuous public relations activity supported by a major corporation. They fall into the category of local community involvement, of which McDonald's Corporation and its individual franchisees are avid proponents.

The now-famous program began 35 years ago in 1974, with the opening of the first Ronald McDonald House in Philadelphia with the help of the Philadelphia Eagles football team. The idea was that of former Philadelphia Eagles linebacker Fred Hill with creative assistance from Elkman Advertising, the ad agency for McDonald's franchisees in Philadelphia.[1] Fred Hill's daughter Kim had been hospitalized with leukemia and he wanted to help other families finding themselves in similar situations. The local franchisees, through a Shamrock Shake promotion, raised $40,000 for the first house. The next house was opened in 1977, in McDonald's home territory—the Chicago area. A major part of the funding for the second house again came through the local McDonald's franchisees, this time through an Orange Shake promotion, one of the colors of the Chicago Bears NFL team. The Chicago Bears football team also helped to promote its development.[2] By 2007, there were 276 houses in 30 countries.[3] Together they contain more than 6,000 bedrooms. The worthy causes in this case are seriously-ill children requiring extended hospital care, and their families. A Ronald McDonald House is a home-away-from-home for the sick children and other family members when the children are receiving treatment.

Courtesy of Ronald McDonald House Charities

The Ronald McDonald House in New Orleans, Louisiana.

RMHC® now has three core programs: (1) Ronald McDonald House®, (2) Ronald McDonald Family Room®, and (3) Ronald McDonald Care Mobile®.

(continues)

(continued)

The mission statement of RMHC® is:

To create, find and support programs that directly improve the health and well being of children. RMHC fulfills its mission by creating innovative, effective programs that address targeted needs, and by supporting these programs and other activities conducted by its local Chapters worldwide. RMHC also awards grants to other nonprofit children's organizations that positively impact the health and well being of children around the world.[4]

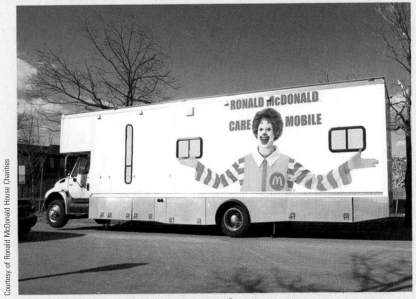

Courtesy of Ronald McDonald House Charities

One of the Ronald McDonald Care Mobiles®.

There is also a RMHC Scholarship Program that awards financial assistance for entering college to high school seniors who are under 21.

Ronald McDonald Houses are owned and operated by local RMHC Chapters. These organizations are eligible to receive start-up funding from the Ronald McDonald House Charities (RMHC®), which was established in 1984, in memory of Ray Kroc. RMHC awards grants to groups that benefit children in the areas of health care and medical research, including Ronald McDonald Houses, education and the arts, and civic and social services.

To oversee day-to-day operations, the local not-for-profit group hires a house manager. Families using the facility pay a small daily donation in the range of $5 to $25, if they can afford it. These donations and any other contributions are all channeled back into the Houses' maintenance and improvement, or into mortgage retirement. Family members also are expected to play the role of temporary volunteers sharing the tasks of cleaning, laundry, cooking, and grocery shopping.

McDonald's believes that the Ronald McDonald House program is a reflection of its business philosophy of giving something back to each

(continues)

(continued)

of the communities in which it does business. There is no doubt that the Ronald McDonald House concept is one of the premier examples of community involvement in our industry. While the corporation and its franchisees fully realize the positive impact of positive public relations, it must be remembered that the Ronald McDonald House idea was someone else's in the first place.

About RMHC

Ronald McDonald House Charities (RMHC®), a non-profit, 501(c)(3) corporation, creates, finds and supports programs that directly improve the health and well being of children. Its programs are grassroots-driven to enable the Charity to offer help where children need it most—right in their own communities. RMHC makes an immediate, positive impact on children's lives through its global network of local Chapters in 52 countries and its three core programs: the Ronald McDonald House®, Ronald McDonald Family Room® and Ronald McDonald Care Mobile®. RMHC and its global network of local Chapters have awarded more than $460 million in grants and program services to children's programs around the world. These programs and grants provide a bridge to assessable health care and allow families more time together which helps in the healing process. For more information, visit www.rmhc.org.[5]

Discussion Questions

1. What are the major public relations benefits that accrue to McDonald's from operating the Ronald McDonald House Program?
2. How does having a program like RMHC potentially impact the motivations of McDonald's employees and what are the possible roles that these employees could perform in furthering the program's goals?
3. What are the main lessons that other hospitality and travel organizations can learn from McDonald's leadership in this area?

References

1. Love, John F. 1986. *McDonalds: Behind the Arches.* Toronto: Bantam Books, 213–214.
2. Kroc, Ray. 1977. *Grinding it Out: The Making of McDonald's.* New York: Berkley Medallion Books, 198–199.
3. *History of Ronald McDonald House Charities.* 2008. http://www.rmhc.org/
4. Ronald McDonald House Charities http://www.rmhc.com/
5. Ibid.

The contact person listed on the release must be ready to answer follow-up questions from the media, and perhaps to be interviewed for a news article or program. How important are news releases in communicating information about organizations? Many stories covered by the media result from news releases.

Nowadays many news releases are posted on an organization's website rather than being sent in the traditional "snail mail" way. For example, in November 2008, the Canadian Tourism Commission (CTC) posted the news release on its media centre site, http://mediacentre. canada.travel/with the headline, *Canada jumps 10 spots to become world's No. 2 ranked country brand as CTC launches new global marketing strategy.* The release announced that Canada was ranked second by Future-Brand of New York only after Australia in its *Country Brand Index.*[7]

b. **News or Press Conferences.** A **news** or **press conference** is a meeting where a prepared presentation is made to invited media people. These conferences are held infrequently, only when an organization has something really important to announce to all the media (Figure 18.6). Press conferences play a key role in pre-opening public relations and when an organization makes major changes to its facilities and

FIGURE 18.6 Press conferences are infrequent but good at getting information out to many media people.

Image copyright R. Gino Santa Maria, 2008. Used under license from Shutterstock.com

services. Good examples are a hotel chain announcing plans to construct a new hotel in a particular city, an attraction owner publicizing a major park addition, a cruise line telling about its plans to build a new ship, or a new travel agency announcing a branch opening.

The persons making the presentations must be carefully chosen. Preferably, they should attract media attention themselves. This could include company presidents, mayors, other important political figures, tourism officials, or sports or entertainment stars. Besides having the opportunity to ask questions after the formal presentation, the media should be given a written summary of the news story. This can be in news release format, or it can be set up as a fact sheet. Think about the precision and planning that go into a president's or prime minister's periodic press conferences. You will soon realize how well these events are orchestrated to get consistent messages to the media.

Once more the Internet has had a big impact on how hospitality and travel organizations handle these types of media events. **Webcasting** or teleconferencing through a website is now used by some organizations to communicate current information. **Podcasts** are another relatively new Web technology, in which people subscribe for the service and then can download audio feeds to their computers or MP3 players. McDonald's Corporation website publicizes its podcasts that can be listened to through **RSS** (Really Simple Syndication) readers.

Did You Know?

Who is Picking the Pods?

- Podcasts are recordings in a digital format of sounds or music, including radio broadcasts, which can be downloaded from the Internet to an MP (MPEG) devices or similar audio players. Podcasts use RSS technology.
- The Pew Internet & American Life Project conducted a survey of Internet users in August 2006 about downloading podcasts.
- Twelve percent of Internet users said they had downloaded a podcast so that they could listen or view it at a later time.
- Males (15%) were more likely to have downloaded podcasts than females (8%).
- More experienced Internet users (13%) were more likely to have downloaded podcasts than those who had used the Internet for three or less years.

Source: **http://www.pewinternet.org/pdfs/PIP_Podcasting.pdf**

c. Ceremonies, Openings, and Events. What is smashed when a newly built ship is launched? What gets cut when a new restaurant is opened? What is broken when construction of a new theme park is announced? You are doing well if you answered a champagne bottle, a ribbon, and the ground. These exercises are parts of traditional ceremonies to introduce new or expanded hospitality and travel facilities or services. All of the hoopla accompanying these events is important in creating a positive first impression. It is also important in building awareness. In among all the balloons, bands, and banners is a very clear public relations and publicity objective—to begin building positive relations with all publics.

Let's take the **pre-opening public relations** of a new hotel as an example. The Gaylord Hotels started its PR work three years before the first guest checked in at the 1,406-room, Gaylord Palms in Orlando, Florida.[8] When the hotel opened in February 2002, the PR and sales efforts had resulted in the pre-sale of one million room nights. From this example it is important to realize that public relations begin months and sometimes years before operations begin. In many ways this is similar to the steps politicians take before they eventually get elected. With almost military precision, they make speeches and appearances, conduct debates and other activities, and then build these activities to near crescendo as election dates approach. Think also about the amount of PR and publicity that's required to support a major theme park development before it opens, and how long a period of time this covers. The plan to develop Hong Kong Disneyland was announced in November 1999, with construction starting during 2003. Almost six years after it was announced, on September 12, 2005, a major Grand Opening ceremony was held in Hong Kong for the official opening of Hong Kong Disneyland.

d. Announcements. Announcements are short news stories, often about one or more of an organization's employees. The events that are typically announced are internal promotions, hiring of new managers, or awards or other accomplishments of management or staff, or by the organization as a whole. The announcement usually features photographs of the individuals involved or of an award ceremony and the organization may be required to pay the print media that publishes the announcement. In addition to helping with public relations, announcements also play an important role in human resources management.

e. Feature Stories. **Feature stories** or features are articles of human interest that entertain, inform, or educate readers, viewers, or listeners. They are longer and have less immediate news value than news releases. In other words, they are unlikely to appear on the front page of a newspaper or at the beginning of a radio or television news broadcast. They are more likely to be published in a newspaper supplement (e.g., the travel, food, or entertainment section), in a magazine, or as a backgrounder or in a feature on a broadcast program.

There are two types of features—sponsor generated and media generated. A sponsor-generated feature is produced by the sponsoring organization; the other is a story idea developed by the media, in which an organization is asked to participate. Examples of media-generated features are the many articles on travel destination areas that appear in such magazines as *Travel + Leisure* and *Condé Nast Traveler*. Figure 18.7 shows the list of contents of *Travel + Leisure's* March 2007 issue with its feature story on San Miguel de Allende. Visitors to http://wwwtravelandleisure.com can also see a slide presentation on San Miguel de Allende. Sponsor-generated stories come in many varieties, including life histories of company founders, company histories and descriptions, backgrounders on interesting or important

FIGURE 18.7 Feature stories on destinations are a great way to get publicity.

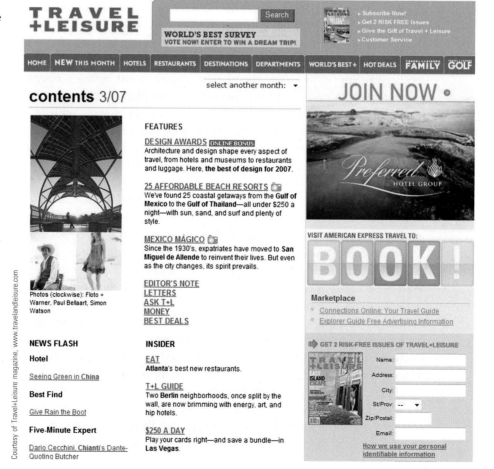

Courtesy of Travel+Leisure magazine, www.travelandleisure.com

customers, continuing contributions to important charities or worthy causes, and other unique organizational features and events.

f. Press and Travel Trade Seminars. These are meetings that last longer than press conferences, where sponsoring organizations communicate detailed information. Although travel trade seminars are definitely a form of sales promotion, they also have public relations value. Here again, the Internet has provided a new way of communicating this more detailed information to the travel trade and the media. For example, Tourism New Zealand offers its *Kiwi Specialist Programme* online in 10 different world regions including North America, Australia, the UK, and Europe.[9]

g. Marketing Research. Marketing research can be used for public relations and publicity purposes when an organization wants to show that consumer polls are in its favor. This was well illustrated by the Canadian Tourism Commission quoting its ranking by FutureBrand in a news release.

3. **Unpredictable, Short-Term Activities.** Not all public relations activities can be carefully preplanned, but every organization must be prepared to deal with them. Management may be asked to do media interviews regarding news events or media-generated feature stories. Additionally, no matter how hard an organization tries, undesirable public relations and publicity are always a possibility. Although the exact nature of these events is certainly unpredictable, an organization should plan ahead and train its staff to handle these situations.

a. **Handling Negative Publicity.** What is the best approach with negative publicity? Should you avoid responding with the typical "no comment," or should you take the offensive and vehemently deny responsibility? Again, you can get a clue from observing politicians and how they react to bad publicity. Their typical response is to acknowledge the rumor or event and do one of the following:

- Say that their staffs are looking into it
- Say that they have set up a special committee or task force to investigate it
- Offer their own or others' help in determining the accuracy of the rumor or event

Of course, politicians can deny rumors outright or criticize the media and political opponents for spreading them. Taking the offensive immediately, however, is seldom the best tack. It does not pay to cover up. Telling the truth pays off in the long run. If the facts are not readily at hand, one of the three previously listed approaches is best.

Hospitality and travel organizations faced with negative publicity must also react with political aplomb. Some of the steps to follow include designating spokespersons and adopting policies of honesty and transparency. How do you plan ahead for these kinds of situations if they are unpredictable? By far the best approach is for the persons responsible for public relations to anticipate the types of negative situations that may be encountered and to frame some possible responses to them. Many larger organizations develop a **crisis management plan** or proactive steps that they will follow in emergency or crisis situations.

A good example of professionalism in handling an adverse situation is how the city of London coped with a series of crises in the early to mid-2000s. The London Development Agency and Visit London produced a guide, *Crisis Management for Tourism Businesses*, to assist businesses through the first few weeks of a major crisis.[10]

b. **Media Interviews.** Although some media interviews are a direct result of preplanned public relations activities, many are not. As you have just learned, some result from negative publicity, whereas others result from media-generated feature stories or from news stories where an organization's manager is asked to give an expert opinion. Media interviews can be nerve-racking for some people, especially under the bright glare of television-camera lights. Being comfortable and articulate during an interview takes both careful planning and practice (Figure 18.8):

- When you are asked for the interview, get as many details as possible on the interview format, the interviewer, and the questions to be asked. Is it a live or taped interview? In which newspaper section or program will it appear? Why have you been chosen for the interview?
- Gather all the facts you need for the interview, and have these at your fingertips during the interview.
- Prepare responses to the questions you anticipate. Keep the answers short and factual. Avoid digressions.

FIGURE 18.8 Media interviews require poise and experience.

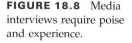
Image copyright Claudia Veja, 2008. Used under license from Shutterstock.com

- Practice your answers by asking someone else to role-play the reporter, and make any adjustments necessary after the role-playing session.
- Make sure that your appearance is neat.
- Establish a rapport with the reporter before the interview starts.

Select Public Relations and Publicity Media (Step 6)

As is true with advertising, many **media vehicles** are available for communicating information to publics. They include the Internet, broadcast media (radio, and network and cable television), newspapers (dailies, weeklies, and business), magazines (consumer and trade), and various in-house vehicles (company newsletters, newspapers, magazines, films, slide presentations, and videotapes). Chapter 15 showed you the relative strengths and weaknesses of most of these vehicles. Again, choosing from among them should be based on the publics targeted and the public relations objectives. For example, if you want to reach several publics in a local community, the broad coverage of a daily newspaper may be best. However, if the target is travel trade intermediaries, then trade magazines such as *Travel Weekly* in the USA, *Travel Press* and *Travel Courier* in Canada, *Travel Weekly* in the UK, and *TTG Asia* in Asia are the right choice. Should you want to communicate with all employees, a company-generated newsletter may be the best route.

The same financial constraints found with advertising are not present when selecting media vehicles and specific newspapers, magazines, and radio and television stations. For example, adding a magazine to the mailing list for a news release costs much less than placing an ad in the same publication. This means that the sponsoring organization does not have to be as selective in placing publicity as it does in placing advertising.

Media Relations

You have already learned about the importance of building long-term relationships with the media and always providing them with honest, factual information (Figure 18.9). Another key to good media relations is not to show favoritism toward any individual stations, newspapers, or magazines. When an organization has a news release or other story, it should generally be given to all the media at the same time. It is then their prerogative to cover the story as quickly and as comprehensively as they choose. There are some situations that warrant releasing an exclusive story to one paper, station, or magazine. The rationale here is that the medium chosen for the exclusive story best fits the publics that an organization is targeting. Which contacts should be developed within different media organizations? You need to understand more about the structure of media organizations to answer this question.

1. **Newspapers.** The newspaper industry is huge. For example, there were more than 2,000 newspapers in 2008 in the U.S. and Canada, according to the Newspaper Association of America.[11] Newspapers now are

FIGURE 18.9 Media relations and meeting the media are an essential part of public relations.

read in both traditional print and in online formats. Major national newspapers such as the *New York Times*, *USA Today*, *Globe & Mail*, *The Australian*, and *The Times* have extensive editorial staffs. Usually a newspaper also has several departments, each with its own editors. For example, there may be a food and entertainment editor, travel editor, sports editor, business editor, women's page editor, family/lifestyles editor, and others. Often these departmental editors are responsible for the special supplements you find inserted into the main newspaper. Additionally, newspapers have feature columnists, both national and local, who write periodic feature stories normally with the same theme. A good example is a local food or wine critic.

It is important to understand the roles of different editors before you approach them. City editors have overall responsibility for covering fast-breaking national, regional, and local news. If a hospitality and travel organization has a story with immediate news value, city editors should be contacted first, not the reporters who work for them. An example is when an important national figure or entertainer uses the organization's services and the individual's permission has been obtained to release this information.

Most stories generated by our industry do not, however, merit front-page news. They often fit better in specialized travel, food, entertainment, weekend, or lifestyle sections. In this case, the appropriate departmental editor should be the first person contacted.

The decision as to whom to contact first is also influenced by the size and the type of newspaper. If it is a small-town paper, the overall editor may be responsible for assigning all reporters. For a large-city daily, the correct procedure is to contact the city editor, as just discussed.

2. **Television.** As Chapter 15 mentioned, there are network, local, and cable television stations. Before you switch channels at the end of a news program, look at the titles and credits. You should see the names of producers, executive producers, news directors, editors, writers, and reporters. The key contacts in getting television coverage are assignment editors. They schedule stories, reporters, and film crews. Getting television stations to cover an event such as a press conference means either directly contacting the stations or having the event listed with a wire service.

3. **Radio.** The key figures at radio stations are the station managers and news directors. Because of the immediacy of placing and airing radio news, radio tends to be a feeder for later coverage by television and newspapers. Again, the wire services, including UPI (United Press International, http://www.upi.com), AP (Associated Press, http://www.ap.org), and Reuters (http://www.reuters.com) play a key role in distributing news stories of national interest. For example in December 2008, Reuters ran the story: "NYC tourists spend record $30 billion in 2008: Mayor." This story reported that 47 million visitors came to New York City in 2008 and spent a total of $30 billion.[12] For local news, direct contact should be made with individual station managers or news directors.

4. **Magazines.** As you know, magazines do not carry the same amount of fast-breaking news as newspapers, television, and radio stations. Many of the pieces they print are feature stories. Some national weekly magazines, such as *Time* and *Newsweek*, have more current news than others published monthly, bimonthly, or quarterly. Several trade magazines, including *Travel Weekly* and *Nation's Restaurant News*, are published weekly and contain more news.

   Appendix 2–4 lists the major consumer and trade magazines in the hospitality and travel field. Each magazine is structured differently, but contact names and titles can usually be found in the first few pages of an issue. Most have a publisher, an editor-in-chief or senior editor, a managing editor, and several departmental editors. Again, choosing the right person for the initial contact depends on the size of the magazine and its editorial departments.

Decide on Timing of Public Relations (Step 7)

You can see from the previous discussion that not all public relations activities can be scheduled precisely, ahead of time. Some situations are unexpected, but they must be dealt with promptly. You have also learned that there is a continuous part to this promotional mix element, including such activities as publishing a monthly employee newsletter, keeping up contacts with the media, and attending regular association and club meetings. Somewhere in between the unexpected and continuous are the preplanned, short-term activities such as news releases, press conferences, announcements, and feature stories.

Did You Know?

How to Develop and Keep Good Media Contacts?

- Know the media's audience, content, and editorial direction
- Know how editors like to be approached (telephone or fax vs. e-mail)
- Be respectful of journalists' time constraints (don't leave long-winded messages and don't call when they're on deadline!)
- If you give an "exclusive," do not share the news with other outlets before first getting a rejection from the first offer
- Know how editors like to receive art (slides vs. digital photos)
- Give editors a speedy, helpful response when they contact you
- Don't badger editors with calls and e-mails and never call simply to determine if they received your press release
- Know that lead times for many magazines are long—sometimes over three months—so if you're looking for immediate feedback, a daily news delivery option is your best bet

Source: Kelly Wisecarver. 2007. *Best Practices: PR Toolkit. Illinois Tourism Alliance News,* **http://www.visitillinois.net/**

Therefore, a public relations plan must include a definite timetable for continuing and preplanned, short-term activities. It must also include a contingency plan to handle the unexpected.

Another important point is that an organization does not have the same control over the timing of publicity as it does with media advertising. For example, when a news release is put on the Internet, follow-up inquiries may be immediate or they may take several weeks to surface. The media control the timing, the volume of coverage, and the position of the news or feature within their programs and publications. As you saw earlier in Chapter 14, this is a drawback of publicity when compared with advertising, but nevertheless it has to be accepted because the organization is not paying for the coverage.

Prepare Final Public Relations Plan and Budget (Step 8)

Now that the activities and media vehicles have been chosen to satisfy public relations objectives, an organization can draft a final plan and budget. Again, it is wise in budgeting and overall planning to anticipate the unexpected by allocating specific persons and funds to handle such situations.

Measure and Evaluate Public Relations Success (Step 9)

Writing the last page of the plan is not the finale of the public relations planning process. It is important to understand how effective the public relations and publicity activities within the plan have been. Has each public's image or opinions of our organization improved, remained stable, or deteriorated? How many and which newspapers, magazines, radio and television stations, and Internet news services covered our news releases and feature stories? What other coverage did we get? What are the circulation rates of these magazines and newspapers, and how many people tuned into the radio and television programs? These are just a few typical questions that can be answered as part of the measurement and evaluation step. The bedrock of effective evaluation of public relations and publicity programs and activities is setting appropriate objectives.[13] You will remember this was Step 1 in developing the public relations and publicity plan.

There are at least six different ways that public relations activities can be evaluated:[14]

1. **Evaluation by Those Responsible.** The evaluation can be based on the opinions and judgments of the public relations director, committee, or agent. This approach is not recommended on its own because the source has a definite interest in a positive evaluation. However, it can be used in conjunction with one or more of the other five methods.

2. **Visibility.** Here the organization measures the amount of publicity it received (e.g., press releases issued and covered, and other positive mentions). This standard is also lacking because it focuses only on the publicity part of public relations, and usually ignores the counteractive effects of negative publicity. Again, it should not be used on its own, but in combination with other evaluation methods.

3. **Organizational Utility.** How available and prepared were public relations staff members when negative publicity or other crisis situations emerged? It is crucial to an organization that its public relations team always be on the spot and ready to handle emergencies. Their ability to cope with the unexpected is definitely one evaluation standard that has great merit.

4. **Artistic Standards.** Did the public relations team follow principles, procedures, and practices generally considered acceptable by public relations professionals? What happens if a well-prepared news release does not get any media coverage? What if a press conference draws very few media companies and people because of an unexpected, competing news story of national significance? In other words, an organization may have followed all the right steps, but because of circumstances beyond its control, the effectiveness of its efforts was not as great as intended. Therefore, evaluation must include consideration of not only what was and was not accomplished, but also how the public relations team tackled each activity.

5. **Change in Opinions, Attitudes, Images, and Issues.** This form of evaluation involves polling publics before and after implementing the plan or individual activities within it. Marketing research, frequently in the form of surveys, is used to determine changes in people's positions on certain issues or in their opinions, attitudes, or images of the organization and its services. This is a particularly valuable measurement and evaluation method, especially when it is used in conjunction with the next one.

6. **Evaluation by Objectives.** Did the plan meet its objectives? This is by far the best way to measure the success of a public relations plan. As this book has emphasized throughout, all objectives should be quantified, and measurements should be made to evaluate success. By how much did we want to improve people's attitudes toward our organization, and did we achieve this amount of change with our public relations plan? As you can see, the best approach to public relations evaluation is using a combination of methods 5 and 6. The other four methods should be used only to supplement these two approaches.

The Institute for Public Relations gives some excellent suggestions for measuring public relations in a publication titled Guidelines and Standards for Measuring and Evaluating PR Effectiveness. This is available through the Institute's website at http://www.instituteforpr.com/. Four specific techniques are identified for measuring PR effectiveness:

a. Media content analysis—studying and tracking what is written and broadcast.
b. Cyberspace analysis—analyzing what is said about the organization in chat groups, forums, and news groups on the Web.
c. Trade shows and event measurement—assessing the benefits of attending trade shows and events.
d. Public opinion polls—determining if target audiences were exposed to particular messages, themes, or concepts, and then assessing their effectiveness through a survey.

Public Relations Consultants

Public relations consultants perform a role quite similar to that of advertising agencies. They employ professionals who are skilled and experienced in public relations and publicity. In the U.S., most of these public relations professionals belong to the Public Relations Society of America and abide by its "Code of Professional Standards for the Practice of Public Relations."

Like an advertising agency, the public relations firm assumes the responsibility for selecting, developing, and implementing all or some of an organization's public relations activities. Because of their size, salary scales, and degree of specialization, they attract and employ some of the best public relations professionals in the country. Some public relations firms are divisions of advertising agencies.

These outside experts help hospitality and travel organizations plan public relations and publicity activities. They do so by:

1. Helping to define public relations objectives
2. Selecting public relations activities and media vehicles
3. Using media contacts to get coverage for their clients
4. Providing creative services to develop various materials, programs, and events (e.g., pre-opening public relations programs, news releases, press conferences, feature stories)

5. Conducting research to measure and evaluate the effectiveness of public relations activities and various aspects of an organization's image among its publics
6. Providing specialized assistance in dealing with specific publics (e.g., preparing an employee newsletter, liaising with the media, handling relations with government agencies, and preparing reports for shareholders)

Should a hospitality and travel organization hire a public relations consulting firm? The answer is exactly the same as it is for an advertising agency—if the organization can afford the firm's fees, it is advisable to retain their services. You should realize that many larger organizations have their own public relations departments with a full-time public relations director, but they still use outside professionals to carry out the work. Organizations choose to do this because the specialized agency has greater objectivity, media contacts, and breadth of experience than an in-house public relations department.

Chapter Conclusion

Public relations activities have a broader focus than other promotional mix elements. They involve an organization's relationships with all its publics, not just customers and travel trade intermediaries. The assumption is made that, in the long run, all the individuals and groups with whom an organization has contact have an impact on its success.

A plan is needed to guide the public relations effort. It should cover three types of activities—continuous; preplanned, short-term; and unpredictable, short-term. A contingency plan for negative publicity, crisis management, and other unexpected situations should be included.

Building positive relationships with the media is the key to getting the right type of publicity. The services of an outside public relations agency may help establish good media relations.

---

1. How are the terms *public relations* and *publicity* defined in this chapter?
2. What are the roles of public relations and publicity in hospitality and travel marketing?
3. How important are public relations and publicity to hospitality and travel organizations? Explain your answer.
4. What are the fourteen publics served by the hospitality and travel industry?
5. What are the nine steps that should be followed in developing a public relations plan?
6. What are the three basic categories of activities covered in a public relations plan?

REVIEW QUESTIONS

7. Which techniques can be used to maintain positive relationships with publics?

8. What media vehicles are available for public relations, and which individuals should be contacted at each of them?

9. How can a hospitality and travel organization develop good media relations?

10. What are the roles and advantages of using public relations agencies and consultants?

CHAPTER ASSIGNMENTS

1. Interview the owner or manager of a hospitality and travel organization in your local area. Ask this person to define public relations or publicity. How does it compare with this book's definitions? What public relations activities does the organization undertake? What techniques and media vehicles are used? Does the organization have a public relations plan? Who is responsible for public relations? Based on your interview, can you recommend improvements in the organization's approaches to public relations and publicity? If so, what are they?

2. You have been asked to put together a public relations plan for an organization in the hospitality and travel industry that is planning to introduce new services in an area (e.g., opening a new hotel, restaurant, travel agency, or car rental agency; or introducing a new air route or cruise excursion). What components would you include in the plan, and what steps would you follow? Which publics would be involved? How would you handle relations with the media? What, if any, special events would you use to publicize the new service or facilities? How would you evaluate the success of the plan?

3. Select a part of the hospitality and travel industry and examine the public relations activities of three of its leading organizations. Do they have a public relations department? How are they organized to handle the public relations function? Are outside agencies or consultants used? What public relations techniques and media vehicles are used? Have any of the organizations had to handle negative publicity recently, and how did they do this? Do you see similarities or differences in their approaches? Which group does the best job of public relations, and why?

4. This chapter suggests that an organization must plan ahead to handle negative publicity. Assume that you are the public relations director for an organization in a specific part of our industry. What are five possible situations that might give your organization bad publicity? Be as specific as possible! Write a set of procedures for each situation that describes how you and others in your organization should handle these situations. In other words, how would you respond?

WEB RESOURCES

Alitalia, http://corporate.alitalia.com/en/
Associated Press, http://www.ap.org/
Chartered Institute of Public Relations (CIPR), http://www.ipr.org.uk/
Condé Nast Traveler, http://www.concierge.com/cntraveler/
Cunard Line, http://www.cunard.com/
Hong Kong Disneyland, http://www.hongkongdisneyland.com/
EURO Chrie, http://www.eurochrie.org/
Institute for Public Relations, http://www.instituteforpr.com/
InterContinental Hotels Group, http://www.ihgplc.com/
International Council on Hotel, Restaurant and Institutional Education (I-CHRIE), http://www.chrie.org/
Las Vegas Convention & Visitors Authority, http://www.lvcva.com/
McDonald's Corporation, http://www.mcdonalds.com/
Marriott International, http://www.marriott.com/
Peninsula Hotels, http://www.peninsula.com/
Public Relations Society of America, http://www.prsa.org/
Reuters, http://www.reuters.com/
Ronald McDonald House Charities, http://www.rmhc.com/
Tourism New Zealand, http://www.newzealand.com/
Travel + Leisure, http://www.travelandleisure.com/
United Press International, http://www.upi.com/

REFERENCES

1. Ketchum Inc. 2008. *Corporate Practice*. http://www.ketchum.com/corporate, accessed December 29, 2008.
2. Associated Press. 2008. *Alitalia strike creates havoc*. http://www.boston.com/business/articles/2008/11/12/alitalia_strike_creates_havoc/, accessed December 29, 2008.
3. Brandenburger, Adam M. and Barry J. Nalebuff. 1997. *Co-Opetition: A Revolution Mindset That Combines Competition and Cooperation: The Game Theory Strategy That's Changing the Game of Business*. New York: Currency.
4. *City of Toronto launches campaign to encourage Torontonians to be tourists in their own town* (July 2, 2003), http://wx.toronto.ca/inter/it/newsrel.nsf/0/b9f1df93684894b085256df60045c911?OpenDocument, accessed December 30, 2008.
5. Improvement and Development Agency (IDeA). 2007. *Six honest serving men*. http//www.idea-knowledge.gov.uk/imp/aio/1033517, accessed December 30, 2008.
6. Travel Industry Association. 2008. Travel Industry Association forecasts stable leisure travel market despite rough economy, http://www.tia.org/pressmedia/pressrec.asp?Item=924, accessed December 29, 2008.

7. Canadian Tourism Commission. 2008. Canada jumps 10 spots to become world's No. 2 ranked country brand as CTC launches new global marketing strategy, http://mediacentre.canada.travel/content/media_ release/future_brand_release, accessed December 29, 2008.

8. Gaylord Entertainment. 2002. *Gaylord Palms Resort poised to become lodging crown jewel in Central Florida's Kissimmee-St. Cloud Resort area; new resort and convention center features 4.5-acre atrium under glass,* accessed December 30, 2008.

9. New Zealand Tourism Board. 2008. *Trade Resources: Training Tools.* http://www.newzealand.com/travel/index.cfm?19F71BB7-FECD-48E8-B13E-5977F69D8E9D, accessed December 30, 2008.

10. London Development Agency. 2005. Crisis Management for Tourism Businesses. http://www.london.gov.uk/mayor/economy/docs/emergency-business-as-usual-jul05.pdf, accessed December 30, 2008.

11. Newspaper Association of America. 2008. *About NAA.* http://www.naa.org/AboutNAA.aspx, accessed December 30, 2008.

12. Reuters. 2008. *NYC tourists spend record $30 billion in 2008: Mayor.* http://www.reuters.com/article/domesticNews/idUSTRE4B-S4UB20081229, accessed December 30, 2008.

13. Watson, Tom and Paul Noble. 2005. *Evaluating Public Relations: A Best Practice Guide to Public Relations Planning, Research & Evaluation.* London: Kogan Page, 157.

14. Crable, Richard E., and Steven L. Vibert. 1986. *Public Relations as Communication Management.* Edina, Minn.: Bellweather Press, 383–393.

chapter 19

Pricing
How Do We Get There?

OVERVIEW

Pricing is the final element of the marketing mix. This chapter begins by explaining that pricing is not only a direct determinant of profitability, but also a powerful promotional tool. Some inherent conflicts in the duality of pricing are identified.

There is a difference between the price of a service and the value for money that customers perceive they are receiving. The concept of value for money is described. The chapter then points out that the hospitality and travel industry uses both unsophisticated and sophisticated pricing approaches. The recommended, cost-based method of pricing is discussed. The chapter ends by reviewing some specific pricing practices in different parts of the hospitality and travel industry.

OBJECTIVES

Having read this chapter, you should be able to:

- Describe the dual role of pricing.

- Explain the role of pricing as an implicit promotional element.

- List and describe the unsophisticated and sophisticated pricing approaches.

- Explain the concept of target pricing.

- Describe break-even analysis and how it is used when making pricing decisions.

- Explain the multi-stage approach to pricing and, in the process, list the nine Cs of pricing.

- Explain the concept of value for money and how this relates to pricing.

KEY TERMS

break-even analysis	leader pricing	rack rate
budget hotels	low-cost carriers (LCCs)	revenue management
competitive pricing	multi-stage approach to pricing	revenue managers
contribution margin	nine Cs of pricing	RevPAR
cost-plus pricing	penetration pricing	target pricing
discounting	price cutting	third-party distributors
discriminatory pricing	price discrimination	traditional (rule-of-thumb)
elasticity of demand	price lining	pricing
fixed cost	price skimming	value for money
follow-the-leader pricing	profit maximization	variable cost
Hubbart Formula	promotional pricing	yield management
intuitive pricing	psychological pricing	

Have you ever watched the popular CBS game show, "The Price Is Right"? If so, you know that contestants try to guess the prices of various products, ranging from groceries to expensive motor homes.[1] Every show has several winners, an obvious necessity for staying on the air. Some people's guesses are surprisingly accurate, while others are way off the mark. What does this show have to do with marketing? The answer may surprise you—very little! When the pricing of hospitality and travel services deteriorates into a guessing game, the price is definitely not right. Prices must be carefully researched. An organization must consider not only the impacts of prices on revenues and profits, but also their effects on other marketing-mix elements (8 Ps).

There are good and bad approaches to pricing, all of which are evident in our industry. You have probably heard the term *price war* used in connection with airline, cruise, and hotel pricing. Like all other participants in wars, some companies are killed, others are wounded, and the fortunate ones return unscathed. Innocent bystanders sometimes are mortally injured in the crossfire. For example, travel agents see their commissions dwindling as airlines and suppliers offer deeper and deeper discounts. As you will see later, however, all price discounting is not necessarily bad if each party has a detailed knowledge of its costs and profit potential.

The Dual Role of Pricing

One of the inherent challenges with pricing is that it fulfills two sometimes contradictory roles. If you have taken a basic accounting or economics class, you already know that, along with costs and volumes of business, pricing is a direct determinant of profitability. The other role of pricing is as an implicit promotional-mix element. In a way, a price acts like a magnet—it attracts some customers and repels others. People tend to base their perceptions of services and products partly on the price. A price offer can also play a central role in an advertising campaign or sales promotion (e.g., a two-for-one sales promotion, looked at another way, is a 50-percent discount on two items).

Some authors say that pricing has both a *transactional* and *informational* dimension.[2] The amount at which a service is offered for sale represents price's *transactional* dimension. Conventional wisdom suggests that the lower the price, the more of the service will be sold. Your economics class has probably described this relationship as a downward-sloping demand curve. As Figure 19.1 shows, the quantity demanded falls as the price increases, but it increases when the price is lowered (Graph A). The slope of the curve in Figure 19.1 varies with the **elasticity of demand** for the service. Demand elasticity measures the sensitivity of customer demand for services, to changes in their price. In an inelastic demand situation, customers are not very price sensitive. The slope of the demand curve is very steep (Graph B). In contrast, customers are much more price sensitive when demand is elastic. Their demand curve is much flatter (Graph C).

The graphs in Figure 19.1 are also based on some very large assumptions. First, it is assumed that customers have full information on all hotels, airlines,

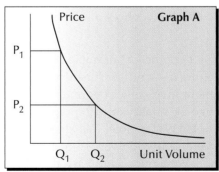

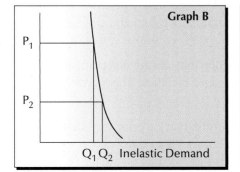

FIGURE 19.1 The transactional view of the price/quality relationship.

restaurants, cruises, tour packages, travel destinations, or any other type of hospitality and travel service. Although this may be close to the truth for experts such as travel agents, most individual customers do not, in fact, have complete information on competitive offerings, even with the help of the Internet. Second, customers gather information without considering the prices of each competitor's services. In other words, a price is a price, and it tells nothing else about the quality or features of services. This is often not the case, because customers tend to read a great deal into the prices of competitive items. A high price is frequently associated with high quality, whereas a low price has the opposite connotation.

Imagine that you are planning a trip to Europe and you are trying to choose a place to stay in London. Other than a long list of hotels with street addresses, numbers of rooms, and room rates, you have not been able to get complete information on the quality and range of services provided by each hotel. You narrow your list to five properties that are closest to the part of the city in which you want to stay. You cannot really tell much about each of these five possible hotels based on the number of rooms each has, and you know nothing about the streets and districts in which they are located. What does this leave you with? The answer, as you have probably already guessed, is the price of each hotel (or room rates in our example).

Let us say that you see the Dorchester Hotel with a **rack rate** (published rate) of over £200 a night, several in the £70 to £80 range, and one at £30. What assumptions would you make about the hotel that charges £200+ and the one that charges £30? Do you expect that each would provide the same quality and variety of services and facilities? What about those charging £70 to £80? Do you think that the services and facilities they offer would differ greatly?

Your answers to this hypothetical example should give you some idea of the *informational* role of pricing, and the function of pricing as an implicit promotional element. Without much other information on the London hotels, you had to use price to gauge the quality of each property. Let us see how you did. Did you think that the Dorchester Hotel that charges £200+ is more luxurious, with top-quality service and a wide variety of facilities and amenities? Was your perception of the lowest priced property that it was of a lower quality and had very few of the frills provided by the most expensive hotel? Were you unable to tell much about the differences between the three hotels that charge £70 to £80?

Research studies have shown repeatedly that customers tend to associate higher prices with higher-quality services and facilities. This is especially true when:[3]

1. Customers do not have sufficient information or prior experiences to compare features of competitive offerings. As in our London example, they are forced to use price as their basis of comparison.

2. Services are perceived as complex, and there is a high risk of making a bad choice. Perhaps you will remember these as the extensive problem-solving or high-involvement decisions mentioned in Chapter 4. Again, our London example is appropriate. For most of us, a trip to London and other parts of Europe involves complex decisions, with a relatively high risk of selecting unsatisfactory accommodations.

3. Services are perceived as having a certain snob appeal and carry social prestige. Can you think of any products that people buy for their snob appeal rather than their inherent qualities? How about Rolls Royce, Porsche, BMW, and Mercedes Benz automobiles? Maybe you thought of Rolex watches. In our London example, the prestige-conscious traveler would probably opt for the most expensive, £200+ per night Dorchester Hotel.

4. The difference between the prices of competitive services is minimal. In this case, customers may choose the highest-priced service because they perceive an added guarantee of quality. In the London example, it is probable that you would select the highest-priced hotel in the £70 to £80 range, if the three hotels charge £75, £77, and £79, for example.

The graphs in Figure 19.1 all suggest that a higher price always results in less demand, and a lower price in greater sales. This is the *transactional* view of pricing. It is hoped that you now see that this is not always true because of the role of pricing as an implicit promotional element (its *informational* role). The demand curve for a prestige product or service looks more like the one shown in the graph in Figure 19.2. Demand actually increases, to a certain point, as the price goes up. The higher the price, the

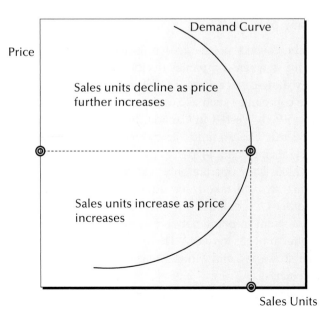

Price

Demand Curve

Sales units decline as price further increases

Sales units increase as price increases

Sales Units

FIGURE 19.2 The demand curve for a prestigious hospitality and travel service.

more exclusive and prestigious the services or products appear to certain customer groups.

The two-sided nature of pricing not only reflects its transactional and informational roles, but can also cause conflicts within hospitality and travel organizations. For example, sales representatives may feel internal pressure to build volumes (e.g., load factors on planes or occupied room nights in hotels) without sufficient regard for profitability. Price can be a powerful promotional tool in getting additional business, but merely having more volume does not necessarily increase an organization's profits. In other words, customers who are bought are not always profitable. A study by the Cornell University School of Hotel Administration in 2004 showed that hotels which discounted room rates achieved higher occupancy rates than competitors who maintained higher prices. However, the hotels that did not discount their prices achieved higher **RevPAR** (revenue per available room).[4] This suggests that cutting prices may increase demand, but not necessarily add to profitability; the graphs in Figure 19.1 need to be interpreted with caution!

Hospitality and travel managers are often uneasy about having half-empty hotels, restaurants, cruise ships, or airplanes. In some ways, their concerns are valid. As you will remember from Chapter 2, inventories of hospitality and travel services cannot be stored. They perish almost immediately. Therefore, is it better for managers and sales representatives to sell empty seats or rooms at any price than to lose their sale and use forever? Let us review the definition of marketing to help you answer this question. Marketing activities, including pricing, are designed to satisfy customers' needs and their organizations' objectives. For many organizations, the primary objective is to make a profit. Having a *fill-empty-spaces-at-any-cost* mentality, therefore, runs contrary to the definition of marketing and shows a sales rather than a marketing orientation. It is often more profitable to have unused inventory than to offer too large or too many price deals.

There's another aspect of the role of pricing that you probably already know about. This is when companies decide to use price as a long-term competitive strategy. **Low-cost carriers (LCCs)** in the airline business are an example and include companies such as Southwest Airlines and JetBlue Airways in the USA (Figure 19.3), WestJet in Canada, EasyJet and Ryanair in the UK and Europe; AirAsia, Air Deccan, and Tiger Airways in Asia; and Virgin Blue in Australia. These airlines had 14 percent of all the flights in the world in the second half of 2006. They operate only one class of service, with a single type of short-haul aircraft, and take reservations mainly through the Internet and by phone.[5] Another LCC definition in the USA context is that these are airlines which operate a point-to-point network, pay employees below the industry average, and offer no-frills service.[6] There are many **budget hotels** that operate with similar strategies, and Motel 6 was one of the earliest brands with the low-price approach.

Courtesy of JetBlue Airways

FIGURE 19.3 JetBlue is a very successful low-cost carrier in the USA.

Pricing and Value for Money

Many leading experts in our industry say that travelers are becoming increasingly value-conscious. Searching online for the best prices has intensified this trend. Travelers want **value for money**. What does this mean? One definition of value for money is the way that customers compare the amount of money they pay to the quality of the facilities and service they receive (Figure 19.4). For something to have value, it does not always have to be a bargain sold at a rock-bottom price. Value is only relevant in the eyes of the beholder. Some services have high perceived value for certain customers, but not for others (Figure 19.5). For example, there are people who pay high prices for luxury-oriented travel services (e.g., the Dorchester Hotel in London), and they perceive that they get exceptional value for their money. Others equate value with economy-oriented or cut-rate travel services (e.g., budget hotels and low-cost carriers).

How does this relate to pricing? The answer is rather simple. A price must convey to customers a feeling that they are receiving value for money. They must be convinced that the quality of the service and facilities they are getting is consistent with the price they are paying. If the two are inconsistent, considerable customer dissatisfaction will result.

FIGURE 19.4 One view of pricing is that it's what the customer pays.

FIGURE 19.5 Luxury travel experiences are unique and have a high price tag.

The Global Perspective: The Big Picture

Pricing by Low-Cost Airline Carriers

Air Berlin, Ryanair, Spring Airlines, Virgin Blue, and Westjet

Courtesy of Air Berlin

Air Berlin is now the second largest airline in Germany.

Low-cost airline carriers (LCC) are companies that use price as a long-term competitive strategy. They operate only one class of service, usually only with a single type of short-haul aircraft (typically the Boeing 737 series), and take reservations mainly through the Internet and by phone. Unlike the major airline carriers that have been unprofitable in recent times, many of the LCCs have enjoyed healthy levels of profit.

Air Berlin, Ryanair, Spring Airlines, Virgin Blue, and WestJet are excellent examples of success in using lower pricing as a competitive strategy in the airline sector. The following is a quick summary on these five airlines, each of which is headquartered in a different country.

Air Berlin, Germany

http://www.airberlin.com

Air Berlin is a German airline which grew out of Air Berlin Inc. founded in 1978 and started operating in 1992 with just two aircraft and 150 employees. In 2007, it carried approximately 27.9 million passengers on more than 120 aircraft. The company flies to more than 140 destinations within Germany, Europe, and around the world, and now has around 8,500 employees. Despite the difficulties caused by rising costs such as aircraft fuel, Air Berlin was profitable in both 2006 and 2007.

(continues)

(continued)

Air Berlin is now the second largest airline in Germany, after the giant global airline of Lufthansa. The Air Berlin Group includes LTU, dba, Belair, and NIKI. The other three airlines were partly or wholly acquired by Air Berlin from 2004 to 2007.

In 2008, Air Berlin's fares began from €29, including all taxes and charges. Like most of the LCCs, Air Berlin's lowest airfares can only be found from the company's website.

Ryanair, Ireland

http://www.ryanair.com

Ryanair commenced operations in 1985 with two small aircraft and 25 staff members; in its fiscal year of 2007–2008, the airline carried around 50.9 million passengers, with a fleet of over 160 aircraft, and over 5,000 employees.

Ryanair was the first low-fare airline to be established in Europe, and is the largest LCC in Europe today. Its cheapest fares are available by booking online at **http://www.ryanair.com**. In early 2009, Ryanair's fares originating from London Stansted Airport to Barcelona and other airports in Spain started from just £15 ($21.70). In fact, Ryanair's average fare (including bag charges) in fiscal 2007–08 was €44 ($62). Unlike many major airlines, Ryanair is a profitable company, and its profits increased by 20 percent from March 2007 to March 2008.

Courtesy of Spring Airlines

Spring Airlines is China's first low-cost carrier.

(continues)

(continued)

Spring Airlines, China

http://www.china-sss.com/index.htm

Spring Airlines is China's first low-fare airline, which was established in 2005 by Spring Travel, China's number one domestic travel agency and tour operator. The airline is based in Shanghai's Hongqiao Airport and also flies out of Shanghai Pudong International Airport as well as Sanya Airport in Hainan. The airline currently owns eight Airbus A320 planes. Spring Airlines has over 20 routes that include flights from Shanghai to Guangzhou, Zhuhai, Xiamen, Kunming, Haikou, Sanya, Guilin, Wenzhou, and Qingdao.

Being the first to successfully establish the low-fare airline business model in China, Spring Airlines' motto is "Making flying affordable for everyone." By selling specially priced tickets costing 1CNY, 99CNY, 199CNY, and 299CNY, Spring passes some of its profits to the consumer. In 2006, the average price of a Spring Airlines ticket was 36 percent lower than the market price, which equated to an average savings of over CNY two billion for the flying public.

Spring Airlines is also the first airline in China to have designed and launched its own ticket sales system and its proprietary Departure Control System which allows passengers to conveniently order, choose their seats, pay, and check in from their home or office via the Internet or mobile phone.

Courtesy of Spring Airlines

The service levels aboard Spring Airlines are excellent.

(continues)

(continued)

Virgin Blue, Australia

http://www.virginblue.com.au

Virgin Blue started its operations in Australia in 2000 with just two planes and 200 staff. Its strategy was to halve the cost of the typical airfares on Australian domestic routes. Virgin Blue has been a huge success; in 2008, the airline had a fleet of 55 aircraft and more than 4,200 employees. The airline carried over 16.67 million passengers for the 12 months up to and including June 2008.

Virgin Blue is a highly profitable airline, and the group now also includes Pacific Blue and Polynesian Blue with flights in New Zealand and within the South Pacific island nations.

Virgin Blue has one interesting promotion called its "Happy Hour." This is the time between 12 noon and 1:00 PM on any day of the week, when the company releases some special low fares on its website that are only available by booking online.

WestJet, Canada

http://www.westjet.com

WestJet is a Canadian airline that was founded in Calgary, Alberta in 1996. It started operations with just three aircraft, flying to five destinations. WestJet carried approximately 13 million passengers and had around 6,700 staff members in 2007. In 2008, it had 76 aircraft with services to 51 destinations in Canada, USA, Mexico, and the Caribbean.

About 68 percent of WestJet's bookings in 2007 came directly through the company's website. The company also has its own reservations center for telephone bookings. Unlike some other airlines, WestJet still pays commissions for bookings through travel agencies.

WestJet Airlines Ltd. was profitable in 2005, 2006, and 2007, with its net earnings increasing each year. This is a very unusual situation among North American airlines for this time period.

There are other successful LCCs that could have been included in this *Global Perspective*. For example, EasyJet (founded in 1995 in the UK), Air Asia (established in 2001 in Malaysia), and Tiger Airways (set up in Singapore in 2004). These companies follow the same basic strategies as the five that have been described above, but have different geographic route systems and slightly different operational and fleet and staff structures.

Not All LCCs Are Successful

Before leaving this topic of low-cost airline carriers, you need to know that this pricing and cost strategy does not absolutely guarantee success and profitability in the airline sector. In fact, several LCCs have failed including Oasis Hong Kong Airlines, ATA, and Frontier Airlines. The high oil prices in 2007 and 2008 hit the LCCs even harder

(continues)

(continued)

than conventional airlines, since LCCs' fuel costs represent a higher portion of their total operating costs. With continuing high oil prices, airline experts were predicting that more of the LCCs would become less profitable and some others would fail.

Not All LCCs Are Exactly Alike

The formula of the LCCs is usually said to involve three items—low fares, low costs, and "no frills." The latter means that very few services are provided to passengers onboard their flights. Some of the LCCs are definitely of the "no frills" variety and charge for every service apart from the basic fare, such as for checked bags and meals and drinks served in-flight. Others provide some level of food and beverage service onboard, and also operate frequent flyer programs similar to the major airlines.

Value Up in the Air

From the marketing perspective, it could be said that these airline companies offer the public greater value for money. It could be argued that this is the main reason for their market success that dates back to the establishment of Southwest Airlines in the USA. However, the major airlines might counter by saying that they offer more convenience and a higher quality of customer service, so their value for money proposition is stronger. You might want to draw your own conclusions about this!

Discussion Questions

1. What are the advantages to consumers in using low-cost airline carriers?
2. What are the advantages to an airline of using a low-cost strategy?
3. Do you think that the current toward LCCs will continue for the next five years? Why or why not?

Planning Pricing Approaches

How do you know when the price is right? From Chapter 8 on, this book has stressed the importance of having objectives, and of basing the plans for each marketing-mix element on these objectives. The right pricing approach, therefore, begins with a set of clear pricing objectives. There are three steps involved in planning prices:

1. Set pricing objectives
2. Select pricing approaches
3. Measure and evaluate pricing success

Price setting, yield and revenue management has become serious issues in hospitality and travel as local and global competition increases. The airlines introduced the concept of **yield management** and hotels followed later

Morrison, A. (2010) Hospitality & Travel
Marketing (London: Cengage)

INTERNET MARKETING

Revenue Management and the Internet: Friend or Foe?

- Revenue management is a concept that makes sense for all service businesses that have a perishable inventory including hotels, airlines, cruise lines, tour operators, car rental companies, and railways. The airlines pioneered this concept as "yield management" and others in hospitality, travel and tourism have followed.

- The basic tasks in revenue management are to: (1) forecast future demand levels for a specific period of time, (2) set prices for that time period, and (3) allocate supply capacity (e.g., rooms, seats, cars, etc.) so as to maximize revenues.

- The Internet now offers many new distribution channels for hospitality and travel, and great opportunities to increase sales. They also tend to be channels with a lower cost percentage. However, the great variety and complexity of online distribution has made revenue management much more difficult.

- Hotels tend to use "bid price" models in their revenue managements systems. This means that if the customer asks for a price equal to or above the "bid price" set by the hotel, the request will be accepted.

- Nowadays customers have become more value conscious and more skilful in seeking out the best deals, both online and offline. In some ways, the Internet offers customers a virtually endless online shopping mall of hospitality and travel services and products. Despite the sophistication of revenue management models, they can shop to their heart's content to find the lowest prices.

Sources: Salerno, Neil. (2006). *Revenue management for dummies.* **http://www.hotelmarketing.com/**; Choi, Sunmee, and Sheryl E. Kimes. (2002). " Electronic distribution channels' effect on hotel revenue management." *Cornell Hotel & Restaurant Administration Quarterly.*

Student Questions

1. How do you think the Internet assists hospitality and travel companies make better use of available supply capacity?

2. What major pricing challenges and issues are involved with selling supply capacity through the Internet?

3. What steps can be introduced in a revenue management system to adapt to the increasing demand from customers via online distribution channels?

4. How do you think new concepts like dynamic packaging (see Chapter 13) will affect revenue management systems in the future?

with **revenue management**. These are similar concepts and can be defined as the application of information systems and pricing strategies to allocate the right capacity to the right customer at the right place at the right time.[6] This involves using computer systems to predict customer demand levels and to match price levels to what certain customer groups are willing to pay at a specific time for a specific duration of service. The trend toward more sophisticated pricing through yield and revenue management has increased the demand for pricing professionals in hospitality and travel organizations. In hotels, these individuals are normally called **revenue managers**, who have been specially trained to contribute to hotel profits and add to the hotel's asset values.[7] There is also now a trade association of these pricing experts, known as the Professional Pricing Society. These professionals are heavily involved in the following steps in planning pricing approaches.

Set Pricing Objectives

Most pricing objectives can be divided into three categories: (1) profit oriented, (2) sales oriented, and (3) status-quo oriented.[8]

1. **Profit-Oriented Pricing Objectives.** Prices can be established either to achieve certain targeted profit levels (**target pricing**) or to generate the maximum amount of profit (**profit maximization**). Target prices are usually expressed as certain percentage returns on investment or sales. Later in this chapter you will learn about a hotel pricing technique called the *Hubbart Formula*, which uses a target return on investment as its base. Target pricing is one of the best approaches to pricing available. With profit maximization, the company sets the price that will give it the greatest profits, based on forecasts of costs and customer demands. Profit maximization objectives tend to be used more in the short term, whereas target pricing is more suitable for long-term application.

2. **Sales-Oriented Pricing Objectives.** Sales-oriented pricing emphasizes sales volumes rather than profits. The company uses price as a tool either to increase its sales to a maximum or targeted level or to get a larger share of the market. This chapter has already alerted you to the fact that sales-oriented pricing does not necessarily lead to increased profits. Despite the real need for caution, sales-oriented pricing approaches have proven extremely successful over several years for some companies.

   Sales-oriented pricing objectives can be either long or short term. In JetBlue's case, low rates are part of their long-term pricing approaches. Short-term applications include many of those involved with sales promotions, which were discussed in Chapter 16. Couponing, for example, usually includes price discounting to increase sales in the short term. Again, the Internet is becoming a more important place for hospitality and travel organizations to announce price deals, and for customers to shop for the best prices. For examples, Hardee's and other restaurant chains are using the Web to distribute coupons on some menu items. The seasonal demand patterns for many hospitality and travel services also force many companies to use price as an inducement in off-peak periods.

3. **Status-Quo-Oriented Pricing.** With status-quo objectives, the company tries to avoid large sales swings and maintain its position relative to competitors and travel trade intermediaries. The most common use of this approach is by companies that try to match competitors' prices closely (the **competitive pricing** approach). In certain parts of our industry, smaller-share companies adjust their prices to match more closely those of the market leaders (e.g., Burger King, Wendy's, and Hardee's following McDonald's price changes—the **follow-the-leader pricing** approach).

Select Pricing Approaches

Once pricing objectives are understood, a company can make an informed choice among several available pricing approaches. These can be divided into three distinct categories—unsophisticated, sophisticated, and multi-stage.

Categories of Pricing Approaches

1. **Unsophisticated Approaches.** The approaches in this category are unsophisticated because they rely less on research and cost considerations than they do on the intuition of managers. They are generally not recommended, but are discussed here because they occur in the hospitality and travel industry.

    a. *Competitive Approach.* As you have already seen, this is a status-quo approach to pricing—companies set prices based on their competitors' prices. It tends to be a reactive or wait-and-see method, because prices are moved up or down as competitors' price changes become known. In today's highly competitive hospitality and travel markets, it is essential to consider one's competitors when pricing, but this should not be the only consideration. Every individual organization has a different cost/profit structure and customer base. A certain price level may produce large profits for one company but result in no profits or a loss for another.

    b. *Follow-the-Leader Approach.* This is a modification of the general competitive pricing approach used mainly by smaller market-share companies. Again, it is a reactive rather than a preplanned method. Smaller companies wait for the new prices introduced by the market leader or leaders, and then they peg their own prices to these. In general, changes follow the direction (either up or down) of the larger firms. Because most smaller organizations operate with more slender profit margins than those of the market leaders (who enjoy considerable economies of scale), it can be dangerous for them to follow the leaders blindly. Market leaders, because of their volume advantage, can generally absorb larger cuts in prices. They also have more to gain from slight increases in prices.

c. **Intuitive Approach. Intuitive pricing** is the least scientific method, because it involves no research on costs, competitive prices, or customer expectations. Some have called it the *gut feel* approach because it relies most heavily on the manager's intuition.[9] You already know how important marketing research is to effective marketing decisions. Thus, you will quickly realize that this is not a good pricing approach.

d. **Traditional or Rule-of-Thumb Approach.** Over the years, certain **traditional** or **rule-of-thumb pricing** has developed in various parts of the hospitality and travel industry. In the lodging sector, it was believed in the 1970s that $1 should be charged for every $1,000 of capital invested per room in each property; this is sometimes called the *building cost room rate formula*. For example, a hotel that cost $100,000 per room to build should have a room rate of $100. Another with a per-room investment of $150,000 should charge $150. Many now believe that this rule of thumb has become obsolete as hotel construction costs have escalated quickly and intense competition has held hotel rates down.[10] Because a 40-percent food cost was quite typical among restaurants in the 1970s, multiplying a dish's food costs by a factor of two and one-half was a common rule of thumb. The mechanics of this approach are very simple—just find out what the rule of thumb is and plug in your own numbers. However, you have probably already spotted serious flaws in this approach. Again, there is no research or consideration of customer expectations and competitive prices.

All four unsophisticated approaches have some common features. First, they are based on little, if any, research. Second, they take into account only one of the factors that influences prices—what competitors are charging. Third, they do not consider an organization's unique cost/profit structure or its customers' expectations and preferences.

Before we discuss the more sophisticated, research-based pricing approaches, you should know more about the variety of factors that influence prices. A discussion of these factors follows.

Customer Characteristics

The characteristics of customers should play a key role in determining prices. Some customers are extremely price-sensitive and will react quickly to even minor price changes (remember elastic demand?). Others do not change their buying habits, even after major price moves (inelastic demand). You will probably recall the discussion of high- and low-involvement purchase decisions in Chapter 4. It is definitely easier to set high prices and to pass along major price increases to high-involvement customers, because they are less price-sensitive.

Based on the target markets served, it may be possible to use **price discrimination** (also sometimes called **discriminatory pricing**). Here, two or more prices are set to appeal specifically to their respective target markets. Economy, business, and first-class airfares are an example, as are the array of rates that most large hotels offer (e.g., regular rack, corporate, tour group, government, and airline crew rates). The yield and revenue management concepts discussed earlier are applications of price discrimination by target market.

Corporate Objectives

Because prices are a direct determinant of profitability, the responsibility for pricing is not usually entrusted solely to the marketing manager; a revenue manager may have greater responsibility for setting prices. Prices must be set in the context of the overall corporate objectives that were discussed in Chapter 3. These objectives may, for example, be stated in terms of profit levels, market share, or sales-volume targets.

Corporate Image and Positioning

Prices should be consistent with the overall company image and positioning approaches. For example, a hotel company or cruise line that chooses to communicate a prestige or deluxe image should set prices well above the average. In contrast, a hospitality and travel organization emphasizing bargains would be advised to take the opposite tack.

Customer Demand Volumes

Another important part of the pricing equation includes the probable volumes of customer demand. The demand for most hospitality and travel services fluctuates widely by season, month, week, day of the week (weekend versus weekday), or even time of day. Added pressure is put on managers to fill off-peak periods because the services are so perishable. (Remember this from Chapter 2?) Price discrimination by time period is a tool heavily used by our industry to smooth out demand patterns. Examples include early-bird specials in restaurants, special weekend rates at city hotels, off-peak airfares on certain routes, pre-season rates on cruise lines and at resorts, and reduced weekend car-rental rates. For example, the Cunard Line in March 2007 offered Early Booking Fares to past guests on cruises on the Queen Mary 2 and Queen Elizabeth 2.

Costs

Although discussed in more detail later, costs are another important consideration in arriving at prices. The weakness of most of the unsophisticated pricing approaches is their lack of regard for potential costs. Research into likely costs is a must in effective pricing.

Competition

Although the competitive pricing approach is not recommended on its own, no company should set prices without some reference to its competitors' price levels. Intensifying competition is expected in all parts of the hospitality and travel industry. Customers are also becoming increasingly value-conscious. Rather than using the wait-and-see or reactive method discussed earlier, it is much more effective for a company to use a proactive approach, anticipating how their organization's price changes will influence those of competitors.

Channels

When establishing prices for services to be sold through travel trade intermediaries, commissions must be taken into account. The actual revenues that airlines, hotels, car rental firms, tour wholesalers, and others realize through travel agent sales are some percentage below the price that the

---

Did You Know?

How much for a Room in Las Vegas or Los Angeles on New Year's Eve?

- The pricing of hotel rooms often goes "sky high" during major holidays and mega-events such as the Olympic Games. There is a huge demand for rooms, but very limited supply.
- New Year's Eve hotel pricing provides a good example, especially in "hot spots" for New Year's celebrations such as New York City, Las Vegas, or Los Angeles.
- A survey done by **HotelChatter.com** on December 26, 2008 found that prices on New Year's for hotels on or near the Strip were mostly above $250 the night of December 31st, and up to $569 at the Wynn Las Vegas. Some hotels were sold out.
- In Los Angeles, the New Year's Eve Package at the Millennium Biltmore Hotel was priced at from $419 (Classic) to $469 (Club), including dinner for two and an invitation to the New Year's Celebration in the Crystal Ballroom.
- In technical terms, it could be said that price is quite "inelastic" during such major holidays like New Year and mega-events. The hotels undoubtedly make more money; but sometimes there is a backlash from some guests who feel they have been "price gouged."

Sources: CondéNet. (2008). "Room rates in Las Vegas get a little steep." **http://www. hotelchatter.com/story/2008/12/26/103035/00/hotels/Room_Rates_in_ Las_Vegas_Get_a_Little_Steep**, accessed December 31, 2008; Millennium Hotels & Resorts. 2008. *New Year's Eve Package.* **http://www.millenniumhotels.com/ millenniumlosangeles/specials/specials_0035.html**, accessed December 31, 2008.

customer sees and pays. **Third-party distributors** are a new channel that has been created through the Internet. These include sites such as Expedia.com, Travelocity.com, Hotels.com, and many others.

Complementary Services and Facilities

How will the price of one item affect the sales of others? This is another important consideration, because most companies in our industry sell a variety of services and facilities at different prices (e.g., different airline routes, cruise destinations, brands of lodging properties, menu items, and classes of automobiles, tours and vacation packages). One typical concern is that lowering the price of one item too much may draw sales away from higher-profit services. In other words, a company must adopt a portfolio approach to pricing, rather than pricing each item individually and ignoring the potential impacts on others.

Consistency with Marketing-Mix Elements and Strategy

Do you remember the traditional four Ps of marketing: product, price, place, and promotion? Throughout this book there is an emphasis on ensuring that these four marketing mix elements are as consistent as possible. For example, higher prices seem appropriate if a company is providing a deluxe or premium service. Economical prices fit better with bare bones service concepts.

Have you noticed anything peculiar about the nine price influencing factors just reviewed? Do you see something that they share in common? Give yourself some applause if you noticed that all nine factors begin with the letter C. You might recall these factors better if you think of them as the **nine Cs of pricing**.

2. **Sophisticated Approaches.** What you have just learned is that pricing involves balancing a variety of factors carefully. You now know that it is insufficient to look at one factor only, such as competitive prices. The more sophisticated pricing approaches are normally used only after a company has carefully researched the consequences of pricing decisions.

   a. *Target Pricing.* Target pricing is an example of a pricing approach based on a profit-oriented objective. The target is usually set in terms of a specific return on investment (ROI) that the company wants to achieve. In some cases, the target may be expressed as a percentage of sales.

   One target pricing method that is popular in the lodging industry is the **Hubbart Formula**. It is used to establish room rates and involves building an income statement up from the bottom to determine the rate that is necessary to provide a predetermined return on investment. Figure 19.6 shows how a Hubbart Formula room rate is calculated. The rate thus calculated does not include travel agent commissions and discounts offered to specific target markets. These two items must be projected before a final, advertised (or rack) rate can be estimated. Figure 19.7 provides a hypothetical example of such a calculation.

+	Desired After-Tax Return on Investment
	Income Taxes
	Interest Charges
	Insurance
	Property Taxes
	Depreciation
	Administrative and General Expenses
	Marketing
	Energy Costs
	Property Operation and Maintenance
−	Food and Beverage Department Revenues
	Telephone Department Revenues
	Other Department Revenues
+	Food and Beverage Expenses
	Telephone Expenses
	Other Department Expenses
=	Required Room Profit
+	Room Expenses
=	Required Room Revenues
÷	Projected Number of Occupied Room Nights
=	Average Rate per Occupied Room Night After Discounts and Commissions

Target pricing methods, such as the Hubbart Formula, are effective because they consider several of the nine Cs of pricing:

- A detailed forecast of costs and profit levels (Costs)
- Estimates of demand (Customer demand volumes)
- Consideration of price preferences of individual target markets (Customer characteristics)
- Specifications of financial objectives (Corporate objectives)
- Estimates of commissions paid to travel trade intermediaries (Channels) Once the target rate is calculated, it may be adjusted slightly in relation to competitors' prices or for better alignment with the corporate image/positioning.

b. *Price Discounting and Discrimination.* **Discounting** is a common practice in certain parts of the hospitality and travel industry.

FIGURE 19.7
Hypothetical Hubbart Formula example for a hotel. How discounts and commissions are handled by the Hubbart Formula.

Required Room Revenues		$555,476
Projected % of Occupied Room Nights = (total rooms × 365/year) × % occ		
Occupancy Rate = 0.65		11863
Target Average Net Rate Per Occupied Room Night =		$46.83

Step Two: Calculate Specific Room Rates for Each Target Market

Target Markets	Occupied Room Nights	Percent	Discounts Offered	Avg. No. of Persons per room
Regular Business	593.13	5%	5.0%	1
Commercial Rate Business	593.13	5%	12.5%	1
Conference/Meeting Groups	4745.00	40%	20.0%	1.5
Motor Coach Tour Groups	1779.38	15%	25.0%	2
Pleasure Travellers	4151.88	35%	15.0%	2.5
TOTAL	11862.50	100%		1.5

Required Average Rate Before Discounting Equals $64.70

Required Average Rates by Target Market	Required Average Before Discount	Less Discount	Average Rate	Single Rate	Double Rate
Regular Business	$64.70	5%	$61.46	$61.46	—
Commercial Rate Business	$64.70	13%	$56.61	$56.61	—
Conference/Meeting Groups	$64.70	20%	$51.76	$49.26	$54.26
Motor Coach Tour Groups	$64.70	25%	$48.52	—	$48.52
Pleasure Travellers	$64.70	15%	$54.99	—	$54.99

Target Markets	Number of Room Nights	×	Average Rate		Revenues
Regular Business	593.125	×	$61.46	=	$36,456
Commercial Rate Business	593.125	×	$56.61	=	$33,578
Conference/Meeting (single)	2372.5	×	$49.26	=	$116,868
Conference/Meeting (double)	2372.5	×	$54.26	=	$128,731
Motor Coach Tour Groups	1779.375	×	$48..52	=	$86,343
Pleasure Travellers	4151.875	×	$54.99	=	$228,331
TOTAL ROOM REVENUES	11862.5	×	$53.13	=	$630,307

Simply stated, it means offering fares, rates, or prices below those advertised. Discriminatory pricing (also sometimes referred to as *price discrimination*) is a form of discounting. In discriminatory pricing and discounting in general, services are sold to some customers at lower prices. However, the price gap does not actually reflect any real difference in the costs of providing the service. Here are a few examples:

- Some fast-food chains offer discounts to schoolchildren. In Hong Kong, Café de Coral offers special meal combinations to school-children if they are wearing their school uniforms.
- Several major national airlines and lodging chains have clubs for older travelers. After paying a modest membership fee, these travelers receive discounts on airfares and related supplier services (e.g., hotels and car rentals). Rail Europe offers people of 60 or over specially discounted fares on trains in the UK and Europe.
- Most major car rental firms have corporate rate plans. Business travelers who join these plans automatically receive discounted rental rates.
- Almost all hotels and resorts have a multi-tiered list of rates. The corporate rate is by far the most common discounted rate, and it works much like the program used by car rental firms. Other below-rack rates often include those for government employees, airline crews, tour groups, convention/meeting guests, seniors, and sports teams.

Discounting and discriminatory pricing can be based on four different criteria. They include target market, form of service provided, place, and time.[11]

- Target market—You have already read several examples of this type of discounting, for example, some target senior citizens, schoolchildren, and business travelers.
- Form of service provided—A few add-on services are not provided, but the discount that is offered is much greater than the cost of the deleted services. For example, an airline offering a discount fare may not issue boarding passes to passengers until check-in time.
- Place—Prices are varied according to the location of the facilities and services. For example, some resorts charge more for beachfront rooms, although other rooms are available at lower prices.
- Time—Discounting according to time period is a very common practice in our industry because of the perishability factor. The weekend packages offered by most city hotels are a good example. Room rates are discounted to attract pleasure travelers on weekends, when business volumes traditionally fall from their weekday highs. Early-bird discounts offered by restaurants are another example; diners are given a price break if they eat before rush periods.

Originated by the airlines, the practice of yield management is an example of discriminatory pricing based upon several of the previously mentioned criteria. You probably know about the advance-booking and non-refundable fares that have become popular. In addition to the standard three-class system (economy/coach, business/club, and first class), typical restrictions include day of departure, minimum length of stay, Saturday stayovers, and the ability to modify or cancel the itinerary.

The types of price reductions involved in discounting are not the **price cutting** (or price slashing) variety used by companies that react quickly and often rashly to competitors' price moves. Discounts are carefully researched and preplanned pricing programs designed to achieve specific objectives. They are based on a thorough review of the impact they will have on costs and profits. Discounting programs are often instituted for several months or years.

One technique that is most useful in establishing discount programs is **break-even analysis**. It involves developing charts that show the relationship of costs, customer demand volumes, and profits. These charts help managers determine the points at which certain prices or customer demand volumes will cover all the fixed and variable costs of providing the services. These are called the break-even points. A **fixed cost** does not vary with the volume of sales (e.g., property taxes on buildings, interest charges on equipment). A **variable cost** changes directly with sales volume (e.g., a 10-percent increase in sales produces a 10-percent increase in the variable cost item). Labor costs and materials used in the production process are normally variable costs. A good example is the cost of food in restaurant meals.

Figure 19.8 shows a break-even chart for a hypothetical situation. As you can see, the total units purchased are plotted on the horizontal

FIGURE 19.8 Break-even chart.

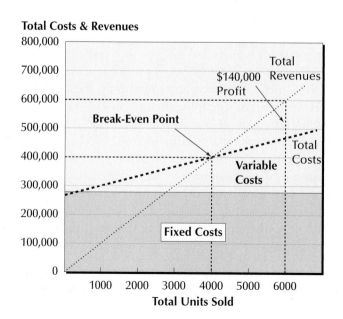

axis. Costs and revenues are measured on the vertical axis. The break-even point is where the total revenue line intersects the total cost (fixed plus variable) line. Figure 19.8 assumes the following:

- The variable cost per unit sold is $30.
- The selling price per unit is $100.
- The **contribution margin** (difference between selling price and variable costs per unit) is $70 (i.e., $100 minus $30).
- Total fixed costs are $280,000.
- The formula for calculating the break-even point is

$$\text{BREAK-EVEN POINT (UNITS)} = \frac{\text{TOTAL FIXED COSTS}}{\text{CONTRIBUTION MARGIN}}$$

$$= \frac{\text{TOTAL FIXED COSTS}}{\text{SELLING PRICE PER UNIT} - \text{VARIABLE COST PER UNIT}}$$

In the Figure 19.8 example, the break-even point is 4,000 units (which could, for example, be occupied room nights in a hotel, or airline or cruise passengers). The 4,000 figure was calculated as follows:

$$\text{BREAK-EVEN POINT (see Figure 19–8)} = \frac{\$280,000}{\$100 - \$30} = \frac{\$280,000}{\$70} = 4,000 \text{ units}$$

What would happen if the selling price in Figure 19.8 was lower than $100 – $65, for example? As you have probably guessed, the break-even volume of units would increase. In fact, it would double from 4,000 to 8,000 ($280,000/$65 – $30).

Besides helping to identify the break-even point, the charts can be used in target pricing. If the company knows how much profit it needs to generate a desired return on sales or investment, it can determine the required sales volumes in units and dollars. Take another look at Figure 19.8 and you will see how this works. Let us say that this company needs a profit of $140,000 to provide its targeted return on investment. To determine the break-even point, the following formula is used:

$$\text{BREAK-EVEN POINT (for \$140,000 profit)} = \frac{\text{TOTAL FIXED COSTS + TARGET PROFIT}}{\text{SELLING PRICE PER UNIT} - \text{VARIABLE COST PER UNIT}}$$

$$= \frac{\$280,000 + \$140,000}{\$100 - \$30}$$

$$= \frac{\$420,000}{\$70} = 6,000 \text{ units}$$

The sales volume required to achieve the $140,000 profit objective is $600,000 (6,000 X $100 per unit).

There are some limitations to a break-even analysis, and you should be aware of them. First, such an analysis assumes that the variable cost per unit sold is exactly the same at every sales volume level. But there are often some cost items that do not vary directly with sales volumes (e.g., a 100-percent increase in unit sales produces a 60-percent increase in costs, not a 100-percent increase). Second, break-even analysis assumes that fixed costs remain constant at all levels of production. This is not always the case, because fixed costs may increase at certain levels of sales (e.g., more equipment is required and the company borrows additional funds to finance the purchase, which results in increased interest charges). Third, a questionable assumption is that price has no impact on market demand. Despite these limitations, break-even analysis is a useful tool for analyzing the relationships of costs, prices, customer demand volumes, and profits.

c. *Promotional Pricing.* **Promotional pricing** involves using short-term price reductions to stimulate temporary sales increases. Many types of sales promotions (which were outlined in Chapter 16) fit into this category, such as two-for-one and percent-off coupon offers.

d. *Cost-Plus Pricing.* **Cost-plus pricing**, also known as *mark-up pricing*, involves adding a certain amount or percentage to the actual or estimated costs of a service to arrive at a final price. This amount or percentage represents the desired contribution margin. For example, Figure 19.8 showed a mark-up of $3\frac{1}{3}$ on variable costs per unit of $30 (the selling price was $3\frac{1}{3} \times \$30$, or $100). Using traditional, rule-of-thumb markups in a particular part of the industry is not recommended, as you saw earlier. In addition, using cost-plus pricing on its own is not the ideal approach. It is much better to combine cost-plus pricing with other techniques, such as break-even analysis, and also to consider other elements of the nine Cs of pricing besides costs.

e. *New-Product Pricing.* Many companies find that they can justify changing prices to correspond to the product life cycles of their services and facilities. Chapter 8 identified four potential strategies to introduce a new service: (1) rapid skimming, (2) slow skimming, (3) rapid penetration, and (4) slow penetration. **Price skimming** refers to the practice of charging high prices for the purpose of maximizing profit in the short run.[12] A skimming price is artificial because the company knows that it will eventually have to reduce the price. For example, the first tourist into space in 2001 paid a premium to do so. **Penetration pricing** uses the opposite approach—introducing a new service at a low price to get a quick stronghold on a significant share of a market. The introduction of Virgin Blue as an airline in Australia discussed earlier is a good example. The company offered lower fares to grab a sizeable share of the domestic airline travel market. A company using the penetration-pricing approach may or may not intend to continue it in the long run.

f. *Price Lining.* **Price lining** is a technique borrowed from the retailing industry, especially retailers of clothing. It involves pre-establishing prices that the company feels confident will attract customers. For example, a restaurant may find from experience that the most popular prices for its entrees are $8.95, $9.95, and $10.95. When it changes its menus, therefore, it looks for dishes that can be sold for these prices and provide a satisfactory profit. Another example is a travel agency that establishes a range of prices for vacation packages that best suits its clients.

g. *Psychological and Odd Pricing.* This is a finishing-touch pricing method, in which a price that has been set by using another pricing technique is modified slightly to provide added appeal. The basic strategy is to avoid prices set in round numbers, such as $10, $100, or $1,000. **Psychological pricing** means using slightly lower prices to give customers the perception of added value.

You will notice many prices that use some odd numbers, rather than only even numbers (e.g., prices of 0.45, 0.49, 0.95, 0.99, or 99.00). These numbers are based on the belief that odd numbers induce greater sales than rounded, even ones such as 0.50, 1.00, or 100.00.[13,14]

h. *Leader Pricing.* **Leader pricing** is a form of promotional pricing in which a company offers one or more services or products for a short time at a price below its actual costs. These items are commonly referred to as *loss leaders.* Very common among retail stores, leader pricing is used by some hospitality and travel companies. For example, some pizza-delivery companies offer free Cokes with the purchase of a pizza (the Coke is the loss leader). The role of the reduced-price items is to induce sales of other items offered by the company (in this example, the pizza).

3. **Multi-stage Approach.** This chapter has outlined a wide variety of pricing techniques, some unsophisticated and others more technically correct. You know that pricing should carefully consider nine factors (competitors, customer characteristics, customer demand volumes, costs, channels, corporate objectives, corporate image and positioning, complementary services and facilities, and consistency with marketing-mix elements and strategy). For effective pricing, therefore, a **multi-stage approach to pricing** is required, including the following steps:

   a. Determine company objectives and specific pricing objectives (Corporate objectives).

   b. Identify and analyze the target market or markets (Customer characteristics).

   c. Consider the company's image and the positioning of services relative to the target market or markets (Corporate image and positioning).

   d. Forecast the demand for services at various price levels (Customer demand volumes).

   e. Determine the costs of providing services (Costs).

   f. Evaluate potential competitive reactions to alternative prices (Competitors).

   g. Consider the impact of prices on travel trade intermediaries (Channels).

   h. Consider the impact of prices on sales of complementary services or facilities (Complementary services and facilities).

   i. Consider the impact of prices on other marketing mix elements and other aspects of the marketing strategy (Consistency with marketing mix elements and strategy).

   j. Select and use a pricing approach to arrive at a final price.

Using the multi-stage approach helps organizations decide which pricing approaches and specific price levels are most appropriate. As each stage is completed, the range of potential prices and pricing approaches narrows, making pricing decisions easier.

Measure and Evaluate Pricing Success

How did the selected pricing approach influence sales? This is the last of three steps in price planning, but no less important than the first two. While both price and sales changes are very measurable, it is often difficult to separate out the impact on sales by pricing alone. Other factors, such as the organization's non-price promotions, changes in customer spending patterns, competition, local industrial activity patterns, and even the weather may also have had an impact on sales. Therefore, it is important when measuring the success of pricing to keep track of these other factors—especially competitors' prices—and to estimate their influence on sales.

The best way to evaluate pricing success is again through marketing research. Research studies can be designed to determine if new customers were attracted by price or whether other factors were more important. Non-customers can be surveyed to find out why a new pricing approach did not appeal to them. Whatever research design is chosen, the most important factor is that thorough research and analysis be done to back up the measurement of price and sales changes.

Chapter Conclusion

Arriving at the right prices for hospitality and travel services is important for marketing as well as profitability reasons. Both unsophisticated and sophisticated pricing approaches are used in the hospitality and travel industry.

The most effective pricing results from a multi-stage approach that considers nine factors (corporate objectives, customer characteristics, corporate image and positioning, customer demand volumes, costs, competitors, channels, complementary services and facilities, and consistency with marketing-mix elements and strategy). Value for money is another important concept to be evaluated in arriving at the optimum prices.

---

1. What are the two major roles of pricing and the inherent conflicts in these?
2. How does price play the role of an implicit promotional element?
3. What are the unsophisticated pricing approaches, and why are they not recommended?
4. What are some more sophisticated approaches, and why are they superior?
5. What does target pricing involve?
6. What is break-even analysis and how is it used in pricing?
7. Are there different pricing approaches that can be used when introducing new services? If so, what are they?
8. What does the multi-stage approach to pricing entail, and what factors are considered?
9. How does the concept of value for money affect pricing?

---

1. Arrange to visit a local hospitality and travel business and interview its manager or owner. Ask this person to describe the pricing approaches that the business uses. Would you classify these as sophisticated or unsophisticated? Which of the nine Cs of pricing are considered? Is the multi-stage approach used? Are discounting, target pricing, or break-even analysis applied? What recommendations would you make to management to improve their pricing approaches?
2. You are the marketing manager responsible for a newly launched hospitality or travel service (e.g., hotel, restaurant, airline route, travel agency, or other service). What steps would you follow in arriving at initial price structures for this operation? What specific factors would you consider? What would your prices be, and how would you justify them to senior management?
3. Select a part of the hospitality and travel industry in which you are most interested. Analyze the pricing approaches used. How would you categorize the approaches you have identified (i.e., unsophisticated or sophisticated)? Which specific approaches are used? Which of the nine Cs seem to have the greatest influence on price levels? Is there room for other organizations to enter the business using different approaches? Explain your answer.

4. Select a local business in our industry and show how it could use either target pricing or break-even analysis to make more effective pricing decisions. Illustrate your recommendations with numerical examples. How would you sell your recommendations to the owners?

WEB RESOURCES

Air Berlin, http://www.airberlin.com/
JetBlue, http://www.jetblue.com/
Priceline, http://www.priceline.com/
Professional Pricing Society, http://www.pricingsociety.com/
Ryanair, http://www.ryanair.com/
Smith Travel Research, http://www.strglobal.com/
Southwest Airlines, http://www.southwest.com/
Spring Airlines, http://www.china-sss.com/
Virgin Blue, http://www.virginblue.com.au/
WestJet, http://www.westjet.com/

REFERENCES

1. CBS. 2008. *The Price Is Right.* http://www.cbs.com/daytime/the_price_is_right//, accessed December 30, 2008.
2. Dommermuth, William P. 1989. *Promotion: Analysis, Creativity, and Strategy.* 2nd ed. Boston: PWS-Kent Publishing Company, 32–34.
3. Dommermuth, William P. 1989. *Promotion: Analysis, Creativity, and Strategy.* 2nd ed. Boston: PWS-Kent Publishing Company, 34.
4. Canina, Linda and Cathy A. Enz. 2006. "Why discounting still doesn't work: A hotel pricing update." *CHR Reports*, Vol. 6, No. 2. Cornell University: The Center for Hospitality Research.
5. Shameen, Assif. 2006. "Asia takes flight on low-cost carriers." *Business Week online.*
6. Najda, Charles. 2003. *Low-cost carriers and low fares: Competition and concentration in the U.S. airline industry*, 8.
7. Smith, B.A., J.F. Leimkuhler, and R.M. Darrow. 1992. "Yield management at American Airlines." *Interfaces*, Vol. 22, No. 1, 8–31.
8. Gregory, Susan, and Jeffrey Beck. 2006. "The activities, training, and reporting relationships of today's revenue managers." *HSMAI Marketing Review*, Fall, 60–64.
9. Stanton, William J., Rosann Spiro, and Richard H. Buskirk. 1998. *Management of a Sales Force.* 10th ed. Boston: McGraw-Hill.
10. The Economic Planning Group of Canada. "Tourism is your business: Marketing management." *Ottawa, Ontario: Tourism Canada*, 92 (1986).
11. Rice, Faye. "Why hotel rates won't take off—yet." *Fortune* (October 4, 1993), 124–128.

12. Kotler, Philip. 2000. *Marketing Management: Millennium Edition*. 10th ed. Upper Saddle River, N.J.: Prentice-Hall, Inc.

13. Small Business Administration. 2008. *The marketing budget.* http://www.sba.gov/smallbusinessplanner/manage/marketandprice/SERV_MSTRAT_MKTBUD.html, accessed December 31, 2008.

14. Evans, Joel R., and Barry Berman. 2000. *Marketing*. 7th ed. Upper Saddle River, N.J.: Prentice-Hall, Inc.

中华人民共和国签证

CHINESE VISA

次 数 01(壹)
ENTRIES

入境后可停留
DURATION OF EACH

天

A79

CONTROLLING AND EVALUATING THE PLAN

WHERE ARE WE NOW?

WHERE WOULD WE LIKE TO BE?

HOW DO WE GET THERE?

HOW DO WE MAKE SURE WE GET THERE?

HOW DO WE KNOW IF WE GOT THERE?

chapter 20

Marketing Management, Evaluation, and Control

How Do We Make Sure We Get There? How Do We Know If We Got There?

OVERVIEW

This chapter discusses the management of marketing activities, often simply called marketing management, and identifies the benefits of effective marketing management. It emphasizes that it is not enough just to have a marketing plan. Even the best plan in the world may need to be changed to adapt to unexpected circumstances. The five components of marketing management (research, planning, implementation, control, and evaluation) are highlighted.

The chapter looks at alternative ways of organizing a marketing department and discusses staffing and supervision. It also explains different ways of arriving at marketing budgets and suggests the best ways of doing this. The last two questions of the hospitality and travel marketing system ("How do we make sure

OBJECTIVES

Having read this chapter, you should be able to:

- Define marketing management and list its five components.

- Explain the benefits of marketing management.

- Describe the five different methods of organizing a marketing department.

- Explain the steps and procedures involved in staffing and managing marketing staff.

- List the unsophisticated and sophisticated approaches to setting marketing budgets and identify the most effective method.

- Describe the building-block procedure for setting a marketing budget and explain its benefits.

- Define marketing control and marketing evaluation.

- Describe the process used to control the marketing plan.

- List and explain the techniques available for marketing evaluation.

KEY TERMS

affordable budgeting
budgeting
building-block procedure
competitive-parity budgeting
conversion rate
e-commerce
efficiency ratios
80-20 principle
iceberg effect
incremental budgeting

integrated marketing
   communications
log file analysis
m-commerce
marginal economic budgeting
market share
marketing audit
marketing control
marketing costs and
   profitability

marketing evaluation
marketing management
metrics
objective-and-task budgeting
percentage-of-sales (rule-of-
   thumb) budgeting
performance measurement
sales analysis
zero-based budgeting

we get there?" and "How do we know if we got there?") are then addressed in an explanation of marketing control and evaluation. The chapter ends by explaining several useful evaluation techniques.

Have you ever started the year with a set of New Year's resolutions, stuck with them for a few weeks or months, but eventually gave them up? Do not feel embarrassed. You are normal, just like the rest of us. Have you ever ended a year knowing that you have kept one or more of your resolutions? How did you accomplish this? It probably took great self-discipline, some encouragement from others, and a constant focus on your objectives. You might also have had to train yourself to modify your behavior—not eat as much, exercise more frequently, stop smoking, or study a certain number of hours each day. Additionally, you probably had to plan and budget your time, money, and other resources. Above all, it took your single-minded determination and dedication to be better disciplined than you were at the beginning of the year. You had to manage yourself.

What does this have to do with marketing and marketing management? New Year's resolutions are very similar to an organization's marketing objectives and plan. They look good on paper and may have been very carefully thought out and researched. But as the Scottish poet Robert Burns wrote, "the best-laid schemes o' mice an' men" often go wrong. Why? Usually, it is because we tend to relax after we have drawn up our objectives and plans. Developing them has sapped so much of our energy that there is not much left after the fact. In marketing, however, managing the marketing plan is every bit as important as thinking it up and writing it down on paper. Just as with New Year's resolutions, successful marketing management involves budgeting, motivation, training, changing people's behavior, and constant checking to ensure that the objectives are always in sight. Of course, marketing plans also sometimes need to be changed due to unexpected or unforeseen circumstances, such as 9-11, the SARS outbreak in East Asia in 2003, and the tsunami in Southeast Asia in 2004, and the so-called "financial tsunami" of 2008.

Marketing management activities are designed to help the organization achieve objectives and to implement and, if necessary, adapt its marketing plan to changing circumstances. It is the way that the organization makes sure it gets where it wants to be. These activities answer the question, "How do we get there?"

Marketing Management—Definition and Components

Marketing management includes all the activities necessary to plan, research, implement, control, and evaluate the marketing efforts of a hospitality and travel organization. Chapters 4 through 19 discussed the first three functions—the PRI of the PRICE model discussed earlier—planning, research, and implementation. These functions together produce marketing strategies, plans, and objectives. However, developing and implementing marketing strategies and plans involves organizing, staffing, and managing the marketing department, its staff, and any outside consultants that are used (e.g., market research specialists, advertising agencies, PR consultants, Internet marketing experts). Marketing managers are also responsible for controlling and evaluating marketing efforts—the CE of the PRICE model—ensuring that strategies and plans are implemented as intended and that success against marketing goals and objectives is measured.

Marketing Management Benefits

Effective marketing management not only provides rich benefits to an organization but is also an absolutely essential part of marketing. The major benefits of sound marketing management include the following:

1. Marketing efforts are accomplished in a well-planned, systematic way.
2. An adequate amount of marketing research and other marketing information is generated.
3. Marketing weaknesses are quickly spotted and corrected.
4. Funds and human resources available for marketing are used as efficiently and effectively as possible.
5. Marketing efforts are always under careful scrutiny. It is always believed that there is room for improvement.
6. The organization is in a better position to adapt to change among customers and competition, and in the industry.
7. Marketing is better integrated into all the organization's activities and within its various departments.

8. Marketing and other staff members are more highly motivated toward achieving marketing objectives.
9. There is a much clearer understanding of marketing results, good and bad, and the reasons for successes and failures.
10. There is definite accountability for marketing.

Marketing Organization

One basic requirement for ensuring the successful achievement of goals, strategies, and objectives is to have the right marketing organization in place. There are several alternative ways to do this, depending mainly on the services provided by the organization, as well as its size and geographic coverage. Marketing departments in hospitality and travel are normally structured using one of the following approaches:

1. *Marketing or Promotional Mix Elements.* Chapters 10 through 19 gave you information on the 8 Ps of marketing and the promotional mix elements. Why not divide an organization's marketing specialists by each of these? For example, you might have individual managers responsible for product development and partnership (Chapter 10), people or services and service quality (Chapter 11), packaging and programming (Chapter 12), place or the distribution mix and travel trade intermediaries (Chapter 13), advertising (Chapter 15), sales promotion and merchandising (Chapter 16), personal selling (Chapter 17), public relations and publicity (Chapter 18), and pricing (Chapter 19). Many marketing departments in the hospitality and travel industry are set up in this way, especially smaller organizations and those with only one unit (e.g., a single hotel property). Some multi-unit chains also organize the head-office marketing department in this way. The individual managers report to a director or vice president of marketing.

   It is very common to find sales departments and public relations (or marketing communications) departments in hotels and DMOs (DMOs). For example, the Kansas City Convention & Visitors Association in Missouri has a Convention Sales Division and a Marketing/Communications Division.[1] Pricing divisions or departments, often identified as revenue management, are also found in many larger hotels.

   Although this is a logical and convenient way to divide the marketing effort, it has some drawbacks. First, as earlier chapters mentioned, all marketing and promotional mix elements are interrelated. They work better if they are planned together. You already know this approach as **integrated marketing communications** (integrated planning for all marketing-promotional mix elements). When an organization allocates marketing responsibility to different managers and their support teams, there is a greater tendency for these groups to "do their own thing," not working together as effectively as they could. Second, many larger companies have more than one product. These may be either various brands (such as with many of the major lodging and restaurant chains, and cruise lines) or completely different types of hospitality and travel businesses (e.g., an airline, a hotel company, and a car rental firm). Each of these products within the parent company may require a different marketing approach and, therefore, merit its own marketing organization.

2. *Brands or Facilities.* The second alternative is to organize marketing by brand or division, each representing a specific type of facility or service. This approach is better suited to larger organizations, including those with several brands (e.g., large lodging and restaurant chains, and cruise lines) and diversified hospitality and travel companies.

    The advantage of this approach over the first is that each brand or division is assured of an individualized and comprehensive marketing program. The potential drawback is that from a total-company standpoint, individual brands and divisions may not capitalize, to the fullest extent possible, on opportunities for joint marketing.

    Marketing may also be organized by facility types. For example, the Fairmont Royal York Hotel in Toronto splits up meeting and event facilities into catering and function space, and bedrooms with meeting space. This is typical in the hotel business where the rooms and the banquet divisions are separated.

3. *Geographic Origins.* A third alternative is to divide the marketing team geographically. This is especially important for hospitality and travel organizations with multi-national operations. Examples include many national government-tourism agencies, such as the Singapore Tourism Board, Canadian Tourism Commission, VisitBritain, and Tourism Australia, each of which has marketing offices in several different countries. Tourism Australia has marketing offices in Australia and in several other key geographic origin countries, including Canada, China, Germany, Hong Kong, India, Japan, South Korea, Malaysia, New Zealand, Singapore, Taiwan, Thailand, the UK, and the USA.[2] In these situations, separate marketing strategies and plans are required for each nation that has an office and for any neighboring countries for which individual offices also have the responsibility. As stated in Chapter 17, geography is also commonly used to organize a sales force. Each sales representative is allocated a territory.

4. *Customer Segments.* A fourth way to divide marketing staff is by assigning them to a specific segments or sets of target markets. This book has emphasized the need for separate approaches for each target market among organizations that choose segmented strategies. One of the best ways to assure the individual attention is by segmenting the marketing organization in this way. For example, several larger hotel properties and DMOs divide up their sales staff by types of convention/meeting groups (e.g., national associations versus state associations).

5. *Combination Approaches.* There are many cases in which some combination of these four approaches is used. One of the most typical arrangements is to organize the marketing department by customer group,

promotional mix element, or brands/facilities, but to have the sales force divided by geographic territories.

Another situation that requires a combination approach is in cases where the parent firm is involved in franchising. Franchising is common in many parts of the hospitality and travel industry, especially among restaurants, lodging facilities, travel agencies, and car rental firms. These companies usually have a national marketing plan that is prepared by a head-office marketing department, as well as individual unit marketing plans. In addition, groups of individual franchisees may get together at a city or regional level and develop marketing plans for their respective geographic areas.

Whatever the organizational approach chosen, there is one principle that must be followed—the marketing organization should have full, or at least shared, responsibility (in the case of pricing) for all the marketing and promotional mix elements. This basic principle is violated in some parts of our industry. As mentioned earlier, some hotel properties have separate sales departments and public relations departments or directors, and DMOs separate sales from other marketing communications. This book recommends placing all promotional mix elements within the same division or department, under the direction of one director or manager.

Staffing the Marketing Organization

Another function of marketing management is hiring and retaining suitably qualified people. Where does the hospitality and travel industry find such individuals? Unfortunately, the answer is unclear, because little research has been done on the subject. However, some generalized comments can be made.

There is a strong tendency in the industry to require sales and marketing staff members to have some previous experience in operations, either with the subject organization or a similar one. Stated another way, this means that sales and marketing jobs tend not to be entry-level positions. Because of the rapid expansion of the industry, some organizations have hired experienced sales and marketing people from unrelated industries. There are few, if any, degrees and professional designations in hospitality and travel marketing, although some schools and professional associations now have them, such as the Education Institute of the American Hotel & Lodging Association and Destination Marketing Association International. However, college and university programs remain strongly oriented toward producing people to fill operational roles, not marketing positions.

The hospitality and travel industry lags behind other industries in accepting marketing and the marketing concept. In other industries, graduates with marketing degrees usually enter directly into organizations' marketing departments without prior operational experience. This will take several years, and perhaps decades, to change in our industry. It demonstrates that operational skills and knowledge are valued more than marketing skills and knowledge.

Managing and Supervising Marketing Staff

Because this is not a book on supervision and human resources management, it is inappropriate to discuss these subjects in great detail. However, it is important to mention that marketing managers at different levels, ranging from senior vice presidents to sales managers, must not only recruit and hire the right people; they must also motivate, coordinate, and communicate with them effectively. They must judiciously delegate authority and responsibility and build a feeling of teamwork directed toward achieving marketing objectives. This sense of common purpose is especially important in the hospitality and travel industry, because our people are so involved in providing customer service. The organizations that excel at motivating and communicating with their own employees are usually the ones that also provide excellent service, including Shangri-La Hotels and Resorts (Figure 20.1).

FIGURE 20.1   Shangri-La Hotels are excellent at motivating and communicating with its employees.

Setting Marketing Budgets

Another important function of marketing management is **budgeting**—allocating human resources and money toward the implementation of the marketing plan. Chapter 19 mentioned that there are sophisticated and unsophisticated approaches to pricing. The same is true with budgeting.

1. **Unsophisticated Approaches.**

    a. *Affordable and Incremental Approaches.* These are budgeting methods involving the personal judgments of marketing managers or business owners. Many smaller businesses use the **affordable budgeting** method, spending only what they think they can afford for marketing. The **incremental budgeting** method means using the current period's budget as the foundation for next year's budget, and adding (or deducting) a certain percentage or specific amount of money.

    b. *Percentage-of-Sales or Rule-of-Thumb Approaches.* With **percentage-of-sales** or **rule-of-thumb budgeting**, marketing budgets are set as a percentage of last year's total sales or next year's expected total sales. The percentage figures are usually chosen because they are rules of thumb for that particular part of the hospitality and travel industry. These recommended percentages are commonly expressed in ranges. For example, for 2006 PKF Consulting found that full-service hotels in the USA spent from 3.9 percent to 6.1 percent on marketing; and an average of 4.7 percent for all full-service hotels.[3] A typical restaurant should allocate from 3 to 6 percent of sales to marketing.[4] These rules of thumb are based on published statistics that represent the averages for the industry segment, such as the PKF Consulting annual report, *Trends in the Hotel Industry* and the National Restaurant Association report, *Restaurant Industry Operations.* As you might already know from statistics, averages (arithmetic means) can be very misleading and often skewed by very high or very low individual figures.

    c. *Competitive-Parity Approach.* **Competitive-parity budgeting** is straightforward—find out what your closest competitors are spending on marketing and set your budget at the same or approximately the same level. How do you find this information? Annual reports are one good source of such statistics on publicly-held corporations. Other sources include published articles on competitive organizations and various annual reports such as *Advertising Age's* series on the *100 Leading National Advertisers* in the United States.[5]

    What are the advantages of using these three budgeting methods? The answer is their simplicity and the speed with which they can be determined. They do not require much research or significant other effort by the marketing manager. Can you spot any problems with using them? If you cannot right away, let us return to Chapter 8 when we began talking about marketing objectives. From that chapter on, this book has suggested that these objectives are the building blocks for the marketing plan. The marketing plan is written with the express purpose of achieving marketing objectives. Now, what is missing from all three unsophisticated budgeting approaches? None of them considers marketing objectives. Why develop a detailed plan based on objectives, and then strike a budget based on sales volumes or competition? It should be obvious by now that what is needed is a budgeting procedure based on marketing objectives.

You might now be questioning the importance of competitors' spending levels and the affordability of marketing. Should organizations completely disregard what competitors are doing? Should they spend as much as it takes to get marketing done, without considering other priorities for funds within the organization? The answer to both questions is a resounding "no." Competition and overall resources available within the subject organization are two factors that must be considered when establishing marketing budgets. They should not, however, be the primary and sole basis used to arrive at marketing spending levels.

2. **Sophisticated Approaches.** You are right in thinking that a sophisticated approach would use marketing objectives as the primary basis for budgeting, but would also consider competition and affordability. In fact, the best budgeting approaches use a **building-block procedure** similar to the one depicted in Figure 20.2. The steps involved in this procedure are as follows:

a. Allocate a tentative, overall budget to marketing or the marketing department.

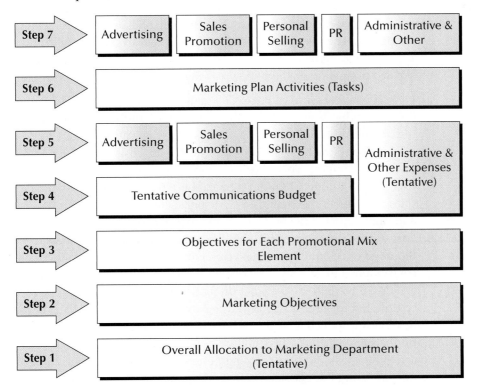

FIGURE 20.2
Building-block procedure for developing a marketing budget.

b. Determine the marketing objectives.

c. Set objectives for each promotional mix element and Internet marketing based on the overall marketing objectives.

d. Tentatively split the overall budget allocation between communications (the promotional mix), and administrative and other marketing expenses.

e. Divide the tentative communications budget on a provisional basis among advertising, sales promotion, personal selling, public relations and publicity, and Internet marketing.

f. Develop the marketing plan, specifying all the activities and tasks required for advertising, sales promotion, merchandising, personal selling, public relations and publicity, and Internet marketing.

g. Determine the final budget allocations for advertising, sales promotion, personal selling, public relations and publicity, Internet marketing, and administrative and other elements, based on the activities included in the marketing plan. Further adjustments may be required to better fit the initial overall budget allocation to marketing or competitive expenditures.

You can see that setting the marketing budget requires a well-researched and carefully planned, step-by-step process. Look again at Figure 20.2. It seems to resemble a brick wall. As you know, a bricklayer starts a wall from the bottom and works up, carefully cementing each new row of bricks to the one below. Establishing the marketing budget is much like wall building—each step builds on the preceding ones, using needed information and guidelines for allocating the amounts of money. Omitting certain steps is similar to the bricklayer leaving out some bricks and not cementing certain layers. The result is obvious—the wall will eventually fall down. Part of the building-block procedure just described reflects the use of a sophisticated budgeting method known as the objective-and-task approach.

a. *Objective-and-Task Approach.* The name given to this approach aptly describes what is involved. With the **objective-and-task budgeting**, the organization sets objectives, figures out what must be done to achieve them (the tasks), and then estimates the costs of completing the tasks (or activities). This three-step approach was recommended in Chapters 15 through 18 to set the final budget amounts for advertising, sales promotion, merchandising, personal selling, and public relations and publicity. It is the budgeting approach recommended in this book.

b. *Zero-Based Budgeting Approach.* There is a tendency in business to repeat activities from previous years without critically evaluating their contributions to achieving marketing objectives. The reason for this is simple—there is some fear that discontinuing the activities that have contributed to success will lower performance. This often results in extending unproductive activities beyond their useful lives. **Zero-based budgeting** challenges this habit by requiring that each marketing-plan activity (or task) for an upcoming period be justified. In other words, the marketing budget starts at zero. There is no guarantee that any of the activities in the previous marketing plan will be continued. The beauty of this approach is that it forces managers to evaluate past activities critically and to consider alternatives that may produce even better results.

You are probably wondering if the objective-and-task and zero-based approaches can be combined. The answer is "yes." In fact, objective-and-task is an application of the zero-based approach. Marketers start with clean slates each period and select activities that are specifically designed to meet chosen objectives.

c. *Other Approaches.* You should be aware that there are other sophisticated budgeting methods, including one known as the **marginal economic budgeting** method. It is an idealistic approach to budgeting in which organizations spend money on promotional mix elements up to the point where the last dollar brings in exactly one dollar in sales. This technique draws from general economic theory. Although considered to be the most technically correct approach, it is difficult to apply in actual practice. Objective-and-task budgeting is an acceptable substitute, and it is far easier to use.

Some experts suggest using various quantitative, statistical models to arrive at budgets. These can be useful in considering the impact of various assumptions, but they are not recommended on their own. What you should realize is that effective budgeting, like pricing, uses a combination of sophisticated and unsophisticated approaches. Using one technique alone is insufficient. The key factors to be considered are marketing objectives, marketing plan activities, affordability (amount of funds that an organization can realistically allocate to marketing), and competitive expenditure levels.

Marketing Control and Evaluation

Why have an elaborate marketing plan and budgeting process if you do not measure its progress and tally the results at the end? **Marketing control** includes all the steps that an organization takes to monitor and adjust the marketing plan as it progresses, as well as the procedures it selects to ensure implementation as planned. **Marketing evaluation** involves analyzing results to determine the success of a marketing plan (Figure 20.3). Marketing control helps answer the question "How do we make sure we get there?" whereas marketing evaluation satisfies the "How do we know if we got there?" question. These are both part of the overall management concept of **performance measurement**.

The 80-20 Principle and the Iceberg Effect

Before discussing control and evaluation techniques, you should know about one common problem with marketing in our industry. This can best be

FIGURE 20.3
Evaluation involves the checking of marketing performance in the previous planning period.

described as the **80-20 principle**, or putting 80 percent of the effort or resources into capturing only 20 percent of the total volume.[6] In other words, there is a tendency to put too much effort and budget into attracting certain types of customers and too little into others. Although the actual percentages may not be 80 percent and 20 percent, the important point is that many organizations in our industry are unaware of the problem in the first place. Efforts are often channeled away from higher- to lower-profit services and customers.

Some also refer to this as the **iceberg effect**, meaning that managers often make decisions based on superficial information (they see only the tip of the iceberg). As every captain knows, it is the larger section of the iceberg under the water that can sink a ship (Figure 20.4). A wide course must be steered around this navigational obstacle. Likewise, a manager must take an in-depth look at a broad range of information to ensure that marketing activities are as effective as possible. How can the 80-20 principle or the iceberg effect be avoided? The answer is by carefully controlling and comprehensively evaluating marketing plan results.

Marketing Control

This book has emphasized two of the major functions of marketing management —research and planning. Controlling what goes on in an organization is another key management function. All systems of control include three steps: (1) establishing performance standards or **metrics** based on plans and the objectives contained in these plans, (2) periodically monitoring actual performance against these standards, and (3) adjusting procedures or activities accordingly (Figure 20.5). In most organizations, controls are devised for production, inventories, product/service quality, and financial resources. Chapter 2 stated that inventory and quality control are made more difficult in our industry because of the perishability and intangibility of services, and by the significant role of people who provide them.

Image copyright Jurgen Ziewe, 2008. Used under license from Shutterstock.com

FIGURE 20.4 The "iceberg effect" means not determining all the reasons behind the marketing results achieved.

How then do managers control their marketing plans? What are their standards or metrics? The two key measurement tools are marketing objectives and budgets. Marketing budgets assist with the financial control of the marketing plan. Periodic checks are made to see whether the budget is being spent according to the plan. Additionally, results are monitored periodically to determine progress toward achieving individual marketing objectives (expressed in numerical terms).

As you probably realize, the success of a marketing plan not only depends on the budget and how it is allocated, but also on the efforts of the many people who work in the organization. Some of these people are employed directly in marketing (e.g., sales representatives and public relations staff). Others are on the front line, providing service to customers. As you saw in Chapter 11, controlling the efforts of all staff members is more difficult than telling them what to do, but is essential to effective marketing.

The main route to success is building a team spirit toward achieving marketing objectives. You read earlier in this chapter about the importance of recruiting and hiring the right people. This must be accompanied by effective

Are we achieving our marketing objectives?

Marketing Control

How Do We Make Sure We Get There
- Performance standards (metrics)
- Monitor performance against standards
- Adjustment of procedures

Did we achieve our marketing objectives?

Marketing Evaluation

How Do We Know If We Got There
- Sales analysis
- Market share analysis
- Marketing cost and profitability analysis
- Efficiency ratios
- Marketing-effectiveness rating review
- Marketing audit

leadership, motivation, orientation and training, and communications. Policies must be established to support individual aspects of the marketing plan, ranging from how employees should dress and wear uniforms to the proper ways of addressing customers. It is often the attention to these seemingly minute details that leads to outstanding success in this industry. Two dazzling examples of such success are the policies of the Disney theme parks and McDonald's. Marketing personnel may not be directly responsible for enforcing these standards and rules, but they must ensure that such systems exist and that compliance is checked periodically.

The marketing department, through the sales manager, is responsible for monitoring and controlling the productivity of sales representatives. Often this is accomplished through systems of sales quotas (the performance standards) and is measured through sales call reports and other reports on sales by representatives. Again, controlling performance is easier if it is preceded by proper orientation and training of sales staff.

It is very unlikely that any marketing plan will proceed exactly as intended, because of the unpredictable nature of the hospitality and travel industry and competitors. The controls that a manager uses provide an "early warning" system, highlighting problem areas and other deviations from the plan. If such situations are spotted early enough, corrective action can be taken.

Marketing Evaluation

Marketing evaluation techniques are used after the marketing plan period has expired. Their two major purposes are to analyze the degrees of success in achieving individual marketing objectives and to more broadly evaluate an entire organization's marketing efforts.

1. *Sales Analysis.* Marketing objectives are frequently expressed in monetary or unit sales volumes (e.g., passenger counts, occupied room nights). Therefore, the most obvious evaluation techniques compare actual sales to desired objectives. The **sales analysis** shows the deviations between actual and desired sales results, and also attempts to explain the reasons for discrepancies. The more detailed the analysis, the better. (Remember the iceberg principle?) For example, larger companies will usually look at sales by target market, brand or division, type of service or facilities, and sales territory.

2. *Market-Share Analysis.* This is a variant of sales analysis, in which the organization compares its sales results to those for everyone in its specific sector of the hospitality and travel industry. **Market share** is the percentage relationship of an organization's sales to total industry or sector sales. It provides useful information on how the organization has performed relative to competition. For example, a drop in market share shows that the industry or sector has outperformed the organization. An increase indicates that the organization has outperformed the industry or sector. In addition to its overall market share, an organization usually is also concerned about its performance relative to specific competitors (e.g., the industry leaders).

3. *Marketing Cost and Profitability Analysis.* Sales and market share analyses provide only part of the required picture. An organization must evaluate the **marketing costs and profitability** associated with various parts of its marketing plan. Only by doing this will the 80-20 problem be detected and corrected. A company analyzes income statements to determine sales, costs, and profits by one or more of the following:

   a. Target markets
   b. Sales territories
   c. Sales representatives
   d. Distribution channels
   e. Travel trade intermediaries
   f. Types of facilities or services
   g. Promotional mix elements and other marketing expense areas

   Income statements are not normally designed so that these figures can be extracted easily. A careful and time-consuming allocation process is required, but the payoffs are worth it. This analysis can lead to dropping unproductive services or facilities, target markets, distribution channels, or specific travel trade intermediaries. It may also highlight the need for major reallocations of promotional expenditures, reorganization of sales territories, or retraining of sales representatives.

4. *Efficiency Ratios.* **Efficiency ratios** are statistical measurements that marketing managers use to evaluate the organization's efficiency in using promotional and distribution mix elements. Figure 20.6 is a selected list of these ratios, which can be used as tools in the evaluation process.

FIGURE 20.6 Selected list of efficiency ratios.

1. SALES-FORCE EFFICIENCY
- Average number of sales calls per sales representative per day
- Average sales-call time per contact
- Average revenue per sales call
- Average cost per sales call
- Sales-force cost as a percentage of total sales

2. ADVERTISING EFFICIENCY
- Number of inquiries generated per ad
- Conversion rate
- Cost per inquiry
- Cost per thousand persons reached (CPM)
- Before-after measures of attitude toward services

3. SALES PROMOTION EFFICIENCY
- Percentage of coupons redeemed
- Number of inquiries generated per promotion
- Cost per inquiry

4. PUBLIC RELATIONS AND PUBLICITY EFFICIENCY
- Number of media organizations using press releases
- Number of mentions in print and broadcast media

5. DISTRIBUTION EFFICIENCY
- Percentage of sales through various distribution channels
- Percentage of sales by specific types of intermediaries

In hospitality and travel advertising, one of the popular measures of efficiency is to calculate the **conversion rate** of a specific advertisement, series of advertisements (advertising campaign), or website. With direct-response advertising and website promotion, in which the customer is given an address, telephone number, e-mail or website address by the hospitality and travel organization, the organization can track the number of customer enquiries or website visits generated. For a tourism destination, the conversion rate of direct-response advertising is the estimated percentage of inquirers who became visitors. The cost per conversion equals the total cost expended on the advertising media divided by the number of converted visitors.[7] The sponsors usually have to conduct special research studies, known as conversion studies, to calculate conversion rates.

Similarly, the efficiency of certain sales promotions, such as coupons, can be measured quite easily by tracking coupon redemption rates (the percentage of the coupons distributed that are used by customers). Other sales promotions are not as easily evaluated. For travel trade and consumer travel shows, exhibitions or fairs, some recommend a procedure like that used in calculating conversion rates of direct-response advertising. For example, Destination Marketing Association International

---

Did You Know?

How to Evaluate a Hospitality or Tourism Website?

- In an interesting application of marketing evaluation, researchers used the *Balanced Scorecard Approach* (BSC) to assess the effectiveness of the websites of convention and visitor bureaus (CVBs) in the USA and Canada. Robert Kaplan and David Norton originally developed the BSC Approach.
- More than 1,000 CVB websites were scored and ranked from the best to the worst.
- The researchers identified four distinct sets of measurement criteria, which they called critical success factors or CSFs:

  - Customer
  - Marketing Effectiveness
  - Technical
  - Destination Information

- Specific criteria and a scoring system were developed for each of the four groups of CSFs. The CVBs' websites were then analyzed and scored.
- The researchers found that there were many ways in which these CVBs' websites could be made more effective.
- The Marketing Effectiveness CSF received the lowest average score.

Source: Destination Consultancy Group, LLC. (2008).

---

recommends keeping track of the number of sales leads generated per trade show.[8] The trade/consumer trade show cost per lead can be calculated by dividing the total costs of exhibiting at the show by the total number of leads received at the organization's booth. The show's converted cost per leads can be found by dividing total show costs by either the number of converted booth leads or the total revenues resulting from these converted leads.

Another newer form of marketing efficiency measurement is **log file analysis** for websites. Computer servers maintain log files for each visitor to a website, and analyzing these log files gives hospitality and travel marketers great information on the characteristics and volume of their website traffic. Many software programs are on the market now to help marketers with these evaluations of websites.

5. *Marketing-Effectiveness Rating Review.* This is an internal survey conducted among the managers of an organization, but it is not restricted to the marketing department. A three-point scale is used to get managers' opinions on five factors that reflect the organization's marketing orientation: (1) customer philosophy, (2) integrated marketing organization,

INTERNET MARKETING

Measuring the Effectiveness of Internet Marketing

- It is very hard and challenge to measure marketing effectiveness; that is the real truth. However, the Internet is one part of marketing where measurement is relatively easy. Here you will find just a few tools of the many that can be used to assess the effectiveness of Internet marketing.
- **Link popularity measures**: Having as many links to a site as possible is very desirable. There are a variety of free programs that let you measure link popularity, including http://www.linkpopularity.com, http://www.seocentro.com/, and http://www.marketleap.com/.
- **Website technical tests**: There are some programs that allow you to test the technical aspects of a website such http://www.netmechanic.com/ and http://www.websiteoptimization.com/services/analyze/.
- **Search engine optimization (SEO)**: Being well positioned with the major search engines is a key to Internet marketing success. Programs such as http://www.instantposition.com/ and http://www.seochat.com/ can help you find out how to get the best SEO.
- **Web traffic analytics**: These are more sophisticated and definitely not free programs that constantly track and analyze the traffic to a website. There are many web analytic software programs on the market, but WebTrends® is a popular one in hospitality and travel, http://www.webtrends.com/. If you go to WebTrends site, you will find testimonials and case studies from several companies there including Virgin Atlantic, La Quinta, Site 59, and STA Travel.

Source: WebTrends®. 2008. WebTrends Analytics™; other websites listed above.

Student Questions

1. What are the benefits to be gained from constantly analyzing a website's effectiveness?
2. What can an organization learn from using a web analytics program like WebTrends?
3. Test out a few of the free programs listed above on three or four websites from one part of hospitality and travel. How do your results compare? Which organization has the most effective website and why?
4. What are the dangers for an organization in having a website but neglecting it for a number of months? What steps can the organization follow to make sure that its website is always updated and maintained?

(3) adequate marketing information, (4) strategic orientation, and (5) operational efficiency.[9] A total point score is calculated based on individual ratings of questions related to these five areas. This evaluation tool is very useful in getting other departments' opinions and perceptions on the strengths and weaknesses of marketing. Conducted annually, it can highlight marketing weaknesses that require further investigation.

6. *Marketing Audit.* The first four evaluation approaches strictly assess a single marketing plan. It is possible to go even further by conducting a full-blown **marketing audit**, which is a systematic, comprehensive, and periodic evaluation of an organization's entire marketing function, including its marketing goals, objectives, strategies, and performance.[10]

Figure 20.7 shows the topics to be considered in the marketing audit. You may notice some striking similarities between the marketing audit

PART I: MARKETING-ENVIRONMENT AUDIT

Macroenvironment

1. Demographic
2. Economic
3. Ecological
4. Technological
5. Political
6. Cultural

Task Environment

1. Markets
2. Customers
3. Competitors
4. Distribution and Dealers
5. Suppliers
6. Facilitators and Marketing Firms
7. Publics

PART II: MARKETING-STRATEGY AUDIT

1. Business Mission
2. Marketing Objectives and Goals
3. Strategy

PART III: MARKETING-ORGANIZATION AUDIT

1. Formal Structure
2. Functional Efficiency
3. Interface Efficiency

PART IV: MARKETING-SYSTEMS AUDIT

1. Marketing Information System
2. Marketing Planning Systems
3. Marketing Control System
4. New Product Development System

PART V: MARKETING-PRODUCTIVITY AUDIT

1. Profitability Analysis
2. Cost-Effectiveness Analysis

PART VI: MARKETING-FUNCTION AUDITS

1. Products
2. Price
3. Distribution
4. Advertising, Sales Promotion, and Publicity
5. Salesforce

FIGURE 20.7
Components of a marketing audit. (Kotler, Philip; Armstrong, Gary, Marketing Management: Millennium Edition, 10th Edition, © 2000; pp. 710–711. Adapted by permission of Pearson Education, Inc., Upper Saddle River, NJ.)

The Global Perspective: The Big Picture

Measuring and Evaluating the Effectiveness of Tourism Marketing Tourism Australia

http://www.tourism.australia.com/home.asp
http://www.australia.com

The rich red colors of the Australia desert outback are a unique feature of this great tourism destination.

Tourism Australia (TA) is recognized as being one of the best destination marketing organizations (DMOs) at the national level. Its marketing and promotional programs are always very upbeat and highly imaginative and colorful. Marketing research is in-depth and applied wisely in TA's marketing plans and programs. In addition, TA has developed outstanding relationship-building programs with travel trade intermediaries. Perhaps less well known—but nevertheless highly impressive—are TA's efforts to determine its marketing effectiveness.

Key Performance Indicators (KPIs)

TA has developed a set of Key Performance Indicators (KPIs) and these are described in the *Tourism Australia Corporate Plan 2008/09 to 2010/11*. These are used to evaluate the overall performance of Australia as a destination and TA's own marketing programs. The KPIs provide the foundation for measurement and evaluation. For 2008/09 to 2010/11 industry performance was evaluated by actual results judged

(continues)

(continued)

against forecasts levels for: (1) inbound (international) arrivals; (2) domestic trips; (3) Tourism Inbound Economic Value (TIEV); (4) Tourism Domestic Economic Value (TDEV); and (5) regional dispersal—visitor nights in regional Australia.

TA measured its own marketing programs with the following KPIs:

Consumer marketing:
- Number of prospective international leisure visitors
- Ensuring that Australia is thought of when considering travel
- Number of prospective domestic leisure visitors
- Number of business event arrivals

Trade development:
- Key agents are knowledgeable about selling Australia (travel trade development)

Australian experiences (international visitors):
- Travelers think key experiences are available in city and regional Australia

Australian experiences (domestic visitors):
- Travelers have knowledge of Australia as a holiday destination

Stakeholder engagement:
- Stakeholders are satisfied with TA's performance

Insights and intelligence:
- Stakeholders are satisfied with TA provision of insights

TA set performance measures for each KPI for evaluation at the end of each operating year. For example, it targeted a specific increase in number of prospective international leisure visitors from its seven *Tier1* markets (UK, Japan, New Zealand, USA, Germany, South Korea, and China). Base level figures were set for the operating year ending in June 2008.

Performance measures were set for these four organizational KPIs. For example, through a stakeholder survey TA will measure the percentage of stakeholders that rate TA's functions as "good" or better.

KPIs were also developed for the *core enabling platforms* of TA:

Information and communications technology:
- TA staff report that technology systems are reliable
- TA staff report that technology systems are highly useful

Finance, governance, administration, and risk:
- TA maintains control of its budgets
- TA complies with Government standards, regulations, internal policies and procedures

People and culture:
- TA staff are motivated to conduct core activities

(continues)

(continued)

TA has 23 markets around the world and within Australia itself. It divides these markets into four *tier* levels.

For example, the top-priority markets (Tier 1) are Australia plus UK, Japan, New Zealand, USA, Germany, South Korea, and China. Tier 2 markets are Canada, France, Ireland, Singapore, Malaysia, India, Taiwan, and Hong Kong.

Image copyright Brooke Whatnall, 2008. Used under license from Shutterstock.com

The koala bear is one of the strong visual icons of Australia

Market Yield Segmentation in Australia

Tourism Research Australia, a branch of TA, has developed a system of "market yield segmentation" for international leisure travelers to Australia. These are measured by what the Australian Bureau of Statistics has called "gross value added" or the total expenditures less the cost of producing the commodities purchased by international

(continues)

(continued)

travelers. Based upon the GVA measure, the following were the key market segments for Australia in 2008–2009:

- USA: Aged 25+ years
- Canada: Aged 35+ years
- Germany: Aged 35+
- Hong Kong: Aged 35+
- UK: Aged 35+
- Hong Kong: 15–24 years

New Marketing Thrust in 2008–2009

In July 2008, TA selected a new creative services agency to guide its advertising and other promotional programs. In October 2008, TA released the new *Walkabout* campaign based on the new movie *Australia* directed by Baz Luhrmann.

The number of international visitors to Australia for the operational year ended June 30, 2008 was 5,629,300, which was down slightly from the 5,641,300 at the same time in 2007. The biggest markets in 2007–2008 were Northeast Asia (Japan, China, South Korea, Hong Kong, Taiwan), Europe (especially the UK and Germany), and Oceania (especially New Zealand).

Discussion Questions

1. What can other DMOs learn for the outstanding example set by Tourism Australia in its marketing evaluation?
2. What are the possible reasons, in your opinion, that other DMOs do not as systematically evaluate their performance as does Tourism Australia?
3. How do you think a highly popular movie affects the number of visitors to a destination like Australia? How can the effects of the movie on tourism be measured?

and the situation analysis described in Chapter 5. In fact, some people in our industry use these two terms interchangeably. Although it is true that all of the topics in a situation analysis are covered in the marketing audit, the audit is more extensive and because of the high level of effort required, may not be performed each year.

The major features of a good marketing audit process are that it is (1) comprehensive, (2) systematic, (3) independent, and (4) periodic.[11] An effective audit analyzes all aspects of an organization's marketing efforts, including planning and strategy setting, organization, marketing management, implementation, performance, and control and evaluation procedures. In other words, the process is similar to placing the entire hospitality and travel marketing system under a microscope. The marketing audit is systematic when it examines each aspect of marketing using the step-by-step procedure described in this book. It starts by investigating the information and decisions outlined in Chapter 5 and then moves chapter by chapter to the present one.

Most experts believe that it is better to get an outside, independent view of an organization's marketing strengths and weaknesses. There is a danger of bias if the marketing department performs the audit itself. Greater objectivity usually results by having the audit conducted by an independent management consulting firm, by another department, or by an internal task force.

In practice, many organizations carry out marketing audits only when they encounter serious problems. This is not the ideal approach because there is always room for improvement, even when things are going well. Because marketing audits are more expensive and time-consuming than situation analyses, they are not done as frequently. However, given the rapid pace of change in the hospitality and travel industry, this book recommends that audits be conducted every three to five years and even more frequently if serious marketing problems arise.

The Future of Marketing

What lies ahead for marketing in the hospitality and travel industry? First, as this book has emphasized, marketing will be a much more important management function in the industry in 2010 and beyond. Marketing budgets will continue to increase as competition grows. More people with marketing backgrounds will head major organizations in our industry. Associations of marketing professionals will grow in size and stature. We may even see specialized, four-year degree programs in hospitality and travel marketing being introduced by major educational institutions. Without question, the industry will become more sophisticated and creative in its marketing practices.

Second, a major trend that has been mentioned throughout this book is the use of new technologies to communicate information among organizations and their customers. There has been rapid growth in the use of the Internet and particularly in the use of e-mail and the Web. Customers are becoming increasingly comfortable buying products and services on the Internet, and **e-commerce** is booming. **M-commerce** or communicating and buying through mobile phones, PDAs and other mobile devices are also on a steep growth rate in many countries around the world. Technological innovations such as wireless Internet access will help accelerate this move to greater online and mobile purchasing. Travel is now one of the most popular items to purchase online, and there are many online travel services available. Travelers have an enormous amount of travel information to surf through on the Web that is both interactive and up to date. Hospitality and travel organizations have invested heavily in ensuring that they have a viable online presence.

Image copyright Ragnarock, 2008. Used under license from Shutterstock.com

FIGURE 20.8 The future of marketing in hospitality and travel will be more global in both market demand and competition.

Third, a trend that can be predicted with confidence is the continued splintering of the market for hospitality and travel services. As Chapter 7 pointed out, both societal factors and the industry's reactions to them are combining to create an ever-expanding range of market segments.

And fourth, another trend is the increasing use of computer technology by the hospitality and travel industry, especially in database marketing and marketing research. As mentioned throughout this book, more marketers are recognizing the vital importance of maintaining detailed relational databases on past and potential customers. When used with direct marketing programs, these databases offer hospitality and travel marketers a more effective and efficient means of achieving objectives. In research, the use of compact- and DVD technologies offers marketers great future potential in the use of research data. For example, many national hospitality/travel survey data sets are now available on CD-ROM and on the Internet.

Nothing is more inevitable than change (Figure 20.8). Through careful management, control and evaluation of marketing activities, an organization is much better equipped to adapt to change when it happens.

Chapter Conclusion

Having a marketing plan is not a prescription for success. Although marketing plans are vital, there are several other marketing management tasks that require attention, including organization, staffing, supervision, budgeting, control, and evaluation. A marketing management process that considers all these tasks is essential in today's competitive environment.

A marketing plan must be monitored carefully during its implementation, and corrective action must be taken when necessary. One of the key tools of control is the marketing budget, which should be developed on the basis of sound budgeting techniques such as the objective-and-task and zero-based approaches. Marketing objectives, stated in measurable terms, also play a key role.

An organization's marketing efforts should always be evaluated critically. There is no room for sacred cows and complacency in modern marketing. Several effective evaluation techniques are available, most notably the marketing audit, that can help an organization improve its marketing in the future.

REVIEW QUESTIONS

1. How is marketing management defined in this book?
2. What are the five components of marketing management?
3. Is marketing management an optional activity or is it essential? What are the benefits of effective marketing management?
4. What are the five different ways of organizing a marketing department, and in which situations does each work best?
5. How do organizations in the hospitality and travel industry recruit marketing staff? Are they ahead or behind other industries in their recruitment approaches?
6. What are the steps and procedures involved in managing and supervising marketing staff?
7. What are the best approaches to developing a marketing budget? Explain your answer by describing unsophisticated and sophisticated approaches.
8. How are marketing control and marketing evaluation defined in this book?
9. What steps are involved in controlling the marketing plan and what roles do the marketing budget and plan play?
10. How important is marketing evaluation to the future success of an organization? Explain your answer by showing how the six evaluation techniques are used.

CHAPTER ASSIGNMENTS

1. Arrange to visit a hospitality or travel organization of your choice, and schedule an interview with the person responsible for marketing. Find out as much as you can about how the organization handles marketing management. How is marketing organized? How are marketing staff recruited? What is done to orient, train, and motivate them? What procedures are used to supervise and control the quality

of service given by marketing and front-line staff? How are marketing budgets developed? Is the organization's control of the marketing plan effective and, if so, how is this accomplished? How does the organization evaluate its marketing efforts? Summarize your conclusions in a report to senior management describing current procedures and including your recommendations on how marketing management could be made more effective.

2. Select three organizations in that part of the hospitality and travel industry in which you are most interested. Do they have marketing departments? How is marketing organized? Why do you think they are organized in this way? What are the advantages and disadvantages of their individual approaches? Which approach is best? Do they satisfy the basic principle that the person or persons responsible for marketing have at least joint responsibility for all marketing and promotional mix elements? How would you improve their organizational setups to increase marketing effectiveness?

3. A local hospitality and travel organization has asked you for help in developing a marketing budget. What approach would you recommend? Who would you involve in developing the budget? What sources of information would you use in developing the budget? Prepare a rough budget based on your analysis and findings.

4. Assume that you have been hired as a consultant by a hospitality and travel organization to improve the effectiveness of its marketing efforts. Explain the procedures you would recommend for using the five-step hospitality and travel marketing system. Make specific suggestions on how the organization should control and evaluate marketing. Describe the benefits the organization can expect from implementing your recommendations.

WEB RESOURCES

Balanced Scorecard Collaborative, http://www.bscol.com/
Balanced Scorecard Institute, http://www.balancedscorecard.org/
College of Performance Management, http://www.pmi-cpm.org/
GSM Association (m-commerce association), http://www.gsmworld.com/
Work Measurement Institute, http://www.workmeasurement.com/

REFERENCES

1. *Kansas City Convention & Visitors Association.* 2008. *Organizational Facts.* http://www.visitkc.com/about-the-cva/organizational-facts/index.aspx, accessed December 31, 2008.

2. Tourism Australia. 2008. *Contact Tourism Australia.* http://www.tourism.australia.com/AboutUs.asp?lang=EN&sub=0388, accessed December 31, 2008.

3. PKF Consulting. 2008. *Annual Trends Reports.* http://www.pkfc.com/store/products.aspx?CategoryID=175, accessed December 31, 2008.

4. Allen, Aaron. 2008. *Restaurant marketing. Restaurant Report*, http://www.restaurantreport.com/departments/biz_restaurant_marketing.html, accessed December 31, 2008.

5. Advertising Age. 2008. *100 Leading National Advertisers.* http://adage.com/datacenter/article?article_id=127791, accessed December 31, 2008.

6. Rosann Spiro, Gregory A. Rich, and William J. Stanton, 2008. *Management of a Sales Force.* 12th ed. McGraw-Hill IrwinBoston, 419–420.

7. Seminole County Convention & Visitors Bureau. 2007. *The ROI of Advertising*, http://www.visitseminole.com/tourism-cvb/local/pdf/2002-2003 MediaConversionStudy%20.pdf, accessed December 31, 2008.

8. Destination Marketing Association International. 2005. *IACVB Recommended Standard CVB Performance Reporting: A Handbook for CVBs. Washington, DC:* Destination Marketing Association International.

9. Kotler, Philip. 2000. *Marketing Management: Millennium Edition.* 10th ed. Upper Saddle River, N.J.: Prentice-Hall, Inc.

10. Rosann Spiro, Gregory A. Rich, and William J. Stanton, 2008. *Management of a Sales Force.* 12th ed. Boston: McGraw-Hill Irwin, 417–418.

11. Kotler, Philip. 2000. *Marketing Management: The Millennium Edition.* 10th ed. Upper Saddle River, N.J.: Prentice-Hall, Inc.

The author and Delmar affirm that the website addresses referenced herein were accurate at the time of printing. However, due to the fluid nature of the Internet, we cannot guarantee their accuracy for the life of the edition.

APPENDIX 1.1A   The Largest Lodging Chains in the World[1]

HOTEL CHAIN	HEADQUARTERS	ROOMS	PROPERTIES
1. InterContinental Hotels Group	Windsor, England	585,094	3,949
2. Wyndham Hotel Group	Parsippany, NJ, USA	550,576	6,544
3. Marriott International	Washington, DC, USA	537,249	2,999
4. Hilton Hotels Corporation	Beverly Hills, CA, USA	502,116	3,000
5. Accor	Paris, France	461,698	3,871
6. Choice Hotels International	Silver Spring, MD, USA	452,027	5,570
7. Best Western International	Phoenix, AZ, USA	308,636	4,035
8. Starwood Hotels & Resorts Worldwide	White Plains, NY, USA	274,535	897
9. Carlson Hospitality Worldwide	Minneapolis, MN, USA	146,600	969
10. Global Hyatt Corporation	Chicago, IL, USA	135,001	721
11. Westmont Hospitality Group	Houston, TX, USA	108,503	703
12. Golden Tulip Hospitality/THL	Amersfoort, Netherlands	86,585	944
13. TUI AG/TUI Hotels & Resorts	Hannover, Germany	83,192	288
14. Extended Stay Hotels	Spartanburg, SC, USA	76,384	686
15. Sol Melia SA	Palma de Mallorca, Spain	75,022	301
16. LQ Management LLC	Irving, TX, USA	69,089	633
17. Jin Jiang International Hotels	Shanghai, PR China	68,797	380
18. Rezidor Hotel Group	Brussels, Belgium	67,000	329
19. Groupe du Louvre	Torcy, France	60,807	848
20. Vantage Hospitality Group	Westlake Village, CA, USA	55,167	798
21. NH Hotels SA	Madrid, Spain	49,677	341
22. MGM Mirage	Las Vegas, NV, USA	42,802	17
23. Interstate Hotels & Resorts	Arlington, VA, USA	42,620	191
24. Barcelo Hotels & Resorts	Palma de Mallorca, Spain	42,173	162
25. Harrah's Entertainment	Las Vegas, NV, USA	38,130	34
TOTALS		4,919,480	39,210

Data source: "Hotels' 325, Corporate 300 Ranking," *HOTELS magazine.*

[1]Ranked by the total number of rooms available in 2007.

APPENDIX 1.1B The 25 Leading U.S. Lodging Brands[1]

HOTEL BRAND	PARENT COMPANY	U.S. ROOMS	U.S. PROPERTIES	FOREIGN PROPERTIES
1. Best Western	Best Western International	173,000	2,100	1,900
2. Holiday Inn Hotels & Resorts	InterContinental Hotels Group	154,213	811	559
3. Hampton Inn/Hampton Inn & Suites	Hilton Hotels Corp.	143,399	1,459	28
4. Marriott Hotels & Resorts	Marriott International	135,611	340	181
5. Days Inn	Wyndham Hotel Group	135,254	1,697	158
6. Holiday Inn Express	InterContinental Hotels Group	122,651	1,503	267
7. Super 8	Wyndham Hotel Group	114,499	1,889	172
8. Comfort Inn	Choice Hotels International	111,505	1,429	552
9. Hilton	Hilton Hotels Corp.	97,154	240	272
10. Courtyard by Marriott	Marriott International	94,830	679	72
11. Motel 6	Accor North America	91,526	902	11
12. Quality	Choice Hotels International	77,515	804	386
13. Sheraton	Starwood Hotels & Resorts Worldwide	77,427	202	197
14. La Quinta Inn & Suites	LQ Management	69,089	633	2
15. Ramada	Wyndham Hotel Group	65,392	576	278
16. Residence Inn by Marriott	Marriott International	61,421	516	18
17. Hyatt Regency/Grand Hyatt/Park Hyatt	Global Hyatt Corp.	59,516	117	97
18. Econo Lodge	Choice Hotels International	50,273	824	44
19. Americas Best Value Inn	Vantage Hospitality Group	47,815	758	12
20. Fairfield Inn by Marriott	Marriott International	46,231	521	7
21. Doubletree	Hilton Hotels Corp.	46,133	180	4
22. Westin	Starwood Hotels & Resorts Worldwide	45,930	100	53
23. Hilton Garden Inn	Hilton Hotels Corp.	45,067	330	19
24. Embassy Suites Hotels	Hilton Hotels Corp.	44,046	181	8
25. Extended Stay America	Extended Stay Hotels	40,426	365	0
TOTALS		2,149,923	19,156	5,299

Data source: "Top Brands." *LH/Lodging Hospitality. December 1,* 2008.
[1]Ranked by the number of U.S. rooms available at December 31, 2007.

APPENDIX 1.1C   The 25 Leading Independent, Third-Party Management Companies in the U.S.[1]

COMPANY	ROOMS MANAGED	PROPERTIES MANAGED
1. InterContinental Hotels Group	125,214	512
2. Interstate Hotels & Resorts	47,157	207
3. Ocean Hospitalities	17,443	117
4. John Q Hammons Hotels and Resorts	16,367	73
5. White Lodging Services Corporation	15,684	115
6. American Property Management Corporation	13,550	47
7. Pyramid Advisors LLC	12,729	39
8. Crestline Hotels & Resorts	11,750	52
9. Outrigger Enterprises Group	10,268	37
10. Janus Hotels and Resorts	9,100	42
11. Sage Hospitality Resources	8,902	47
12. Davidson Hotel Company	8,427	29
13. Driftwood Hospitality Management	7,866	37
14. Swissotel Hotels & Resorts	7,824	21
15. Destination Hotels & Resorts	6,662	32
16. Winegardner & Hammons	6,415	26
17. Concord Hospitality Enterprise Company	6,200	50
18. Dimension Development Company	5,927	37
19. Richfield Hospitality	5,927	26
20. Windsor Hospitality Group	5,920	28
21. Horizon Hotels Ltd.	5,692	25
22. Sonesta International Hotel Group	5,456	26
23. Marcus Hotels & Resorts	5,096	20
24. Marshall Management	4,644	34
25. Kinseth Hospitality	4,580	32
TOTALS	374,800	1,711

Data source: "H&MM's Top Independent, Third-Party Management Companies." *Hotel & Motel Management*, June 4, 2007.

[1]Ranked by the number of U.S. rooms available in 2006.

APPENDIX 1.2A   The 25 Leading U.S. Foodservice Chains[1]

CHAIN NAME	PARENT COMPANY	CONCEPT	NUMBER OF UNITS	TOTAL SALES ($ MILLIONS)
1. McDonald's	McDonald's Corporation	Sandwich	13,862	$28,576.10
2. Burger King	Burger King Holdings Inc.	Sandwich	7,210	8,916.00
3. Subway	Doctor's Associates Inc.	Sandwich	21,195	8,225.00
4. Wendy's*	Wendy's International Inc.	Sandwich	5,936	7,924.00
5. Starbucks Coffee	Starbucks Corporation	Coffee	10,183	7,250.00
6. Taco Bell	Yum! Brands Inc.	Sandwich	5,580	6,100.00
7. Aramark Food & Support Services	Aramark Holdings Corporation	Contract	3,486	6,090.00
8. Pizza Hut	Yum! Brands Inc.	Pizza	7,515	5,400.00
9. KFC	Yum! Brands Inc.	Chicken	5,358	5,300.00
10. Dunkin' Donuts	Dunkin' Brands Inc.	Beverage-Snack	5,670	4,750.00
11. Applebee's Neighborhood Grill & Bar	DineEquity Inc.	Casual Dining	1,864	4,505.40
12. Chili's Grill & Bar	Brinker International Inc.	Casual Dining	1,305	3,880.00
13. Sonic Drive-In	Sonic Corporation	Sandwich	3,342	3,607.00
14. Domino's Pizza	Domino's Pizza Inc.	Pizza	5,155	3,208.00
15. Arby's*	Triarc Cos. Inc.	Sandwich	3,564	3,160.00
16. Olive Garden	Darden Restaurants Inc.	Casual Dining	647	3,048.00
17. Jack in the Box	Jack in the Box Inc.	Sandwich	2,132	3,020.00
18. Chick-fil-A	Chick-fil-A Inc.	Chicken	1,356	2,640.90
19. Outback Steakhouse	Bain Capital LLC	Casual Dining	795	2,637.00
20. Red Lobster	Darden Restaurants Inc.	Casual Dining	651	2,567.00
21. Dairy Queen	Berkshire Hathaway Inc.	Sandwich	4,660	2,500.00
22. International House of Pancakes/IHOP Rest.	DineEquity Inc.	Family	1,330	2,317.00
23. Denny's	Denny's Corporation	Family	1,471	2,315.00
24. Panera Bread	Panera Bread Company	Contract	1,115	2,105.00
25. TGI Friday's	Carlson Cos. Inc.	Pizza	595	2,028.90
TOTALS			115,977	$132,070.30

Data source: "NRN Foodservice Top 100, 2008," *Nation's Restaurant News.*

[1]Ranked by total U.S. Sales volume in either 2007 or 2008 depending on year end.
*Wendy's and Arby's were merged in 2008 into the Wendy's/Arby's Group. Inc.

APPENDIX 1.2B **The Top Five Restaurant and Foodservice Chains By Total U.S. Sales in Each Category[1]**

CATEGORY/CHAIN	CATEGORY/CHAIN
1. SANDWICH CHAINS • McDonald's • Burger King • Subway • Wendy's • Taco Bell	**6. FAMILY CHAINS** • International House of Pancakes/IHOP • Denny's • Cracker Barrel Old Country Store • Bob Evans Restaurants • Waffle House
2. CHICKEN CHAINS • KFC • Chick-fil-A • Popeyes Chicken & Biscuits • Church's Chicken • Boston Market	**7. CONTACT CHAINS** • Aramark Food & Support Services • Canteen Services • Sodexho Health Care Services • Sodexho Campus Services • Sodexho Corporate Services
3. PIZZA CHAINS • Pizza Hut • Domino's Pizza • Papa John's Pizza • Little Caesars Pizza • CiCi's Pizza	**8. HOTEL CHAINS** • Marriott Hotels, Resorts & Suites • Hilton Hotels • Sheraton Hotels • Holiday Inn • Radisson Hotels & Resorts
4. CASUAL DINING CHAINS • Applebee's Neighborhood Grill & Bar • Chili's Grill & Bar • Olive Garden • Outback Steakhouse • Red Lobster	**9. GRILL-BUFFET CHAINS** • Golden Corral • Ryan's Grill Buffet & Bakery • Ponderosa Steakhouse
5. BEVERAGE/SNACK CHAINS • Starbucks Coffee • Dunkin' Donuts • Krispy Kreme Doughnuts • Baskin-Robbins • Cold Stone Creamery	

Data source: "NRN Foodservice Top 100, 2008." *Nation's Restaurant News.*

[1]Ranked by total U.S. sales volume in either 2007 or 2008 depending on year end.

APPENDIX 1.2C The Estimated Market Shares of Restaurant Chain Brands in the U.S.[1]

CHAIN BRAND/CATEGORY	MARKET SHARE
SANDWICH	
1. McDonald's	34.94%
2. Burger King	10.85%
3. Wendy's	10.05%
4. Subway	9.92%
5. Taco Bell	8.11%
6. Sonic Drive-In	4.27%
7. Arby's	3.98%
8. Jack in the Box	3.62%
9. Dairy Queen	3.10%
10. Quiznos Sub	2.29%
PIZZA	
1. Pizza Hut	41.54%
2. Domino's Pizza	25.76%
3. Papa John's Pizza	15.70%
4. Little Caesars	8.41%
5. CiCi's Pizza	4.32%
6. Chuck E. Cheese's	4.27%
CHICKEN	
1. KFC	43.90%
2. Chick-fil-A	18.88%
3. Popeyes Chicken & Biscuits	12.31%
4. Church's Chicken	6.70%
5. Boston Market	5.64%
6. El Pollo Loco	4.38%
7. Bojangles' Famous Chicken 'n Biscuits	4.22%
8. Zaxby's	3.89%
CASUAL DINING	
1. Applebee's Neighborhood Grill & Bar	14.95%
2. Chili's Grill & Bar	11.57%
3. Olive Garden	9.22%
4. Outback Steakhouse	8.62%
5. Red Lobster	8.39%
6. T.G.I. Friday's	6.39%

(Continued)

APPENDIX 1.2C   Continued

CHAIN BRAND/CATEGORY	MARKET SHARE
7. Ruby Tuesday	6.05%
8. The Cheesecake Factory	3.81%
9. Red Robin Gourmet Burgers & Spirits	3.19%
10. Texas Roadhouse	3.06%
COFFEE/SNACK	
1. Starbucks	49.97%
2. Cold Stone Creamery	35.71%
3. Dunkin' Donuts	5.81%
4. Baskin-Robbins	4.60%
5. Krispy Kreme Doughnuts	3.91%
HOTELS	
1. Marriott	21.69%
2. Hilton	19.61%
3. Sheraton	16.49%
4. Holiday Inn	12.12%
5. Radisson	11.59%
6. Hyatt	9.57%
7. Ramada Inn	8.93%

Data source: "NRN Foodservice Top 100, 2007." *Nation's Restaurant News.*

[1]Ranked by total U.S. sales volume within category in either 2006 or 2007 depending on year end.

APPENDIX 1.3 The Major Cruise Lines Serving North America[1]

CRUISE LINE	NUMBER OF SHIPS	NUMBER OF LOWER BERTHS
1. Royal Caribbean International	22	52,838
2. Carnival Cruise Lines	22	50,882
3. Princess Cruises	16	34,110
4. Norwegian Cruise Line	12	25,326
5. Costa Cruise Lines	12	23,265
6. Holland America Line	13	18,915
7. MSC Cruises USA	8	13,548
8. Celebrity Cruises	8	13,388
9. Cunard Line, Ltd.	3	6,411
10. Hurtigruten ASA (Norway)	13	5,923
11. Disney Cruise Line	2	3,508
12. Regent Seven Seas Cruises	5	2,422
13. Oceania Cruises, Inc.	3	2,052
14. Crystal Cruises	2	2,014
15. Majestic	7	1,588
16. Azamara	2	1,420
17. Silversea Cruises	4	1,356
18. AMA Waterways	9	1,294
19. Uniworld River Cruises	9	1,206
20. Orient Lines, Inc.	1	826
21. Seabourn Cruise Line	3	624
22. Windstar Cruises	3	608
23. American Cruise Line	4	302
24. SeaDream Yacht Club Luxury Cruises	2	110
TOTALS	185	263,936

Data source: 2008 CLIA Cruise Market Overview. Cruise Lines International Association, 2008.

[1]Ranked in number of lower berths available at the end of 2007.

APPENDIX 1.4   The Major U.S. Car Rental Companies[1]

COMPANY	FLEET SIZE (CARS) Aug. 2006	U.S. LOCATIONS	2007 REVENUES (in $ millions)
MAINLY AIRPORT SALES			
1. Hertz	327,200	2,850	$3,940.00
2. National Car Rental/Alamo Rent A Car	232,892	662	$2,900.00
3. Avis Rent A Car	204,200	1,200	$3,100.00
4. Dollar Thrifty Automotive Group	167,000	606	$1,580.00
5. Budget Rent A Car	143,600	850	$1,600.00
6. Advantage Rent-A-Car	20,000	108	$220.00
7. Payless Car Rental System Inc.	10,000	41	$100.00
8. ACE Rent A Car	9,000	85	$92.00
9. Fox Rent A Car	8,700	29	$78.72
MAINLY LOCAL SALES			
1. Enterprise	643,289	6,131	$7100.00
2. U-Save Auto Rental of America Inc.	11,800	390	$102.00
3. Rent-A-Wreck America	7,280	280	$52.00
4. Triangle Rent-A-Car	6,000	30	$47.50
5. Affordable/Sensible	5,000	225	$36.00
INDEPENDENTS	65,500	3,275	$59.00
TOTALS	1,861,461	16,762	$21,007.22

Data source: "2007 US Car Rental Market." *Auto Rental News.* **http://www.fleet-central.com/**

[1]Ranked by the fleet size (total number of vehicles) in 2007.

APPENDIX 1.5A   The Top 25 Amusement/Theme Parks Worldwide[1]

RANK	PARK AND LOCATION	ATTENDANCE
1. Magic Kingdom	Walt Disney World, Lake Buena Vista, FL, USA	17,060,000
2. Disneyland	Anaheim, CA, USA	14,870,000
3. Tokyo Disneyland	Tokyo, Japan	13,906,000
4. Tokyo Disney Sea	Tokyo, Japan	12,413,000
5. Disneyland Paris	Marne-La-Vallée, France	12,000,000
6. EPCOT at Walt Disney World	Walt Disney World, Lake Buena Vista, FL, USA	10,930,000
7. Disney's Hollywood Studios	Walt Disney World, Lake Buena Vista, FL, USA	9,510,000
8. Disney's Animal Kingdom	Walt Disney World, Lake Buena Vista, FL, USA	9,490,000
9. Universal Studios Japan	Osaka, Japan	8,713,000
10. Everland	Kyonggi-Do, South Korea	7,200,000
11. Universal Studios Florida	Orlando, FL, USA	6,200,000
12. SeaWorld Florida	Orlando, FL, USA	5,800,000
13. Disney's California Adventure	Anaheim, CA, USA	5,680,000
14. Pleasure Beach	Blackpool, England, UK	5,500,000
15. Islands of Adventure	Universal Studios, Orlando, FL, USA	5,430,000
16. Ocean Park	Hong Kong SAR, PR China	4,920,000
17. Hakkeijima Sea Paradise	Yokohama, Japan	4,770,000
18. Universal Studios Hollywood	Universal City, CA, USA	4,700,000
19. Busch Gardens Tampa Bay	Tampa Bay, FL, USA	4,400,000
20. SeaWorld California	San Diego, CA, USA	4,260,000
21. Hong Kong Disneyland	Hong Kong SAR, PR China	4,150,000
22. Tivoli Gardens	Copenhagen, Denmark	4,110,000
23. Europe-Park	Rust, Germany	4,000,000
24. Nagashima Spa Land	Kuwana, Japan	3,910,000
25. Port Aventura	Salou, Spain	3,700,000
TOTAL		187,622,000

Data source: *TEA/ERA Attraction Attendance 2007 Report.* TEA and Economics Research Associates (ERA).

[1]Ranked by the estimated attendance in 2007.

APPENDIX 1.5B The Top 20 North American Amusement/Theme Parks[1]

RANK	PARK AND LOCATION	ATTENDANCE
1. Magic Kingdom	Walt Disney World, Lake Buena Vista, FL, USA	17,060,000
2. Disneyland	Anaheim, CA, USA	14,870,000
3. EPCOT at Walt Disney World	Walt Disney World, Lake Buena Vista, FL, USA	10,930,000
4. Disney's Hollywood Studios	Walt Disney World, Lake Buena Vista, FL, USA	9,510,000
5. Disney's Animal Kingdom	Walt Disney World, Lake Buena Vista, FL, USA	9,490,000
6. Universal Studios Florida	Orlando, FL, USA	6,200,000
7. SeaWorld Florida	Orlando, FL, USA	5,800,000
8. Disney's California Adventure	Anaheim, CA, USA	5,680,000
9. Islands of Adventure	Universal Studios, Orlando, FL, USA	5,430,000
10. Universal Studios Hollywood	Universal City, CA, USA	4,700,000
11. Busch Gardens Tampa Bay	Tampa Bay, FL, USA	4,400,000
12. SeaWorld California	San Diego, CA, USA	4,260,000
13. Knott's Berry Farm	Buena Park, CA, USA	3,630,000
14. Canada's Wonderland	Maple, Ontario, Canada	3,250,000
15. Busch Gardens Europe	Williamsburg, VA, USA	3,157,000
16. Cedar Point	Sandusky, OH, USA	3,120,000
17. Kings Island	Kings Island, OH, USA	3,050,000
18. Hershey Park	Hershey, PA, USA	2,940,000
19. Six Flags Great Adventure	Jackson, NJ, USA	2,720,000
20. Six Flags Great America	Gurnee, IL, USA	2,630,000
TOTAL		122,827,000

Data source: TEA/ERA Attraction Attendance 2007 Report. TEA and Economics Research Associates (ERA).

[1]Ranked by the estimated attendance in 2007.

APPENDIX 1.5C The Top 25 Fairs in North America[1]		
FAIRS	**LOCATION**	**ATTENDANCE**
1. Texas State Fair	Dallas, TX	2,052,000
2. Houston Livestock Show & Rodeo	Houston, TX	1,806,129
3. Minnesota State Fair	St. Paul, MN	1,681,678
4. Los Angeles County Fair	Pomona, CA	1,365,026
5. San Diego County Fair	Del Mar, CA	1,265,997
6. Calgary Stampede	Calgary, ALB	1,251,105
7. Canadian National Exhibition	Toronto, ONT	1,240,000
8. Eastern States Exhibition	Springfield, MA	1,227,889
9. Arizona State Fair	Phoenix, AZ	1,214,442
10. San Antonio Livestock Show & Exhibition	San Antonio, TX	1,204,417
11. Western Washington Fair	Puyallup, WA	1,182,937
12. Oklahoma State Fair	Oklahoma City, OK	1,100,000
13. Orange County Fair	Costa Mesa, CA	1,090,122
14. Erie County Fair	Hamburg, NY	1,009,122
15. Iowa State Fair	Des Moines, IA	1,002,464
16. Tulsa State Fair	Tulsa, OK	987,057
17. New York State Fair	Syracuse, NY	936,399
18. Pacific National Exhibition	Vancouver, BC	906,808
19. Evergreen State Fair	Monroe, WA	882,095
20. Southwest Exposition & Livestock Show	Fort Worth, TX	875,300
21. North Carolina State Fair	Raleigh, NC	858,611
22. Ohio State Fair	Columbus, OH	806,301
23. Wisconsin State Fair	West Allis, WI	801,420
24. Capital EX	Edmonton, ALB	772,692
25. Indiana State Fair	Indianapolis, IN	751,218
TOTAL		28,271,229

Data source: 2007 Top 50 Fairs. **Carnivalwarehouse.com.** (2008).

[1]Ranked by the estimated total attendance in 2007.

APPENDIX 1.6A   The World's Leading International Airlines[1]

AIRLINE	INTERNATIONAL
1. Air France	118,112
2. Lufthansa	116,838
3. British Airways	110,320
4. Singapore Airlines	90,901
5. Emirates	90,530
6. American Airlines	81,324
7. United Airlines	77,709
8. Cathay Pacific	74,987
9. KLM	74,488
10. Delta Airlines	63,202
TOTAL	898,411

Data source: World Air Transport Statistics. IATA. (2008).

[1]Ranked by number of passenger kilometers flew on international flights in 2007.

APPENDIX 1.6B The Domestic Performance and Market Shares of Major U.S. Airlines[1]

AIRLINES	PASSENGERS[2]	RPM[3]	MARKET SHARE[4]	LOAD FACTOR
1. American Airlines	75,339	86,366	14.63%	83.0%
2. Southwest Airlines	104,451	74,547	12.63%	73.1%
3. United Air Lines	54,409	65,790	11.14%	82.7%
4. Delta Airlines	60,642	63,375	10.73%	82.7%
5. Continental Air Lines	36,694	45,732	7.75%	84.1%
6. US Airways	43,887	40,337	6.83%	81.4%
7. Northwest Airlines	42,317	38,968	6.60%	84.6%
8. JetBlue Airways	20,716	24,862	4.21%	79.8%
9. AirTran Airways	24,496	18,224	3.09%	77.0%
10. Alaska Airlines	15,455	16,182	2.74%	77.0%
TOTALS	478,406	474,383	80.35%	

Data source: *Research and Innovative Technology Administration.* (2008). U.S. Department of Transportation.

[1] Figures are for the year ending May 31, 2008.
[2] Figures are in thousands.
[3] Figures are in millions.
[4] Market share is based on Revenue Passenger Miles (RPMs).

APPENDIX 1.7   The Leading Hospitality, Travel and Tourism Advertisers in the U.S.

	RANK	TOTAL U.S. ADVERTISING ($ millions)	U.S. MEASURED MEDIA ADVERTISING ($ millions)
COMPANY[1]			
McDonald's Corporation	16	1748.30	785.00
Yum! Brands	46	902.00	719.40
Doctor's Associates/Subway	71	539.80	361.70
Wendy's International	85	435.20	361.20
Burger King Holdings	90	379.50	285.70
PARENT COMPANIES[1]			
Walt Disney Company	8	2320.00	1438.40
American Express Company	43	928.70	534.00
BRANDS[2]			
McDonald's	7		776.40
Subway	31		361.40
Wendy's	32		360.40
Burger King	47		285.20
Taco Bell	53		260.20
KFC	55		251.40
Pizza Hut	80		206.40
Southwest Airlines	98		177.60
Applebee's	103		174.20
Domino's	123		152.30
Chili's	150		125.00
Olive Garden	172		111.90
Sonic	179		108.70
Dunkin' Donuts	183		107.90
Red Lobster	188		103.70
Arby's	189		103.00

Data source: "100 Leading National Advertisers." *Advertising Age.* (2007).

[1]Ranked by brand measured media spending in U.S. in 2006.

APPENDIX 1.8 The Advertising Expenditures by Hospitality, Travel and Tourism Companies by Media Type[1]

	TOTAL	MAGAZINE	NEWS PAPERS	OUT-DOOR	TV	CABLE NETS	RADIO	INTERNET
INDUSTRY CATEGORIES								
Airline, hotels, car rental, travel	5,415.6	1,484.1	1,412.9	331.9	876.1	515.4	342.9	452.2
Restaurants	5,291.5	134.9	183.8	240.2	3,339.2	810.6	534.2	48.5

		Mcdonald's	Yum!	Subway	Wendy's	Burger King		
MEASURED MEDIA TYPES								
Magazines	64,658	37,868	2,203	2,665	19,989	1,933		
Sunday Magazines	2,506	1091				1,415		
B2B Magazines	583	147		52	22	362		
Local Magazines	20	20						
Spanish-language Magazines	2,122	2,080				42		
Total Magazines	*69,889*	*41,206*	*2,203*	*2,717*	*20,011*	*3,752*		
Newspapers	5,426	2,768	1,637	493	143	385		
National Newspapers	2,065	1,098	897	70				
Spanish-language Newspapers	377	198	79	11	43	46		
FSI (free-standing inserts)	3,704	757	2,207	278	76	386		
Total Newspapers	*11,572*	*4,821*	*4,820*	*852*	*262*	*817*		
Network TV	984,434	252,136	294,275	155,233	164,092	118,698		
Spot TV	520,872	150,581	223,289	101,995	37,702	7,305		
Syndicated TV	116,260	37,388	6,267	26,971	27,217	18,417		
Spanish-language TV	124,751	66,743	15,428	7,594	18,524	16,462		
Cable TV Networks	418,570	89,820	157,913	43,260	60,009	67,568		
Total Television	*2,164,887*	*596,668*	*697,172*	*335,053*	*307,544*	*228,450*		
Network Radio	11,442	7,964	215	2,655	70	538		
National Spot Radio	38,597	4,741	8,742	781	3,542	20,791		
Local Radio	145,206	66,955	26,953	12,542	16,553	22,203		
Total Radio	*195,245*	*79,660*	*35,910*	*15,978*	*20,165*	*43,532*		
Outdoor	*72,967*	*48,735*	*5,778*	4,755	6,319	7,380		
Internet	*27,764*	*13,917*	*2,815*	2,306	6,924	1,802		
Total Measured Media	*2,542,324*	*785,007*	*748,698*	*361,661*	*361,225*	*285,733*		
Unmeasured Media	*1,462,527*	*963,338*	*153,348*	*178,130*	*73,985*	*93,726*		
Total Media Advertising	*4,004,851*	*1,748,345*	*902,046*	*539,791*	*435,210*	*379,459*		

Data source: "100 Leading National Advertisers." *Advertising Age.* (2007).

[1]Advertising spending in 2006.

APPENDIX 1.9A   The Top 25 U.S. Travel Agencies[1]

COMPANY	HEADQUARTERS	TOTAL SALES ($ million)
1. American Express Business Travel	New York, NY	26,400.00
2. Carlson Wagonlit Travel	Minneapolis, MN	24,900.00
3. Expedia.com	Bellevue, WA	20,000.00
4. Hogg Robinson Group (HRG)	New York, NY	16,000.00
5. BCD Travel	Wassenaar, Netherlands	12,000.00
6. Orbitz.com	Chicago, IL	10,800.00
7. Travelocity.com	Southlake, TX	10,000.00
8. Priceline.com	Norwalk, CT	4,800.00
9. AAA Travel	Heathrow, FL	4,150.00
10. Liberty Travel	Ramsey, NJ	1,770.00
11. Omega World Travel	Fairfax, VA	1,450.00
12. STA Travel	Dallas, TX	1,180.00
13. Travel and Transport	Omaha, NE	1,000.00
14. Travel Acquisitions Group	Eden Prairie, MN	862.30
15. Tzell Travel Group	New York, NY	858.00
16. Travizon	Woburn, MA	776.00
17. World Travel Holdings	Port Washington, NY	735.00
18. Travel Solutions	Columbus, OH	604.70
19. Protravel International	New York, NY	590.00
20. World Travel Inc.	Douglasville, PA	554.00
21. Altour International	New York, NY	535.00
22. Boeing Travel Management Group	Hazelwood, MO	515.20
23. Ovation Corporate Travel/The Lawyers' Travel Services	New York, NY	490.00
24. Travelers Advantage	Nashville, TN	460.00
25. Garber/FCm Travel Solutions	Chestnut Hill, MA	426.00
TOTAL		141,856.20

Data source: "Travel Weekly's Power List 2008." *Travel Weekly.* (2008).

[1]Ranked by estimated total sales in 2007.

APPENDIX 1.9B   The Leading North American Full-service Meeting and Incentive Companies[1]

COMPANY	HEADQUARTERS	INCENTIVE PROGRAMS[2]	CORPORATE MEETINGS	ROOM NIGHTS	FULL-TIME STAFF
Advantage Performance Network	Savage, MN	48	78	50,000	115
Ambassadors, LLC	Newport Beach, CA	105	82	535,000	137
American Express Business Travel	New York, NY		9,000	1,000,000+	300+
BCD Meetings & Incentives	Chicago, IL	339	3,202	378,408	185
BI	Edina, MN	125	725	425,000	925
Bucom International Inc.	Chicago, IL	8	55	25,000	16
Carlson Marketing Worldwide	Minneapolis, MN	387	896	360,000	2,526
Creative Group Inc.	Appleton, WI	68	321	150,000	116
Enterprise Events Group	San Rafael, CA	18	69	94,770	96
Excellence in Motivation	Dayton, OH	84	20	86,000	300
Experient	Twinsburg, OH		1,363	483,549	698
Fox Premier Meetings and Incentives	Oshkosh, WI	85	62	20,000	17
Gavel International inc.	Lincolnshire, IL	75	115	212,000	48
George P. Johnson	Auburn Hills, MI	100+	550+	240,997	1,319
Gray Consulting International Meetings & Incentives	Philadelphia, PA	2	205	25,216	53
Maritz Travel Co.	Fenton, MO	395	2,124	876,000	855
McVeigh Associates, Ltd.	Amityville, NY	22	425	125,000	86
Meeting Alliance	Robbinsville, NJ	6	75	68,000	19
Meeting Expectations	Atlanta, GA	20	220	30,000	70
Meridian Group Travel	Hazelwood, MO	180	32	155,000	100
Motivaction, LLC	Minneapolis, MN	28	64	56,000	145
R/A Performance Group	San Francisco, CA	48	26	53,000	30
SDI Travel and Incentives	Chicago, IL	48	40	23,700	15
TBA Global, LLC	Los Angeles, CA	76+	547+	164,550	210
USMotivation	Atlanta, GA	62	30	91,176	137

Data source: "The CMI 25." *Corporate Meetings & Incentives,* 2008.

[1] Listed in alphabetic order; not ranked.
[2] Approximate number of programs in 2007.

APPENDIX 1.10A   **The Budgets of Leading National Tourism Offices**[1]

COUNTRY	ORGANIZATION	LOCAL CURRENCY	US$ EQUIVALENT
Australia	Tourism Australia	A$ 161,054,000	$145,269,326
Austria	Austrian Tourist Office	€50,778,000	$74,307,320
Canada	Canadian Tourism Commission	C$ 104,362,000	$104,419,427
France	Direction du Tourisme	€172,720,000	$252,757,678
Hong Kong	Hong Kong Tourism Board	HK$ 711,999,513	$91,299,114
Ireland	Tourism Ireland	€78,769,000	$115,283,929
New Zealand	Tourism New Zealand	NZ$ 77,410,000	$60,780,240
Singapore	Singapore Tourism Board	S$ 176,692,000	$124,752,526
South Africa	South African Tourism Board	592,100,870	$77,142,036
Spain	Turespana	€148,000,000	$216,589,073
United Kingdom	VisitBritain	£55,100,000.00	$108,495,201

Data source: Annual reports on NTOs, author's research.

[1]Listed in alphabetic order; not ranked, for 2006 or 2007.

APPENDIX 1.10B The Top 25 State Tourism Budgets for 2007–2008

STATE	BUDGET
1. Hawaii	$85,100,000
2. Texas	$63,169,169
3. California	$57,987,914
4. Illinois	$50,400,000
5. Florida	$42,123,203
6. Pennsylvania	$31,840,000
7. Louisiana	$28,963,382
8. South Carolina	$28,097,267
9. Arizona	$24,986,829
10. Colorado	$22,671,508
11. Tennessee	$20,782,300
12. Missouri	$20,659,810
13. Utah	$19,583,500
14. Nevada	$19,279,583
15. Virginia	$18,499,923
16. New Mexico	$16,853,100
17. Arkansas	$16,425,158
18. New York	$16,000,000
19. Kentucky	$15,830,500
20. Wisconsin	$15,142,500
21. North Carolina	$13,684,291
22. Alabama	$12,642,405
23. Georgia	$12,614,321
24. Oklahoma	$12,426,380
25. Michigan	$11,993,725
TOTALS	$677,756,768

Data source: 2007–2008 Survey of State Tourism Offices. U.S. Travel Association. (2008).

APPENDIX 1.11   The Leading Tourism Destinations in the World by Country[1]

COUNTRY	2005 (millions)	2006 (millions)	2007 (millions)
INTERNATIONAL TOURIST ARRIVALS			
1. France	75.9	78.9	81.9
2. Spain	55.9	58.2	59.2
3. United States	49.2	51.0	56.0
4. China	46.8	49.9	54.7
5. Italy	36.5	41.1	43.7
6. United Kingdom	28.0	30.7	30.7
7. Germany	21.5	23.5	24.4
8. Ukraine		18.9	23.1
9. Turkey		18.9	22.2
10. Mexico	19.9	21.4	21.4

COUNTRY	2005 ($ billions)	2006 ($ billions)	2007 ($ billions)
INTERNATIONAL TOURIST RECEIPTS			
1. United States	$81.8	$85.7	$96.7
2. Spain	$48.0	$51.1	$57.8
3. France	$42.3	$42.9	$54.2
4. Italy	$35.4	$38.1	$42.7
5. China	$29.3	$33.9	$41.9
6. United Kingdom	$30.7	$33.7	$37.6
7. Germany	$29.2	$32.8	$36.0
8. Australia	$16.9	$17.8	$22.2
9. Austria	$16.0	$16.6	$16.9
10. Turkey	$18.2	$16.9	$18.5

Data source: "Tourism Highlights, 2007 and 2008 Editions." *UN World Tourism Organization.*

[1]*Ranked by the data for 2007.*

APPENDIX 1.12 **The Most Visited Travel Websites in the U.S.**[1]

BRAND OR CHANNEL	UNIQUE AUDIENCE (thousands)	ACTIVE REACH (%)	TIME PER PERSON
1. MapQuest	15,940	11.92	12:07:38 AM[2]
2. Google Maps	9,544	7.14	0:02:12
3. Expedia	4,939	3.69	0:11:05
4. Southwest Airlines	3,979	2.98	0:11:21
5. Travelocity	3,843	2.87	0:10:32
6. Orbitz	3,005	2.25	0:06:40
7. Google Earth	2,870	2.15	0:20:54
8. American Airlines	2,470	1.85	0:17:54
9. Yahoo! Travel	2,344	1.75	0:02:14
10. AOL Travel	2,127	1.59	0:06:33

Data source: Nielsen//NetRatings AdRelevance, October 29, 2007.

[1] Ranked by the number of unique visitors to the sites for the week ending October 29, 2007.
[2] Time is shown in minutes and seconds.

Industry Resources

The author and Delmar affirm that the website addresses referenced herein were accurate at the time of printing. However, due to the fluid nature of the Internet, we cannot guarantee their accuracy for the life of the edition.

APPENDIX 2.1 Travel Trade Intermediaries and Trade Publications

INTERMEDIARY/PUBLICATION	WEB ADDRESS
RETAIL TRAVEL AGENTS, CORPORATE TRAVEL MANAGERS, AND AGENCIES	
ACTE Global Business Journal	http://www.acte.org/
Business Travel News Online	http://www.btnonline.com/
Cruise Trade Magazine	http://www.cruisetrade.com/
Frequent Flyer	http://www.frequentflyer.oag.com/
JAX FAX Travel Marketing Magazine	http://www.jaxfax.com/
Travel Agent Magazine	http://www.travelagentcentral.com/
Travel Daily News	http://www.traveldailynews.com/
Travel Trade	http://www.traveltrade.com/
Travel Weekly	http://www.travelyweekly.com/
TOUR WHOLESALERS AND OPERATORS	
Courier (NTA)	http://www.ntaonline.com/
The Group Travel Leader	http://www.grouptravelleader.com/
INCENTIVE TRAVEL PLANNERS	
CIM	http://www.cim-publications.de/
Corporate Meetings & Incentives	http://meetingsnet.com/
Incentive	http://www.incentivemag.com/
Motivation Strategies	http://www.info-now.com/
Potentials	http://www.potentialsmag.com/
Promo Magazine	http://www.promomagazine.com/
CONVENTION AND MEETING PLANNERS	
Association Meetings	http://meetingsnet.com/
Associations Now	http://www.asaenet.org/
Association Meetings International	http://www.meetpie.com/
Financial & Insurance Meetings	http://meetingsnet.com/
Journal of Association Leadership	http://www.asaenet.org/
Medical Meetings	http://meetingsnet.com/
Meetings & Conventions	http://www.mcmag.com/
Meetings & Incentive Travel	http://www.meetpie.com/
Meeting News	http://www.mimegasite.com/
Religious Conference Manager	http://meetingsnet.com/
Sales & Marketing Management Magazine	http://www.salesandmarketing.com/
Successful Meetings	http://www.mimegasite.com/

(continues)

APPENDIX 2.1 (continued)

INTERMEDIARY/PUBLICATION	WEB ADDRESS
Training	http://www.trainingmag.com/
Training & Development	http://www.astd.org/
NICHE AND SPECIAL INTEREST TRAVEL	
Bank Travel Management	http://www.banktravelmanagement.com/
Going on Faith	http://www.goingonfaith.com/
InfoHub	http://www.infohub.com/
Specialty Travel Index	http://www.specialtytravel.com/
TravelBound!	http://www.travelboundmagazine.com/

APPENDIX 2.2   Major Directories of Hospitality and Travel Facilities and Services

DIRECTORY NAMES	WEB ADDRESS
Berlitz Complete Guide to Cruising & Cruise Ships	http://www.berlitzbooks.com/
Cruise Industry Source Book	http://www.cruising.org/
Hotel & Travel Index Worldwide	http://hotelandtravelindex.travelweekly.com/
OAG Pocket Flight Guide	http://www.oag.com/
OAG Flight Guide North America	http://www.oag.com/
OAG Airport Guide	http://www.oag.com/
Official Meeting Facilities Guide (omfg.com)	http://www.omfg.com/
World Travel Guide	http://www.worldtravelguide.net/

APPENDIX 2.3 Key Trade Associations in the North American Hospitality and Travel Industry

INDUSTRY GROUP	WEB ADDRESS
1. CARRIERS	
Air Transport Association	http://www.air-transport.org/
Airlines Reporting Corporation	http://www.arccorp.com/
American Automobile Association	http://www.aaa.com/
American Bus Association	http://www.buses.org/
Amtrak	http://www.amtrak.com/
International Air Transport Association	http://www.iata.org/
International Airlines Travel Agency Network	http://www.iatan.org/
Recreation Vehicle Industry Association	http://www.rvia.org/
Regional Airline Association	http://www.raa.org/
United Motorcoach Association	http://www.uma.org/
Via Rail Canada	http://www.viarail.ca/
2. SUPPLIERS	
American Bed & Breakfast Association	http://www.abba.com/
American Gaming Association	http://www.americangaming.org/
American Hotel & Lodging Association	http://www.ahla.com/
American Resort Development Association	http://www.arda.org/
Canadian Restaurant and Foodservices Association	http://www.crfa.ca/
Convention Industry Council	http://www.conventionindustry.org/
Cruise Lines International Association	http://www.cruising.org/
Hotel Association of Canada	http://www.hotelassociation.ca/
Hotels Sales and Marketing Association International	http://www.hsmai.org/
International Association for Exhibitions & Events	http://www.iaee.com/
International Association of Amusement Parks and Attractions	http://www.iaapa.org/
International Association of Assembly Managers	http://www.iaam.org/
International Association of Conference Centers	http://www.iacconline.com/
International Association of Fairs and Expositions	http://www.fairsandexpos.com/
International Festivals & Events Association	http://www.ifea.com/
National Association of RV Parks and Campgrounds	http://www.arvc.org/
National Park and Recreation Association	http://www.nrpa.org/
National Restaurant Association	http://www.restaurant.org/
Professional Association of Innkeepers International	http://www.paii.org/
Society of Independent Show Organizers	http://www.siso.org/
World Waterpark Association	http://www.waterparks.org/

(continues)

APPENDIX 2.3   (continued)

INDUSTRY GROUP	WEB ADDRESS
3. THE TRAVEL TRADE	
Adventure Travel Trade Association	http://www.adventuretravel.biz/
American Society of Association Executives	http://www.asaenet.org/
American Society of Travel Agents	http://www.asta.org/
Association of Canadian Travel Agencies	http://www.acta.ca/
Association of Corporate Travel Executives	http://www.acte.org/
Association of Destination Management Executives	http://www.adme.org/
Association of Retail Travel Agents	http://www.artaonline.com/
Canadian Institute of Travel Counsellors	http://www.citc.ca/
Meeting Professionals International	http://www.mpiweb.org/
National Association of Commissioned Travel Agents	http://www.nacta.org/
National Business Travel Association	http://www.nbta.org/
National Tour Association	http://www.ntaonline.com/
Professional Conference Management Association	http://www.pcma.org/
Receptive Services Association of America	http://www.rsana.com/
Religious Conference Management Association	http://www.rcmaweb.org/
Reunion Friendly Network	http://www.reunionfriendly.com/
Society of Government Travel Professionals	http://government-travel.org/
Society of Incentive & Travel Executives	http://www.site-intl.org/
The Travel Institute	http://www.thetravelinstitute.com/
U.S. Air Consolidators Association	http://www.usaca.com/
U.S. Tour Operators Association	http://www.ustoa.com/
4. DESTINATION MANAGEMENT AND SUPPORT SERVICES	
Association of Travel Marketing Executives	http://www.atme.org/
Destination Marketing Association International	http://www.iacvb.org/
International CHRIE	http://www.chrie.org/
International Society of Travel and Tourism Educators	http://www.istte.org/
Society of American Travel Writers	http://www.satw.org/
The International Ecotourism Society	http://www.ecotourism.org/
The Travel and Tourism Research Association	http://www.ttra.com/
Tourism Industry Association of Canada	http://www.tiac-aitc.ca/
U.S. Travel Association	http://www.tia.org/
Western Association of Convention & Visitors Bureaus	http://www.wacvb.com/

APPENDIX 2.4 Major Consumer, Academic, and Trade Magazines in the Hospitality and Travel Industry

1. CONSUMER MAGAZINES

Arthur Frommer's Budget Travel Magazine	*Outdoor Life*
Backpacker Magazine	*Outside Magazine*
Blue	*Pathfinders*
Caribbean Travel & Life	*Resorts & Great Hotels*
Condé Nast Traveler	*Southern Living*
Cruise Travel	*Travel 50 & Beyond*
Endless Vacation	*Travel + Leisure*
Gourmet	*Travel + Leisure Golf*
Islands	*Travel Holiday*
Midwest Living	*Travel America*
National Geographic Traveler	*Vacations Magazine*

2. TRAVEL TRADE JOURNALS

Club Management	*Nation's Restaurant News*
Hotel & Motel Management	*Restaurant Business*
Hotels	*Restaurants and Institutions*
LH/Lodging Hospitality	*Restaurants USA*
Lodging	

3. ACADEMIC JOURNALS

ACTA Turistica	*Journal of Restaurant & Foodservice Marketing*
ANATOLIA	*Journal of Sports Tourism*
Annals of Tourism Research	*Journal of Sustainable Tourism*
Asia Pacific Journal of Tourism Research	*Journal of Teaching in Travel & Tourism*
Australian Journal of Hospitality Management	*Journal of The American Dietetic Association*
China Tourism Research	*Journal of Travel Research*
Cornell Hotel and Restaurant Administration Quarterly	*Journal of Travel & Tourism Marketing*
Current Issues in Tourism	*Journal of Travel & Tourism Research*
Event Tourism	*Journal of Vacation Marketing*
FIU Hospitality Review	*NACUFS Journal*
Gaming Research & Review Journal	*Pacific Tourism Review*
Journal of Information Technology & Tourism	*PRAXIS: The Journal of Applied Hospitality Management*
International Journal of Contemporary Hospitality Management	*Scandinavian Journal of Hospitality and Tourism*
International Journal of Hospitality Management	*School Foodservice Journal*
International Journal of Hospitality and Tourism Administration	*Teoros International*
Journal of Convention & Event Tourism	*The Tourist Review*
Journal of Ecotourism	*Tourism Analysis*

(continues)

APPENDIX 2.4 (continued)

3. ACADEMIC JOURNALS

Journal of Foodservice Systems	*Tourism: An International Interdisciplinary Journal*
Journal of Gambling Studies	*Tourism, Culture & Communication*
Journal of Hospitality & Leisure Marketing	*Tourism Economics*
Journal of Hospitality Financial Management	*Tourism Geographies*
Journal of Hospitality Marketing & Management	*Tourism and Hospitality Research*
Journal of Hospitality & Tourism Education	*Tourism Management*
Journal of Hospitality & Tourism Research	*Tourism Recreation Research*
Journal of Human Resources in Hospitality & Tourism	*Tourismus Journal*
Journal of Nutrition for the Elderly	*Tourist Studies*
Journal of Nutrition in Recipe & Menu Development	*Travel & Tourism Analyst*
Journal of Quality Assurance in Tourism	

GLOSSARY

Accountability research Research done to measure the results of a marketing plan, particularly, to determine if marketing objectives were achieved.

Accreditation The recognition of travel agencies, DMOs, or other hospitality and travel organizations by specific associations as meeting certain criteria.

Advertising (1) Any paid form of non-personal presentation or promotion of ideas, goods, or services by an identified sponsor. (2) The placement of announcements and persuasive messages in time or space purchased in any of the mass media by business firms, non-profit organizations, government agencies, and individuals who seek to inform and/or persuade members of a particular target market or audience about their products, services, organizations, or ideas. (American Marketing Association definitions).

Advertising agency A specialized company that provides advertising services to hospitality and travel organizations. Also may now be called creative service agency.

Advertorial An advertising message that is presented in an editorial format and is usually lengthier than a standard advertisement.

Affinity cards Credit cards issued by a bank or other financial institution that are linked with a specific hospitality and travel company, attraction, tourism destination, or non-profit organization.

Affinity group packages Vacation/holiday packages or tours arranged for groups that share some form of affinity, usually a close social, religious, or ethnic bond.

Affordable budgeting A method of budgeting for marketing, often used by small businesses, in which only what can be afforded, is spent.

AIDA formula An acronym for attention, interest, desire, action. This is a formula approach to personal selling. It is also used to describe the functions that advertisements need to play (get attention, create interest and a desire, and cause action).

AIOs Activities, interests, opinions.

All-inclusive packages A generic term for packages that include all or nearly all the elements that travelers require for their trips including airfare, lodging, ground transportation, taxes, and gratuities.

American Plan (AP) A rate that includes accommodation and three meals per day—typically breakfast, lunch, and dinner.

Appointed A retail travel agency receives a designation from an association, airline, cruise line, or other supplier or carrier to act as a sales agent for them.

Approach This is part of the second step in the sales process. It includes various activities leading up to the sales presentation including making appointments with prospects, establishing rapport, and checking out preliminary details.

Arbitrary budgeting Allocating a marketing budget of approximately the same size as previous years.

Attitude(s) Predisposition to evaluate some symbol, object, or aspect of the world in a favorable or unfavorable manner.

B2B (business to business) The business transacted among suppliers, carriers, travel trade intermediaries, and DMOs.

Baby Boomers A demographic segment of the population consisting of people born between 1946 and 1964.

Balanced Scorecard Approach (BSC) A performance measurement approach for a company that was originally developed by R. Kaplan and D. Norton.

Banner advertisements Advertisements placed on a website, usually by an organization other than the one that owns the site.

Bed and Breakfast (B & B) A rate that combines a night's accommodation with a breakfast the following day that can be either a full or continental breakfast.

Behavioral segmentation Divides customers by their usage rates, usage status and potential, brand loyalty, use occasions, and benefits sought.

Benefit segmentation A type of behavioral segmentation. It groups customers according to similarities in the benefits they look for in specific products or services.

Bid A proposal submitted by a hotel, destination, or other organization in response to an RFP.

Blind prospecting Involves the use of telephone directories, the Internet, and other published lists to find sales prospects. The sales representative has no prior knowledge of the people on the lists and has no idea if they are true sales prospects.

Blocking space Reserving groups (blocks) of rooms or seats for tour wholesalers or other group customers.

Blogs (Web logs) Newer ways to communicate among and with customers. They are written by customers, corporate executives, or marketing/public relations officers.

Brand extension Using the leverage of a well-known brand name in one category to launch a new product in a different category.

Brand loyalty The extent to which a customer repeatedly buys a specific brand of product or service.

Brand segmentation Developing brands that are designed to appeal to a specific target market or sets of target markets, e.g., broad types of hotels that are aimed at different customer profiles.

Branding Developing a mark (logo), symbol, set of words, or combination of these to differentiate an organization from others.

Break-even analysis A technique used in pricing based on the consideration of fixed and variable costs, customer volumes, and profit margins.

Broadcast media Advertisements displayed by means of electronics, encompassing television (including cable), radio, videotape, and computer-generated graphic presentations.

Budget hotel A hotel which operates with the low-price approach.

Budgeting Allocating human resources and money toward the implementation of marketing plans.

Building-block procedure (for marketing budgets) A carefully sequenced, step-by-step process for developing a marketing budget. Also known as the objective-and-task approach.

Business travel market One of the two main divisions of the hospitality and travel market. This includes people traveling and dining out for business purposes, and those attending conventions and meetings, and on incentive travel trips.

Buying process Stages customers go through before and after making a purchase. The stages are need recognition, search for information, pre-purchase evaluation of alternatives, purchase, consumption, post-consumption evaluation, and divestment.

Call centers A department operated by several large airlines and lodging companies for trained telephone reservationists to provide information and accept bookings.

Canned sales presentations Methods for making sales presentations in which sales representatives know exactly what they will say beforehand. All or parts of the presentations are memorized.

Cannibalize A situation where one of an organization's brands takes customers away from one or more of the organization's other brands.

Capital budget A projection of the capital investment expected in a new hospitality and travel business.

Carriers Airlines, railways, ferries, bus and motor coach companies, and canals.

Case studies A primary research technique that produces in-depth, qualitative information on comparable hospitality and travel organizations or other specific situations relating to marketing hospitality and travel services.

Celebrity testimonials A type of advertising message format in which a well-known celebrity recommends or otherwise endorses the service or product.

Change As one of the five Cs of marketing research, this refers to trends that have occurred among customers and competitors.

Channel-of-distribution segmentation Dividing up travel trade intermediaries (the travel trade) by function and by common characteristics shared by functional groups.

Channels of distribution Direct or indirect (through the travel trade) distribution arrangements used by suppliers, carriers, and DMOs.

Charter tour A trip or package where the aircraft or other equipment is chartered (rented) by a tour wholesaler, tour operator, or another individual or group.

Circulation The number of households who subscribe to a given magazine or newspaper. It is one of the measures of reach in advertising.

Click-through rate A measurement to track the number of people that follow a hyperlink within an advertisement or editorial content to another website or frame within a website.

Closing Getting a sales prospect's agreement on the objectives of the sales call, normally implying a definite sale or reservation.

Clutter This is a factor considered when evaluating advertising media alternatives. It represents the number of ads in one newspaper or magazine issue, or one radio or television program.

Co-branding Also sometimes referred to as dual branding, this is the offering of two or more brands at one location, e.g., combining a KFC restaurant with a Taco Bell.

Co-production Various self-service options in the hospitality and travel industry that include salad and buffet bars, cafeterias, airline boarding card and e-ticket dispensing machines, and so on.

Cognitive dissonance Also sometimes called post-purchase doubt, this is a feeling of anxiety that a person experiences after making a purchase.

Cold calling or canvassing A type of blind prospecting in the field. Sales representatives call on individuals or organizations with no idea if these people will turn out to be true sales prospects.

Combiners Organizations that recognize that they serve different market segments but choose to ignore these differences when marketing. This is one of four alternative marketing strategies available to organizations.

Comment cards In-house, self-administered surveys that typically generate a low response rate.

Commercial information sources The advertising and other promotional materials designed by corporations and other organizations.

Commercial sources   (See commercial information sources.)

Commission caps   First initiated by Delta Air Lines in 1995, these caps placed a maximum amount in dollar terms on the amount of commission paid by the airlines.

Commissionable (packages)   Packages where suppliers, carriers, and DMOs agree to pay the travel agent a commission.

Communications process   The process through which hospitality and travel marketers communicate with customers consisting of nine elements—source, encoding, message, medium, decoding, noise, receiver, response, and feedback.

Community involvement   Various activities undertaken by a hospitality and travel organization and its employees to help or serve the local community. This is considered part of the public relations effort.

Comparative advertising   An advertising message format in which direct comparisons are made between the sponsor and specific competitors.

Competition   For hospitality and travel organizations, this includes: (1) direct competition, (2) substitute services, and (3) indirect competition.

Competitive budgeting   (See competitive-parity budgeting.)

Competitive pricing   A marketing approach in which companies try to match competitors' prices closely.

Competitive-parity budgeting   An unsophisticated approach to setting a marketing budget. Marketing expenditures are set at approximately the same amount as competitors.

Competitors   Organizations with similar services or products competing to satisfy the needs of the same customer groups. Also, this is one of the marketing environment factors.

Concentrated marketing strategy   An approach to marketing where a few market segments are chosen from among several and attention is concentrated on these selected market segments.

Conclusive research   Information gained through research that helps solve a business problem or assess a marketing opportunity.

Confidence   One of the five Cs of marketing research in which the marketer believes that a prediction or decision is more likely to be accurate or successful.

Consultative selling   It is a customized sales presentation approach in which the salesperson is viewed as an expert and serves as a consultant to the customer. The salesperson identifies the prospects' needs and recommends the best solution even if the best solution does not require the salesperson's products or services.

Consumer advertising   Advertising aimed at the customers who will actually use the services being promoted.

Contests   A sales promotion technique where entrants win prizes on the basis of some skill requirement that they are asked to demonstrate.

Contextual differences   Unique characteristics of organizations in the service industries, including hospitality and travel, that exist because of the ways they have been managed and regulated.

Continental Plan (CP)   A meal and accommodation package that includes a room and a cold breakfast.

Contingency planning   This is where some flexibility is built into marketing plans and budgets to allow for unexpected events.

Continuity programs   Sales promotions that require people to make several purchases, sometimes over a long period of time.

Contribution margin   The difference between the selling price and the variable costs per unit.

Convention and visitors bureau (CVB)   A term coined in North America for an organization, typically non-profit, that is responsible for marketing a specific destination. A CVB is a type of DMO. In the United States, the majority of funding comes through room taxes.

Convention/meeting packages   Special packages offered by resorts, hotels, and conference centers to attract conventions and meetings. Normally, they include accommodation and meals, but they may also incorporate local tours, attraction admissions, special events, or programs.

Convention/meeting planners (MICE market)   Persons who plan and coordinate meetings and conventions. Some belong to major national associations, large non-profit organizations, government agencies, educational institutions, and large corporations. Others work for specialized convention management consulting firms.

Conversion rate   Used with direct-response advertising, this is the percentage of customers who enquire that actually buy or use the sponsor's advertised hospitality and travel service.

Cookie   A type of software technology that enables marketers to recognize return visitors to websites.

Cooperative advertising   A situation where two or more organizations share the costs of an advertisement or advertising campaign.

Cooperative promotion (partnership)   A situation where two or more organizations share the costs of a promotional effort (advertising, sales promotion, personal selling, public relations or publicity, or website development/maintenance).

Co-opetition   Communication channels with competitors are opened to allow for the exploration of areas of mutual interest in the future.

Copy platform   A statement that fully describes the (advertising) message idea and serves as the foundation for the copy (text) within an advertising campaign.

Core principles of marketing   The seven basic principles of marketing: the marketing concept, marketing or customer orientation, satisfying customers' needs and wants, market segmentation, value and the exchange process, product life cycle, and marketing mix.

Corporate travel agencies   Also known as outplants, these are retail travel agencies specializing, either partly or wholly, in handling corporate or government accounts.

Corporate travel managers   Individuals employed by corporations, associations, government agencies, and other types of organizations to coordinate the organization's travel arrangements.

Cost per thousand (CPM)   This is a criterion used to evaluate alternative advertising media and vehicles based on the cost per thousand readers, viewers, or listeners reached.

Cost-plus pricing   Also known as mark-up pricing, this pricing approach involves the addition of a certain monetary amount or percentage to the actual or estimated costs of a service to arrive at a final price.

Coupon redemption rates   The percentages of total coupons issued that are used (redeemed) by customers.

Coupons   Vouchers or certificates that entitle customers or intermediaries to a price cut on the couponed product or services.

Credibility   One of the five Cs of marketing research referring to the level of believability attached to the marketer's information or facts.

Crisis management plan   A contingency plan drawn up by a DMO, hotel, or other organization to deal with unexpected emergency situations, e.g., a major natural disaster.

Critical success factor (CSF)   A characteristic, strategy, or approach that industry experts believe is required for success in a particular area of business.

Cruise-only agents   Retail travel agencies involved exclusively in selling and booking cruises.

Culture   A combination of the beliefs, values, attitudes, habits, traditions, customs, and forms of behavior that are shared by a group of people.

Customer behavior   The ways in which customers select, use, and behave after they have purchased hospitality and travel services.

Customer mix   The combination of customers that use or are attracted to a specific hospitality and travel organization or destination.

Customer needs   Gaps between what customers have and what they would like to have.

Customer relationship management (CRM)   A strategy used by a hospitality and travel organization to select customers and to maintain relationships with these customers to increase their lifetime value (LTV).

Customer wants   Needs of which customers are aware.

Customers   One of the five Cs of marketing research referring to the importance of gathering and analyzing data on past and potential guests.

Customer trends (Changes in demand)   Changes in the demand from hospitality and travel customers as a result of: (1) demographic and socio-economic trends; (2) geographic trends; (3) purpose of trip trends; (4) psychographic trends; (5) behavioral trends; (6) product-related trends on the demand side; and (7) distribution channel trends on the demand side.

Database marketing   An approach by which computer database technologies are harnessed to design, create, and manage customer data lists containing information about each customer's characteristics and history of interactions with the company. The lists are used as needed for locating, selecting, targeting, servicing, and establishing relationships with customers in order to enhance the long-term value of these customers to the company. The techniques used for managing lists include: 1. database manipulation methods such as select and join, 2. statistical methods for predicting each customer's likelihood of future purchases of specific items based on his/her history of past purchases, and 3. measures for computing the lifetime value of a customer on an ongoing basis (American Marketing Association definition).

Databases   Detailed information on individual customers maintained in computerized systems by individual hospitality and travel organizations.

Decline stage   This is the final stage in the product life cycle when the sales of a service begin to fall.

Decoding   Part of the communications process. This is when customers interpret promotional messages in such a way that the messages have real meaning for them.

Demographic segmentation   Dividing up markets based on population statistics.

Destination management companies (DMCs)   A professional services company possessing extensive local knowledge, expertise, and resources, specializing in the design and implementation of events, activities, tours, transportation and program logistics.

Destination marketing organizations (DMOs)   Government agencies, convention and visitors bureaus (CVBs), travel associations, and other bodies that market travel to their respective destination areas.

Designated market area (DMA)   The geographic area composed of all the counties that a specific television station influences.

Destination mix   A unique relationship found in the hospitality and travel industry involving attractions and events, facilities, infrastructure and transportation amenities, and hospitality resources.

Destination package   A travel package characterized by the destination it features.

Differential pricing   (See price discrimination.)

Differentiated marketing strategies   Marketing approaches that recognize differences between target markets by using individualized marketing mixes.

Digital marketing   All the types of marketing communication that involve digital technologies, including the Web, e-mail, CD-ROM, and other forms of transmission of text and images in a digital format.

Direct distribution   Where the organization itself assumes the total responsibility for promoting, reserving, and providing services to customers.

Direct mail   An advertising medium involving the mailing of promotional materials to customers and intermediaries.

Direct marketing   A form of hospitality and travel promotion in which no intermediaries are used. Booking is made or information requested directly from the sponsoring organization. The major elements of direct marketing are direct mail, telemarketing, and home shopping through television and by personal computer.

Direct-response advertising   A form of direct marketing which encourages the hospitality and travel customer to take immediate action or make an immediate response directly to the advertiser (American Marketing Association definition).

Director of Sales (DOS)   The individuals whose task is preparing sales plans. The sales management functions for which these individuals are responsible include (1) sales-force staffing and operations, (2) sales planning, and (3) sales performance evaluation.

Discounting   A common pricing practice in the hospitality and travel industry in which fares, rates, or prices are below the advertised figures. This is usually done by target market.

Discriminatory pricing   (See price discrimination.)

Disintermediation   Giving the customer direct access to information or reservations, often electronically. This enables the customer to bypass travel trade intermediaries.

Distribution channel   A particular direct or indirect distribution arrangement used by a supplier, carrier, or DMO.

Distribution mix   The combination of direct and indirect distribution channels used by a hospitality and travel organization to make customers aware of its services and to reserve and deliver them.

Dominance   The ability of an advertising sponsor to dominate a particular medium at a specific time.

Double occupancy basis   A rate for a lodging property that is based on the assumption that two persons will be sharing the room or unit.

Dynamic packaging   This is an interactive online feature that allows customers or travel trade intermediaries to assemble their own packages by selecting those elements that meet their own or clients' needs.

E-commerce   The online purchasing of hospitality and travel services, mainly through the Web and by e-mail.

Economic environment   The overall condition of the economy at the local, regional, national, and international levels.

Economic feasibility   The analysis of a development project to determine if it will produce a sufficient return on investment (ROI).

Efficiency ratios   Statistical measurements that marketing managers use to evaluate their organizations' efficiency in using promotional and distribution mix elements.

Eight Ps (8 Ps)   Product, place, promotion, price, people, packaging, programming, and partnership—the eight elements of a hospitality and travel organization's marketing mix.

80-20 principle   A common problem found in marketing in which 80% of the effort or resources are put into capturing 20% of the total sales volume.

Elasticity of demand   The sensitivity of customer demand to changes in the prices of services.

Empowerment Giving hospitality and travel employees the authority to identify and solve guest problems or complaints on the spot and to make improvements in work processes when necessary.

Encoding Part of the communications process in which the sponsor translates the message to be communicated into an arrangement of words, pictures, colors, sounds, movements, and even body language.

Escorted tours Packages that follow a predetermined itinerary and provide tour escorts and guides to accompany the travelers.

European plan (EP) An accommodation-only rate that includes no meals.

Evaluation research Research that is completed to determine the effectiveness of a hospitality and travel organization's marketing efforts, also referred to as accountability research.

Event packages Packages developed around special, one-time events, festivals, entertainment and cultural performances, or other occurrences.

Evoked set The set of hospitality or travel brands, or destinations, from which the customer selects for a specific purchase occasion.

Exchange process A process through which suppliers of hospitality and travel services and their customers trade items of value.

Executive summary A few pages usually positioned at the beginning of a marketing plan that sum up the plan's main sections. It is for the organization's executives to quickly review.

Experience clues Customers cannot see, sample, or self-evaluate services because of their intangibility, but they can see and sense various experience clues associated with these services.

Experimental research A category of primary research in the hospitality and travel industry. It involves tests of various kinds to determine the

likely reactions of customers to new services or products.

Explicit communication Promotional messages explicitly (clearly and intentionally) given to customers through the use of language, either orally (e.g., via television, radio, telephone, or personal selling) or in a written format (e.g., via direct mail, magazine or newspaper ads, websites, or sales proposals).

Exploratory research Information collection techniques that shed more light on a research problem or opportunity but that do not help solve or assess the problem or opportunity.

Exposure A term used in advertising to describe the numbers of customers who read, see, or hear advertisements.

External customers The guests or customers of a hospitality and travel organization.

External environment Events (marketing environment factors) that are completely beyond the control of the marketing manager and that shape the way business is done.

External secondary research data Previously published information obtained from sources outside the hospitality and travel organization, including government agencies, DMOs, magazines, journals and newspapers, research companies and private consulting organizations, and universities.

Familiarization (fam) trips or tours Free or reduced-priced trips given to travel agencies, tour wholesalers and operators, travel writers, and other intermediaries by suppliers, carriers, and DMOs.

Family life-cycle Predictable stages that families pass through over a period of time.

Family vacation or holiday packages Vacation or holiday packages that provide something for everyone in parent-children households.

FAQs (frequently asked questions) A set of predetermined questions and answers that are supplied on a website.

Fear appeal   An advertising message format that uses a negative emotional appeal to arouse or shock the customer into a purchase or change of attitude.

Feasibility analysis   A study of the potential demand and economic feasibility of a business or other type of organization.

Feature stories   Also known as features, these are articles or stories of human interest that entertain, inform, or educate readers, viewers, or listeners.

Feedback   An element of all systems, feedback is used in two slightly different ways in this book. First, it is said that there must be feedback mechanisms in the hospitality and travel marketing system. Second, feedback is said to be an element in the communications process (a system itself); the response message that the receiver (customer) transmits back to the source (sponsor).

Field sales   Also known as external selling, these are selling efforts taking place in person outside the hospitality and travel organization's place of business.

Five Cs of research   The five major reasons for doing marketing research including customers, competition, confidence, credibility, and change.

Five Ds of positioning   These are five sequential steps that an organization should follow for effective positioning—documenting, deciding, differentiating, designing, and delivering.

Fixed costs   Costs that remain the same no matter how many customers buy the package or other services.

Fly-cruise packages   Mostly offered by cruise line companies, these are packages that include round-trip airfare to a port of departure plus a cruise.

Fly-drive packages   Single-price packages with round-trip airfare and car rental at destinations.

Fly-rail packages   A type of hospitality and travel package that includes air and railway travel.

Focus group   A form of personal interviewing in which the researcher directs questions to a small group of people.

Follow-the-leader pricing   A pricing approach where, if one company (e.g., Burger King) raises its prices, others (McDonald's and Wendy's) also do so.

Foreign independent tour (FIT)   Custom-designed packages arranged by travel agents or other foreign independent travel specialists that fit individual client's needs while traveling in foreign countries.

Four Ps   The four factors traditionally considered to comprise an organization's marketing mix—product, price, place, and promotion.

Free-standing inserts (FSIs)   Separate, pre-printed, and multi-page sections that fit into a daily or Sunday editions. These may or may not incorporate coupons.

Frequency   A criterion for evaluating alternative advertising media based on the average number of times potential customers are exposed to a given advertisement or advertising campaign.

Frequent flyer programs   Continuity recognition programs first introduced by U.S. airlines in the early 1980s. This sales promotion technique awards free trips, upgrades, and other prizes to passengers after they have logged certain numbers of air miles with the airline.

Frequent guest award programs   Continuity recognition programs, similar to frequent flyer programs, first introduced by lodging chains in the early 1980s. This sales promotion technique awards free accommodation, upgrades, and other prizes to guests after they have spent certain numbers of room nights with the chain.

Frequent travelers   People, especially business travelers, who make more than the average number of trips.

Frequently asked questions (FAQs)   A set of predetermined questions and answers that are supplied on a website.

Full-coverage marketing strategy   A marketing strategy, often followed by industry leaders, where the company appeals to all market segments in the total market with a tailor-made approach for each market segment.

Games   Sales promotion events, very much like sweepstakes, that involve the use of game pieces, such as scratch-and-win cards.

Gaming   It is defined by the AGA as the action or habit of playing at games of chance for stakes.

GDSs (Global Distribution Systems)   These include Sabre, Travelport, and Amadeus, and are electronic systems for booking and reserving hospitality and travel services. They have existed for around 50 years and are mainly used by retail travel agencies.

General positioning approach   An approach to creating an image for an organization or destination that promises more than one benefit. These benefits may not be very obvious to the customer.

Generation X   A demographic segment of the population consisting of those people born between the early 1960s and early 1980s.

Generic differences   Unchangeable differences shared by all services that affect the marketing of services.

Geo-demographic segmentation   A two-stage market segmentation approach using the geographic and demographic characteristics of customers.

Geographic segmentation   Dividing the market into groups of customers who share the same geographic location.

Gift certificates   Vouchers or checks that are either selectively given away by the sponsor or sold to customers who, in turn, give them to others as gifts.

GIS (Geographic Information System)   GIS maps demographic and socio-economic characteristics of potential customers within trading areas.

Green marketing   These are marketing programs for which hospitality and travel organizations develop actions to protect the environment and communicate these actions to customers.

Gross rating point (GRP)   An exposure measure used in evaluating advertising success. It is calculated by multiplying the reach percentage (percent of target market customers exposed to advertising) by the frequency (average number of exposures per target market customer reached).

Group inclusive tour (GIT)   An all-inclusive package with a specified minimum size (number of travelers) involving one or more groups traveling on scheduled or chartered air service.

Growth stage   The second stage of the product life cycle when sales climb rapidly and profit levels improve.

Guests   The customers of a hospitality and travel organization.

Handling objections   Techniques that sales representatives use to address objections that prospects raise or indicate about sales presentations. This is a step in the sales process.

Heavy-half or use-frequency segmentation   Dividing the overall market based on the number of times a service is purchased or upon each segment's share of total demand.

Historical budgeting   A form of arbitrary budgeting that involves taking last year's marketing budget and adding a certain monetary amount or percentage to it.

Home-based agents   A special group of travel agents that has emerged due to the ability to use the Internet from the agent's home.

Horizontal integration   Developing or acquiring similar businesses.

Hospitality and travel industry   A group of interrelated organizations providing personal services to customers who are away from home.

Hospitality and travel marketing environment   All the factors to be considered when making marketing decisions.

Hospitality and travel marketing system   A five-step, systematic process for marketing a hospitality and travel organization based on answering the questions: (1) Where are we now? (2) Where would we like to be? (3) How do we get there? (4) How do we make sure we get there? (5) How do we know if we got there?

Hosts   The people who work within hospitality and travel organizations and that serve guests.

Hotel revenue manager   Individuals who have been specially trained to contribute to hotel profits and add to the hotel's asset values.

Hubbart Formula   A target-pricing method used by lodging facilities. This involves building an income statement up from the bottom to determine the room rates necessary to provide a predetermined return on investment.

Iceberg effect   When marketing managers make decisions based on superficial information.

Implementation plan   One of the main parts of the marketing plan, this details the marketing budget, staff responsibilities, activities, timetable, and methods of controlling, measuring, and evaluating activities.

Implicit communication   Promotional cues or messages conveyed through body language or other non-verbal means.

Inbound tour operator   Tour operators that specialize in providing local services to other tour operators in specific countries or destinations.

Incentive packages   All-inclusive packages given by corporations and other organizations as a reward for outstanding performance from employees, dealers, and others.

Incentive travel   Travel by persons who have received incentive packages as a reward for outstanding performance.

Incentive travel planners   Specialized tour wholesalers who assemble incentive packages for sponsoring organizations.

Incremental budgeting   Using the current period's budget as the foundation for next year's budget, and adding (or deducting) a certain percentage or specific amount of money.

Indirect distribution   A situation in which part of the responsibility for promoting, reserving, and providing services is given to one or more other hospitality and travel organizations especially travel trade intermediaries.

Individual customers   Individual people or families who make their own hospitality and travel decisions.

Individual depth interviews   A qualitative research technique involving a meeting of one interviewer and one interviewee for about 45 minutes to one hour.

Infomercial   A form of direct marketing including responses generated by television.

Inplants   An office of a retail travel agency located on the premises of a corporate client.

Inseparability   Some hospitality and travel services (e.g., restaurants and tennis camps) are closely associated with the individuals who provide them. Without these individuals, the services would not have the same appeal.

Inside sales   Also known as internal selling, these are personal selling efforts within an organization's place of business to either increase the likelihood of a sale or to add to customers' average spending levels.

Institutional advertisements   An advertising message format in which the philosophy or goodwill of an organization or industry sector is promoted.

Intangibility   A generic difference shared by all services. It means that most services have to be purchased in order to experience them.

Integrated marketing communications (IMC) The planning and coordination of all the promotional mix elements and Internet marketing so that they are as consistent and mutually supportive as possible. This is also used to refer to the closer coordination of a hospitality and travel organization's promotional consultants and advisors (advertising agencies, sales promotion firms, public relations consultants). A planning process designed to assure that all brand contacts received by a customer or prospect for a product, service, or organization are relevant to that person and consistent over time.

Interactive marketing Using interactive media to enable buyer-seller electronic communications in a computer-mediated environment. The customer controls the type and amount of information that is received from the organization.

Interactive media A combination of electronic and communication devices (e.g., television, personal computers, phone lines) that permit customers to interact with a hospitality and travel organization's information or reservation services. Includes all the features of the Internet and mobile technologies.

Interdependency (interdependent) This unique characteristic of the hospitality and travel industry occurs because several organizations usually contribute to satisfying customers' needs and wants.

Interests Things that people spend time on and that get their attentions including families, homes, jobs, hobbies, recreational pursuits, communities, clothes, food and drink preferences, and other items.

Intermediaries Also known as the travel trade and channels of distribution, these include retail travel agents, tour wholesalers and operators, corporate travel managers and agencies, incentive travel planners, convention/meeting planners and online travel companies.

Internal customers All of the employees of a hospitality and travel organization.

Internal marketing Includes all the efforts in which an organization engages to communicate with its employees in support of its customer marketing efforts.

Internal secondary research data Customer databases and other information contained within a hospitality and travel organization's own records.

Internal sources Information stored in a person's mind, including past experiences with a service and recollections of related promotions.

Internet A system connecting millions of computers around the world. The Internet's main elements include the Web, e-mail, File Transfer Protocol (FTP), and Gopher.

Interpersonal factors The outside influence of other people on customer behavior including factors such as cultures and subcultures, reference groups, social classes, opinion leaders, and the family.

Introduction stage The first stage in the product life cycle when a new service is first offered to the public.

Intuitive pricing An unscientific pricing approach based solely on management's intuition.

Laws and government regulations Legislation that dictates how business is done. They directly affect the ways that services and products can be marketed, and they are constantly changing. It is an uncontrollable factor in the hospitality and travel marketing environment.

Lead prospecting Techniques used by sales representatives to pinpoint leads or potential sales prospects.

Lead time The space of time between the design of an advertisement and its actual appearance in the selected medium.

Leader pricing A form of promotional pricing where one or more services or products is offered for a short time at a price below its actual costs.

Learning A personal factor that influences customer behavior and that develops through a combination of factors including needs, motives, objectives, cues, responses, and reinforcement.

Lifestyle The way people live based on their activities, interests, and opinions (AIOs).

Lifestyle hotel An umbrella term for town house, boutique, designer, and themed hotels. These are usually small, specialized properties that fill a niche within the luxury hotel segment. Their main features are individual and contemporary character, smaller properties, high levels of personal service, reflective of the personality/style of their designers or owners/operators, and stylish, carefully designed buildings and interiors.

Lifestyle segmentation   Also known as psychographic segmentation, this is a market segmentation approach that divides the market by lifestyle categories.

Lifetime value (LTV)   A concept associated with relationship marketing and customer relationship management (CRM) in which the lifetime value of individual customers is considered. The customer is viewed as a long-term asset of the organization rather than as a one-time transaction.

Location and community analysis   A step followed in market, feasibility, and situation analyses to determine how a given site and community will contribute to a business' success.

Log file analyzer programs   Programs that analyze the traffic to websites.

Log files   Server files that record the traffic patterns for a website.

Long-term planning   Also known as strategic planning, this involves planning for a period of three or more years into the future.

Low-cost carriers (LCCs)   Airlines which operate only one class of service, with a single type of short-haul aircraft, and take reservations mainly through the Internet and by phone.

Loyalty programs   Programs to build loyalty to the company among frequent customers. These programs identify and build databases of frequent customers to promote directly to them, and to reward and provide special services for those frequent customers.

Macro-system   Every organization in the hospitality and travel industry.

Management contract   A contract between the owners of a hotel and a hotel management company that specifies the duties of each party and the formula for sharing revenues and profits.

Marginal economic budgeting   An idealistic approach to budgeting in which sponsors spend money on promotional mix elements up to the point where the last dollar spent brings in exactly one dollar in sales.

Market analysis   A study of the potential demand for a new hospitality and travel business.

Market potential analysis   A research component of a market or feasibility analysis that determines if there are enough potential customers for a new hospitality or travel business.

Market segment   An identifiable component group of an overall market, whose members have something in common, and to which a specific service appeals.

Market segmentation   The division of the overall market for a service into groups of customers with common characteristics.

Market segmentation analysis   A two-step process in which a hospitality and travel organization first segments the market and then selects its target markets from among the resulting market segments.

Market share   The percentage relationship of an organization's sales to total industry or sector sales.

Marketing   A continuous, sequential process through which management in the hospitality and travel industry plans, researches, implements, controls, and evaluates activities designed to satisfy customers' needs and wants, and their own organization's objectives. To be most effective, marketing requires the efforts of everyone in an organization and can be made more or less effective by the actions of complementary organizations.

Marketing audit   A systematic, comprehensive, and periodic evaluation of the entire marketing function in an organization including its marketing goals, objectives, strategies, and performance.

Marketing-company era   The second stage of the marketing-organization era when companies realized that marketing was a long-term organizational concern and not just the responsibility of the marketing department.

Marketing-company orientation   The view that marketing is a long-term, organized concern where the success of the company hinges not only on satisfying the customers' short-term needs, but the long-term needs as well.

(The) marketing concept   Acting on the belief that satisfying customers' needs and wants is the first priority in business.

Marketing control   Steps that an organization takes to ensure that its marketing plans are successful. This includes setting standards, measuring performance against standards, and correcting deviations from standards and plans.

Marketing cost and profitability analysis   A marketing evaluation technique in which income statements are analyzed to determine sales, costs, and profits.

Marketing-department era   The first stage in the marketing-orientation era, this was a period when manufacturing and packaged-goods companies began to accept the need to set up new departments to coordinate all marketing activities.

Marketing environment analysis   A step completed in a situation, market or feasibility analysis examining the organization's marketing environment (i.e., the economy, society, culture, government, technology, and population/demographics) that will affect its direction and success. This analysis provides a foundation for the organization's marketing plans and strategic market plans.

Marketing environment factors   Events and other factors completely beyond the direct control of the marketing manager, but which must be analyzed in marketing planning. There are six factors

in this part of the hospitality and travel marketing environment: competition, laws and government regulations, economy, society and culture, technology, and organizational priorities and goals. They are also often referred to as the uncontrollable factors.

Marketing evaluation   Techniques used after the marketing plan period to analyze success in achieving individual marketing objectives and to more broadly assess the entire organization's marketing efforts.

Marketing management   All the activities necessary to plan, research, implement, control, and evaluate the marketing efforts of a hospitality and travel organization.

Marketing manager   The person with overall responsibility for marketing in an organization or individual unit.

Marketing mix   Includes the controllable factors, including product, price, place, promotion, packaging, programming, people, and partnership (8 Ps), that an organization selects to satisfy customer needs.

Marketing myopia   A term coined in 1960 by Theodore Levitt to describe many of the thirteen symptoms of production and sales orientations.

Marketing objective   A measurable goal for a target market that a hospitality and travel organization attempts to achieve within a specific time period—typically one to two years.

Marketing orientation   This means acceptance of the marketing concept—that customer needs are the first priority in a hospitality and travel organization.

Marketing-organization era   The second stage in the marketing-orientation era, this was the period after the marketing-department era when manufacturing and packaged-goods companies began to see marketing as not only one department's responsibility, but as a long-term organizational concern.

Marketing plan A written, short-term plan—for a period of two years or less—that details how a hospitality or travel organization will use its marketing mix(es) to achieve its marketing objectives.

Marketing plan rationale Explains the facts, analyses, and assumptions upon which the marketing plan is based. It describes the marketing strategies, target markets, positioning approaches, and marketing objectives selected for the period.

Marketing position and plan analysis A step followed in market, feasibility, and situation analyses to determine how best a new or existing organization should be positioned and marketed.

Marketing research The function of marketing that links the consumer, customer, and public to the marketer through information (American Marketing Association definition).

Marketing research process The sequential steps for marketing research projects that include: defining the research problem, developing an approach to the research problem, formulating the research design, conducting the data collection or fieldwork, preparing the data and analysis, and preparing and presenting the research report.

Marketing research program A plan developed by an organization to investigate several opportunities or problems.

Marketing research project An individual element of a marketing research program where a specific problem or opportunity is investigated.

Marketing strategy The selection of a course of action from among several alternatives that involves specific customer groups (target markets), communication methods, distribution channels, and pricing structures.

Marketing strategy factors The elements of the hospitality and travel marketing environment that a marketing manager can control. These factors are the elements of a hospitality and travel organization's marketing mix (8 Ps). They are also often referred to as the controllable factors.

Market-share analysis A marketing evaluation technique that analyzes an organization's market share and the market-share performance of its competitors.

Maturity stage The third stage in the product life cycle when there is a slowdown in the rate of sales growth.

M-commerce A new way of purchasing hospitality and travel services mainly through mobile phones, PDAs, and other mobile devices.

Media (press) kits A selection of press releases, articles, and photographs assembled for use by the press.

Media vehicles Specific newspapers, magazines, journals, directories, websites, and television and radio stations where advertising can be placed.

Medium A means of communicating, including print and broadcast, with customers through advertising. In the broader context of the communications process, media are the communication channels that sources (sponsors) select to pass their messages to receivers (customers).

Mega-carriers A term commonly used in North America to refer to the major domestic airlines such as United and American Airlines.

Menus Merchandising tool used in restaurants and other food and beverage operations that list all food and beverage items available.

Merchandising Also sometimes referred to as point-of-purchase advertising, this includes all in-house materials used to stimulate sales (menus, wine lists, tent cards, posters, displays).

Message Part of the communications process, it is what the source (sponsor) wants to communicate in the hope that the receivers (customers) understand.

Message format Broad creative approaches in advertising to communicate the message idea to customers.

Message idea   The main theme, appeal, or benefit communicated in an advertisement.

Message strategy   The way an advertising message is communicated including the message idea, copy platform, and message format.

Metrics   The marketing control standards based on plans and the objectives contained in these plans to monitor the actual performance and adjust procedures or activities accordingly.

MICE   Meetings, incentives, conventions, and exhibitions.

Micro-systems   Individual organizations in the hospitality and travel industry. The hospitality and travel marketing system is a micro-system.

Milestones   Sub-objectives with specific time deadlines that are established within a marketing plan.

Mission statement   A broad statement about a hospitality and travel organization's business and scope, services or products, markets served, and overall philosophy. It summarizes the organization's role in society.

Modified American Plan (MAP)   Packages that include accommodation and two meals per day, normally breakfast and dinner.

Moments of truth   A term used to describe service encounters or when a customer directly interacts with an employee of a hospitality and travel organization.

Mood   The added enhancement or feeling of excitement that a particular medium or vehicle gives to an advertisement.

Motivation   Inner drives that customers have that cause them to take action to satisfy their needs.

Motives   Individual drives or desires that customers have to satisfy their wants.

Multi-branding   It is another name for co-branding, as is brand bundling and brand alliances. Multi-branding is a strategy in which a firm puts more than one of its brands into the same restaurant in hopes of raising sales and improving operating efficiency.

Multi-stage approach to pricing   The pricing approach this book recommends based on step-by-step consideration of nine factors—corporate objectives, customer characteristics, corporate image and positioning, customer demand volumes, costs, competition, channels, complementary services and facilities, and consistency with marketing mix elements and strategy.

Multi-stage segmentation   An approach to market segmentation in which more than two segmentation characteristics are used.

Need recognition   The customer's perception of a difference between the desired state of affairs and the actual situation that is sufficient to arouse and activate the decision process.

Needs   (See customer needs.)

News (press) conferences   A meeting where a prepared presentation is made to invited media people.

News (press) releases   Short articles about organizations that try to attract media attention, leading to media coverage of the materials contained within the releases.

Newsworthy   This means that a story is of enough interest and with sufficient recentness that the media are likely to cover it.

Nichers   Organizations that choose the marketing strategy of appealing only to one target market (single-target-market approach).

Niching   Using a strategy to appeal only to small or narrow target markets.

Nine Cs of pricing   Nine factors that influence prices including customer characteristics, corporate objectives, corporate image and positioning, customer demand volumes, costs, competition, channels, complementary services and facilities, and consistency with marketing mix elements and strategy.

Noise   This is a factor that affects the communications process and includes the distractions (other promotional messages) that draw the customer's attention away from the sponsor's message.

Non-commercial sources   Independent, objective assessments of hospitality and travel services such as ratings by the American Automobile Association, Mobil, Michelin, and restaurant critics.

Non-probability sampling   A subjective sample-selection approach used in marketing research where every person in the group does not have a known probability of being in the sample.

Objective-and-task budgeting   A sophisticated approach to setting the marketing budget where the actions (tasks) required to achieve marketing objectives are determined and then cost-estimated.

Objective criteria   Factors that the customer uses to choose between alternative hospitality and travel services or destinations that include prices, locations, physical characteristics of facilities, and services offered.

Objectives (for customers)   The services that the hospitality and travel industry supplies—hotel accommodations, restaurant meals, destinations, cruises, flights, travel counseling, inclusive tours, and entertainment.

Observational method   A category of primary research in the hospitality and travel industry that involves watching and noting how customers behave.

Observational research   Includes both human and mechanical observational research methods. Human observation is watching and noting how customers behave. The other method uses mechanical or electronic devices to collect data.

Occasion-based segmentation   A form of behavioral segmentation in which customers are categorized according to when they buy and the purpose of their purchases (e.g., honeymoon vacationers).

Online advertising   Generally considered to involve advertising on the Internet, particularly the Web.

Online marketing   Marketing of a hospitality and travel organization or destination using the Internet, mainly the Web and e-mail.

Online prospecting   A type of prospecting for sales leads by hospitality and travel organizations through the Internet.

Online research   Marketing research conducted using the Internet.

Online surveys   Surveys conducted on the Internet.

Online travel companies   Sites on the Web that provide travel information and that enable the customers to book travel, including Travelocity.com, Expedia.com, Kayak.com, and others.

Open systems   The micro-systems or individual organizations in the hospitality and travel industry which are dynamic, constantly undergoing change.

Opinion leaders   People in various social groups who exert an above-average influence, through word-of-mouth communication, on the behavior of their peers.

Opinions   Beliefs that people have, accurate or inaccurate, about a variety of subjects, including the political scene, the economy, the educational system, products, future events, sports, countries, and so on.

Organizational buying behavior   The ways in which people in organizations select, use, and behave after they have purchased hospitality and travel services.

Organizational priorities and goals   Overall, long-term goals and priorities of an organization—usually in for-profit companies—set as profitability, market share, and sales volume targets. They are an uncontrollable factor in the marketing environment.

Outlined presentations   Systematic sales presentations that list the most important sales points that the salesperson needs to make.

Outside sales A term used mainly in the travel agency business for people who sell the agency's services outside of its retail location.

Packaging The combination of related and complementary hospitality and travel services into a single-price offering.

Partnership Cooperative promotions and other cooperative marketing efforts by hospitality and travel organizations.

Pass-along rate An element in the reach of a medium, it is the rate at which magazines and newspapers are passed along from primary to secondary audiences.

Penetration In common usage this means the share of the total market available that an organization captures. It also is used to describe a low price set to capture a large share of the market.

Penetration strategies Strategies used when a new service is first introduced involving setting low prices to capture as much of the market as possible.

People All of an organization's employees (hosts) who provide services to customers. It also includes the customers (guests).

Percentage-of-sales (rule-of-thumb) budgeting An arbitrary, unsophisticated approach to setting a marketing budget based on industry-average percentages of sales.

Perception The mental process customers employ using their five senses—sight, hearing, taste, touch, and smell—to size up hospitality and travel services and the industry's promotional messages.

Performance measurement The tools used to evaluate the success of an organization's marketing efforts.

Perishability A generic difference shared by all services in which services cannot be stored. If they are not sold when they are available, that sale is lost forever.

Permanence The lifespan of a promotional message and its potential for repeated exposures to the same customers.

Personal factors Psychological characteristics of individual customers that influence their behavior—needs, wants, and motivation; perception, learning, personality, lifestyle, and self-concept.

Personal selling Involves oral conversations, either by telephone or face-to-face, between salespersons and prospective customers.

Personality All the things that make a person unique—motivation, perception, learning, and emotions—and the different ways that every person thinks and acts.

Persuasive impact The ability of an advertisement to convince customers in accordance with the advertiser's objectives.

Place (distribution) The plan that the organization makes to allow it to work with other complementary groups in the distribution channel.

Plan The outcome of the process of planning. In this text, a plan is defined as a written document that details how a hospitality or travel organization has decided to try to achieve its marketing objectives.

Planning The process that produces plans. Planning is a management activity in which choices are made between alternative marketing approaches.

Pleasure and personal travel market One of the two main divisions of the hospitality and travel market, this includes people traveling and dining out for pleasure and other personal, non-business reasons.

Podcasts A recent web technology in which people subscribe for a service and then can download audio feeds to their computers or MP3 players.

Positioning The development of a service and marketing mix (8 Ps) to occupy a specific place in the minds of customers within target markets.

Positioning statement   Phrases reflecting the image the organization wants to create.

Post-testing   The use of marketing research techniques to determine the effectiveness of an advertisement after it has been run.

Pre-approach   A step in the sales process; this is the review of each sales prospect's files and other relevant information in preparation for the sales call.

Preferred suppliers or vendors   An example of relationship marketing in which airlines, hotel companies, rental car firms, cruise lines, and tour operators try to increase their shares of selected travel agencies' business by offering extra commission percentage points or other incentives.

Premiums   Items of merchandise offered at a reduced price or free with the purchase of services or products.

Pre-opening public relations   A program of public relations activities used before the opening of a new hospitality and travel business.

Press (or news) conferences   Prearranged meetings where prepared presentations are made to invited media people.

Pre-testing   The use of marketing research techniques to find out whether an advertisement or other promotion communicates information to customers in the manner the sponsor intended.

Price   The monetary value at which services are offered.

Price cutting   This is not the same as discounting but happens when companies react quickly and rashly (without careful analysis) to competitors' price moves.

Price discrimination   Also known as discriminatory or differential pricing, this is where services are set to appeal to specific target markets with some markets receiving rates lower than others.

Price lining   Pre-establishing price lines (levels) that the company feels confident will attract customers.

Price-offs   A type of special-offer sales promotion where there is an advertised price reduction that does not involve using a coupon.

Pricing   One of the marketing mix elements (8 Ps) that is a marketing technique and a major profit determinant. Pricing should include all special rates and discounts in addition to regular pricing.

Pricing objectives   The first step in price planning, these fall into three categories: (1) profit-oriented, (2) sales-oriented, and (3) status-quo-oriented.

Primary competitor analysis   A step followed in market, feasibility, and situation analyses to determine the strengths and weaknesses of primary competitors (competitive organizations who market similar services to some or all of the subject organization's target markets).

Primary groups   Customers' family and friends who influence what they purchase.

Primary research   Data collected for the first time by a method other than secondary research, to answer specific questions.

Primary segmentation base   The characteristic that is most important in determining the customer's choice of a service.

Print media   Newspapers, magazines, direct mail, outdoor advertising, and other printed materials in which advertising can be placed.

Probability sampling   A sampling procedure used in marketing research where every person in the group to be researched has a known probability of being in the sample.

Product   The range of services and facilities (product/service mix) a hospitality and travel organization provides to customers.

Product adoption curve   A concept suggested by Everett M. Rogers that divides the population into five groups known as the innovators, early adopters, early majority, late majority, and laggards.

Product life cycle (PLC) A concept that suggests that all hospitality and travel services pass through four predictable stages: (1) introduction, (2) growth, (3) maturity, and (4) decline.

Product-related segmentation A market segmentation approach that uses some aspect of the service to classify customers.

Product/service mix The assortment of services, facilities, and products that an organization provides to customers.

Product/service mix length The number of related services provided by an organization.

Product/service mix width The number of different services provided by an organization.

Production orientation A production-oriented organization puts most of its emphasis on producing and selling services that are the easiest and most efficient to produce, and not on satisfying the needs and wants of its customers.

Production-orientation era The first evolutionary stage in the development of marketing among manufacturing and packaged-goods companies. This was a period when the concept of mass production began.

Profit maximization Setting a price to achieve the maximum amount of profit.

Pro forma (projected) income statement A forecast of the income and expenses for a hospitality and travel organization or development project for 5 to 20 years in the future.

Programming The development of special activities, events, or programs to increase customer spending or give added appeal to a package or other hospitality/travel service.

Promotion All the techniques that hospitality and travel organizations use to promote their services.

Promotional mix The combination of advertising, sales promotion, merchandising, personal selling, public relations-publicity approaches used by a hospitality and travel organization for a specific time period. It also includes Internet marketing.

Promotional pricing The use of short-term price reductions to stimulate temporary sales increases, particularly as part of sales promotion efforts.

Prospecting A step in the sales process, these are the various techniques that sales representatives use to identify sales prospects.

Psychographic segmentation A market segmentation approach based on psychographics.

Psychographics The development of psychological profiles of customers and psychologically based measures of distinctive modes of living or lifestyles.

Psychological pricing Using slightly lower prices to give customers the perception of added value.

Public relations All the activities that a hospitality and travel organization uses to maintain or improve its relationships with other organizations and individuals.

Public relations consultants Specialized companies that provide public relations and publicity services to hospitality and travel organizations.

Public relations plan A written plan that outlines all the public relations and publicity activities to be carried out over a specific period of time.

Publicity Non-paid communication of information about an organization's services.

Publics All those individuals and groups with whom an organization interacts.

Purpose-of-trip segmentation A market segmentation approach based on dividing hospitality and travel markets according to the customer's primary trip purpose.

Qualifying This is a sales process step and involves using pre-selected criteria to identify the best sales prospects.

Qualitative data or information Data that are non-numerical; non-numerical market research information.

Questionnaire   A printed form used in surveys that lists questions and provides spaces for answers.

Rack rate   The published rate of a hotel.

Rail-drive packages   A type of hospitality and travel package that includes travel by railway and car or other vehicle.

(Marketing Plan) Rationale   The part of the marketing plan that explains the facts, analyses, and assumptions on which the plan is based.

Reach   The number of potential customers exposed to a given advertisement at least once.

Rebating   A certain percentage of the commissions that a travel agency earns that it pays back to a corporate client.

Receiver   An element in the communications process; this is the person who notices or hears and decodes the source's (sponsor's) encoded message.

Recognition programs   A sales promotion technique that makes awards to travel trade intermediaries, sales representatives, or customers for providing certain levels of sales or business.

Reference groups   Groups with which customers identify.

Relationship marketing   A marketing principle that emphasizes the importance of building long-term relationships with individual customers and with other organizations in the distribution chain.

Relationship selling   The practice of building ties to customers based on a salesperson's attention and commitment to customer needs over time. This is an element of the relationship marketing and customer relationship management concepts.

Repositioning   Using various promotional programs and physical changes in the product/service mix to change the image of an organization in customers' minds.

Response   An element in the communications process. This is the manner in which receivers (customers) react to sponsors' messages.

Response rate   The percentage of all people surveyed who supply answers to the researcher's questions.

Retail travel agents   A specialized travel trade intermediary that sells the services of carriers, suppliers, other travel trade intermediaries, and DMOs, earning commissions for providing the service.

RevPAR   This is the revenue per available room and is an important metric in the hotel industry.

Revenue management   The application of information systems and pricing strategies to allocate the right capacity to the right customer at the right place at the right time. This involves using computer systems to predict customer demand levels and to match price levels to what certain customer groups are willing to pay at a specific time for a specific duration of service.

RFP   This means a request for proposals and is an invitation to submit a proposal on a service or commodity.

RSS   This means "really simple syndication" and represents XML file formats suitable for providing real-time information via Internet subscription.

Rule-of-thumb budgeting   (See percentage-of-sales budgeting.)

Sales analysis   A marketing evaluation technique that compares actual sales with sales objectives.

Sales blitz (blitzing or concentrated canvassing)   An approach in which several sales representatives cold call in the same, specified geographic area.

Sales call   An in-person visit by a sales representative to a sales prospect.

Sales demonstration   The sales representative demonstrates the ability of the organization's services to meet the prospect's needs.

Sales leads   Another name for sales prospects or customers who may be interested in purchasing the organization's services.

Sales management   The management of the sales force and personal selling efforts to achieve desired sales objectives.

Sales management audit   A periodic analysis of the sales department's policies, objectives, activities, personnel, and performance.

Sales missions   Most often used by DMOs, and when doing personal selling abroad or at a long distance from the destination. Also sometimes called road shows.

Sales orientation   A sales-oriented organization places most of its emphasis on outselling the competition, and not on satisfying the needs and wants of its customers.

Sales-orientation era   The second evolutionary stage in the development of marketing among manufacturing and package-goods companies. This was a period—beginning in the 1930s and lasting through the 1940s—when the emphasis switched from production to outselling the competition.

Sales plan   A detailed description of personal selling objectives, sales forecasts, sales-force responsibilities, activities, and budgets.

Sales presentation   A presentation, either verbal, written or both, through which a sales representative tries to convince a prospect to make a purchase.

Sales process   The step-by-step process used in conducting personal selling efforts.

Sales promotions   Approaches other than advertising, personal selling, and public relations and publicity where customers are given a short-term inducement to make an immediate purchase.

Sales prospects   The prospective customers of an organization.

Sales quotas   Performance targets periodically set for individual sales representatives, branch offices, or regions.

Sales representative   A person who works in the sales department of a hospitality and travel organization and who is directly involved in personal selling.

Sales territories   Specific areas of responsibility, usually geographic, that are assigned to individual sales representatives or branch offices.

Sampling   A sales promotion technique in which free samples are given away or another type of arrangement is made so that people can try out all or part of a service. It has another means when used in marketing research.

Satellite ticket printers (STPs)   A travel agency branch that has an attended or unattended airline ticketing machine.

Secondary groups   Groups to which customers belong including churches, workplaces, clubs, and societies.

Secondary research   Published marketing research information available from other sources, either internal or external.

Segmentation characteristics   The characteristics used to divide a market into segments.

Segmentation criteria   The specific criteria or techniques that a hospitality and travel organization uses to divide up markets into subgroups.

Segmented marketing strategy   Also known as differentiated marketing strategies, these are approaches that recognize differences between target markets by using individualized marketing mixes.

Segmenters   Organizations that use segmented marketing strategies.

Self-concept   Mental pictures that customers have of themselves, consisting of four different elements: the real self, ideal self, reference-group self, and self-image. These are personal factors that influence how customers behave.

Self-liquidating premiums   Merchandise items sold at a reduced price that recovers the sponsor's costs.

Service encounter   A period of time when a customer directly interacts with a service.

Service fees   Fees that travel agencies charge their clients for making bookings of airlines and other travel. Service fees have become common among U.S. travel agencies as a result of airline commission cuts.

Service industries   Organizations, including those within the hospitality and travel industry, primarily involved in the provision of personal services.

Services analysis   A step followed in market, feasibility, and situation analyses to determine what new or improved services can be provided to better match the needs of customers.

Services marketing   A concept based on the recognition of the uniqueness of all services. It is a branch of marketing that specifically applies in the service industries.

SERVQUAL   A technique developed by Parasuraman, Zeithaml, and Berry to measure service quality.

Seven core principles (of marketing)   The basic principles of marketing comprising the marketing concept, marketing orientation, satisfying customers' needs and wants market segmentation, value and the exchange process, product life cycle, and marketing mix.

Shared room basis   (See double-occupancy basis.)

Short-term planning   The process of preparing plans for a period of two years or less.

Simulation   A category of primary research that involves using computers to simulate marketing situations.

Single-stage segmentation   A market segmentation approach where only one of the seven segmentation characteristics is used.

Single supplement   An added charge to packages and tours for people who book on a single-occupancy basis.

Single-target-market strategy   A marketing strategy approach where the organizations select only one target market from several market segments and market exclusively to the chosen target market.

Situation analysis   Similar to a market analysis, this is a study of the marketing strengths, weaknesses, and opportunities of a business or other type of organization.

Skimming strategies   Strategies used when a new service is first introduced involving high prices to achieve the highest possible gross profit.

Slice-of-life   An advertising message format that shows a short mini-drama or playlet from everyday life where the sponsor's service or product solves customers' problems.

Social classes   A system of classifying the population based on such factors as occupation, sources of income and accumulated wealth, highest level of education achieved, place of residence, and family history.

Social information sources   Interpersonal channels of information—also known as word-of-mouth—that influence customer behavior.

Social sources   Interpersonal channels of information.

Society and culture   An uncontrollable factor in the hospitality and travel environment, these are the changes in society and culture that affect organizations and individual customers. The societal and cultural norms and environment affect people's thoughts and actions.

Societal-marketing-orientation era   Beginning about the 1970s, this is the fourth evolutionary era of marketing. It is when organizations started to recognize their social responsibility in addition to their profit and customer-satisfaction objectives.

Source   An element of the communications process. This is the person or organization (sponsor) transmitting the information to customers.

Special communication methods This is one of the two main groups of sales promotion techniques—the other being special offers. It includes specialty advertising, sampling, trade/travel show exhibits, point-of-purchase displays and demonstrations, educational seminars and training programs, and sales representatives' visual aids.

Special-interest packages The primary attraction in these packages is the special activities, programs, and events—e.g., sports instruction, hobbies, and continuing education topics—arranged by one or more of the providers.

Special offers This is one of the two main groups of sales promotion techniques—the other being special communication methods. It includes coupons, price-offs, premiums, contests, sweepstakes and games, travel trade inducements, recognition programs, and continuity programs. They offer short-term inducements to customers, travel trade intermediaries, and sales representatives.

Specialty advertising A sales promotion technique in which free items are given to customers or travel trade intermediaries displaying the sponsor's name, logo, or advertising message.

Specific positioning approach An approach to creating an image for an organization or destination. Only one customer benefit is selected and the concentration is on that one benefit.

Spots and spot advertising Local and network radio and television advertisements that are aired between programs.

Stimulus response A sales presentation method that emphasizes the importance of saying the right things at the right time by means of a well-prepared sales presentation (stimulus) in order to elicit the desired response (sale).

Strategic alliances A form of relationship marketing; these are special long-term relationships formed between two or more hospitality and travel organizations or between a hospitality and travel organization and one or more other types of organizations.

Strategic market plan Also known as long-term planning, this is a written plan for marketing a hospitality or travel organization covering a period of three or more years in the future. It supports the organization's vision for the long-term, and is consistent with its mission.

Strategic marketing planning The process that produces strategic (long-term) market plans. It is a management activity in which long-term choices are made between alternative marketing approaches.

Strategic plan The more general and long-term plan of an organization.

Subcultures Cultures within a broader overall culture. In the United States, subcultures include ethnic minorities (Black-, Hispanic-, and Asian-Americans) and religious-based groups.

Subjective criteria Intangible factors used by the customer to choose among alternative hospitality and travel services, or destinations, such as the image of the organization or destination.

Suggestive selling Also known as up-selling, this is where employees suggest or recommend additional or higher-priced items or services.

Suppliers Organizations that operate facilities (lodging, restaurant and food service), attractions and events, cruise lines, car rental agencies, casinos, and other support services in or between travel destinations.

Surrogate cues Product/service features that provide no direct benefits in use but convey a message about what is being offered, e.g., a company name like Econo Lodge.

Survey research The most popular of the four primary research categories. This includes personal interviews, mail, telephone, and online surveys.

Sustainable development Developing hospitality and travel in such a way as not to harm the environment or the culture and lifestyles of local people, so that future generations may enjoy them as they are today.

Sweepstakes (lucky draws)   Sales promotions in which entrants submit their names and addresses, and where winners are chosen on the basis of chance and not skill.

SWOT analysis   An abbreviation for strengths, weaknesses, opportunities, and threats, this is an analysis technique used as the foundation of an organization's strategic market plan and marketing plan. Often it is used interchangeably with situation analysis.

Synergism   An outcome of partnership (cooperative marketing). It is the combined action of two or more organizations producing a result that individually would not have been possible.

System   A collection of interrelated parts that work together to achieve common objectives.

Tactical planning   The process by which short-term (2 years or less) marketing plans are developed, implemented, controlled, and evaluated. Marketing plans are what most experts call tactical or short-term plans.

Target market   A market segment selected by a hospitality and travel organization for marketing attention.

Target pricing   A sophisticated pricing approach where the target is usually set in terms of a specific return on investment that the company wishes to achieve.

Technology   Methods or processes for handling specific technical problems.

Telemarketing   Personal selling efforts conducted via the telephone.

Telephone selling   Any communications via the phone that lead directly or indirectly to sales. This is one of the three main categories of personal selling.

Test marketing   An experimental research technique in which new services or products are tested in locations thought to be representative of the population as a whole.

Testimonial advertisement   An advertisement in which a celebrity, authority figure, satisfied customer (real or fictitious), or continuing character recommends or otherwise endorses the service or product.

Third-party intermediaries   Same as online travel companies.

Tone   The way an advertising message is communicated based on choices between rational and emotional appeals, dealing with competitors' services versus not mentioning them, and the strength of the message.

Total quality management (TQM)   A process designed to cut down on an organization's defects, to determine its customer requirements, and to satisfy those requirements.

Tour operator   A tour wholesaler, other company, or individual who operates packages or tours, i.e., provides the necessary ground transportation and guide services.

Tour wholesaler   A company or individual who plans, prepares, markets, and administers travel packages, usually combining the services of several suppliers and carriers.

Trade advertising   Advertising to travel trade intermediaries who will influence customers' buying decisions.

Trade-area analysis   A research study that analyzes the market within an organization's surrounding trading area.

Trade promotions   Sales promotions directed at travel trade intermediaries including trade show exhibits, recognition programs, sweepstakes and contests, price offs, and other trade inducements.

Trade shows   Events where all parts of the industry (suppliers, carriers, intermediaries, and DMOs) are brought together to share information.

Trading area   The geographic area from which an organization (or similar organizations) tends to attract the majority of its customers.

Traditional (rule-of-thumb) pricing   An unsophisticated pricing approach based on traditional ways of arriving at prices—usually using some sort of formula—in various parts of the hospitality and travel industry.

Travel agency appointments   Processes by which travel agencies are approved to sell and receive commissions by specific supplier and carrier associations.

(Retail) travel agent   A person or organization who sells and reserves the services of suppliers, carriers, other travel trade intermediaries, and DMOs to individual and group customers, and receives commissions for these efforts.

Travel demand generators   The primary reasons for travel including attractions, events, and business-related facilities.

Travel management   According to the National Business Travel Association (NBTA), it is the practice of approaching corporate travel strategically.

Travel trade   A term commonly used in the hospitality and travel industry to describe all intermediaries.

Travel trade intermediary   One of several specialized indirect distribution channels, including retail travel agents, tour wholesalers and operators, corporate travel managers and agencies, incentive travel planners, convention/meeting planners, online travel companies, and GDS in the hospitality and travel industry.

Two-stage segmentation   A market segmentation approach in which a primary segmentation base is chosen and then customers are further subdivided using a second segmentation base.

Undifferentiated marketing (strategy)   A marketing strategy approach that overlooks segment differences, using the same marketing mix for all target markets.

Up-selling   (See suggestive selling.)

Use-frequency segmentation   (See heavy-half segmentation.)

VALS™   A lifestyle segmentation system approach developeed by SRI Consulting Business Intelligence.

Value or value for money   Mental estimates that customers make of a hospitality or travel service's ability to satisfy their needs and wants.

Variability   A generic difference shared by all services. This results from the difficulty of standardizing services because of the heavy involvement of different people in their provision.

Variable (direct) costs   Costs that vary in direct proportion to the number of customers buying the package or other hospitality/travel service.

Vertical integration   Expansion up and down the distribution channel by a hospitality and travel organization (e.g., a travel agency chain acquiring a lodging company).

Vision   A broad and long-term marketing objective describing the organization's view of where it would like to be in the future.

Vision statement   A formal step in the marketing plan comprised of a written statement outlining the organization's view of where they would like to be in the future.

Wants   (See customer wants.)

Waste   The number of customers exposed to an advertisement that are not part of an organization's target markets.

Web   The collection of text, graphics, video, and sound that can be accessed on the Internet through the use of URLs or website addresses.

Webcasting   A Web technology to handle media events and communicate current information through a website.

Word-of-mouth   Information about a service experience passed orally from past (and other social information sources) to potential customers.

Yield management A revenue-management approach used by airlines, hotels, cruise lines, car rental firms, and others to maximize the sales of their perishable inventories by controlling prices and capacity.

Zero-based budgeting A sophisticated approach to setting a marketing budget that requires that each marketing plan activity (task) for an upcoming period is justified, i.e., the budget begins at zero.

Zip-code demographics analysis An analysis of the demographic characteristics of the people living within a specific zip code area.

INDEX

Note: Page numbers followed by "f" are Figures